NO HOLDING BACK

Our Little Army in the Field: The Canadians in South Africa 1899-1902, Vanwell, St. Catharines, 1996

With G.D. Mitchell and W. Simcock, *RCHA – Right of the Line, An Anecdotal History of the Royal Canadian Horse Artillery from 1871,* Royal Canadian Horse Artillery, Ottawa, 1986

"Prepare for Cavalry! The Battle of Ridgeway, 2 June 1866" and "'For God's sake … save your guns!' Action at Leliefontein, 7 November 1900" in Donald E. Graves (ed.), *Fighting for Canada: Seven Battles, 1758-1945,* Robin Brass Studio, Toronto, 2000

"A Most Dashing Advance: Paardeberg, 27 February 1900" in Donald E. Graves (ed.), *More Fighting for Canada: Five Battles, 1760-1944,* Robin Brass Studio, 2004

NO HOLDING BACK

OPERATION TOTALIZE, NORMANDY, AUGUST 1944

Brian A. Reid

Foreword by
Brigadier-General E.A.C. Amy,
DSO, OBE, MC, CD

Maps and illustrations by
Christopher Johnson

ROBIN BRASS STUDIO
Toronto

Published 2005 by Robin Brass Studio Inc.
www.rbstudiobooks.com

Printed and bound in Canada

Library and Archives Canada Cataloguing in Publication

Reid, Brian A.
    No holding back : Operation Totalize, Normandy, August 1944 / Brian A. Reid ; maps and illustrations by Christopher Johnson.

Includes bibliographical references and index.

ISBN 1-896941-40-0

    1. Operation Totalize, 1944. 2. World War, 1939-1945 – Campaigns – France – Normandy. 3. Canada. Canadian Army – History – World War, 1939-1945. 4. Simonds, Guy Granville, 1903-1974. I. Title.

D768.15.R47 2005   940.54'2142   C2004-905596-8

CONTENTS

MAPS

My first task is to watch for the opportunity when the Boche weakens that pivot and then crack through. Once this takes place his whole position in Normandy collapses. This is the time when there will be no holding back, because it will be the finish of the enemy as far as this phase of the war is concerned, unless he decides upon a general withdrawal.

LIEUTENANT GENERAL GUY SIMONDS,
GENERAL OFFICER COMMANDING, 2ND CANADIAN CORPS,
30 JULY 1944

From: Main Headquarters, Supreme Headquarters Allied Expeditionary Force

To: HQ First Canadian Army

29 July 1550 Hours

Top Secret. Code Words from 21 Army Group Pool for Operational Use by First Canadian Army. TALLULAH, TOTALIZE, TRACTABLE

FOREWORD

Brigadier-General (Retd.) E.A.C. Amy,
DSO, OBE, MC, CD

Lieutenant-Colonel Brian Reid and I served together in Germany in the 1960s in Canada's NATO Brigade. I retain lasting memories of Operation TOTALIZE in 1944 and I am delighted he asked me to write the foreword for this book.

Prior to the Normandy campaign, I had served for seven months in Sicily and Italy with the 1st Canadian Armoured Brigade, commanded by Brigadier R.A. Wyman. I landed in Sicily with the Ontario Regiment and later was posted to command a squadron with the Calgary Tank Regiment. With this background, I took part in TOTALIZE in August 1944 as a squadron commander in the Canadian Grenadier Guards of 4th Canadian Armoured Brigade.

At 2200 hours on 7 August 1944, less than two hours before H-Hour for Phase 1 of the operation, Lieutenant-Colonel Bill Halpenny, our commanding officer, briefed us for the first time on TOTALIZE. He explained that in Phase 2 the Regiment was to lead 4th Armoured Brigade's advance south through a breach to be created in the German defences by the troops taking part in Phase 1. My squadron, with a company of the Lake Superior Regiment and detachments of anti-tank guns and flails, was to lead the Grenadier Guards' advance and we were to be ready to cross the Phase 2 start line by first light on 8 August. In his text, the author aptly describes the chaotic circumstances under which these orders were given.

After a hasty and distressing night move described in the narrative below, my squadron was in the assembly area by 0500 hours, but not yet married up with the infantry company or the detachment of flails. After this occurred, we were told we could not move forward until the Commander of the 2nd Canadian Infantry Division declared Rocquancourt clear. There followed a very long wait due to the USAAF bombing program, about which I was now informed for the first time.

Finally, between 1500 and 1600 hours on 8 August, we were ordered to cross the start line. During this interminable delay I had no contact with Phase 1 units ahead of us, nor had I any idea of their locations or that of the enemy with whom they were in contact. I deemed this information essential to avoid firing accidentally on our own troops, including those in the Polish Division on our left. To me, therefore, the persistent commands to "bypass all opposition" were nonsensical. While feasible in the North African campaign, this was not possible in the narrow corridor in which we were operating and, not knowing the location of either the enemy or our own troops, I was determined to wait until someone came forward with this information in order to make a sensible decision on how to proceed. This did not happen, and the unfortunate incident described in the narrative concerning Lieutenant Craig Smith was one of the results. He considered that the frantic commands to bypass the enemy were directed at him, and with only two tanks left in his troop he charged forward. His tank was hit, he was severely wounded and two members of his crew were killed.

There has been criticism in some written accounts of TOTALIZE of us not bypassing the opposition, to which the author notes, "a criticism that definitely was not based on any knowledge of the tactical situation." My squadron was inexperienced but I was not. However, without sleep for 32 hours, I was stressed and angry that troops were being committed to their first battle in this manner and I was not prepared to commit them further without the information I needed.

Reid's extensive research and analysis of the issues which shaped the development and training of the Canadian army and its leadership in the half century leading up to the invasion of Normandy, including the lengthy period in England where its training was influenced by the North African campaign, leads him to conclude that the Canadian army and its leaders were ill prepared to cope with an operation as complex as TOTALIZE. This was particularly so given that a battle against an experienced enemy, second to none, was being fought on ground of their choosing, not ours.

The success of Phase 2 of the operation rested with two inexperienced armoured divisions, neither of which were given adequate time for preparation and deployment for their very first battle. The plan for TOTALIZE failed to accommodate this reality.

Lieutenant-General Guy Simonds's planning for Operation TOTALIZE, including his appreciation, plan, orders and special briefings for his armoured brigade commanders, suggests a remarkable orderliness in a very compressed time-frame. Reid's research reveals that this orderliness was not present on the battlefield and, to my recollection, it definitely was not present on 8 August 1944.

There are passages in the narrative that reveal a conflict between the leaders at the higher levels of command and their subordinates. The Commander of 2nd Canadian Corps allegedly accused commanding officers of his armoured regiments of cowardice and incompetence. This calls into question the nature of the relationship with troops at the higher and lower levels of command. It may suggest a diminished memory by those in high command of the unique relationship that each of them once had with their soldiers as a regimental commanding officer. Reid's work suggests some commanding officers were not given reasonable time to brief and ready their soldiers for the battle, and this shortcoming has to rest with one or other of the three higher levels of command.

The ongoing controversy over the successes and the failures of Operation TOTALIZE continues to challenge historians. Much has been written on the subject by Canadian and British authors and *No Holding Back,* with its mission to replace fiction with facts, and its inclusion of material heretofore unrecorded, is an excellent and worthy addition to this literature. In his prologue, Reid states that when he began his examination he knew "some of the more extreme criticisms of the battle were based on frighteningly shallow research and much of what had been written was more in the nature of urban legend than military history." His book does a great deal to clarify a difficult chapter of Canadian military history and there is certainly no holding back on his part as he calls a spade a spade and attributes blame and praise impartially to generals and lesser mortals. His study delves into virtually every aspect of the planning and execution of the operation, and he opines that much of the fault for the lack of success of TOTALIZE lies in faulty British and Canadian doctrine, and not with the quality of the troops who did the fighting in August 1944.

As a knowledgeable gunner, Brian Reid's comments on the use of artillery *vis-à-vis* aerial bombing are insightful and reveal that Simonds's steadfast commitment to the latter removed whatever flexibility he might otherwise have had to take advantage of unforeseen successes on 8 August.

The clarity of the narrative is achieved with well-ordered chapters and its epilogue encapsulates much of what went wrong and what went right. Based on what actually was achieved, the author concludes that "Totalize was a great success, although it could and should have achieved more, more quickly." Notwithstanding faults real or imagined, he expresses the view that "Simonds clearly was by far the best Canadian senior commander of the war, and one whose performance does not suffer when compared to his Allied contemporaries."

The 8th of August 1944 was the worst day of my entire war and the enemy was not the problem. For half a century, I have hoped that one day someone would undertake a more critical examination of TOTALIZE. Brian Reid's *No Holding Back* does this and, to use a Hollywood idiom, chronicles "the good, the bad and the ugly."

BRIGADIER-GENERAL (RETD.) E.A.C. AMY, DSO, OBE, MC, CD

Halifax, Canada, 23 October 2004

INTRODUCTION

OTALIZE was both the first major operation conducted by First Canadian Army and its first attempt to employ armour in mass. The recognition of these firsts has been overshadowed by the "sexier" aspects of the battle – the introduction of the armoured personnel carrier, the use of armour at night and the replacement of artillery by heavy bombers in support of an attack. Even with these flashy distractions, it does seem passing odd that so much of the treatment of such a momentous occasion has been, on one hand, both shallow and rarely original and, on the other, so glaringly wide of the mark.[1] In one of the more extreme cases, a writer claimed in a recent article that TOTALIZE failed because the two Phase 1 divisions got lost while attempting to advance at night and the Phase 2 forces were devastated by a misplaced attack by British heavy bombers.*

While TOTALIZE did break the German defence line south of Caen, ultimately it failed to reach its final objective, the ground that protected the city of Falaise. In fact it took another week and a second Canadian offensive to actually capture the old seat of the Dukes of Normandy, which had seemed so ripe to fall on the dawn of TOTALIZE. This is often cited as the cause of the delay of several days in closing the Falaise Gap, thus allowing many thousand Germans to escape and perhaps even denying the Allies victory in the

---

* Flint Whitlock, "Imperfect Victory at Falaise," *World War II Presents Normandy Campaign,* (Leesburg, VA, 2004), 68.

west in 1944. It must be added that the gap did not exist when TOTALIZE was mounted, and in early August the Allied armies still were working under the original concept for the Normandy campaign that envisaged trapping the retreating enemy against the Seine River. While other factors contributed to the failure to close the gap, not least of all some questionable decisions on the part of Montgomery and Bradley, the failure to capture Falaise in a timely manner certainly contributed.

One theory has it that the inexperience of two Allied armoured divisions, one Canadian and the other Polish, was the root cause, both formations stopping to clear pockets of resistance instead of bypassing them and going for the final objectives. This theory was first put forward by Lieutenant General Guy Simonds, the Commander of 2nd Canadian Corps, and there is a grain of truth to it, although he modified his views in a 1968 interview, in which he stated that rather than being too cautious, the Poles were too impetuous.[2] Another theory is that the wait for the heavy bomber strike allowed the Germans time to build up sufficient forces to contain and then defeat the Allied attack.

Some observers have opined that a relatively junior German officer defeated the Allies by his tactical brilliance and the competence and skill of his troops; a subset of this theory is that the Canadian army was poorly-trained and incompetently-led, and thus unable to brush aside weak German forces. This theory conveniently ignores the advantage held by the Germans in the quality, if not the quantity, of their tanks and anti-tank guns over those of the Allies, as well as in tactical doctrine and the ability to employ combined arms teams of infantry, tanks and anti-tank weapons. It also fails to recognize that the Canadian army in the Second World War was trained to British standards, used British doctrine and British training methods, was assessed on British exercises by British officers and was largely equipped with British equipment. In any case I have included a comparison of German and Allied tactics, doctrine and equipment at Appendix A, while the Allied and German and orders of battle can be found at Appendices B and C.

This book originally was planned to cover the Canadian attacks – Operations TOTALIZE and TRACTABLE – that culminated in the capture of Falaise on 16 August 1944. However, as the manuscript grew, it soon became apparent that each operation merited a complete book of its own. In truth, both operations were complex and, while there were some similarities, quite different in concept and execution. *No Holding Back,* therefore, is the first instalment of a two-part study of the Canadian offensive down the road to Falaise in Normandy six decades past.

A word about methodology: distances and measurements are in the Imperial system in use during the Second World War. For those brought up in the metric system, a yard is roughly 90 per cent of a metre while a foot is one third of a yard. More precisely, a half-mile is about 800 metres while a mile is about 1.6 kilometres. A North American ton is 2,000 pounds, while 2.2 pounds equal a kilogram. For the sake of simplicity I have avoided delving into the complexities of British long tons and hundredweight – which was not a hundred pounds. As for titles I have used italicized German and Polish ranks and unit and formation names whenever possible. Thus 12th SS Panzer Division and 1st Polish Armoured Division are 12. *SS-Panzerdivision* and 1. *Dywizji Pancernej* respectively. However the titles of French-Canadian units such as Les Fusiliers Mont-Royal, in accordance with Canadian practice, appear in plain print.

While we are on the subject of unit titles, a brief explanation is in order for those not familiar with Commonwealth military terminology, as this is often a source of some confusion. In the Commonwealth, the word "regiment" is part of a unit's title and does not indicate its size. Thus an armoured regiment, an infantry regiment and an artillery regiment are respectively, a tank battalion, an infantry battalion and an artillery battalion (although the Second World War Commonwealth artillery regiment had more guns than the American field artillery battalion). The Commonwealth equivalent to an American regiment is a brigade. To avoid confusion, the American reader should simply substitute "battalion" for "regiment" and "regiment" for "brigade" every time these terms are used in the text.

A Commonwealth armoured squadron is an American tank company and a Commonwealth armoured troop is an American tank platoon.

Finally, in the Commonwealth the private soldier can be referred to by a number of different titles according to his unit, corps or trade – "trooper," "gunner," "sapper," "guardsman," "rifleman," and "craftsman" and others – but they all are the equivalent of "private." If that were not enough, in the artillery the lowest non-commissioned rank is "bombardier," not "corporal."

While solely responsible for every word that appears in these pages, I have relied on the contributions of many in reaching my conclusions. The staff of both the National Archives of Canada and the Department of National Defence Directorate of History and Heritage provided a great deal of assistance and both proved to be, as ever, willing to go the extra mile. I was also able to make use of the resources of the British National Archives, the former Public Records Office, and the Sikorski Institute in London thanks to Dianne Graves, who took time from her visits to her family to gather stacks of source material from both. The staff of the Canadian Land Forces Command and Staff College library kindly allowed me free access to their collection, for which I am truly grateful. I was fortunately able to interview a number of veterans of "the night push," as TOTALIZE was known at the time. Of particular help were Brigadier-General Sydney "Rad" Radley-Walters, Lieutenant Colonels Norman R. Donogh, W. Edward "Chick" Sills, James C. "Jamie" Stewart and Lockhart R. "Lockie" Fulton. Regrettably Chick and Jamie passed away before this book went to print. Both were fellow gunners and mentors of mine in my military career; both were good friends and great Canadians.

I am especially grateful to Brigadier-General "Ned" Amy, who, like Rad, commanded a squadron of Shermans in TOTALIZE, both for the material he collected on the operation over the years and for agreeing to write the foreword to this book. I must admit that he was very kind when he stated that we had served together in the Canadian army in Germany in the sixties; he was the brigade commander and I but a lowly subaltern.

Mike McNorgan, Bob Caldwell, Steve Harris and John Grodzinski all read and commented on drafts of my manuscript, while Jody Perrun provided some valuable insights into the relationship between the Allied armies and air forces in Normandy. John also found time despite the pressures of his day job as a history professor at the Royal Military College of Canada to prepare the study of the Polish army in exile in the Second World War found at Appendix F. The reader may notice differences in the spelling of Polish titles between the main text and John's work, as I used the spellings found in the documents of the time, while he has used more modern terminology. Robin Brass was a pillar of support for my largest book project to date while Christopher Johnson truly served above and beyond the call of duty in translating my scribbles into his magnificent maps, charts and drawings. Their combined expertise in the technicalities of the presentation of material is truly amazing. Donald E. Graves, a self-admitted brutal editor, spent countless hours on my manuscripts. My book is by far the better for it, and I have almost forgiven him for threatening to consign one of my chapters to his cats' litter box. Many thanks to Dianne Graves for her thorough index as well as her useful suggestions for corrections.

The demands of Casey, who went from a seven-week-old ball of yellow fluff to a large, enthusiastic Labrador during the latter stages of this project, provided a handy excuse for temporarily abandoning the studio to enjoy long walks together. The change of routine, the exercise and the fresh air were just what the doctor ordered both creatively and physically. Last but by no means least, my wife, Patricia, maintained her enthusiastic support for my efforts, going so far as to voluntarily surrender her large, airy studio for my use. Her efforts may not have improved my filing system, but at least I now have more space to indiscriminately pile stuff.

When I began my examination I was not sure what I would find; what I did know is that some of the more extreme criticisms of the battle were based on frighteningly shallow research, and much of what had been written was more in the nature of urban legend than military history. That above all else led me to take on this study. While I am reasonably confident that my conclusions are sound, I learned long ago to gladly surrender claims of infallibility to egoists and those with axes to grind. Having said that, if I have contributed to our knowledge of the Normandy campaign, then I have accomplished my aim.

BRIAN A. REID
January 2005

NOTE TO READERS: In the picture credits, NAC stands for National Archives of Canada.

PART ONE

THE ROOTS
OF TOTALIZE

THE CRAMESNIL SPUR – 0615 HOURS, 8 AUGUST 1944

"We had more Germans behind us than we had in front of us."

LIEUTENANT COLONEL M.B.K. GORDON,

COMMANDING OFFICER, THE SHERBROOKE FUSILIER REGIMENT

ieutenant Colonel Melville Gordon, the commanding officer of the Sherbrooke Fusilier Regiment, found it hard to credit what he was seeing. After a terrible night of noise and confusion, of smoke and dust, of wild streams of tracers and the sudden flashes of shell bursts, of fear and blood and death, the rapidly-brightening light of dawn revealed … nothing, or at least nothing of the highly dangerous, black-cross variety. From the very first moment when there was barely enough light to capture an image in his binoculars, Gordon had been carefully searching the fields and copses that sloped upwards to the south, starting with the area of greatest danger, the ground closest to his Sherman, then repeating the process, working progressively farther out until finally he had swept the horizon a few thousand yards to his front, and then he did the whole thing over and over and over again. Moreover, he knew that the crew commanders in the three squadrons of his regiment were all doing the same thing, and none had reported sighting any Germans. What finally convinced him that the impossible had occurred – and that the Canadian army had achieved a complete breakthrough of the German defence line south of Caen – was the appearance of an enemy *staff* car of all things driving north up Route Nationale 158, the Caen–Falaise road. Suddenly the vehicle braked abruptly, turned about and sped away to the south with indecent haste. There could be only one conclusion: 2 Canadian Armoured Brigade group* and their British comrades to the east of the Route Nationale in 33 Armoured Brigade and 154 Highland Brigade had fought through the mud and the blood to the green fields beyond. Operation TOTALIZE, the first attack mounted by the First Canadian Army, had broken through the German lines and the road to Falaise was open. Surely if there was a time to throw caution to the winds and order a general advance, it was now.

In a few minutes Gordon was joined by Brigadier Robert A. Wyman, his brigade commander, who rolled up in his Sherman in response to an urgent plea to come forward and see for himself. Gordon wasted no time in telling Wyman that the way ahead was clear and urged that he be allowed to advance up the Route Nationale towards Falaise.** But Wyman would have none of it and emphasized that their orders were to hold the present location as a firm base for 4th Canadian Armoured Division to pass through. Besides, Wyman explained, the advance guard of that division was only a few minutes away, although he apparently did not tell Gordon that he had already passed the report to his superiors that "the area was securely held by our forces and that the situation appeared to be entirely suitable for further op[eration]s to begin."[1] It is an open question whether Gordon might have been able to convince Wyman that the opportunity was worth seizing, especially when the tanks of the 4th Division did not appear in "a few minutes," but it was not to be. While the two officers were discussing the situation, they had attracted the attention of a lurking German straggler, who knocked the brigadier out of the war with a bullet that rendered him incapable of exercising command; although his deputy, Colonel J.F. Bingham, was able to make his way forward within a few hours, the opportunity had been lost. Gordon later estimated that Wyman was wounded at about 0630 hours, while the leading elements of the 4th Division did not pass through his location until 1615 hours, or nearly ten hours later. As it proved impossible to evacuate Wyman until 1300 hours, he was probably right in concluding ruefully that at that time "we had more Germans behind us than we had in front of us."[2]

---

* Group is not capitalized as the force was an *ad hoc* arrangement, and not a permanent organization as is the case for a modern Brigade Group.

** According to then-Major Sydney Radley-Walters, commanding A Squadron of the Sherbrooke Fusilier Regiment, Gordon had actually issued radio orders to his regiment to be prepared to advance in anticipation of receiving authority to exploit the breakthrough.

At about the same time that Gordon was arguing his case to Wyman, Lieutenant General Guy Granville Simonds, commanding 2nd Canadian Corps, was on the phone with Brigadier Churchill Mann, the Chief of Staff of Headquarters, First Canadian Army. From the 0645 hours entry in the army operations log that recorded the gist of the conversation, it was apparent that the 41-year-old Simonds was well satisfied with the developments as he reported that the operation was progressing satisfactorily, although he added that he expected to be counterattacked in two or three hours. He then reported that 1. *Dywizji Pancernej* and 4th Canadian Armoured Division, the two follow-on formations, were starting to infiltrate their way forward, and ended by confirming with Mann that the heavy bomber support for the second phase of the operation should be scheduled to end at 1345 hours.[3] Thus, as the Canadian plan was built around this bombing, there could be no advance for seven hours, and in mobile operations seven hours is an eternity.

In the case of TOTALIZE, the delay of seven hours was more than an eternity; it was time enough for the Germans, who were rarely slow off the mark, to frustrate the Allies' carefully crafted plans and to delay the liberation of Falaise by more than a week. What happened? How had an attack that had started with so much promise achieved so little? Or did TOTALIZE actually succeed beyond the norm for major operations by the British and Canadian armies in Normandy? In the following pages we shall study the development of the plan for the operation and then follow the bitter struggle across the verdant fields south of Caen. But to truly understand the ways and whys of the TOTALIZE, it is first necessary to trace the development of the Canadian army in the years before the Second World War.

CHAPTER ONE

THE CANADIAN ARMY

"The idea that every twenty years this country should automatically and as
a matter of course take part in a war overseas for democracy or self-determi-
nation of other small nations, that a country which has all it can do to run
itself should feel called upon to save, periodically, a continent that cannot
run itself, and to these ends risk the lives of its people, risk bankruptcy and
political disunion, seems to many a nightmare and sheer madness."

PRIME MINISTER WILLIAM LYON MACKENZIE KING,

HOUSE OF COMMONS, 30 MARCH 1939

I n 1919, at the end of the First World War, Canada found itself with two
distinct military establishments: the magnificent Canadian Expeditionary Force (CEF) and a voluntary militia with roots in virtually every
community in the country. On one hand many veterans of the CEF were
keen on seeing their units live on in the postwar army – in the words of a wartime divisional commander, it was "better that a dozen Peace [militia] Regiments should go to the wall than the C.E.F. units be lost"[1] – while on the other
the politically powerful militia saw no reason why it should be penalized so
that upstart CEF units, with no claim to fame other than having whipped the
best the Kaiser could throw at them, might survive. The challenge facing the
government and its military advisers was to integrate the CEF and the militia
into a structure that met peacetime constitutional responsibilities such as aid
to the civil power but also provided a mobilization base for future conflicts.

Leaving aside the vexing issue of the transfer of CEF battle honours to
militia regiments, which would consume several forests of trees over the
next several years, the committee headed by the geriatric Major General Sir
William Otter, which was formed on 23 April 1919 to consider the shape of
the postwar army, indulged in some politically-naive wishful thinking and
went so far as to suggest a large regular army and a system of universal mili-

tary service, a concept that was and still is anathema to most Canadians. Sickened by war and with no apparent external threat other than the remote possibility of a conflict with the United States, Canadians saw no virtue in paying for a large defence establishment, and while the government was prepared to entertain a modest increase in the size of the permanent force, it rejected the Otter Committee's proposal for a regular army of 20,000 or more officers and men. At the same time, it accepted the suggested militia structure of eleven infantry and four cavalry divisions proposed by the committee, which was an assessment of the forces needed to hold the Americans at bay for two years in the unlikely event of war with the United States.[2] Cabinet's approval of this force structure, however, did not extend to spending the funds necessary to equip and man it, and the militia was forced to make do with equipment for four infantry divisions and a cavalry brigade transferred to Canada by the British government to replace materiel left behind in Europe by the CEF.

With little possibility of war Prime Minister Mackenzie King's government, which had replaced Arthur Meighen's Conservatives in the 1921 election, calculated that wilful neglect of the military was a political strategy least likely to offend voters. Thus, while the government approved a permanent force establishment of 10,000, it was only prepared to fund less than half that number, a situation that would prevail literally up to the day German troops invaded Poland on 1 September 1939. Canada's defence spending was ludicrously small in the interwar period. In 1923-1924, for example the Canadian government spent $1.46 per person on defence, compared to $24.06 in France, $23.04 in Great Britain, $6.51 in the USA, $4.27 in South Africa, $3.30 in Australia and $2.33 in New Zealand.[3] With war looming, the situation improved somewhat in the late 1930s. The defence appropriation in fiscal year 1938-1939 was $36,345,000, while the next year's amounted to $66,666,874, or slightly more than $6 per person, with most of the funds devoted to the Royal Canadian Navy and Royal Canadian Air Force.[4]

This wilful and parsimonious shortfall in defence expenditure did nothing to dissuade Lieutenant Colonel James Sutherland Brown, Director of Military Operations and Plans, from preparing Defence Scheme One, in the event of a war between the British Empire and the United States. Brown's thinking was audacious; he recognized that the key to the independence of Canada was the arrival of reinforcements from the rest of the Empire, and it therefore was essential at the very least to keep the port of Quebec in Canadian hands. Ergo, the only feasible course was to buy time by sending columns drawn from the 15 militia divisions deep into the northern states to delay the American forces until reinforcements from overseas could arrive. While Brown was not the paranoid lunatic he has been painted, and many Canadians of the time shared his distrust of America, his plan ignored the realities of geopolitics and the existence of the United States Navy, especially after Britain accepted the principle of naval parity with the Americans – which translated into naval inferiority in the Western Atlantic – following the Washington Naval Treaty of 1922.[5] Indeed his ignorance of this fundamental shift in international affairs is even more remarkable as Canada had played a leading part in the negotiations that led to the treaty, an accomplishment that has been described rather ambiguously as her "single most important endeavour towards the end of her own national security" in the period between the wars, as the agreement with the Americans isolated and antagonized the Japanese and led to its increasingly militaristic stance in Asia and the Pacific.[6]

Perhaps unwittingly, the three illustrations on facing pages of the history of the Royal Canadian Armoured Corps capture the end of one era and the beginning of another. One shows rows of dead horses of C Squadron, Lord Strathcona's Horse (Royal Canadians), cut down by German machine gun fire in the bloody charge at Moreuil Wood on 30 March 1918; the others are of Armoured Autocars of the Canadian Motor Machine Gun Brigade, including one shown near Amiens in August 1918.[7] It was apparent in the 1920s and 1930s, at least to the more visionary, that the introduction of armoured fighting vehicles signalled the end of the usefulness of the horse soldier on the battlefield. According to conventional wisdom, the reactionary Canadian army ignored the developments in armour and mechanization and remained firmly wedded to the horse. For example, historian George Stanley, writing of the peacetime structure adopted after the Great War, claimed that Canada returned to reliance on a partly-trained, poorly equipped and, above all, cheap militia, rather than absorbing the lessons of the war and stressing mechanization and mobility.[8]

Besides mixing apples of mechanization with oranges of defence policy, Stanley's claim is quite unfair. While the Otter committee avoided recom-

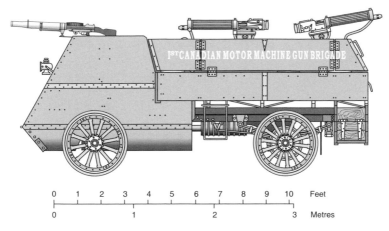

1ST CANADIAN MOTOR MACHINE GUN BRIGADE

0	1	2	3	4	5	6	7	8	9	10	Feet

0			1			2			3	Metres

Armoured Autocar

After serving with the 1st Motor Machine Gun Brigade through the First World War, several Armoured Autocars were brought back to Canada at the end of hostilities. They equipped the Permanent Force Motor Machine Gun Brigade in the immediate postwar years. One example survives and is on display at the Canadian War Museum.

Country of origin: Canada
Crew: 8
Length: 14 feet 9 inches
Width: 3 feet 7 inches
Height: 6 feet
Weight: 3 tons
Engine: 2 cylinder
Maximum speed: 25 mph
Range: Unknown
Armament: 2 x .303 inch Vickers MG, .303 inch Lewis MG (optional)
Armour – Maximum: 9.5 mm

mending the inclusion of tanks in the postwar army,[9] and Canada was hardly a hotbed of military innovation and experimentation, the army was well aware of the military revolution that was underway. In fact, the first signs had been recognized much earlier; it had been difficult in the later years of the Great War to obtain enough horses to meet the needs of the British armies in the field,[10] and in 1920 the accelerating replacement of animals by motorized vehicles in civilian life had led to the recognition of the necessity of using trucks instead of horses to draw artillery. That same year the Chief of the General Staff circulated a paper on the future of armoured vehicles, which led to the (very poorly received) submission of a proposal by Lieutenant Colonel E.W. Sansom[11] of the Canadian Machine Gun Corps for the creation of a separate tank corps to "facilitate shock tactics and manoeuvre."[12] In 1924 Major General J.H. MacBrien, the Chief of the General Staff, commenting on British experiments with mechanization, noted that major economies resulted from replacing horses with vehicles. The next year militia field artillery training at Camp Petawawa, Ontario, used rented vehicles to tow the guns, although this was because of an unexpected lack of horses (the Royal Canadian Horse Artillery Brigade* was in Cape Breton on aid of the civil power duties) rather than any grand design. In 1928 what probably were the earliest trials of military transport in Canada were carried out at Rockcliffe Air Field in Ottawa and at Petawawa, although, ironically in the same year, Major General H.C. Thacker, the new Chief of the General Staff, summed up the prospects of mechanization with the too familiar lament of the Canadian peacetime soldier that "while we are long in sympathy, we are short in cash." Still, early in 1929 the 3rd Medium Battery RCA became the first regular unit to be mechanized when it received four Leyland six-wheeled trucks to tow its 6-inch howitzers and a Morris six-wheeled "car" to carry the battery staff. In 1930 the Royal Canadian Horse Artillery Brigade in Kingston, Ontario, bade a sad farewell to its horses and the three regular infantry regiments were each issued four tiny Carden-Loyd tracked machine gun carriers, dubbed "tankettes," in 1931-1932.[13]

While the cavalry sometimes seemed more intent on bickering over which of its regiments would be issued swords (enabling these units to provide mounted escorts for visiting dignitaries) than clamouring for mechanization or even conversion to tanks,[14] the situation was not quite as grim as it seemed, at least by the horribly low Canadian standards. By 1936 the structure of what was still classed as "cavalry" boasted 15 horsed, three mechanized and four armoured car regiments, while the infantry establishment included six (tankless) tank battalions. Lest one be so naive as to imagine that this was an indication of national resolve to counter the threat posed by an increasing militant Germany and the failure of the League of Nations to curb Fascist aggression, the Canadian inventory of armoured fighting vehicles in that year consisted of the 12 Carden-Loyd tankettes and two prototype armoured cars, one with each regular cavalry regiment. Not all the news was bad, however; in a major step forward, the Canadian Tank School (later renamed the Canadian Armoured Fighting Vehicle Centre) was formed in November of that year at Wolseley Barracks in London, Ontario. Still, equipment remained in short supply; in 1939 on the eve of the Second World War the inventory had grown slightly to two armoured cars, six reconnaissance

---

* The regular Royal Canadian Field Artillery was titled the Royal Canadian Horse Artillery in 1905 in recognition of its service in South Africa, a designation that survives to this day.

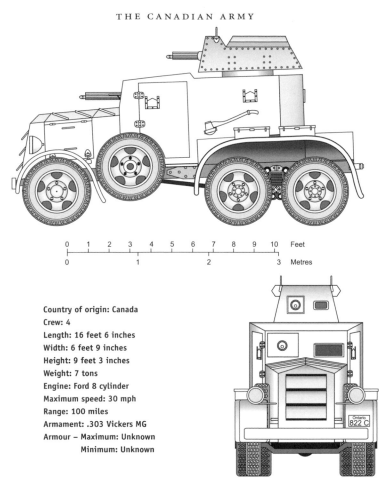

0 1 2 3 4 5 6 7 8 9 10 Feet

0 1 2 3 Metres

Country of origin: Canada
Crew: 4
Length: 16 feet 6 inches
Width: 6 feet 9 inches
Height: 9 feet 3 inches
Weight: 7 tons
Engine: Ford 8 cylinder
Maximum speed: 30 mph
Range: 100 miles
Armament: .303 Vickers MG
Armour – Maximum: Unknown
Minimum: Unknown

Ford Canada 1935 armoured car – experimental

In 1934, Ford and General Motors were each invited to build an experimental armoured
car to undergo testing by the Permanent Force. As an incentive, the government paid
for the materials and chassis while the companies bore the cost of the design work
and assembly. In the end, the government paid only $2,500 while Ford and GM each
ended up investing $9,000 to build their respective cars. The Ford design differed
from the Chevrolet in that it had dual wheels on the second and third axles, an eight-
cylinder gasoline engine, and the armour plating was welded rather than riveted and
bolted. Both armoured cars had a maximum speed of 30 mph. Plans called for arming
the vehicles with the Vickers Mk. VI medium machine gun but these were delayed as
their feed mechanisms were on the wrong side, having been designed by the British
for right-hand-drive vehicles. The cars underwent testing at Petawawa, Ontario, with
the Royal Canadian Dragoons, where both performed satisfactorily. The ten-wheel Ford
excelled in the off-road tests while the six-wheel Chevrolet performed well on roads.
Orders for further cars failed to materialize due to budgetary limitations and the Ford
experimental car was shipped to Winnipeg for service with the Lord Strathcona's Horse.
The Chevrolet remained with the Royal Canadian Dragoons.

vehicles converted from Ford cars, one 1928 Dragon tracked artillery gun tower and the 12 Carden-Loyd tankettes and 16 Vickers Mark VIB light tanks at the Canadian Armoured Fighting Vehicle Centre, now located at Camp Borden, near Barrie, Ontario, along with four 2-pounder anti-tank guns and four 3-inch anti-aircraft guns manned by the permanent force artillery. (The move to Borden came about, not because the London area was unsuitable for armoured training, which it clearly was, but because the horse barns at Wolseley Barracks were burned down by two children playing with matches, prompting the centre's commandant to quip that the errant boys "did more to advance the cause of armoured forces ... than any other single event.")[15]

As a group, Canadian officers seemed content to avoid grappling with difficult issues of organization and tactics, and waited for guidance to appear from the "old country." That this was considered to be proceeding down the right path by the majority was indicative that the army was firmly wedded to uniformity and standardization with not only the British army but those of the rest of the Empire and Commonwealth. Given the social and political climate of the time, this was understandable and not a bad thing.

Within the defence establishment there were some, however, who recognized the merit in discussing the very doctrine that Canadians would be using in the next war. Many historians have noted in particular the debate in 1938-1939 in the *Canadian Defence Quarterly* between two regular officers, Lieutenant Colonel E.L.M. Burns[16] and Captain G.G. Simonds,[17] on the organization and tactics of tanks in support of an infantry division.[18] While the debate demonstrated a healthy understanding of the issues on the part of the two officers, it was more in the nature of applied, rather than basic, research into the form of a future war. In other words, both were talented tinkerers, not innovators, and neither demonstrated any real appreciation of the use of armoured forces in manoeuvre warfare, although Simonds appeared to have grasped the advantages of using tanks *en masse* in exploitation. It is also noteworthy that Burns was an engineer and Simonds a gunner; the cavalry and the infantry, while aware of the emergence of armoured forces, largely stayed out of the debate, and anecdotal evidence suggests that at least one regular regiment discouraged its officers from wasting their time in bookish pursuits.

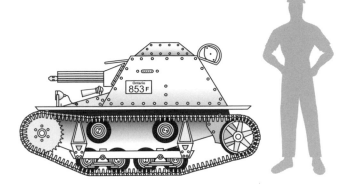

Carden-Loyd Mk VI A machine gun carrier

Entering Canadian service in 1933, the Carden-Loyd was designed to carry the Vickers medium machine gun to a firing position where it was dismounted and remounted on a tripod. The vehicle provided protection to the two-man crew against shell splinters and small-arms fire. It was a cheap and practical design for the period and was useful for training but was replaced in the early years of the Second World War as more modern vehicles became available.

Country of origin: Great Britain
Crew: 2
Length: 8 feet 1 inch
Width: 5 feet 7 inches
Height: 4 feet
Weight: 3.5 tons
Engine: Ford
Maximum speed: 28 mph
Range: Unknown
Armament: .303 inch Vickers MG
Armour – Maximum: 9.5 mm
            Minimum: 6 mm

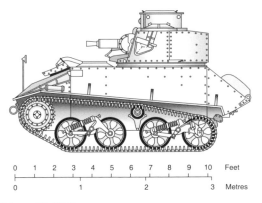

Country of origin: Great Britain
Crew: 3
Length: 12 feet 11 inch
Width: 6 feet 9 inches
Height: 7 feet 3 inches
Weight: 6 tons
Engine: Meadows six cylinder
Maximum speed: 25 mph
Range: 130 miles
Armament: .5 inch Vickers MG in
            turret, .303 inch Vickers MG
            co-axial
Armour – Maximum: 14 mm
            Minimum: 4 mm

Vickers Mk VI B

This robust light tank was developed from the Carden-Loyd series of machine gun carriers after Vickers took control of the Carden-Loyd company in 1928. The Mark VI B was the largest and heaviest of the series and entered production in 1936. First entering Canadian service in small numbers in September 1938, the Mk VI B was used for training the fledgling Canadian Armoured Corps well into the war, until it was replaced by more modern tanks.

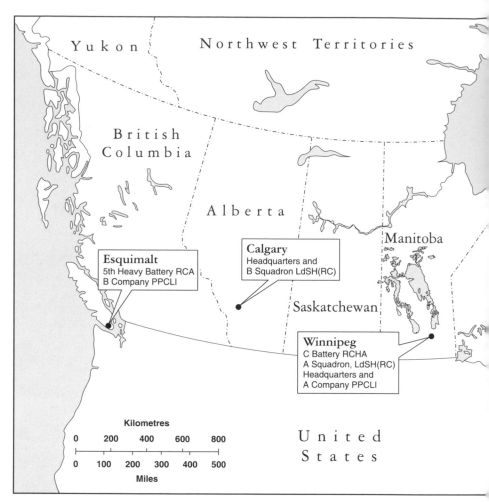

Yukon

Northwest Territories

British
Columbia

Alberta

Manitoba

Esquimalt
5th Heavy Battery RCA
B Company PPCLI

Calgary
Headquarters and
B Squadron LdSH(RC)

Saskatchewan

Winnipeg
C Battery RCHA
A Squadron, LdSH(RC)
Headquarters and
A Company PPCLI

Kilometres

| 0 | 200 | 400 | 600 | 800 |

| 0 | 100 | 200 | 300 | 400 | 500 |

Miles

United
States

No matter how often one does the sums, the stark, cold truth was that the prewar Canadian army was not a real army, no matter how much one watered down the definition. It could hardly be otherwise, given the three perennial limiting factors of population, geography and climate, as well as the general indifference of Canadian governments towards matters military and the personal antipathy of Prime Minister Mackenzie King towards overseas entanglements. The reality was even worse than it appeared on paper. The permanent force was made up of two cavalry regiments; a three battery brigade (regiment) of field artillery; one medium, one anti-aircraft and three coast artillery batteries; a field company of engineers: and three infantry regiments, each of one battalion. None were organized on a war establishment,

14

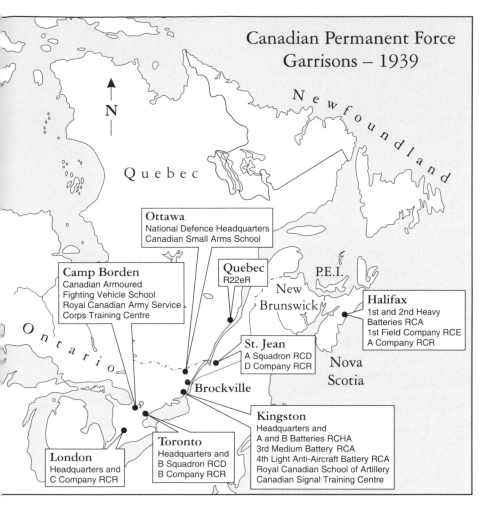

Canadian Permanent Force Garrisons – 1939

N

Ottawa
National Defence Headquarters
Canadian Small Arms School

Camp Borden
Canadian Armoured
Fighting Vehicle School
Royal Canadian Army Service
Corps Training Centre

Quebec
R22eR

Halifax
1st and 2nd Heavy
Batteries RCA
1st Field Company RCE
A Company RCR

St. Jean
A Squadron RCD
D Company RCR

Brockville

London
Headquarters and
C Company RCR

Toronto
Headquarters and
B Squadron RCD
B Company RCR

Kingston
Headquarters and
A and B Batteries RCHA
3rd Medium Battery RCA
4th Light Anti-Aircraft Battery RCA
Royal Canadian School of Artillery
Canadian Signal Training Centre

and even the peace establishments were severely restricted.* In all of Canada, there were four squadrons of cavalry (two in each of the regular regiments), eight artillery batteries, a field company of two sections of engineers, and seven infantry companies (four in the Royal Canadian Regiment (RCR), two in the Princess Patricia's Canadian Light Infantry (PPCLI) and one in the Royal 22e Regiment (R22eR)). To make matters even worse, many of the sub-units were separated from their parent headquarters by more than a day's travel by train, and travel by air was almost non-existent. For example, one of the PPCLI companies was stationed with the regimental headquarters

---

* According to the RCHA history, a PF field battery had a strength of about 70 all ranks as opposed to a war establishment of 160.

in Winnipeg, while the other was 1,500 miles to the west at Esquimalt on Vancouver Island, and the other Western-based regiment, Lord Strathcona's Horse (Royal Canadians), was split between Calgary and Winnipeg. In fact Winnipeg was the only garrison in the country that could boast representation from regular cavalry, artillery and infantry: A Squadron of the Strathconas; C Battery RCHA; and Headquarters and A Company of the PPCLI. The four RCR companies were stationed in London and Toronto, St. Jean in Quebec and Halifax, while in the case of the Royal 22e Regiment, according to the *Defence Forces List* of August 1938, only the commanding officer, Lieutenant Colonel P. Flynn, the adjutant, Lieutenant J.P.E. Bernatchez, Captains J.P.E. Poirier and A.A. Larue and Lieutenants F. Trudeau and D. Menard were serving with the regiment in Quebec City.[19] In early 1939 the three regular infantry regiments boasted a grand total of eight captains and 19 lieutenants under the age of 40. An army this tiny was hard-pressed to develop a solid cadre of potential commanders and staff officers for the next war, whenever that might occur. It is to the credit of the permanent force that, despite the handicaps, it produced officers who took their professional responsibilities very seriously and proved able to meet the test of war.

While many regular officers, especially those who had completed staff college, had a theoretical grounding in their profession, this was not matched by the practical knowledge that could only be gained by all-arms field training at the brigade or higher level. This had been driven home vividly in 1938, when the regulars based in eastern Canada concentrated in Camp Borden for a month to train as a "skeleton infantry brigade" for three weeks, and then, augmented by two Toronto militia regiments, the Royal Regiment of Canada and the Toronto Scottish, to exercise as an all-arms force for the last four days. Not surprisingly, the exercise, which was the first training concentration for the regulars since 1929, was a disaster. Simply put, the regular army, which was responsible for training the militia in the science of war, did not have a clue.[20]

And above all else, the existence of the militia with its ill-equipped and under-manned battalions and regiments, but little of substantive worth in terms of brigades and divisions, clouded the issue as the mobilization plan ignored the militia command structure in order to provide representation from across the country in each stage of any future expeditionary force. The militia, the backbone of Canada's defence structure, besides being chronically ill-trained and poorly equipped, was at about half of its established strength; in the last years of peace when it was clear that war was coming, the number of officers and men who attended the annual camps provided an indication of its condition. A few examples will suffice: the Governor General's Foot Guards, 200 all ranks in 1937; the Royal Regiment of Canada, 34 officers and 266 men in 1939; the Royal Hamilton Light Infantry, 27 officers and 139 men in 1937; the Lincoln and Welland Regiment, 37 officers and 196 men in the same year; and the Algonquin Regiment, 250 officers and men in 1939, while the war establishment for an infantry battalion in 1939 was 21 officers and 641 men.[21] Even local training was constrained under these conditions, and with most men in the country working a five and a half day week, it was only possible to carry out field training on Sunday. In 1936 this led to the public admonishment of the Royal Hamilton Light Infantry by Archdeacon W.F. Wallace for conducting exercises on the Sabbath, and another cleric wholeheartedly supported his stand in the pages of a local newspaper.[22]

Furthermore, in the years between the wars these camps hardly provided a training environment suitable for the development of battlefield commanders. During one camp in the Cypress Hills of southwestern Saskatchewan, Captain Harry W. Foster[23] of Lord Strathcona's Horse spent two weeks drilling a newly amalgamated mounted regiment in cavalry tactics – squadron drill at the gallop, charges and the like – after, that is, he had tamed the mustangs rounded up to provide mounts for the regiment, and this while the Germans were experimenting with the organization and tactics of the first panzer divisions.[24]

Despite its major shortcomings, the army entered the Second World War in a relatively coherent and ordered manner as, unlike the First World War when the Minister of Militia and Defence scrapped the mobilization plan more or less on a whim, the existing defence scheme was used as the basis for the expansion. While it was ostensibly designed for the defence of Canada in the event of war, the army staff had carefully crafted the plan to provide an expeditionary force, and in fact the plan, Defence Scheme Three,* had been approved by the defence minister in January 1932 as part of a real-

---

* Defence Scheme Two was a plan to protect Canadian neutrality in the event of a war between Japan and the United States.

istic appreciation of Canada's potential to support a field force in a European war. Thus the 11 infantry and four cavalry divisions that formed the basis for Sutherland Brown's Defence Scheme One were replaced by an expeditionary force of a corps headquarters and one cavalry and two infantry divisions, along with corps, army and line of communication units. The plan also referred to the mobilization of a further four infantry divisions and ancillary troops.

While the restructuring of the militia to align it with Defence Scheme Three did not take place until 1936, the plan had provoked howls of outrage from the now-retired Sutherland Brown about the horrors of an "artillery-oriented army" and the "intrigue of the Artillery Association,"[25] although it seems that he was more concerned over the abandonment of his Defence Scheme One and its 15 divisions than any perceived empire building by the gunners. While the number of artillery, engineer and service units was increased to fit the requirements of a seven-division army, primarily by disbanding, consolidating or redesignating surplus infantry and cavalry regiments, the reorganization included the addition of six tank battalions (which were infantry units) to the order of battle.

In 1937 the plan was revised to provide greater emphasis on home defence in light of the government's reluctance to consider any overseas commitment, while retitling the expeditionary force the "Mobile Force." This force was further subdivided into Forces A and B, each of an infantry division and a portion of the corps, army and line of communication troops. While both would be mobilized simultaneously, Force B would not be concentrated until Force A was sent overseas or committed to operations in Canada. (In the spring of 1939 the cavalry division was dropped from the mobile force.) When it became clear during the summer that war was imminent, additional funds were allotted to the defence budget and troops were called out to guard vital points across Canada. On 1 September the German invasion of Poland prompted the cabinet that same morning to authorize "the organization forthwith of a Canadian Active Service Force" and at noon army headquarters telegraphed the military districts "Reference Defence Scheme Number Three Mobilize Entire Mobile Force."[26]

Canadian militia on parade
This photo shows the Essex Scottish regiment of Windsor, Ontario, on parade at
some time during the 1930s. Note the First World War uniforms. The officer on the
right of the picture is Lieutenant Douglas Aitchison, who in civilian life worked as a
transmission designer for Ford. (Courtesy Colonel (retd) W.J. Aitchison)

CHAPTER TWO

CANADA GOES TO WAR

"G.S. 201 Reference Defence Scheme Number Three.
War has broken out with Germany."

CHIEF OF THE GENERAL STAFF TO DISTRICT OFFICERS

COMMANDING, ALL MILITARY DISTRICTS,

10 SEPTEMBER 1939.

The German invasion of Poland on 1 September 1939 found the Canadian army woefully unprepared for war. Two decades of government neglect had left the tiny permanent force dysfunctional, while the militia was a collection of poorly trained and ill-equipped cadres. The story of the shortages in material, equipment and supplies has been told many times, in the words of Colonel, Temporary Brigadier, H.D.G. Crerar, the Commandant of the Royal Military College, the militia "possessed neither armoured fighting vehicles, supplies of modern transport of approved design, nor modern weapons."[1]

The Royal Regiment of Canada from Toronto provides an example of the situation in those early days. Although the regiment reached its war establishment in personnel on 19 September, the situation was far different in clothing, weapons and equipment. There were practically no uniforms, either of the prewar pattern or the new battle dress, and there was an acute shortage of boots. Most of the men had only thin civilian shoes that could not bear the strain of foot drill and route marches. What kit was available usually came in dribs and drabs: 20 wedge caps might arrive one week and some sweaters or fatigue trousers the next. On one glorious day the regiment received 60 service uniforms, but as the tunics had been manufactured in Montreal and the trousers in Toronto, the shades of khaki did not match. Nevertheless training was conducted, even if a considerable amount of ingenuity was often required. The only weapons available were rifles and obsolete Lewis guns, and even these were in short supply. By December the unit was able to began range practices and to stage a tactical scheme in High Park, although the only means of passing orders was by bugle calls, "a means of communications which proved no more successful in 1939 than it had at the Battle of Ridgeway in 1866." That same month the regiment was able to obtain the loan of a 3-inch mortar and three Bren guns for a few days; if the troops were unable to train on them, at least they could gaze with awe at the hallowed weapons. In February 1940 the Royal Regiment of Canada received its first vehicle, a 15-cwt truck, which allowed driver training to commence. And so went the mobilization; slowly and perhaps not very steadily Canada began to develop a war machine after years of indifference and neglect.[2]

What was less often discussed was the simple truth that Canada's greatest deficiency in 1939 was capable senior officers, and this sad state of affairs persisted throughout most of the Second World War. German *General der Panzertruppen* Heinrich Eberbach, who commanded in turn *Panzergruppe West*, 5. *Panzerarmee* and finally *Panzergruppe* Eberbach in Normandy, opined in captivity that the Canadian "peace-time army probably was too weak for the training of a sufficient number of higher commanders and their assistants without the support of a strong military power."[3] Certainly the standard of Canadian generalship, which included a Boer War veteran commanding the 2nd Division, during the build-up of forces in the United Kingdom left something to be desired.[4]

In one area at least the army was in better shape than in 1914; that was in the pool of officers who had completed the staff college course conducted by the British army at Camberley in England and Quetta in India (now Pakistan). It has been argued that the most difficult part of staff college was getting there in the first place[5] as selection was by means of a set of comprehensive examinations, with the successful candidates nominated for the course based on their order of standing. Headquarters was meticulous in ensuring that this principle was maintained as it was realized that any attempt to bypass officers who stood higher on the list in order to apply other criteria would have provoked a wave of outrage for perceived favouritism.[6] This emphasis on the entrance exams as a selection tool, a British requirement by the way, has been ignored by critics of the process, including Sutherland Brown,

who accused the army leadership of favouring officers from the more technical arms such as the artillery and engineers to the detriment of the cavalry
and infantry.* (One historian has debunked this theory by suggesting the
only way the Chief of the General Staff could have increased the number
of cavalry and infantry officers attending staff college would have been by
writing their entrance examinations for them.[7]) Thus, as the theory went,
the army found itself without qualified tacticians to command the divisions
and brigades mobilized in 1939. Attractive as the theory is, and many very
intelligent people have embraced it wholeheartedly, to point the finger of
blame at the method used to select officers to attend staff college for the lack
of competent battlefield commanders is, in a word, nonsense.[8]

While 62 Canadian officers had completed the British army staff college
course in the interwar period, which was a marked improvement over the
12 staff-trained officers in the permanent force in 1914, in fact there were no
more than 36 staff college graduates available to fill the required appointments. This number proved to be a tiny part of the total requirement for staff
officers to man the myriad of field and static headquarters required to command and control a large, modern army.[9] Furthermore, the mobilization
plan included the appointment of commanders drawn from both the permanent force and the militia who had proven themselves in the First World
War, in line with both existing defence policy and the expectations of the
government, the people and the army alike.[10] No amount of fiddling with appointments to staff college was going to change that! One must also remember that with promotion based largely on seniority, in peacetime even the
most brilliant staff college graduate would have to wait years before he was
in a position to command even one of the truncated companies, squadrons
or batteries of the permanent force. Given the prevailing political, financial
and military climate in interwar Canada, even if the senior leadership of the
army somehow had experienced an overnight conversion in their attitude
and thinking, there was little they could have done to groom the next generation of senior commanders, and no less a personage that Major General

---

* According to the table on page 274 of John Macdonald's MA thesis, "In Search of Veritable:
Training the Canadian Staff Officer, 1899 to 1945," 28 officers trained at the British staff colleges
in the period 1930-1939. The breakdown by corps was cavalry two, artillery seven, engineers
three, signals ten, infantry five and service corps one. With the exception of the signals officers,
the proportion for the corps was not out of line with their number of officers.

A.G.L. McNaughton,[11] the dominant personality in the Canadian army in the years between the wars, seemed to deny the existence of a profession of arms that required concentrated, career-long education and study on the part of its members. Instead McNaughton believed that

> the art of military command could be developed just as easily in civilian life as in a professional army, and that given a quick and basic military education after mobilization, successful businessmen would "prove very adaptable to military life in war" and probably become good senior officers.[12]

Events would prove him terribly wrong, but the damage was done. As for the permanent force and the militia, it was unfortunate that in the 20 years that had passed since Canadians had last fired shots in anger, the generation that had ably led the CEF in battle had for the most part atrophied, while the next generation had been forced to learn their craft largely in theory and without practical experience to develop the professional background found in larger armies. It was like trying to field a championship ice hockey team made up of "old timers" and tyros who had learned to play the sport by correspondence course.

The mobilization ordered on 1 September 1939 envisaged the creation of one division immediately, while the units of the second division* would be recruited more slowly and would not be concentrated until the first division had moved to confront an enemy invasion or proceeded overseas. Virtually overnight the Canadian Active Service Force (CASF) would be brought into being and a host of new units created; even if every officer and man in the permanent force were to be embodied in it, which was by no means the case, the first division alone was two and one half times the size of the regular component, and that did not cater for the requirement to man the ancillary units, the second division, the defences on both coasts and the training and reception centres required to handle the influx of manpower. In fact, even if every unit in the militia had been drained of its medically-fit manpower,

---

* What may not be apparent to the non-Canadian reader is that there would not be sufficient time to construct heated, covered accommodation for the mobilized troops before the onset of winter; thus they could not concentrate as a formation or even conduct other than very limited training outdoors.

which was clearly impractical, there still would have been a considerable shortfall to be made up off the street. And that was only the start!

Although none could have foreseen it at the time, the situation developed in marked contrast to the First World War, when the CEF was in action early and grew progressively from one division to a two-division corps, which added a third and then a fourth division. At each stage except the first, the army was able to draw upon officers who had proven their abilities in battle, so that by the summer of 1917 the Canadian Corps was a meritocracy commanded at all levels by men of proven ability and courage. There was another factor; in the First World War the 1st Division and then the Canadian Corps were commanded by British officers until Canadian officers had gained enough experience to take on the responsibilities of high command in battle. Furthermore, throughout the war the Canadian Corps was fortunate in that it had a cadre of excellent British staff officers, two of whom, Lieutenant Colonels Edmund Ironside and Alan Brooke, rose to become the Chief of the Imperial General Staff, the professional head of the British army.

The wartime Canadian army expanded rapidly to an extent that has not been fully appreciated by either its fans or its critics. While the British army increased roughly 15 times from its 1939 strength and the United States Army (including the Army Air Forces) by 44 times (although to only six times of its pre–Pearl Harbor level because of a partial mobilization in 1940-1941), by 1944 the Canadian army had exploded to 119 times the number on full-time service in 1939.[13] Not surprisingly the experience level plummeted, although this was true in all wartime armies; what was surprising, and this is not meant facetiously, was just how good the Canadian army became despite all the handicaps it faced.

To compound matters, the bulk of the army overseas spent much of the war stagnating on guard duty in the British Isles, while other armies fought in the Middle Eastern theatre. The consequences were twofold: first, without the experience of battle to act as a filter, too much of what was practised stood the danger of being inappropriate or at least not properly appreciated; and potential commanders could not be tested in battle. It took the intervention of Major General H.D.G. Crerar,[14] who had assumed acting command of the Canadian Corps while McNaughton was on sick leave in Canada, to address the situation when he asked Lieutenant General B.L. Montgomery

Lieutenant General H.D.G. Crerar, CB, DSO
Harry Crerar served as the senior Canadian officer overseas during the last two years of the war. He had commanded I Canadian Corps in Italy and took over First Canadian Army for the Normandy command. In the months after the D-Day landings, his army included Guy Simonds's II Canadian Corps, I British Corps and the 1st Polish Armoured Division. (Painting by T.R. MacDonald/ Canadian War Museum 13151)

to assess the Canadian officer corps down to the unit level in early 1942.[15] Monty's comments were, as one would expect, brutally frank and led to a wholesale housecleaning of the old, the ill and the addled, most of whom, it must be emphasized, had done well in the First World War.

While necessary and perhaps long overdue, this resulted in further turmoil and accelerated the rapid progression of a number of officers through the system to fill the key appointments in army, corps and division headquarters. The same Captain Guy Simonds who had debated the employment of tanks in the pages of the *Canadian Defence Quarterly* went overseas in 1939 as a major on the operations staff of the 1st Canadian Division. In July 1940 he was promoted lieutenant colonel and appointed commanding officer of the 1st Field Regiment, RCHA; a few months later he was handpicked by McNaughton to organize and run the first Canadian war staff course. This was followed by his appointment as the GSO 1 of the 2nd Canadian Division from May to August 1941. In August Simonds was promoted to brigadier and appointed chief of staff of the Canadian Corps, a post he held for nearly a year until he became the commander of 1 Canadian Infantry Brigade for a few months, followed by a posting as chief of staff at Headquarters First Canadian Army. In April 1943 he was promoted major general to command 2nd Canadian Division, a position he held for only a few weeks before he moved sideways to take over 1st Canadian Division for the invasion of Sicily following the death of its commander in a plane crash. Simonds then led his division in Sicily and Italy, until he was appointed to command 5th Canadian Armoured Division on 1

November 1943. On 30 January 1944 he was promoted to the rank of lieutenant general and returned to England to command 2nd Canadian Corps. Thus in 41 months of war, from September 1939 to January 1944, Simonds was promoted five times and held 11 different command or staff appointments, with time out for an attachment to the Eighth Army in North Africa in early 1943. While Simonds's rapid upward progress was exceptional, and he enjoyed the patronage of both Montgomery and McNaughton, the "musical chairs" nature of his appointments was not unique.

Guy Simonds was a brilliant man with a compulsion to succeed in anything he set his hand to. At the same time he was somewhat introverted and withdrawn and had learned to keep his fiery temper under control. As a result he gave the impression of coldness and lacked the human touch of any number of British and American (and even a few Canadian) senior commanders. Simonds had patterned himself on Montgomery and firmly believed his role as a commander included making his own plans, or at the very least, giving firm, detailed direction to the staff. When faced with a tactical dilemma, for example, he retired to his caravan and chain-smoked until he had worked out the details himself. Like Montgomery, he brought a number of commanders and senior staff officers back from Italy to fill positions in 2nd Canadian Corps; most notably he cleaned house in the upper echelons of 4th Canadian Armoured Division, replacing the divisional commander and the command-

Lieutenant General G.G. Simonds
Guy Simonds led the 1st Canadian Division in Sicily and Italy and subsequently commanded II Canadian Corps in Northwest Europe. He was, in the view of British and American officers, the best of the Canadian generals. In 1951, he became Chief of the General Staff (Painting by C.F. Comfort/Canadian War Museum 12384)

ers of the divisional artillery and both 4 Armoured and 10 Infantry Brigades, a move he later may have had cause to regret. Simonds was right far more often than he was wrong and a strong case can be made that he was the best corps commander in 21st Army Group, and among the best of the war. Certainly, like Sir Arthur Currie in the First World War, he was able to concentrate on the task at hand to such an extent that he would seize upon an unorthodox but workable solution to a seemingly insurmountable challenge, as he would demonstrate in the series of operations he mounted south of Caen.

Turning to the too frequent changes in senior officers, the 2nd Canadian Division,* for example, had six different commanders from when it was organized in April 1940 until it went into action in July 1944, and it then experienced a further change of command in November.[16] A number of battalions and regiments had officers appointed as their commanding officer for a few months for "ticket-punching purposes," that is, to gain command experience before moving onwards and upwards, while the average length of command of the nine brigade commanders in 2nd Canadian Corps in the spring of 1944 before they led their formations into action was seven months, although this was skewed as Brigadier Kenneth G. Blackader, the commander of 8 Infantry Brigade, had held his appointment for 29 months. The average for the other eight brigadiers was slightly over four months.[17] Of the nine, Blackader and Young of 6 Brigade were Great War veterans, as was Lett of 4 Brigade, who had been wounded at Dieppe (and on 25 July would be wounded again in Normandy), Wyman of 2 Armoured Brigade had commanded an armoured brigade in Sicily and Italy, Booth of 4 Armoured Brigade and Jefferson of 10 Brigade had led an armoured regiment and an infantry battalion respectively in that same theatre, while Foster of 7 Brigade had commanded 13 Brigade in the unopposed invasion of Kiska in the Aleutians, and Cunningham of 9 Brigade had been the brigade major of 4 Brigade at Dieppe; thus eight of the nine – Megill of 5 Brigade being the odd man out – had at least a taste of operational experience. But it was not enough.

Other than the militia officers, professionals such as doctors, lawyers and

---

* In the First World War, the 2nd Division had a total of three commanders in its four years of existence. Furthermore, the four Canadian divisions that made up the Canadian Corps on the Western Front had a total of ten commanders, compared to the 28 officers who commanded the five divisions that served outside Canada in the Second World War.

chaplains, the Canadian Officer Training Contingents found at Canadian universities and the fewer than 300 gentlemen cadets commissioned from the Royal Military College of Canada between October 1939 and July 1942,[18] there was no obvious "officer class" in Canadian society, and any potential officers would have to be found within the overall manpower pool. The Minister of National Defence admitted that no coherent system had existed during the first year of the war in the House of Commons on 15 November 1940 when he acknowledged that the standard of officers "varied considerably, depending on different units and formations." He added that a number of steps were being taken to improve the standard of officer qualification and that "for the future every candidate for a commission in the Canadian Army must first pass through the ranks," and that "the system was based on a study of the experiences of the last war and on the present practice in the British Army."[19] In fact, of the 43,244 individuals granted commissions in the Canadian army in the Second World War, less than half – 20,723 – rose from the ranks.[20]

Whatever their source, all non-specialist officers progressed through essentially the same training system and were required to qualify for their rank through a process of formal military education and training. While the system produced the desired numbers, the quality of the graduates has been questioned, although it seems that the root of the complaint was the officer who, for a period of time, commanded the Brockville Officer Training Centre and apparently gave more importance to mess etiquette – mastery of table manners for example – than to performance in the field. As the commandant considered how candidates ate their peas at mess dinners a matter of overriding importance in determining if they were officer material, candidates invariably left their peas untouched.[21] However, there was more than one Officer Training Centre in Canada, and regardless of the blimpish idiosyncrasies of one senior officer, the program called for four weeks spent on common-to-all-arms skills, four weeks on special-to-corps subjects and two weeks devoted to infantry platoon tactics *before* the candidate proceeded to an advanced training centre for qualification as an officer in a corps such as infantry, armour or artillery. Furthermore, after graduation from the advanced training centre, many newly commissioned officers spent a period of time in the reinforcement stream, where they commanded and trained new soldiers, thus gaining confidence and experience in the performance of their duties.[22] The system worked.

Over a period of more than three years the Canadian army in the United Kingdom steadily grew in size. First overseas of course was the 1st Canadian Division, which sailed in two flights from Halifax on 10 and 22 December 1939, followed by a third flight composed mostly of ancillary units which left Canada on 30 January 1940.[23] In the meantime the 2nd Division languished in Canada with recruiting suspended, its headquarters not yet formed and its commanders unnamed, and even elementary training hampered by winter and a lack of accommodation. While Prime Minister Mackenzie King had announced in the House of Commons on 25 January 1940 that a second division would be sent overseas "as soon as may be possible," recruiting for the 2nd Division did not resume until late February, with better weather more or less around the corner. Under the impetus of the German victories in the west, the formation moved overseas in the early summer of 1940, although it was not complete in England until December 1940, as some of its units had been sent to Iceland.[24]

On 17 May 1940 the Cabinet War Committee authorized the formation of the corps of two infantry divisions envisaged in Defence Scheme Three as well as the raising of a third infantry division for service at home or overseas. With German armour ranging at will across northern France and Belgium, this was followed ten days later by the announcement of the mobilization of the infantry battalions for a fourth division, although it was well into 1941 before the organization of the division was complete, as the mobilization of armoured formations was given a higher priority.[25] What eventually became the Canadian Corps had been formed in England as 7th Corps on 21 July 1940, with the newly-promoted Lieutenant General Andrew McNaughton, who had been commanding the 1st Canadian Division, as its first commander, and his old division, the 1st British Armoured Division and a New Zealand Force of two infantry brigades and some artillery under command. On Christmas Day 1940 the corps was renamed the Canadian Corps with the two Canadian divisions and the British armoured division under command.[26]

As the corps was now larger than the one planned for in Defence Scheme Three, Major General Henry Crerar, the newly-appointed CGS, proposed to the government that the Canadian Corps of three divisions should be completed in the UK by the early spring of 1941, and it should be reinforced by an armoured brigade group as soon as possible thereafter. He added that the 4th Division should be prepared for despatch in the latter part of 1941, and that any further additions to the forces overseas should be armoured rather than infantry formations.[27]

In fact the first steps to form an armoured force had already been taken, as on 13 August Colonel J.L. Ralston, the Minister of National Defence, had approved the institution of the Canadian Armoured Corps and the organization of the 1st Canadian Armoured Brigade at Camp Borden, Ontario. Following prolonged discussions with British authorities by Colonel Ralston and Crerar, the 1941 Army program approved by Cabinet on 28 January 1941 included the formation of an army tank brigade (which was not the same as an armoured brigade) to join the corps in England, and the organization and dispatch overseas of an armoured division, which eventually was titled 5th Canadian Armoured Division, while the movement of the 4th Division to England was now to be delayed until the summer of 1942.[28]

At this stage the government had agreed to the provision of a corps of three infantry divisions, an armoured division and an army tank brigade overseas as well as an infantry division at home. While Crerar was thinking in terms of a field army of four infantry and two armoured divisions, he had yet to raise the matter with Ralston, although he had apprised McNaughton of his intentions. In late July 1941 the Cabinet War Committee had agreed to mobilize the 6th Division for service at home and further to maintain four divisions plus the army tank brigade overseas. That was as far as it was prepared to go at the time.[29]

In September 1941 Crerar underwhelmed the Minister by suggesting an ambitious expansion of the army for 1941 and 1942 that included

(a) Conversion of the 4th Canadian Division to armour for service overseas.

(b) Eventual formation overseas of a Canadian Armoured Corps of two divisions.

(c) Creation of a Canadian Army Headquarters overseas to command and administer the Canadian Corps of three divisions and the Canadian Armoured Corps of two Armoured Divisions.[30]

On 18 November Crerar submitted a formal proposal to Ralston for the remainder of 1941 and for 1942 which omitted the formation of an army headquarters, but included the creation of a large number of corps and army units, the conversion of the 4th Division to armour and the organization of a second army tank brigade, which would "permit the constitution of a Canadian Armoured Corps of two armoured divisions." Following a Christmas Day conversation with General Sir Bernard Paget, the C-in-C Home Forces in England, McNaughton wired Ralston that the British had raised the subject of Canada providing an army headquarters, while on his part he stressed the need for a second corps headquarters. It should be noted that there was a great deal of difference between a "conversation" with a field commander, albeit one who commanded the operational British land forces in the United Kingdom, and a formal request from the British government.

It is true that a personal note from Alan Brooke, the new Chief of the Imperial General Staff, to McNaughton shortly before he departed to Canada on leave had broached the subject of forming a force or army headquarters to take over the running of all the "rear services, workshops, base organizations, etc., and free the Corps Commander's hands for the job of commanding & training the fighting formations," but it hardly was a pressing demand for Canada to provide a complete field army. Still, the matter was now on the table at the ministerial level and it could reasonably become the subject of debate by the War Committee. In the meantime, the committee had been examining the Army Programme for 1942 carefully when the Japanese attacks in the Pacific brought the United States into the war. On 26 January 1942 the Prime Minister announced in the House of Commons that "a Canadian army of two corps would be created overseas in 1942."[31]

First Canadian Army Headquarters came into existence on 11 April 1942 with McNaughton as the commander, while Crerar's acting command of the Canadian Corps, which was renamed 1st Canadian Corps, was made permanent. (He had relinquished the position of CGS and had been posted to the United Kingdom to command the 2nd Division in December, although he was almost immediately made the acting corps commander when McNaughton became ill.) The expansion from one headquarters to three, a major undertaking for an army that had perhaps three dozen staff-trained officers 30 months before, probably had a serious effect on the training of the field formations, as it could only have diluted the efficiency of the staff and tied down a very large number of troops in ancillary roles. However, given that the number of field formations that the government had authorized required two corps headquarters, it probably was an inevitable development for a country still wrestling with the realities of full independence. The activation of a field army proved more difficult than expected as, despite having introduced war staff courses in 1940, there were not enough trained staff officers available to fill the vacancies in both of the new headquarters, and the Headquarters 2nd Canadian Corps was not formed until 14 January 1943.[32]

Given the conflicting national demands on the available manpower, it soon became clear that it would be impossible to man all the army, general headquarters (GHQ) and line of communications units required to support an army in the field, which actually represented a larger number of troops than the fighting formations. On 19 November 1942 McNaughton discussed the matter with Alan Brooke and the Director of Military Operations at the War Office,* along with a suggestion that the possibility of operating as an army could be abandoned in favour of providing "individual formations to specific theatres or to break up divisions if this were the proper and best solution." The CIGS responded that the project to field a Canadian army should continue and that he hoped a second army tank brigade would be sent to the United Kingdom in due course.[33] The result of these discussions was that the British, who were faced with serious manpower shortages themselves, finally agreed to make up the difference between what Canada was prepared to provide and the actual establishment figures for the army, GHQ and lines of communications troops, up to a ceiling of 9,000 men per division, or 45,000 men.

Thus the final form of the Canadian army was a two corps army made up of three infantry and two armoured divisions and two independent armoured brigades. Unfortunately, after all the effort that had gone into the creation of a field army, it was both tragic and ironic that it did not fight as an entity until the last few weeks of the war.

Given all the turmoil generated by the wartime expansion, as well as the requirement to fill the extra positions created by the establishment of an army headquarters and another corps headquarters, it should not sur-

---

* British army headquarters.

prise anyone that the field formations experienced difficulties in preparing for war. While the official historian of the Canadian army opined that the major problem was regimental officers who took too casual an approach to training, the stark truth was that the responsibility for training fell on commanders at all levels, and that did not exclude army, corps and division commanders, and a *laissez faire* approach was not restricted to the Canadian army.[34] Harry W. Foster, who in the 1930s had trained a militia regiment in mounted cavalry tactics and who was now a brigadier and would command one of the assaulting brigades on D-Day and later successfully lead a division in battle, admitted that he and his colleagues were greenhorns without battle experience, ruefully adding that senior officers might get top marks on exercises yet wind up as a disaster in action,[35] while Lieutenant G.D. Adams, of the South Alberta Regiment, captured the sharp end's assessment of the state of affairs with refreshing Western Canadian candor: "We were the greenest bloody army that ever went to war."[36]

Given the shortages of equipment and restrictions on training, especially in the number and size of training areas and in the opportunities to practise

Field Regiment
Canadian Infantry Division

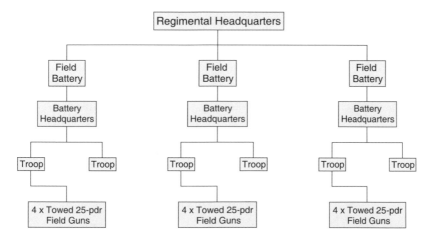

This organization was adopted in the Commonwealth artilleries after the 1940 campaign in France revealed serious shortcomings in the provision of artillery support. Combined with the "Parnham" system of fire control, the artillery was able to literally concentrate the fire of every gun within range on a target when required, although the normal response was the fire of a field regiment.

Armoured Regiment
Canadian Armoured Brigade

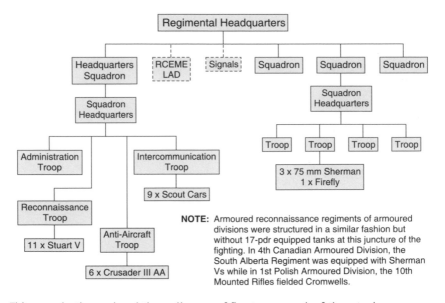

NOTE: Armoured reconnaissance regiments of armoured divisions were structured in a similar fashion but without 17-pdr equipped tanks at this juncture of the fighting. In 4th Canadian Armoured Division, the South Alberta Regiment was equipped with Sherman Vs while in 1st Polish Armoured Division, the 10th Mounted Rifles fielded Cromwells.

This organization replaced the earlier one of five troops, each of three tanks, per squadron. While this was used by British and Canadian regiments, the Poles adopted one of four platoons, each of three troops, per squadron.

cross-country movement in the English countryside, the decision to move partially-trained formations to the United Kingdom to complete their training seems, with the benefit of hindsight, to have been wrong. But that is too simplistic: after Dunkirk there was a definite possibility of the Germans crossing the channel, and the Canadian army had an anti-invasion role, at least up to 1943. Be that as it may, reports on training exercises show that the Canadian divisions in the United Kingdom, despite claims to the contrary made as early as 5 June 1940, were not really combat-ready before late 1941 at the very earliest. A report prepared in September 1941 indicates that after two years of war there still were severe shortages in virtually all types of equipment, as the following examples of holdings versus establishments demonstrate: anti-tank guns, 96 of 198; Bofors light anti-aircraft guns, 20 of 137; Bren light machine guns, 2,241 of 2,961; 2-inch mortars, 234 of 466; Universal Carriers 528 of 770; and infantry tanks, 45 of 192, while the 13 Canadian field artillery regiments in the United Kingdom had only 112 25-pounder guns (along with 92 obsolete weapons in lieu) of the 312 authorized.[37]

What was the state of training of the Canadian army on the eve of the invasion? While space does not permit a detailed examination, and the 3rd Canadian Infantry Division and 2 Canadian Armoured Brigade were transferred to the command of 1st British Corps on 30 January 1944, a short study on this very subject was produced in 1954,[38] while an earlier study dealt with the training of the two Canadian armoured divisions in the United Kingdom.[39] First Canadian Army Training Directive No. 18 dated 15 December 1943 significantly included: "it must be realized by all unit com[man]d[er]s that this will be their last opportunity to make the men of their units fighting fit, and fit to fight." Specifically, as the 4th Division recorded

Individual training was to receive top priority. Collective training was to proceed up to platoon level in January 1944 and to company and battalion levels in February and March, except in the case of 4 Cdn Armd Div, which would "continue with bde and div trg". Both before and after the

Infantry Battalion
Canadian Infantry Brigade

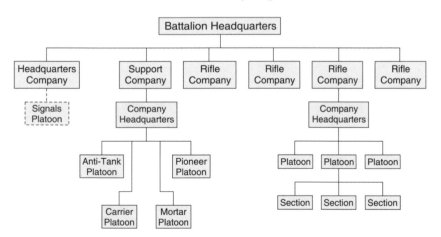

This organization, which came into effect in the spring of 1943, remained in place basically unchanged until the end of the war. At the time of TOTALIZE nearly all the battalions in 21st Army Group were severely under-strength because of a shortage of infantry replacements.

turn of the year, however, in 4 Cdn Armd Div – as well as in First Cdn Army as a whole – the emphasis was on individual training, notably range work, specialist training under unit arrangements, and anti-gas training. Preparations for ceremonial parades, occasioned by a series of visits and inspections, accounted for additional training hours. Sports and recreation also received considerable attention.[40]

A great deal of effort was expended, although one might question whether the best use was made of the limited training time available to the armoured brigade of 4th Canadian Armoured Division by tasking it to participate in tank *cum* infantry training with 2nd Canadian Infantry Division in late April 1944, given later comments about the state of training of the 4th Division in Normandy. Other than that, First Canadian Army focused on studying the breakout from a bridgehead followed by a fighting advance to an objective some 40 miles away in accordance with instructions issued by Headquarters 21st Army Group on 1 March 1944. This later was expanded to include the assault crossing of a tidal estuary and the capture of Le Havre and Rouen. Unfortunately not only had the 4th Division changed its divisional, divisional artillery and brigade commanders on 26 February, but it was not until mid-May 1944 that it was brought up to its operational war establishment. It should also be noted that the division had not had an opportunity to exercise as a complete formation since early November 1943, and certainly not under its new and untried commander.[41] South Alberta Regiment Lieutenant G.D. Adams commented,

> We didn't have the best training... ... Never had any exercise with our infantry. We had no drills, we just decided that we'll attack this village... ... We got no bloody training, we were green as grass and if you survived, you knew how to do things... ... We learned as we went along.[42]

It should be understood that at that time structured operational evaluations prior to committing formations to action were not used in either the British or Canadian armies. Rather, both seemed to rely on intuition as a management tool.

After his retirement, Charles Stacey, who had been famously critical of the unprofessional approach of some commanding officers, commented on the training of the Canadian army that, although it was

> Canadian-controlled, it followed British lines throughout. The Canadian formations were to fight under higher British command alongside British formations; uniformity of training practices was highly desirable. So Canadian training followed the same sequence of stages as British training, culminating in the major exercises staged across England by the British command, in which the Canadian formations played their parts and their senior officers shared with their British counterparts the pain and profit of the comments made by British umpires and directors in the post-exercise conferences.[43]

Furthermore, Stacey noted:

> All the Allied armies committed to the battle had one thing in common: a high proportion of the formations used had never fought before – and those that had fought had operated under conditions very different from those of the North-West Europe theatre. It is probably true, in these circumstances, that all the Allied forces had very similar problems, and the comments upon Canadian formations which follow could doubtless be applied with little change to the British and American forces also.[44]

If his statement in the last sentence is correct, and there is no evidence that Stacey was being other than objective, the Canadian army shared the strengths and weaknesses of its Allies. However, in one area at least, he had muddied the waters; *none* of the Canadian formations had fought before, which was not the case in either the British or the American armies, although in both those armies events would show that experience in itself was not necessarily a guarantee of combat effectiveness. While it could be argued that the professional development of Canadian senior officers may not have been all it should have been, the same charge could be levelled at the British and Americans, although perhaps to a lesser extent.

At the unit level the officers and men – volunteers all – were fit, keen and motivated – and this assessment was held by no less a personage than

Montgomery. On 8 March 1944 Lieutenant General Kenneth Stuart, who was the acting commander of First Canadian Army at the time, wrote Colonel Ralston that he had

> recently completed a five day tour of Canadian troops with General Montgomery in his private train.... General Montgomery met and talked individually with every one of our senior commanders and staff officers. He looked over the men in groups of about 5000... We did as many as five groups in one day and altogether we saw and he spoke to more than a hundred thousand all ranks.
>
> Frankly I have never seen such a splendid body of men in my life and as Montgomery said to me you would not see such a body of men in any other army in the world. Their turn out was excellent but what impressed me most was the very fine type of men we now have throughout the Army... . To see and study the faces of thousands of grand young Canadians as they listened to Montgomery was the most impressive and inspiring sight I have ever witnessed.
>
> Montgomery was tremendously impressed with what he saw. He was most complimentary and he not only told the men what he thought of them but also wrote letters of appreciation to each of our formation commanders.[45]

While Lieutenant Adams of the South Albertas was critical of the state of training of his formation, a veteran of one of the D-Day assault battalions had a different opinion. Norman R. Donogh, who was a lieutenant in the Royal Winnipeg Rifles, found "the unit training in England to be both interesting and vigorous: much field work, mainly at platoon and company level, some competitions between platoons and companies with 7th Bde [sic], some cliff-scaling on the Isle of Wight, and some assault landing training."[46]

If the training proved inadequate, and no amount of training can replace the shock of battle, it was less the fault of the trainers and more because the methodology and practices of the time were unscientific. And that was before one factored in the doctrine and equipment, which were clearly inferior to those of the German army.

CHAPTER THREE

FIRST CANADIAN ARMY
IN THE FIELD

"When we first went into battle at Caen and Falaise we found that
when we bumped into battle-experienced German troops
we were no match for them."

MAJOR GENERAL CHARLES FOULKES, 2ND CANADIAN INFANTRY DIVISION

The assault troops of the 3rd Canadian Infantry Division and 2 Canadian Armoured Brigade landed on Juno Beach shortly after dawn on D-Day, 6 June 1944, and after short but bloody battles moved inland. While progress on D-Day was not as great as had been planned, the 3rd Division was the first Allied formation to reach its objectives, although attempts to increase the size of the bridgehead on 7 June were stalled by elements of 12. *SS-Panzerdivision,** which had been belatedly moved forward from its depth position as *Oberkommando der Wehrmacht* (high command of the armed forces) reserve.[1] During the first fortnight of the invasion there were successes and failures on both sides, and by D+14 (14 days after 6 June) the front had stabilized along a line far enough inland to allow the landing of follow-up forces to proceed unimpeded, but without the capture of the key objectives in the area of Caen and Carpiquet. It is also worth emphasizing that while there had been examples of Canadian tactical bungling, including the disastrous attempt to seize the hamlet of Le Mesnil-

---

* The division was formed in 1943 from a cadre of experienced officers and NCOs from 1. *SS-Panzerdivision Leibstandarte Adolf Hitler* and 17- and 18-year-old products of the *Hitler Jugend* (Hitler Youth, a program of political indoctrination and military training that had replaced the Boy Scouts) commanded by officers and NCOs who had been brutalized on the Eastern Front. The mixture produced a lethal combination of fanaticism and brutality rare even in other *Waffen SS* units and rarer still in the German army.

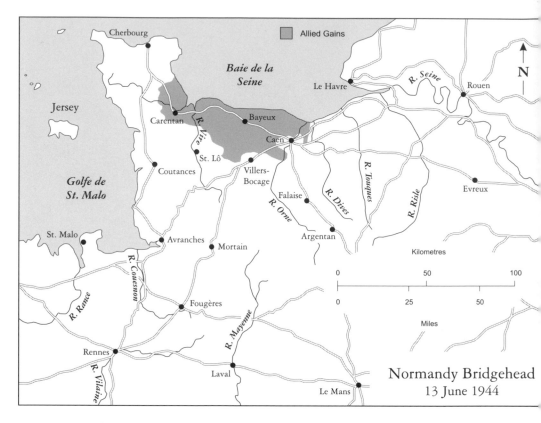

Baie de la Seine

Allied Gains

Cherbourg

Le Havre

R. Seine

Rouen

N

Jersey

Carentan

R. Vire

Bayeux

Caen

St. Lô

Coutances

Villers-Bocage

Falaise

R. Orne

R. Dives

R. Touques

R. Risle

Evreux

Golfe de St. Malo

St. Malo

Avranches

Mortain

Argentan

Kilometres

0   50   100

0   25   50

Miles

R. Couesnon

R. Rance

Fougères

R. Mayenne

Rennes

Laval

Le Mans

R. Vilaine

Normandy Bridgehead
13 June 1944

Patry, German performance was by no means flawless, and while the Germans had stopped the Allied advance on Caen, they also had failed in their most critical task of the war, as defined in a 12. *SS-Panzerdivision* operation order of 7 June, "to attack the landed enemy and throw him back into the sea."[2] These early encounters, especially the murder of Canadian prisoners on a number of separate occasions in the first two weeks after D-Day, set the tone, and throughout the Normandy campaign the Canadians and the SS panzer division waged a semi-private "ask no quarter, give no quarter" war with a ferocity that was rarely equalled in the west.[3]

For a variety of "big picture" reasons, the line was to remain more or less static for the remainder of June 1944, much to the chagrin of the senior British air force commanders, who had counted on the availability of the open terrain about Caen for use as airfields. Other than that, Montgomery's overall strategy for the development of the battle in Normandy was unfolding in line with the broad outline of his original concept, and the Germans had

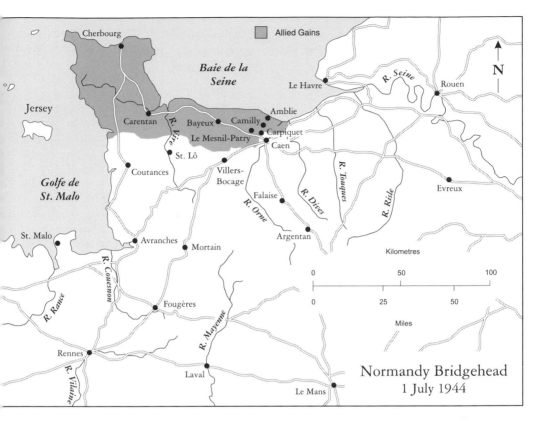

Normandy Bridgehead
1 July 1944

obligingly danced to his tune so that by the end of June they had deployed
seven and a half of the eight panzer divisions in Normandy as well as about
half of their other divisions against the Second British Army,[4] thus allowing the First United States Army to make relatively steady, if costly, progress
through the difficult *bocage* country. Not surprisingly, this lack of gains by
the British and Canadians was criticized by many, including senior British
members of the staff of General Dwight D. Eisenhower, the Supreme Allied
Commander, and the media.[5] Montgomery, a truly great general but not one
apt to be seized by attacks of humility, felt it unnecessary to explain himself
to lesser beings, and as a result his actions have been criticized ever since.

While Lieutenant General H.D.G. Crerar had landed in France on 18 June
and set up his small First Canadian Army tactical headquarters at Amblie,
the congestion caused by the failure to expand the British bridgehead as
well as the delays resulting from the great storm of 19 June prevented his
headquarters from becoming operational for several more weeks. On 24

Senior commanders
Displaying the disregard for conformity of dress typical of senior British and Canadian officers of the time are, left to right, Lieutenant General Miles Dempsey, Second British Army, General Bernard Montgomery, 21st Army Group, Lieutenant General Guy Simonds, II Canadian Corps, and an unidentified British general officer. (NAC/PA 142101)

June Crerar learned from Montgomery that the move of both the Guards Armoured and the 4th Canadian Armoured Divisions to France would be delayed in favour of the deployment of 12th British Corps and the 53rd and 59th Infantry Divisions followed by the 2nd Canadian Infantry Division and the headquarters and corps troops of the 2nd Canadian Corps. The army group commander also told Crerar that he had informed Lieutenant General Miles Dempsey, commander of Second British Army, to place the 3rd Canadian Infantry Division under the 2nd Canadian Corps as soon as the latter could take over operational responsibility, thus getting the two Canadian infantry divisions under Canadian command.[6]

This was easier said than done. Lieutenant General Guy Simonds, the commander of 2nd Canadian Corps, had opened his tactical headquarters at Amblie on 29 June and his main headquarters at Camilly a week later, although the corps had yet to be given an operational role, while the leading units of 2nd Canadian Infantry Division disembarked on 7 July.[7] In the meantime the 3rd Canadian Infantry Division and 2 Canadian Armoured Brigade had taken part in two major operations, WINDSOR and CHARNWOOD, as part of the liberation of Caen. The first was the attack on the village of Carpiquet and its adjacent airport on 4 July 1944 by 8 Canadian Infantry Brigade reinforced by the Royal Winnipeg Rifles from 7 Brigade and the Fort Garry Horse from 2 Canadian Armoured Brigade as well as a squadron each of Crabs, Crocodiles and AVREs from 79th British Armoured Division. Unfortunately WINDSOR, the first set-piece attack mounted by the 3rd Division, was barely successful, as the Germans remained in possession of the airport itself, and thus forced the withdrawal of the British 43rd Infantry Division from positions it had just captured south of the airfield. What probably should have been a two-brigade attack controlled by the divisional headquarters was executed as an attack by one brigade on the village itself with the attached Royal Winnipeg Rifles directed across open fields on a cluster of hangars on the southwest end of the airfield. For whatever the reason, the main attack received the bulk of the artillery, air and naval gunfire support, while the Winnipeg battalion had to make do with whatever crumbs were left over. Despite this, and despite

Commuting to work, Juno Beach, 6 June 1944
Major General R.F.L. Keller, 3rd Canadian Infantry Division, with a duffel coat over his arm, is accompanied by Brigadier R.A. Wyman, 2 Canadian Armoured Brigade, who is wearing a steel helmet and carrying a briefcase, shortly after landing in Normandy. (NAC/PA 115534)

being subjected to heavy fire from two sides, the Rifles assault companies actually fought their way into the hangars and were clearing them when they were ordered to withdraw, and this happened not once, but *twice*, during what was a long, bloody day. The main attack managed to capture the village itself as well as a group of hangars on the north end of the airport, but without the rest of the airfield in Canadian hands, this result was a dangerous salient which was repeatedly attacked over the next few days.[8] Unfortunately the lack of positive results raised serious doubts in the minds of his British superiors about the fitness of the divisional commander, Major General R.F. L. Keller,[9] for command of his formation.

While WINDSOR was being mounted, the preparations for CHARNWOOD, a three-division attack to capture Caen, were already underway; this may be why Keller had delegated so much of the planning and execution of the former operation to Brigadier K.G. Blackader,[10] the commander of 8 Canadian Infantry Brigade. The operation order for CHARNWOOD, which was issued on 5 July, envisaged three divisions advancing on the city – 3rd Canadian Division on the right, the newly-arrived 59th Infantry Division in the centre and the 3rd British Division on the left, supported by the artillery of both 1st and 8th British Corps and naval gunfire from the battleship *Rodney*, the monitor *Roberts* and the cruisers *Belfast* and *Edinburgh*. In addition, for the first time heavy bombers of RAF Bomber Command supported the ground troops by attacking a rectangle some 4,000 yards long by 1,500 wide on the northern outskirts of Caen. While it is a basic military principle that a bombardment should be followed up as quickly as possible by the ground troops, this was not the case in CHARNWOOD. Instead the bombing attack took place between 2150 and 2230 hours on the 7th, while the ground operations began at 0420 the following morning. Unfortunately the area selected for the bombing was largely unoccupied by the Germans, although it caused many civilian casualties and heavy damage in parts of Caen.[11]

Unlike WINDSOR, the Canadian part in CHARNWOOD went reasonably well, although Keller's reading of the battle was not as sure as it should have been. In particular he was critical of Brigadier D.G. (Ben) Cunningham, the commander of 9 Canadian Infantry Brigade, for his lack of drive, even though the brigade had suffered 616 casualties in two days of heavy fighting in the area north of Carpiquet.[12] Be that as it may, the 3rd Canadian Division fought its way into Caen and reached the Orne River, which formed the boundary with the factory suburb of Vaucelles south of the river. Total Canadian casualties for the two days of CHARNWOOD totalled 1,194, of which 330 were fatal, a higher toll than D-Day. On the other side of the ledger, 12. *SS-Panzerdivision* also had suffered heavy casualties and was withdrawn to rest and refit on 11 July.[13]

That same day a new phase of Canada's battle in Normandy began. At 1500 hours Lieutenant General Simonds's 2nd Canadian Corps took over responsibility for about eight thousand yards of the front in the Caen area* with the 2nd and 3rd Canadian Infantry Divisions and 2 Canadian Armoured Brigade under command.[14] Simonds's first task had little to do with fighting the Germans; he was called upon to arbitrate in a dispute over the future of Keller and Cunningham. On the 10th Keller had gone directly to Crerar in an attempt to have Cunningham relieved for his lack of drive on a number of occasions dating back to the D-Day landing, while on that very day Montgomery had passed Crerar letters from himself, Crocker and Dempsey recommending that Keller be sacked. Throughout his career the commander of the 3rd Division had enjoyed a reputation as a tough "soldier's soldier"[15] (one of his nicknames was "Captain Blood," which apparently predated the swashbuckling pirate in the 1935 Errol Flynn action movie of the same name; another was "Killer Keller") and he was a favourite of Crerar, who had considered him a potential corps commander.** Lieutenant General John Crocker,[16] the GOC of 1st British Corps, his immediate superior at the time, damned Keller as "not standing up to the strain" and showing "signs of fatigue and nervousness (one might almost say fright) which were patent for all to see." Dempsey agreed, stating "[Keller was] not fitted to command a Division" while Montgomery wrote that "Keller has not proved himself quite fit to com[man]d a Div[ision]; he is unable to get the best out of his sol-

---

* It would remain under command of Second British Army until 31 July.

** This appreciation of his abilities was not shared by Lieutenant General K.L. Stuart, the Chief of the General Staff, who advised Colonel J.L. Ralston, the Minister of National Defence, that Keller was "pompous, inconsiderate of others. Anything but brilliant and much over-rated. Consider that he has not the ability to command a brigade in the field, let alone a division."

Fit to command?
Major General R.F.L. Keller, left, in conversation with Lieutenant General J.T. Crocker, 1st British Corps. Shortly after the invasion the latter concluded that Keller was unfit to command a division, but Crerar, supported by Simonds, allowed him to retain his post. (NAC/PA 129170)

diers – who are grand chaps." In fact, when Simonds confronted Keller with the adverse comments on his performance prepared by Crocker, Dempsey and Montgomery, he was quite taken aback when Keller responded that "he did not feel that his health was good enough to stand the heavy strain and asked that he be medically boarded as he felt he would be found to be unfit." While he declined to recommend Keller's relief and Crerar concurred in this decision (neither general had first-hand knowledge of the circumstances), Simonds had based his decision on the effect on the division's morale rather than any concern for Keller's career and reputation.[17]

In the meantime, the Germans had succeeded in stabilizing their front south of Caen, at least to a certain extent; as we have seen the Hitler Youth division had been withdrawn to rest and refit, while the *Panzerlehr Division* moved to the west and came into action against the First United States Army. Clearly, this was a setback for Montgomery's strategy and any further transfer of panzer divisions must be prevented.[18] This set the stage for the corps' first offensive operation, ATLANTIC, and the parallel operation, GOODWOOD, carried out by 8th British Corps with three armoured divisions under command. While the intention of the operation was limited, and certainly did not signal a change in his campaign strategy,[19] Montgomery unfortunately had raised the expectations of Eisenhower and his senior staff that the stalemate on the east half of the bridgehead would be broken and his armour launched down the highway towards Falaise.

Operation ATLANTIC, unlike its better known partner, GOODWOOD, achieved most of its objectives and carved out a foothold south and west of Caen along the Bourguébus Ridge. Moreover, much of this success was gained by the inexperienced 2nd Division, which was fighting its first battle since Dieppe, while the 3rd Division, which was tired and in serious need of a rest, crossed the Orne and cleared the suburbs of Vaucelles and Cormelles. In the later days of the operation as the 2nd Division attempted to expand the bridgehead it had seized south of Caen onto the Verrières Ridge, it was caught off balance by German counter-strokes and forced off the crest of the ridge in some disorder. That much of the responsibility for the reverse lay with two battalion commanders whose units had broken should not obscure the fact that basic battle procedure at the division and brigade level had broken down. ATLANTIC had been costly, especially to the 2nd Division, which had had a "very nasty baptism of fire." In all, the nine infantry battalions of the division suffered 1,149 casualties, including 254 dead.[20] Regrettably two common features of the division's operations in Normandy appeared in these early battles: Major General Charles Foulkes,[21] the dour division commander, blamed his troops for the slow progress on the ground; and he was prone to temporarily shifting battalions between brigades with the results one would expect when unfamiliar units are forced to fight together. Foulkes later attempted to obfuscate the situation by claiming

Welcome to Normandy
Major General R.F.L. Keller (left) welcomes Major General Charles Foulkes, 2nd Canadian Infantry Division, to Normandy. This is one of the rare instances where Foulkes displayed anything other than displeasure or perhaps the effects of chronic acid indigestion. (NAC/ PA 129134)

[w]hen we first went into battle at Caen and Falaise we found that when we bumped into battle-experienced German troops we were no match for them. We would not have been successful had it not been for our air and artillery support. We had had four years of real hard going and it took about two months to get that Division so shaken down that we were a machine that could fight.[22]

If his explanation is to be accepted, then the 2nd Division was ineffective during the Normandy campaign – almost two months – and it only became really effective later during the clearing of the Channel ports and the Scheldt. Foulkes was a rather unimaginative commander and one who tended to act as a postal clerk in merely passing along orders without much amplification. As already noted, he also tended to shift battalions between brigades far too frequently for it not to have been a tactical aberration. In my opinion, while the various components of the division were performing well in a much shorter time than two months, it really only came into its own after Foulkes was promoted and sent to Italy to command the 1st Canadian Corps. The old adage about "a poor workman always blaming his tools" was not out of place here.

First Canadian Army became operational on 23 July 1944 with what can only be termed a very shaky start. "The basic cause was Harry. I fear he thinks he is a great soldier, and he was determined to show it the moment he took over command at 1200 on 23 July. He made his first mistake at 1205 and his second after lunch."[23] These words of Montgomery's in a letter to Alan Brooke have been used to bash Crerar's reputation for nearly 60 years, and there is some truth to the allegation. However on closer examination it is apparent that, as was far too common in Montgomery's dealings with others, he both exaggerated Crerar's sins and conveniently ignored his own role in the matter. A brief review of the events that led to these words is in order. On 21 July Montgomery had issued a directive to his four army commanders, Dempsey of Second British Army, Bradley of First U.S. Army, Patton, whose Third U.S. Army was about to go into action, and Crerar, who at long last was about to assume an operational role for First Canadian Army. After noting that the general situation on the eastern flank of the bridgehead had improved since Operation GOODWOOD/ATLANTIC on 18 July, as the Allies now had a sizeable bridgehead over the Orne south of Caen, he directed that operations in this sector were to be "continued intensively" until the British forces were on the general line of the River Dives from the sea southwards to Bures, and then along the Muance River to St. Sylvain, and then eastwards across country to Evercy and Noyers to Caumont. Montgomery then issued the following instruction to Crerar:

> 9. The immediate task of First Canadian Army will be to advance its left flank eastwards so that Ouistreham will cease to be under close enemy observation and fire, and that use can be made of the port of Caen. To achieve this it will be necessary to push the enemy back to the east side of the R. Dives, and to occupy such positions as will ensure that all territory to the west of the river is dominated by our troops.[24]

While First Canadian Army did not become operational until noon on 23 July, initially with only 1st British Corps under Crerar's command, on 22 July Crerar had sent the corps commander, Lieutenant General J.T. Crocker, a letter of instruction based on the directive he had received from Montgomery. This letter included the following direction

> 3. The immediate task of First Cdn Army ... is to advance its left flank Eastwards so that Ouistreham will cease to be under close enemy observation and fire, and so that use can be made of the Port of Caen. This operation will be carried out by 1 Corps... ...
>
> 5. A firm hold on the high ground within the triangle Bures–Troarn–Trouffreville is a preliminary essential to any operations further North or NE. If Troarn itself can be seized without undue casualties, this should be done. In any event, it is essential to obtain and retain domination of the immediate approaches to Troarn and to deny their general use to the enemy.[25]

On the morning of 24 July Crerar and his Chief of Staff, Brigadier Churchill Mann,[26] visited Crocker's headquarters to discuss the above operation. To their surprise, Crocker, who had a reputation for bluntness, was not only rude, he crossed the line into insubordination when he refused to carry out the operation on the grounds that not only would it accomplish nothing, but it would cost 500 or 600 casualties. Crerar terminated the discussion after asking Crocker to put his views in writing. Later that day, having received the letter he had requested, the army commander forwarded it to Montgomery with a memorandum of the morning's discussion in which he stated that Crocker had given him the impression that "he resented being placed under my command and receiving any directive from me." He then added, "I do not know whether the attitude is personal, or because of the fact that I am a Canadian – but it certainly showed itself." Crerar closed by requesting that Crocker be transferred to the 12th or 30th British Corps and one of these commanders be put in Crocker's place.

The next morning (25 July) Crerar discussed the incident with Montgomery at the latter's headquarters. The army group commander was in Crerar's words "very friendly and helpful," but did make the valid observation that the situation had been caused by the manner in which Crerar had handled an operational requirement with Crocker, who required to be brought around to see the virtue in a course of action, rather than being ordered to carry it out. (Coming from Montgomery, who was not one to brook criticism of his orders from anyone very far removed from the Almighty in the chain of command, and then only grudgingly, this was a bit much. Furthermore, it was unlikely that Crocker would have dared to question any direction he had received from the army group commander, and he probably would have adopted a different approach with Dempsey. There may well have been, as Stacey has suggested, overtones of the lingering inability of many in both armies to overcome the perception that Canada was a colony, not an independent nation, and hence some reluctance on the part of Crocker to accept with good grace being placed under the command of a Dominion officer.[27]) Be that as it may, the situation was eventually resolved, and an amicable working relationship evolved which appears to have been sustained through the remainder of the war.

What is less satisfactory is the subsequent treatment of the incident by Montgomery. We have already seen "the spin" in his account of the incident to Brooke; he used essentially the same line during an interview on 8 October 1944 with Colonel J.L. Ralston, the Canadian Minister of National Defence. The minister's notes of the conversation showed that not only did Montgomery not leave him with any inkling that the orders Crocker had

The fall of Caen
A Sherman Observation Post tank of the 19th Army Field Regiment drives through Caen. The RC (signifying the troop commander of C Troop) on the front of the hull bottom and the barely visible 4 of the 45 unit sign behind the spare road wheel on the right front of the hull identifies this as an artillery vehicle. (NAC/PA 162667)

failed to carry out were in fact his own, but that the general had clearly attempted to create the impression that the fault was almost totally that of Crerar.[28] As the record of the events prepared by Crerar, including an account of the criticism of his approach by Montgomery during their interview on 25 July, and the treatment of the incident in the Canadian official history[29] have rarely been cited by non-Canadian historians, it was Montgomery's one-sided and, one must add, distorted version that historians of the Normandy campaign have followed, but perhaps that was the army group commander's intention. There also may be more than a grain of truth to the theory that Montgomery disliked Crerar, not only for any shortcomings, real or imagined, as a commander, but because of his unwavering position that his first loyalty lay to Canada and not to the Commander of 21st Army Group.[30] In truth the incident did not reflect well on all three officers: Crocker for his pugnacious response to a legitimate order; Crerar (who had a born bureaucrat's love of paper) for not having made a point of calling on Crocker to discuss the transfer of command and the forthcoming operations; and Montgomery for failing to acknowledge his responsibility as the originator of the order, and then for belittling Crerar for simply trying to follow his instructions.

While this bureaucratic battle was being fought in the caravans of power, another more deadly battle was being fought by 2nd Canadian Corps, still under the command of Second British Army, on the slopes of Verrières Ridge. If one drives south from Caen along Route Nationale 158, as the highway crests the feature between Ifs and Bras, the eye is struck by a long, flat crest running from the left (east) side of the road away to the west for about five kilometres towards the Orne River.* This feature, the Verrières Ridge, which culminates in an irregularly shaped hump of ground running southwest to northeast from Caillouet to Point 122 and Cramesnil – the "Cramesnil Spur" – was the scene of Operation SPRING, probably the most poorly conceived and executed battle fought by the Canadians in Normandy, and one which controversy still swirls around. While perhaps not as impressive physically as higher ground near it, the ridge was a feature of major importance to both sides; as long as the Germans held it, they could observe and fire on any Allied movement south of the general line Fleury-sur-Orne–Ifs –Bras–Soliers. Thus the Allies were hemmed in to a narrow belt south of the suburbs of Caen; if the Allies could take the Cramesnil Spur, then they would have advanced their line close to five miles, and even if they reached no further than the first crest running east and west from the hamlet that gave its name to the ridge, they would have gained precious room to build up their force free from German observation and to launch a massive offensive towards Falaise and beyond.

A brief review of the background to the operation is in order. First, Montgomery in his directive of 21 July, which we have seen above, declared:

4. It is now vital that the western flank should swing southwards and eastwards, and that we should gain possession of the whole of the Cherbourg and Brittany peninsulas. The whole weight of the Army Group will therefore be directed to this task; we require the Brittany ports so that we can develop the full resources of the Allies in Western Europe, and we must get them soon.

---

* This point was first made by Stacey several decades ago; the ridge is an imposing feature that catches one's eye.

And while carrying out this task we must improve, and retain firmly, our present good position on the eastern flank, and be ready to take quick action on that flank…

And as for Second British Army, he directed:

13. The army will operate intensively so as to secure the general line [from St. Sylvain to Caumont], within the army boundaries, and to hold it firmly. Having gained this line, that part of the army front east of the R. Orne will be kept as active as is possible with the resources available; the enemy must be led to believe that we contemplate a major advance towards Falaise and Argentan, and he must be induced to build up his main strength to the east of the R. Orne so that out affairs on the western flank can proceed with greater speed.[31]

While paragraph 13 certainly was direction to continue offensive operations east of the Orne, it is also clear that the main effort would be at the western end of the front. Even so, it was apparent that Dempsey was expected to push the Germans back some five to six miles, which would necessitate one or more major operations involving several divisions. After that, it would be a case of continuing to threaten the enemy, thus inducing him to build up his main strength east of the Orne River. Montgomery clearly intended to continue developing the situation on the eastern flank with an ultimate objective of launching "a very large scale operation by possibly three to four armoured divisions" towards Falaise.[32] As for Simonds, while he certainly planned to capture the Cramesnil Spur and perhaps more, the over-riding aim of SPRING was to deter the Germans from thinning their defences in the area south of Caen. That is not to say that if a breakthrough had occurred, it would not have been exploited; however, the aim of the operation was to deter the Germans from moving armoured formations eastwards against Operation COBRA, the American breakout from the bridgehead into open country scheduled to commence on 24 July. It is also clear that to hold German forces in place, the "holding attack" would have to have enough offensive punch to pose the threat of breaking the German defence line south of Caen. It was a clear case of the semantics becoming blurred and there should

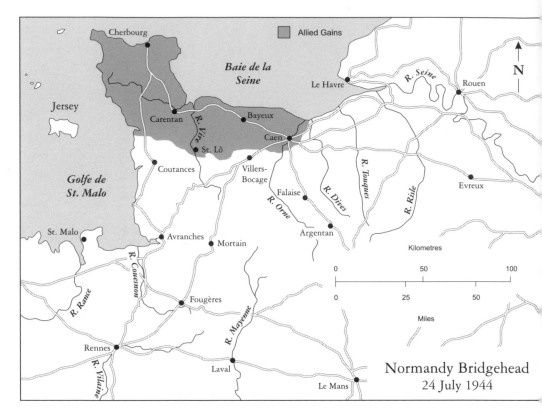

Normandy Bridgehead
24 July 1944

be no doubt that any substantial degree of success would have drawn German reserves away from the American front.

Operation COBRA had been delayed for several days by heavy rains and low clouds that grounded the Allied air forces, but on 24 July 1944 conditions were such that the order to commence the attack was issued. The air support for the offensive had already taken off when the weather suddenly deteriorated again and the operation was postponed. While some aircraft returned to base and others refused to bomb because their targets were obscured, a number released their loads on their own ground forces with devastating effect, killing 25 and wounding 131 members of the 30th U.S. Division. Moreover, the raids indicated to the Germans that the Americans planned an offensive in the St. Lô–Périers area.[33]

On 25 July flying conditions had improved and the offensive commenced, somewhat unusually, with the forward American troops apparently abandoning their forward positions to the astonishment of the Germans. The reason for this apparent withdrawal became clear when the *Wehrmacht* was attacked first by fighter bombers and then by a massed raid of Fortresses and Liberators. Unfortunately, good visibility was not a guarantee of accurate bombing and the Americans suffered a further 111 men killed, including Lieutenant General Lesley J. McNair, the provisional commander of the 1st U.S. Army Group. However the majority of the bombs fell on German positions south of the St. Lô–Périers road, killing more than 1,000 men, wrecking three command posts of the *Panzerlehr Division* and effectively destroying *Kampfgruppe* Heinz of that formation. Even with the setback caused by the short bombing, 7th U.S. Corps launched a heavy attack across a front 7,000 yards wide and made slow but steady progress until it broke through the German defence line, and by the morning of 26 July American formations were starting to fan out across the country against rapidly-crumbling resistance. By 28 July the advance had progressed 20 miles, and three days later, on 31 July, 8th U.S. Corps, on the right flank of 7th Corps, had liberated Avranches and was on the verge of exploding into Brittany and the French interior. It was the beginning of the end of the enemy's hold on Normandy.[34]

On 24 July what was the enemy situation south of Caen? First, the Germans expected a major attack east of the Orne: on 24 July *Heeresgruppe B* reported that "The 2nd British Army will try to obtain a breakthrough in the general direction of Falaise in order to create the conditions required for the thrust on Paris," and their deployment reflected this; on the eve of SPRING and COBRA there were seven armoured divisions facing Second British Army, with the equivalent of five east of the Orne, while only two opposed the Americans. Second Canadian Corps was faced by strong German forces with ample reserves: 1. *SS-Panzerdivision* held the line from Cagny to Verrières; from there to the Orne 272. *Infanteriedivision,* reinforced with a tank battalion and a panzer grenadier battalion from each of 2. *Panzerdivision* and 9. *SS-Panzerdivision* and the reconnaissance battalion of 10. *SS-Panzerdivision,* was in the front line. In reserve were the remainder of 9. *SS-Panzerdivision* northwest of Bretteville-sur-Laize, 116. *Panzerdivision* near St. Sylvain and the main body of 2. *Panzerdivision* northwest of Tournebu.[35]

Simonds decided to seize the ridge using his two Canadian infantry divisions and then exploit to Point 122 in the third phase with the 7th British Armoured Division. Subsequently he would expand his lodgement using

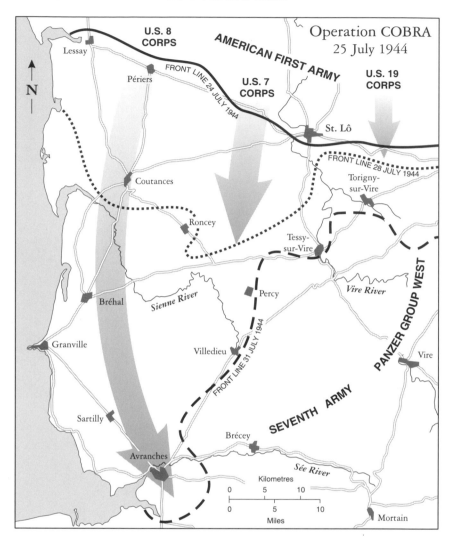

the Guards Armoured Division and the 3rd Canadian Infantry Division. It is noteworthy that 5. *Panzerarmee* had deduced by 0845 on the first day of the operation that it was not a major effort because "the enemy air arm has not yet appeared in sizeable dimensions."[36] While the operation is perhaps best known for the disastrous attack by the Black Watch (Royal Highland Regiment of Canada) on the west end of Verrières Ridge, the root cause of the debacle was the extremely poor execution of the mission by the commanders of 2nd Canadian Division and 5 Canadian Brigade, although a too-rigid plan imposed by Simonds certainly contributed. At the other end of the ridge, Major General Rod Keller managed to dilute the effort against what in fact was his division's only objective in the opening phases of SPRING until one Canadian infantry battalion was attacking Tilly-la-Campagne, which was held by a panzer grenadier battalion, a company of Mk IV tanks and a company of engineers. Not surprisingly the attempt to capture the fortified village turned into a bloodbath, until Brigadier Ben Cunningham, the commander of 9 Brigade (the same officer Keller had tried to fire after CHARNWOOD), and two of his battalion commanders flatly refused to continue the attacks. In fact, only one Canadian unit, the Royal Hamilton Light Infantry of 4 Brigade, was able to capture and hold its objective, and that was more the result of a good plan by its dynamic commanding officer, Lieutenant Colonel John M. Rockingham, carried out by well-trained troops, than adherence to the rigid timetable imposed from above. (This was the only battle he fought as a battalion commander, as Rockingham was soon promoted and moved to replace Cunningham in command of 9 Brigade.) What is often overlooked is that the 2nd Division had managed to seize a foothold on the ridge from the village of Verrières to St. Martin-de-Fontenay, and this would allow the attacking troops in TOTALIZE to assemble in the lee of the ridge free from German observation. Furthermore, while the Germans withdrew one of the panzer divisions that had been defending the ridge, this formation was redeployed against Second British Army, not against the Americans. In this regard, SPRING was a strategic victory, in that it achieved its part in the overall scheme of things, but it certainly was a tactical stalemate, if perhaps not the outright defeat it has been painted as for the last 60 years.

After SPRING groaned to its bloody conclusion, Simonds must have been a frustrated man. Never one to suffer fools gladly, he had just seen an incredibly inept performance by Major General Charles Foulkes and his 2nd Canadian Infantry Division. Foulkes, who made the cold, remote Simonds appear positively bubbly and charismatic, characteristically placed the blame on the inexperience of his troops.* In Simonds's only other Canadian division, the 3rd, he was faced with an apparent loss of nerve by Cunningham of 9 Brigade and two of his battalion commanders, all of whom Simonds relieved

---

* While Simonds is often described as young and dynamic, few would have used those terms to describe Foulkes. However, although he appears old and toad-like in photographs, Foulkes was only three months older than Simonds. Both were 41 in 1944.

from command for refusing to continue the attack on Tilly-la-Campagne. (In fact, the three officers had refused to continue to throw their men into the cauldron under what they perceived as Keller's incompetent direction.) Simonds and his Canadian superiors must have retained some confidence in Cunningham as he was appointed to command the Canadian War Staff College, not usually a job reserved for an officer accused of a breach of discipline, or worse, a loss of nerve. On his deathbed in 1974 Simonds confessed to a close friend and fellow Normandy veteran that he still agonized over whether he should have fired Keller instead of Cunningham.[37]

What he saw as a breakdown in battlefield discipline in the 3rd Division must have been particularly disturbing, for Simonds knew that for some time his British superiors (he was still operating as part of Second British Army) had been dissatisfied with Keller. While Simonds had mounted a vigorous defence to save Keller more for the sake of the division than for concern for his subordinate's reputation, apparently he was prepared to see Foulkes go because of his demonstrated incompetence as a commander in his first battles. Like Simonds, both Keller and Foulkes were members of the tiny, elite group of permanent force officers who had passed the prewar British Army Staff College course.

His third divisional commander, Major General George Kitching,[38] whose 4th Canadian Armoured Division was in the process of moving into the beachhead from Britain and would soon come under Simonds's command, had been a British regular junior infantry officer who had resigned his commission and emigrated to Canada in 1938 and quickly joined the Royal Canadian Regiment in September 1939. Not surprisingly, as a one-eyed man in an army of the blind and near-blind, Kitching had risen rapidly and served as Simonds's chief operations officer in Sicily and Italy. Unlike Foulkes and Keller, he had at least commanded a brigade, 11 Infantry of 5th Canadian Armoured Division, in Italy in action, albeit briefly and not very successfully, before taking command of his division.[39] The unpalatable reality was that after more than four years of war the Canadian pool of capable senior commanders was shallow and any criticism of Simonds's too strict control of his subordinate commanders must be viewed with this factor in mind. It also raises the question of what would have happened if Simonds had become a casualty, as he nearly did on at least two occasions in Normandy.

PART TWO

PREPARING
FOR TOTALIZE

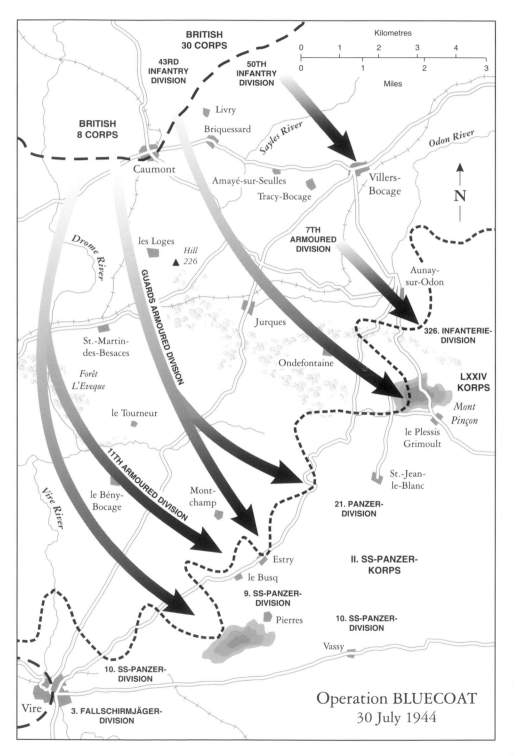

BRITISH
30 CORPS

43RD
INFANTRY
DIVISION

50TH
INFANTRY
DIVISION

Livry

BRITISH
8 CORPS

Briquessard

Sayles River

Odon River

Caumont

Amayé-sur-Seulles

Villers-
Bocage

Tracy-Bocage

N

Drome River

les Loges

7TH
ARMOURED
DIVISION

Hill
226

Aunay-
sur-Odon

GUARDS ARMOURED DIVISION

Jurques

326. INFANTERIE-
DIVISION

St.-Martin-
des-Besaces

Ondefontaine

LXXIV
KORPS

*Forêt
L'Eveque*

*Mont
Pinçon*

le Tourneur

le Plessis
Grimoult

11TH ARMOURED DIVISION

St.-Jean-
le-Blanc

Vire River

le Bény-
Bocage

Mont-
champ

21. PANZER-
DIVISION

Estry

II. SS-PANZER-
KORPS

le Busq

9. SS-PANZER-
DIVISION

Pierres

10. SS-PANZER-
DIVISION

Vassy

10. SS-PANZER-
DIVISION

Vire

3. FALLSCHIRMJÄGER-
DIVISION

Operation BLUECOAT
30 July 1944

Kilometres

0   1   2   3   4

0   1   2   3

Miles

60

CHAPTER FOUR

MAKING THE PLAN

*"A matter of the highest importance is to get the infantry over and through
the enemy's prearranged zones of defensive fire in the shortest possible time
after the intention to attack has been revealed."*

LIEUTENANT GENERAL HENRY CRERAR, FIRST CANADIAN ARMY

With the U.S. forces charging out of the hole they had blown
in the German lines at the western end of the bridgehead,
Montgomery now directed Lieutenant General Miles
Dempsey, the commander of Second British Army, to
shift his effort from the 2nd Canadian Corps area east of the Orne River to
an advance farther west through the difficult *bocage* country to conform to
the American advance. While this move has been criticized in recent years
– with the benefit of rather more hindsight than strategic insight – it is clear
that the army group commander was anticipating the pursuit across France
to trap the Germans against the Seine River and was beginning to pivot his
land forces through 90 degrees.

On 30 July 1944 the planned attack, Operation BLUECOAT, began with
8 and 30 British Corps advancing south-southeast to secure the line from
just east of Vire through Estry and Mont Pinçon to Aunay-sur-Odon. To the
east 12 British Corps would advance southeast, driving the Germans from
the west bank of the Orne River and eventually seizing crossings over that
river in the area of Thury-Harcourt. The operation also had the subsidiary
purpose of holding the bulk of the German panzer divisions against Second
British Army, thus allowing the U.S. forces the opportunity to exploit their
superior mobility. While the operation was generally successful, the progress
of 30 Corps in the centre was disappointingly slow and Montgomery sacked
Lieutenant General G.C. Bucknall, its commander, as well as Major General

W.R.J. Erskine, the commander of 7th British Armoured Division.[1] By 6 August, on the eve of TOTALIZE, the British forces had pushed the Germans steadily back, while the Americans continued their advance against negligible opposition eastwards towards the Seine and Paris.

By the morning of 30 July 1944 Simonds had decided, at least in outline, how he would attack up Route Nationale 158, when the order finally did come. At 1000 hours he briefed Foulkes, Keller and Kitching, his three divisional commanders, along with the senior staff from their and his own headquarters on the strategic picture and how he intended to break the deadlock south of Caen. In his briefing he emphasized that

> the main pivot of [the German] defences and the determining points between an orderly [enemy] withdrawal or a rout rested with the strength with which he [the enemy] held the Caen sector. A glance at the map revealed that so long as he held Caen in spite of his weakening position on the American front he was still able to swing back northeastwards and later, if need be, commence a gradual withdrawal to the North [sic] keeping control at all times. This explains his sensitivity in this particular sector, and it was more important to him to keep concentrated as much armour and heavy weapons as he could…
>
> Our immediate task is to make the threat to this pivot so serious that he will not dare reduce the strength of the force which he now holds there… [My] task is to watch for the opportunity when the Boche weakens that pivot and then crack through. Once this takes place his whole position in Normandy collapses. This is the time when there will be no holding back, because it will be the finish of the enemy as far as this phase of the war is concerned, unless he decides upon a general withdrawal.

Simonds then went on to say that, if all continued to go well on the American front, to look for instructions for a breakthrough to Falaise. He felt that for this operation he should employ not less than three infantry and two armoured divisions with an armoured brigade with each infantry division and with possibly a third armoured brigade in reserve. The main problem, as he saw it, was how to get the armour through the line made up of anti-tank guns and tanks with long effective fields of fire. Simonds would not mount the operation without complete air support, by which he meant both fighter-bombers and heavy bombers, as this provided the means to neutralize the anti-tank screen. The commander of 2nd Canadian Corps was certain in his own mind that

> the best solution to the problem would be to employ armour at night, although he knew that the armour people would be reluctant to attempt this. He felt that if effectively carried through, it could be possible at night to bring armour up forward at least 5,000 yards... He was not minimizing the risk of such an operation but risks had to be accepted if armour was to be brought to the line of guns. For air support, he would call for a heavy bomber force such as that used in the attack on Caen and this would be employed at dusk. He would then arrange for these bombers to make a return trip and resume their attack as soon after first light as it was possible for the bombers to refuel and return. The whole bomber effort would depend a great deal on this "turn around."[2]

While Simonds pondered the task of breaking through the German defences, his immediate task was to continue to maintain pressure on the enemy so as to prevent him from reducing his forces south of Caen to reinforce the western flank of their line. To this end, he proposed to introduce 4th Canadian Armoured Division to action by mounting a small-scale operation to take Tilly-la-Campagne. The capture of the village, which from a low rise overlooking the Allied lines provided observation nearly to Caen itself, would minimize enemy observations of movements, and thus provide a better opportunity to concentrate forces for the planned major attack to come.[3]

By now Tilly was largely reduced to rubble, craters and panzer grenadiers. In fact the area about the tiny hamlet was held by two battalions of SS panzer grenadiers and two companies of armour, all of 1. *SS-Panzerdivision*.[4] While all were seriously under-strength, the inescapable fact was that Tilly and its surrounding area were defended by the equivalent of a Canadian brigade, and the Germans could have had little doubt that the Allies would continue to keep attacking Tilly, as during the night of 29-30 July the Essex Scottish of

4 Brigade of 2nd Canadian Infantry Division had captured a small group of farm buildings northwest of Tilly on the Caen–Falaise Road from I. *Bataillon, SS-Panzergrenadierregiment* 1 after a bitter, costly fight. Now this farm would be used as the jumping off point for the next attack.[5] The first of a renewed series of attacks on Tilly-la-Campagne was made by the Calgary Highlanders of 5 Brigade of 2nd Canadian Infantry Division at 0230 hours in the morning of 1 August. This battalion was supported by a squadron of the Royal Scots Greys of 4 British Armoured Brigade as well as the divisional artillery of 2nd Infantry Division and 4th Armoured Division and 2 Canadian AGRA.* A diversionary attack at 0100 hours by D Company of the Lincoln and Welland Regiment of 10 Brigade of 4th Armoured Division from the direction of Bourguébus was brought to a halt and the troops were forced to dig in. It was hoped somewhat optimistically that an attack launched the same night on the church in St. Martin-de-Fontenay at 0400 hours by the Fusiliers Mont-Royal of 6 Brigade would divert attention away from the main event. While three successive attacks by the Calgary Highlanders supported by tanks, the last at 1430 hours across open ground, had failed, the Fusiliers Mont-Royal were in possession of the church by 0645 hours.[6]

At 0950 hours on 1 August Lieutenant General Henry Crerar (Simonds's 2nd Canadian Corps had come under the command of his First Canadian Army from Dempsey's Second British Army at noon the previous day)[7] recorded that General Montgomery had telephoned to say it was "very important to keep Boche worried on our front" and inquired if Simonds could continue to keep the Germans occupied.[8] Crerar spoke to Simonds, who responded that it would be impossible to mount another attack before the next night (1-2 August) because of planned reliefs. However, the Corps Commander must have had second thoughts because the Lincoln and Welland Regiment was ordered to capture Tilly that same night.[9]

The unit's first battalion attack of the war, and the first set piece attack by 4th Canadian Armoured Division, was not a success. While III. *Bataillon, SS-Panzergrenadierregiment* 2 had been redeployed to cover the area between Rocquancourt and May-sur-Orne, the remaining defenders were able to beat off the attack readily.[10] One can detect more than a little displeasure

---

* Army Group Royal Artillery. A brigade-sized formation of medium and heavy artillery regiments.

over the planning and conduct of the operation in the Lincoln and Welland Regiment's history. After mounting a frontal diversionary attack from Bourguébus with D Company at 0100 hours, the regiment received orders at 1800 hours to attack Tilly that night. The commanding officer spent from 2000 to 2200 hours issuing his orders, and this for a battalion attack scheduled to begin at 2345. His plan saw A and B Companies taking up a position between La Hogue and Tilly to block an anticipated armoured counterattack on the latter place from La Hogue, which was sensible and showed a degree of tactical awareness. C Company would then seize an intermediate objective as a firm base for D Company, and then follow D Company into Tilly.[11] Despite having available the support of five field regiments and an AGRA, it was decided to forgo any artillery bombardment in an attempt to surprise the defenders by means of a silent night attack. When all is said and done, a company without artillery support was assaulting a strong defensive position held by a reinforced battalion, and not surprisingly the attack failed with a cost of 58 Canadian casualties.[12]

On 3 August Brigadier James C. Jefferson, the commander of 10 Brigade, tore a strip off the surviving officers of the battalion, telling them "insufficient determination had been shown in attacking what should have been a two company objective," thereby demonstrating for posterity his dubious grasp of the situation.[13] In Jefferson's defence, given the size of Tilly, it would have been difficult to deploy more than one or two companies against it at any one time unless the village could have been sealed off from relief or reinforcement, which implied more tactical sophistication than had been evident to date. In fact the plan used by the Lincoln and Welland Regiment recognized this, but failed more for lack of resources than resolve. If there was one common negative characteristic of Canadian tactics at this stage of the war, it was the failure to assign sufficient resources to tasks. This was remarked upon by *General Der Panzertruppen* Eberbach in his interrogation, where he stated the Canadian "attack methods were different from the British. Although their advance was also preceded by bombing attacks and a heavy barrage, the forces committed to follow up rarely exceeded one regiment [brigade] and up to 50 tanks. Attacks on a large scale were rare."[14] There now was a pause in the attacks on Tilly for a few days and we shall turn to the planning for the breakthrough south of Caen.

By 30 July the German situation at the western end of the Normandy front was critical. The Americans were about to capture Avranches and there were no reserves to prevent an American breakout and exploitation. It was appreciated that the British meant to advance in contact with the Americans and compel the Germans to withdraw additional formations from the area south of Caen. *Generalfeldmarschall* Gunther Hans von Kluge, the German Supreme Commander in the West (*OBW*), who was only too aware that only quick major withdrawals could save his two armies from destruction, appealed once again for either *Generalfeldmarschall* Wilhelm Keitel, *Generaloberst* Albert Jodl or *General Der Artillerie* Walter Warlimont from the High Command of the Armed Forces (*OKW*) to come to his headquarters to get a clear picture of the situation.[15]

By 31 July the situation at the extreme western end of the Normandy front had become desperate. The Americans had taken Avranches and the bridge at Pontaubault; it was obvious that the next stage would be mobile warfare on a grand scale as a torrent of Shermans poured through the breach. The day before, Jodl had submitted a draft order for a withdrawal from the coastal front to Hitler and the next day the Führer had seemed prepared to authorize it, while at the same time mentioning he was "looking for a new O.B. West."[16]

During the day, 84. *Infanteriedivision*, then en route to *Panzergruppe West*, was redirected to the Condé–Flers area of Seventh Army. Since the reserve divisions of the panzer group had moved westward, to compensate for the loss of that division, 89. *Infanteriedivision* was alerted for immediate transfer from the Rouen–Le Havre sector to the Bretteville area, south of Caen.[17]

The situation worsened again on 1 August. In the area of Pontaubault (south of Avranches) the weak German forces were withdrawing towards the south and southwest, leaving the way to the south and southeast open. On the extreme left of *Panzergruppe West* the orderly withdrawal was being threatened by British armour. The reserve was unable to deliver a decisive counter-blow and 74. *Korps* reported that it was unable to restore the situation. With Le Bény-Bocage now in British hands and American tanks roaming freely between Avranches and Rennes, 7. *Armee* was in danger of being enveloped and trapped. Closing the gap south of Caumont was imperative; 2. *SS-Panzerkorps* with 9. and 10. *SS-Panzerdivisionen* was ordered to move to the gap during the night of 1-2 August to offer resistance to the British concentration of armour and to re-establish contact with 2. *Fallschirmjägerkorps* of 7. *Armee*.[18]

The situation on 2 August on the right and centre of the Panzer Group was uneventful; on the left wing the situation was stabilized to some extent. Nevertheless the British advancing from Le Bény-Bocage had come close to Vire, while 7. *Armee* was falling back to the line Garville–NW St. Sever–Fontenermont. 2. *SS-Panzerkorps* had not been able to make contact with 7. *Armee*; a new attempt would be made on 3 August. The Germans realized that British Second Army seemed to be attempting to split the two German armies and that a thrust from Caen towards Falaise might occur at any time. Last, the American First Army apparently intended to seal off the Brittany peninsula and throw its main weight to the southeast.[19]

The German reaction to the twin blows of the American Operation CO-BRA and the British Operation BLUECOAT opened the way for the encirclement of the bulk of their forces in the west. However, the Germans might have been able to carry out a fighting withdrawal to the Seine had not Hitler and his lackeys intervened with a stroke of their unique brand of military genius. On 2 August the *OKW* determined that "the enemy breakthrough on the western wing of the beachhead front can only be parried by a decisive counterattack of strong German Panzer forces" and that

> Our superior tactical experience must be used to return the situation to a positive state. The combat-inexperienced and difficult-to-move Infanterie Divisions must not be brought into this torn wing, while the bulk of the Panzer units is tied down at the still coherent main line of defence in infantry defence further to the east and remains there.

Therefore, orders were issued to move the remaining panzer units from the eastern end of the front in order to participate in an operation designed to

> destroy the enemy tank forces which have broken through to the east, southeast and south. Without any regard to the enemy breakthrough in Brittany, contact must be established with the western coast of the Cotentin peninsula near Avranches or north of it.

In effect, this meant that the remaining panzer divisions in the east, 1. and 12. *SS-Panzerdivisionen*, were to be pulled out, stripping the Caen sector of armoured forces.[20] The record of the meeting held the next day in the *Panzergruppe West* war diary confirmed that the German commanders actually engaged in combat were not as confident or sycophantic as the toadies at *OKW*, who were not inclined to question Hitler's strategic genius and operational brilliance, although there probably was a strong element of self-preservation involved as well following the turmoil of the failed attempt on the Führer's life. Despite strong protests about the danger of stripping the Caen front, *OKW* persisted in the exasperating "orders are orders" mode of the "my hands are tied" school of the professional bureaucrat, military or civilian. The main participants in the 3 August[21] conference were *Generalen* Heinrich Eberbach, the commander of *Panzergruppe West*, Sepp Dietrich, the commander of 1. *SS-Panzerkorps*, and Walter Warlimont, acting chief of the *Wehrmacht* operational staff at *OKW*. Their discussion included the following telling exchange of views

> Eberbach: It seems that ultimately the situation of the two Armies will become untenable.
>
> Warlimont: But you have been able to hold out until now. If you can do this for another month or two, this summer's fighting will not have been in vain. The British people have been assured that the war will end this year. If this fails to happen, there exists for us one more great opportunity (serious effect of V1 on morale).
>
> Eberbach: The situation of Seventh Army makes it necessary to arrive at a big decision.
>
> Warlimont: If the Normandy front in its extent of 120 km cannot be held, it will certainly not be feasible further back (Seine–Marne–West Wall). It is also out of the question because no supply arrangements have been made there. It is necessary to withdraw now from the zone of Panzer Army West four panzer divisions for a thrust to Avranches and to cut off the Americans.
>
> Diettrich: If the SS Divisions are pulled out south of Caen, the enemy will attack there and break through.
>
> Warlimont: However, the SS Divisions are not in their proper place there;

they are employed in an immobile role and not at the focal point of the enemy's effort.

Eberbach: The infantry divisions now approaching will be committed as soon as possible, but the SS divisions must be held ready in the rear to support the front. The main question remains how the front can be held in the long run against an enemy so far superior in materiel.

Warlimont: Two more SS brigades can be moved in from Denmark; the homeland and occupied France are being combed through for all available material.

Eberbach: Moving in the SS brigades will take from eight to ten days; that is too long. Pulling out the SS divisions and launching them in the direction of Avranches takes at least three to four days. And we do not know what the situation then will be there.

Warlimont: The enemy now has his first great success. He is now attaining that which he had set as the objective [to be reached] within the first few days of the invasion. Within a measurable period the commitment of completely new weapons will have its effect. Here too the culprits of 20 July have caused delay. But one may count on it that everything will move faster now. The first thousand of new fighter planes will brought into action in the second half of August. There will be hope then of breaking the enemy's complete supremacy of the air.[22]

The stage was set for the defeat of the German forces east of the Orne River south of Caen, even if Warlimont seemed to be incapable of grasping that obvious fact. The question now was, could the Allies capitalize on the opportunity?

On 31 July Simonds presented his appreciation of the situation and outline plan to Crerar, his immediate superior, and on the next day confirmed them in written form. The appreciation, a key military planning tool, was a logical and disciplined process designed to organize a mass of detail so as to come to a reasoned conclusion. Commonwealth officer training at virtually all levels devoted considerable time to teaching the appreciation both as a drill and as an intellectual exercise in deductive thinking. Despite the apparent contradictions, the two were not mutually exclusive. The 1944 *British Field Service Pocket Book* summarized the format and process of the appreciation as follows,

1. **Sequence**. Whether written or mental, appreciations will be in the following accepted logical sequence :-
   (a) The object to be attained.
   (b) Factors which affect attainment of the object.
   (c) Courses open to
       (i) own side   The order in which these are considered
       (ii) the enemy   will usually vary logically according to
                         which side has the initiative
   (d) The plan...
3. **The Object** – A correct definition of the "object" to be attained is essential. It must be clearly and accurately stated. The object is a purpose or aim NOT to be confused with the "objective", *e.g.*, a locality the capture of which will most rapidly and economically result in the attainment of the [object]. The object will frequently be defined in the orders of the superior commander. Objective(s) will emerge as a result of the appreciation.
4. **Factors** – All factors which may affect the attainment of the object must be considered, and a *deduction* [emphasis in original] made from each. If no deduction is possible, omit that factor. Factors should be considered in order of importance, and should lead logically from one to the next. Important factors must be stressed in order that the appreciation may be balanced...
5. **Courses** – The arguments for and against each course should be summarized. It will normally be best to discuss last the course to be adopted. This section must end with a statement making clear which course is to be adopted.
6. **Plan** – The plan to implement the course adopted must be the logical outcome of previous argument. It must be definite and clear, concisely stated in outline, but in sufficient detail to form a basis for orders.[23]

Simonds's appreciation, which was completed on 31 July, eight days before the operation commenced, and well before Montgomery directed Crerar on

4 August to "launch a heavy attack from the Caen sector in the direction of Falaise no later than 8 August and, if at all possible, the day before" is the clearest indication of how he perceived the tactical situation and how he intended to deal with it. It also demonstrates the considerable difficulties which faced Simonds, as well as some of the limitations and constraints imposed upon him. The first impression is one of conciseness and clarity. Formal written appreciations tended to cover every detail in excruciating detail both to ensure all the factors were considered and to demonstrate the author's knowledge and brilliance. There is no reason to believe that the preliminary work that led to this document was not comprehensive and detailed, but clearly Simonds did not feel it necessary to lay out his complete thought process for his superior – nor did Crerar feel a need for it – and instead submitted a summary to explain the rationale underlying his outline plan. While some features of the plan were unique, if not radical, Crerar and his staff would have had no trouble grasping its underlying logic after examining the outline plan and the marked maps submitted with it.[24]

The appreciation, reflecting as it does the thinking of both Simonds and Crerar, is of such importance to an understanding of TOTALIZE that is reproduced in full below. Each paragraph of the appreciation appears in (my) bold face followed by a discussion of its content.[25]

1. **"Object – To break through the German positions astride the road CAEN–FALAISE."**

This was based on Crerar's direction of 29 July – to plan a major operation on the axis Caen–Falaise to break through the German positions astride the main road – and is a clear indication that neither officer was focused on advancing any further south than Falaise in this operation. In fact, when Montgomery did direct Crerar to advance towards Falaise, it was to "cut off the enemy forces … facing Second Army." This in turn would have forced the retreating Germans to move through the difficult country south of Falaise, thus slowing their withdrawal. The overall strategic objective of the Allied armies was to trap the Germans in a so-called "long envelopment" against the Seine river. At the end of July there was no intention of completing a more limited short envelopment, in what became known as the "Falaise pocket," as the Germans were being forced back under pressure, and the launch of Hitler's foolhardy Mortain counteroffensive, which created the opportunity to trap his panzer divisions, was still a few days in the future.[26] Crerar's order, and thus the object of Simonds's appreciation, also fixed his axis of advance as the Route Nationale 158 and excluded any indirect approach such as a "left hook" through St. Sylvain, Rouvres and Epancy. What the object did not do was establish Falaise as the objective of TOTALIZE, and in fact the final objectives of the operation were to be north of that city. This distinction has been missed by a distressingly large number of the historians who have written about the forthcoming battle.[27]

2. The Germans have a forward prepared defensive position with its F[orward]D[efended]L[ocality] on the general line MAY SUR ORNE 0259–TILLY LA CAMPAGNE 0760–LA HOGUE 0960 and a rearward partially prepared position on the general line HAUTMESNIL 0852–ST SYLVAIN 1354. The high ground point 122 in 0756 is the key to the first and the high ground about HAUTMESNIL 0852 the key to the second. Both are obvious objectives and ones for which the Germans will fight very hard.

This paragraph summarized a combination of both the enemy and ground factors and delineated them as objectives. The first objective was essentially the same as that of the ill-fated Operation SPRING, while the second was considered to be the last defensible ground before the highway passed the village of Quesnay and its nearby wood and climbed to the heights behind Potigny. Even without the outline plan, it would have been obvious to Crerar that each objective must be assaulted by at least two divisions, and that the distance between them meant that the artillery must be moved forward to support the second attack. However, at this time 2nd Canadian Corps had only three divisions, two infantry and one armoured, so Simonds would require reinforcement. It is noteworthy that Simonds omitted any reference to the Quesnay–Potigny area from his discussion of possible enemy defensive positions. As we shall see with the benefit of hindsight, this was a major oversight which would have disastrous consequences.

3. The positions are manned by as good troops as the German Army possesses. The area is the pivot, which, from the German point of view must be held as long as they fight West of the River ORNE. The position is presently manned by 1 SS [Panzer Division] Right and 9 SS [Panzer Division] Left. Available information indicates that each division has one infantry regiment forward, supported by all the available tanks and SPs, whilst the other infantry regiment works on the rear position, and is available to form the nucleus of a defence in the event of a "break in" forward. The Germans apparently rely on being able to get tanks and SPs back, but ensure that some infantry will be available in the rearward positions from the onset, in the event of forward positions being over-run. Two "break in" operations are required to penetrate the German defence. 12 SS [Panzer Division] Div may be regarded as in close reserve opposite our front and counterattack against our East flank must be expected.

The identifications of the German divisions holding the line opposite 2nd Canadian Corps were correct at the time the appreciation was written. Before TOTALIZE commenced, all three SS Panzer divisions would be replaced in the line by other formations, all of which was dutifully tracked by Canadian intelligence. Perhaps of primary importance, by the night of 3-4 August, 12. *SS-Panzerdivision* would be relieved by 272. *Infanteriedivision* and established as 1. *SS-Panzerkorps* reserve behind the forward divisions and east of Route Nationale 158.[28] The relief of 1. *SS-Panzerdivision* by 89. *Infanteriedivision* caused some consternation as the information gained from the interrogation of a deserter from the latter was that the former had pulled back to Bretteville-sur-Laize, in the area of the second defensive line. As we shall see, this was to cause a major change in the corps plan 36 hours before the battle. It is important to remember that when the appreciation was completed, Canadian intelligence cannot be faulted for deducing from the information available that the second line probably was held by elements of two panzer divisions.[29]

On the face of it Simonds was faced with an insurmountable challenge. In the two previous attacks against similar German defensive lines – Operations GOODWOOD-ATLANTIC and SPRING – the *Wehrmacht* had been able to absorb the momentum of the Allied attack and then stabilize and defeat the assault. In more concrete terms, the Germans were holding Verrières ridge with six battalions supported by tanks and self-propelled guns that totally outclassed the Allied tanks, as well as a significant number of towed anti-tank guns. If and when the attackers were able to bludgeon their way through the first position, they would then be faced by another position held in nearly equal strength to the first. In the best case, after mounting two major attacks the Allies would gain perhaps 10 to 15 kilometres down the road to Falaise, but at a dreadful cost in lives and time. In the worst case, they would have been sent reeling back to their start lines, after suffering heavy losses and a catastrophic setback. Furthermore, not only would the first operation mounted by First Canadian Army be a failure, but 2nd Canadian Corps had yet to win a major battle in Normandy, although it had achieved some local successes, but at too heavy a cost, in ATLANTIC and SPRING. Last, the presence of 12. *SS-Panzerdivision* on the eastern flank of the advance posed a very real threat as a potential counterattack force. In all, the German defensive posture reflected the importance of the Caen "hinge" to both sides.

4. **The ground is ideally suited to full exploitation by the enemy of the characteristics of his weapons. It is open, giving little cover to either infantry or tanks and the long range of his anti-tank guns and mortars, firing from carefully prepared positions, provides a very strong defence in depth. This defence will be most handicapped in bad visibility – smoke, fog or darkness, when the advantage of long range is minimized. The attack should therefore be made under such conditions.**

Both Crerar and Simonds were very aware of the advantages enjoyed by the defenders over the attackers in the ground south of Caen. The ground between Falaise and Caen was open and rose and fell in a series of "steps" or ridges and plateaus. The going was generally good with a well developed system of hard-surface roads connecting the villages and hamlets. However, there were some obstacles to movement in the form of sunken roads and a major north-south railway that roughly parallelled Route Nationale 158 as well as the Laison River, which ran in a southwest to northeast direction across the area of operations about three-quarters of the way to Falaise. There were two approaches that would support the advance of a division, although Crerar's selection of his object largely eliminated the more easterly, which ran east of Tilly-la-Campagne, Garcelles-Secqueville and St. Aignan-de-Cramesnil and then between Cauvicourt and St. Sylvain and on to Estrées-la-Campagne. This route provided a good axis for a tank advance against light or neutralized opposition; however, if the enemy was not neutralized and was given time to establish a defence, it was a death trap. The other approach ran along the Route Nationale, with the apparent best going east of the road along the open ground, and with all the advantages and disadvantages of the other approach; conversely the area west of the road was more restricted and suited to a methodical all-arms operation using fire and movement and moving a tactical "bound" at a time. If one accepts the premise that the best tank approach was one that would allow an advance against opposition to succeed, then this was the preferred approach, despite the limitations it imposed in terms of speed and shock action.

The crops were lush and ripe and the harvest was underway; this provided cover for the defending infantry and armoured vehicles, and the numerous haystacks and stooks had the nasty habit of suddenly erupting with machine gun or anti-tank fire. The network of woods and small villages made up of fortress-like stone buildings also provided good cover and protection for the enemy; perversely the shape of the ground allowed the defenders to provide accurate mutual support by direct fire weapons, while the British and Canadian tanks, armed, as the majority were, with the short-range 75 mm gun, usually could not effectively engage armoured targets in the next possible defensive position from the protection of the one just occupied. In short, while open and with broad vistas, it was apparent to the professional military eye that it was not good country to mount an armoured advance across against determined opposition.

The simplest and most effective way to neutralize this advantage was to attack during a period of what military jargon terms "reduced visibility," that is smoke, fog, haze or darkness. Simonds may have ruled out smoke as technically and logistically impractical and it was obviously impossible to order up fog or haze when and where required. This left a night attack. During the opening stages of GOODWOOD Simonds, after watching with horror as the Germans "brewed up" 20 or 30 British tanks in a matter of seconds, had remarked to Captain Marshall Stearns, his aide, "when my turn comes, we will do it at night." Moreover, in early August (Caen lies just north of the 49th parallel) there were hardly more than six hours of complete darkness, so it would be necessary to attack late in the evening if the troops were to be on or near their Phase 1 objectives by dawn. A night attack also would confuse the defenders and perhaps dilute the effects of the inevitable counterattacks.[30]

5. During the last few days we have attacked, and done everything possible to indicate that we intend to continue attacking, the positions opposite us. Tactical surprise in respect to objectives or direction of attack is therefore impossible. Tactical surprise is still possible in respect to time and method, but very heavy fighting must be expected.

This paragraph reinforced the one preceding and set the scene for Simonds's introduction of another innovation, the transport of the attacking infantry in armoured vehicles. It also served to reinforce his conclusion that a normal tactical approach would not suffice.

6. If all available air support is used for the first "break in" there will be nothing for the second except diminished gun support, unless a long pause is made with resultant loss of speed. If on the other hand the first "break in" is based upon limited air support (heavy night bombers), all available gun support and novelty of method, the heavy day bombers and medium bombers will be available for the second "break in" at a time when gun support begins to decrease, and it should be able to maintain a high tempo to the operations.

This was one of the most important paragraphs of the appreciation. To maintain the tempo of the advance, Simonds made a case for the use of heavy and medium bombers to compensate for his artillery, which would have to move forward after supporting the attacks on the Phase 1 objectives. Unfortunately, his reasoning was based on an incorrect understanding of the capabilities and limitations of air power; in short, he was asking more of the air force than it could deliver.

7. In essence, the problem is how to get the armour through the enemy
    gun screen to sufficient depth to disrupt the German anti-tank gun
    and mortar defence, in country highly suited to the tactics of the
    latter combination. It can be done by:-

    (a) Overwhelming air support to destroy or neutralize enemy
        tanks, anti-tank guns and mortars.

    (b) Infiltrating through the screen in bad visibility to a sufficient
        depth to disrupt the anti-tank gun and mortar defence.

    It requires practically the whole day-bomber lift to effect (a) and
    if two defence zones are to be penetrated, a pause with loss of speed
    and momentum must be accepted. It is considered that this may be
    avoided if the first zone is penetrated by infiltration at night but this
    can only be attempted with careful preparation by troops who are to
    do the operation.

In this one short paragraph Simonds introduced a radically new concept
to an attack against a position prepared for defence in depth and held by
excellent troops. His plan played to his own side's strong points and to the
enemy's weaknesses, especially the relative reluctance of the Germans to
fight at night and their inability to interfere with the Allied air forces. In effect he was proposing to bypass the German battalions holding the forward
positions and drive hard to the ground about Point 122 with his leading
troops, and then assault the second, partially prepared position with fresh
troops, leaving the bypassed forces to be mopped up later. At the same time
Simonds reinforced his case for the use of the day bomber force in place of
massed artillery to eliminate the delay between phases. Unfortunately, as we
have seen, this substitution of aircraft bombs for artillery shells was based
on a false assumption, albeit one that was fostered by the air force. It was a
daring, verging on radical, approach and could only have come from a man
who possessed absolute confidence in his own abilities.

Simonds also made a case for time to prepare his troops for the forthcoming operation. This clearly would have struck a chord with Crerar, who
understood from first-hand experience that much of the success of the
Canadian Corps in 1917-1918 was due to innovative tactics and detailed

preparations, including rehearsals by the attacking troops.[31] Last, a plea for time to prepare for a difficult operation involving untried tactics was both basic common sense and a reminder that, while surprise is a recognized principle of war, the aim is to surprise the enemy, not your own troops.

> 8. The plan is submitted on the assumption that the Right wing of Second Army has secured, or imminently threatens to secure, a bridgehead East of the River ORNE, thus loosening the enemy grip on the Northern pivot.

There was little scope for manoeuvre east of the Orne and the series of frontal attacks in July had produced little in the way of progress. Simonds might be implying in this paragraph that under the conditions prevailing on 1 August, the German position was too hard to crack with the forces available to him. Probably, but he also may have deduced that the attack should be timed to coincide with the operations of Second Army in order to lessen the ability of the Germans to concentrate reserve formations against both First Canadian Army and Second British Army, or to fire into the Canadian flank as the attack progressed.

The appreciation for TOTALIZE was a remarkable document. In eight short paragraphs Simonds neatly summed up the strength of the German position south of Caen and then proposed ways and means to defeat it. It is worth emphasizing that it was hardly a "take it or leave it" document sprung upon a compliant Crerar. Simonds, who had been studying the problem since the failure of SPRING, had already discussed a number of its features with him, even though 2nd Canadian Corps did not come under Crerar's command until noon on 31 July. As we have seen, on 29 July Crerar had instructed him to plan a major operation on the Caen–Falaise road, although both the written record in Crerar's diary and the entry in the corps war diary are dated the next day. On the 30th, the same day he briefed his divisional commanders, Simonds had requested one additional infantry and one additional armoured division, and the fullest possible air support for a period of 24 hours, while in the evening of 31 July Crerar had directed Brigadier G.M. Grant, the Deputy Director, Mechanical Engineering at Headquarters First Canadian Army (the officer responsible for maintaining and repairing the army's equipment), to create an organization to complete the conversion of "Priest" self-propelled guns to armoured personnel carriers by 9 August.[32]

Last, Simonds's concept was certainly in tune with Crerar's thinking. On 22 July the latter had sent a tactical directive to his prospective corps commanders which, in turn, echoed his address of 14 May in which he had emphasized "a matter of the highest importance is to get the infantry over and through the enemy's prearranged zones of defensive fire in the shortest possible time after the intention to attack has been revealed."[33]

Two supporting documents (and marked maps) were submitted with the appreciation – an outline plan and a summary of Simonds's requirements to execute the operation. While not cross-referenced, the plan followed logically from the appreciation; for example, the assignment of tasks by formation and phases was developed from paragraph 3 of the appreciation. Hence, based on the object to break through the defences along the Caen–Falaise road and the German defensive layout as determined by his intelligence staff, Simonds decided that a three-phased operation was required. These phases were to be:

Phase 1. Two infantry divisions, each supported by an armoured brigade, would "break in" through the forward German defence line and capture the ground around Point 122 at the rear of the position to form a firm base for the second phase. The divisions would also mop up bypassed German positions.

Phase 2. One armoured and a fresh infantry division would "break in" the second defence line. Simonds saw the initial attack mounted by the armoured division while the infantry division would follow along and widen the area of the penetration of the defensive position.

Phase 3. Having penetrated the German defences, the attackers would exploit towards Falaise. The Phase 2 armoured division would capture the high ground west of Quesnay village that dominated the axis of advance while a fresh armoured division would advance along the Caen–Falaise road past the heights south of the river Laison and seize the high ground northeast of the city. The infantry divisions would follow on and occupy the ground vacated by the armoured divisions.[34]

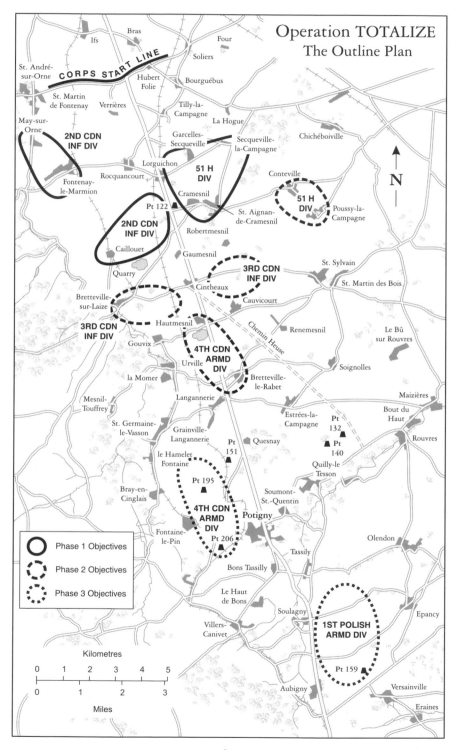

Operation TOTALIZE
The Outline Plan

N

2ND CDN INF DIV

51 H DIV

51 H DIV

2ND CDN INF DIV

3RD CDN INF DIV

3RD CDN INF DIV

4TH CDN ARMD DIV

4TH CDN ARMD DIV

1ST POLISH ARMD DIV

○ Phase 1 Objectives
⬭ Phase 2 Objectives
⬭ Phase 3 Objectives

Kilometres

0   1   2   3   4   5

0   1   2   3

Miles

Anti-Tank Regiment
Canadian Infantry Division

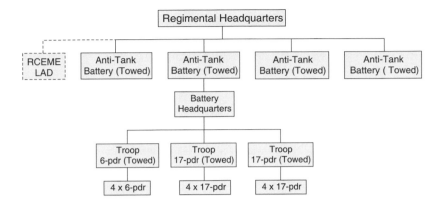

The regimental commander was responsible for coordinating the divisional anti-tank plan, which was based on the guns of his regiment, while the infantry anti-tank platoons were used to defend battalion areas. The 3rd Anti-Tank Regiment of the 3rd Canadian Infantry Division had replaced its 6-pounder troop with American self-propelled M10s for the invasion.

Simonds, with the encouragement of Crerar, had identified some variations on the usual tactics that had the potential to shift the balance in the Allies' favour. First, the attack would go in shortly after nightfall. While Canadians had successfully attacked under the cover of darkness before, this time tanks would be part of the assault force. Furthermore, the infantry would ride in armoured vehicles travelling with the Shermans and thus the tanks would not be restricted to the pace of marching infantrymen, but would move at a rate dictated by their ability to find their way forward at night. While the use of tanks at night was discouraged, not least of all by the Armoured Corps itself, the tactic had been employed successfully in North Africa. Simonds was well aware of this as he had visited the British forces in North Africa shortly after the battle of El Hamma, which is often touted as the model for TOTALIZE.[35]

Indeed the El Hamma battle, which turned the Axis forces out of a very strong "Maginot" type defensive position constructed by the French to guard their frontier with Libya, did have a number of features in common with TOTALIZE. These included the use of bombers in support of the ground forces and the employment of tanks at night. It must be added that there was

Machine Gun Battalion
Canadian Infantry Division

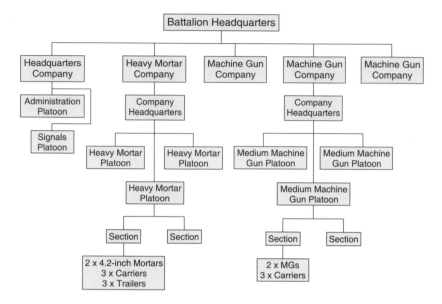

The machine gun companies usually supported the infantry brigades and the platoons tended to be affiliated with battalions to foster cooperation and cohesion. The venerable Vickers water-cooled medium machine gun, while both more cumbersome and slower-firing than its German counterpart, was a reliable and effective weapon.

another feature that would appear again in TOTALIZE. Just as the German front was collapsing, one of those combat leaders with the tactical flair and energy so characteristic of the German officer corps took charge. A *General-major* von Liebenstein hastily cobbled together a grab bag of remnants into an anti-tank screen and halted a British armoured brigade that threatened to cut the German line of retreat. Again, as would be the case with TOTALIZE, there were two interpretations of El Hamma, both fully justifiable based on the evidence. On the one hand, thanks to von Liebenstein the Axis forces escaped to fight again another day; on the other, the British broke through the enemy line and drove them deep into Tunisia.[36]

As we have seen, besides calling for all available air support, Simonds had realized that there were not enough troops, guns and tanks available in 2nd Canadian Corps for the task he had been given. At the end of the outline plan, he summarized his requirements as

1 Three infantry divisions.

2 Two independent armoured brigades. NOTE: Of the above, two infantry divisions and the two armoured brigades must have had special training in a deep advance at night and had ample time to study the ground, their special problems and equipment. I consider these troops must be earmarked a week ahead as a absolute minimum.

3 Two armoured divisions.

4 Armoured infantry carriers to carry infantry through to deep objectives with the tanks in First Phase. I strongly recommend that "Priests" released by conversion of field regiments have their guns and equipment "lifted" and be converted for this purpose. They could be reconverted to their normal role after the operation, if still serviceable.

5 One searchlight battery for movement lighting, if low cloud obscures the moon.

6 Two squadrons of C[anal]D[efence]L[ight]s, one to work on the outer flank of each armoured bde in First Phase – if trials confirm claims for this equipment.[37]

7 Two squadrons of flails – one with each armoured brigade.

8 Crocodiles to assist in mopping up during darkness.

9 The whole of the available air effort (Heavy night and day bombers as well as tactical air forces).

10 Two complete AGRAs in addition to divisional artilleries and support of two additional AGRAs, one with each 1 and 12 Corps.

The concept of carrying troops in specially adapted tanks had been tried by the Canadian Corps during the Amiens offensive on 8 August 1918, but the troops had been so sickened by the nauseous and claustrophobic environment that they were incapable of fighting when they dismounted. In 1942-1943 there had been experiments with the use of armoured sleds towed by tanks to carry infantry, and these had been used operationally by the Americans at Anzio. In early 1944, 1st Canadian Corps in Italy had proposed using gutted Universal Carriers in the same manner.[38] And, of course, both the Germans and the Allies used half-tracks to transport some of the infantry in their armoured divisions. On rare occasions, Commonwealth troops had assaulted while mounted in the small, lightly-armoured Universal Carriers found in the carrier platoon of infantry battalions and divisional reconnaissance regiments. These occasions were so rare that they usually merited special mention, with terms like "cavalry charge" and "daring and imaginative" being used to describe them, along with an implication that this sort of thing was not quite "on." However TOTALIZE would be the first time that troops in infantry divisions would ride into battle mounted in vehicles with the same armoured protection and mobility as the tanks they accompanied.[39] It was the dawn of the widespread mechanization of armies as a whole as opposed to the narrower confines of the armoured community.

Obviously specialized armoured troop-carrying vehicles of this sort did not exist and would have to be improvised, since, as Simonds noted, no one at this stage of the war was inclined to develop a specialized armoured troop carrier. He explained in a 1947 battlefield study tour of Operation TOTALIZE that he had been watching some Priests one day when it occurred to him that if the vehicles were stripped, they would have sufficient space and protection to carry infantry into battle. As these Priests properly belonged to the U.S. Army, Simonds had asked Crerar to obtain their permission to convert the vehicles and use them for this operation.[40] Hence, in his statement of requirements submitted with the outline plan Simonds had strongly recommended "that 'Priests' released by conversion of field regiments have their guns and equipment 'lifted' and be converted for this purpose."

The "Priests" (the American nomenclature was M7) were 105 mm self-propelled guns on adapted Sherman tank chassis that had been loaned to the British and Canadian armies by the Americans to equip the field artillery regiments in the assaulting divisions. Four Canadian artillery units – the 12th, 13th and 14th Field Regiments of the 3rd Division and the 19th Army Field Regiment – had exchanged their 25-pounders for Priests in the fall of 1943 as part of their equipment for OVERLORD. The time was now ripe, with the 3rd Division withdrawn from the line for a well deserved rest, for the three divisional regiments to exchange their borrowed guns for towed 25-pounders as part of a program to re-equip the field regiments of 21st Army Group. (The 12th and 13th Field Regiments began to turn in their Priests on 1 August, followed by the 14th Field Regiment on 3 August. The 19th Army

84

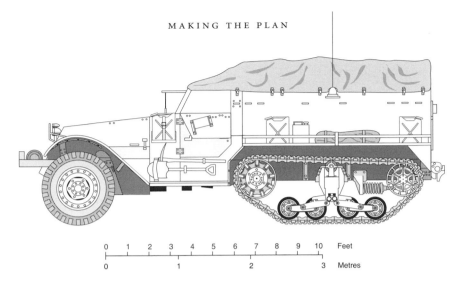

```
0  1  2  3  4  5  6  7  8  9  10  Feet
0          1          2          3   Metres
```

Half-track – M5

The half-track design was employed by both the Allies and the Germans as armoured personnel carriers throughout the war. The M5 was an American design that had seating for an infantry section of 10 men in the rear, plus three seats in the cab. Armour protection was proof against shell splinters and small-arms fire but there was no overhead protection for the occupants. The half-track was a popular vehicle in Canadian service and served as the basis for many specialized conversions.

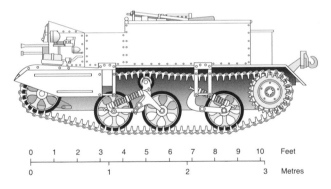

```
0  1  2  3  4  5  6  7  8  9  10  Feet
0          1          2          3   Metres
```

Universal Carrier No 3, Mk II*

The ubiquitous Universal Carrier served in many different guises in Canadian units. Some 29,000 were built in Canada alone, together with 40,000 in Great Britain. Carriers were also built in Australia and New Zealand. Although there was no overhead protection for the crew, the armour plate was proof only against shell splinters and small-arms fire and the engine occupied the centre of the cargo compartment, the Universal Carrier remained popular throughout the war for its versatility.

Country of origin: Great Britain
Crew: 4–5
Length: 12 feet 4 inches
Width: 6 feet 11 inches
Height: 5 feet 3 inches
Weight: 3.95 tons
Engine: Ford 8 cylinder
Maximum speed: 32 mph
Range: 160 miles
Armament: .303 Bren MG
Armour – Maximum: 12 mm
Minimum: 7 mm

Field Regiment (SP) did not exchange its Priests for 25-pounder self-pro-pelled Sextons until 24 August.) On 31 July Crerar had anticipated that the Americans would agree and had directed Brigadier Grant to be prepared to convert the SP guns to armoured infantry carriers by 9 August, although this date was later moved forward to 6 August.[41] Wiggan, the officer commanding 2 Tank Troops Workshop, set up an *ad hoc* Advanced Workshop Detachment nicknamed "Kangaroo," which eventually numbered some 250 tradesmen drawn from Royal Electrical and Mechanical Engineers and Royal Canadian Electrical and Mechanical Engineers units plus a Royal Canadian Ordnance Corps stores section and a Royal Canadian Army Service Corps unit. Among the equipment pooled were electric and gas welding equipment, while vir-tually unlimited access to welding rods, armour plate, radial engine parts, oxy-acetylene welding sets and gases and radial engine overhaul stands was required. Authority to adapt the vehicles was not received from HQ 21st Army Group until the early afternoon of 2 August. While officially work did not begin actively until the next morning, a recent history of the RCEME stated that the first tradesmen reported for duty on the afternoon of the 2nd and had stripped 15 vehicles by last light.[42]

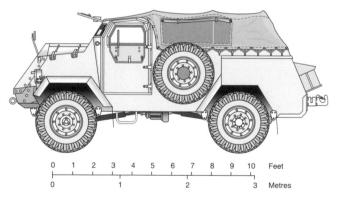

GMC armoured truck

Produced by General Motors at Oshawa, Ontario, the GMC Armoured Truck was a wheeled, open-topped personnel carrier with full frontal protection against .303 rounds and shell splinters. It could carry eight men, including the driver, and their equipment. The armoured side plates were designed to enable the troops to fire over the sides of the vehicle but that entailed limiting armour protection to shoulder height for the passengers. The GMC Armoured Truck could be converted to an ambulance for two stretcher cases by folding down the seats and moving stretcher brackets into place. By removing the seats altogether the truck could be used as an armoured load carrier.

The first order of business on 3 August was to complete the pilot model, both to obtain formal approval of the design and to work the bugs out of the production schedule. At 1830 hours that evening Lieutenant Green and a driver of D Squadron, 25 Canadian Armoured Delivery Regiment (Elgin Regiment), delivered the vehicle to Headquarters 2nd Canadian Corps for inspection by Simonds. The actual conversion entailed removal of the gun, mantlet, seats and ammunition bins and then welding armour over the aperture left when the gun and mantlet were absent. When the supply of armour plate was exhausted, sheets of mild steel plate were welded on the inside and outside of the space and the intervening gap filled with sand. (At one stage the enterprising craftsmen even cut strips of plating from landing craft stranded on the beaches, which provoked howls of outrage from the navy. Other steel was collected from a metal works in Caen.) As well, a complete check-up and overhaul of each vehicle's chassis was performed and all the engines were pulled and either overhauled or replaced. Brigadier H.V.D. Laing, the senior administrative officer at Simonds's headquarters, estimated that the conversion required about 100 man-hours per vehicle based on the strength of the detachment and a 15-hour working day. This may well have been a conservative estimate as at least one soldier reported working from 0400 to 2300 daily tightening tracks or changing engines using his Diamond-T wrecker. By 2200 hours on Saturday 5 August, 72 Priests had been converted and a further four were completed the next morning to end the production run. As the last step between the Advanced Workshop Detachment and end users, D Squadron of the Elgin Regiment organized the delivery and issue of the vehicles, described colourfully if inaccurately in the squadron's war diary as "specially converted tanks designed to carry a battle platoon of infantry each."[43]

There was another aspect of the introduction of the armoured carriers that has largely been ignored, perhaps because the historical record is so sparse. Even the recently published history of the 1st Canadian Armoured Carrier Regiment was unable to provide more than the barest outline. What seems clear however is that there was an *ad hoc* organization created to take over the vehicles from the Workshop Detachment and to train with and then carry the troops of the two assaulting divisions into action. The available evidence suggests this organization was under the control of 3rd Canadian

Infantry Division and based on E Squadron of the Elgin Regiment, responsible for the supply of armoured vehicles to 2nd Canadian Corps troops. The drivers would have needed a place to eat and sleep and collect their pay and pick up their mail and learn what was going on and just hang out, in other words a home. As well, the vehicles would have required fuel, minor repairs and maintenance. All this could not have happened automatically and it appears that a small number of officers and NCOs from the Elgin Regiment provided the nucleus of a squadron-sized unit, while the drivers came from a variety of sources, including the recently converted artillery regiments, armoured corps reinforcements and the ranks of the Elgin Regiment itself.[44]

The available Kangaroos (Kangaroo, the nickname for Major Wiggan's detachment, was so appropriate that it transferred itself more or less automatically to the vehicles, although initially they were also called "Unfrocked Priests" and "Holy Rollers") could lift only one infantry battalion's equivalent of troops in each of the two divisions. The remaining lift was found from the divisions' holdings of half-tracks, including some earmarked as replacements that were rushed over from England, Universal Carriers and Canadian-built armoured 15 cwt trucks. The latter, a strong contender for the "ugliest military vehicle of all time" award, was a workhorse that could carry ten infantrymen while affording some degree of protection from small-arms fire and shell and mortar fragments.[45]

None of this would matter if the troops were unable to exploit the advantages provided by the cover of darkness and the protection provided by the vehicles' armour. Simonds had realized the first step was to sell the two assault divisions on the opportunities. As he explained during the postwar battlefield tour,

> It was obviously going to be quite useless to mount the infantry if they felt like a lot of sardines in a tin and had no likelihood of the operation succeeding. So I quickly suggested to 2 Cdn Div that we might be able to produce some form of Armoured Personnel Carrier in order to get them thinking about its possibilities. As soon as the operation began to harden and I had received definite orders, I at once asked that my second [phase one] infantry division be detailed. The Highland Division was nominated and I was a bit worried as to how the Scots would like it, because they had

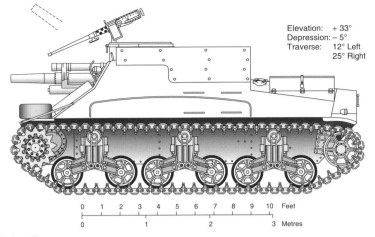

Elevation: + 33°
Depression: − 5°
Traverse: 12° Left
25° Right

M7 "Priest"

Based on the chassis of the American M3 medium tank, the M7 was armed with a 105 mm howitzer. The ammunition load totalled 69 rounds, which compared favourably with contemporary German designs. The 33 lb HE projectile had a maximum range of 11,500 yards. The M7 suffered from an open-topped crew compartment as did most self-propelled howitzers of the period, but was well regarded due to its roomy design and the effectiveness of its weapon. Canadian and British users added extra armour plating along both sides of the fighting compartment for additional protection.

Country of origin: United States
Crew: 7
Length: 19 feet 9 inches
Width: 9 feet 5 inches
Height: 8 feet 4 inches
Weight: 25.3 tons
Engine: Continental R-975
Maximum speed: 25 mph
Range: 125 miles
Armament: 105 mm Howitzer, .50 calibre MG HB M2 in
     flexible mount in pulpit
Armour – Maximum: 62 mm
          Minimum: 12 mm

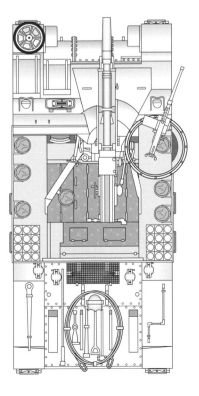

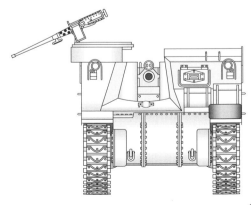

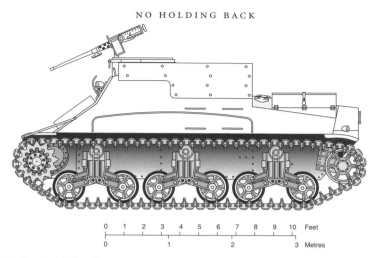

M7 "Unfrocked Priest"

As the M7 "Priest" was being phased out of Canadian service in Normandy, it proved to be well suited for conversion into an armoured personnel carrier. The 105 mm howitzer and all other artillery-related equipment, with the exception of the gun mount, was removed. This resulted in a spacious vehicle capable of lifting a section of infantry. While it lacked overhead protection for the occupants, the "Unfrocked Priest" performed so well in its role that the establishment of Canadian and British armoured carrier regiments followed in short order. Instead of "Unfrocked Priests" though, these regiments were equipped with surplus Ram tanks with their turrets removed and the interiors stripped out to provide room for the troops.

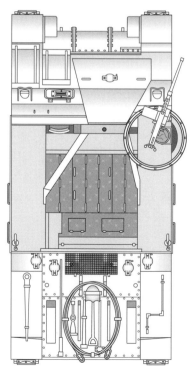

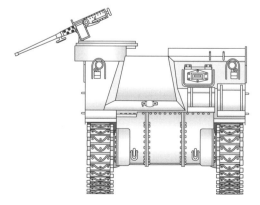

the reputation of being rather canny and having their own ideas about things. General RENNIE, who was unfortunately later killed at the Rhine crossing, came over to see me as soon as they had been nominated and I had a talk with him. He was very taken with the idea and I knew from that first talk that I had his support one hundred per cent and subsequently 51 (H) Div took to it with great enthusiasm.[46]

All this happened quickly. Simonds had briefed Crerar on 31 July and the 2 Canadian Corps General Staff war diary recorded on the following day that detailed planning for Operation TOTALIZE had commenced. During that day his divisional commanders were brought into the picture by Simonds, who then met with Major General Rennie at 1700 hours[47] and again at 1500 hours on the 4th, although Rennie's division did not come under Simonds's command officially until late in the afternoon of 4 August.[48] Brigadier Elliot Rodger, the chief of staff of 2nd Canadian Corps, described the reaction when Simonds outlined his plan to his division commanders in a letter to Simonds's biographer

I well recall his O Group [Orders Group] before Totalize when the several division commanders sat in a circle under the pine trees (all being much older than GGS [Simonds] and some with desert sand in their ears) to whom he opened "Gentlemen, we will do this attack at night with armour." Their jaws dropped noticeably. Prior to then I believe that not I nor any of the Corps HQ Brigadiers knew of the plan. Perhaps he had some prior discussion with [Brigadier SF] Clark (CSO) on the considerable plans needed to help the tanks and defrocked priests keep direction in the dark. But the whole plan poured forth complete and crystal clear.[49]

Rodger's description was clear and vivid, if somewhat misleading. As noted above, this meeting was attended by his three Canadian division commanders, while the commander of 51st Highland Division was briefed separately.[50] The only commander present with sand in his ears was Simonds, who had been attached to the Eighth Army in the desert in early-1943. As for their being much older, Keller was three years his senior and Foulkes was only three months older, while Kitching was seven years younger than Simonds.

Simonds may have been dissembling a bit when in 1947 he claimed during the battlefield tour that originally he had considered that the troops involved "would have something like a month's training because a great deal of work was needed to rule out the likelihood of very serious hitches." This clearly was impossible to achieve, but Simonds was on firmer ground when he had asked for a week to prepare his forces. In the end he was forced to settle for much less, although he did contribute to the shortfall by agreeing to move the attack ahead 24 hours based on a "request" from Montgomery. As it was, many units had time for less than two full days of training and the last vehicles were delivered the day before the attack, and Major Sydney Radley-Walters of A Squadron, the Sherbrooke Fusilier Regiment, recalled that the infantry battalion he was attached to trained with 3-ton trucks initially until the armoured carriers arrived.[51]

When was TOTALIZE to be mounted? The situation in the western part of the bridgehead was developing rapidly and the American break out was well underway. Montgomery had telephoned Crerar on the evening of 31 July to direct that 3rd British Infantry Division be detached from 1st British Corps, the other corps in First Canadian Army, and sent to reinforce Second British Army. This left the corps with two divisions, 6th Airborne and 49th (West Riding) Infantry, in the line and 51st (Highland) Division in reserve north of Caen. The corps was obviously incapable of mounting any offensive operations, and Montgomery confirmed with Crerar that he did not anticipate initiating any major operation with First Canadian Army for at least a week. Crerar had anticipated this pause when, on 29 July, he had directed Simonds to plan an attack down the Caen–Falaise road, and he had been briefed in outline on Simonds's plan earlier on the 31st. (As we have seen, on 31 July Crerar had ordered Brigadier Grant to be prepared to complete the conversion of the Priests to armoured carriers by 9 August.) On the evening of 3 August, the same day that the first Priest was unfrocked, Montgomery phoned Crerar again to tell him that planning for the operation "should go on actively" and giving him a target date of 8 August.[52]

On 4 August at 2100 hours Crerar received Montgomery's Directive M 516. It began with his usual vivid clarity of language: "The general situation is very good and we have unloosed the shackles that were holding us down and we have knocked away the key rivets. The enemy front is now in such a state that it could be made to disintegrate completely." Montgomery then elaborated on the situation. The Second Army had broken through the German defences and was pivoting southward and eastward on its left corps (12) while the centre corps (30) had the task of securing the general area around Mont Pinçon and then thrusting towards Thury-Harcourt on the Orne. The right corps (8) was directed on the area Condé-Vassy and then on in the direction of Argentan. The American 12th Army Group operations were to follow the lines already laid down, but with decreased emphasis on the Brittany peninsula. First U.S. Army was swinging to the east round the southern flank of Second British Army, and its left was to advance on the axis Domfront-Alençon. Patton's Third U.S. Army had sent a corps to clear the Brittany peninsula while its remaining corps were directed towards Laval and Angers. The portion of Montgomery's directive dealing with First Canadian Army read as follows:

Task of First Canadian Army [all italics in original]
8. To launch a heavy attack from the Caen sector in the direction of Falaise.
9. *Object of the operation.*
    (a) To break through the enemy positions to the south and south-east of Caen, and to gain such ground in the direction of Falaise as will cut off the enemy forces now facing Second Army and render their withdrawing eastwards difficult – if not impossible.
    (b) Generally to destroy enemy equipment and personnel, as a preliminary to a possible wide exploitation of success.
10. The attack to be launched *as early as possible* and in any case not later than 8 August – dependent on good weather for air support. Every day counts, and speed in preparing and launching the attack is very necessary.

    Every endeavour will be made to launch the attack on 7 August if this is in any way possible.[53]

Late that evening (4 August), Brigadier Churchill Mann, the Chief of Staff at Army Headquarters, called Brigadier Elliot Rodger, his counterpart at Simonds's Headquarters, at 2300 hours to ask if D-Day could be moved forward 24 hours. After some deliberation, Simonds agreed and it was decided that TOTALIZE would be mounted on 7 August.[54]

The Canadian official history recounts that on 5 August the villages in the enemy's front line were quieter than for many days.[55] Brigadier Rodger recorded in his diary that Mann phoned at 1330 hours to say 1. SS-*Panzerdivision* seemed to be pulling away "on our front." Rodger added that "both our divisions were ordered to push their necks out and found it softer but [there were] still some Boche there."[56] In fact, the two forward Canadian divisions made probing attacks to determine if the Germans might be abandoning their forward positions. Late in the afternoon the Black Watch of 5 Brigade and a squadron of the Fort Garry Horse advanced south from St. André-sur-Orne towards May-sur-Orne. Their reception and that accorded to Le Régiment de Maisonneuve, who passed through the Black Watch and continued the attack, proved that the village was still strongly held. A further attempt by the Maisonneuves the next morning also was unsuccessful. West of the Route Nationale, 4th Canadian Armoured Division sent patrols during the afternoon against Tilly-la-Campagne and La Hogue that captured some prisoners from 1. SS-*Panzerdivision.* That evening the Argyll and Sutherland Highlanders of Canada, supported by a squadron of the South Alberta Regiment, attacked the former, while a company of the Lake Superior Regiment (Motor) and a squadron of the Canadian Grenadier Guards assaulted the latter.[57] Both were costly failures that proved beyond a shadow of a doubt that the front was strongly held. The original plan would still have to be executed.

We now know, which the official historian did not, that Ultra had reported that the *Flivo* (*Fliegerverbindungsoffiziere*, air liaison officer) with both 1. SS-*Panzerkorps* and 1. SS-*Panzerdivision* had made reference to a pending move in reports on both 4 and 5 August, but other intelligence, including the prisoners mentioned above, indicated the division was still in place. For example on 4 and 5 August, Hut 3 at Bletchley Park, the home of Ultra, informed Crerar and Simonds that the panzer division air liaison officer had signalled "transfer in view soon" on the morning of the 4th and the next day had reported at 1630 hours "Division beginning that night would be relieved stage by stage by 89 Inf div and would assemble in area north of Falaise." On that day Hut 3 signalled at 1137 hours that "Main body of 1 SS Panzer division relieved by 0350 hrs Aug 5 according to Flivo I SS Panzer Corps" and then reported at 1805 hours from the same source that the Allies seemed to be unaware of the German withdrawal movements and were following up only hesitantly. [58] (It should be understood that the time of each Ultra message was when it was logged into the message centre at Bletchley Park. Depending upon a number of factors, it might not be in the hands of commanders in the field until much later.) A significant amount of Ultra was based upon interception of *Flivo* messages, which tended to provide summaries of the locations and intentions of German ground forces, but not necessarily anything in the way of detailed plans. *Luftwaffe* signals security and procedures were terribly lax compared to the other German services, a vulnerability the code breakers had identified and targeted.[59]

What exactly was Ultra? For our purposes, it was intelligence derived by analysing deciphered German radio messages along with a system to ensure its secure dissemination on a need-to-know basis to a few selected individuals at the upper levels of the Allied command structure. It is important to understand that it was not raw intercept data, which in most cases would be of limited worth to most users. Hut 3, which served the Allied armies and air forces, had built up a large, efficient system of cross-referencing information and assigning indications of reliability to its individual products. In short, Ultra was a sophisticated intelligence service. While extremely valuable and important, it was not infallible, especially as it depended upon deciphered radio messages, often intercepted in difficult atmospheric conditions. Many messages remained unbroken while others could be read only partially. Any information that was passed by courier or land line could not be intercepted by Ultra, or other signals intelligence systems for that matter.[60] Moreover Ultra was not universally accepted; General Omar Bradley, for example, believed that too much reliance was placed on it.[61]

It is important to note that these attacks on Tilly and La Hogue were not mounted to disguise the Ultra message of 1137 hours as a source in the event the Germans were abandoning their forward positions. The intercept regarding the relief of 1. *SS-Panzerdivision* by 89. *Infanteriedivision* was not received until well after the assaults had been launched. In the absence of any firm information that pointed to a major counter-offensive at this time, although there were a number of reports of westward movement of panzer divisions, Canadian intelligence appreciated that the most likely course of action by the Germans would be to develop their defences in depth. In view of what might have been a withdrawal, not necessarily a relief in the line, at approximately 2040 hours Gerald Beament, the Colonel General Staff, phoned Mann, the Chief of Staff, who had flown to England to attend a conference at the headquarters of the Allied Expeditionary Air Forces regarding the TOTALIZE air plan. As Mann was unavailable, Beament spoke to Brigadier Charles Richardson,[62] the Brigadier General Staff Plans at 21st Army Group, who had accompanied Mann, to explore the amendment of the air plan to cater for such a possibility.[63] This conversation will be discussed later as part of the development of the air plan. In fact the relief of 1. *SS-Panzerdivision* by 89. *Infanteriedivision* was underway while Beament was talking to Richardson, although this was far from an abandonment of the German forward position. In any case both Crerar and Simonds would have been remiss if they had not developed a contingency plan once the first indications of a possible withdrawal from the forward position were detected, and if they had not attempted to verify the information by other means.

In its June 1945 after-action report, the First Canadian Army intelligence staff somewhat ruefully admitted that they had committed a classic error during the planning of TOTALIZE, in that it is the role of intelligence staffs at all levels to report what is known of the enemy and to aggressively search out more. Often this includes making an appreciation of the situation from the enemy's point of view to determine a likely course of action, but unfortunately these two functions sometimes work at cross purposes. From this point forward it appears that Crerar and Simonds, perhaps taking their guidance from their intelligence staffs, assessed the possible enemy actions based on an appreciation of what they would do if they were in the Germans' boots, not what the evidence, including some very precise Ultra intelligence, indicated they were actually doing.[64] While his biographer claims that Simonds was ill served by army intelligence,[65] the truth is that he accepted it at face value. However, Crerar and Simonds were not the only Allied commanders who were not thinking critically at the time.

There are indications that this pre-judging was going on as early as that very day (5 August). At 1100 hours Crerar assembled the subordinate commanders who would be involved in TOTALIZE down to brigade level to deliver his assessment of the importance of the operation.[66] He gave what only could be termed a rather ponderous "pep talk," comparing the operation with Amiens, which was launched on 8 August 1918, 26 years before. Crerar took care to stress the importance of maintaining the momentum and emphasized the importance of foresight and initiative by his commanders.[67] However, and this was the indication that he had decided the Germans would not be so foolish as to leave the Caen front under-defended, he pronounced that one thing was certain, and that was that the German High Command "will not unduly weaken the vital northern hinge of the German line." Crerar ignored indications to the contrary[68] and his conclusion guided Canadian thinking virtually up to the time the troops crossed the start line.

Other intelligence confirmed that 89. *Infanteriedivision* was replacing 1. *SS-Panzerdivision* in the line. In fact, this untried and supposedly low-quality formation was now holding the front from the area of Tilly-la-Campagne and La Hogue west to the banks of the Orne, an area that at one time had been held by two SS panzer divisions. No sooner had this formation completed its changeover than a Yugoslav deserter from III. *Bataillon, Grenadierregiment* 1055, one of its two infantry regiments, arrived in Canadian lines with news of the relief. He thought that 1. *SS-Panzerdivision* had withdrawn to the area of Bretteville-sur-Laize, on the western flank of the Phase 2 objective. Later the same night an ambulance drove into the Canadian lines at St. Martin by mistake, and its two occupants, members of an ambulance platoon attached to *Grenadierregiment* 1056, the other infantry regiment of 89. *Infanteriedivision,* were captured. This intelligence, in the absence of news of the Mortain offensive, convinced Crerar and Simonds that not only were the Germans not abandoning their forward positions, but they had managed to establish a strong defence in depth. To their minds, it seemed the Phase 2 objective would now be held by 1. and 12. *SS-Panzerdivisionen,* a formidable prospect indeed, and one that strengthened the defence.[69]

In the meantime, on 6 August Crerar communicated his direction to his two corps commanders for post-TOTALIZE operations by letter. Echoing Montgomery's directive, he confirmed that the object of the operation was to break into, and through, the enemy positions SOUTH and south east of CAEN, and to gain such ground in the direction of FALAISE as will cut off large numbers of the enemy now facing Second Brit Army, thus rendering the withdrawal Eastwards difficult, if not impossible.

Crerar also issued directions regarding the transfer of 51st Highland Division and the extra armoured brigade Simonds had requested, 33 British Armoured Brigade, back to the command of 1st British Corps on 9 August, and detailed the Highland Division's activities to protect the left flank of 2nd Canadian Corps. He then laid out the specific post-TOTALIZE tasks and guidance for the drive eastward to the Seine. All of this was based on the existing 2nd Canadian Corps plan as Crerar understood it.[70] What he did not know was that Simonds had changed his plan because of the perceived change in the German defensive layout and especially the reinforcement of the second position.

Simonds appreciated that the weight of the German defences had shifted to the rear and that this required modification to his original plan. At a conference held at corps headquarters at 1000 hours on 6 August he issued revised orders to his commanders. He explained that the forward position was now held by 89. *Infanteriedivision* bolstered by whatever tanks and assault guns 1. *SS-Panzerdivision* had left in position, while the two SS panzer divisions were deployed on or near the Phase 2 objective. Without the necessity of battering a way through the tough panzer grenadiers of 1. and 9. *SS-Panzerdivisionen*, the two infantry divisions attacking in Phase 1 could be handled more boldly than was originally planned. He did, however, make some minor changes to his Phase 1 plan. The tasks of seizing Bretteville-sur-Laize on the right and the woods south of Robertmesnil on the left, were now to be carried out by the assaulting divisions, leaving 3rd Canadian Infantry Division free to follow up behind the armour in Phase 2.[71] On the other hand, he noted that,

the second break through attack might meet stronger resistance than originally anticipated, as in the redisposition of the enemy forces, it was possible that neither 1 SS Pz nor 12 SS Pz Divs would be involved on the May-sur-Orne–La Hogue position, but would be found on the next defensive line. Consequently a widening of the frontage and an increase

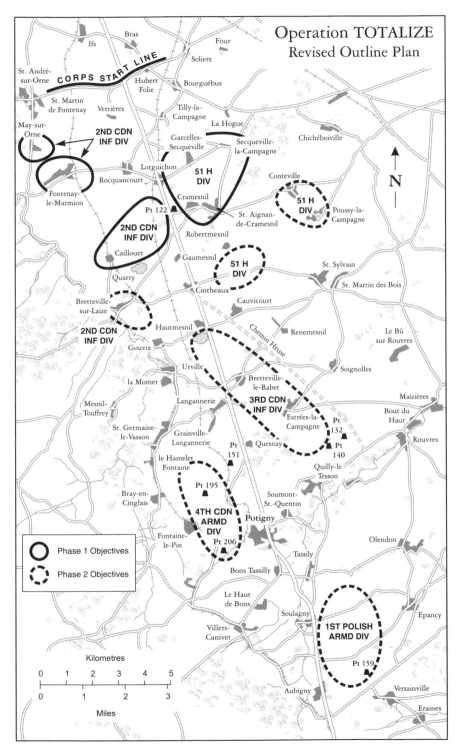

Operation TOTALIZE
Revised Outline Plan

Bras

Ifs

Four

St. André-
sur-Orne

CORPS START LINE

Soliers

Hubert
Folie

Bourguébus

St. Martin
de Fontenay

Verrières

Tilly-la-
Campagne

La Hogue

May-sur-
Orne

**2ND CDN
INF DIV**

Garcelles-
Secqueville

Secqueville-
la-Campagne

Chichéboiville

N

Fontenay-
le-Marmion

Lorguichon

Rocquancourt

**51 H
DIV**

Conteville

Cramesnil

**51 H
DIV**

Poussy-la-
Campagne

Pt 122

St. Aignan-
de-Cramesnil

**2ND CDN
INF DIV**

Robertmesnil

Caillouet

Gaumesnil

**51 H
DIV**

St. Sylvain

Quarry

Cintheaux

St. Martin des Bois

Bretteville-
sur-Laize

Cauvicourt

**2ND CDN
INF DIV**

Hautmesnil

Chemin Heuse

Renemesnil

Le Bû
sur Rouvres

Gouvix

Urville

Bretteville-
le-Rabet

Soignolles

la Momer

Maizières

Mesnil-
Touffrey

Langannerie

**3RD CDN
INF DIV**

Estrées-la-
Campagne

Pt
132

Bout du
Haut

St. Germaine-
le-Vasson

Grainville-
Langannerie

Quesnay

Pt
140

Rouvres

le Hamelet
Fontaine

Pt
151

Quilly-le
Tesson

Pt 195

Bray-en-
Cinglais

**4TH CDN
ARMD
DIV**

Soumont-
St.-Quentin

Potigny

Fontaine-
le-Pin

Pt 206

Olendon

Tassily

Bons Tassilly

Le Haut
de Bons

Soulagny

**1ST POLISH
ARMD DIV**

Epancy

Villers-
Canivet

Pt 159

Versainville

Aubigny

Eraines

○ Phase 1 Objectives

◌ Phase 2 Objectives

Kilometres

0   1   2   3   4   5

0   1   2   3

Miles

in the weight of attack for Phase II was required. He had decided therefore to launch the Polish Armoured Division simultaneously and parallel with 4th Canadian Armoured Division, and to direct these two divisions straight to their final objectives.

As this attack had been planned to take place during daylight, the weight of the available air support had been arranged to suppress the anticipated strong enemy positions before the Allied artillery could complete its move forward. Therefore, Simonds decided that no alteration to the air plan was necessary,[72] although, as we shall see, his confidence in the air plan may have been based on some false assumptions. Simonds explained his appreciation and the reasoning behind his changes to the plan in a letter to Crerar signed at 2100 hours that evening. In it, he reiterated the points expounded above, and concluded with the assurance that "these modifications have been embodied in an amendment to the original operation instruction."[73]

As this alteration of the plan would have the greatest effect on 4th Canadian Armoured Division and the Polish 1. *Dywizji Pancernej*, the differences in the tasks assigned to the two divisions must be examined. First, 4th Canadian Armoured Division had originally been assigned the mission in Phase 2 of attacking along the Route Nationale and capturing Hautmesnil and the high ground northwest of Bretteville-le-Rabet. In the next (third) phase, the division was to advance on the axis Hautmesnil–Point 180–Point 206. It was then to position itself facing west and south on the high ground Point 180–Point 195–Point 206 and send out patrols to maintain or gain contact with the enemy to the south and west. In Phase 2 the Polish division was to move to a forward concentration area on the order of the corps commander, and in Phase 3 was to advance on the axis Quesnay–Point 165–Point 150 and position itself facing east and south on the high ground Point 170–Point 159. The division was then to patrol east and south to maintain or gain contact with the enemy. It was a rather conservative plan, but one that had a good chance of success against what were anticipated to be elements of two panzer grenadier regiments supported by a few tanks and assault guns.[74]

In Simonds's revised plan, both divisions were be positioned on the corps start line by the morning of D plus 1, 4th Canadian Armoured Division behind 2nd Canadian Infantry Division and 1. *Dywizji Pancernej* behind 51st

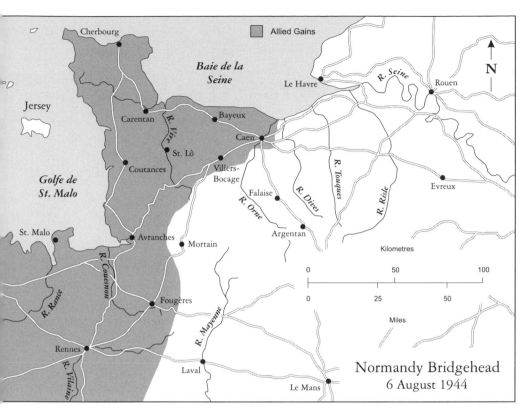

Normandy Bridgehead
6 August 1944

Highland Division. In Phase 2, 4th Canadian Armoured was to go directly to its final objective and position itself and patrol as directed in the original plan. The effect of the change was more profound for the Polish division. It was no longer to advance along the Caen–Falaise highway behind 4th Armoured Division and 3rd Infantry Division; it was now to pass through the Highlanders and advance southwesterly to its final objective. There was a potentially major element in the plan that could sabotage the Polish mission: the 51st Highland Division axis was too constrained to allow the passage of an armoured regiment, let alone a brigade or division, and any movement to the west would interfere with the 4th Canadian Armoured Division advance. Therefore 1. *Dywizji Pancernej* would have to advance between the eastern Phase 1 bombing targets and the 51st Highland Division Phase 1 positions. This in itself was not necessarily a bad thing, that is until the Poles neared the forward position of the Highlanders. If 51st Highland Division had not yet secured the ground forward of St. Aignan-de-Cramesnil and southeast to St.

Panther

This Panther of *SS-Panzerregiment* 12, which was knocked out early in the campaign, provides an indication of the formidable capabilities of one of the best tanks of the Second World War. (NAC/PA 130149)

Sylvain, the Polish formation might be presenting its left flank to the enemy as it passed through the British division's lines.[75]

At this stage, with preparations at army and corps nearly complete, there was time to consider eventualities. For example, Lieutenant Colonel P.E.R. Wright, Crerar's chief intelligence officer, signed an appreciation to Crerar at 1320 hours on 7 August that described the latest information on enemy dispositions. While it had been known that 1. *Panzerdivision* had been replaced by 89. *Infanteriedivision* for at least a day, it was now becoming clear that the panzer division had moved west to take part in the Mortain offensive. Although most of 12. *SS-Panzerdivision* was thought to be southwest of the Caen–Mézidon railway, elements were known to be as far west as the road from Falaise to Bretteville-sur-Laize. Later on this same day, these elements would be identified fighting against a British bridgehead across the Orne near the Forêt de Grimbosq. The fighting strength of 12. *SS-Panzerdivision* was estimated at 2,500 front-line troops and 45 Mk IV and 35 Panther tanks. Wright alerted Crerar to the possibility that some tanks of *SS-Panzerregiment* 1 may have been left to support 89. *Infanteriedivision* and that as many as 25 Tiger tanks of *schwere SS-Panzerabteilung* 101 must be considered to still be in the area. He predicted that the Germans would not be able to react in time to the

Phase 1 advance in conjunction with the bombing and he also had deduced that, if 12. *SS-Panzerdivision* was not deployed on the Phase 2 objectives, it would not be able to defend the second line effectively until after first light. He, however, discounted the fighting power of 89. *Infanteriedivision* and underestimated the potential of 12. *SS-Panzerdivision* to block the Canadian offensive.[76] It may be an unduly harsh judgement, but this was the second time in as many days that Lieutenant Colonel Wright appeared to be telling his boss what he wanted to hear, rather than what the evidence suggested.

At 1700 hours 7 August Montgomery called on Crerar and discussed the general situation. Crerar kept a record both of this meeting and his subsequent telephone conversation with Simonds regarding the army group commander's appreciation of the situation and instructions. Suddenly, instead of talking about breaking through the German defences on the Caen–Falaise Road, the generals were not only thinking and talking about capturing Falaise, they were actually talking about pushing light armoured forces east, south and west of Falaise. Crerar and Simonds also discussed using 1. *Dwyizji Pancernej* to clear the enemy forces from the area west of the River Dives from St. Pierre-sur-Dives north to the sea.[77] While they were correct to have been considering their next steps, one cannot help but wonder if over-confidence was not setting in. Certainly there was nothing to indicate that Crerar had not accepted Wright's predictions as perfectly valid and reasonable, or that Montgomery had done anything to restrain his enthusiasm, and it was only human nature for both Simonds and Crerar to have become convinced that success in TOTALIZE would crown their efforts.

Count the holes

If there was any doubt that the Sherman was terribly vulnerable, this photo should indicate the challenge that Simonds attempted to nullify by advancing at night. (Courtesy Mr. Roy T. Leslie, formerly 1st Hussars)

CHAPTER FIVE

BULLETS AND BOMBS –
THE FIRE PLAN

*"The essential conditions of this operation may therefore be summarized as
follows:- (a) the provision of overwhelming air support both by night and by
day until completion of the break-through, and (b) the existence of suitable
weather to ensure the full effectiveness of such overwhelming air support."*

OPERATION TOTALIZE, REQUEST FOR AIR SUPPORT

With the manoeuvre plan developed in outline, it fell to the specialist organizations such as artillery, engineers, signals and air as well as the administrative staffs to develop their own plans, and work on these would have proceeded concurrently with the fleshing-out of the manoeuvre plan. While all were vital to the successful outcome of the operation, the artillery and the air plans merit examination in detail.

The artillery fire plan for TOTALIZE is one of the least understood elements of the operation, perhaps because few of the historians who have written on the operation have had the background knowledge or the inclination to make sense of the details.[1] Most have relied on the table in Appendix L of the BAOR *Battlefield Tour* and limited their comments to noting that there were 720 guns involved in the plan and that it included a barrage in Phase 1. At this point it is best to reiterate a simple statement of principle. Artillery affects battle by the application of guns and ammunition, and there is much more to that statement than a blinding flash of the obvious. Where and how commanders employ the available guns and ammunition to best support forward troops is more than a simple *pro forma* exercise of filling in the blanks. The making of the artillery plan, like the manoeuvre plan, begins with an appreciation by the artillery commander; the difference is that the object is always to support the formation carrying out the operation. It would have been normal for the supported formation commander, in this case Simonds, to give further guidance to his artillery commander on such matters as the weight and distribution of fire, the policy on softening up enemy positions before H-Hour, the form of the supporting fire, etc. For TOTALIZE, as he noted in his appreciation, Simonds decided to dispense with any preparatory and counter-battery program before H-Hour in order to gain surprise in the timing and form of the attack, if not its direction and objectives.

Within the framework of the manoeuvre plan, the artillery appreciation considered three major factors: guns, ammunition and targets. These had to be balanced with the requirements to support the various phases of the operation, to take on enemy artillery in a counter-battery and perhaps a counter-flak program, to cater for unforeseen events while still supporting the attacking troops and to maintain a reserve of ammunition at all levels. In the case of TOTALIZE, the appreciation and plan were the responsibility of Brigadier A.B. Matthews,[2] the Commander Corps Royal [Canadian] Artillery (CCRA) of 2nd Canadian Corps, while Brigadier H.O.N. Brownfield, the Brigadier Royal [Canadian] Artillery (BRA) of First Canadian Army, coordinated the overall details, supervised the provision of the ammunition, arranged for support from the two flanking corps (one of which, in an indication of the sophistication of the British and Canadian artillery system of fire control, was part of Second British Army) and grouped extra artillery resources under Matthews's control. While Matthews was responsible for working out the details, final approval of the plan rested with Simonds as the commander responsible for conducting the operation.

When Simonds submitted his requirements to Crerar, he had specifically requested substantial artillery resources. These included a searchlight battery (yet to arrive on the Continent) for movement light* and "two complete AGRAs (Army Groups, Royal Artillery) in addition to divisional artilleries and support of two additional AGRAs, one each with 1 and 12 Corps." An

---

* Movement Light or, as it was dubbed by the press, "Monty's Moonlight," was created by "bouncing" searchlight beams off low clouds. It was a bit of a hit-or-miss effort and was not all that popular with the troops, who believed that it silhouetted them to enemy observation and fire. On occasion, such as during Operation SPRING on 25 July 1944, it did just that. Commanders and staffs, however, thought it was just the thing, and perhaps it was, compared to the CDL.

AGRA was for all intents and purposes an artillery brigade provided on the scale of one per corps, although there were six AGRAs and five corps in 21st Army Group. Within First Canadian Army at this time there were three of these formations: 2 Canadian and 4 British, which supported 2nd Canadian and 1st British Corps respectively, and 9 British AGRA.

There has been considerable confusion displayed over the organization of an AGRA, probably because order of battle tables published in both the Canadian official history and Volume 2 of *The Gunners of Canada* show only Canadian units. The table for an AGRA published for study purposes at wartime staff courses shows its composition as an army field regiment, four medium regiments and a heavy regiment – a total of 24 field, 64 medium and 16 heavy guns.[3] In Normandy, 2 Canadian AGRA was made up of 19 Army Field Regiment (Self Propelled); 3, 4 and 7 Medium Regiments; 15 British Medium Regiment; and 1 British Heavy Regiment (although 19 Army Field Regiment operated as part of 4th Canadian Armoured Division); while 9 AGRA fielded only three medium regiments (with a heavy anti-aircraft regiment of 24 3.7-inch guns attached). The two supporting AGRAs from the flanking corps, 3 and 4 British AGRA, each provided one heavy and four medium regiments for the fire plan. An Army Group Royal Artillery was a powerful, flexible organization that could both thicken the fire of the divisional artilleries and take on tasks on its own such as harassing fire, attacking targets in depth and

Medium Regiment
2nd Canadian AGRA

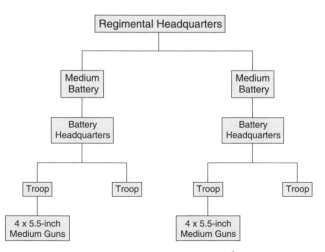

Unlike the field regiments, medium (and heavy) regiments retained their 1940 organization. The 5.5-inch was a reliable, modern design that entered service in 1942-1943 and stayed in British first-line service into the 1960s.

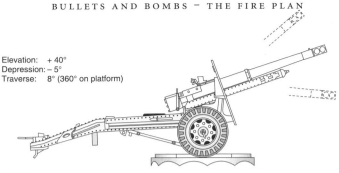

Elevation: + 40°
Depression: – 5°
Traverse: 8° (360° on platform)

25-pdr field gun

One of the most effective artillery pieces of the war, the 25-pdr gun equipped Canadian and British field artillery regiments throughout the conflict. It fired HE, AP, smoke and carrier rounds. Carrier rounds were usually filled with propaganda leaflets and were derived from the smoke round. In a two-stage loading sequence, the projectiles were loaded separately from the cartridges. With four charges to choose from and a muzzle velocity of 1,700 feet per second, the 25-pdr had a maximum range of 13,400 yards. The hollow box trail design permitted the breech of the gun to depress between the trails, enabling a 40° elevation. When coming into action, the platform, often seen slung under the trail, was released under the gun, which would then be pulled on top of it by the tractor. This permitted the 25-pdr to be rotated through a full 360° by one man, which was of great benefit when the gun was forced into an anti-tank role. The 25-pdr was served by a detachment of six men.

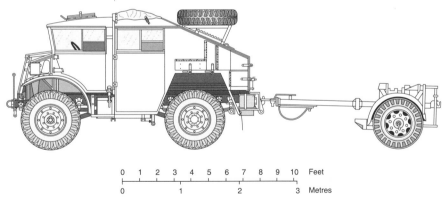

```
0   1   2   3   4   5   6   7   8   9   10   Feet
|---|---|---|---|---|---|---|---|---|---|
0                1                2                3   Metres
```

Field artillery tractor – (FAT)

The FAT was the standard tractor for the 25-pdr field gun and was based on the prewar British "Quad" design. Over 22,000 were built by Ford and General Motors in Canada during the war. It had a specially built body for the gun detachment members and their equipment. The main benefit in having a purpose-built vehicle, rather than using a common truck as a tractor, was that artillery regiments were virtually assured that their tractors wouldn't be redeployed to other duties when not hauling their guns. The FAT drew a No. 27 ammunition limber which in turn was connected to the 25-pdr. The limber stored 32 rounds of ammunition, tools and other equipment and supplies.

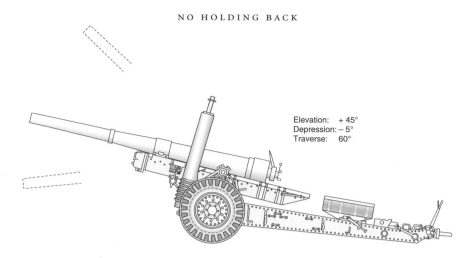

Elevation: + 45°
Depression: − 5°
Traverse: 60°

5.5-inch medium gun

A British artillery design, the 5.5-inch gun had a conventional split trail carriage with detachable spades and upright spring-balanced cylinders on both sides of the barrel. It originally fired a 100-pound HE projectile, which was superseded by a lighter 80-pound version in 1943 with a maximum range of 18,000 yards. There were four charges for the projectile plus a supercharge. Served by a gun detachment of 10 men, the 5.5-inch gun was capable of a sustained rate of fire of 2 rounds per minute.

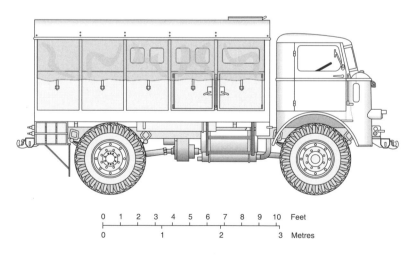

0   1   2   3   4   5   6   7   8   9   10   Feet

0   1   2   3   Metres

Medium artillery tractor – (MAT)

Built by the Four Wheel Drive Auto Company in Canada, this tractor had an open-topped, canvas-covered body with transverse seating arrangements for the 5.5-inch gun detachment of 10 men. It was also fitted with a 15-ton winch. In addition to the gun detachment, it could also carry a limited quantity of 5.5-inch ammunition and assorted other equipment.

counter-bombardment. It was normal practice for medium regiments to deploy observation posts and forward observation officers with the armoured regiments and infantry battalions of the attacking formations. Brownfield, the BRA of First Canadian Army, also arranged to have the support of the three field regiments of 49th (West Riding) Division, the flanking division of 1st Corps, and two heavy anti-aircraft regiments that were in the process of moving to France from the United Kingdom. In subsequent phases, artillery planning would also include the two field regiments of 1. *Dywizji Pancernej*, which was slated to exploit towards Falaise during Phase 3.

A medium regiment had two batteries, each with eight 5.5-inch guns. These were excellent guns (actually gun-howitzers) that fired a 100-pound shell 16,000 yards or an 80-pound round 18,500 yards. In its effect on the ground, a salvo from a medium battery was roughly equal to the rockets from a single Typhoon aircraft or a salvo from a light cruiser, except that a medium battery could maintain this fire more or less indefinitely in all weather. The concentrated fire of Scale One (one round per gun on establishment) from the four medium regiments of an AGRA, using the 100-pound shell, would land over three tons of steel on the target in a matter of seconds. It bears emphasizing that such concentrated fire was the ideal as the effect of a large number of shells bursting on the target in a few seconds was much more devastating than the same number of rounds from a lesser amount of guns delivered over a longer time.

The heavy regiments, one of which was found in most AGRAs, were made up of four batteries, each of four guns. Two batteries manned the British 7.2-inch howitzer while the other two batteries were equipped with the U.S. 155-mm gun. The 7.2-inch fired a useful 202-pound shell 16,000 yards, roughly the same range as the 100-pound round of the 5.5-inch gun and the 200-pound shell of the comparable American weapon, the 8-inch howitzer. The 155 mm gun, was a modern, well-designed piece of equipment that fired a 95-pound round 26,000 yards.

There was an additional resource that strictly speaking was not an army, let alone an artillery resource, the Royal Air Force AOP (Air Observation Post) squadrons. These squadrons, equipped with light single-engine aircraft and manned by a combination of air force and army personnel with artillery pilots, were provided on a scale of one per corps and army headquar-

Air Observation Post
An Auster Air OP aircraft of C Flight 661 AOP Squadron RAF about to take off on a mission. Observing from behind the friendly lines, the pilots were able to engage the enemy with artillery several miles deep into German territory. (NAC/PA 162286)

ters, and usually were allocated on the basis of one flight per division and AGRA.[4] The AOP extended the view into enemy territory by a considerable amount and was able to direct fire onto German positions that would be invisible to ground-based observers. The light aircraft used could operate from unimproved fields and, because of their low speed and manoeuvrability, were almost invulnerable to attack by enemy fighters.

While on paper 720 guns were available for TOTALIZE, that figure is misleading. First, nearly a quarter of these guns were employed solely on the front of the flanking corps or on pre-selected targets in depth for a limited period: 3 AGRA (64 medium and 16 heavy guns) in 12th Corps west of the Orne, and 49th West Riding Division (72 field guns) and part of 4 AGRA (16 medium and 16 heavy guns) in 1st Corps. Second, neither 3rd Canadian Infantry Division artillery (only 48 field guns as the 14th Field Regiment was still converting to 25-pounders) nor 1. *Dywizji Pancernej* artillery (48 field guns) were used in the Phase 1 fire plan. Third, the two heavy anti-aircraft regiments (48 guns) were only used on targets in depth. Fourth, there were restrictions on the employment of the 155 mm batteries in the heavy regiments because of the limited amount of ammunition. Thus, the guns available for the opening phase of the battle totalled 392, of which the greater part of the firing to cover the movement of the assaulting troops would be by nine field (216 guns) and nine medium regiments (144 guns), 360 guns in all. Many of the medium, heavy and heavy anti-aircraft guns were reserved largely for counter-bombardment. In the second and third phases, relatively fewer guns would be available to support the forward troops as some, such as those of 49th West Riding Division and 3 and 4 AGRAs, would gradually run out of range after the end of Phase 1, while the 2nd Canadian Corps divisional artilleries and the guns of 2 Canadian and 9 AGRA would be moving forward. This was accepted – indeed it was a major feature of the plan – as the lack of artillery was offset by the use of heavy bombers in support of the second phase attack and it was assumed that German resistance would lessen considerably once the assault troops fought through the crust of the defences and advanced south along the Route Nationale.

Brigadier Brownfield would have to seek authorization to draw and expend the hundreds of thousands of rounds of ammunition needed for the TOTALIZE fire plan. While all guns carried a first line of ammunition, this was based on three days normal expenditure, not on the ammunition required to support a major operation. The BRA and CCRA staffs had calculated the following ammunition requirements: 25-pounder (and 105 mm) high explosive, 500 rounds per gun (rpg); 5.5-inch high explosive, 300 rpg; 155 mm, 30 rpg; 7.2-inch, 170 rpg; and 3.7-inch HAA, 150 rpg, and 90 rounds of red flare and 60 rounds of green flare for 25-pounders to mark the Phase 1 bombing targets.[5] These were average figures; the planning figures for 25-pounders, for example, ranged from 650 rpg for the field regiments of 2nd Canadian Infantry Division and 51st Highland Division down to 250 rpg for those of 49th West Riding Division.[6] Once the authorization was received, it fell to the senior administrative officers at army and corps headquarters, Brigadiers A.E. Walford and H.V.D. Laing respectively, to arrange a program to deliver the ammunition, some 205,000 rounds in all, directly to the gun positions, some of which were not yet occupied.[7] This formed part of a major administrative operation that included the delivery of fuel and rations as well as ammunition and the establishment of a reserve of ammunition and fuel on wheels. This task was completed in 36 hours, the drivers working night and day without rest,[8] in itself a testimony to both the efficiency of the administrative services and the tangible benefits of air superiority.

Before the plan for the dumping program could be prepared, however, artillery staffs had to clear deployment areas with the divisional and corps staffs who actually controlled the ground. It would have been worse than useless, for example, to have decided to put a medium regiment in a certain area and make arrangements to deliver several thousand rounds of 5.5-inch ammunition there, only to discover that the particular piece of ground was occupied by a division headquarters. The deployment plan entailed not only pushing the new gun areas as far forward as possible to squeeze every inch of range from the supporting artillery, but also selecting and reserving gun areas still in enemy-held territory to support the second and third phases.

With the matters of guns, ammunition and deployment areas considered, it now fell to the CCRA and his staff to create a coordinated fire plan for Simonds. Artillery fire in support of an attack in 1944 fell into four general areas:

a. preparatory fire to soften up the enemy positions prior to the actual attacks on these positions;

b. counter-battery fire to neutralize or destroy enemy gun and mortar positions. These targets could be engaged prior to or during the attack. Counter-flak was an element of counter-battery designed to suppress enemy anti-aircraft fire during Allied air attacks;

c. covering fire on enemy positions to keep the Germans from interfering with our troops during the actual attack; and

d. defensive fire, usually abbreviated as DF, tasks selected on likely enemy approaches to break up counterattacks.

Leaving aside preparatory, counter-battery and defensive fire tasks for the time being, there were two basic ways that the artillery could support the Phase 1 divisions with covering fire. The first was for the divisions to select a series of targets along their axes of advance and then engage these during the advance as "on call" targets when the need arose. There were some advantages to this approach: it saved ammunition that otherwise would be fired into areas not occupied by the enemy, and it reduced the possibility that the fire plan would leave the advancing troops behind. However, it had some significant disadvantages. First, accurate and timely intelligence was required about the German positions and this could not take into account any enemy movement during the attack. Second, the radios used in 1944 were adversely affected by atmospheric conditions during the hours of darkness, and voice communications at night was at best a slow and difficult business. The other approach was to fire a timed program using either the same targets selected by the divisions or a barrage, a moving wall of fire that advanced ahead of the troops at a predetermined rate. Preselected targets posed many of the same advantages and disadvantages as on call targets, but tended to be less complicated to control.

Simonds favoured the barrage. It had the advantage that it could be prepared easily as a drill using standard operating procedures. However, a barrage was expensive in ammunition and could indicate the direction and frontage of the attack to the Germans. Given the amount of ammunition expended, the number of rounds that actually fell on an individual target during a barrage was rather limited. Finally, it was inflexible and once underway was difficult to modify in terms of altering the rate or duration of fire to allow the supported troops to deal with opposition or to catch up to the fire.[9] Whichever method he selected, a proportion of the guns could be taken off the program to engage targets of opportunity and, in the case of the Phase 1 fire plan, each divisional commander could order his own field guns to engage other targets, while the mediums continued to fire on the original program.[10]

The barrage planned for TOTALIZE would have a frontage of 4,050 yards and advance 6,000 yards at a rate of 100 yards a minute, or roughly 3.5 miles per hour. This rate of advance was three times that normally used for dismounted infantry in an attack and the length was much greater than normal. The TOTALIZE barrage would progress in steps of 200 yards with the mediums moving 400 yards ahead of the field guns. Thus the guns would fire for two minutes on each of 30 lines, before lifting to the next. With a frontage of 4,050 yards, the gun density worked out to 11 yards per gun. It was, however, not that simple. The allotment of artillery support to the two attacking divisions was weighted in favour of the 51st Highland Division, perhaps because its area included the strong point of Tilly-la-Campagne. Thus only its own 72 25-pounders and the four medium regiments of 2

AGRA would support 2nd Canadian Infantry Division, while 51st Highland Division would be supported by the six field regiments of its own artillery and 4th Canadian Armoured Division and five regiments of mediums from 4 and 9 British AGRAs.[11] This worked out to densities of 15 and 9 yards per gun respectively.[12]

In his appreciation, Simonds had stressed that while it was impossible to disguise the direction and objectives of the attack, it was important to disguise its form and timing. He therefore decided to forgo any preparatory softening-up of the German positions and any counter-battery program before H-Hour. This was in accordance with the principle long held by Crerar that "to attain the greatest possible surprise in a battle to break into a strong system of defences, it was necessary to eliminate prolonged preliminary bombardment prior to movement."[13] However, a special counter-flak program was arranged by 2nd Canadian Corps in conjunction with the air and artillery staffs at First Canadian Army. All known German anti-aircraft batteries were to be engaged from the start of the night target-marking until shortly before the main fire plan began, with the exception of batteries within 1,000 yards of the bombing targets, which might have been because of fears of obscuring the target markers.[14] In the case of counter-battery, 2nd Canadian Corps had been deployed in the area south of Caen for nearly three weeks and 1st British Corps had been holding the "airborne bridgehead" even longer. In that time both corps counter-bombardment officers had built up a comprehensive picture of the German artillery opposite them through air observation, reports from survey regiments and forward troops, and the information had been collated, sifted, analysed, filed and cross-referenced. Slowly and methodically the enemy's main gun areas had been accurately located and classified by calibre and function.[15] After the barrage ended, 310 guns would be available to fire two intensive prearranged programs each of 20 minutes duration at H plus 100 minutes and H plus 7 hours. Meanwhile other guns on the fronts of 1st and 12th Corps would deal with hostile batteries in their own areas east and west of 2nd Canadian Corps respectively.[16]

It should be noted that there was more to the covering fire program than just the barrage. The two attacking divisions had submitted targets along their axes of advance to be engaged while the barrage was being fired, either as part of a timed program or as on call targets. The divisions also stated

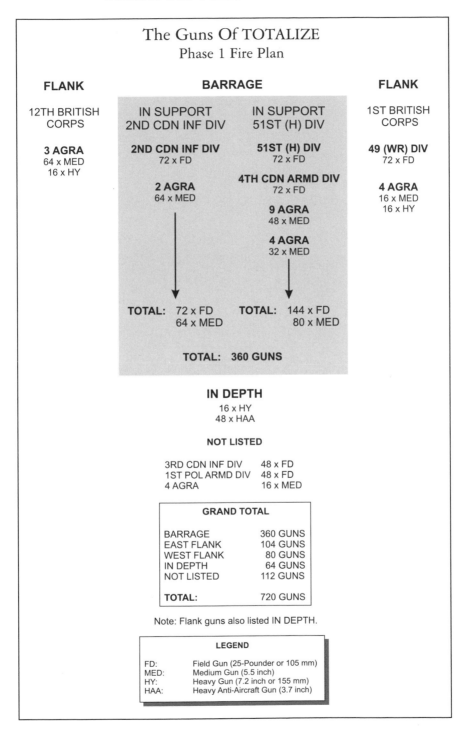

The Guns Of TOTALIZE
Phase 1 Fire Plan

FLANK	BARRAGE		FLANK
12TH BRITISH CORPS	IN SUPPORT 2ND CDN INF DIV	IN SUPPORT 51ST (H) DIV	1ST BRITISH CORPS
3 AGRA 64 x MED 16 x HY	**2ND CDN INF DIV** 72 x FD	**51ST (H) DIV** 72 x FD	**49 (WR) DIV** 72 x FD
	2 AGRA 64 x MED	**4TH CDN ARMD DIV** 72 x FD	**4 AGRA** 16 x MED 16 x HY
		9 AGRA 48 x MED	
		4 AGRA 32 x MED	

TOTAL: 72 x FD / 64 x MED   **TOTAL:** 144 x FD / 80 x MED

TOTAL: 360 GUNS

IN DEPTH
16 x HY
48 x HAA

NOT LISTED

3RD CDN INF DIV	48 x FD
1ST POL ARMD DIV	48 x FD
4 AGRA	16 x MED

GRAND TOTAL	
BARRAGE	360 GUNS
EAST FLANK	104 GUNS
WEST FLANK	80 GUNS
IN DEPTH	64 GUNS
NOT LISTED	112 GUNS
TOTAL:	**720 GUNS**

Note: Flank guns also listed IN DEPTH.

LEGEND	
FD:	Field Gun (25-Pounder or 105 mm)
MED:	Medium Gun (5.5 inch)
HY:	Heavy Gun (7.2 inch or 155 mm)
HAA:	Heavy Anti-Aircraft Gun (3.7 inch)

Brass, brass, brass
This picture was taken shortly before the conference to plan the air support for TOTALIZE at First Canadian Army headquarters on 4 August 1944. Front row, left to right, Crerar (First Canadian Army), Coningham (Second Tactical Air Force), Montgomery (21st Army Group) and Leigh-Mallory (Allied Expeditionary Air Force), who has his cigarette dangerously near the tobaccophobic Montgomery. (NAC/PA 129122)

their requirements for defensive fire tasks.[17] The complete Phase 1 fire plan included the counter-flak program, the covering fire program, that is, both barrage and concentrations, the two counter-battery programs and defensive fire tasks on call. On top of that, the Phase 2 fire plan consisted on a series of on call targets selected by the Phase 2 divisions along their axes of advance and defensive fire tasks around their objectives. All components of the plan had to be checked and double-checked to ensure that a regiment had not been allotted two targets at the same time or even worse a target that was out of range. The artillery planning process involved considerable input from the attacking divisions and both 2nd Canadian Infantry Division and 51st Highland Division were tasked to submit prearranged timed concentrations for the artillery of the flanking formations as well targets for their own guns and their supporting AGRAs after the barrage. The CCRA staff would arrange the distribution of lists of these targets as well as the task tables for the counter-bombardment programs, the on call targets for Phase 2 and the barrage.[18]

While it was not strictly speaking part of the fire plan, Brigadier Matthews, the CCRA, was also responsible for coordinating details for the move forward of the guns detailed to support both Phase 2 divisions. In the case of the 4th Division, arrangements were made to expedite the reconnaissance and preparation of gun positions for their field regiments in the newly occupied areas near Rocquancourt, while the Poles authorized each brigade commander to move his supporting field regiment. Both of these divisions were also allotted an AGRA – 2 Canadian AGRA for the Poles and 9 British AGRA for 4th Canadian Armoured Division – in support and were delegated authority to move one medium regiment without reference to the CCRA's headquarters.

The fire plan had been arranged over two days and there must have been some scrambling when on the morning of 6 August, or D minus 1 day, Simonds changed his plan from three to two phases. The completed plan was presented to him at 1800 hours that day for approval, and the consolidated fire plan was issued by the CCRA's headquarters at noon on 7 August, or just 11 hours before the first rounds were to be fired in the counter-flak program.[19]

As the use of heavy bombers in place of artillery was a keystone of Simonds's plan for TOTALIZE, we must examine the development of the air planning for the operation.* It is important to remember that the heavy bomber force of 1944 was very much an "area weapon" and the bombing pattern covered an area roughly at least a thousand yards in diameter around the aiming point, regardless of the number of aircraft employed and their bomb load. Simonds understood this and intended to exploit this characteristic to blast his way through the second defence zone.

Simonds had decided to use heavy bombers to seal off the corridor down which his troops would advance in Phase 1. He envisaged that heavy bombers would attack five targets, two to the west of the advance at the strong points of Fontenay-le-Marmion and May-sur-Orne and three on the east flank running some 2,000 yards on a northwest to southeast axis from La Hogue through Secqueville-la-Campagne to a woods roughly 1,000 yards

---

* An examination of Commonwealth air support doctrine is at Appendix D.

to the southeast. The type of attack requested on all five targets was blast and fragmentation with cratering accepted – in other words, heavy bombs. The attack on the latter three targets, if successful, would have produced a "moonscaped" barrier impassable to wheeled and tracked vehicles about 3,000 yards long by 1,000 yards wide running along the boundary between 1. and 12. *SS-Panzerdivisionen*. In fact 272. *Infanteriedivision* had replaced 12. *SS-Panzerdivision* in the front line during the night of 3/4 August, but this had not been confirmed by Canadian intelligence at the time the request for air support was submitted. This, however, would not have altered the requirement to block counterattack routes into the area of 51st Highland Division's objectives until the ground could be occupied.

The two western targets were painted as strong defensive positions capable of striking at the right flank of 2nd Canadian Infantry Division as it advanced. May-sur-Orne had proven itself to be a tough nut to crack on a number of occasions and it was suspected that Fontenay-le-Marmion would prove equally difficult, especially as it was held by SS panzer grenadiers. As each lay outside the area covered by the barrage, and was to be attacked by a Canadian infantry battalion immediately after the bombing ended, it is clear that the bombing of these targets also was intended as a substitute for artillery fire.

It is important to remember that Canadian intelligence had deduced that the Phase 2 objective was held by elements of two SS panzer divisions. In fact, on 1 August First Canadian Army intelligence reported that work appeared to have begun on a *third* defensive line 2,000 yards long two miles north of Potigny. It would have been unthinkable for any western general, let alone one like Lieutenant General Guy Simonds with an artillery background, to mount an unsupported attack under those conditions. The traditional means of support, of course, was massed artillery, which would have to move forward to new positions after supporting the Phase 1 attacks. A basic principal of defensive planning was to site subsequent positions far enough apart so the attackers would be forced to move their guns between attacks, thus reducing the momentum of the attack and providing time for the defenders to regroup. The German positions south of Caen were clearly planned with this principle in mind. The redeployment of artillery was more than a simple exercise in road movement, although that would take several hours in itself. Once the move forward was completed, even if details of the targets to be engaged had been circulated in advance, firing data for the guns would have to be worked out and checked. If a formal timed artillery program was planned to support the operation, the Phase 2 attack could not have been mounted until the evening or perhaps even the next day. This was the diminished gun support – 88 guns or perhaps a third to a half of the normal support for a divisional attack on a prepared position – Simonds referred to in his appreciation and illustrates why he believed the use of heavy bombers would decrease the pause between phases.[20]

The details of the air plan for Phase 2 developed by Simonds, that is the break-in of the second defensive position, were more general than for the first phase and included the use of four different air elements:[21]

a. medium bombers to lay a "fragmentation carpet" [the quotation marks appear in the original] over an area about 3 kilometres wide astride the Caen–Falaise road from Cintheaux in the north to Bretteville-le-Rabet in the south.

b. heavy day bombers (Fortresses) to deliver attacks with high-explosive bombs on Bretteville-sur-Laize, Gouvix, Hautmesnil and the large quarry south of the village and Cauvicourt and attacks with fragmentation bombs to neutralize gun positions in the area bounded by Urville, Point 180, Quesnay, Estrées-la-Campagne and Bretteville-le-Rabet, in other words an area to the south of the medium bomber targets. The high-explosive targets were specifically requested at H-Hour.

c. air reconnaissance by fighter bombers with principal targets guns and tanks in the battle area beyond the bombline.

d. tactical reconnaissance to look for and second lift of mediums [bombers] to deal with moves and concentrations of 12th SS [Panzer] Division. While 12th SS Panzer Division had been shown still in the line by Allied intelligence on the previous day, this task is in line with Simonds's appreciation that the Hitler Youth division would be made available as a counterattack force.

While the requirement as stated was too much of a "big hand, little map" approach to be used by the air forces, or anyone else for that matter, for targeting purposes, it confirms that Simonds intended to use bombers as a substitute for massed artillery in a very specific way. His Phase 2 air plan was essentially an extension of the Phase 1 artillery barrage along with engagement of specific targets in depth. Even the selection of weapons was suggestive of a fire plan, with lighter fragmentation bombs taking the place of the 25-pounders of the field regiments and heavier high-explosive bombs in place of medium and heavy guns to soften up specific strong points and objectives in depth.

With the enemy second defence line smashed, Simonds believed that the road to Falaise would be open. He intended to exploit up the Caen–Falaise highway onto the high ground north of the city as a prelude to future operations, either to capture Falaise or to begin the turn to the east as part of a drive on the Seine. With the situation anticipated to be fluid and hard intelligence lacking, he could only request "Med[ium] and fighter bombers on call to leading b[riga]des. In particular, to attack any movement of 12 SS [Panzer] Div[ision]."

It has been suggested by some commentators that after a long, bureaucratic struggle to obtain the requested heavy bomber support, Lieutenant Generals Crerar and Simonds were reluctant to cancel the Phase 2 bombing when a breakthrough was achieved on the morning of 8 August. Whether they were aware that this breakthrough had been achieved will be discussed later, but the negotiations for the heavy bomber support were approached by both sides in a positive manner. At 1700 hours on 4 August, the same day that Montgomery formally directed First Canadian Army to attack "from the Caen sector in the direction of Falaise," an army–air force conference was held at HQ First Canadian Army to develop the bombing air support plan in detail. The air force officers in attendance included the commanders of the Allied Expeditionary Air Force (Air Marshal Trafford Leigh-Mallory), Second Tactical Air Force (Air Marshal Arthur Coningham) and 83 (Air Vice Marshal Harry Broadhurst) and 84 (Air Vice Marshal Leslie Brown) Composite Groups. The minutes reflected healthy discussion and the provision of sound advice regarding the employment of heavy and medium bombers.

As a result of this meeting, on the same day HQ First Canadian Army produced a detailed request for air support including accurate locations and target intelligence for the aiming points for each of the Phase 1 and 2 targets. While the Phase 1 targets remained essentially as requested, the Phase 2 program was modified considerably. For example, the Phase 1 target of May-sur-Orne, which was to be "obliterated" in the request for air support, was now identified as Target 3, located by an accurate map grid reference and description of the cross roads to be used as the aiming point and described as a forward company area with "at least 9 A[rmoured] F[ighting] V[ehicle]s seen dug in in vicinity." In other words, like the other Phase 1 targets it was refined, not modified. Turning to Phase 2, St. Sylvain, a village lying at the east end of the Phase 2 objectives, was added to the list of heavy bomber targets for attack at the suggestion of the air force as Target 7.

The greatest change, however, was in the planned carpet bombing by the mediums and the attacks by the Fortresses along the Caen–Falaise road. This area was designated as Targets 8, with eight distinct aiming points (8A to 8H), and 9 (Urville). Leigh-Mallory agreed that the more southerly targets could be engaged last, if necessary, although surely he was, or should have been, aware that this would depend upon the prevailing wind direction and speed. The last three targets, 10, 11 and 12, were to be attacked with fragmentation bombs at H plus 30 minutes for 45 minutes. Unlike the other targets identified by aiming points on the ground, these were described as areas; for example, Target 11 ran southwest for two and one half-miles from Bretteville-le-Rabet to St. Hilaire Farm. At this time it was determined that H-Hour for the Phase 2 bombing would be 1400 hours on D plus 1 and that no change to the plan could be made after 0900 hours, that is five hours before H-Hour. And there is one last item that bears mentioning. All references to the use of medium and heavy bombers on specific targets were deleted in favour of a blanket statement that "[t]his part sets out the requirements for air support beyond the resources of 83 Group RAF." It is most likely that this change was made at the request of the air force using an argument along the lines of "tell us what you want us to do and let us decide on the best way to do it."[22]

It was decided that an army/air force delegation that included Brigadier C.C. Mann, Chief of Staff (C of S), First Canadian Army, and Brigadier C.A. Richardson, the Brigadier General Staff (BGS) (Plans), 21st Army Group, Lieutenant Colonel P.E.R. Wright, the General Staff Officer (GSO) 1 (Intelligence), First Canadian Army, and Major R.G. Marks, the GSO 2 (Air), 2nd Canadian Corps would fly to England the following afternoon to work out details at the headquarters of the Allied Expeditionary Air Force at Stanmore on the outskirts of London. The planning envisaged the use of heavy bombers, which were controlled by Eisenhower's Supreme Headquarters Allied Expeditionary Forces (SHAEF), and as yet no representative of that headquarters or of the heavy bomber force had been involved in the development of the air support plan.

The conference convened at 1800 hours on 5 August with a bevy of senior air force officers in attendance including Eisenhower's deputy commander British Air Chief Marshal Tedder, Leigh-Mallory, Lieutenant General Spaatz of the U.S. Strategic Air Forces, Broadhurst of 83 Group and Air Vice Marshal Oxland, representing Air Marshal Harris of RAF Bomber Command. Brigadier Mann outlined the object and details of the corps plan, taking care to emphasize the vital role to be played by the heavy bombers. While he used a rather heavy brush and may have deliberately overstated the strength of the German forces *vis à vis* the Allies, Mann succeeded in making the case to the airmen for the requested air support and its integration with the ground plan. The remainder of the conference was spent in working out the details of the attack on each target and reconciling the inevitable conflicts. It is almost axiomatic that there always are more targets than resources to hit them, whether one is dropping bombs or firing guns.

During the presentation Brigadier Richardson was called to the phone to take a call from Colonel G.E. Beament, the Colonel General Staff (GS) of First Canadian Army. Despite a bad line and several broken connections, the message was finally passed by Beament and checked back by Richardson. Its gist, as recorded by Beament in note form, was

Present indications that enemy thinning out on our own front. Therefore, possible that we may gain objectives for Phase I by D Day without any major op. In this event we would commence op on D Day at the same phase I H hr but with an advanced [Start Line] incl the Phase I objectives. Air s[u]p[port] plan must be considered in light of this possibility. Present air target plan stands. In the event of possibility set out above, targets 1 to 5 incl would NOT be required and remainder of targets would be at appropriate timings for Phase I.

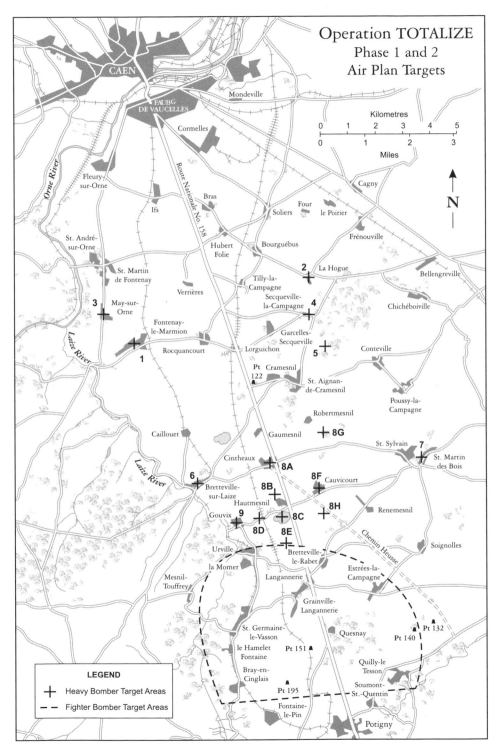

Operation TOTALIZE
Phase 1 and 2
Air Plan Targets

LEGEND
+ Heavy Bomber Target Areas
- - - Fighter Bomber Target Areas

He then went on to ask for answers to the following questions

> What, if any, implications would arise if 1 to 5 incl were omitted and
> remainder of targets were engaged at appropriate timings as for Phase I
> H hr?
>
> What are the limitations in time under which this alternative might be
> put into effect?[23]

Shortly after the conference ended, Mann called Beament at approximately 2130 hours to brief him on its results. While the Phase 1 program was approved as requested, albeit with some technical reservations, the air officers considerably modified the Phase 2 plan. Most importantly, the RAF would now deal with all the targets. While Mann had reported that there would not be deliberate cratering in the area known as Target 8, the report on the meeting prepared by HQ Allied Expeditionary Air Force stated categorically that "Cratering not acceptable in Area 8." Originally it had been planned that the USAAF would attack Target 8 with fragmentation bombs while at the same time RAF Bomber Command took on Targets 6, 7 and 9 with high-explosive weapons. As the dust and smoke from these heavy weapons would likely obscure the American aiming points, Tedder suggested that

> in view of the difficulty of arranging the timing in order to allow the smoke
> to clear from the target between the bombing of Bomber Command and
> the 8th Air Force, and in view of the doubt whether cloud conditions would
> be suitable for high level bombing by 8th Air Force, it would be better for
> Bomber Command to take on all the bombing in the phase 2 area.[24]

In fact, the possibility of targets being obscured began to drive the development of the air plan from this point onwards. To allow the smoke and dust from Targets 6 and 7 to clear, the attacks on them would have to be completed at least 60 minutes before H-Hour* and then Targets 8 and 9 would be hit beginning at H-Hour, which was set at 1400 hours. There was one more

---

* In this case H-Hour signified the time at which the first bomb was to hit the target and not the time the troops crossed the start line. In fact, in an apparent violation of doctrine, there were negative timings in the bombing plan; that is, some targets would be hit before H-Hour.

point, the import of which seems to have missed the attention of most historians who have written on TOTALIZE. The air force flatly refused to attack Targets 8A and G, that is Cintheaux and the feature a thousand yards south of Robertmesnil respectively, as they would be too close to the positions of the troops who had captured the Phase 1 objectives.[25]

Finally, the consensus among the airmen was that hard intelligence about Targets 10, 11 and 12 was too scanty to justify their inclusion in the heavy bombing plan. While the AEAF record indicates that these would be allotted to 2 TAF, Mann's impression was rather different.[26] Beament recorded him as reporting that

> Owing to the absence of recorded targets, the Bomber Com[man]d reps and other RAF Comds concerned will NOT deal with Targets 10, 11 and 12. They feel it can be better and adequately dealt with by art[iller]y and an increased fighter bomber effort from RAF and US sources. The AOC 83 Group agrees.[27]

Still the 39-year-old Brigadier Mann could be well satisfied with the progress made. The majority of the targets, including all five in Phase 1, had been accepted virtually as proposed. Two had been turned down for reasons of troop safety, the fusing option had been changed for others and the targets farthest south had been allotted to tactical air resources, although there was a notable difference between the AEAF interpretation (2 TAF) and Mann's (increased fighter bomber effort from RAF and USAAF sources). None of that appreciably changed the plan, at least to someone who had been engaged in lengthy negotiations over a period of three days, and the implications of dropping Targets 8A and G from the list of bomber targets went unnoticed, perhaps because Mann believed that fighter bombers would be available to take them on.* Little did he know that, within half a day, the carefully crafted air plan would run afoul of the stern, uncompromising "Bomber" Harris, and that ubiquitous nemesis of airmen, the weather "gremlins."

---

* This indicates that Mann and perhaps even a number of the senior airmen did not understand the fundamental differences between the effects of bombers, which were area weapons, and fighter bombers, which had to identify and aim at individual targets. To produce the equivalent effect in terms of bomb weight of just one squadron of heavy bombers on either Target 8A or 8G would have exceeded the capability of all the Typhoons in 2 TAF in one lift.

The next morning, 6 August, Mann and Richardson met with Harris at Bomber Command Headquarters at High Wycombe. Harris had a reputation for being crusty and he certainly did nothing to dispel it during the meeting. As Mann wrote in his report, the proceedings got off to a very shaky start,

12. At approximately 1100 hours we gathered in the C in C's office. The C in C stated that he was not prepared to bomb at night as plan[ned] and agreed upon at the meeting of the night before, and that there was no question of deviating from this policy. He gave, briefly, the reasons and explained that bombing in close proximity to the troops was done by Oboe [a radar aid to navigation] and markers dropped by path-finders with a check of the position of the Pathfinder Oboe Marker by the "Master Bomber" who flies down sufficiently low to identify the target on the ground, drops another marker and orders "bombs away." The C in C explained that this could NOT be done at night.

13. The situation thus became extremely unsatisfactory! I stated that since orders were now being arranged on the basis of the agreements reached and notified that night that if the C in C was not prepared to support the arrangements made on his behalf by his SASO (SB) that it would be necessary for me to telephone this information to my Army Commander at once and that I considered it appropriate that the C in C Bomber Command should telephone the C in C 21 Army Group and inform him of his decisions since the tactical and strategic situation in Normandy had reached the point where a delay in mounting this operation Totalize might have most regrettable consequences as it seemed we were on the threshold of a great strategic opportunity.

14. The C in C stated that he had no intention of phoning the C in C 21 Army Group. Silence reigned for approximately a minute, and then we got down to discussions as to what Bomber Command could do. From this point onward the matter proceeded in a very satisfactory way and with evident desire on the part of the C in C Bomber Command to assist with his resources in the Operation.[28]

The atmosphere in the office must have been glacial! Harris could dish it out with the best of them, but he certainly was not used to taking it, least of all from an *army* officer three ranks his junior, and a "colonial" to boot. Mann had refused to be intimidated, but he had come perilously close to insubordination when he accused Harris in so many words of reneging on a commitment. With the matter off their chests and their blood pressure returning to normal, the three officers began to work on solutions to the dilemma. It is important to stress that Harris was not being an obstructionist, a point he successfully had managed to conceal from Mann and Richardson. He had been directed to support the land forces and he would do it. However, he understood all too well the limitations of his force, which was neither designed nor trained for this sort of task; his motivation was a real concern for the safety of the forward troops. Matters proceeded swiftly and two possible solutions were developed in less than an hour. Neither Mann nor Richardson, of course, had the authority to accept these, and Mann phoned Crerar from Harris's office.[29]

Crerar took the call at 1213 hours and listened as his chief of staff explained Harris's concerns regarding target identification and marking for his main force crews. Mann explained the requirement for the "master bomber" to identify the target before ordering the attack to start. Clearly this required at least some light and would be impossible if the H-Hour for the Phase 1 bombing was at 2300 hours. However, Harris was willing to participate in a trial that night to see if marking the targets with 25-pounder flare shells was identifiable by his master bombers. If these skilled and experienced pilots were satisfied, then the mission would proceed at the planned time on 7 August; otherwise H-Hour would be advanced with the bombing commencing at 2130 hours and ending at 2210 hours. Simonds, who was present at Crerar's headquarters, was consulted and replied that "while he very much hoped to retain 2300 h[ou]rs as 'H' Hour for the operation, he would, if proven necessary, phase back 'H' Hour for the operation to 2130 hrs."[30]

Brigadier Richardson was already on the phone to the Major General Royal Artillery at 21 Army Group arranging the details of the trial. That night 25-pounders of 150 Field Regiment of 4 AGRA engaged targets near Ouistreham on the 6th Airborne Division front, the place in the First Canadian Army that was about the farthest possible from the TOTALIZE target areas, with one-minute bursts of red or green flares fired to burst in the air above each according to plan at precisely 2300, 2305, 2310 and 2315 hours.

The master bombers reported that the flares could be easily seen and the original H-Hour was confirmed some hours later.[31]

Beament signed First Canadian Army Operations Instruction Number 11 at 0418 on 7 August. In this document H-Hour for the Phase 1 bombing was 2300 hours if Bomber Command agreed to bomb on night marker shells or 2130 hours if Bomber Command did not agree to this procedure. The instruction noted that the decision would be passed to First Canadian Army Headquarters by 1300 hours. At 1100 hours Beament chaired a conference at army headquarters to tie down the final details of the air plan for TOTALIZE. While most of those in attendance were from his headquarters, among the other representatives were Richardson, officers from both the general staff and the artillery of Headquarters 2nd Canadian Corps and the Group Captains Operations from 83 and 84 Groups. Among the key matters discussed were

> The operation will commence at 2300 hours on the first night suitable for air operations.
>
> H-Hour for Phase 2 at present is fixed for 1400 hours, D plus 1. This may be altered by Commander 2 Canadian Corps subject to Bomber Command being notified of change by H minus 5 hours.
>
> Targets 8A and 8G [the two most northerly targets across the axes of advance] which had been turned down by Bomber Command due to safety considerations will be attacked by fighter bombers if considered practical by 83 Composite Group. Attack will be carried out from H minus 30 to H-Hour D plus 1 [8 August].[32]

At some time between 1100 and 1535 that day the decision was made to substitute American heavy bombers for Bomber Command aircraft in the Phase 2 attacks. The record of a message phoned by Colonel McKinnon of AEAF to Brigadier Richardson at Headquarters First Canadian Army, including Richardson's annotation, reads

> H-Hour for Phase II is 1300 hrs 8 Aug. Bombing of Targets 6 and 7 will probably commence before H-Hour. Bombing of Targets 8 and 9 will commence at H-Hour. All bombing will be completed by H-Hour plus

45 minutes. 8th Air Force and First Cdn Army will complete detailed arrangements through 83 Group.

"Brig Richardson enquired what the situation would be if Canadian Army could not accept 1300 hrs. Col McKinnon said that on the met forecast, 8th Airforce appreciated that there was little chance of the weather being suitable after 1300 hrs owing to cumulus clouds, but that the 8th Airforce would, of course, try to carry out the operation if the weather turned out to be better than expected. Brig Richardson promised to send a reply by telephone (AEAF Extn [letters illegible]) after referring the question to 2 Cdn Corps."[33]

It seems likely from the tone and content of the above that Crerar *et al* already knew that the substitution had been made, but this cannot be confirmed. As for the reason for the substitution, an American study claimed that "because of bad weather at RAF bases the night before, many of the heavy bombers were required to land at other than home airdromes on returning from their previous missions."[34] While the wording is ambiguous, the author could only have been referring to the night of 6/7 August, and not 7/8 August as has sometimes been assumed. However, there is a British document that clarifies the matter:

The settled fair weather was marked by the absence of wind which resulted in persistent morning fogs. This entailed the risk of R.A.F. Bomber Command's forces having to land away from their bases after a night operation and thus it would be impossible to guarantee a sufficiently strong force for the second phase of the bombing operations on the following day.[35]

There still were a few loose ends to tie up before the air planning was complete. Richardson phoned 83 Group immediately to bring that headquarters into the picture regarding the changes in the Phase 2 bombing, although one might have thought the information flow should have been the other way around. He also emphasized that the army wished to review the situation at 0800 hours on the 8th, and to receive the views of the 8th Air Force on this matter. In the event that weather prevented the American bombers from operating, he requested that 83 Group attack targets 6, 7, 8 and 9 with fighter bombers. In his record of the conversation he then requested 83 Group "to take on targets 8A and 8G with fighter bombers, working the timings in with the programme of 8th Airforce." Richardson ended his record of the call by noting that "the Army does not favour adoption of any last min[ute] frills such as coloured smoke, and is depending on 83 G[rou]p RAF to present any 8th Airforce requirements."[36]

It is important to note that Richardson had *requested* 83 Group to take on targets 8A and 8G with fighter bombers, working the timings in with the program of the 8th Air Force. In army staff language the verb "request" had a specific meaning. Basically, a staff officer did not have the authority to issue an order to a headquarters commanded by an officer of higher rank (or of another service) so "request" was used, with the understanding that the officer was speaking for his commander. The headquarters receiving the request was expected to either comply or to reply giving the reasons for non-compliance as soon as possible. While it must be taken as a given that HQ First Canadian Army understood the two targets *would* be attacked by fighter bombers, there are no indications that 83 Group would have considered the request to be anything but another request for air support to be considered along with all the others.

In so many words Richardson had confirmed the timing for the "go/no go" decision for the Phase 2 bombing as 0800, or five hours before the nominal air force H-Hour. The record of a telephone conversation with 8th USAAF in the Headquarters 2 TAF operations log implies that the Americans may have been more flexible than Bomber Command:

> Asked what time is the latest by which 8th must be informed to cancel attack if necessitated by 8th A.F. advance [sic] – answer 0800 hours to prevent bomber being airborne and 1100 hours if bombers are airborne. Request for red smoke to be put down by Arty on N. Edges of 8B and 8F from 1255-1330 [It is] important that smoke is put down on time and no earlier as 8th is putting down red markers on Targets 6 and 7. (83 Group informed and will confirm.)[37]

There is no indication that 83 Group passed the latter time, i.e. 1100 hours, to First Canadian Army. In any case, it was unlikely that Simonds would have cancelled the bombing without compelling information that the Germans had withdrawn. Despite the reservations already expressed about target marking, as we shall see, target marking was carried out on time by 4th Canadian Armoured Division.

That same morning Colonel Beament signed First Canadian Army Operations Instruction Number 11 which detailed the air arrangements as they then existed. With a major change in the Phase 2 bombing, it was now vital that the new arrangements be circulated to the land forces post haste. At 1840 he signed Operation Instruction Number 12, which included the admonition "This Op Instr cancels and supersedes Op Instr Number 11 (less Trace 'P') which will be destroyed AT ONCE by fire." It appears that details of the Phase 2 plan were still not clear as the timings for targets 6 and 7 indicate that bombing would probably begin before 1300 hours and end not later than 1345 hours, while the timings for targets 8 and 9 indicate that the first bombs were to fall at 1300 hours with the last bombs not later than 1345 hours. In fact, as we have seen above, at the meeting at AEAF on 6 August the air force had insisted on 60 minutes to allow the smoke and dust to clear between the attacks on targets 6 and 7 and targets 8 and 9. This had been accepted by Mann and Richardson and was reflected in the minutes, but was not made clear in this operation instruction.

For the first time the ground and air forces appear to have considered the possibility that the heavy bombers might not be able to hit the Phase 2 targets. Under the heading "Alternative Plan" arrangements for the attack on some or all of these targets by tactical aircraft in that event were detailed. In addition targets 8A and 8G were added to this list. While the effect of fighter bombers would not have been as devastating as that of bombers, the substitution would have provided a degree of flexibility that was lacking from the previous arrangements.*

If this prearranged fighter bomber programme is required following timings will apply. Time and sequence of attacks will be as requested by 2 Cdn

---

* Perhaps surprisingly, there are no indications that arrangements were made for the artillery to also have these targets "on call." After all, if the weather was bad enough to force a cancellation of the bombing, the possibility, while unlikely, existed that flying conditions might deteriorate enough to ground the fighter-bombers.

Corps through G Air channels on 2 hrs notice. Exact ETAs for each attack will be notified by G Air First Cdn Army in normal manner.

While the army had been reluctant to get into target marking for the 8th Air Force, perhaps because of a desire to avoid a repetition of the last-minute objections raised by Harris, there seem to have been no such objection to marking targets for the fighter bombers. The instruction directed 2nd Canadian Corps to "be prepared on demand to fire RED smoke on centre of targets at ETA notified, 4 r[oun]ds interval 20 sec[onds]."[38]

The instruction included two other points that the air force had stressed continually during the planning process. The first was troop safety. It was emphasized that troops, including those in the British Second Army and 1st British Corps sectors, must be withdrawn beyond the safety lines shown on the trace issued with Operation Instruction Number 11. The second point had to do with the blast and concussion effects of the bombing. Any troops who would be within 3,000 yards of the target aiming points were to wear ear plugs.[39]

The procedure for obtaining air support had proven to be slow and cumbersome. While this was partially because 84 Group was not yet operational, and First Canadian Army Headquarters was fighting its first battle, there can be no doubt that Brigadier Mann, the Chief of Staff, was kept away from his proper place in action for two days because he was negotiating the details of Simonds's air support plan in England. While his presence was necessary on one day, the second day was directly attributable to "bloody mindedness" on the part of Harris of Bomber Command. After all, if Harris had expressed his reservations earlier and as forcefully as he had showed himself capable of doing, much heartache and scrambling on 6 August could have been avoided.

However, the commanders and staff of both First Canadian Army and 2nd Canadian Corps made an egregious mistake in planning. At no time was the air force plan presented to Simonds by a senior air force officer along with an exposition of the things that might go wrong and the contingencies the air force had developed in that event. For example, no one seems to have explained how fighter bombers were expected to provide the effect of several hundred heavy bombers on a target. It also is evident that no thought was given to the development of an alternate plan if the bombing had to be cancelled because of weather or if it proved to be ineffective. Rather it appears everyone blithely accepted the air plan as a done deal as if it operated on the same basis as artillery support, and failed to realize that the differences between air and artillery support identified in a postwar study included:

(a) Artillery support was not dependent on weather; air support was absolutely dependent on it. This fact made it impossible for commanders, in their planning to count on air support to the same extent as artillery support.

(b) Aircraft in flight from base to target were quite different from artillery projectiles in flight from gun to target. Pilot error or enemy anti-aircraft fire, or a host of other factors, could affect air support to a much greater extent than artillery support.

(c) Air support was vastly more expensive than artillery support. There was, in consequence, a correspondingly greater need for economy in its use.

(d) Air support outranged artillery support. In planning air support, therefore, it was necessary to search for the best targets in an area much wider than normally dealt with by the staff of a headquarters such as HQ First Canadian Army.

(e) The primary task of the tactical air force was, *and had to be* [emphasis in original], the winning of the air battle. As a result, use of this support on ground targets was always conditional on a favourable air situation. However, artillery support, though affected by counter-bombardment, was not committed to responding to it as its top priority.[40]

It is surprising that Simonds would have gone along with it, unless he had become fixated on the plan as he had conceived it, and not as it really was. He, of course, had also seen the effects of heavy bomber attacks and had been briefed many times on the kills claimed by the fighters and fighter bombers of 2 TAF. It is likely that at this stage he would have had no reason to think that the Allied air forces might prove incapable of living up to his expectations. This was perhaps his major failing as a commander in that he consistently demanded more from his subordinates, or in this case the air force, than they were capable of delivering, regardless of the circumstances.

PREPARING FOR BATTLE

"It obviously was going to be quite useless to mount the infantry
if they felt like a lot of sardines in a tin and had no confidence
in the likelihood of the operation succeeding."

LIEUTENANT GENERAL GUY SIMONDS, 2ND CANADIAN CORPS

The two previous attempts to crack the German defences south of Caen, Operations GOODWOOD and SPRING, had been costly failures. Considering that an advance of this distance had rarely been attempted before at night, and certainly not with infantry in armoured carriers accompanying the tanks, TOTALIZE, as conceived by Lieutenant General Guy Simonds, was a risky operation that could easily turn into a major disaster. Furthermore, it was an apparent abandonment of the "balance" that was a feature of the Montgomery school of offensive planning – lengthy preparations, limited objectives and no risk of surrendering the initiative – that allowed that general to claim, and perhaps even to believe, that he never lost a battle or was forced to alter a plan.

Before the training and other preparations for this operation are examined, it is appropriate to follow the development of the detailed plans by the two commanders of the divisions detailed for the attack, Major General Charles Foulkes of the 2nd Canadian Infantry Division, who would assault west of the Route Nationale, and Major General Thomas Rennie[1] of 51st (Highland) Division, who would do the same east of the road. It is interesting that the two commanders adopted tactical solutions that, while similar in outline, were different in detail. Both, of course, were forced to make last-minute changes to their plan because of the sudden withdrawal of 1. *SS-Panzerdivision* from the front, but this did not alter the details of the armoured night advance. As their task was the less complicated of the two, we will begin with Rennie and his Scots.

During the war the fortunes of the 51st Highland Division, one of the first Territorial* divisions mobilized in 1939, had swung pendulum-like between triumph and humiliation. In June 1940, while attached to the French army for training, it had been trapped and forced to surrender at St. Valery-en-Caux. It re-arose phoenix-like (by renaming the 9th Scottish Division) and had been sent to Egypt in August 1942. At El Alamein the 51st Division was one of the assault formations that breached the German minefields, making room for Montgomery's armour to fan out on the far side. It had fought with the Eighth Army through the rest of the North African campaign, and then, in the invasion of Sicily, had landed next to the 1st Canadian Infantry Division commanded by Major General Guy Simonds. The 51st Highland Division was one of the three veteran divisions from the Eighth Army that returned to the United Kingdom to take part in the invasion and liberation of Northwest Europe.

Once home, however, a feeling had developed within the division that it had done its share and it was time for others to take up the torch. This was not to be and it landed in Normandy as a second-wave formation on the heels of the invasion. It failed badly in an attempt to capture Caen from the northeast on 10 June and Montgomery, deciding it was not "battleworthy," had considered returning it to England for further training. The critical manpower situation would not allow this, and not surprisingly the divisional commander was fired. Montgomery correctly decided that a Highlander was needed to turn the formation around and had appointed Major General Thomas Rennie as its General Officer Commanding. He was no stranger as he had commanded the division's 5th Battalion, Black Watch, at El Alamein and 154 Highland Brigade in Sicily, and in Normandy had been wounded and evacuated on 18 June while commanding the 3rd British Infantry Division. In some ways Rennie's appointment seemed a bit incongruous as he had been criticized for the lacklustre performance of the 3rd Division, especially for its failure to capture Caen on D-Day. If his roots had not been in a

---

* The Territorial Army was the British equivalent of the Canadian Militia and the U.S. Army Reserve and National Guard.

Highland regiment, he might have sat out the remainder of the war in a rear echelon appointment. Whatever his previous failings, Rennie's reputation and presence did the trick. As one of his brother Scots put it, "Aye, he was a guid general. He wasna' a shouting kind of man. The men liked his style and they had great confidence in him."[2] TOTALIZE would be the first test of the "new" 51st Highland Division since its public humiliation.[3]

As the left forward division, the 51st would be required to advance south-east on a frontage of some 2,000 yards through the enemy forward defences and seize objective areas in both the depth position of I. *Bataillon Grenadier-regiment* 1055 and the gun and *nebelwerfer* area of 89. *Infanteriedivision*. The total distance to be covered was nearly five miles at its farthest extent. This route, which was to be traversed at night, ran from the unit assembly areas, across the corps start line, through the enemy defences and on to debussing areas, where the assaulting troops would leave their vehicles and advance on foot to capture three battalion objectives more or less simultaneously. The actual tasks given to the HD were to

(a) Capture as first objective Lorguichon Wood–Cramesnil–St. Aignan-de-Cramesnil and the woods to its south–Garcelles-Secqueville, then
(b) after the first objective was captured, capture in succession Secqueville-la-Campagne and the woods to its east and south. These objectives included targets 4 and 5 of the Phase 1 bombing program.

Other Highlanders would follow on foot to seize intermediate objectives, including the blood-soaked rubble of Tilly-la-Campagne. Obviously, large bodies of Germans would have been bypassed by the armoured columns; the division would be responsible to clear up any remaining pockets of resistance and collect the stragglers.

Rennie appreciated it would take four infantry battalions to capture the first objective, but there were only enough armoured carriers to lift three battalions. Therefore, one of the battalions would be required to advance on foot to its objective. He decided to allot Cramesnil, St. Aignan-de-Cramesnil and Garcelles-Secqueville to the mounted battalions; these therefore became the objectives of an infantry brigade, in this case 154 Brigade, which would be supported by 33 Armoured Brigade. This meant that while the infantry brigade and battalion commanders would be supported by tanks, it was up to the armoured commanders to decide how this support would be provided and in theory they could refuse orders they considered unsound.

The area of Lorguichon where a railway line crosses the Route Nationale was given to 152 Brigade to capture, mop up and hold, as was Tilly. While the battalion that attacked Tilly would be able to take advantage of the barrage, the battalion directed on Lorguichon would not have any artillery support. In lieu, the 4.2-inch mortar company of the divisional machine gun battalion would be on call to support it. With these objectives secure, the brigade was then to occupy and clear Secqueville-la-Campagne and the woods around the village. As the first two objectives were to be held after their capture, there would be only one infantry battalion available for this task, although a squadron of flame-throwing tanks would be on call to support the operation.

The third brigade, 153 Brigade, was to hold a firm base to cover the deployment of the other battalions. After Secqueville-la-Campagne was captured by 152 Infantry Brigade, 153 Brigade was to be prepared to clear the large wooded area east of Secqueville.

Finally, in Phase 2, 152 Brigade was to be prepared to exploit to secure the area Poussy-la-Campagne–Billy–Conteville.[4] Rennie's concept of operations was to seize the three forward objectives with one brigade, then fill in behind them and expand the area of the penetration to the east with a second brigade and then, as a last step, push a bulge to the east of the initial objectives with the third brigade.

The Highland Division, unlike 2nd Canadian Infantry Division, did not have to deal with the large, well-defended strongholds of May-sur-Orne and Fontenay-le-Marmion, which lay outside the main thrust line, thus posing a major problem to the Canadian division. It is true that Tilly-la-Campagne would prove to be a major hindrance to Rennie and his men, but it lay within its main point of effort. The expansion of the area of the assault to the east and south would only take place after the main assault was successful. As the division was to revert to the command of 1st British Corps shortly after Phase 1 was complete, the expansion was in many ways a refinement to prepare for future operations by that British corps, and not a move that necessarily contributed to the attainment of the main objective. However, it did provide additional security to the south and east where intelligence believed the ever-dangerous 12. *SS-Panzerdivision* was lurking.

As for the night advance and attack on the main objectives, virtually the first thing to be decided was how to get the assaulting forces through the defences and onto their objectives. At first glance, the obstacles appeared difficult and insurmountable. However, as Rennie studied the mission, solutions began to appear and the components of the plan fell into place. First, the layout of the objectives and the number of flail tanks available for breaching minefields dictated that two routes would be used. Considering the location of the objectives, perhaps that seems glaringly obvious, but there was the possibility that three columns might have been a viable option. This was now ruled out, while the only other option, that of restricting the advance to one route, was fraught with danger besides being just too slow. From this deduction then, there must be two battalions on one route and two (one mounted and one on foot) on the other. The question was which route would receive the second carrier-mounted battalion, that is the one directed on Garcelles-Secqueville. The village and the adjacent woods that made up the objective lay behind and roughly midway between the two forward objectives and about a mile southwest of Tilly-la-Campagne. Perhaps in the end, the decision to put the two columns on the west route was based on nothing more than that it may have been judged to be the more secure of the two.

This would not have been an easy task on a peacetime exercise in a familiar training area against an "exercise enemy" firing blanks and throwing fireworks to simulate grenades and artillery and mortar fire. Any division that could have done it after weeks of preparatory training would have been showered with praise, and its commander marked for bigger and better things. To carry it out successfully with no more than two or three days preparation over unknown terrain against a well-armed and resolute enemy was a daunting prospect. The most complex task was for 154 Infantry Brigade and 33 Armoured Brigade to navigate in darkness through enemy country, arrive at the correct points selected from maps and then dismount from their vehicles, form up in battle formation – which is much harder than it sounds – and attack and secure their objectives. With that little task completed, they would then be expected to repel all manner of counterattacks from irate German forces. It was quite a job to give a commander deemed too cautious and plodding and a division that was pulled out of the line as unfit to fight a few weeks earlier.

The supporting armoured brigade, 33 Armoured Brigade, commanded by Brigadier H.B. Scott, had been formed in the United Kingdom on 30 August 1941. The brigade, which was made up of 1st Northamptonshire Yeomanry and 144 and 148 Regiments, Royal Armoured Corps (RAC), had landed in Normandy on 13 June 1944, and had supported a number of different divisions. The Northamptonshire Yeomanry was a locally-organized reserve regiment which pre-dated the territorial army, the British equivalent of the Canadian militia, while the two RAC regiments were wartime infantry battalions converted to armour in 1941 and 1940 respectively.[5]

The armoured attack was to be undertaken by two columns, the left made up of an armoured regiment accompanied by an infantry battalion carried in unfrocked Priests, half-tracks and carriers, while the right column was to consist of two of these groups, one following the other. In all cases the column was to be commanded by the armoured regimental commander, who would be responsible for the navigation of the column and getting the infantry forward to the objective. The composition of the columns was

Left (East) Column	Right (West) Column
1st Northamptonshire Yeomanry (1 NY) with Flails and one troop AVREs (armoured engineer vehicles)	144th Regiment Royal Armoured Corps (144 RAC)
1st Battalion The Black Watch (Royal Highland Regiment) (1 BW)	7th Battalion The Argyll and Sutherland Highlanders (7 A&SH)
	148th Regiment Royal Armoured Corps (148 RAC)
	7th Battalion The Black Watch (Royal Highland Regiment) (7 BW)

As each column arrived at its objective, command would pass to the infantry battalion commanding officer, and the armoured regiment would support the infantry; the tasks for the tanks included repelling any armoured counterattacks that might develop during the day. Finally 33 Armoured Brigade would command the flails, AVREs and flame-thrower tanks. The Highland Division's machine-gun battalion, less one machine-gun company and its 4.2-inch mortar company, which was supporting 152 Infantry Brigade,

Left Route Assault Column – 51 (H) Division
1st Northamptonshire Yeomanry, 1st Battalion The Black Watch and Supporting Elements 79th Armoured Division

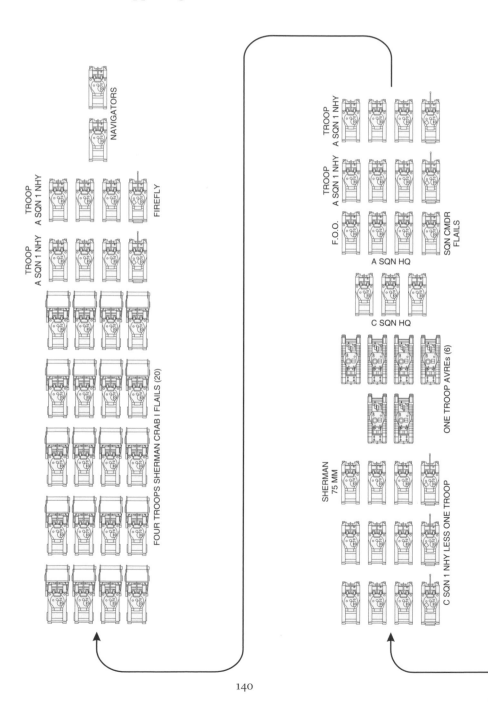

NOTE:

This illustration shows the organization of one of the two British columns. It is an approximation as sources differ in regards to the composition. Infantry battalion lift was distributed between Defrocked Priests, Half-tracks, Universal Carriers and assorted other armoured vehicles as available. Space limitations prevent illustrating the column as one continuous line.

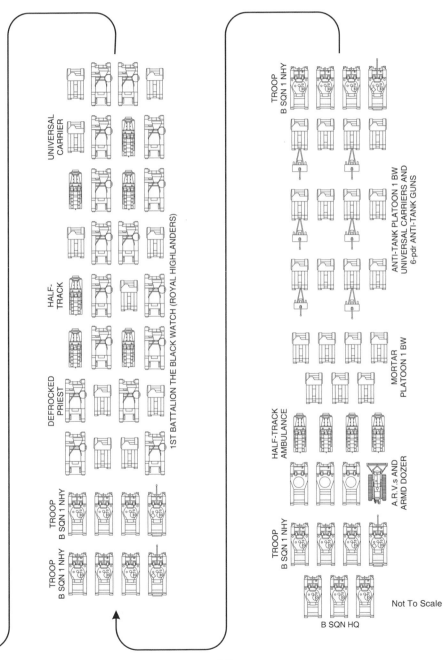

Not To Scale

would cover the left flank during the advance to the first objectives from positions east of Bourguébus. The divisional reconnaissance regiment, which had provided its carriers and scout cars to 154 Infantry Brigade for use as armoured carriers, would remain north of Caen until called forward by division headquarters.[6]

The scope of the mission given Major General Charles Foulkes, the commander of 2nd Canadian Infantry Division, was more complex and, it can be argued, would have strained the capabilities of any infantry division and its supporting armoured brigade. In fact, the 2nd Division had done little to date that would justify it being given a difficult task. It had been mobilized on 1 September 1939, but it was not concentrated until the spring of 1940. Following the German invasion of western Europe, the division sailed to England, where it formed part of 7th Corps and then the Canadian Corps. On 19 August 1942 the 2nd Division suffered extremely heavy casualties in the raid on Dieppe. On 6 July 1944 its leading elements arrived in Normandy, where it came under command of 2nd Canadian Corps. In the ensuing battles, especially Operation SPRING on 24 July 1944, Foulkes had shown himself to be a mediocre divisional commander at best, and Simonds was actively considering relieving him. The difficulty of the tasks facing Foulkes's division actually increased after the corps plan was revised on 6 August as it was given the additional task of guarding the corps' right flank by clearing and forming a firm base about Bretteville-sur-Laize. The tasks as ultimately assigned were to

(a) capture as the first objective the area from Caillouet running east past a quarry including both Point 122 and the area about Gaumesnil;

(b) mop up the area May-sur-Orne–Fontenay-le-Marmion–Caillouet–Gaumesnil–Rocquancourt;

(c) reorganize in the above area, but this time including the ground up to Verrières to protect the right flank of the Corps and to form a firm base for the launching of phase two; and

(d) finally protect the right flank by clearing and forming a firm base in Bretteville-sur-Laize.[7]

Mopping up the two defended villages of May-sur-Orne and Fontenay-le-Marmion was an additional mission that complicated the task for Foulkes and his soldiers. The little places, now largely reduced to rubble, lay outside the area of the barrage and had been assigned to Bomber Command as Phase 1 targets.

In fact, a case could have been made that the assigned tasks warranted the temporary assignment of a fourth infantry brigade to the division.[8] That, of course, did not happen and it was unlikely that Foulkes, who already was on shaky ground with Simonds because of his division's poor performance in SPRING and knew it, would have ventured to propose such a course of action. Simonds had decided that the job could be handled by 2nd Canadian Infantry Division and 2 Canadian Armoured Brigade, and likely that was enough to stifle any complaints from anyone outside the Corps Commander's small circle of trusted advisers. In Simonds's defence, the other side of the argument was that he would not have wished to dissipate his second phase forces in this way. Furthermore, once it appeared the Germans were thinning out and then replacing their elite SS panzer divisions in the front line with low-calibre army formations, he would have been even less likely to listen to any such plea from either Foulkes or Rennie.

The geography of the 2nd Division's main objective area was quite different from that faced by 51st Highland Division. Whereas the Scottish objectives lay in the form of an inverted triangle in relation to the front line, the Canadian objectives were in a line roughly perpendicular to the front. All were close enough together that the defenders could provide mutual support to one another. The objective farthest to the east was Point 122, the key terrain in Simonds's appreciation. Last, in a contradiction that never was resolved satisfactorily, Gaumesnil, the forward edge of one of the objective areas, was inside the planned safety distance for the Phase 2 bombing. This meant that it could not be assaulted and captured until after the bombing ended, which was just when the Phase 2 divisions should have been passing through the area.

The four objective areas each called for a battalion-sized organization to capture it. However, even when supplemented by half-tracks, scout cars and armoured 15-cwt trucks, there only was enough transport to lift three battalions. Rather than dissipate the strength of his assault force, Foulkes decided to allot the divisional reconnaissance regiment, the 14th Canadian Hussars, to take on the fourth objective. While not an infantry battalion, this regiment, which included a platoon-sized assault troop in each squadron, could capture and hold lightly defended areas for a limited period of time. As the Point 122 area was adjacent to the objective area that included Gaumesnil, it was allotted to the Hussars.

Rennie of the Highland Division had opted for a simple solution with 33 Armoured Brigade in support of 154 Highland Brigade, whose commander, Brigadier J.A. Oliver, would command the operation. Foulkes opted for a different solution; however, given the circumstances he faced, his solution was entirely justifiable. In the commander of 2 Armoured Brigade, Brigadier R.A. Wyman, Foulkes had available the most experienced brigade commander in the Canadian army, with nearly a year in command of a brigade in action in both Italy and Normandy under his belt. By comparison, Foulkes's own brigade commanders were inexperienced, including two prewar regular officers, both from the signal corps, who were posted to the division on 27 February 1944. The third had just taken over his command on 3 August, on promotion and posting from a staff appointment in the headquarters of 4th Canadian Armoured Division.[9] While Wyman may have had his faults, he was far and away the best, if not the only, choice for the job.

The 2nd Canadian Armoured Brigade had originally been formed as the 3rd Armoured Brigade in the 4th Armoured Division on 26 January 1942, and on 1 January 1943 was redesignated as the 3rd Army Tank Brigade. On 22 July 1943, following a reorganization of Canadian armoured resources in the United Kingdom, it became the 2nd Canadian Armoured Brigade, with three armoured regiments, the 1st Hussars from London, Ontario, the Fort Garry Horse from Winnipeg and the Sherbrooke Fusilier (no "s") Regiment from the Eastern Townships of Quebec. It landed on Juno Beach on 6 June 1944 and had been almost continually in action ever since.[10]

Foulkes tasked Wyman to command the advance and capture the first objectives, with both 4 Infantry Brigade and 8 Canadian Reconnaissance Regiment as well as the flails, AVREs and an Air Support Signals Unit tentacle (a vehicle-mounted station that could communicate with 83 Composite Group HQ and airfields) under his command.[11] Given the "under command" relationship, and even with one of his armoured regiments detached, Wyman would be leading an organization not much smaller than an armoured division, although with a much smaller headquarters and staff. On first glance, this seemed to be a case of giving Wyman too much to do, but in fact the forces and tasks he was given were similar in scale to those given to Oliver of 154 Highland Brigade. Where Wyman took a different approach was in the organization and structure he used. While the method Wyman adopted appeared cumbersome, in fact it was a doctrinaire approach taken from the War Office manuals on the employment of armoured forces. It also reflected the more difficult nature of the tasks allotted 2nd Division, in particular the addition of Bretteville-sur-Laize as an objective. Simply, General Foulkes had calculated that he would require an infantry brigade and an armoured regiment to seize that objective; that left Wyman with two armoured regiments, which did not allow the one-to-one grouping used by the Highlanders. It appears Wyman also was very concerned about the safety of the infantrymen being carried in unfrocked Priests and half-tracks in the column, as he opted to separate the leading tanks from the main body of each column.

The troops that Wyman, as commander of what he termed 2 Canadian Armoured Brigade group, was composed of his brigade, less the 1st Hussars, one of his armoured regiments, which was detached to 5 Infantry Brigade, and

(a) 4 Brigade (in armoured troop carriers)

(b) 14 Canadian Hussars

(c) one MMG company Toronto Scottish

(d) one 4.2-inch mortar platoon Toronto Scottish

(e) 56 Anti-Tank Battery (Self Propelled)

(f) 74 Anti-Tank Battery (17-pounder anti-tank guns, Ram towed)

(g) 1 Lothians (Flail tanks)

(h) 79 Assault Squadron, Royal Engineers (AVREs)

(i) one platoon, 2 Canadian Field Company, Royal Canadian Engineers

(j) one Air Support Signal Unit tentacle

as well as artillery FOO parties carried either in their own transport or in the observation post tanks held by the brigade headquarters squadron for that purpose. Wyman decided that his force would advance on two separate axes, three parallel columns on the right axis directed on the main objectives, and

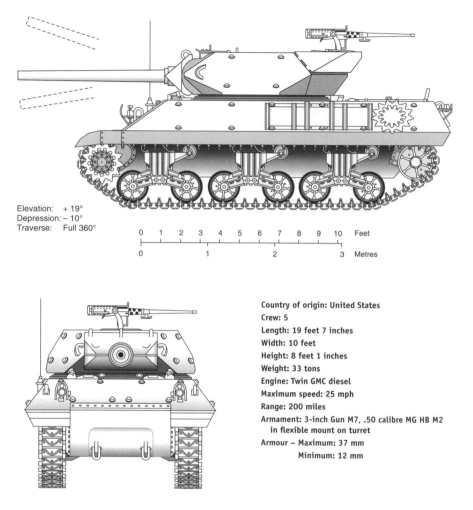

Elevation: + 19°
Depression: − 10°
Traverse: Full 360°

| 0 | 1 | 2 | 3 | 4 | 5 | 6 | 7 | 8 | 9 | 10 | Feet |

| 0 | | 1 | | 2 | | 3 | Metres |

Country of origin: United States
Crew: 5
Length: 19 feet 7 inches
Width: 10 feet
Height: 8 feet 1 inches
Weight: 33 tons
Engine: Twin GMC diesel
Maximum speed: 25 mph
Range: 200 miles
Armament: 3-inch Gun M7, .50 calibre MG HB M2
     in flexible mount on turret
Armour – Maximum: 37 mm
           Minimum: 12 mm

M10 self-propelled gun

An American design, the M10 was equipped with a high-velocity 3-inch gun in an open-topped, 360° rotating turret. It was based on the robust hull and chassis of the M4A2 Sherman, but incorporated a sloped hull design. The British upgraded the M10 by installing their high-velocity 17-pdr gun and this version gradually found its way into the anti-tank regiments in Northwest Europe as increased numbers of the 17-pdr gun became available. The M10 armed with the 3-inch gun was a familiar sight in Canadian service from the D-Day landing through Normandy. While the provision of a turret-mounted gun was superior to restricted-traverse German tank destroyer designs, the M10 suffered from excessive height, thin armour and a lack of overhead protection for the crew.

a single column on the left for Point 122, which he termed the Cramesnil feature.[12]

Instead of grouping the troops that would move in each column under a separate commander, Wyman formed his command into four task-organized groups. The first, "Gapping Force," was under the command of Lieutenant Colonel M.B.K. Gordon, the commanding officer of the Sherbrooke Fusilier Regiment. Gordon would be responsible for navigation on the right-hand axis and marking the route for the troops that would follow along that route. Once at the debussing area, Gapping Force would cover the three 4 Brigade battalions as they formed up and assaulted their objectives. The Gapping Force for each battalion column was made up of two troops of the Sherbrookes commanded by the squadron second-in-command, two troops of Sherman flails from 1 Lothians and a troop of AVREs of 79 Assault Squadron, RE.

On the right axis Brigadier J.E. Ganong, the commander of 4 Infantry Brigade, would command "Assault Force," the group responsible for capturing and securing the objectives. Each of his battalion groups consisted of a Sherbrooke squadron less two troops, an infantry battalion mounted in armoured carriers, two troops of anti-tank guns, one self propelled and the other towed by turretless Ram tanks, a platoon of Vickers machine guns of the Toronto Scottish and a section of engineers.[13]

On the right route, a separate Gapping Force organized similarly but with tanks from C Squadron, the Fort Garry Horse, operated under the direct control of Lieutenant Colonel Bruce Alway, commanding officer of the reconnaissance regiment. In fact, unlike the troops on the right axis, Alway commanded the entire column on the left axis. His assault force, or main body, was made up of one squadron of the Garries less two troops, his own unit, that is, his headquarters and three reconnaissance squadrons wholly mounted in carriers and half-tracks for the operation, a troop from each of 56 and 74 anti-tank batteries, a platoon of MMGs and a section of engineers.[14]

Last, Wyman detailed the Fort Garry Horse, less the squadron with Alway's column, as "Fortress Force." The regiment would follow Assault Force on the right axis and secure the debussing area. Later it would form Wyman's reserve. The tactical headquarters of 2 Armoured Brigade, that is, the commander, brigade major and four liaison officers in brigade headquarters tanks, and the headquarters 4 Brigade were to advance on the right axis at the rear of the centre column's assault force. On arrival in the objective area, they would set up in the debussing area. Captain J.E. Fuger, the GSO III, and another officer, would take "Tactical Headquarters Two," consisting of an Armoured Command Vehicle and a scout car, to join the tactical headquarters of 2nd Canadian Infantry Division at Ifs. Meanwhile 2 Armoured Brigade main headquarters would return to an old location near Cormelles adjacent to the headquarters of 3rd Canadian Infantry Division.[15]

Wyman's third armoured regiment, the 1st Hussars, was detached to 5 Infantry Brigade, which was tasked with assisting 2 Armoured Brigade if required, mopping up the division area and acting as division reserve. When the forward objectives were secured, the brigade was to be prepared to capture and secure Bretteville-sur-Laize on Foulkes's order.

When the planning and preparations for TOTALIZE had started, the attacking formations had been informed that the operation would be mounted on the evening of 8 August 1944. At 0905 hours on the morning of 5 August, however, 2 Canadian Corps informed "all concerned" that the H-Hour for the operation would now be 2300 hours on 7 August.[16] It is now necessary to examine the detailed preparations, which were compressed to adjust to that new timing. As we shall see, while it may have seemed of little consequence to Simonds and his staff, who had agreed to advance the operation 24 hours after conducting some hurried checks with the staff, the change caused mad scrambling in the Phase 1 divisions, especially 2nd Canadian Infantry Division.

On 1 August, when Simonds's headquarters began detailed preparations for TOTALIZE, the formations that would carry out the operation were in what was basically a defensive posture. This was in line with Montgomery's direction to Crerar of 29 July that "no large scale effort was immediately required."[17] The corps sector was held by 4th Armoured Division on the left facing Tilly-la-Campagne and La Hogue, while 2nd Infantry Division faced 1. and 9. *SS-Panzerdivisionen* from the Route Nationale highway to the Orne. At long last, 3rd Infantry Division had been withdrawn across the Orne to rest and rebuild after 55 days in the line,[18] while Wyman's 2 Armoured Brigade had done the same in the area of Louvigny, the formation War Diary

Gapping Force
The Sherbrooke Fusilier Regiment
with Elements of 79th Armoured Division

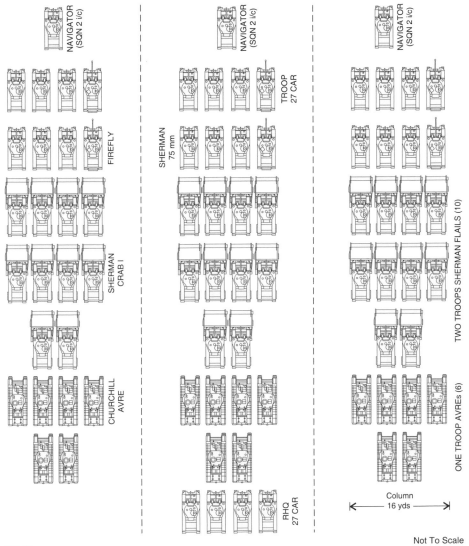

Not To Scale

NOTES:

1) This chart is an approximation as sources differ in regards to the composition of a column. Main fighting vehicles illustrated.

2) Gapping Force was based on six troops of the S.F.R. (two troops per column) with six troops of Crab I Flails of 1st Lothians (two troops per column) and three troops of AVREs (one troop per column) of 79 Assault Squadron R.E.

3) Organization applies to the three right side Canadian columns.

reflecting the positive effects of this, both in the tone of its reports during the period of rest, and in more concrete terms, by reporting a 24 percent increase in its number of serviceable Shermans in the period 1 to 5 August.[19]

One of the first physical preparations was to re-posture for the upcoming battle. For 2nd Division, which held its part of the front with 4 Brigade left and 6 Brigade right, it was a case of staying in place while replacing 4 Brigade with 5 Brigade on the night of 3-4 August. Regrettably this relief did not start well and the Royal Hamilton Light Infantry of 4 Brigade suffered some casualties from a surprise *Luftwaffe* bombing raid as it made its way to the rear.[20] The rest of the relief went well and by dawn the brigade completed its move back across the Orne to join 2 Armoured Brigade in the area of Louvigny.[21] As for the other Phase 1 troops, 51st Highland Division was still in a concentration area north of Caen while 33 British Armoured Brigade had moved to Cazelle in the same area on 3 August.[22] The Highlanders would replace 4th Armoured Division in the line opposite Tilly-la-Campagne during the night of 6-7 August with the two follow-on brigades forward. The Canadian armoured division concentrated on the southern outskirts of Caen while 1. *Dywizji Pancernej* would remain south of Bayeux until ordered forward.

Simonds had been definite in his appreciation of 31 July that the attacking troops would need at least a week to train, to gain confidence in rolling through the German defences in the "newfangled" armoured carriers and in navigating cross country at night in mixed columns of tanks and carrier-borne infantry. In the event, this time was not available and then, on the morning of 5 August, while the tradesmen were still converting Priests to Kangaroos, Simonds exacerbated the problem by agreeing to move the attack ahead 24 hours. This posed particular problems for the 2 Armoured Brigade group, which had only received the bulk of its carriers after 51st Highland Division and thus had a day less to train with them. In his defence, Simonds would have found it difficult to prove to the satisfaction of Montgomery and Crerar, and perhaps even to himself, that he could not attack on the night of 7-8 August even if he had been inclined to turn the request down. At this stage he seemed to agreeable to Montgomery's requests for early action, as he demonstrated on 1 August by ordering 4th Armoured Division to mount a short-notice attack on Tilly-la-Campagne. Moreover, any appreciation from the "big picture" point of view would have demonstrated the advantages of

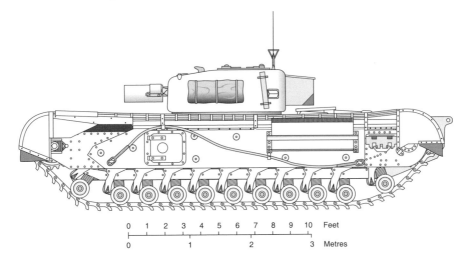

0 1 2 3 4 5 6 7 8 9 10   Feet

0   1   2   3   Metres

Churchill AVRE (Armoured Vehicle Royal Engineers)

Developed as a result of lessons learned from the Dieppe raid of August 1942, the AVRE provided engineers with the protection of an armoured vehicle when they were clearing obstacles under enemy fire. The Churchill infantry tank was a logical choice as the parent vehicle for the conversion because of its heavy armour and roomy interior. The AVRE was fitted with a 290 mm Petard spigot mortar in place of the turret gun and the interior stowage was converted to carry Petard rounds and engineering equipment. The Petard fired a 40-pound projectile which contained a 26-pound demolition charge. The round was commonly known as a "Flying Dustbin" among AVRE crews and had an effective range of only 80 yards. Loading the mortar was accomplished outside the confines of the tank by the hull gunner who "broke" the mortar, much as with a shotgun, and inserted the projectile. A sliding hatch was supplied in the top of the hull at his station so that his exposure to enemy fire was kept to a minimum. A well trained crew was capable of firing two to three rounds per minute.

an early attack. Still, the nagging thought remains that Simonds may have given more weight to the factor of staff preparations and battle procedure, and less to the challenges of training, than was warranted.

Of all the difficulties inherent in Operation TOTALIZE, the most serious was – excepting the Germans – navigation. The ground had been battered by bombing and shelling since the days of GOODWOOD in mid-July, and the villages and woods tended to look the same, especially at night. Moreover, navigation was hard enough in a tank under ideal conditions, let alone in one moving cross country in close formation in the dark and under fire. The moon would rise after midnight, but given the chances of clouds, to rely on it for enough illumination to find one's way was out of the question. The alternative was artificial light. There were not enough artillery flares available to provide even a fraction of the light needed, and even if there had been, the only guns with flare ammunition, the 25-pounders of the divisional artilleries, were committed to the barrage. Simonds, however, arranged for light anti-aircraft guns to fire tracers to indicate the direction of the advance along each route. He then turned to mechanical means and got the use of 344 Searchlight Battery to provide "Monty's Moonlight" as was used in the desert.

Simonds's signals officer had been conducting trials to develop a radio navigation aid that could be used in a moving tank. (Similar devices were in use by the air forces of both sides to guide bombers to their targets with some success, so the idea was not as far-fetched as it seems.) The idea was to direct signals on two beams that navigating officers could pick up in their radio headsets along the axis of each column. If a navigating officer's tank veered too much to the west, he would hear loud dots; if he veered to the east, he would pick up loud dashes. By staying in the centre of the beams, the naviga-tor would hear a series of dots and dashes that would continue as long as his tank was following the beam down the correct route. The accuracy achieved was about 200 yards either side of the axis at six miles from the transmitter site. On the down-side, the navigating officer would have to concentrate on listening to this signal and ignore whatever was going on around him, which could not have appealed to the officers detailed for the job. While it worked in trials and seemed to perform satisfactorily in training, the commander of 33 British Armoured Brigade decided there had not been enough time to become proficient in its use and decided to rely on other methods.[23]

Finally, there were the tried and true "low technology" methods: Bofors anti-aircraft guns of the 3rd Light Anti-Aircraft Regiment were sited to fire bursts of tracer in prearranged patterns to indicate the axis and boundary for each column. The British also fitted magnetic compasses to some of their tanks, despite the conventional wisdom that this would not work. (This was an expedient at best, as the turret could not be traversed without affect-ing the accuracy of the compass.) Perhaps the most successful device, along with the tracer, was the issue of air photos with the grid lines and other data printed on them. And naturally, there was no substitute for the old stand-by of studying the map and getting a look at as much ground as possible from

Marshalling
A column of Allied Shermans moving into position between Hubert Folie and Tilly-la-Campagne. (NAC/PA 132904)

vantage points within the Allied lines. Last, the Highland Division built a large three-dimensional model of the area with the details of the objectives and routes marked on it. It was first used by Rennie for planning and briefing his brigade and battalion commanders, and was later studied by all officers of the attacking units.

Perhaps because they had longer to prepare, as well as having been through this sort of thing before in three different theatres, the Highland Division seems to have adopted a more systematic approach than 2nd Division. They did, however, have some advantages, including having their flails and AVREs available earlier than was the case for the Canadians. Their preparations were detailed in the booklet prepared for a 1947 battlefield tour of TOTALIZE:

154 Highland Bde (the brigade detailed to conduct the mounted night advance) selected a local area for training and 33 British Armoured Brigade joined it there on 3 August. The armoured transport for the infantry arrived the next day, and was organized so that each battalion had one mixed platoon of thirty Priests, half tracks and carriers. Conferences and practice runs took up all available time, day and night, between 4 and 6

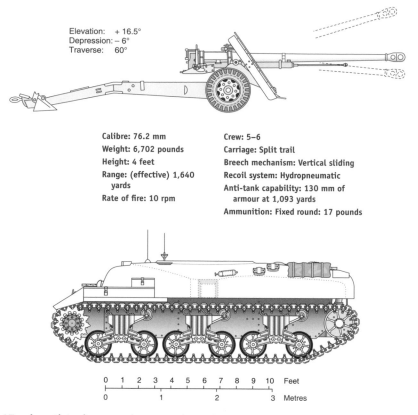

Elevation: + 16.5°
Depression: – 6°
Traverse: 60°

Calibre: 76.2 mm
Weight: 6,702 pounds
Height: 4 feet
Range: (effective) 1,640 yards
Rate of fire: 10 rpm

Crew: 5–6
Carriage: Split trail
Breech mechanism: Vertical sliding
Recoil system: Hydropneumatic
Anti-tank capability: 130 mm of armour at 1,093 yards
Ammunition: Fixed round: 17 pounds

| 0 | 1 | 2 | 3 | 4 | 5 | 6 | 7 | 8 | 9 | 10 | Feet |

| 0 | | | 1 | | | 2 | | | 3 | Metres |

17-pdr anti-tank gun and armoured gun tower
First coming into service in early 1943, the 17-pdr was the most effective anti-tank gun in service with British and Canadian anti-tank regiments in Normandy, be it towed or self-propelled. Towed 17-pdr batteries in armoured divisions utilized converted, turretless Canadian Ram tanks as tow vehicles to keep pace with the other armoured vehicles, while those in infantry divisions were often towed by the 25-pdr Field Artillery Tractor.

August, and last minute adjustments such as fitting dimmed tail-lights and reorganising the stowage so that crew were below the level of the armoured sides of the half tracks had to be completed. Great attention to detail was paid in the precautions against straying and in the instructions for commanders and drivers of vehicles. A very close liaison was established and the various practices carried out were most successful. The squadron and company commanders, who were to work together once the objective was reached, got to know each other ...[24]

2 Canadian Armoured Brigade and 4 Canadian Infantry Brigade concentrated at Louvigny on 5 August, although the AVREs did not arrive until the following morning and the flails only in the afternoon. To make matters worse, one of the anti-tank batteries actually joined the group in the assembly area only a few hours before the attack, having missed all the training.[25] This obviously hampered rehearsals and training and no doubt contributed to some of the difficulties experienced in the advance. The problem was made more difficult as Assault Force was to move five minutes, or 500 yards, behind Gapping Force. The unfrocked Priests arrived during the day on 6 August and were allotted to battalions. In the meantime, 3-ton trucks were used in lieu to practise moving in formation by at least one battalion.[26]

In short, 2 Armoured Brigade group had a very limited time to get ready for TOTALIZE; for example, the gapping parties were only able to rehearse on the evening of 6 August, about 24 hours before the operation was to begin. Training was conducted up to the last possible moment, and the units of the last column in the move to the assembly area were actually still rehearsing

Allied armour at dawn
The tank on the right can be identified as a Sherman Firefly armed with a 17-pounder gun. While this gun could kill any German tank, it was inaccurate and a hit at over 1,000 yards range was a matter of luck. (NAC/PA 162391).

while the other columns were on the road to their assembly area. Still, even with the limited time, the columns were able to practise embussing and debussing drills, and runs were made to an exercise dispersal area, where the troops debussed and attacked objectives while Fortress Force secured the dispersal area.[27]

PART THREE

THE
NIGHT PUSH[1]

Unfrocked Priests
Infantrymen of 4 Canadian Infantry Brigade kill time while waiting for the Phase 1 advance to begin. In this photo the modifications to the original SP guns are clearly apparent. Note that the .50 calibre machine guns have been removed, someone probably concluding that unpractised men firing these weapons at night would be as least as dangerous to their own troops as to the enemy. (NAC/PA 129172)

CHAPTER SEVEN

PHASE 1 TOTALIZE

*"Not particularly highly trained Canadian troops
are holding the general line St. Martin–Tilly."*

GRENADIERREGIMENT 1056 OPERATION ORDER

Even as Crerar's staff were confirming with Bomber Command that Operation TOTALIZE would actually start on the evening of 7 August 1944,[2] the troops of the assault divisions were moving forward to their assembly areas. While 154 Highland Brigade and 33 British Armoured Brigade had moved to the factory area of Cormelles during the night of 6/7 August[3] and now faced a relatively short drive, 2 Canadian Armoured Brigade group had to slowly snake its way in a long train of vehicles across the Orne River by the bridge at Fleury-sur-Orne and then south to its assembly areas on either side of Ifs. The day was hot and dry and the Canadian convoy, while out of direct German observation, raised towering clouds of dust. Surprisingly, perhaps because of the inexperience of 89. *Infanteriedivision*, no enemy air attacks or shelling resulted.

In the assembly area each unit had to form up into its own column, four vehicles wide and no more than a pace or two apart, the total column width being 16 yards, which was the maximum that could be swept for mines by the flail tanks. Behind the first four vehicles, another four closed up to within a yard or two of those ahead, and behind them another four, and another, and another all the way back to the last vehicles, more than 25 rows in all.[4] Within the columns, Gapping Force was made up of two troops of tanks commanded by the squadron second-in-command as navigator, the flails and AVREs, while the Assault Force was led by the tank squadron less two

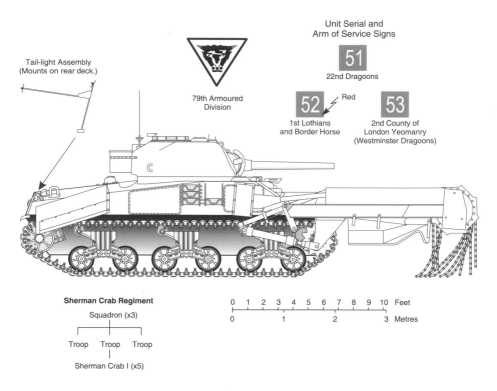

Tail-light Assembly
(Mounts on rear deck.)

Unit Serial and
Arm of Service Signs

51

22nd Dragoons

79th Armoured
Division

52 Red

1st Lothians
and Border Horse

53

2nd County of
London Yeomanry
(Westminster Dragoons)

Sherman Crab Regiment

Squadron (x3)

Troop   Troop   Troop

Sherman Crab I (x5)

0 1 2 3 4 5 6 7 8 9 10 Feet

0   1   2   3 Metres

Sherman Crab Mark I

The Sherman Crab was the most successful mine-clearing tank of the war. It equipped Britain's 79th Armoured Division throughout Northwest Europe. The Crab Mark I consisted of a standard Sherman V (M4A4) with a forward-mounted revolving flailing device. It was as wide as the tank itself and was mounted on two pivoting arms attached to the sides of the hull. A series of chains attached to the rotating drum beat the ground as the drum revolved. The engine of the tank drove the rotating drum by means of a power takeoff connected to a transmission on the right arm of the flail. This in turn was coupled to chains that rotated the drum. Lights facing the rear were fitted to arms at the back of the Crab. These assisted a trailing Crab to maintain station while flailing. Lane markers were carried in boxes on both sides of the hull. Flailed lanes were initially marked with powered chalk but the chalk was superseded by markers that could be illuminated during periods of low visibility or night operations. Flailing was effective to a depth of 4–5 inches and proved to be an efficient means of destroying teller mines. As would be expected, the flailing chains took a terrific pounding from beating the ground. As detonating a mine put further strain on the chains, each Crab carried replacements so the crew could change them as required.

Country of origin: British conversion of U.S.-built Sherman M4A4

Crew: 5

Length: 27 feet

Width: 11 feet 6 inches

Height: 9 feet

Weight: 35 tons

Engine: Chrysler Multibank

Maximum speed: 25 mph

Range: 100 miles

Armament: 75 mm Gun M3, .30 calibre MG M1919A4 co-axial, .30 calibre M1919A4 MG in bow mount

Armour – Maximum: 75 mm
Minimum: 12 mm

Mine Clearing by two Troops of Sherman Crabs

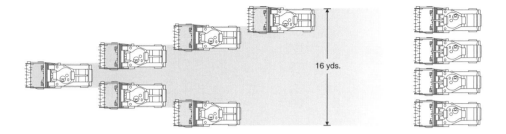

Mine clearing by two troops of Sherman Crabs

The assault columns in Phase I of Operation TOTALIZE each had two troops of Sherman Crab tanks from 1st Lothian and Border Horse, 79th Armoured Division. Unlike a standard four-tank troop, a troop of Crabs consisted of five tanks. A single Crab was capable of flailing an eight-foot lane. Standard operating procedure for the troop was for three Crabs to flail a 24-foot lane while the remaining two tanks supported them with covering fire as necessary, and simultaneously acted as reserves should they be required to replace one of the flailing Crabs.

Had a minefield been encountered during the advance, the two troops of Crabs would have moved to the front of the column, where six of the Crabs would flail a lane 48 feet (16 yds.) wide – the width of the column itself. Note that the turrets on the flailing Crabs were traversed to the rear in an effort to avoid the dust, dirt and debris that was churned up by the revolving chains.

troops followed by the infantry battalion and the support weapons.[5] Behind the three battalion columns came Fortress Force of the Fort Garry Horse, the Shermans and Stuarts of 2 Canadian Armoured Brigade's Tactical Headquarters and the headquarters of 4 Infantry Brigade. The three battalion groups on the west axis covered a frontage of 150 yards, so there was about 50 yards between each of the unit columns. Finally, all vehicles were in place and there was time to stretch, catch a quick smoke, have a pee and then wait as the sun lowered in the west.

A thousand yards or so to the east, the reconnaissance regiment formed its own column, similar in outline but rather different in composition. Behind its own Gapping Force, the Assault Force was made up of C Squadron of the Fort Garry Horse less two troops, the reconnaissance regiment in three parallel squadron columns with the anti-tank guns, bulldozers, and half-tracked

Fortress Force
The Fort Garry Horse Less One Squadron

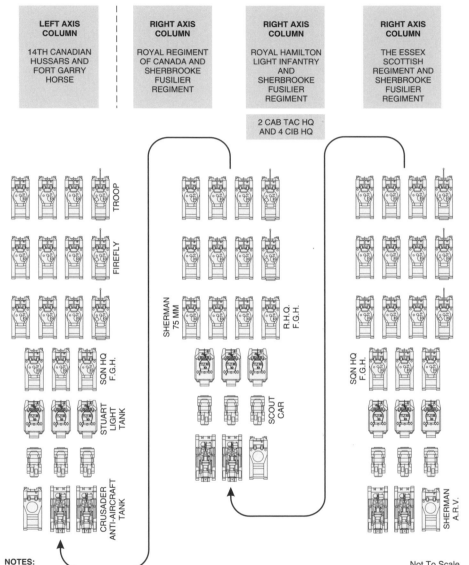

LEFT AXIS COLUMN	RIGHT AXIS COLUMN	RIGHT AXIS COLUMN	RIGHT AXIS COLUMN
14TH CANADIAN HUSSARS AND FORT GARRY HORSE	ROYAL REGIMENT OF CANADA AND SHERBROOKE FUSILIER REGIMENT	ROYAL HAMILTON LIGHT INFANTRY AND SHERBROOKE FUSILIER REGIMENT	THE ESSEX SCOTTISH REGIMENT AND SHERBROOKE FUSILIER REGIMENT

2 CAB TAC HQ AND 4 CIB HQ

NOTES:

Not To Scale

1) This chart is an approximation and illustrates the main fighting vehicles. Space limitations preclude illustrating Fortress Force as a single long column.

2) Fortress Force followed behind the Gapping and Assault Forces of both the left axis (one column) and right axis (three columns).

3) Support vehicles (not illustrated) which didn't form a part of Gapping, Assault or Fortress Forces followed in echelon behind Fortress Force.

ambulances and fitters' vehicles bringing up the rear. To their left could be seen the two British columns, one just east of the Caen–Falaise Highway and the other beyond it. To Sergeant C.W. Wilson, a carrier section commander of B Squadron, "all that could be seen for miles around were great masses of tanks, equipment and men, all waiting for zero hour."[6] To the gunners in the field regiments of 2nd Canadian Infantry Division the magnitude of the assault was driven home when the slopes to the south and west of their gun areas around Ifs began to fill with armoured vehicles of all shapes and sizes, while the sound of more could be heard coming from the "dead ground"* in the direction of Fleury-sur-Orne.[7] For the staff of Headquarters 2 Canadian Armoured Brigade in the château at Cormelles, it was possible to see vast formations of armour and armoured infantry vehicles drawn up in the final assembly area in preparation for the night breakthrough.[8]

The two columns of 51st Highland Division were organized in a different form from the Canadian columns. First, Brigadier J.A. Oliver, the commander of 154 Highland Brigade, had decided to dispense with a separate Gapping Force, while the shape of the ground and the objectives precluded any requirement for a Fortress Force. Second, the shortage of manpower that was beginning to seriously affect British operations had forced Oliver to reduce the number of rifle companies in his three battalions from four to three. It was a case of opting to attack with three companies with rifle sections that averaged seven men instead of going with four weak ones.[9] This restored the ability to perform the most basic of infantry tactics, fire and movement, to the sections with a rifle group of five men and a Bren group of two. While the detailed order of march of each British column varied slightly, in general it was made up of the navigating party, a squadron of tanks with the flails and AVREs, the armoured regimental headquarters and a tank squadron, the infantry battalion and support weapons, with the third tank squadron as rear guard.[10] There was another difference in the composition of the columns. The commanding officer of the Northamptonshire Yeomanry had decided to arrange the vehicles in four rows, 10 yards apart left to right and with 15 yards spacing between nose and tail, while the commanding officer of 144th Regiment RAC opted for 6 yards between each of

---

* The military term for ground hidden from view by other terrain features such as ridges or woods.

Reconnaissance Regiment
Infantry Division

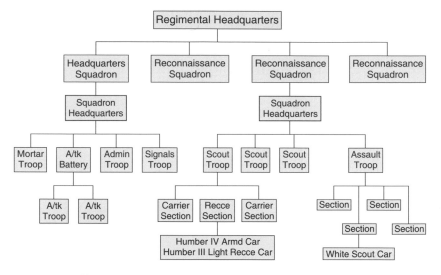

Note: Humber IV replaced by Daimler armoured car after September 1944

By 1944 the infantry divisional reconnaissance regiment had evolved into an "economy of force" unit that tended to be given tasks that did not fall neatly into the infantry or armoured camp. Thus, in British service the regiments belonged to a wartime creation, the Reconnaissance Corps, while the Canadians allotted them to the Canadian Armoured Corps.

his four rows and the same distance front to rear.[11] At 2110 hours the right British column moved through the narrow streets from the Cormelles factory complex to its forming-up point. By 2210 hours 144 RAC and 7 Argyll and Sutherland Highlanders were formed up in a tightly packed column of over 150 vehicles, just on the edge of the last ground that could not be observed from the German lines. As there was not sufficient space between the crest and the built-up areas, 148 RAC and 7 Black Watch column formed up on their left, while 1 Northamptonshire Yeomanry and 1 Black Watch waited on the other side of Bras.

Even before the columns began to form, there was an alteration to the basic plan. Major General Thomas Rennie had decided that it was too risky for his left column to pass to the east of Bourguébus, as it would come too close to the bombing target at La Hogue. On the morning of 6 August, Captain Tom Boardman, the second-in-command of A Squadron, 1st North-amptonshire Yeomanry, the navigating officer of the column, accompanied by an engineer officer, scouted a route skirting Bourguébus to the west. This brought them close enough to Tilly to provoke a violent enemy response. Nevertheless, the reconnaissance discovered two sunken roads lying across the axis of advance with banks steep enough to be obstacles for half-tracks. That night the divisional engineers made gaps in the banks of both of the roads. When the navigating officer checked the roads on the morning of 7 August, he reported that he thought the half-tracks would now be able to pass through the gaps.[12]

With the assault forces assembled and the clock ticking down to H-Hour at 2345, it fell to Crerar to brief the assembled Allied war correspondents on TOTALIZE and explain how the battle was to be fought. Ross Munro, a veteran Canadian journalist, noted that Crerar made a point of emphasizing the significance of 8 August. Twenty-six years before, 8 August 1918 – the day Ludendorff called the "Black Day" of the German Army in the First World War – the Canadian Corps attacked out of the mist at Amiens on what was the first of Canada's Hundred Days that ended on 11 November with Canadian infantry in the town square of Mons. This time, in TOTALIZE the assaulting troops would attack at night, with massive heavy bomber and artillery support. If they succeeded in breaking through the German defences and gained the heights behind Rocquancourt and Tilly-la-Campagne, Crerar said, then 4th Canadian Armoured Division and 1. *Dywizji Pancernej*, followed by 3rd Canadian Infantry Division, would charge through the breach and carry the advance towards Falaise.[13]

As the assault troops rested and the press began to mentally compose their stories, there were several thousand other men whose work had yet to reach its fullest tempo – the gunners. During the week ammunition had been accumulating in ordered piles on the gun positions. Now, on 7 August the rounds were sorted and arranged in the order they would be used in the fire plan. During the day the gun position officers in each troop had briefed their gun detachment commanders, usually sergeants. For the 25-pounders in 2nd Canadian Infantry Division and 51st Highland Division, 400 or more rounds would be fired that night, while the 5.5-inch medium guns in the AGRAs would shoot half that amount; most of the ammunition would be expended in the short period of an hour during the barrage. To ensure that the rate of fire could be maintained required a considerable amount of preparation on the guns. The gunners ran lightly-oiled brushes through the bores, stripped and cleaned the breeches and tested the accuracy of the sights. The gun fitters came around to check the recoil mechanisms and just before last light, the guns' sights were aligned on the night aiming points. An hour or so before the H-Hour for the barrage, the completed gun programs, sheets of paper with actual timings, sight settings and ammunition to be expended on each line of the barrage, were distributed to the gun detachments.[14]

H-Hour for the barrage was 2345 hours,* but some guns would open fire before that time. First, single guns would mark targets for the Pathfinders just before the main force bombers arrived, while other batteries would engage known German anti-aircraft positions to suppress their fire during the bombing run. With the RAF Pathfinders and Master Bombers only a few minutes away and inbound, and the guns laid and loaded on their first targets, it is time to turn our attention to the troops who would face the onslaught, the men of 89. *Infanteriedivision.*

Ever since Kurt Meyer of the *Hitlerjugend* Division first libelled its reputation by claiming that it broke and ran and played no further part in the battle, 89. *Infanteriedivision* has received less than its due.[15] The assessments delivered before the battle by Allied intelligence were no more flattering. On 7 August Lieutenant Colonel P.E.R. Wright, the GSO 1 Intelligence at First Canadian Army, summed up its capabilities: "Once the initial morale or line has been broken, it can be counted out as a formation although separated groups may continue to fight with SS or other strong German backing." After commenting on its lack of battle experience, the author of an assessment published by 2nd Canadian Infantry Division concluded that "the battle experience which the formation will gain will be short, sharp and unhappy, for it is most unlikely that it will stand long against determined and aggressive attacks. We must be prepared for a large number of PW and deserters."[16] In view of these harsh words, what kind of formation was 89. *Infanteriedivision*?

---

* In fact the guns on the British portion of the barrage opened fire at 2341 hours, or H-4 minutes as the barrage had two extra lines on their front.

The Allies actually had amassed a fair amount of useful intelligence about it. According to their information, they believed, for example, that it had been formed in February 1944 and was immediately sent to Norway. On 12 June 1944 it left Norway and had been located near Rouen at the start of July. Both of its infantry regiments, *Grenadierregimenten* 1055 and 1056, of three battalions each, had been identified in the line between May-sur-Orne and Tilly-la-Campagne on the night of 5/6 August. The division had two additional units that could fight effectively as infantry, a bicycle-mounted fusilier (reconnaissance) company and a two-company engineer battalion. The following qualitative assessment of its personnel was derived from the interrogation of a prisoner

> Amongst its personnel will be a large number of foreigners. Our first PW, who incidentally deserted, being a Yugoslav, spoke little German. This deserter also stated that the German personnel was comprised chiefly of men over 40 and under 18 years of age…

It was believed that the division was close to its establishment in personnel, weapons and equipment, including 18 75 mm and 12 88 mm guns in its combined anti-aircraft/anti-tank battalion. The division also had a large number of machine guns and mortars, although it had proportionally fewer field guns than was the case in British and Canadian infantry divisions. Last, the divisional commander was identified as Lieutenant General Heinrichs, an infantryman with a distinguished combat record and winner of the Knight's Cross as a regimental commander, who had performed well commanding an infantry division on the eastern front.[17]

Actually, Allied intelligence on 89. *Infanteriedivision* was fairly accurate, at least in the details of numbers and types of weapons and equipment. The division had been formed in January 1944 in Bergen, Germany, and was almost immediately sent to Norway. Its commander was indeed 52-year-old Lieutenant General Konrad Heinrichs; it had two regiments each of three battalions, but a fusilier battalion, not a company, and was in good shape for personnel and equipment. As for its manpower, it was a relatively "young" division with 64 per cent of its strength aged 19 or less, which is a different matter than what was implied by the claim that its German personnel were "comprised chiefly of men over 40 and under 18 years of age." It was, of course, designed to fight defensive battles and, as it relied on horse-drawn transport, not terribly mobile. The division was known as the *Hufeisen* (Horseshoe) Division from its sign, which was interpreted by some as recognition of its main transport resource but could have been related to the names of its two regimental commanders, *Obersts* Rossman and Roesler, as *"Ross"* meant a steed or horse in German. The troops were no less realistic or cynical than their Allied counterparts and preferred to call themselves by the sardonic nickname "Wheelbarrow Division" because of the primitive nature of much of their equipment.[18]

The division had some additional resources allotted to it from corps and army troops, including two extra motorized artillery battalions, *Artillerieabteilung* 1151, equipped with 12 captured Russian 122 mm howitzers, and *Artillerieabteilung* 1193, with 12 Italian 149 mm howitzers. As well *Werferregiment* 83 of *Werferbrigade* 7 was present, as were the 20, 37 and 88 mm anti-aircraft guns of III *Flakkorps*, a German air force formation commanded by *General Der Flaktruppen* Wolfgang Pickert. As well there may have been a company of StuG III self-propelled anti-tank guns of *Sturmgeschützabteilung* 1344, although this assumption was based on no more than reports of the capture of at least 10 prisoners from that unit in the opening stages of the coming battle. Last 13 *Sturmpanzer IVs Brummbärs* of *Sturmpanzerabteilung* 217 supported the division. The *Brummbär* or Grizzly Bear was a 150 mm short-barrelled infantry gun mounted on a tracked chassis; while of little use as an anti-tank gun, its large round was quite effective against other targets.[19]

89. *Infanteriedivision* had taken over a heavily fortified front held by two SS panzer divisions. On 6 August *General* Heinrichs appreciated that he was faced by 2nd and 4th Canadian Infantry Divisions [sic], and that 3rd Canadian Infantry Division had been withdrawn from the line after receiving heavy punishment. He also expected to encounter units of 2 Canadian Armoured Brigade. As for reading Allied intentions, as this murky assessment showed, German intelligence officers could come down firmly on both sides of a question just as readily as their Allied counterparts[20]

It is thought that the enemy has drawn tank units from areas south and southeast of Caen for operations in other places and that at the present moment no heavy tank concentrations are left in this area. It must be expected however, according to reliable reports, that these tank units can quickly be replaced from reserves in near areas. The purpose of these reinforcements might be to effect a break-through from the Orne bridgehead towards south and southeast, or to establish a firm screen of tanks at the front line.

Intelligence is never an easy or straightforward matter and it inevitably leads to second guessing and finger pointing. Many intelligence officers, and not just in the German army, had learned the hard way the folly of making definite predictions. The German intelligence system also laboured without the benefit of Ultra and reliable aerial reconnaissance. While 1. *SS-Panzerdivision* had warned 89. *Infanteriedivision* that "a major enemy attack from Caen [was] immediately imminent," in this case it appears that no one east of the Orne recognized the signs of the pending attack (remember the lack of response to the dust clouds from the marshalling columns late on 7 August) or at least drew the appropriate conclusions and alerted the commanders of I. *SS-Panzerkorps* or 5. *Panzerarmee*.[21] Moreover, the lack of Canadian success south of Caen had led *Oberst* Roesler, the commander of *Grenadierregiment* 1056, to write in his operation order of 4 August the unflattering assessment that "not particularly highly trained Canadian troops are holding the general line St. Martin–Tilly."[22] And based on the performance of 2nd Canadian Corps to date, who could blame him?

Heinrichs disposed his division with *Grenadierregiment* 1055 right and *Grenadierregiment* 1056 left with the inter-regimental boundary running just east of Verrières and southerly just west of Rocquancourt. In the right sector, II. *Bataillon Grenadierregiment* 1055 was responsible for La Hogue and Lorguichon while III. *Bataillon Grenadierregiment* 1055 held Tilly-la-Campagne and Rocquancourt. I. *Bataillon Grenadierregiment* 1055 was deployed in depth, including Cramesnil and St. Aignan-de-Cramesnil. To the west, III. *Bataillon Grenadierregiment* 1056 in the area from the inter-regimental boundary to Fontenay-le-Marmion, and I. *Bataillon Grenadierregiment* 1056 around May-sur-Orne, were the two forward battalions. II *Bataillon* was in a depth position from just south of Fontenay-le-Marmion through Caillouet to the quarry south of an abandoned airfield. The fusilier battalion formed the division reserve in its position near Bretteville-sur-Laize, while

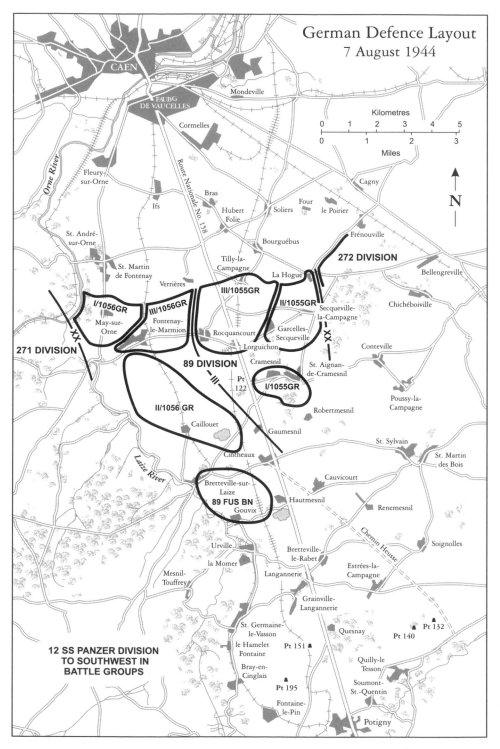

German Defence Layout
7 August 1944

the headquarters of 89. *Infanteriedivision* was in a mine near Urville. There were two corps self-propelled gun *Abteilungen* allotted to the division while its anti-aircraft battalion formed a screen from Caillouet to Gaumesnil.[23]

Behind the forward infantry battalions, the three battalions of *Artillerie-regiment* 189 and the infantry guns of 13 *Kompanie* of the two infantry regiments were deployed from just south of Fontenay-le-Marmion through St. Aignan-de-Cramesnil to Secqueville. The artillery of 89. *Infanteriedivision* was reinforced by the launchers of *Werferregiment* 83 as well as *Artillerie-abteilungen* 1151 and 1193. Most of these had been located and classified by the 2nd Canadian Corps Counterbombardment Office, but no one on the Allied side was aware of the presence of a number of 88 mm guns of III. *Flak-korps* south of the general line from Bretteville-sur-Laize to St. Sylvain.[24]

On the right of *Grenadierregiment* 1055, 272. *Infanteriedivision* held the line running eastward from just to the east of La Hogue, while, on the other flank, 271. *Infanteriedivision* was fighting hard to contain the Second British Army bridgehead over the Orne near Grimbosq. Both 89. and 272. *Infanteriedivisionen* were under the command of *SS-Obergruppenführer* Sepp Dietrich's I. *SS-Panzerkorps.* In fact the only armour the corps controlled on 7 August were the depleted tanks and *jagdpanzers* of *SS-Oberführer* Kurt Meyer's 12. *SS-Panzerdivision* and *schwere SS-Panzerabteilung* 101 and the *Hitlerjugend* division had been split into three groups, only one of which was yet uncommitted to battle. While First Canadian Army Intelligence still believed 12. *SS-Panzerdivision* was in the area, the only confirmed location was against the British near Grimbosq. The Allies did not know that another part of the division was facing the British and Americans near Vire, or that what was left as well as part of *schwere SS-Panzerabteilung* 101 was located south of Bretteville-sur-Laize.

The division that would bear the brunt of the hailstorm of thousands of bombs and shells and the massed armoured onslaught was probably representative of German infantry divisions in Normandy. It could fight from prepared positions and was well supplied with infantry and anti-tank weapons and ammunition, but, even with its attached troops, it was at a severe disadvantage in both the quality and quantity of its artillery, and in the numbers, if not the quality, of its anti-tank weapons. Like the rest of the German army, it was unable to match the amount of artillery ammunition the Allies were prepared to fire in support of an attack; the name the Germans used to describe this type of Allied bombardment was *Trommelfeur* or "drumfire." However, it had a combat-proven commander of unquestioned bravery under fire and a cadre of experienced officers and NCOs. Perhaps Canadian intelligence, after fighting high-quality army and SS panzer formations since the first days in Normandy, tended to downgrade normal enemy infantry divisions by comparison. If so, it was a serious error in judgement as most put up a good fight, although they lacked the ability to regroup and fight a mobile battle.

A s the sky finally darkened into night, the first of 1,019 heavy bombers neared the French coast in two parallel north-to-south streams. The bombing itself was to last from 2300 to 2340 hours, with May-sur-Orne and La Hogue to be struck first at 2300, followed by Fontenay-le-Marmion and Secqueville-la-Campagne at 2320 and finally Mare-de-Magne at 2340. The targets were to be marked by flare shells, green for the western targets and red for the eastern targets, fired at an interval of ten seconds between rounds for five minutes ending at the time the first bomb dropped on each target. At 2255 hours, 2nd Canadian Infantry Division 25-pounders began firing green flare shells at May-sur-Orne, while farther east the guns of 51st Highland Division began to burst red flares over La Hogue.[25] To the approaching aircraft the red flares would appear to their port or left and the green to their starboard or right, similar to the lighting system used on ships and aircraft. It might be added that anything that could be done to avoid confusing airmen, or anyone else for that matter, was always a good idea. The sky was relatively clear, but the presence of low winds hinted that smoke and dust would not clear as quickly as desired. The master bombers, flying at four to five thousand feet, identified the targets and marked them with target indicators of the same colour, although they later reported the green artillery flares ended before Targets 1 and 3 could be marked accurately.* With the targets identified and marked, the main bomber force was called in and the attack commenced.[26]

---

* The target marking aircraft also could have been late, a possibility the air force did not explore. To hit a point exactly on time was a very difficult task, even for the highly trained pathfinder crews.

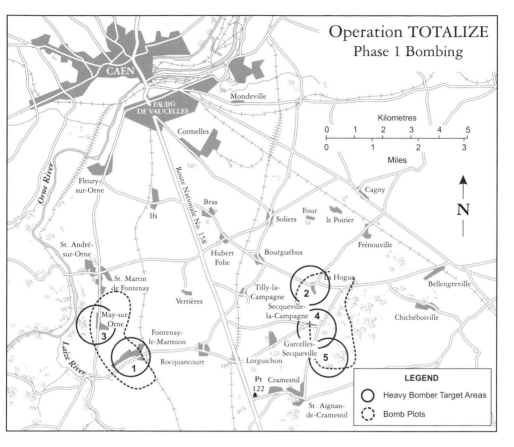

Operation TOTALIZE
Phase 1 Bombing

LEGEND

○ Heavy Bomber Target Areas

◌ Bomb Plots

To Simonds, with the planning completed and the operation underway, the situation seemed to be under control. He described the bombing as, "like the worst thunderstorm you have ever been in in your life, only worse. The ground was shaking beneath us." After confirming that the attacking columns were moving forward, he went to bed. In his own words,

You see, people have a mistaken idea of what a general does. I'd spent several days planning the operation. After I'd sent it in, there was nothing to do except to wait for morning. When you send in an operation of that size, there's nothing you can do to influence the course of it until you can see what's taking place, and then, of course, you can do a great deal. I knew that there'd be plenty of decisions to make the following day, so I decided to get some sleep.[27]

To some of the Germans on the ground the effect was immediately apparent and highly gratifying. Some members of *Grenadierregiment* 1055 apparently mistook the bombing for a *Luftwaffe* attack on Allied positions, and left their trenches to enjoy the rarely seen spectacle. Optimism is usually considered a positive asset in soldiers in wartime, but in this case it was perhaps more in the nature of a combination of inexperience and refusal to come to grips with reality, like the man who fell off a hundred-storey building and remarked, as he passed the fiftieth floor, "So far, so good." However, *Grenadierregiment* 1056 reported "a massive [Allied] bombing attack on the [Canadian] main line of resistance and well into the main battlefield." When the bombs began to fall on May-sur-Orne, the tanks and vehicles in Fontenay-le-Marmion withdrew and the troops in trenches north of the village were told to hold on and wait as there would be a counterattack in the morning.[28]

Without a brisk wind to dissipate the smoke and dust, the targets soon became obscured and the master bombers ordered more than a third of the aircraft to bring their bomb loads home. In all, 642 aircraft actually attacked the five targets, dropping a total of 3,456 tons of high explosive. The air force later claimed that the bombing was both accurate and effective, citing both its own optimistic damage assessment and Crerar's glowing message to Harris sent while bombs were still falling:[29]

> Timing and accuracy of tonight's programme heavy bombers now in progress reported 100%. Greatly appreciate outstanding contribution your command. We shall hope to continue and complete this battle as well as you have commenced it.

Harris later acknowledged that "[k]nowing the limitations of the force I was originally horrified at this proposal." He must have been greatly relieved by Crerar's message as he replied[30]

> Thanks for the message. Regret lack of wind and accumulating smoke made it unsafe to put down last third of tonnage on each objective but hope two thirds did the trick. Don't be shy of asking. Good luck.

In fact while the bombing of two of the eastern targets, La Hogue and Mare-de-Magne, was effective and the third, Secqueville-la-Campagne, lay inside the cratered area, this was not the case in the west. Target 1, Fontenay-le-Marmion, was struck only slightly, the weight of the bombing falling about a half mile to the west and obliterating the small hamlet of Le Val. Target 3, May-sur-Orne, was largely untouched despite being attacked by 89 Halifaxes and 3 Lancasters, and while some bombs fell in fields near St. Martin-de-Fontenay, no evident bomb pattern could be identified during an investigation by No. 2 Operational Research Section shortly after the battle. In fact, a few bombs even fell among the Fusiliers Mont-Royal companies of 6 Canadian Infantry Brigade waiting for the order to advance.[31] It is possible that the poor results on Targets 1 and 3 resulted from the gap between the 25-pounder flares burning out and the arrival of the marking aircraft, although other factors may have played a part, including the tendency for the bomb pattern to creep backwards as the crews dropped on the rear of the marker pattern.

This bombing attack was designed to seal off the flanks of the advance but the strong points like Tilly-la-Campagne and Rocquancourt were still untouched. The result was that, after a major attack by Bomber Command resulting in the dropping of 3,456 tons of bombs and the loss of ten aircraft shot down and another destroyed on landing, the main German defences were left largely intact and fully alert. It now fell to the attacking troops and the artillery to batter a way through six battalions of German infantry in prepared positions.

As the last of the light faded into darkness, the silence was broken by the sudden rumble of hundreds of engines starting in unison. The distances from each of the forming-up places had been measured precisely and the column commanders had been ordered to move off so as to cross the start line at exactly 2330 hours. At the same time Bofors from the light anti-aircraft regiments of the two assaulting divisions began to pump out 40 mm rounds to mark the direction for the advancing troops.[32] The lead vehicles crawled ahead in low gear, their way marked by illuminated markers placed on either side of the route. The troops had been warned about the dangers of the bombing and had been issued ear plugs to protect their ears. However, as Lieutenant Colonel Alan Jolly, the commanding officer of 144 RAC, explained, except for a few flashes in the distance, "the noise of the tanks was so great that we hardly realised it [the bombing] was on."[33] The columns all seemed to have crossed the start line at 2330 hours without serious incident or enemy interference. In the case of the two British columns, each moved as a single formed body. While the Canadian gapping forces crossed at 2330 hours, the remainder of each column allowed a gap of 500 yards to develop before following the tapes and illuminated markers planted by the AVREs bringing up the rear of the Gapping Force.[34]

Once past the start line the columns increased their speed to 5 mph to cover the one mile to the opening line of the barrage, which was due to begin at 2345 hours.[35] The navigators listened for the dots and dashes in their headsets, officers tried to relate ground details to their gridded and annotated air photographs, and everyone peered into the dark and the dust kicked up by the lead vehicles. If it was difficult for the tank crews and the drivers of the armoured vehicles, the infantrymen crammed in the Kangaroos, half-tracks and carriers, must have been going through hell as all they could do was hang on and pray. Other men, the marching infantry in the four battalions detailed to capture Tilly-la-Campagne and Rocquancourt and May-sur-Orne and Fontenay-le-Marmion, waited on the start lines in battle formation for the order to advance and do the dangerous, dirty job that is the lot of the infantryman and no one else – to close with and destroy the enemy.

Meanwhile, while thousands of men entered battle, other thousands checked their watches and waited and checked their watches again as the minutes ticked away. These were the gunners, all too aware of the peril their comrades faced and bound by their own creed that demands they give their all for the troops they support – trite as it may sound. The men by the guns waited with tense anticipation in nearly a hundred positions arrayed in a great arc stretching nearly two miles around the southern verges of Caen. Finally, as the second hand on their watches neared the vertical, at each of these gun positions a young officer bellowed "Fire." The crash and roar and flash from hundreds of guns firing suddenly was something few had experienced before in Normandy, and the continuous roar on the gun positions made conversation impossible.[36] This was inconvenient, but not critical as once fire had been ordered on the first line of the barrage, each Number 1 controlled the fire of his own gun during the rest of the barrage by referring to his own gun program and wrist watch. The sky pulsated and flashed like a gigantic electrical storm. Perhaps more guns had been employed in the giant Alamein barrage of October 1942, but not crowded into as small an area as this. With 360 guns firing on the barrage, at an average rate of fire of better than two rounds per gun a minute, and as some guns invariably lagged behind their neighbours, the firing became more of a rumble than a distinct series of roars.[37] No wonder the Germans called it "drum fire." On it went, the guns roaring, cordite fumes filling the nostrils and the mounds of spent cartridge cases steadily growing beside the field guns, until the last round on the last line of the barrage whistled down-range 60 minutes later.

All at once, the silence was all-consuming. Men with ringing ears and dazed senses looked around and shook their heads and waited for whatever would come next. But something was different. Before, when fire plans had ended, the sound of fierce firefights often could be heard on the gun positions and the FOOs had almost immediately begun to call down fire on counterattacking Germans. This time, while there were scattered shots, the usual sounds of pitched battle were missing. Instead, the sound of tank engines and the clank of tracks could be heard receding faintly in the distance. With the FOOs operating under orders of radio silence, except in the direst emergency, to avoid causing interference with the radio beacons, there were not even the usual reports to indicate what was happening at the sharp end. Clearly TOTALIZE was not going to be like the other battles, at least not yet.[38]

For the men in the assault columns, especially those in the navigating parties concentrating on their work, the sound of the guns was drowned out by the sound of their own engines. All at once, their forward horizon erupted in fountains of smoke and dust, and the men with their heads out of their turrets or above the sides of their carriers and half-tracks felt the blast on their faces. Alan Wood, a war correspondent for the British *Daily Express* newspaper, described the barrage from his vantage point in the Allied lines:[39]

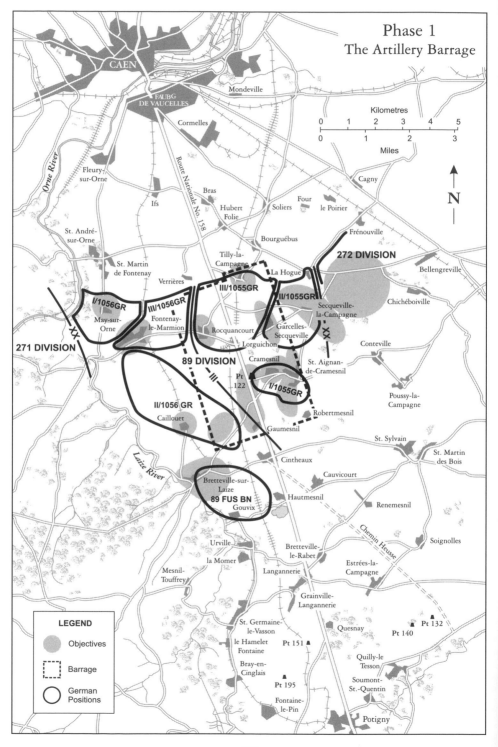

Phase 1
The Artillery Barrage

CAEN

FAUBG
DE VAUCELLES

Mondeville

Cormelles

Kilometres
0 1 2 3 4 5
0 1 2 3
Miles

Fleury-
sur-Orne

Orne River

Route Nationale No. 158

Bras

Ifs

Hubert
Folie

Soliers

Four
le Poirier

Cagny

N

St. André-
sur-Orne

St. Martin
de Fontenay

Verrières

Tilly-la-
Campagne

La Hogue

Bourguébus

Frénouville

272 DIVISION

Bellengreville

Chichéboiville

III/1055GR

II/1055GR

I/1056GR

III/1056GR

May-sur-
Orne

Fontenay-
le-Marmion

Rocquancourt

Lorguichon

Garcelles-
Secqueville

Secqueville-
la-Campagne

Conteville

XX

271 DIVISION

89 DIVISION

Cramesnil

Pt
122

I/1055GR

St. Aignan-
de-Cramesnil

Poussy-la-
Campagne

II/1056 GR

Caillouet

Robertmesnil

Gaumesnil

St. Sylvain

St. Martin
des Bois

Laize River

Cintheaux

Cauvicourt

Bretteville-sur-
Laize

89 FUS BN

Gouvix

Hautmesnil

Renemesnil

Chemin Heusse

Soignolles

Urville

Mesnil-
Touffrey

la Momer

Bretteville-
le-Rabet

Langannerie

Estrées-la-
Campagne

Grainville-
Langannerie

LEGEND

Objectives

Barrage

German
Positions

St. Germaine-
le-Vasson

le Hamelet
Fontaine

Bray-en-
Cinglais

Pt 151

Quesnay

Pt 140

Pt 132

Quilly-le-
Tesson

Soumont-
St.-Quentin

Pt 195

Fontaine-
le-Pin

Potigny

We watched the shells bursting in an irregular twinkling row on the German ridges opposite, moving onward into a hollow, then up on high ground again. Once it seemed that a supply dump had been hit. A great purple ball of fire puffed up for a second.

Occasionally the Germans, groping in the dark and wondering where our tanks were and what they were doing, shot up a star shell.

Before midnight a blood red moon, just past the full, could be seen rising when the lurid flashes from our guns died down momentarily. Above was starlight.

The moon climbed up and brightened, and with it, at about quarter to one, came a heavy ground mist filling the hollows in the ground.

As the barrage began, Bofors light anti-aircraft guns began to pump tracers in prearranged patterns along the axis of advance, and the beams of movement light began to brighten the sky. For the navigators in 33 British Armoured Brigade trying to read their magnetic compasses, the barrage had another, unexpected consequence: the dials on their compasses began to spin madly.[40] As for the radio beacon that their brigadier distrusted, the navigator of 144 RAC was unable to pick up any signal at all, while his counterpart in 1 Northamptonshire Yeomanry found that it distracted him from his task as he lost the signal completely when he veered to make his way around bomb craters or searched for passages across sunken roads and hedges.[41] In the Canadian columns, some navigators discovered that the radio beams faded once the tanks started down the far side of Verrières Ridge,[42] while Captain M.H. "Bomber" Bateman of the Sherbrooke Fusilier Regiment was more positive:[43]

As a point of interest we ran into terrible visibility very soon there after. I never did find out if it was caused by our own bombing or artillery or the enemy but if we hadn't had the radio direction method we would have been lost very quickly. The bofors of course was useless in the smoke and the movement light did not, under the circumstances, help very much. We reached our objective south of Roqunacourt [sic] on time, three and a half miles behind the enemy, all with no casualties.

With the 1940s version of "high tech" *hors de combat* and the British compasses gyrating uselessly, the navigators were forced to rely on their brains and their maps and their gridded air photographs and to take their bearing from the lines of Bofors tracer winging overhead. Visibility had been quickly reduced to near zero by clouds of dust thrown up by the barrage. The situation was made even more confusing by the smoke shells some alert German had ordered fired behind the barrage along with the shell and mortar fire of their defensive fire. The artificial moonlight created by the eight searchlights of 344 Searchlight Battery may have increased the brightness a bit, but when the visibility was near zero, a bright dust cloud was not much more useful than a dark dust cloud for the drivers in the columns, straining their eyes to keep the dimmed tail lights of the vehicles ahead of them in sight.[44] And finally there was another remarkably simple aid to keeping station that worked. In the Canadian sector the crews of the AVREs of 79 and 80 Assault Squadrons laid giant trails of the woven white tape normally used to mark minefields and threw out red and green lights to mark the flanks of the route.[45]

The forward move soon became worse than difficult. It could hardly have been otherwise with visibility virtually nil and drivers and navigators (and everyone else) dreadfully inexperienced at this sort of thing. No one, after all, had tried anything like this before TOTALIZE, and no one who had not attempted it could have anticipated just how difficult and confusing cross-country night movement in tanks would be. At least in a night administrative move by roads, there were guides and signs and proper maps and route cards, but here everything looked the same and nothing seemed to match the map. Simonds may have given advance warning to his commanders that he intended to use tanks at night, and he had done his best to provide navigation aids, but without time for the troops to experiment and practise, it was very much a matter of trusting to luck – like the proverbial brave man who first ventured to taste a raw oyster. And then, there were the Germans with their artillery and their smoke and their machine guns and their mortars and their Panzers and their anti-tank guns lurking somewhere in the dark.

CHAPTER EIGHT

THE 51st HIGHLAND DIVISION ADVANCE

"As soon as the barrage started the column was immediately enveloped in a dense cloud of dust which reduced visibility to a few yards."

LIEUTENANT COLONEL ALAN JOLLY,

144 REGIMENT ROYAL ARMOURED CORPS

T he left Phase 1 column in the advance, that of 1 Northamptonshire Yeomanry and 1 Black Watch, led by Captain Thomas Boardman as the navigator with Captain Kenneth Todd immediately behind him in another Sherman acting as the assistant navigator, crawled forward behind the barrage at 1½ miles per hour, a slow walking pace. The air was thick with dust and smoke, making visibility bad for the next few hours. With the compasses spinning uselessly, the radio navigation beam silent and map reading near impossible, it was a case of groping forward behind bursting shells. In fact, even at that glacial pace, as the flails and some of the half-tracks had difficulty negotiating the gaps through the sunken roads, the column fell behind the barrage. While the flails and engineers reported that no mines were discovered, inspection of the route in daylight showed the column had missed two minefields, by six feet and 12 feet respectively, which proves the old adage that sometimes it is more important to be lucky than it is to be good.[1] Boardman fired a series of green flares from his Verey pistol as a prearranged signal as he puzzled his way forward. When he ran out of flares somewhere between Bourguébus and St. Aignan – he was not sure where – he halted his tank and walked back to Captain Todd's Sherman to replenish his supply. On the way he encountered a group of Germans huddled in a trench, petrified with terror. As his tank moved off, he noted thankfully that the enemy were still in their trench and staying very still.[2]

Other Germans were made of sterner stuff. A number of Shermans and three Priests were lost to enemy action during the move and there were clashes with isolated posts of infantry.[3] As his No. 2 Troop of A Squadron of the Yeomanry groped its way ahead along in the right file of the column, Lieutenant Wyn Griffith-Jones detoured to the right to bypass some flails that had fallen behind the main body. He had just crossed through a gap in a hedge when there was a blinding, green flash 50 yards to his left and a round brewed up Corporal Howard's tank, which had followed him. Lance Corporal S. Symes, Griffith-Jones's gunner, swung the turret left and put two rounds into what appeared to be an enemy tank, setting it on fire. He saw two more dim shapes 25 yards to his front and, while he was trying to identify them as enemy, two shots hit the front of his Sherman, one glancing off the front armour and the other lodging in the transmission gear, without putting the vehicle out of action. Sergeant Burnett, who had moved up just to the right and forward of his troop leader, brewed one of the enemy tanks. In the meantime, Griffith-Jones's tank was hit again, this time in the engine compartment, and the whole tank was engulfed by flames that went 50 to 60 feet in the air, forcing the crew to bale out and take cover in a potato patch. Burnett managed to knock out the second of the two tanks to the front, but the fierce flames from the burning vehicles silhouetted the 2 Troop Tanks for the surviving German tank, invisible in the darkness, which then knocked out the Sherman of Corporal Ferrier. After Griffith-Jones ordered Burnett to proceed on to the objective, he collected his dismounted crews and they spent the remaining hours of darkness pinned down by machine gun fire, listening to the guttural voices of Germans unsuccessfully searching for them. After the event, when he was asked to describe what had happened, all Griffith-Jones could say was that in his letters home he had always told his mother not to worry, but during what he described as a shambles, he found himself saying aloud, "For goodness sake, Mother, start worrying now."[4] (He may have cleaned his language up a bit for posterity.)

After what the authors of the 1947 British Army of the Rhine Battlefield Tour booklet on TOTALIZE described, with typical British understatement, as "an eventful journey," Boardman arrived within 50 yards of his debussing point, to his and everyone else's surprise and relief. Lieutenant Colonel John Hopgood, commanding 1 Black Watch, who was never quite convinced that

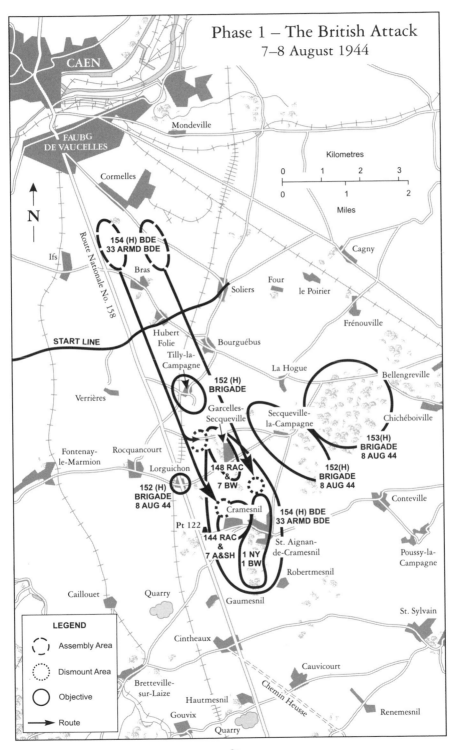

Phase 1 – The British Attack
7–8 August 1944

CAEN

FAUBG
DE VAUCELLES

Mondeville

Cormelles

Kilometres

0   1   2   3

0   1   2

Miles

N

Ifs

154 (H) BDE
33 ARMD BDE

Cagny

Bras

Soliers

Four

le Poirier

Frénouville

Route Nationale No. 158

Hubert
Folie

Bourguébus

START LINE

Tilly-la-
Campagne

La Hogue

Bellengreville

152 (H)
BRIGADE

Verrières

Garcelles-
Secqueville

Secqueville-
la-Campagne

Chichéboiville

Fontenay-
le-Marmion

Rocquancourt

153(H)
BRIGADE
8 AUG 44

Lorguichon

148 RAC
&
7 BW

152(H)
BRIGADE
8 AUG 44

Conteville

152 (H)
BRIGADE
8 AUG 44

Cramesnil

154 (H) BDE
33 ARMD BDE

Pt 122

144 RAC
&
7 A&SH

1 NY
1 BW

St. Aignan-
de-Cramesnil

Poussy-la-
Campagne

Robertmesnil

Caillouet

Quarry

Gaumesnil

St. Sylvain

LEGEND

Cintheaux

Assembly Area

Cauvicourt

Dismount Area

Objective

Bretteville-
sur-Laize

Route

Hautmesnil

Chemin Heusse

Renemesnil

Gouvix

Quarry

the operation was feasible, commented pithily, "Fuck me! We've arrived." There were many signs of recent activity by German tracked vehicles in the area, and he and Forster, the commanding officer of the Yeomanry, decided to remain mounted and drive forward closer to the village of St. Aignan-de-Cramesnil. As carriers straggled in, they were collected and the infantry companies were formed over the next three quarters of an hour. The advance over the last half mile up to the edge of St. Aignan was made under the cover of a 20-minute prearranged artillery concentration and the fire of the Shermans of A and B Squadrons of the Yeomanry. The Black Watch dismounted and entered the village from the north end against limited opposition, most of the enemy seeming to be intent on leaving town via the south end. A and B Companies of the Black Watch "smashed through taking 79 prisoners and killing many Boches [from *Grenadierregiment* 1055], also capturing some 7.5 [cm] Atk guns and some mortars." With the village cleared, the tanks were brought up and by first light the objective was secure and the tanks were ready for the anticipated counterattack.[5]

The other British column got off to a shaky start when the lead navigator's Stuart tank drove into a large bomb crater. No sooner had that happened than the two tanks carrying the alternate navigators drove into another crater while trying to avoid the first one. Things went from bad to worse quickly. The dust was so thick it was impossible to see more than a few feet in any direction. One crew commander was startled to find himself driving down the main street of a village that had suddenly appeared where his map told him it had no right to be. He drove through it as quickly as possible and was mightily relieved when he picked up the Bofors tracer that marked the way ahead. It was not until later that he and his crew realized that they had driven right through the German stronghold of Tilly-la-Campagne, to their surprise, and judging by the lack of German reaction, to the surprise of the defenders as well.[6] The vehicle of the commanding officer of 7 Argyll and Sutherland Highlanders broke down and was left behind by the rest of the column, leaving the command group quite alone in the darkness. Fortunately the passengers transferred to another vehicle and, by driving at top speed, were soon able to rejoin the column.[7]

The tanks of 144 RAC had become disoriented in the smoke and dust and elements of the two leading squadrons and regimental headquarters became intermingled.

Great shapes of tanks loomed up out of the fog and asked who you were. Flails seemed to be everywhere and their enormous jibs barging about in the dark seemed to add to the confusion. It was not until you chanced on the road or railway that you had any idea of your position. Even so, this was no check on the distance travelled and it was possible to go over the main road in the gloom without noticing it. In fact some of the Canadians [from the 8 Reconnaissance Regiment column] became mixed up with part of our column and one Canadian tank spent the rest of the night with us.[8]

It soon became a case of small groups making their way forward more or less independently. Somehow during the march 144 RAC picked up Sergeant George Duff's Sherman from C Squadron of the Yeomanry as well as the Canadian tank mentioned above.[9] Enemy activity was fortunately light except for a machine gun post that was taken out by the Argylls, resulting in several German casualties at the cost of one officer wounded. Lieutenant Colonel Alan Jolly, the commanding officer of 144 RAC, had been concerned about a railway line that crossed his axis diagonally, and his foreboding was not misplaced. As the lead tanks reached the railway and attempted to cross it, they were fired at

Flail tanks
The chains used to detonate mines are clearly visible in this photo of two British flail tanks. These vehicles could also function as normal 75 mm gun tanks if required and were employed in a supporting fire role in Phase 2 of TOTALIZE. (NAC/PA 116518)

by enemy troops armed with *Panzerfausts.* The troop leader of 1 Troop of the AVRE squadron destroyed a building suspected of harbouring German troops with two massive rounds from its Petard demolition gun. Two tanks were lost and several Germans killed and wounded in the ensuing fire fight.

After the armoured regiment found its way across the railway to the north, the column attempted to reform on the east side, but things were hopelessly confused and all semblance of tactical integrity among the tanks had been lost. Small parties were collected by squadron and troop commanders and the advance continued, although the commander of B Squadron spent some time near the Caen–Falaise highway trying to disentangle some of his tanks from part of the 8 Canadian Reconnaissance Regiment column which was moving along on the east side of the Route Nationale. This time, the lead tanks took no chances and anything suspicious was shot up with machine gun fire. This included at one time the 1 Northamptonshire Yeomanry/1 Black Watch column, which rather testily demanded to be left alone. At about 0330 hours, long after the barrage had finished – the dust had cleared, the moon was out and stars were shining, so visibility was not too bad – the tanks arrived at what the commanding officer estimated to be the debussing area by comparing the number of hedges he had crossed with the air photo. Major Thomas Lovibond, his second-in-command, who had taken a slightly different route, was a bit ahead on the left with a small group of tanks and reported he was entering the last field before the objective. No sooner had Lovibond done so than he was killed when his tank was hit by a *Panzerfaust* and brewed up. Enough was enough. Jolly called the others tanks back and passed a message to the infantry battalion commander that it was time to dismount. The infantry came forward, dismounted and attacked Cramesnil, which lay only 200 yards ahead. By about 0700 hours the village was secured and 47 prisoners taken, the tanks had deployed to protect the objective and contact was made with the Canadians on the right and 1 Black Watch on the left.[10]

It will be remembered that a second regimental group, that of 148 RAC and 7 Black Watch, was following on this route. Unlike the 144 RAC and 7 Argyll and Sutherland Highlanders group, it was able to advance fairly easily and crossed the railway and moved to its debussing area without heavy opposition once the column had begun to move again. The infantry suffered only one casualty, a toll described in the battalion war diary as "surprisingly light." In fact the major difficulty encountered was in passing through the single vehicle crossing over the railway. By 0400 hours the Black Watch had dismounted and 90 minutes later had completed clearing Garcelles-Secqueville.[11]

In the 51st Highland Division area, 152 Highland Brigade was given the task of clearing Tilly with one battalion, while another battalion was to follow the right British column and clear Lorguichon Wood.[12] Later, with the main objectives secure, the brigade would expand the penetration to the east by securing the village of Secqueville-la-Campagne and the woods to the southeast.[13] Once again, the Highland Division had what appeared to be the simpler task, if any task could be termed easy that night. Not only was its area much narrower, but the battalion assigned to Tilly-la-Campagne would advance between the two British columns, thus having the advantage of the barrage and the demoralization of the defenders caused by large armoured columns passing on both sides. The other battalion would follow the right column of two regimental/battalion groups, itself also taking advantage of the psychological effect of a large armoured column rolling over the unfortunate defenders. The third battalion was to be held in readiness to support 154 Highland Brigade if required, but Major General Rennie agreed to allow the brigade commander to use one company as his brigade reserve.

Both Rennie and the commander of 152 Highland Brigade, Brigadier A.J.H. Cassels, had appreciated that Tilly-la-Campagne would not be a tough nut to crack as the garrison would realize it had been bypassed and cut off. Therefore they assumed that not only could one battalion do the trick, although two strong Canadian attacks had failed, but the covering artillery fire need not be as heavy as usual for an infantry attack. Thus, the other two battalions of the brigade were given other tasks quite apart from Tilly. Cassels later admitted:[14]

It will be seen that these factors seriously affected the plan and nearly caused its failure; because our main premise was entirely false as, in the general din, the enemy in Tilly had no idea that armoured thrusts were encircling them and merely regarded the whole performance as yet another attack which must be defeated.

There was no artillery support other than three lines of the barrage, or six minutes of fire, that would cross Tilly-la-Campagne, although the 4.2-inch mortars of the heavy mortar company of the divisional machine gun battalion were available. Because of the large area covered by their shelling pattern, however, the mortars could not be used to lead troops onto the objective. As the barrage was to start at 1241 hours (the British barrage had two extra lines added to cover the forward area of Tilly-la-Campagne), and the opening line was 1,500 yards from the start line, it was obvious that the attacking battalion, 2 Seaforth Highlanders, could not reach the objective before the barrage moved on. A request for the battalion to cross the start line at H-15 minutes was refused, but eventually authority was granted for it to move at H-5.[15]

As was the case in 154 Highland Brigade, the battalions in 152 Highland Brigade were under strength. While the former had opted for three strong companies, the battalions of 152 Highland Brigade decided on a different solution. In the case of 2 Seaforths, four companies were retained, each with a normal headquarters and two up-to-strength platoons. In place of the third platoon, a support group of seven or eight men armed with 2-inch mortars and automatic weapons was formed to operate under the control of company headquarters. The solutions adopted by the other two battalions in 152 Highland Brigade were similar.[16]

The commander of 2 Seaforths decided that D and A Companies would capture the west and northeast edges of the village, respectively. Next, B Company would skirt D Company as it was attacking the western part and seize the southern end of Tilly-la-Campagne. Finally C Company would establish a block on the road from Tilly to Garcelles-Secqueville. Major A.M. Gilmour, who commanded C Company, noted that "the village would therefore be closely surrounded by infantry and further cut off by the advance of the armoured columns. The centre of the village was to be cleared at first light and companies had been given definite sectors for which they were responsible."[17]

The Seaforths' attack started well but in attempting to negotiate the railway the barrage was lost. D Company, attacking the west side of Tilly, managed to finally clear its objective after about an hour of confused fighting, but any attempt to enter the village was met by heavy fire. The company finally reported its objective was secure at 0130 hours, but in fact had been held up west of the village. Unfortunately A Company had even worse luck. One of its two platoons had come under heavy small-arms fire at short range from Germans dug in north of the village and was virtually wiped out, while the rest of the company also took some casualties. The company could not get any closer to the village than about 400 yards. B Company, meanwhile, had begun to attempt to work its way around the west side. The battalion commander realized that while matters seemed to be in hand on the west side, the northern end had to be taken as it commanded the approaches to Tilly. He therefore ordered his last remaining troops, C Company, to assist the pinned-down A Company in taking its objective and then move on to its own at the road junction.

C Company had already been mortared when it attempted to cross the railway. It was about 0300 hours before this company was ready to attack. The plan was simple: a platoon would outflank the enemy position to the left and then assault from the rear. Unfortunately, the platoon did not sweep wide enough and hit the end of the enemy position. It came under heavy fire and was repulsed after losing the platoon commander and five men killed and several others wounded. By this time it was beginning to get light and both companies were in the open within a few yards of the enemy and short of ammunition. After a hurried consultation between the two company commanders, they withdrew to the cover of the railway in good order. B Company was slow in moving up and was held up by determined fire from German troops who had infiltrated back into positions that had been cleared by D Company, and went to ground behind the railway line and stayed there for the remainder of the battle.[18] Once again, the defenders of Tilly had been able to frustrate and hold off an attack by an Allied battalion.

Once it became clear that the attack on Tilly was bogged, the brigade commander released his brigade reserve, D Company of 5 Seaforth, to the CO of 2 Seaforth. Unfortunately, owing to incorrect information from B Company, this company was committed in the wrong place. It ended up being held up beside D Company of 2 Seaforth and suffered very heavy casualties. The whole operation was turning into a costly fiasco. It was clear that the stalemate must be resolved so at about 0330 hours the brigade commander received authority from the divisional commander to use the remainder of 5 Seaforth, which had been earmarked for other tasks, to capture Tilly. As Brigadier Cassels explained:[19]

This of course was alright in theory, but not so hot in practice, as 5 Seaforth had made no study whatsoever of the problem, having been given two other tasks later in the battle. I saw the Commanding Officer at about 0400 hours and told him the situation and ordered him to take his battalion forward to capture Tilly-la-Campagne in conjunction with 2 Seaforth from the West. Naturally, he was somewhat taken aback but, after a justifiable moan or two, he set off to reconnoitre and ordered his battalion to a RV. I warned the Commanding Officer of 2 Seaforth of the form.

The two left companies of 2 Seaforth, that is A and C Companies, which were now down to a combined total of 40 to 50 men, or the equivalent of not more than a small platoon each, were placed under the command of 5 Seaforth. Soon after, they were pulled further back so that artillery and machine gun fire could be brought down on the east edge of the village. H-Hour for the renewed attack was set for 0610 hours, or in just over an hour's time, but was postponed because ground mist had prevented the CO of 5 Seaforth from conducting a proper reconnaissance.[20] The battle procedure was being hurried, 2 Seaforth as well as D Company 5 Seaforth had suffered very heavy casualties and no one had a clear idea of the situation, other than that is was imperative that Tilly be taken by first light. As first light was already past, and desperation may have been overruling common sense, it probably was fortunate that mist forced a postponement.

Brigadier Cassels had also asked for some tanks to support the attack by 5 Seaforth. Rennie approved the request and 148 RAC, which was with 7 Black Watch in Garcelles-Secqueville, was ordered to send a squadron back to support the attack. The appearance of this squadron (B) from the south seems to have had a devastating effect on the resolve of the defenders, especially when it began to sweep the rubble with fire from its machine guns. It was 0740 hours when the leading tank "went into Tilly, and by 0805 hours they had reached northern edge and contacted our own infantry holding line north of town. B Squadron then proceeded to sweep through town from East to West." The mist cleared at abut 0900 and 5 Seaforth began to move forward into the village. A number of Germans had surrendered to the tanks and at 1015 hours a German officer offered to arrange the surrender of the rest of the troops in the village. The squadron remained with the infantry during the morning as they cleared the village, and later claimed 25 Germans killed, 85 prisoners (turned over to the infantry) and three German SPs knocked out.[21] Tilly finally passed into Allied hands around 1200 hours, 8 August, nearly 12 hours behind schedule and well after first light.

In the meantime 5 Queen's Own Cameron Highlanders of 152 Highland Brigade had advanced on foot behind 7 Black Watch at the rear of the right British column. As we have seen, this column was held up when 144 RAC had to clear a German position over the railway line that ran north-south from the eastern outskirts of Caen. In fact, the battalion had only advanced 500 yards in two hours. At 0130 hours the battalion was ordered to swing to the right of the column and advance towards Lorguichon, and at 0330 hours "it was thought that 5 Camerons were on their objective but this was

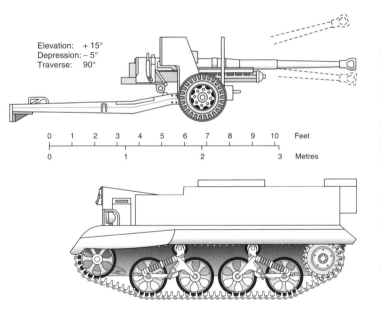

Elevation: + 15°
Depression: – 5°
Traverse: 90°

0 1 2 3 4 5 6 7 8 9 10 Feet
0   1   2   3 Metres

Calibre: 57 mm
Weight: 2,698 pounds
Height: 4 feet
Range: (effective) 1,093 yards
Rate of fire: 15 rpm
Crew: 4–5
Carriage: Split trail
Breech mechanism: Vertical sliding wedge
Recoil system: Hydropneumatic
Anti-tank capability: 118 mm of armour at 519 yards
Ammunition: Fixed round weighing 6 pounds

6-pdr anti-tank gun and T 16 Universal Carrier

The 6-pdr anti-tank gun entered service in late 1941 and first saw action in North Africa, where it acquitted itself well. In addition to the towed anti-tank version, it also equipped British tanks and the Canadian Ram series until it was superseded by the dual-purpose 75 mm gun and the 17-pdr. The towed 6-pdr continued to equip anti-tank platoons in British and Canadian infantry and motor battalions to the end of the war. The T 16 Universal Carrier, of which 14,000 were built in the United States, was the preferred tractor for the 6-pdr. The T 16 was initially in short supply in Normandy and was supplemented by the regular Universal Carrier in anti-tank platoons.

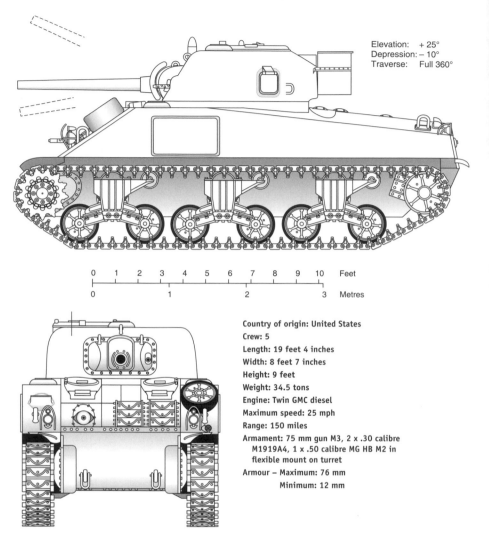

Elevation: + 25°
Depression: − 10°
Traverse: Full 360°

```
0   1   2   3   4   5   6   7   8   9   10   Feet
0               1               2          3   Metres
```

Country of origin: United States
Crew: 5
Length: 19 feet 4 inches
Width: 8 feet 7 inches
Height: 9 feet
Weight: 34.5 tons
Engine: Twin GMC diesel
Maximum speed: 25 mph
Range: 150 miles
Armament: 75 mm gun M3, 2 x .30 calibre
    M1919A4, 1 x .50 calibre MG HB M2 in
    flexible mount on turret
Armour – Maximum: 76 mm
          Minimum: 12 mm

Sherman III – M4A2

To step up production of the Sherman tank, American manufacturers employed several
different engines, one of which was the twin diesel that powered the Sherman III.
As the diesel engine never enjoyed much popularity in the U.S. Army in the Second
World War, the Sherman III was largely allocated to the U.S. Marine Corps and
Allied nations to equip their armoured forces. In Normandy, 2nd Canadian Armoured
Brigade was almost exclusively equipped with the Sherman III. At the time, it was
erroneously believed that diesel-powered tanks burned less frequently than gasoline-
engined tanks, so the Sherman III was perhaps the more popular of the Shermans that
equipped Canadian and British armoured units.

not firm as fighting was still in progress." By 0445 hours the village and the level crossing on the Caen–Falaise road had been captured, but the company attempting to clear the woods to the southeast of the village was held up by enemy fire. By 0600 hours the battalion reported that Lorguichon Wood had been cleared and it was consolidating on its position.[22]

While there had been some setbacks, and in particular the men of III *Bataillon Grenadierregiment* 1055 in Tilly had shown that Allied intelligence had seriously underestimated their mettle, by first light the British division had four infantry battalions and three armoured regiments on their Phase 1 objectives. Major General Rennie's tasks were now to stand firm in the face of the expected German counterattacks and mop up his divisional area, while waiting for 1. *Dywizji Pancernej* to pass through his lines in Phase 2.

CHAPTER NINE

THE CANADIAN ADVANCE

*"One of the points that went wrong in the assault was that we seemed
to veer to the left a little bit and that seems to be an actual tendency
in movement at night that you do to move."*

MAJOR SYDNEY RADLEY-WALTERS,

SHERBROOKE FUSILIER REGIMENT

To the west of the Highlanders, in the 2nd Canadian Infantry Division area, the situation had developed differently. The right Canadian column lost two tanks to mines before it reached its start line. The left Canadian column, 8 Canadian Reconnaissance Regiment and C Squadron, Fort Garry Horse, ran into trouble as it advanced just west of the Route Nationale and halted until a number of machine gun positions were cleared. Two flails were destroyed by mines, and some tanks were brewed up while others lost their way and strayed east of the highway,[1] and one Sherman spent the night with the 144 RAC column. Sergeant C.W. Wilson, a carrier section commander in B Squadron of the reconnaissance regiment, recalled that:[2]

An intense artillery barrage was laid down to soften the enemy positions. When we moved off an hour later it was pitch black and the flails were raising a terrific dust. As they moved forward they laid white tapes on either side to mark the lane for the following vehicles. Every 150 yards, a green light was placed on the right of the lane and a red light on the left. Bofors were firing to the front, just above our heads, to indicate the direction in which we were to travel. Batteries of searchlights were used to provide artificial moonlight. At midnight we were in the thick of it. The noise was deafening, artillery, machine guns and vehicle motors in a crescendo

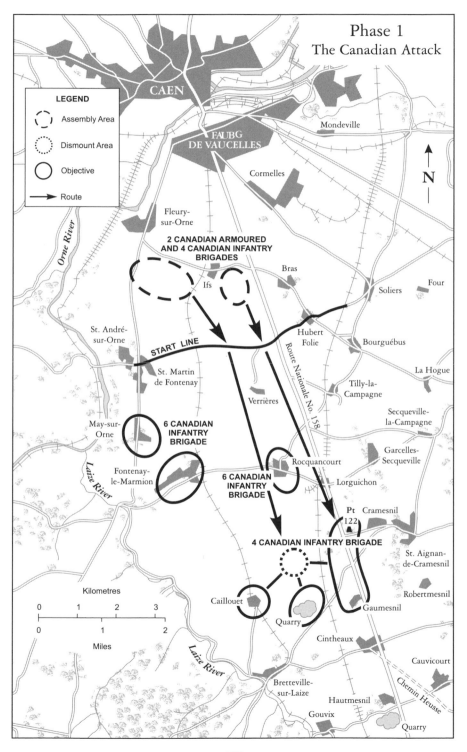

Phase 1
The Canadian Attack

LEGEND
- - - Assembly Area
····· Dismount Area
◯ Objective
→ Route

CAEN

FAUBG DE VAUCELLES

Mondeville

Cormelles

N

Fleury-sur-Orne

2 CANADIAN ARMOURED AND 4 CANADIAN INFANTRY BRIGADES

Bras

Ifs

Soliers

Four

St. André-sur-Orne

START LINE

Hubert Folie

Bourguébus

St. Martin de Fontenay

Verrières

Tilly-la-Campagne

La Hogue

Route Nationale No. 158

Secqueville-la-Campagne

May-sur-Orne

6 CANADIAN INFANTRY BRIGADE

Garcelles-Secqueville

Fontenay-le-Marmion

Rocquancourt

6 CANADIAN INFANTRY BRIGADE

Lorguichon

Laize River

Pt 122 Cramesnil

4 CANADIAN INFANTRY BRIGADE

St. Aignan-de-Cramesnil

Robertmesnil

Kilometres

0   1   2   3

0   1   2

Miles

Caillouet

Quarry

Gaumesnil

Cintheaux

Cauvicourt

Laize River

Bretteville-sur-Laize

Chemin Heusse

Hautmesnil

Gouvix

Quarry

Orne River

195

of sound. A tank on our right went up in a burst of flame and then another to our front. We were 'bogged down' it seemed. "A" Squadron on our right was having a field day shooting into the German masses.

Major [Donald J.] Scott, our Squadron leader, had jumped out of his vehicle and was directing the troops to dig-in. While doing so, he was caught in a burst of machine gun fire and was killed.

By morning, we had managed to get down roughly three feet into the hard chalk. When we looked about it was the weirdest sight we ever hope to see. The vehicles were in a slight depression roughly in a circle, as the caravans of the old west might form up while under attack by Indians.

The column had halted and dug in as it was estimated that the unit was very close to Point 122. It was not until much later that they were able to establish that the leading elements were on the railway bridge northeast of some mine buildings near Rocquancourt and farther from the objective than they had estimated.[3]

The most westerly column, which, it will be recalled, included three parallel battalion columns, had not proceeded far past the start line when effective enemy fire on the right battalion column, the Essex Scottish, forced the Gapping Force and the battalion columns more to the east. The plan had been to pass just to the west of Rocquancourt, but the columns struck the village more or less head on. Considerable confusion resulted and the barrage was lost. As a result the Gapping Force did not reach the debussing area until 0210 hours, over an hour after the barrage had ended. The left column, the Royal Regiment of Canada, swung up the east side of the village. To Major Radley-Walters of A Squadron, Sherbrooke Fusilier Regiment, the unexpected change of plan did not pose a large problem:[4]

My column, as we came through Rocquancourt was supposed to come out through here on [the west of] Rocquancourt. We all got pushed out to the east and once we got through, I realized that Rocquancourt was on my right. I had to get down into Gaumesnil. I got next to the railroad track and had to find a place to cross over. Then I had the railroad track on my right and the road on my left and I couldn't get lost.

While one of Radley-Walters's gapping troops somehow joined up with B Squadron, and B Company of the Royal Regiment of Canada ended up with the Royal Hamilton Light Infantry, the former unit's assault force was together in the low ground between the railway tracks and Point 122. An eerie silence had fallen over the battlefield and no one was sure of the situation. It was not the time to take counsel of one's fears. The Royal Regiment of Canada's commanding officer, Lieutenant Colonel J.C.H. Anderson, who had won a Military Cross with the regiment at Dieppe, ordered A Company to move onto its original objective as quickly as possible, while D Company would capture the objective originally allotted to the missing B Company. C Company, whose commander had been killed by shellfire during the move, would remain in reserve. The two companies remained mounted and drove onto their objectives, dismounted and consolidated. By 0600 hours, although the other battalions of 4 Brigade were not yet on their objectives, attempts were being made to contact the British to the east. By this stage there was considerable evidence that there were lots of unsubdued enemy to the rear of the Royals.[5]

The centre column, the Royal Hamilton Light Infantry, crossed the start line on time and was met only by small-arms fire. However five or six hundred yards south of Verrières, two Kangaroos became disabled after driving into bomb craters. The passengers abandoned the vehicles and clambered into other carriers. This column too had veered left during the march and instead of bypassing Rocquancourt to the west, hit it dead on. A German anti-tank gun took the combined columns under fire at point-blank range, fortunately for the RHLI concentrating on the Essex Scottish. After considerable difficulty, the column got underway again. The Royal Hamilton Light Infantry drove right through the village, much to the surprise of itself, the German defenders and the South Saskatchewan Regiment of 6 Brigade, which was following the advance on foot to capture the village.

Captain Leonard Harvey's FOO party from 4th Field Regiment was making its way through the village in its carrier when it found that the passage was narrowing inexplicably. Harvey reached out to feel the way, but felt the warm, vibrating steel of a German armoured vehicle instead of the cold brick wall he expected. To his horror, he found himself looking at a large black cross painted on a vehicle at close eyeball range. His driver floored the accelerator and the carrier leapt ahead and left the unwary German in its wake.[6] Once

Left Axis Column
14th Canadian Hussars with The Fort Garry Horse and Supporting Elements, 79th Armoured Division

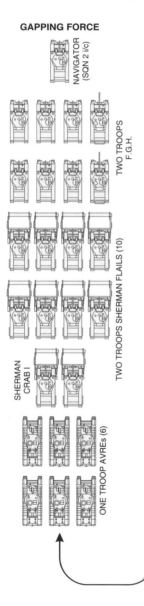

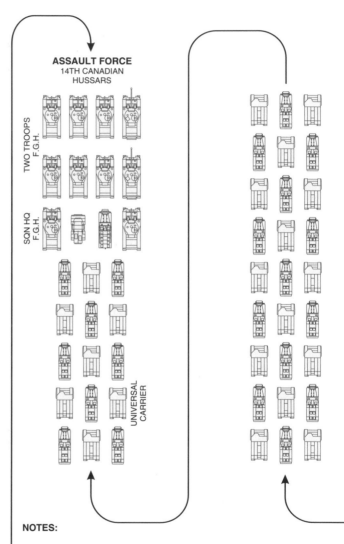

NOTES:

1) This order of battle is an approximation showing the main fighting vehicles. Space limitations prevent illustrating the column as one continuous line.

2) 14th Canadian Hussars lift was distributed between Universal Carriers, White Scout Cars and assorted other armoured vehicles as available.

3) Supporting elements included two troops 6th Canadian Anti-Tank Regiment, one platoon Medium MGs of The Toronto Scottish Regiment and one section Royal Canadian Engineers.

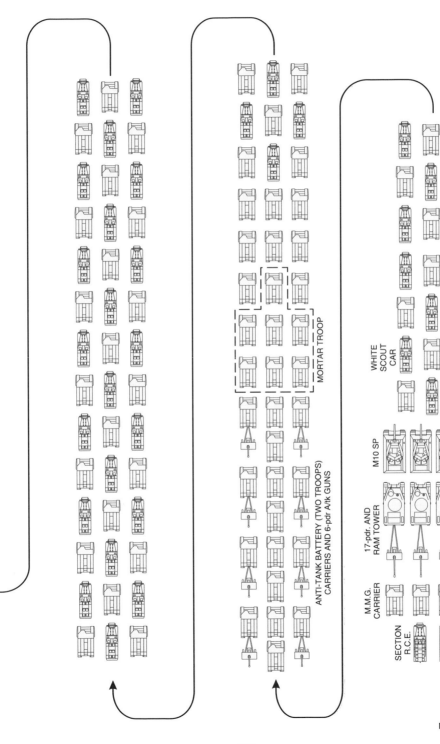

MORTAR TROOP

ANTI-TANK BATTERY (TWO TROOPS)
CARRIERS AND 6-pdr A/tk GUNS

WHITE
SCOUT
CAR

M10 SP

17-pdr. AND
RAM TOWER

M.M.G.
CARRIER

SECTION
R.C.E.

Not To Scale

Assault Force
Lifting the Royal Hamilton Light Infantry Column
with Supporting Elements

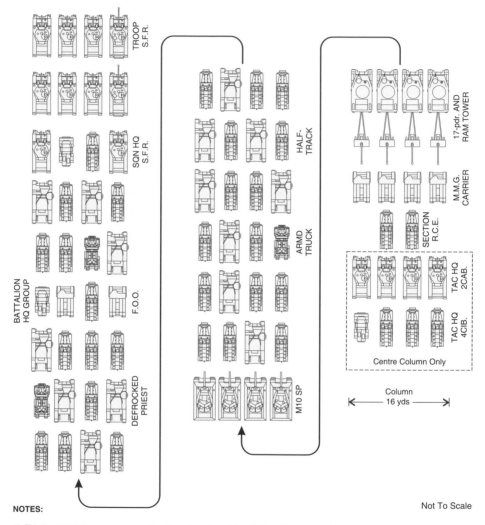

NOTES:

Not To Scale

1) This illustration shows the organization of one of the three right side Canadian columns. It is an approximation as sources differ in regards to their composition. Main fighting vehicles illustrated. Space limitations prevent illustrating the column as one continuous line.

2) Infantry battalion lift was distributed between Defrocked Priests, Half-tracks, Armoured Trucks and assorted other armoured vehicles as available. Two additional columns lifting the Essex Scottish and Royal Regiment of Canada organized as above. Each Assault Force column followed a Gapping Force column.

3) Supporting elements included two troops 6th Canadian Anti-Tank Regiment, one platoon medium MGs of The Toronto Scottish Regiment and one section Royal Canadian Engineers.

clear of the village, the RHLI column drove across the abandoned German airfield under machine gun and small-arms fire along with the occasional anti-tank and mortar round. At about 0400 hours the objective was recognized ahead. As the companies had become intermingled, a halt was called and the order of march sorted out. Fortunately the area had been abandoned by the Germans and the companies moved quickly onto their positions. The commanding officer decided, after seeing the ground, not to occupy Point 46, the battalion consolidating some 200 yards to the north instead.[7]

The Gapping Force for the third battalion group, the Essex Scottish, made generally good progress at the start, although the lead troop of the Sherbrooke Fusilier Regiment became scattered before Rocquancourt was reached. Shortly later, the right and centre columns converged, halted while the mess was sorted out and the Gapping Force moved off again, followed by the Essex Scottish assault force, which had closed the gap. In the words of the flail squadron commander, "At this point the column was engaged by an 88 and a 3rd T[roo]p crab in the rear was hit but the crew was unhurt. The tank was burnt out." In the meantime Assault Force had halted to re-orient itself close to an enemy defensive nest, while Gapping Force moved on, in the process destroying an anti-tank gun which had knocked out a half-track and an M10 SP anti-tank gun. The flails continued to move forward slowly until shortly before the dispersal point was reached, where another flail was destroyed by an anti-tank gun. Gapping Force eventually rallied in the area of the debussing point, but it was not until first light that all elements were reunited.[8] However, the Essex Scottish had been unable to break contact with German defenders of Rocquancourt as

they had come under fire from an anti-tank gun: some of their half-tracks and tanks were hit and burst into flames. Other vehicles turned or backed and collided with those behind, throwing the column into a disorder which was increased as vehicles straying from another column tried to join company. A platoon sent to deal with an 88-mm gun was driven off by machine-gun fire. By this time the commanding officer [Lieutenant Colonel T. Jones] was missing, and Major J.W. Burgess, acting second-in-command, took charge and ordered the infantry to get out of their vehicles, deploy and dig in while the column was reformed. This situation was reported to

Brigade at 0327 hours. Major Burgess then walked into Rocquancourt, and there learned for the first time that the battalion was 3000 yards short of their objective. There, too, he found his Commanding Officer wounded, but safe, in the hands of the S. Sask R. Not until 0845 hours, in broad daylight, was the battalion finally re-formed south of the village.[9]

The losses to the battalion in a night of confusion, gunfire and dust were considerable, not only in men but especially in equipment. One of the rifle companies was reduced to 30 men, 14 half-tracks had been destroyed or were missing, two of the self-propelled anti-tank guns were missing[10] and the only tank to be seen belonged to the FOO. And that worthy gentleman, who earned the praise of the battalion for staying with them and shepherding them forward, had dared not tell the Essex Scottish that not only was he mounted in an observation post tank fitted with a dummy gun, but he had lost contact with the rest of the tanks and had no idea where he was and where he was going.[11]

Behind the armoured columns other troops moved forward on foot to clear bypassed areas and mop up the villages of May-sur-Orne, Fontenay-le-Marmion, Rocquancourt and Tilly-la-Campagne. The first three were the responsibility of 6 Canadian Brigade, which allotted a battalion to each. All three of its battalions would advance at H-Hour and assault the three objectives, although the task given it in the division operation order was to mop up the area between the Caen–Falaise road and the Orne River as far south as an east-west line running about 500 yards south of Fontenay-le-Marmion and Rocquancourt. As was the case with 152 Highland Brigade, 6 Canadian Brigade did not have the benefit of any artillery support except for the barrage, and that only in the area of Rocquancourt. However the brigade did have a machine gun company and the heavy mortar company from the division machine gun battalion, two batteries of the division anti-tank regiment and a squadron of flame-throwing Crocodiles of 141 RAC.[12]

As May-sur-Orne and Fontenay-le-Marmion had been sentenced to be obliterated by the bombing, it was thought that it would be a case of following along and collecting any Germans who had managed to survive the

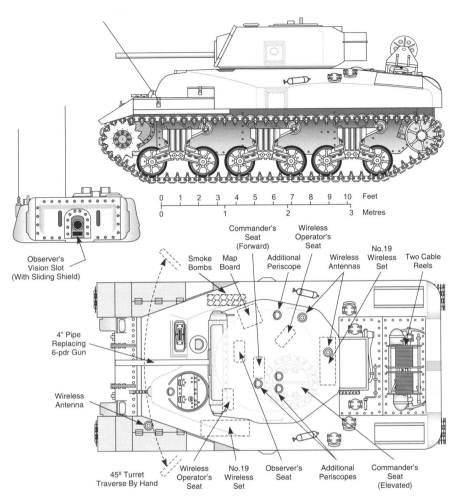

0 1 2 3 4 5 6 7 8 9 10 Feet

0 1 2 3 Metres

Observer's
Vision Slot
(With Sliding Shield)

Commander's
Seat
(Forward)

Wireless
Operator's
Seat

No.19
Wireless
Set

Two Cable
Reels

Smoke
Bombs

Map
Board

Additional
Periscope

Wireless
Antennas

4" Pipe
Replacing
6-pdr Gun

Wireless
Antenna

45° Turret
Traverse By Hand

Wireless
Operator's
Seat

No.19
Wireless
Set

Observer's
Seat

Additional
Periscopes

Commander's
Seat
(Elevated)

Ram observation post – OP

Designed as an armoured artillery observation post or for use as a command vehicle, the regular Ram's 6-pdr gun and ammunition bins were dispensed with to increase interior space. A dummy gun barrel was fixed to the turret for camouflage. An observer's seat, a second No. 19 wireless set, line communication equipment and map board were installed in the fighting compartment for use in an observation or command role. Additional periscopes were fitted to the turret roof and an observation vision slot was cut into the face of the turret under the dummy gun barrel. Two telephone cable reels were mounted on the engine deck.

Country of origin: Canada
Crew: 6
Length: 19 feet
Width: 9 feet 1 inch
Height: 9 feet
Weight: 32 tons
Engine: Continental R975-C1
Maximum speed: 25 mph
Range: 144 miles
Armament: Browning .30 cal
    M1919A4 MG in bow mount
Armour – Maximum: 76 mm
    Minimum: 12 mm

aerial onslaught. Two days before, on the afternoon of 5 August, an attempt to capture May-sur-Orne by 5 Canadian Brigade supported by artillery and a squadron of tanks had been a costly failure.[13] This time, with hundreds of tons of bombs due to fall on the village, the Fusiliers Mont-Royal would attack without the support of either, relying on the bombing to destroy the enemy resistance. The reliance on air power was misplaced because May-sur-Orne

> appeared to have received only a slight attack; some bombs had obviously fallen in the fields near St. Martin de Fontenay to the north of the target but even so the number of craters was nowhere near the 1112 which was the number of bombs said to have been used in this attack.
>
> The following points were made by officers who were concerned in the attack. The flares had just faded out when the bombers arrived. Some bombs fell short among the men who were waiting to advance; this caused confusion and did not improve their morale. It was suggested that, whereas in daylight attacks our forward troops are able to see the planes unload their bombs and fire their rockets on the enemy, at night they do not see any such heartening spectacle but merely hear the bombs descend and wonder where the next one will fall.[14]

Be that as it may, the Fusiliers, which were already considerably below strength, were hit by heavy fire from mortars and artillery as they moved through St. André-sur-Orne which killed and wounded so many that the battalion was halted while the companies were reorganized. When the advance was resumed, the unit came under heavy fire again and was able to struggle forward for a few hundred yards supported by the 4.2-inch mortars. One company managed to fight its way into the outskirts of May-sur-Orne, but it was cut off and communications with it were lost. At about 0150 hours, artillery concentrations were called for and fired, but the Fusiliers were unable to make any headway against heavy enemy fire.[15] The battalion now reorganized again and renewed the attack at about 0430 hours. This attack fared little better:

> While "A" and "B" Coys advanced down the r[oa]d "C" and "D" were to try and infiltrate quietly without fire s[u]p[port] around by the left and were

to attempt to enter the village from the direction of the quarries [southeast of the village]. In this attack "C" Coy had about 35 men. They advanced to [a point about 300 yards east of the village] where they ran into enemy MG posns firing on them from both flanks. The silent attack had so far been successful but at this p[oin]t a German off[ice]r or NCO was observed going around putting his sleepy men on alert and the adv[ance] was halted with considerable cas[ualties].

After these attacks failed, the battalion was consolidated in its former positions under continual German fire during the morning.[16]

Like the FMR, the Queen's Own Cameron Highlanders of Canada from Winnipeg expected to gain some advantage from the bombing. Again, the bombing largely missed the target and prisoner reports indicated that when the bombing of May-sur-Orne alerted the defenders of Fontenay-le-Marmion, the tanks and vehicles in the village were pulled out, while "the troops in the trenches north of the town were told to hold on as a counter attack would be launched in the morning."[17] It fell, therefore, to the Manitobans to advance 2,000 yards without artillery support and attack an alert enemy on a reverse slope, most of whom had been untouched by the bombing. The situation was made worse by the low effective fighting strength of the rifle companies, only 60 to 70 men each.[18]

As they advanced over the ridge astride the road from Ifs, the Camerons were blinded by the dust and smoke from the bombing (the Canadian Army Historical Section's suggestion that this was from the armour on their right and smoke laid by the enemy does not seem credible) as well as some local mist. It was difficult to keep formation, especially as mines were encountered and the troops came under heavy shelling as well as machine gun fire from the flanks. The companies reached the village with very few men actually present, perhaps 20 at most, although others who had become separated in the confusion eventually rejoined their sub-units. Despite the low numbers, the Camerons fought their way into Fontenay-le-Marmion. There were considerable numbers of enemy still holding out to their rear. Lieutenant Colonel John Runcie, the commanding officer, had been wounded shortly after crossing the start line and the companies had lost physical contact with one another.[19]

Without a commanding officer and with their numbers depleted, the three surviving Cameron company commanders decided to hold the north end of the village around the church and its yard, rather than to fight their way through to the south edge. Major C.W. Ferguson, the Brigade Major of 6 Brigade, and formerly the second-in-command of the Highland battalion, came forward to take command at some time between 0500 and 0700 hours (accounts vary). Major Cavanagh, the commander of A Company, recalled that Ferguson ordered him

> to move south and to take the group of buildings which formed a clear rectangular block of buildings south of the village. By 0700 hrs, 8 August, the dust had settled sufficiently so that visibility was good and we pushed off sending back word about 0800 hours that were reasonably well established in our area. Counter attacks soon developed on us from south and east. As I arrived on the position with only 50 men, with which I had to hold an area about half a mile, I asked for assistance. The enemy were infiltrating through the town and between us and the town so that information got through very slowly. Counter attacks continued all that morning. We were able to hold on only with the small arms fire which we had even though we received no reinforcements and heard that Battalion Headquarters had been wiped out.[20]

In fact, the Germans, who had been bypassed by the advance, began to attack from the north with tanks. Their first shell indeed knocked out battalion headquarters, mortally wounding Major Ferguson, wounding the support company commander, the adjutant and the anti-tank platoon commander as well as the artillery FOO, and cutting off wireless communications with brigade headquarters. The FOO's assistant, Bombardier Peter Pearce, carried his wireless set to another building and throughout the day directed artillery fire while under continuous machine gun and mortar fire. He also provided the only link with brigade headquarters, as road communications were cut off for much of the day,[21] although the carrier platoon commander was able to take his carriers out to Ifs under heavy fire and return with ammunition and "all available reinforcements, including shoemakers and other administrative personnel."[22]

Lieutenant John Graham, the battalion intelligence officer, attributed the failure of the first (and heaviest) counterattack to succeed because "the [enemy] infantry did not have guts enough to follow up the tank attack with an attack to retake the village. Hence we were able to hold on despite the disorganization caused by the direct hit on Battalion HQ." The situation, however, was still serious as

All during the day 8 Aug the [German] infantry made minor counter-attacks from every direction. Since we had passed through them the attacks could come from almost any direction. The biggest attack, consisting of two platoons, came in at once but was driven off. The tanks followed the infantry, but left an 88 mm gun on the hill and at least one 75 mm infantry gun plus mortars, which sniped at us continually. Finally the scout platoon sent patrols forward which infiltrated into the long grain and sniped at the gun crews which stopped the fire of all of them but the 88 mm. This was about mid-morning. Then we directed medium artillery on the 88 mm although it was too close for safety. The first round broke the barrel off the 88 mm and stopped its fire.

Up to this time the battalion strength was probably at best 150 men, occupying an area in the town itself, mostly north of the lateral road running by the church. "A" Coy was detached somewhat and was fighting pretty well on its own because of its bad communications. Wireless was poor, there was no line, and LOs [Liaison Officers] found it difficult to reach "A" Coy, which had moved SE to the enclosed and somewhat detailed [fenced field lying about 200 meters from the village.][23]

Unlike the other two battalions, the South Saskatchewan Regiment, which had been holding Verrières, expected to gain some advantage from the barrage as well as the presence of the armoured columns. Before H-Hour the Westerners moved back behind the bomb line and formed up behind their start line at Troteval Farm. The battalion attacked with A Company right, D Company left, C Company following and B Company in reserve. The artificial moonlight worked well until the dust and smoke from artillery fire obscured it, but the Bofors tracer proved to be useful in showing the direction to be taken. Despite the rate of advance of the barrage being extremely fast for dismounted troops advancing at night, the forward companies were able to follow the barrage and arrive at the north end of the village while rounds were still falling on

The perils of war
A Sherman, possibly of the Sherbrooke Fusilier Regiment, in a bomb crater somewhere north of Cintheaux. Recovery of this vehicle would have posed little problem for the skilled RCEME tradesmen of the unit Light Aid Detachment. (NAC/PA 113707)

its south end. According to Major Courtneay, the commander of A Company, who was interviewed by a historical officer shortly after the battle:

> to support the attack an artillery barrage lifting 200 yards every two minutes was laid down beginning just in front of ffERRI RES at 2345 hours. The battalion rushed off from the start line at 2330 hours, the position being taped to the bomb line. Thus we caught up with the barrage at its first lift. "A" Company hit the village right on the nose touching at the northwest corner of the orchard which left room for manoeuvre. A lot of prisoners were taken inside the orchard along the centre wall. "D" Company passed through and we consolidated on our position waiting until the moon rose later on to do the final mopping up. Digging continued and by dawn everyone was tied into a close-knit defence... The attack was extremely successful in that the battalion stayed so close behind the barrage that enemy heads were still under ground when we arrived... This permitted us to get into town and be consolidated and reasonably well organized at 0045 hours. Once we were settled the enemy at once opened

up on us with mortars, moaning minnies, 88 mm and so forth, but caused few casualties.

About 0430 hrs an enemy patrol apparently returning to its base, although it knew that something was up, nevertheless stumbled into one of our platoon positions near a gap in the orchard wall. One of our troops was killed by Schmeisser fire, but the enemy usually surrendered quietly. Most of our prisoners were from the orchard where six mortars had been set up and where much ammunition and small arms were obtained. The resistance we met was not as heavy as had been expected.

The reason for the success of this attack lay in the barrage which was very closely followed. One must ignore machine gun fire unless it is very close and hug to [sic] own artillery shells... On the whole the attack went through according to plan just like a well rehearsed exercise.[24]

While the advance did not go as planned, especially on the western flank of 2nd Canadian Infantry Division, by early morning the better part of two infantry brigades and two armoured brigades, along with their supporting arms, were on their objectives. Behind them, another three infantry battalions, two British and one Canadian, had also taken their objectives. As an indication of the success, five armoured regiments – about 300 tanks in all – had lost between them less than 20 tanks in a penetration of nearly 6,000 yards into the enemy's rear. This was unheard of for a major attack in Normandy, or for that matter anywhere else in 1944. Along with the tank losses, casualties among the carrier-borne infantry had been lighter than anticipated and, unless the Germans could pull a miracle out of their hats, the Caen hinge appeared broken for good.

The fact was that, for every horror story of vehicles colliding or falling into bomb craters or going astray and joining other columns or being brewed up, the vast majority arrived at their objective areas after having driven through the prepared main defensive zone of an enemy infantry division. Although there were serious incidents, for many drivers and their passengers in the columns it was a case of following the tracks and lights and keeping alert, until somebody in authority at the end of the movement told them where to go and what to do. That is not to say it was a cakewalk. It must have been a

After daybreak
A group of tanks of the Sherbrooke Fusilier Regiment "near Cintheaux" on 8 August.
The third tank is a Ram observation post tank. Note the scout car in the rear. (NAC/PA
114062)

terrifying experience, especially for those who were not occupied navigating
or driving or trying to maintain some sort of grip on the situation.

Whatever the difficulties the visibility made for the attackers, it was worse
for the defenders. Most had not the slightest idea what was going on and
were powerless to do anything about it. The darkness, the dust and smoke,
the crashing explosions of the barrage and the concentration of the columns, meant that all many members of 89. *Infanteriedivision* knew was that
something large and dangerous was out there. If it had been a terrifying and
confusing night for the attacking troops, it was worse for the Germans, most
of whom were fighting their first battle.

Even the two strongholds of May-sur-Orne and Fontenay-le-Marmion
were on the verge of changing hands for good, although the Canadian hold
on them was precarious, while Rocquancourt and Tilly no longer posed a
serious threat. The intervening countryside was still infested with German
troops and would have to be mopped up, but this formed part of the overall
plan. As for the Horseshoe Division, on the whole its members had fought
bravely and well, but the units that had born the brunt of the attack had
been hard hit and the division's command structure and cohesion badly disrupted.

CHAPTER TEN

8 AUGUST 1944 –
THE GERMAN REACTION

"I realized that if I failed now and I did not deploy my division
correctly, the Allies would be through to Falaise and the
German armies in the west completely trapped."

SS-OBERFÜHRER KURT MEYER, 12. SS-PANZERDIVISION

itler's insistence on mounting the Mortain offensive had resulted in a dangerous thinning-out of the German forces south of Caen. As we have seen, 1. *SS-Panzerdivision* had begun its move west on the night of 6 August. The next evening the *Heeresgruppe* issued orders at 2240 hours (2140 hours German time) to 5. *Panzerarmee* (*Panzergruppe West* had been raised to army status on 5 August) that 12. *SS-Panzerdivision* was to withdraw from its position north and west of Falaise to an assembly area northwest of Condé as a first step before moving to the west to reinforce the offensive. At this stage two battle groups from the division were already in action, *SS-Sturmbannführer* Erich Olboeter's[1] *Aufklärungsgruppe* in the area of Vire and *SS-Obersturmbannführer* Max Wünsche's[2] *Kampfgruppe* against the Grimbosq bridgehead. In response to this order, *Oberstleutnant* von Kluge, the chief of staff of 1. *SS-Panzerkorps*, reported that one battalion of panzer grenadiers, a battalion each of artillery and *Nebelwerfers*, a company of tanks, a battery of 88 mm flak and a panzer grenadier regiment light anti-aircraft company could be available as early as that night, while Wünsche's force should be available at 1000 hours on the 8th once the British bridgehead at Grimbosq had been eliminated.[3]

At 2345 hours on & August 1. *SS-Panzerkorps* reported to 5. *Panzerarmee* that heavy artillery fire was falling on the main defence line south of Caen in what were probably preparations for a major attack and the corps requested that 12. *SS-Panzerdivision* not be withdrawn at this time. By 0145 hours the chief of staff of the *Panzerarmee* reported that Army Group B "had decided 12th SS Pz Div would stand at the disposal of Pz Army as heretofore. Nevertheless, all measures were to be taken for a speedy transfer to the zone of Seventh Army."[4] The decision to cancel the move would, in the words of 12. *SS-Panzerdivision's* historian, have significant consequences; a relatively strong armoured force under a dynamic leader was now available, albeit one split into three groups, two of which were in action, one a considerable distance to the west. The only elements that could be immediately employed against the attackers were a battalion of Mk IV tanks, the headquarters and *Nr. 3 Kompanie* of *schwere SS-Panzerabteilung* 101 with a total of eight to ten Tigers, a battalion of panzer grenadiers (*Kampfgruppe* Waldmüller), a company of *jagdpanzers* of *SS-Panzerjägerabteilung* 12, the division and corps escort companies (*Begeleitkompanien*), the three divisional artillery battalions less one 105 mm *Wespe* battery and the *Nebelwerfer* battalion.[5] In addition elements of III. *Flakkorps* and *Nebelwerferregiment* 83 were available in the corps area.[6]

During the evening *SS-Oberführer* Kurt Meyer,[7] the divisional commander, was alerted by the bombing that a major Allied offensive was in motion even before the first reports arrived. Certainly he knew that the Allies could attack down Route Nationale 158 at any time, even if the German high command seemed incapable of grasping the peril inherent in the breaching of the line south of Caen. Furthermore, the movement of his division would mean that 1. *SS-Panzerkorps* would be without any meaningful reserve or defence in depth until the untried and immobile 85. *Infanteriedivision* commanded by *Generalleutnant* Kurt Chill[8] arrived, and that would be the following night at the earliest. The sky to the north flashed with explosions, followed soon by the rumble and roar of literally thousand of bombs, signalling the entry of RAF Bomber Command to seal off the flanks of the axis of advance, and within minutes hundreds of Allied guns firing in support of a major attack added to the tumult of death and destruction.

Meyer was not a soldier to wring his hands in despair or wait for orders in a crisis. He recognized a *schwerpunkt* when he saw it, and he swung into action. The first thing to do was to warn his subordinates, and he did that. The next task was to get as much information as possible; he therefore despatched what the divisional historian called scouting parties, but we would

Organization – 12. *SS-Panzerdivision*
1100 Hours, 8 August, 1944

Commander: *SS-Oberführer* Kurt Meyer
Operations Officer: *SS-Sturmbannführer* Hubert Meyer

Kampfgruppe Waldmüller

I. *Bataillon, SS-Panzergrenadierregiment* 25
II. *Abteilung, SS-Panzerregiment* 12 (less 8. *Kompanie*)
HQ and 3. *Kompanie, schwere SS-Panzerabteilung* 101
1. *Kompanie, SS-Panzerjägerabteilung* 12
Divisionbegleitkompanie 12
Korpsbegleitkompanie

Kampfgruppe Wünsche

HQ and 3. *Kompanie,* I. *Abteilung, SS-Panzerregiment* 12
8. *Kompanie,* II. *Abteilung, SS-Panzerregiment* 12
2. *Kompanie, schwere SS-Panzerabteilung* 101
I. *Bataillon, SS-Panzergrenadierregiment* 26
III. *Bataillon, SS-Panzergrenadierreigment* 26
(less 9. *Kompanie*)

Aufklärungsgruppe Olboeter

2. *Kompanie,* I. *Abteilung, SS-Panzerregiment* 12
9. *Kompanie,* III. *Bataillon, SS-Panzergrenadierregiment* 26
1. *Kompanie, SS-Aufklärungsabteilung* 12
I. *Batterie,* I. *Bataillon, SS-Artillerieregiment* 12

Under Divisional Command

SS-Panzeraufklärungsabteilung 12 (less 1. *Kompanie*)
SS-Panzerjägerabteilung 12 (less 1. *Kompanie*)
SS-Panzerartillerieregiment 12 (less 1. *Batterie*)
SS-Werferabteilung 12
SS-Flakabteilung 12
SS-Panzerpionierbataillon 12

likely call liaison officers or contact patrols, to make contact with units of 89. *Infanteriedivision* so as to report developments as they happened. Gaining information was not as easy as it seems. The first reports may have said little other than that forward areas well east and west of the Route Nationale were being bombed. Later the "Horseshoe Division" could report that its forward positions astride the Caen–Falaise road were under heavy artillery fire and perhaps pass on confused messages that hundreds of enemy armoured vehicles were driving through and around their positions. Meyer must have appreciated from what information there was that the Allied attack was confined to a relatively narrow front astride the Caen–Falaise road.

Somehow the Allies had managed to launch a surprise breakthrough attack on the critical point of the German line, and he appreciated that this was not a diversion to draw troops away from Mortain – it was the real thing and it was in juggernaut proportions. It spurred Meyer to order his division to prepare to move forward from its concentration areas south of the battle area. In fact, his subordinates had not been idle and were already preparing for action. *SS-Sturmbannführer* Waldmüller,[9] for example, had already ordered a platoon of *Panzerjägers* from his battle group to Cintheaux.

In the meantime, it was time to see for himself. Unlike the British and Canadian armies, which believed that a commander's place was in his headquarters where he could gain an accurate picture of the battle from studying the situation map and reading wireless reports, the Germans felt a commander must be able to make crucial decisions based on what he could see and feel, not on information filtered through two or more levels of command. Even in the *Waffen SS*, which emphasized leading from the front, Kurt Meyer stood out for his audacity and his uncanny ability to show up at the right place at the right time, and then make the right decision.

By the time Meyer left his headquarters before dawn on the morning of 8 August to drive to the front to get a first-hand understanding of the situation, reports had painted a bleak picture. As he neared Bretteville, he was able to supplement his knowledge by talking to *SS-Obersturmbannführer* Wilhelm Mohnke,[10] the commander of *SS-Panzergrenadierregiment* 26, who was in Urville.[11] It appeared that the Allies had broken through across the front of 89. *Infanteriedivision,* and while some strongpoints seemed to be holding out, contact with these positions had been lost. The Germans still held Garcelles but there were reports of Allied tanks in St. Aignan, while the situation in Rocquancourt and May-sur-Orne was muddled. Meyer had the advantage of knowing the ground well as he had been stationed in the area in 1941 when he commanded a reconnaissance battalion. Thus, if the enemy had broken through to the extent it seemed, he realized that the next possible main defensive position was behind the natural tank obstacle of the Laison River and on the heights near Potigny. However, there were no troops to hold that line and there would not be until 85. *Infanteriedivision* arrived over the next couple of nights. Clearly the enemy advance had to be contained for another 24 to 48 hours.[12]

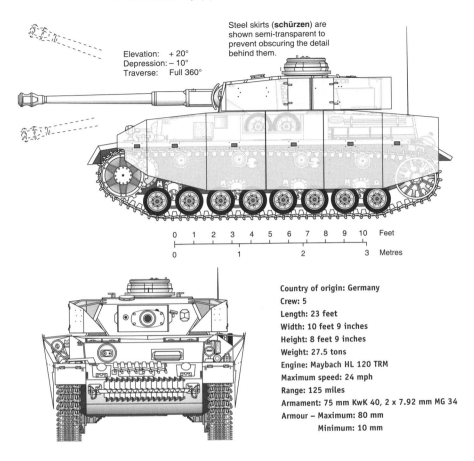

Steel skirts (**schürzen**) are shown semi-transparent to prevent obscuring the detail behind them.

Elevation: + 20°
Depression: − 10°
Traverse: Full 360°

Country of origin: Germany
Crew: 5
Length: 23 feet
Width: 10 feet 9 inches
Height: 8 feet 9 inches
Weight: 27.5 tons
Engine: Maybach HL 120 TRM
Maximum speed: 24 mph
Range: 125 miles
Armament: 75 mm KwK 40, 2 x 7.92 mm MG 34
Armour – Maximum: 80 mm
Minimum: 10 mm

PzKpfw IV – Ausf. H

The PzKpfw IV series turned out to be the mainstay of the German panzer arm throughout the war. Continually up-gunned and up-armoured throughout its service life, this tank equipped one of the two tank battalions in a 1944 panzer regiment. At least the equal of the Sherman, the PzKpfw IV was a reliable, robust design upon which many specialized German armoured vehicles were based.

Protection in the Frontal Arc – A Comparison

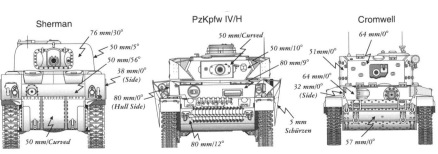

Sherman

76 mm/30°
50 mm/5°
50 mm/56°
38 mm/0°
(Side)
80 mm/0°
(Hull Side)
50 mm/Curved

PzKpfw IV/H

50 mm/Curved
50 mm/10°
80 mm/9°
5 mm
Schürzen
80 mm/12°

Cromwell

64 mm/0°
51mm/0°
64 mm/0°
32 mm/0°
(Side)
57 mm/0°

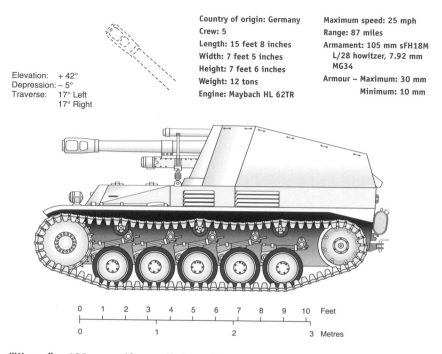

Country of origin: Germany
Crew: 5
Length: 15 feet 8 inches
Width: 7 feet 5 inches
Height: 7 feet 6 inches
Weight: 12 tons
Engine: Maybach HL 62TR

Maximum speed: 25 mph
Range: 87 miles
Armament: 105 mm sFH18M L/28 howitzer, 7.92 mm MG34
Armour – Maximum: 30 mm
Minimum: 10 mm

Elevation: + 42°
Depression: − 5°
Traverse: 17° Left
17° Right

| 0 | 1 | 2 | 3 | 4 | 5 | 6 | 7 | 8 | 9 | 10 | Feet |

| 0 | | 1 | | 2 | | 3 | Metres |

"Wespe" – 105 mm self-propelled howitzer

The Wespe was based on the chassis of the obsolete PzKpfw II. It mounted a 105 mm howitzer in an open-topped fighting compartment. The design entailed extending the hull slightly, moving the engine forward and constructing a fighting compartment at the rear of the vehicle from sloped armour plating. The maximum range of the 32 pound 105 mm HE round was 13,450 yards. The vehicle carried an ammunition load of 32 rounds. Small in size and easily concealed, the Wespe proved to be a successful design and it served as a light self-propelled howitzer in panzer artillery regiments of panzer and panzer grenadier divisions from early 1943 until the end of hostilities.

The road through Bretteville-sur-Laize was impassable due to heavy shelling. Meyer left it and bounced cross-country in his *Kubelwagen* towards Cintheaux, which also was under shell fire. (While Meyer described it as bombing, that had ended before midnight.) The transcript of his interrogation captures the sense of the situation:

[Meyer:] I got out of my car and my knees were trembling, the sweat was pouring down my face, and my clothes were soaked with perspiration. It was not that I was particularly anxious for myself because my experiences of the last five years had inured me against fear of death, but I realized that if I failed now and if I did not deploy my division correctly, the Allies would be through to Falaise and the German armies in the west completely trapped. I knew how weak my division was and the double task which confronted me gave me at that time some of the worst moments I had ever had in my life. [Interrogator:] At the same time Meyer was up on that road alone, groups of 89 Division scattered in panic by the bombing, were making their way down the Caen–Falaise Road as quickly as possible. Meyer, on perceiving this serious situation, calmly lit a cigar, stood in the middle of the road and in a loud voice asked if they were going to leave him alone to cope with the allied attack when it came. One look at the young commander was enough and the men turned around and began to take up defensive positions. He must certainly have looked an impressive figure, this 35 year old divisional commander, wearing the highest decorations the Germans could bestow on him, quietly but confidently facing this disorderly mob and by his example and sheer determination influencing the whole division to turn back into line and take up the fight once more.[13]

The next stop for Meyer was Urville, the site of the headquarters of 89. *Infanteriedivision*, where Meyer and Mohnke met with *Generalleutnant* Konrad Heinrichs, the commander of 89. *Infanteriedivision*, and the commander of 5. *Panzerarmee*, *General Der Panzertruppen* Heinrich Eberbach, who also had come forward to see for himself rather than waiting in his headquarters for reports. The army commander concurred with Meyer's assessment of the situation and approved Meyer's decision for a counterattack to block and then delay the Allied advance. Little more could be expected given the disparity of forces, and any attempt to restore the front line was clearly beyond the capability of Meyer's division. In the meantime, 1. *SS-Panzerkorps* had ordered the *Hitlerjugend* division to stop the enemy breakthrough with a counterattack and, if possible, to throw it back. Clearly the presence of Eberbach resulted in a realistic plan being adopted without the necessity of debate with the next higher headquarters and his conference with Meyer in Urville at a critical point undoubtedly saved a crucial few hours in the decision-making cycle.

Meyer's plan was simple and straightforward. There were two possible routes that were large enough for an Allied division to advance along. The first and most obvious was south along Route Nationale 158, the Caen–Falaise

General der Panzertruppen Heinrich Eberbach

Eberbach is shown (left) with a Canadian interpreter sometime after his capture by the British. Eberbach's prompt and decisive action on the morning of 8 August probably delayed the liberation of Falaise and the closing of the gap by at least a week. (NAC/PA 189586)

highway, to Bretteville-le-Rabet, Potigny, Soulagny and on to Falaise. The second, and in fact the better of the two, was from St. Aignan-de-Cramesnil to Estrées-la-Campagne, then either southeast across the Laison in the area of Rouvres and through Olerdon and Epancy to Falaise, or southwest through Quesnay and Potigny and then south to Soulagny and Campagne. He planned to block both possible Allied axes as far forward as possible, which was the only feasible option given his limited forces. First, *Kampfgruppe* Waldmüller reinforced by II. *Abteilung, SS-Panzerregiment* 12 and *Nr. 3 Kompanie, schwere SS-Panzerabteilung* 101, which was to prepare for the attack from the area of Bretteville-le-Rabet, would capture the hills south of St. Aignan-de-Cramesnil. The acting commanding officer of the Tiger battalion, *SS-Hauptsturmführer* Michael Wittmann,[14] and the unit operations and signals officers would all take part in the attack mounted in Tigers. (The Tigers were actually in Cintheaux and would attack from there north along the Caen–Falaise highway.) The *Korpsbegleitkompanie* (Corps Escort Company) would form part of the battle group and move on its right during the attack while the *Divisionbegleitkompanie* (Division Escort Company), also operating as part of Waldmüller's battle group, with *Nr.* 1 *Kompanie* of *SS-Panzerjägerabteilung* 12, was to advance via Estrées-la-Campagne to capture the hill west of St. Sylvain. At the same time the small remnant of the *Panzeraufklärungsabteilung* (Divisional Reconnaissance Battalion) not deployed to the west, was to maintain contact with the left wing of 272. *Infanteriedivision* and probe into the gap assumed to exist from there to the west. The actual objectives covered a fairly wide area, nearly the whole of Simonds's Phase 1 objectives in fact, and effectively blocked the two main approaches to Falaise.

The three battalions (less the *Wespe* battery with Olboeter's group) of the divisional artillery and *SS-Werferabteilung* 12 would support the attack from gun positions near Route Nationale 158, while *SS-Flakabteilung* 12 would deploy an anti-tank screen on both sides of the Route Nationale in line with Bretteville-le-Rabet. In the meantime, *Kampfgruppe* Wünsche would break off its counterattack near Grimbosq, disengage from the British, occupy the hills west and northwest of Potigny and defend the passage between the Laize and Laison Rivers. The divisional command post was to be set up in La Breche-du-Diable below Tombeau-de-Marie about a mile east of Potigny. Meyer would stay with Waldmüller's battle group. H-Hour would be 1230 hours (1330 hours Allied time).[15]

Still, and this is important, Meyer and Eberbach both understood that they could only delay the Allies, and that the strong defensive position that had held firm since GOODWOOD nearly three weeks before was no more. It would take extraordinary measures to prevent the eastern hinge of the front from snapping. There were no reserves and no troops to prepare a defensive position in depth until *Kampfgruppe* Wünsche got into position near Potigny. The heights beyond the Laison River would remain open until Chill's 85. *Infanteriedivision*, whose leading elements were in the area of Trun, began to arrive in the early hours of the next morning. Accordingly, the planned counterattack was an all-or-nothing effort and defeat would spell disaster for the German forces in the west. With this clearly in their minds, Meyer continued with the preparations for his counterattack, while Eberbach set out for his headquarters, where he would plead with his superiors for reinforcements from the forces engaged in the Mortain offensive.

SS-Oberführer Kurt Meyer, 12. SS-Panzerdivision
Kurt Meyer possessed an uncanny ability to read a battle. His presence on the battlefield on the morning of 8 August was key to the effective execution of Eberbach's orders. (Michael Reynolds Collection)

CHAPTER ELEVEN

MOPPING UP

"I thought a great opportunity was lost and that we could have been in Falaise in an hour or so, had we started soon after first light."

LIEUTENANT COLONEL MELVILLE GORDON,

SHERBROOKE FUSILIER REGIMENT

A s the day brightened and the ground mist began to thin, Lieutenant Colonel M.B.K. (Mel) Gordon, the very able commanding officer of the Sherbrooke Fusilier Regiment, found it hard to credit his senses. His Gapping Force of six troops of his own regiment as well as the two squadrons of flails of the Lothian & Border Horse and a squadron of AVREs had arrived on their objectives more or less intact, if a bit scattered. He also knew that the remainder of A and B Squadrons of his regiment had made their way forward with only light losses. Behind him the Royal Regiment of Canada had captured Point 122 and was digging in while the Royal Hamilton Light Infantry had halted a few hundred yards from the quarry that was its main objective.

If Gordon had any cause for concern, it was to his right. The Essex Scottish, along with part of his C Squadron, were still bogged down on the other side of Rocquancourt and had suffered a number of casualties, although not as many as originally believed. Behind him, his regimental headquarters and two squadrons of Lieutenant Colonel Robert Morton's Fort Garry Horse ringed the fortress area, providing protection for Brigadier R.A. Wyman's tactical headquarters of 2 Canadian Armoured Brigade and Brigadier J.E. Ganong's 4 Canadian Infantry Brigade HQ. Thus there were nearly seven squadrons of gun tanks – the flails were capable of engaging targets with both their main armament and their machine guns – and four troops of anti-tank guns in an area of perhaps two square miles with, as far as he could determine, nothing to shoot at.

Gordon realized that an opportunity beckoned for a further advance but, as described in the prologue, it was not to be. Years after that morning the failure to take advantage of that opportunity still bothered Gordon. In a letter to the Director of the Army Historical Section he wrote

I led the three tank and cut-down Priest columns and we were on our objectives before first light. At first light, my then Brigadier, Bob Wyman, came along and in a very few minutes was wounded, the wound resulting in him going out of the war for good, but I was unable to get him back until about 1 o'clock in the afternoon as *we had more Germans behind us than we had in front of us.* [author's emphasis] At about the time he was wounded a German staff car drove up the highway, turned quickly and went back at full speed before we were able to get our guns on it. It seemed to me that if a German staff car drove up the road as that one did, the road into Falaise should be wide open and I asked for permission to start down the highway to Falaise. The Brigadier said that our orders were to form a firm base and that, in any event, the 4th Armoured Division would be passing through us in a few minutes. My memory of this is that it was about 6.30 a.m. when I made the request. It was about 4.15 p.m., according to my memory, when the 4th Armoured [Division] came along and, of course, by that time the Germans had had an opportunity to set up their guns to stop the break-through. I thought a great opportunity was lost and that we could have been in Falaise in an hour or so, had we started soon after first light.[1]

Across the Route Nationale the three infantry battalions of 154 Highland Brigade and the three armoured regiments of 33 British Armoured Brigade were in an even better position. Their move forward had gone well, with the only major engagement having been at the crossing over the railway between Rocquancourt and Garcelles-Secqueville. That there were few if any Germans to their front seemed apparent to at least the tank crews in the forward squadrons. At this time, however, Tilly was still holding out and, according to the orders received from 2nd Canadian Corps, the next task for the division was to capture Secqueville-la-Campagne and the woods adjacent to it.

Gordon's letter encapsulated the situation as he saw it. Was he right? Was the road to Falaise open? Should Wyman or Foulkes or Simonds or perhaps even Crerar have taken a risk and grabbed at the main prize? The critics of TOTALIZE certainly seem to think so. Historian John English blames Crerar for not cancelling the bombing and ordering his subordinate to continue the advance, but then dismisses the Commander of First Canadian Army as not knowing as much as Simonds. Both he and Roman Jarymowycz suggest that Crerar may have been reluctant to tell Harris of Bomber Command that the Phase 2 bombing was not needed after all the difficult and detailed staff work over the past few days. After both misstating the tactical situation and missing the obvious point that Lieutenant General James Doolittle, not "Bomber" Harris, commanded 8 USAAF, they fail to grasp the point that Simonds and Crerar were forced to conform to the working of the not-very-responsive air force command structure.[2] Both historians, it appears, may have been overly influenced by Kurt Meyer's comments expressed in his memoirs about an Allied armoured division sitting on its start lines for several hours, waiting for the heavy bombers to arrive. And, after all, Meyer's likening pauses in an armoured offensive to a cavalry charge with meal breaks and averring that "you just cannot command a tank battle from behind an office desk" are classic military criticisms![3]

Before addressing the matter of whether the road was as open as Gordon thought, it is important to determine what Crerar and Simonds knew and what they were doing. First, when was Brigadier Wyman wounded? Gordon estimated that it had happened at about 0630 hours, while the 2 Armoured Brigade report on TOTALIZE put the time at 0615.[4] However the news was not entered in the 4 Brigade Operations Log until 0730 hours when the brigade commander reported "2 CAB Comd is casualty" with no other details.[5] There are no indications that Wyman had passed on Gordon's assessment of the situation or that he would have seen any reason to do so if he had not been wounded. However, this also establishes the earliest time that anyone above the regimental commander level was informed that the way ahead seemed clear. At 0645 hours the Headquarters First Canadian Army Operations Log recorded the following summary of a telephone conversation between Simonds and Brigadier Churchill Mann, the Army Chief of Staff.

1. Ops seem to be progressing satisfactorily but of course we must expect the usual counter attack during the next two or three hours. 2. Enemy still fighting in Fontenay le Marmion and May-sur-Orne, and enemy still holds Tilly-la-Campagne. 3. 51 Brit (H) Div have reached Garcelles and Lorguichon. 4. 4 Cdn Armd Div and 1 Polish Armd Div are to be started f[or]w[ar]d to infiltrate as far as possible prior to their assembly for Phase Two. 5. Com[man]d[er] 2 Cdn Corps confirmed to Chief of Staff that bombing for Phase Two should if weather permits be based on the completion of bombing on targets 8 and 9 at 1345 hrs but that it was acceptable earlier if necessary. He stated that if it was earlier that they would try to take advantage of the situation and to adv[ance] beginning 45 mins after the commencement of the second portion of the bombing for Phase Two. 6. This was conveyed to Op[eration]s Room 83 G[rou]p RAF by tele[phone] m[e]ss[a]g[e] number GS 91 by the Chief of Staff who asked them to pass it verbatim to ensure it is understood beyond doubt. 7. 83 G[rou]p RAF Ops phoned back at 0730 hrs to say it had been passed.[6]

This rarely-quoted entry indicates that Simonds and Mann – and by extension Crerar – were aware of the general situation, but not that, in at least one experienced officer's opinion, the road to Falaise was open. Indeed, there was absolutely nothing recorded in the logs that would have led them to such a conclusion. As we have seen, these officers all believed that the key task was to confirm H-Hour with 8 USAAF by 0800 hours, and therefore Mann had ensured that First Canadian Army's part in it had been completed by 0715 hours. Furthermore, if Gordon's report had reached them, none were likely to have acted on one assessment and would have wanted confirmation from Foulkes and/or Rennie. Given the prevailing British and Canadian doctrine that a commander's place was, in Kurt Meyer's dismissive phrase, behind an office desk, and that both had to have been concentrating on mopping up their divisional areas, as per Simonds's orders, it would have been impossible for either Foulkes or Rennie to have supported such a radical change in plan without better information than was available to them at the time. Gordon may have been right, but he was powerless to change the ponderous execution of the corps plan.

The problem with all this is that while he was essentially correct in his

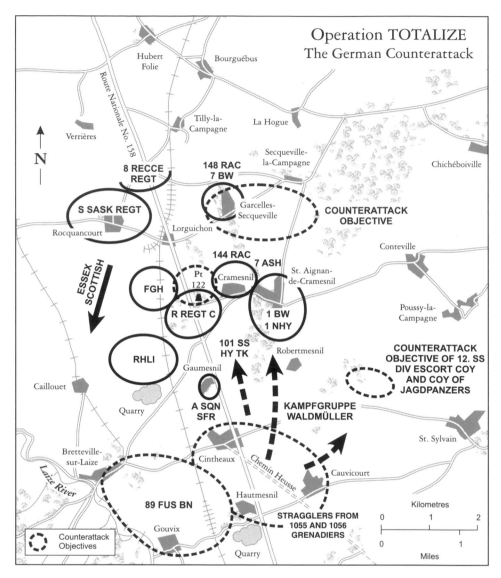

Operation TOTALIZE
The German Counterattack

assessment, there were German forces within 2,000 yards of him, and some were of the highly dangerous variety, although their presence is often downplayed in accounts of the battle fought by 12. *SS-Panzerdivision*. First, contrary to Kurt Meyer's claim, 89. *Infanteriedivision* had not disintegrated completely. At least 50 per cent of its forward troops as well as a number of armoured vehicles had made their way back and were being regrouped into coherent fighting units, while the fusilier battalion had been deployed as the division reserve in its position near Bretteville-sur-Laize. In fact, later that morning troops from the division would actually mount local counterattacks, accompanied by a few tanks and assault guns, on the Royal Regiment of Canada and Royal Hamilton Light Infantry. Third, the division's flak battalion had formed a screen from Caillouet to Gaumesnil and one of its batteries was deployed in the woods southwest of Gaumesnil along with a battery of 150 mm *Sturmpanzer* IVs of *Sturmpanzerabteilung* 217, while Cintheaux held a platoon of three self-propelled anti-tank guns of *Kampfgruppe* Waldmüller and perhaps five Tiger tanks of *Nr.* 3 *Kompanie, schwere SS-Panzerabteilung* 101. Other infantrymen from 89. *Infanteriedivision* were preparing to defend that village against attack from Canadian infantry and tanks.[7] As well, elements of *Nebelwerferregiment* 83 and III. *Flakkorps* were also in action in the area.

The presence of the 88 mm guns of the latter unit would come as an unpleasant surprise to Canadian intelligence officers, who had consistently failed to produce realistic assessments of the German strength and capabilities during TOTALIZE. Still, while the Route Nationale was by no means as open as it seemed, and any attempt to exploit forwards down it probably would have come to a sudden halt, there was the possibility that some additional progress might have been made. If Cintheaux and/or Hautmesnil could have been captured, which was within the realm of possibility, it would have badly upset the German plans for their counterattack. The possibility also existed that a real success could have been achieved, and the German attempts to hold the Allies north of the Laison River forestalled. All of this, however, is speculation, because Crerar and Simonds never received even a hint that the way ahead was clear.

Even if Simonds knew, would he have changed his plan and ordered the infantry divisions and their armoured brigades to exploit towards Falaise? There are some factors that suggest he would not have, and the first is the location of the artillery of his two forward divisions. While they had been pushed as far forward as possible to support the barrage, they could not have been able to engage targets much beyond Cintheaux. The medium guns of the two supporting AGRAs could reach out a few thousand yards farther, but their ammunition supply was limited. There is a well known story of the commander of 5 Canadian Armoured Brigade running afoul of Simonds, and thereby losing his command, by claiming he did not need to wait for the guns to move up during a 5th Canadian Armoured Division training session in Italy, and the approved solution to a similar appreciation exercise at the Canadian Junior War Staff Course was to wait for the guns.[8] It should also be remembered that Simonds was a disciple of Montgomery and, like the 21st Army Group Commander, was a strong advocate of "balance," that is, avoiding risks whenever possible during the conduct of a battle. In Simonds's mind, his plan was going to work and there was no need to imperil success by venturing onto unknown ground.

Even if Simonds had been predisposed to disregard all his inclinations, there would have been more to it than merely grabbing a handset and ordering "move now" over the wireless, no matter how many times Hollywood depicts just that on the silver screen. It easily could have taken two or more hours for Foulkes and Rennie to have organized any sort of an organized exploitation, although the tanks could probably have moved a couple of thousand yards forward. By that time, by Simonds's reckoning, 4th Canadian Armoured Division and 1. *Dywizji Pancernej* would have closed up behind the present forward positions, and he might have opted to let the fresh formations take up the chase.

As for ordering the reconnaissance units to probe forward, 8 Reconnaissance Regiment of 2nd Canadian Infantry Division was still attempting to sort itself out near Rocquancourt, and was without its armoured cars and half-tracks, while its counterpart in 51st Highland Division, 2 Derbyshire Yeomanry, still had its armoured cars but had been stripped of its carriers and was waiting north of Caen, with many miles and a horrendous traffic jam between it and the battle. The 4th Armoured Division reconnaissance regiment, the South Alberta Regiment, was operating as an armoured regiment with 10 Canadian Infantry Brigade (but was capable of operating in a reconnaissance role) and 10. *Pułk Strzelców Konnych*, the Polish reconnaissance regiment, was still on the road, and finally the Corps armoured car regiment, 12 Manitoba Dragons, was sandwiched in the 4th Division convoy. And remember, Simonds had seen how quickly German counterattacks could materialize, and it would have taken a lot of convincing to make him order his troops out of what were essentially positions calculated to repel the inevitable counterattack in order to chance a slugging match between out-

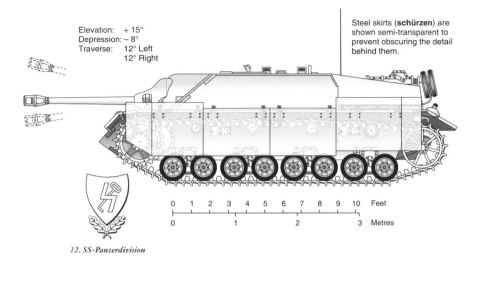

Elevation: + 15°
Depression: – 8°
Traverse: 12° Left
12° Right

Steel skirts (**schürzen**) are shown semi-transparent to prevent obscuring the detail behind them.

| 0 | 1 | 2 | 3 | 4 | 5 | 6 | 7 | 8 | 9 | 10 | Feet |

| 0 | | | 1 | | | 2 | | | 3 | | Metres |

12. SS-Panzerdivision

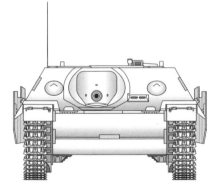

Country of origin: Germany
Crew: 4
Length: 28 feet 1 inch
Width: 9 feet 7 inches
Height: 6 feet 5 inches
Weight: 28.5 tons
Engine: Maybach HL120TRM
Maximum speed: 22 mph
Range: 133 miles
Armament: 75 mm PaK 39 L/48 gun, 2 x 7.92 mm
MG34
Armour – Maximum: 80 mm
Minimum: 11 mm

Jagdpanzer IV tank destroyer

Developed as a replacement for the successful Sturmgeschütz III series of assault guns, the Jagdpanzer IV was based on the lower hull and chassis of the reliable PzKpfw IV tank. The vertical plate front end of the PzKpfw IV was changed to a ballistically superior sharp-nose profile, while the upper hull was built with well sloped armour plating. Armour protection for the front of the upper hull was initially 60 mm and this was increased to 80 mm beginning in May 1944. The Jagdpanzer IV provided all-round protection for its crew with an extremely low silhouette. Combined with a powerful 75 mm gun, these features served it well in the defensive battles most often fought by German forces in Normandy. As with the Sturmgeschütz series of assault guns though, the Jagdpanzer IV suffered from a limited traverse for its main gun.

gunned Shermans and panzers in the open. Last, there was no guarantee that the bombing by 8 USAAF that had just been confirmed could be diverted or cancelled and there was no guarantee that any tactical air support would be available earlier than that previously requested, that is, at the same time as the heavy bombers.

I n the meantime, Foulkes still had to complete the mopping up of his divisional area, especially the two running sores of May-sur-Orne and Fontenay-le-Marmion, as well as complete the capture of his forward objectives. His first priority was for the Essex Scottish to capture Caillouet and accordingly, at 0705 hours Foulkes ordered 4 Brigade to direct 8 Reconnaissance Regiment "to move on and directly to ROBIN [Caillouet] to clear that up."[9] It will be recalled that during the previous night the regiment had run into trouble and had halted and circled its carriers in a hollow to wait for morning.[10] The regiment reported to 4 Brigade Headquarters at 0856 hours that it was located about 1,000 yards northeast of Rocquancourt with a strength of approximately 140 men and that it proposed to move via that village and then follow the track southwest to Caillouet. The message ended with a statement that it should be moving soon, but it apparently had difficulty crossing the intervening ground because of the number of bypassed German troops who were still holding out behind the forward objectives.[11]

One could sense Foulkes's growing irritation. At 0910 he ordered that Caillouet was to be cleared of enemy and occupied by the Essex Scottish assisted by the reconnaissance regiment. At 1025, while German counterattacks were going in against the Royal Regiment of Canada and the Royal Hamilton Light Infantry, the Essex reported that on "approaching our objective [we] find it is picketed with tiger tanks[. W]e saw 4 tks with inf [. W]e withdrew to approx 1500 yds of our obj[ective] and are engaging with our guns. May we have tks to support us before we go in." Shortly after, at 1045 hours, 8 Reconnaissance Regiment announced it was moving to a new location south of Rocquancourt."[12] The Essex Scottish finally completed securing Caillouet at 1300 hours, while 8 Reconnaissance Regiment occupied the abandoned airfield between Rocquancourt and the Essex's objective. Conflicting information about the identity of the "Tigers" reported on the objective had contributed

to the delay and it required both artillery concentrations and a squadron of
Sherbrooke Fusiliers in support before Caillouet was finally captured.[13]

Meanwhile, the capture of May-sur-Orne and Fontenay-le-Marmion was
progressing slowly. As we have seen, the Fusiliers Mont-Royal had been unable to fight their way into May-sur-Orne despite having mounted two night
attacks; for the third attempt this battalion was reinforced by a squadron of
flame-throwing Churchill tanks from 141 RAC.[14] This time C and D Companies with about 60 men would attack on the west of the road running into
the village from St. André-sur-Orne, supported by one troop of tanks, while
A and B Companies, 90 men in all, would attack east of the road with two
troops of tanks, and an H-Hour of 1545 hours. It is not going too far to say
that this operation was a textbook example of the clearance of a built-up area
by infantry supported by flame-throwing tanks as the 2nd Canadian Corps
chemical weapons staff described it:

> The general plan was that behind each tank would move two sections fol-
> lowing very closely on the trailer behind the tank. As the tank approached
> a house it would fire [its 75 mm gun], knock a hole in the house, then
> squirt the liquid flame into the opening thus created. Immediately the
> section directly behind the tank would dash for the doorway and clear
> the house as quickly as possible. This sound[ed] very dangerous but the
> fire once ignited is not dangerous. The thing to beware of is getting in the
> path of the flame thrower itself for everything touched by the liquid is
> ignited. The tank meanwhile moves forward down the line to the second
> house and turns its turret against it. Gun and flame thrower repeat their
> actions and the second section of infantry following the tank is available
> for clearing this house. These two sections thus alternate in entering the
> buildings set ablaze by the tank and the sections of the reserve platoon
> following further in rear occupying the buildings already searched.[15]

Other Crocodiles, with two companies of infantry, moved on the east and
southeast edge of the village, flaming copses and buildings as they progressed.
The report prepared by the chemical weapons staff at 2nd Canadian Corps
noted that "the objective was gained without difficulty. A few enemy wounded
were captured. Apparently the enemy ceased all resistance and withdrew when

the flame action commenced."[16] The Fusiliers felt that the effect on the enemy was shown by his abandonment of five mortars, some field telephones, one 88 mm and at least one field gun, and the French-Canadian infantrymen had nothing but the highest praise for the British Crocodile crews,[17] and who could blame them after the dreadful experiences of the two attacks earlier that day?

In the meantime, Major D'Arcy Marks, commanding C Squadron of the 1st Hussars, which was under command 5 Infantry Brigade for the capture of Bretteville-sur-Laize, was waiting to cross the start line at 1200 hours when

Major George Hees, B[rigade]. M[ajor]. of 6 Canadian Infantry Brigade drove up in a scout car and said the Commander of 2nd Canadian Infantry Division had ordered that the first armour he met was to be taken off whatever job they were doing, and together with S[outh]. Sask[askatchewan] R[egiment]. were to relieve the pressure on the Camerons. S. Sask R. were right in Rocquancourt itself, a most unpleasant spot. Lt-Col Clift said all he could spare was two companies. Lt-Col Clift wanted to drive from Rocquancourt to Fontenay-le-Marmion but we had been told there was an anti-tank gun there. Accordingly the two companies and my squadron made an encircling movement, swung in on Fontenay-le-Marmion from the north. While we were waiting for S. Sask R. to march out of Rocquancourt, Lt-Col Clift was sitting on my tank when we saw some Germans to the south of us on the skyline perhaps 600–800 yards away. We decided to have a shot at them, and moving my tank forward twenty yards or so, we opened up with the Brownings. We sprayed the whole field, and Germans kept popping up to surrender all over the place. We left the prisoners to be looked after by the infantry and got on with the attack. We came in from the north. One of the leading troops dealt with the anti-tank gun and from there on it was pretty clear sailing. We were ordered back to the regiment at last light, or possibly we would have taken more prisoners south of Fontenay-le-Marmion. By next day they had pretty well all pulled out. There were no casualties in "C" Sqn that day.[18]

In Fontenay-le-Marmion itself, Lieutenant John Graham, the intelligence officer of the Camerons of Canada, noted that at about 1200 the enemy counterattacks which had been mounted from all directions slackened off consid-

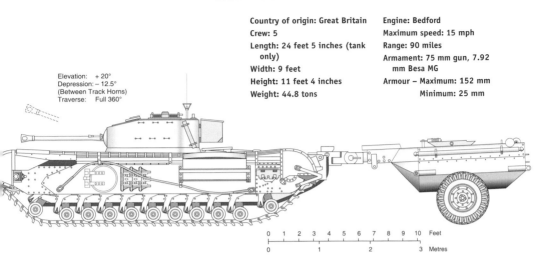

Elevation: + 20°
Depression: − 12.5°
(Between Track Horns)
Traverse: Full 360°

Country of origin: Great Britain
Crew: 5
Length: 24 feet 5 inches (tank only)
Width: 9 feet
Height: 11 feet 4 inches
Weight: 44.8 tons

Engine: Bedford
Maximum speed: 15 mph
Range: 90 miles
Armament: 75 mm gun, 7.92 mm Besa MG
Armour − Maximum: 152 mm
Minimum: 25 mm

Crocodile–Churchill VII with flame-throwing equipment

The first of the flame-throwing Churchill tanks was the "Oke," employed by the Calgary Regiment in the abortive Dieppe raid. It was a rudimentary, relatively inefficient design but it paved the way for the Crocodile, one of the most fearsome weapons to emerge from the Second World War.

The Crocodile evolved from trials initially carried out with Valentine infantry tanks in 1942. As with the experimental Valentine conversions, it made use of pressurized nitrogen as the flame propellant. The Crocodile was based on the Churchill VII, a design particularly well suited for specialized conversions because of its spacious interior. While the Crocodile was fitted with flame-throwing equipment, it also retained its 75 mm main gun. As the flaming fuel was carried in a two-wheeled armoured fuel trailer, rather than in the tank itself, the danger of fire and explosion for the crew was minimized to some degree.

In a flaming operation, the fuel was piped from the trailer along the underside of the tank to the flame projector, which replaced the hull machine gun. When the flame gun was fired, liquid fuel squirted from the projector and was ignited by an electrical charge. When flaming a target, the effective range of the Crocodile was some 80–120 yards. As the system was based on pressurization, the more the Crocodile flamed, the more the pressure dropped. Eventually, the propellant pressure dropped to the point where the flame projector became inoperable. Therefore, standard operating procedure was to "pressure up" the Crocodile immediately before going into action. When the Crocodile could no longer flame due to a low-pressure condition, the trailer could be jettisoned and the Churchill VII could operate as a regular gun tank if required. The Crocodile proved to be such a success that all late-production Churchill VIIs were built for quick conversion to flame-throwers. A total of 250 Crocodiles were originally ordered but some 800 conversion units had been produced by May 1945.

erably, but there still was heavy enemy fire, especially on the right (west) flank and the Germans were beginning to withdraw two or three at a time from their positions six to eight hundred yards away. As a result the Camerons

> got a lot of pleasure from sniping at them as they withdrew. A few P[risoners of] W[ar] gave themselves up and a few were driven out of the buildings. We sent forward one or two German speaking members of the battalion to shout at the remainder to give themselves up. A group of about 30 came forward almost at once to surrender. Then our own armour appeared to usher forward two companies S Sask R who were to sweep and clear the fields. The tanks went well forward of the infantry with the German speaking lads and obtained large groups of prisoners. One group was of about 153 men and at about 1800 hrs a second group of approximately the same size surrendered. During the afternoon very close to 400 PW were taken. By this time it was obvious that the enemy were withdrawing in strength and that the dangerous time for our battalion was over. From then on we were free of fire except from mortars.[19]

All things considered, the clearance of the two villages that had cost so much Canadian blood over the past few weeks, had ended with the collapse and demoralization of the defenders from I. and III. *Bataillonen, Grenadier-regiment* 1056. Despite their spirited defence during the confusion and chaos of the night, the realization that they were in danger of being trapped behind Canadian lines by a major advance, and the presence of the Crocodiles and the Shermans of Marks's squadron, proved to be too much for troops fighting their first battle.

Lieutenant General Guy Simonds had expected that his troops on the forward objectives would be counterattacked by 1000 hours and, in fact, both the Royal Regiment of Canada and the Royal Hamilton Light Infantry were hit by infantry, tanks and SP guns, with the attack on the latter battalion apparently coming in perhaps as much as a half hour before the second.[20] According to a report prepared by the latter battalion's adjutant, the enemy had attacked viciously after the morning ground mist lifted at about 0800 hours

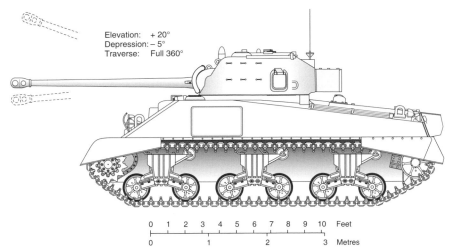

Elevation: + 20°
Depression: − 5°
Traverse: Full 360°

```
0   1   2   3   4   5   6   7   8   9   10   Feet
0            1            2            3    Metres
```

Sherman Vc "Firefly"

The Firefly Vc was based on the Sherman V (M4A4) with the 75 mm gun replaced with the British high-velocity 17-pdr gun. To accommodate this change a hole was flame cut in the turret bustle and the wireless set was moved into an armoured box welded on the outside of the bustle. This provided more room for the larger gun breech and for handling the 17-pdr rounds. The crew was reduced to four by eliminating the assistant driver position together with the hull machine gun, which provided more room for the ammunition load. In Normandy, the Firefly was issued on a scale of one per troop in an armoured regiment.

Country of origin: British conversion of American M4A4
Crew: 4
Length: 25 feet 9 inches
Width: 8 feet 7 inches
Height: 9 feet
Weight: 36.5 tons
Engine: Chrysler multibank
Maximum speed: 25 mph
Range: 100 miles
Armament: 17-pdr Gun Mk IV or VII, 1 x .30 calibre M1919A4, 1 x .50 calibre MG HB M2 in flexible mount on turret
Armour – Maximum: 76 mm
Minimum: 12 mm

with between eight and ten tanks and SP guns and some infantry. They could not have anticipated the strength of the Canadian defence, and withdrew after losing two tanks and an SP, while the defenders had a Sherman and an M10 SP anti-tank gun destroyed and a second Sherman damaged.[21]

This attack, which included infantry from *Grenadierregiment* 1055, apparently came from the southwest. While the history of the Royal Regiment of Canada states that they were attacked at 0830 hours, the brigade operation logs records the first report of any attack at 1020, but this timing may, however, have been far too late. The thrust against the Royals seems to have come from two directions; one thrust, reported as two Panthers and two Tigers with a couple of self-propelled anti-tank guns, came north along the Route Nationale, while the second was mounted from the woods south of

Cramesnil. The Germans enjoyed some initial success and were able to take the carriers of the attached medium machine guns of the Toronto Scottish as well as the battalion's mortar platoon under direct fire. The tanks began to methodically knock out the carriers and spray the area with machine gun fire until several tanks of the Sherbrooke Fusiliers engaged the enemy and drove them off, leaving four German armoured vehicles blazing within the Royals' area. According to an eyewitness account, Captain William Waddell, the FOO from the 4th Field Regiment, RCA, pinpointed the location of the tanks and then sought out a troop of Sherbrooke Shermans and led them into a position where they were able to knock out one or two SP guns and two tanks. A number of prisoners were taken, including the major who had commanded the attack and had been wounded.[22]

Many commentators have claimed that it was Meyer's counterattack on 4th Canadian Armoured Division and 1. *Dywizji Pancernej* waiting on their start lines for the bombing that disorganized them and bought the Germans the time they needed to establish a defence line. In fact, neither division was anywhere near the front lines during the morning of 8 August. Just as it was in Meyer's aggressive nature to exploit tactical advantages to the last degree, so it was in his character to claim more for his troops than was their due, and it is odd that so many historians have failed to subject his claims to the critical scrutiny they apply as a matter of course to Allied commanders.

While things looked serious, Meyer seems to have retained a grip on the realities of the situation and allowed his subordinate commanders ample time to complete their preparations. He, Eberbach and Heinrichs could not have completed their deliberations much before 0730 or 0800 hours, and it would have taken him some time to complete his own plan and prepare and issue his orders, even in an abbreviated form. It would have required several hours for his commanders to complete their own reconnaissances and issue their orders, and for their troops to move into position and prepare for battle. There was sufficient time, for example, for the tank crews of II. *Abteilung, SS-Panzerregiment* 12, to actually move forward from their tanks to examine the ground over which they would attack.[23]

Meyer had met Waldmüller north of Bretteville-le-Rabet and they drove together to Cintheaux, where they assessed the situation and observed large numbers of Allied tanks on both sides of the Caen–Falaise Highway. While they believed these tanks to be an Allied armoured division,[24] we now know that they were the Shermans of 2 Canadian Armoured Brigade and 33 British Armoured Brigade. If Gordon was frustrated, the two German officers were perplexed. Where were the fighter bombers? Why had the Allies not kept going? If they had pushed on, they could have steam-rolled their way to Falaise and the German hold on Normandy would have been lost. When the counterattacking units were given their original tasks, Meyer designated the woods southeast of Garcelles as the final objective. It is interesting that he also decided that the large quarry south of Cintheaux had made a tank attack there unlikely, so took no special preparations other than to ensure that town was defended.[25]

In the meantime, it must have been frustrating for the Canadians, and especially for Lieutenant Colonel Mel Gordon, to stand by as the opportunity slipped away. The first counterattacks had been beaten off, but they could now see indications that the Germans were building up their forces as far north as Cintheaux. Meanwhile, where was 4th Armoured Division? Wyman had told Gordon that it would be here in a few minutes, and that was four hours ago.[26] At this time, at about 1030 hours, Caillouet had not yet been captured and there were parties of Germans holding out around Rocquancourt and elsewhere across the 89. *Infanteriedivision* area. Gordon could only look on as the momentum slipped away because his superiors seemed to be more concerned about tidying up the battlefield than getting on with the battle. He, of course, was not aware that the timing of the bombing, which could not be changed or cancelled, was driving the operation. In fact, Gordon may not even have known of the bombing.

East of the highway, the two forward battalions of 154 Highland Brigade with their supporting armoured regiments were consolidating. In the St. Aignan-de-Cramesnil area, Lieutenant Colonel Douglas Forster, the commanding officer of 1 Northamptonshire Yeomanry, was wounded by shellfire at 0830 hours; about two hours later the unit repulsed a counterattack by

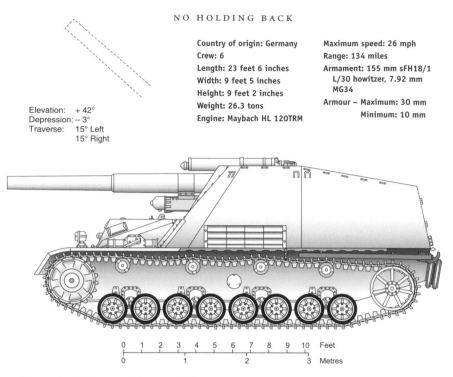

Country of origin: Germany
Crew: 6
Length: 23 feet 6 inches
Width: 9 feet 5 inches
Height: 9 feet 2 inches
Weight: 26.3 tons
Engine: Maybach HL 120TRM

Maximum speed: 26 mph
Range: 134 miles
Armament: 155 mm sFH18/1
  L/30 howitzer, 7.92 mm
  MG34
Armour – Maximum: 30 mm
  Minimum: 10 mm

Elevation: + 42°
Depression: – 3°
Traverse: 15° Left
  15° Right

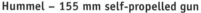

0 1 2 3 4 5 6 7 8 9 10 Feet
0   1   2   3 Metres

Hummel – 155 mm self-propelled gun

Designed to fill the role of a heavy self-propelled howitzer, the Hummel was based on a lengthened hull and chassis of the PzKpfw IV. The engine was moved forward to a central position and the fighting compartment was relocated at the rear. The 155 mm gun fired a 96-pound high-explosive round to a maximum range of 14,490 yards. The Hummel suffered from several design shortcomings, chief of which was its high silhouette due to the 155 mm gun being mounted directly over the engine compartment. Secondly, its ammunition load was restricted to a mere 18 rounds. To alleviate that problem, some Hummels were built as ammunition carriers, which simply involved removing the howitzer and blanking off the aperture with armour plating. The Hummel equipped the heavy SP batteries of panzer divisions.

about a company of infantry and two tanks.[27] During the morning glimpses could be caught of German troop and tank movement south of the British position. Clearly a major counterattack was being prepared and both the Yeomanry and 144 RAC reported enemy contacts at 1136 hours.[28]

In the meantime, the British and Canadians in the forward positions could do little except direct artillery fire onto the German build-up and continue to work on their defences. Once again, the Allied air forces were strangely absent, although the comment by 2 Canadian Armoured Brigade that their attached air support vehicle could do little as the visibility forward was restricted, may provide at least part of the answer.[29] It probably was, if the vehicle had not moved into a position where it could observe to the south, for there soon would be more than enough targets around that morning to satisfy even the keenest Typhoon pilot. Perhaps because of the warning against crossing the bomb line the forward troops stayed in their objective areas, with one exception; at about 1030 hours or slightly later Major Radley-Walters, commanding A Squadron of the Sherbrooke Fusiliers, took his squadron, which was down to no more than 10 or 12 tanks (the troop that had joined up with B Squadron the previous night had not yet returned), and leaving the woods near Point 122,

> skirted the woods to the west until I reached the railway line, then turned south past Jalousie until we reached the rear of Gaumesnil … … The village was small but at its eastern edge near the Caen [-Falaise] Highway was a large château with a large stone and cement wall completely around the property, giving good fire positions to the south and south east.

Here the crews moved their Shermans into concealed positions behind the wall, knocking down parts of it to create firing ports like the battlements of a medieval castle. It was about 1115 hours by the time the squadron was finally in this new position. It is worth noting that, according to Radley-Walters, the village was not occupied other than by a few German stragglers.[30] Meanwhile, across the fields in an orchard southwest of St. Aignan-de-Cramesnil Lieutenant A. James had his troop of Shermans of A Squadron, Northamptonshire Yeomanry, posted covering the Caen–Falaise Road and the approaches from Cintheaux.[31] These British and Canadian tanks formed two sides of a pocket and a mile to the north the tanks of B Squadron 144 RAC made up the bottom.[32] It was a trap, perhaps an unplanned one, but a trap nevertheless, for any German tanks that might venture into it, even more so because the Shermans were well hidden and some at least may have not been spotted by Meyer's troops.

Running west to east, the Allied defensive layout was, by about 1200 on 8 August, in the 2nd Canadian Division area, the Royal Hamilton Light Infantry, with C Company of the Royal Regiment of Canada, in the open ground on perhaps a slight reverse slope north of Point 46 and the Royal Regiment of

Major S.V. Radley-Walters
Radley-Walters of the Sherbrooke Fusilier Regiment receives the Military Cross from Montgomery. "Rad" probably ranked in ability with the best German panzer officers, but he was hobbled by an inferior tank. (NAC/PA 128092)

Canada in the woods around Point 122. There were perhaps two and a half squadrons of Sherbrooke Fusiliers in their area, including Radley-Walters's tanks in the château grounds, with another armoured regiment and the flail regiment a half mile or so behind them in the fortress area. Both battalions also had their own 6-pounder anti-tank guns plus two troops of 17-pounders from the corps anti-tank regiment. The third battalion, the Essex Scottish, had reorganized and would soon occupy its objective at Caillouet, while 5 Brigade and the 1st Hussars were preparing to move on Bretteville-sur-Laize and Quilly.

East of the Route Nationale, 7 Argyll and Sutherland Highlanders held Cramesnil, with two squadrons of 144 RAC in the area of the village, while B Squadron of the regiment was on the high ground to the west, and this squadron had made contact with the Canadians west of the road. To the immediate left of the Argylls, 1 Northamptonshire Yeomanry and 1 Black Watch held St. Aignan-de-Cramesnil, with B Squadron of the Yeomanry providing rear protection and contact with 144 RAC. A and C Squadrons were forward of the village, with the latter in a semi-circle facing east, southeast and south, while A Squadron, down to three troops after the loss of three tanks from Lieutenant Griffith-Jones's troop during the night advance, was in a large orchard facing south with, as we have seen, a troop on the right guarding the Caen–Falaise road.[33] Behind the two forward Scottish battalions, 7 Black Watch with 148 RAC held Garcelles-Secqueville and the woods to its south, while 5 Queen's Own Cameron Highlanders defended the area around

The Master Race
German prisoners
formed up waiting for
the next step in their
march to a POW camp.
By the badges of
rank, it appears that
this group includes a
number of NCOs and
perhaps an officer
at the extreme left.
(NAC/PA 161992)

Lorguichon. These woods near Garcelles-Secqueville, it will be remembered, were Meyer's indicated objective in the plans for his counterattack.

Both 2nd Canadian and 51st Highland Divisions had the support of their own divisional artillery as well as an AGRA. Potentially, as the situation developed, they could expect the support of every gun in 2nd Canadian Corps, although the guns of 4th Armoured Division were just coming into action in new positions south of Rocquancourt. They could also request air strikes but without a cab rank of aircraft waiting overhead the response time would have been about two hours or longer.

While Meyer levelled criticism at Simonds and his corps for not following up on their initial advantage, he also disguised the fact that he was not able to mount a counterattack until several hours after 2nd Canadian Corps seized its forward Phase 1 objectives. Because he had to move into position over a restricted road network under the constant threat of air attack, Meyer was unable to build up his forces until late morning. If he had his forces where Simonds expected them to be, he might have been able to launch a coordinated counterattack earlier in the morning using his own division and the forces from 89. *Infanteriedivision.* That might have achieved some success, and clearly that was Simonds's main concern. As a result of the delay by 1200 Meyer was preparing to attack with a weak infantry battalion, a company of Mk IV tanks, seven or eight Tigers, the two escort companies (small all-arms groups that included anti-tank guns) and a company of SP anti-tank guns against two infantry and two armoured brigades on ground of their own choosing, backed up by a powerful artillery that outgunned the German artillery by at least five to one. While many German counter-attacks against Allied forces had succeeded, these more often than not had been against troops caught in the open or still attempting to reorganize on an objective after their own attack. When the British and Canadians were given the time to bring up their anti-tank guns, coordinate their defences and then lash the attackers with massed artillery fire, the German counter-attacks failed, or at best succeeded only at a terrible cost. As historian Marc Milner put it in his analysis of the Normandy campaign, "it worked, but it wasn't fancy and analysts have carped about it ever since."[34]

From his position on the northern edge of Cintheaux with Waldmüller and Wittmann, the acting-commanding officer of *schwere SS-Panzerabteilung* 101,* Meyer continued to wonder about the Allied inaction. Why were the tanks he could see arrayed across his front doing nothing? Why were there no fighter bombers circling overhead and methodically attacking his troops with rockets and bombs? As he continued to tie up details with his two subordinates, they noticed a large four-engine bomber circling overhead. To their experienced eyes, it was obviously an airborne command post and surely would be followed by others within minutes, although it may have been the aircraft flown by Lieutenant General James Doolittle, the commander of 8 USAAF, who would observe the effects of the bombing.[35]

Meyer was not nicknamed *SchnellMeyer* (literally "Fast Meyer") for nothing; he ordered "an immediate attack" to get his troops near the enemy and thus away from the bombing. In practice "an immediate attack" probably meant in 10 to 20 minutes at the earliest. Most of his troops in fact were in the area of Bretteville-le-Rabet and Estrées-la-Campagne and would be attacking almost straight north. In Cintheaux itself were eight Tigers** of the

---

* Wittmann was the top scoring German tank "ace" of the war with 143 enemy armoured vehicles to his credit. He was a winner of the Knight's Cross and a minor celebrity in Germany.

** There were eight Tigers in the area but only seven attacked, three from the headquarters and four from Number 3 Company. Despite its formidable reputation, the Tiger was mechanically unreliable and the eighth tank well may have been out of action.

headquarters and *Nr. 3 Kompanie* of *schwere SS-Panzerabteilung* 101 and the platoon of three *jagdpanzers* of *Kampfgruppe* Waldmüller. Meyer remembered that he personally talked to Wittmann once again and stressed how critical it was that the counterattack succeed. In response, Wittmann guffawed with boyish laughter and climbed into his Tiger, although members of his battalion staff remarked after the event that he had been nervous and may have joined the attack only because the new company commander was inexperienced.[36] Meyer was unusually reticent in describing these troops' part in the battle other than to allude to Wittmann leading his tanks along with Waldmüller's panzer grenadiers into "the steely inferno."[37]

The approaching bombers were the first wave of a three-wave major effort by 8 USAAF. While Meyer claims that he ordered the troops he was with in Cintheaux to run north into the open fields to escape the hail of bombs that rained down on the village, this was probably pure embellishment.[38] First, this wave of bombers was attacking Bretteville-sur-Laize and St. Sylvain, not Cintheaux, which was not even a target for the heavy bombers. Second, given the large area covered by a heavy bomber attack, an attempt to escape by running a few hundred yards would have been fruitless, and might even have been counter-productive if it meant leaving the protection of trenches and basements to face the hail of bombs in the open, not to mention fire from the British and Canadians.

The focus of the German attack fell on the Northamptonshire Yeomanry and 1 Black Watch south of St. Aignan-de-Cramesnil, although both the Canadian battalions and other units of 154 Highland Brigade also came under heavy shelling and mortaring. Before the counterattack actually moved forward, the Yeomanry were attacked by a most unusual source. Some B-17s on their run to bomb St. Sylvain dropped their sticks of high-explosive bombs across the regimental area. As the bombs rained down, the earth shook, everything went black and stones and dirt showered down across the regimental area. To Trooper Ken Tout and his mates in C Squadron, each bomb set off a minor earthquake,[39] while the unit adjutant, Captain L. Llewellyn, remarked

I was sitting in my tank when I heard a rumbling noise like an express train. Suddenly the tank rocked, everything went completely black and we were smothered by a shower of earth and stones, which continued to rain down on us for some seconds. Everything was covered with dust. I thought the end of the world had come.[40]

As the bombs fell on the two towns, and, inadvertently, the Northamptonshire Yeomanry, the German tanks broke from cover and rolled forward with Wittmann's seven Tigers leading on the left flank. The first report on the Yeomanry radio net electrified the unit; Sergeant Gordon, commanding the lone Firefly in the orchard watching the highway, reported three Tigers moving slowly north in line ahead (single file) along the Caen–Falaise Road at about 1,200 yards range. Captain Thomas Boardman, the second-in-command of A Squadron and erstwhile regimental navigator, came on the net and ordered Gordon to hold fire. Boardman then moved into the orchard and took charge of the engagement. The Tigers seemed to be concentrating on the Canadians, as their turrets were traversed facing to the left. When the range had closed to 800 yards, Boardman gave the order to fire. Sergeant Gordon engaged the rear tank and his gunner, Trooper Elkins, hit it with two rounds and set it on fire. Time, 1240 hours. In this sort of engagement a stationary Sherman was a dead Sherman and Gordon's tank wasted no time reversing into cover. The second Tiger, however, had rapidly traversed to the right and fired three rounds at the disappearing Sherman. Either a near miss from one of these rounds or contact with an overhanging branch dislodged the crew commander's hatch, which crashed down on Gordon's head, dazing him. He dismounted from the tank and was almost immediately wounded by shrapnel, for the position was under heavy shell fire. Lieutenant James ran over to the Firefly and took command. He moved the tank into a new fire position and Trooper Elkins fired a round at the second tank, which exploded. Time, 1247 hours. By this time, the third Tiger was in a panic, scurrying about in an attempt to get away. Captain Boardman peppered away at it with his 75 mm, hitting it in the tracks and bringing it to a halt. At 1252 hours two more shots from Elkins brewed this one as well.[41] This was good shooting by anyone's standards.

Meanwhile across the fields A Squadron of the Sherbrooke Fusiliers had detected the Tigers as they broke cover at Cintheaux. To Major Radley-Walters's recollection, the time was between 1215 and 1230 hours. The visibility was bad as the air was thick with smoke and the Germans were laying down heavy concentrations of artillery and mortar fire. The attack came as a group with five Tigers well spaced with four at the front and the fifth leading a number of Mk IVs and half-tracks and *Jagdpanzers.* One of the Tigers was running close to the highway while two *Jagdpanzers* were driving on the highway itself. As the attacking enemy tanks neared, Radley-Walters recalled,

I just kept yelling, "Hold off! Hold off!" until they got reasonably close. We opened fired at about 500 yards. The lead tank, the one nearest the road, was knocked out. Behind it were a couple of SPs. I personally got one of the SPs right on the Caen–Falaise road.

The other Tigers were engaged not only by my Squadron, but also by two Fireflys from B Squadron that had moved over to the La Jalousie area when the counterattack started. Once we started to fire, the German column turned to the north-east and headed for the wooded area south of St. Aignan [de Cramesnil] … … It is my recollection that we destroyed two Mk IVs before the rear of the German column veered too far to the east…

… When the action was over we claimed the Tiger beside the highway, a second Tiger which was at the rear of the advancing column, two Mk IVs and two SPs.[42]

At the bottom of the pocket, B Squadron of 144 RAC also took the advancing Germans under fire. Subsequently the regiment claimed a Tiger and a Mk IV for two Shermans destroyed.[43] In fact five Tigers, including that of Wittmann, who was killed in this action along with his crew, had been knocked out, three by Trooper Elkins alone, but the total claimed was eight, five by 1 Northamptonshire Yeomanry, two by the Sherbrooke Fusiliers and one by 144 RAC. As in aerial combat, claims nearly always exceeded the actual score. It should be understood that several tanks may have engaged the same target before and, if it had not brewed up or exploded, after it was knocked out. That in itself was a common occurrence and undoubtedly was done by both sides for very obvious reasons, not the least being self-preservation.

In recent years the question of which unit actually killed Wittmann and his crew and destroyed their Tiger has been a matter of controversy. A French civilian who examined his tank a few months after the battle thought that it had been destroyed by a rocket from a Typhoon, while the medical officer of *schwere SS-Panzerabteilung* 101 noted Wittmann's tanks were under heavy 15 cm anti-tank fire [sic]. Other writers claim he fell to Polish or Canadian Shermans. For nearly 20 years, the Northamptonshire Yeomanry have been considered the front runners, but Radley-Walters's account has never been factored into the equation. While the most important matter was that the counterattack was defeated, not who killed Michael Wittmann, an examination of the evidence for the competing claims will be found at Appendix E.

This short, little action, lasting no more than 45 minutes from the time that the first Tigers appeared east of Cintheaux to the end of the German advance up the road, tilted the odds against the counterattack reaching its objectives – the woods south of Garcelles-Secqueville. No matter what kind of spin is put on it, the immutable truth is that Wittmann drove into an ambush. As a result, the action cost the Germans five Tigers and crews they could ill afford to lose. One cannot but question if a double standard has not been applied over the years since 1944. If an Allied tank commander had done something this tactically unsound, it would have told and retold over the years as a typical example of American, British or Canadian tactical incompetence. Wittmann's action, however, has survived in popular lore as an example of courage and audacity; he may have been a dead hero, but the key word is dead, not hero. And that applied not only to him, but also to most of his men.

The left prong of the German counterattack may have failed, but on the centre and right there still was a chance of success. On the extreme right flank *Divisionbegleitkompanie* 12 and a company of *Jagdpanzers* from *SS-Panzerjägerabteilung* 12 was able to move into the small woods midway between St. Sylvain and Robertmesnil, effectively blocking any Allied advance east of St. Aignan-de-Cramesnil.

In the centre, the ground provided excellent covered approaches that led into the Northamptonshire Yeomanry/ Black Watch position. *Kampfgruppe* Waldmüller attempted to force their way into the British position by what essentially was an arc-shaped frontal attack that attempted to overwhelm A and C Squadrons of the Yeomanry. The battle began with tank-on-tank engagements between tanks of roughly similar capability, Shermans and Mk IVs, followed by a series of dismounted assaults by panzer grenadiers. Shortly after the demise of Elkins's third Tiger, a Yeomanry A Squadron tank reported a large number of tanks, estimated as 15 to 20 in number, passing from east to west just forward of the Robertmesnil ridge. Sergeant Gordon's Firefly, now commanded by Lieutenant James, knocked out a Mk IV to go with its three Tigers. Shortly after, this tank was brewed by another Mk IV which methodically knocked out six A Squadron tanks one after the other in short order. Justifiably angry, Major Gray Skelton, the squadron commander, called Sergeant Finney on the radio, "We are not going to let this bastard pick off the Squadron one by one. You go left and I will go right, one of us must get him." He then stalked and killed the Mk IV, but not before it brewed up Finney's Sherman. Captain Boardman also managed to work up to within 200 yards of a Mk IV, which he killed.[44] The British lost tank after tank, but so did the Germans.

On the east of the village, C Squadron of the Yeomanry was also fighting for its life. This squadron was deployed in a semi-circle with No. 2 Troop on the right in contact with A Squadron, No. 1 Troop in the centre and No. 4 Troop on the left. No. 3 Troop formed a reserve with squadron headquarters in the centre of the position. At about 1030 hours No. 2 Troop pushed across the gully that lay to their front to improve its position. Sergeant R. Thompson moved his tank up on the right of a wood from where he could observe Robertmesnil, while the other tanks moved to positions from where they could cover the gully. At 1115 Corporal J. Stanley moved his tank forward to join Thompson, but his tank was put out of action by an anti-tank gun firing from the area of the Robertmesnil farm. This gun, however, had disclosed its position and was destroyed in turn by return fire from virtually every tank that saw its muzzle flash.

When the German attack came in against A Squadron, C Squadron also found itself heavily involved. The engagement had started well. Corporal T. Giles of No. 2 Troop spotted four Mk IVs crossing a gap between two woods, and in another example of brilliant shooting, Trooper E. Wellbelove, his gunner, knocked out the last three. However, another Mk IV, which had been diverted by A Squadron fire, had worked through a woods and took up position behind a small rise, where it found itself on the right rear of No. 2 Troop. It wasted no time in putting the remaining three tanks out of action. At this, Major David Bevan, the C Squadron commander, ordered No. 3 Troop to move over and fill the gap left by the loss of No. 2 Troop. One of its tanks knocked out a Mk IV on arrival although it is unknown if this vehicle was No. 2 Troop's nemesis. Shortly later two SP guns firing from a crest

1,000 yards to the south brewed Captain Kenneth Todd's Sherman but were driven off by return fire. A number of SPs soon made their presence known by opening fire from the ridge. One brewed up the tank of Lieutenant A.W. Faulkner, the troop leader of No. 1 Troop, but Sergeant Sydney Hulme's No. 1 Troop tank was able to kill two of the anti-tank guns, while another SP was destroyed by the squadron second-in-command. Following this engagement, No. 1 Troop was pulled back even with B Squadron. This short but bloody battle had only taken about 45 minutes, from 1300 to 1345 hours.[45]

Just before 1400 hours, the Germans mounted a frontal attack with massed dismounted infantry in line abreast on a front of about 1,000 yards. They were in such strength that they seemed to blacken the standing crops in the fields they were advancing through. The FOO called down artillery fire and the remaining tanks of the two forward Yeomanry squadrons began spraying the enemy with machine gun fire, forcing them to go to ground and attempt to crawl to safety. In the meantime A Squadron was reinforced by two troops of B Squadron. No. 4 Troop of B Squadron moved into the position that been held by Lieutenant James's troop, now all destroyed; no sooner did the troop arrive than one of its tanks knocked out two Mk IVs on a ridge 1,500 yards away.

By 1500 hours the counterattack had shot its bolt and for the rest of the day the Germans were content to shell and mortar the British positions. At the end of the day the Northamptonshire Yeomanry claimed 15 tanks, including five Tigers, and five SP guns, as well as a large number of infantry killed and wounded. In return, it had lost 20 Shermans (including 5 Fireflys) as well as two officers and 10 men killed and 11 officers, including both the commanding officer and the commander of B Squadron, and 40 men wounded.[46] The Black Watch estimated the attackers as 20 tanks and 200 infantry, adding that the Yeomanry had knocked out 11 tanks and inflicted heavy casualties on the infantry. The Highlanders themselves admitted to having lost two officers and 11 men killed and three officers and 43 men wounded by the day-long shelling.[47]

If any event during Operation TOTALIZE can be said to have finally doomed the German hold on the area north of the Laison River, it was the defence of St. Aignan-de-Cramesnil by 1 Northamptonshire Yeomanry and 1 Black Watch. For all their vaunted skill in the coordinated employment of all-arms teams, the Germans had failed to do precisely that while mounting their attacks. If the panzer grenadiers had been able to close with the British position while the tanks were slugging it out, the result might have been quite different. As it was they were caught in the open and proved that the SS camouflage smocks were no more bulletproof than battle dress. Despite the skill and courage of these German soldiers, the feckless manner in which they were thrown into battle meant that the attempt to capture the Garcelles-Secqueville woods ultimately failed, a matter which Meyer, characteristically, omitted to mention in his memoirs. On the other hand, the Germans were in a strong position to delay any further advance by the Allies east of St. Aignan-de-Cramesnil, and, as we shall see, that is exactly what they did.

The reader may recall that both of the Phase 1 Divisions were also to be responsible for expanding their objective areas; in the case of 51 Highland Division, 153 Highland Brigade was to clear the large wooded area east of Secqueville-la-Campagne as far as La Hogue. This was accomplished by a series of single battalion attacks supported by tanks, Crocodiles and artillery and heavy mortars, with the enemy only offering any degree of resistance in Secqueville-la-Campagne, where 65 prisoners from *Grenadierregiment* 1055 were taken and a number of other Germans killed, the remainder of the garrison withdrawing to the east.[48]

On the other flank 5 Canadian Infantry Brigade supported by the Shermans of the 1st Hussars, less Major D'Arcy Marks's squadron which was mopping up the defenders of Fontenay-le-Marmion, was ordered to capture Bretteville-sur-Laize, thus blocking the approach from west of the Orne into the corps area. While the operation was postponed until 1600 because the artillery was engaged in supporting 6 Brigade in completing its capture of May-sur-Orne and Fontenay-le-Marmion, it involved two battalions, the Calgary Highlanders directed on the village itself, while Le Régiment de Maisonneuve attacked Quilly.[49] The latter operation involved an advance across open fields for some 2,000 yards, and as the artillery had set the crops afire, the Montreal unit's commanding officer described it as a dramatic attack from a "flaming desert."

The Maisonneuves had been shelled during their march south from their positions securing the start line near Troteval Farm through Rocquancourt and on to the objective, where they then came under fire from the west side

After the battle
A street in St. André-sur-Orne, 9 August 1944. The damage was typical of the condition of many liberated towns in Normandy. A knocked-out German tank is to the left of the jeep. (NAC/PA 145562)

of the river. The objective itself was lightly held and a few snipers and the single machine gun encountered were soon silenced, but a pesky *Nebelwerfer* then opened up from a position behind a stone wall until it was silenced by artillery fire. When the area was cleared by the Maisonneuves, two damaged and one abandoned *vaches** were captured.[50] In the meantime, the Calgary Highlanders advanced in open order down a long slope and into Bretteville-sur-Laize, taking it without incident. Unfortunately, the commanding officer then began to have second thoughts and later that evening convinced the brigade commander that he should withdraw to positions back up the slope. While attempting thus to redeploy, the Highlanders were caught by shellfire and needlessly suffered heavy casualties, which the official history puts at 14 killed and 37 wounded.[51]

---

* The *Nebelwerfer* was called the "moaning minnie" for the sound its round made in flight; however, this did not translate into French, so the Maisonneuves referred to it as *la vache*, the cow, for its sound was not unlike the mooing of cattle.

PART FOUR

FROM THE JAWS
OF VICTORY

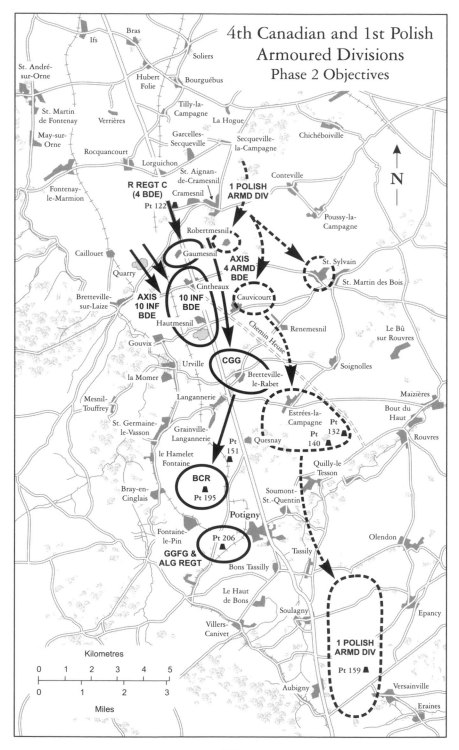

4th Canadian and 1st Polish Armoured Divisions
Phase 2 Objectives

N

Ifs
Bras
Soliers
St. André-sur-Orne
Hubert Folie
Bourguébus
St. Martin de Fontenay
Verrières
Tilly-la-Campagne
La Hogue
May-sur-Orne
Garcelles-Secqueville
Secqueville-la-Campagne
Chichéboiville
Rocquancourt
Lorguichon
St. Aignan-de-Cramesnil
Conteville
Fontenay-le-Marmion
R REGT C (4 BDE)
Cramesnil
1 POLISH ARMD DIV
Poussy-la-Campagne
Pt 122
Robertmesnil
Caillouet
Gaumesnil
AXIS 4 ARMD BDE
St. Sylvain
Quarry
Cintheaux
AXIS 10 INF BDE
10 INF BDE
Cauvicourt
St. Martin des Bois
Bretteville-sur-Laize
Hautmesnil
Chemin Heuse
Renemesnil
Le Bû sur Rouvres
Gouvix
Urville
CGG
Bretteville-le-Rabet
Soignolles
la Morer
Langannerie
Maizières
Mesnil-Touffrey
Estrées-la-Campagne
Bout du Haut
St. Germaine-le-Vasson
Grainville-Langannerie
Pt 132
le Hamelet Fontaine
Pt 151
Quesnay
Pt 140
Rouvres
Bray-en-Cinglais
BCR
Pt 195
Quilly-le-Tesson
Soumont-St.-Quentin
Potigny
Fontaine-le-Pin
Pt 206
Olendon
GGFG & ALG REGT
Bons Tassilly
Tassily
Le Haut de Bons
Villers-Canivet
Soulagny
Epancy
1 POLISH ARMD DIV
Pt 159
Aubigny
Versainville
Eraines

Kilometres

0 1 2 3 4 5

0 1 2 3

Miles

250

CHAPTER TWELVE

PHASE 2 COMMENCES

*"If you have no opposition you must push on. I want to get
all the rest forward as far as possible. We have air support.
Where are enemy tanks reported? Outflank and push on."*

BRIGADIER LESLIE BOOTH, 4 CANADIAN ARMOURED BRIGADE

For half a century after he made it, Simonds's decision to compress his plan for Operation TOTALIZE from three phases to two and especially to launch his two armoured divisions "side by side" has been the source of unrelenting criticism of his generalship. Much of this criticism has echoed Major General George Kitching's comments in his memoirs that both he and *Generał brygada* Stanisław Maczek,[1] the commander of 1. *Dywizji Pancernej,* had asked Simonds to extend their frontages to give them room to manoeuvre. While Kitching did not mention where and when he and Maczek requested the alteration in plans, in other correspondence he indicated that this was at 1000 on 7 August.[2] According to Kitching, Simonds refused as he would have had to widen the objective area for one of his Phase 1 divisions. Kitching went on to say that this not only restricted the room available for both divisions to manoeuvre but allowed the Germans to concentrate their force against the single thrust.[3]

Unfortunately few historians who have written on the subject have bothered to analyse Kitching's criticisms, particularly the contradictions in his argument. Reginald Roy, for example, seems to have accepted his argument that neither general was particularly happy with the new plan which gave both an extremely narrow front. While he did not say so explicitly, Roy left the impression in his 1984 book on the Normandy campaign that both divisions were to attack together down the Route Nationale, but that in the original plan there had been sufficient room for 4th Canadian Armoured Division to manoeuvre as it was the only division attacking down that road.[4] John English also seems to have accepted the same premise for he noted that the 4th Division frontage was only 1,000 yards and, between Gaumesnil and the quarry to the west, it was even more narrow.[5] The authors of the Royal Canadian Armoured Corps history have fallen into the same trap, claiming that 1. *Dywizji Pancernej* was substituted for the 3rd Canadian Infantry Division in an advance on the east side of the Route Nationale.[6] All these commentators were unfortunately mistaken as can be seen by referring to the comparison of tasks in the original and revised plans in Chapter 4 above.

At 1000 hours on 6 August Simonds gave revised orders for TOTALIZE at a conference at his headquarters because he had amended his plan when it became clear that 1. *SS-Panzerdivision* had been replaced by 89. *Infanterie-division* in the forward position. At this time, however, Simonds still believed, based on the available intelligence, that he would be faced with one or two SS panzer divisions on the Bretteville-sur-Laize–St. Sylvain position.[7]

Despite the change in the number of phases, essentially there was no change in the route, tasks and the final objective assigned to 4th Canadian Armoured Division – that formation would have to control and cross the same piece of ground, no matter the number of phases. Turning to General Keller's 3rd Division, it can be seen that there was no reference in the first plan to this formation advancing on the east side of the Route Nationale, and certainly not at the same time that 4th Armoured Division was attacking south along it, as is alleged in the Royal Canadian Armoured Corps history.[8] Nor was there at any time, as Kitching claimed in his memoirs, a plan to use 3rd Division to punch a hole in the German lines for 4th Division to pass through.[9] While Simonds had chaired a conference with his division and armoured brigade commanders at his headquarters at 1500 hours on 3 August to discuss TOTALIZE,[10] and it is possible but unlikely that this option was discussed, the orders issued on 5 August reflected the concept and tasks that were in the outline plan presented to Crerar verbally on 31 July and confirmed in writing the next day. In fact this plan specifically included the phrase "Following in rear of 4th Canadian Armoured Division" in the tasks assigned to Keller's formation.[11]

The controversial point is the role assigned to 1. *Dywizji Pancernej*. The confirmatory notes regarding the revised plan did not specifically assign a route to this formation, other than to pass through 51st Highland Division and go directly to its final objective. It has been assumed by many who have written about TOTALIZE, especially after noting Kitching's comments about too narrow frontages, that the two armoured divisions attacked together with the Route Nationale as the boundary between them. Nothing was further from the truth. As shown in Maczek's report on the battle, the Polish formation advanced southwards past the east side of the 154 Highland Brigade area with an aim of capturing the ground south of Estrées-la-Campagne across to point 140.[12] However, there were two places where the axes narrowed. In his 1947 lecture to the BAOR battlefield tour Simonds drew attention to the first, between Cintheaux and Robertmesnil,[13] and while the gap was quite narrow, there was room to manoeuvre on either side of these villages. What Maczek may have been referring to is where the two divisions' axes coincided south of Bretteville-le-Rabet. Here the 4th Division was nearing its final objective, while 1. *Dywziji Pancernej* still had to move past Quesnay and Quilly-le-Tesson, then swing south past Potigny and move south along the Route Nationale to its final objective. Essentially 1. *Dywziji Pancernej* had to arrive at Quesnay in sufficient strength – that is, without losing too many tanks and infantry – to be able to advance another six miles to its final objective. Simonds had given Maczek at least two extra brigade-sized objectives, in other words areas that could be defended by up to a battalion, to move across. It would not have been an easy task for an experienced armoured division; it might have been too much for one fighting its first battle, even with soldiers as determined to kill Germans as were the Poles.

What if Simonds had agreed to the request to widen the front from Kitching and Maczek? The object as given to him was to break through the German defences astride the Route Nationale. Presumably he and Crerar had discussed this and were comfortable with it in view of the overall Allied objectives. Remember that, at this time, Montgomery was thinking in terms of First Canadian Army and Second British Army linking up near Falaise to cut off the German forces to the west. With the Germans sandwiched between 21 Army Group on the north and the American armies to the south, the Allies would then swing west and advance to the Seine in the "long envelopment" that formed part of the original SHAEF strategy for the Normandy campaign. If, for argument's sake, Simonds had been predisposed to accept this request, how could the frontage have been widened for the Phase 2 divisions? The only possible variation would have been for Maczek's formation to head southeast from Soignolles to Rouvres, Olendon and onto Soulagny and Point 159. It was a possible, if unlikely, option given the object of the operation and Simonds's propensity for narrow frontages and concentration of force.

Apparently the two generals had also questioned the decision to wait for the Phase 2 bombing before launching their armoured divisions. They were apprehensive that the momentum of the attack might be lost in the eight hours between the capture of the Phase 1 objectives and H-Hour for Phase 2. Furthermore, Kitching and Maczek argued this pause would allow the Germans to collect their forces in sufficient strength to halt the attack.[14] In retrospect they were correct, but at the time the objection was raised, shortly after 1000 hours on 7 August, they could not have known that 1. *SS-Panzerdivision* was moving west to join the Mortain offensive. Simonds also had no idea at this time that this move was underway, and whether or not he was let down by his intelligence staff, he was prepared to accept a delay based on three premises:

a. that the two attacking Phase 1 divisions might still have had to fight hard for their final objectives and this might not be completed until late in the morning;

b. that the bombing would render the German defenders of the Phase 2 objectives temporarily unable to oppose the advance; and

c. that the two Phase 2 armoured divisions would be able to move forward quickly before the Germans recovered from the effects of the bombing.

It should be emphasized, and re-emphasized, that Simonds had watched the virtual destruction of three British armoured divisions attacking in daylight in Operation GOODWOOD. That experience had surely coloured his thinking and actions during TOTALIZE.

Once the two generals had presented their case to Simonds, and he had declined to alter his new Phase 2 plan, it fell to them to get on with it. In the case of 4th Canadian Armoured Division, which had fewer adjustments to make than 1. *Dywizji Pancernej*, Kitching had decided to capture the area up to Hautmesnil with 10 Infantry Brigade and at the same time launch 4

Kitching and Simonds
Major General George Kitching, 4th Canadian Armoured Division (left), with Lieutenant General Guy Simonds in England a few months before the invasion. The nearby gaggle of headquarters-type troops would probably have preferred to be somewhere else. (NAC/PA 132650)

The Polish general
Generał brygada S. Maczek, 1. *Dywizji Pancernej,* fields the usual penetrating questions from Allied war correspondents, while two of his officers view the proceedings with the slightly bemused mien of combatants towards a necessary evil. (NAC/PA 129199)

Armoured Brigade onto the final objective, the Point 206 feature. The infantry brigade would then follow along, advancing through Bretteville-le-Rabet and onto Point 180–Point 195–Point 206 to relieve the armour for exploitation. Unfortunately, after his complaints about being forced to attack on too narrow a frontage, Kitching decided to attack with Jefferson's 10 Brigade right of the Route Nationale and Booth's 4 Armoured Brigade on the left, thus narrowing the frontage available to each. Both brigades would close up to the corps start line by first light on 8 August and, after the field regiments of the divisional artillery had deployed in the area of Rocquancourt, move forward to the division start line behind the Phase 1 objectives.

For this operation 10 Brigade with the South Alberta Regiment attached, but less the Algonquin Regiment which was detached to 4 Armoured Brigade, would pass through 4 Infantry Brigade and capture Cintheaux and Hautmesnil, including the quarry to the south of it.[15] It was a straightforward task for an infantry brigade and well within its capabilities, even with only two infantry battalions. While this was going on, 4 Armoured Brigade would advance to the final objective in a three-phased operation. In the first phase the Canadian Grenadier Guards with the Lake Superior Regiment, 96th Anti-Tank Battery and a squadron of flails was to secure Bretteville-le-Rabet. In the next phase the British Columbia Regiment was to move onto point 195 and finally the Governor General's Foot Guards was to capture point 206.[16] The Algonquins, mounted in half-tracks and reinforced with a battery of anti-tank guns and a troop of flame-throwing Churchill tanks, were available to support the armoured regiments and to clear and hold the final objectives. The corps armoured car regiment, the 12th Manitoba Dragoons, had been placed under command of 4th Armoured Division. Its regimental headquarters and D Squadron were to follow 4 Armoured Brigade, while B Squadron was to do the same behind 10 Brigade so that, in the case of a breakthrough, they could pass through the forward troops and fan out across the front to screen the drive south.[17]

So much for the plan but, unfortunately, the battle procedure used by 4th Armoured Division in what was to be its first major operation broke down in 4 Armoured Brigade. While the blame for this has been attributed to Simonds's decision to change his plan, this seems to be more of a case of looking for an excuse to let Brigadier E.L. Booth,[18] the commander of 4

Armoured Brigade, off the hook than a valid reason.[19] The major failure was in not issuing orders and passing information to subordinate levels of command in a timely manner, so that they were unable to make proper use of the time available; furthermore the other formations in 2nd Canadian Corps were all able to cope with the change in plans. In this regard both Booth and Lieutenant Colonel W.W. Halpenny, the commanding officer of the Canadian Grenadier Guards, erred badly. General Kitching briefed his brigade commanders at 1900 hours on 6 August, and he noted that 10 Brigade began preparations for TOTALIZE on the morning of the 7th.[20]

It is possible that this delay in the armoured brigade may have been no more than a reflection of the current published doctrine that cautioned commanders against wasting their subordinates' time by issuing orders too early. Under the heading "Time of Issue of Orders," readers were advised "to avoid rousing individuals unnecessarily from sleep if the order can be issued at a later hour without prejudice to the success of the operation," in what can only be termed a highly unrealistic example.[21] Clearly whoever had allowed that to be appear in an official manual had a rather tenuous grip on reality; what is astonishing is that an officer like Booth, who had considerable command experience in Sicily and Italy, might have bought into such utter hogwash. Certainly this was not the practice in 2 Armoured Brigade, where the units were given ample time to study a problem and rehearse their roles. Major E.A.C. Amy, the commander of No. 1 Squadron of the Canadian Grenadier Guards, who had served in Italy, later noted that good deployment procedures are absolutely essential, and that both 4 Armoured Brigade and his regiment had such procedures in place, but failed to follow them in any way during TOTALIZE.[22]

He went on to recount how on the morning of 7 August, as was normal, he and his fellow members in the regiment stood to at first light. At that time they had no idea they were to be going into battle the next morning. The Grenadier Guards' war diary started its account of the day's activities by noting that Brigadier Booth briefed his commanding officers and unit intelligence officers at 1100 hours or no less than 16 hours after he had attended Kitching's Orders Group. If the sequence of events as detailed in the war diary is to believed, the details of the brigade plan were known by Halpenny by noon, but nothing more than a warning of an impending move and the

Briefing
Members of 1 Protective Troop, Headquarters Squadron 4 Canadian Armoured Brigade, are briefed on Phase 2 of TOTALIZE. Unfortunately the troops who were ordered to spearhead the advance did not receive the same information. (NAC/PA 131364)

information that they would be going into action on the next day was passed on to the squadrons. Later in the afternoon, the Grenadiers redeployed to another location closer to their assembly area. On arrival, the squadron commanders were immediately called to regimental headquarters, where, for the first time, they were issued with maps marked with boundaries, code words, etc. In Amy's opinion, "all was confusion in the unit": the new area had been bombed heavily and, in any case, none of the squadron commanders were sure of their present location. Furthermore he had been issued an enormous 1:25,000 scale map of the area of operations, which he was certain he would be unable to manage in his tank turret. It is important to emphasize that the squadron commanders had no idea where their troops were now located and absolutely no way of passing on any of this information to them.[23]

Finally, after attending what seems to have been an unnecessary second brigade orders group held by Booth at 1800 hours, Lieutenant Colonel Halpenny issued his orders for the operation at what the Grenadier war diary said was 2200 hours. However, it must have been later, or his orders went on for far too long, for it was interrupted by the roar of the Phase 1 bombers passing overhead. Someone panicked and extinguished the lights, which threw the group into confusion. By the time the colonel finished it was after dark, which fixes the time as well past 2300 hours, and the squadron commanders had to stumble around looking for their squadrons, and then assemble their troop leaders and give orders. Many, if not all, had only a vague idea of what was planned for the next morning and what his particular role was to be. As the historian of the Lake Superior Regiment put it in his description of the orders group, all could now appreciate the meaning and significance of the familiar phrase, the fog of war. For Major Ned Amy, who was to command the vanguard, his task was not made easier, after he finally did manage to find his squadron, by the need to maintain blackout conditions so only small, shaded lights could be used, and by the noise of a nearby artillery regiment firing on the barrage which made even conversing by shouting in people's ears very difficult. As it was well nigh impossible for his troop leaders to either study the 1:25,000 map or hear what he had to say, Amy quite rightly described his orders group as "a shambles." As the

Lieutenant Colonel W. Walton Halpenny
Halpenny, the Commanding Officer of the Canadian Grenadier Guards, was forced to compress his battle procedure unsuccessfully because of the delay in issuing orders by 4 Canadian Armoured Brigade.

Major E.A.C. Amy
"Ned" Amy of the Canadian Grenadier Guards led the vanguard of the Canadian Phase 2 advance without receiving timely orders or being able to brief his troops. He assumed command of the regiment in February 1945.

regiment was to move off at 0030 hours, he limited his orders to an order of march and a direction to mount up and follow him. Amy had been told he was allotted a company of the motor battalion, a FOO, a section of the regimental reconnaissance troop, a troop of anti-tank guns and a section of engineers. Due to the darkness and the confusion, none of these supporting troops arrived to join his squadron until well after first light.[24] It was not an auspicious start for an officer who had been ordered to be prepared to lead the 4 Armoured Brigade vanguard across the corps start line at 0500 hours.

The move forward itself was *pro forma*, thanks in no small part to the movement light and the Bofors tracers indicating the axis for 2 Armoured Brigade group. However as his squadron was moving into its forming-up place near the corps start line, trouble struck. Lieutenant Douglas Macdonald of Amy's squadron, whose tank was leading the brigade, remembered that

at one point they [unnamed] told us to stop and park "over there." I climbed out of the turret to direct the driver from the ground but not before telling him to advance. But for him having trouble with his gears I would have been a goner because the delay gave me time to get 10-15 feet ahead of the tank. It moved six inches onto a mine. Socket [sic] completely disappeared along with two treads from the side I jumped off. Small piece in my finger but radio silence so no MO [visit to Medical Officer].

It should be remembered that two tanks of 2 Armoured Brigade had also hit mines in the same area before they crossed the same start line. Other tanks were guided through a position of Le Régiment de Maisonneuve in the darkness, always a frightening experience for the infantry and one that provoked angry (and largely unprintable) shouts in French.[25]

As we have seen, Simonds had reported to First Canadian Army at about 0615 hours on 8 August that 4th Canadian Armoured Division and 1. *Dywizji Pancernej* were to be started forward to infiltrate as far as possible prior to their assembly for Phase 2.[26] At this time, while 2 Armoured Brigade group was still consolidating on its forward objectives and 5 Brigade was involved in clearing the routes – what the orders termed "mopping up" – 4th Canadian Armoured Division began its move forward, or at least Simonds thought it had.

Rocquancourt was reported to be firmly in Canadian hands at 0700 hours on 8 August, but in fact it was not finally completely cleared until shortly after noon. Furthermore there still were many Germans lurking in the farms and copses outside the village who would have to be killed or captured. That was not apparently clear when the leading troops of 4th Canadian Armoured Division, the reconnaissance parties of the three field regiments of the divisional artillery, were ordered to move forward to prepare their new gun areas in the area of that village. As they did so, they observed battles between German and Canadian troops attempting to mop up the area, while their new gun areas were being shelled from three directions. They themselves became the targets of sniper fire from Rocquancourt, and German anti-tank guns displayed an unhealthy interest in any vehicles that ventured onto higher ground. Nevertheless, under mortar and small-arms fire the preparation of the gun positions began and was well underway, but then was cancelled as the areas were deemed to be too exposed. As a result the deployment of the guns was put off until new positions were selected and prepared. The German resistance had imposed so much delay that the last regiment, 15 Field, did not report ready until 1400 hours. In fact, the gunners were forced to act as infantry and clear the areas adjacent to the gun positions of enemy, one battery capturing more than 100 prisoners.[27] This, of course, also did little to clear the way for 4 Armoured Brigade and 10 Brigade to move forward. So much for the theory that the armoured divisions should have been unleashed early in the morning to take advantage of the momentum of the breakthrough.

While one may question if the senior commanders of 4th Canadian Armoured Division might not have been able to find a way forward for the two brigades, it also appears that Major General Charles Foulkes of 2nd Canadian Infantry Division had become fixated on tidying up his area and getting the Essex Scottish onto its objective at Caillouet at the expense of expediting the passage of the armoured division. It might well have been preferable to picquet May-sur-Orne and Fontenay-le-Marmion and delay the capture of Bretteville-sur-Laize, to concentrate on clearing routes forward for 4th Division. Later commentators may have hit the mark, but they were aiming at the wrong target altogether, when they criticized the armoured division for not bypassing strongpoints, at least in this part of the battle.[28]

As a result, 4 and 10 Brigades spent a long, frustrating morning strung out on the road north of Rocquancourt waiting for the village and the ridge it sat on to be cleared. While 10 Brigade was to pass through or close to the village, 4 Armoured Brigade was to have swung onto the RN, following the route taken by 8 Reconnaissance Regiment. In fact the advance did not resume until after 1200 hours (the operations log of Headquarters 4 Armoured Brigade logged "Rocquancourt now clear. You can get cracking," at 1224 hours) but even then, only limited progress was made. At least some of this may have been attributable to the fact that Gaumesnil had not yet been cleared. However, as we have seen, that village, really a collection of buildings near a château, lay on the far side of the bomb line and 2nd Canadian Infantry Division had been cautioned not to capture it until after the Phase 2 bombing was completed at 1355 hours. As this also was H-Hour for the Canadian Grenadier Guards to cross the start line, a horrendous tactical muddle promptly resulted. At 1315 hours, the 2nd Division logged a message from 4th Armoured Division that it would now capture Gaumesnil,[29] and at 1515 hours 2nd Canadian Corps logged a report from Phantom Signals* that 10 Brigade was attacking Gaumesnil at 1430 hours; but this did not happen and the original plan came back into force.[30] At 1400 hours the Royal Regiment of Canada was ordered to occupy the village, A and D Companies moved into Gaumesnil at 1530 hours and the battalion reported it had cleared and consolidated the place at 1700 hours.[31]

Why did it take so long to capture what was a largely enemy-free collection of buildings and orchards that had grown up around a château? First, there is the obvious point that any attack could not start until after 1355 hours when the bombing ended, or that was the plan. Also, ripe as the little hamlet may have been for the plucking, this could not have been known by Lieutenant Colonel John Anderson, commanding the Royal Regiment of Canada. Therefore, he would have rightly treated his task as another battalion attack against unknown opposition. One of his companies had gone astray during the night move and was still with the Royal Hamilton Light Infantry. This meant that he could employ no more than two companies in the initial stages of the task if he was to maintain any sort of a reserve, which was all the more reason for Anderson to be prudent.

---

* Phantom Signals was a unit designed to provide up-to-date information to higher headquarters about current operations without the delays caused by passing messages through intermediate layers of command.

Returning to the sequence of events, Anderson would have issued orders including tasks and the H-Hour of the attack to his company commanders, supporting arms representatives and the like, and this may well have taken place before 1355 hours. After that he would have expected them to get on with the job, which included personal reconnaissances by the company commanders. In fact, Major Radley-Walters of the Sherbrookes recalled meeting these officers in his position on the château grounds when they came forward to take a look at the terrain they would advance over and at their objectives.[32] By the time they had returned to Point 122, briefed their platoon commanders and allowed them time for their own reconnaissance and orders, it would have been close to 1500 hours before the Royals were in a position to move on Gaumesnil. It all this seems slow to the casual reader, it should be remembered that all movement was on foot, and the reconnaissance close to enemy positions was often done by crawling. It perforce took time, but on the other hand the "move now, orders later" school of tactics rarely, if ever, worked against the *Wehrmacht*. And finally, to secure even as small a place as Gaumesnil took time, for in clearing the hamlet each and every room in each and every building, be it a château or a chicken coop, had to be physically checked.

Unfortunately, the delay was fatal. If any one thing can be said to have doomed Phase 2 of TOTALIZE, it was the failure of 2nd Canadian Corps Headquarters to have realized that by including Gaumesnil as a Phase 1 objective, while arranging to have it captured by 2nd Canadian Infantry Division after the Phase 2 bombing, or at the same time as the vanguard of 4th Canadian Armoured Division crossed its start line, the result would only be confusion and delay. Since Gaumesnil lay south of the safety line for the bombing, it probably should have been made a Phase 2 objective. In any case, the result was that the Germans had several hours grace to reinforce their defences south of Hautmesnil, which became the rock on which TOTALIZE foundered. It was a fundamental error that did not reflect well on Simonds and his staff – in the army jargon of the time, it was bloody poor staff work.

As the afternoon of 8 August wore on, for reasons that will become apparent later, the tone of the radio transmissions from Brigadier Leslie Booth of 4 Armoured Brigade to the Lieutenant Colonel Halpenny of the Canadian Grenadier Guards became more and more frantic, rising to the near-hysterical in tone. At 1504 hours: "If you have no opposition you must push on. I want to get all the rest forward as far as possible. We have air support. Where are enemy tanks reported? Outflank and push on." At 1617: "You are reporting no opposition so push on. If there is opposition then I should know about it. By pass any opposition the momentum must be carried on." At 1700: "Advance must continue immediately." At 1702: "What is hold up? Push them, on the hour, phase 2 [presumably of the 4 Armoured Brigade plan] in 3 hours time – I want phase 1 in 1 hour – no opposition in front, yet the going is very slow. I'm not waiting any longer. I want you to move fast."[33]

I n the meantime the bombing had come and gone hours before. The 8 USAAF plan was neither complicated nor confusing. Its heavy bombers were organized in three "bombardment divisions," two of which, the 1st and 3rd, were equipped with B-17 Flying Fortresses, while the 2nd Division flew B-24 Liberators.[34] For this mission, only the 1st and 3rd Bombardment Divisions were tasked, although six GEE-H-equipped* Liberators for pathfinder duties from the 2nd Bombardment Division were placed under operational control of the 3rd Division. Unlike Bomber Command, the Americans flew in tight formations designed to act as a defensive "box" against fighter attacks and to deliver a concentrated bomb pattern on the target. This formation had another purpose. Over time during a "prolonged period of intensive strategic operations" the standard of experience and training of the crews had deteriorated due both to casualties and to the policy wherein a crew had to "only" complete 30 missions before it rotated back to the United States. As a result, crews were briefed to maintain formation at all costs and to release their bombs in concert when the lead aircraft, flown by an experienced crew, was seen to drop its bomb load.

The Americans had planned to bomb using combat wing formations because the "nature, size and shape of the targets were well suited to this tactic and because only a few wings would have been necessary to make the attack."** Unfortunately, when it was realized that the northern half of the

---

* A British electronic navigation system designed to enable pathfinders to accurately locate their targets.

** A combat wing was the level of command between a bomb group and a bombardment division. Using wing formations probably would have increased both the accuracy and the concentration of the bombing.

target was to be bombed first because of friendly troops advancing towards that area, it became necessary to group the bombers in boxes of 12 or 13 aircraft each – 55 boxes in all. It seems there were not enough experienced crews available to lead all of these boxes, which may have contributed to what followed. It seems unfortunate that 8 USAAF was a late substitution after having been taken off the mission on 5 August by Air Chief Marshal Arthur Tedder, Eisenhower's deputy supreme commander, and thus excluded from much of the detailed planning. Crerar and Simonds might have agreed to a simultaneous bombing of Target 8 if the realities had been explained to them. After all, 5 or 10 or even 30 minutes difference in bombing is not what Simonds had in mind when he asked for a barrage-like carpet of bombs advancing in front of his armour south along the Route Nationale. One must conclude that the air force planners got caught up in the literal interpretation of the wording of the request, and not the intent of the originator.

As can be seen from the timings, the bombing was to take place in two formations. The first, which was further subdivided into two raids tasked for Targets 6, 7 and 8, would pass over the target area for 29 minutes from 1226 to 1255 hours. The second, and smaller, wave would hit Targets 8 and 9 from 1335 to 1355 hours. In all 678 or 681 B-17s (accounts differ) were despatched on the missions, of which 497 actually dropped 764.8 tons of high explosive and 723 tons of fragmentation bombs – or roughly three tons per aircraft.

The Americans took off from England, soared in great sweeping circles like so many hunting eagles until they had assembled into their boxes, and then flew southwest over the Atlantic before turning back to cross over the French coast. The bomb run was made parallel to the Canadian front so the aircraft approached from west to east, starting their approach at Vire and continuing over the targets and back to England. Unfortunately, this route also brought them parallel to the German front line, exposing them for a long time to enemy anti-aircraft fire, especially since the bombing altitude was lower than usual. The unfortunate result was that German flak shot down ten bombers and damaged a further 294 aircraft to varying degrees, an incredible figure. Whatever might be said about the American aircrews' lack of training and experience, which after all was beyond their control, no one should question the courage of these young airmen. The disorganization caused by the anti-aircraft fire as well as the haze and low clouds and the smoke and

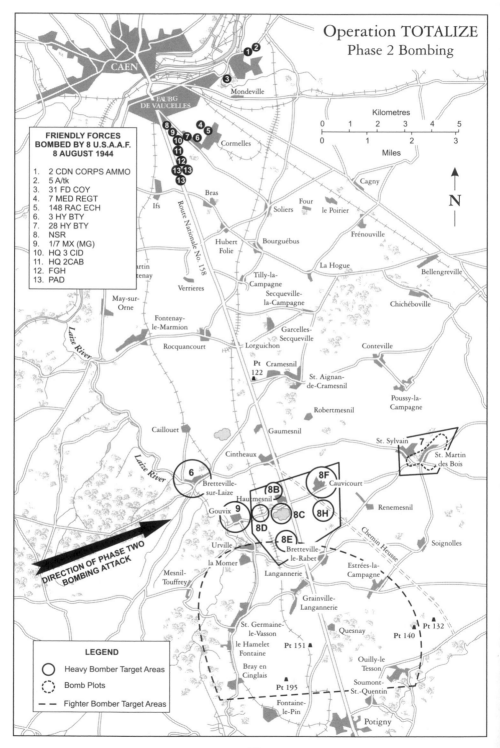

Operation TOTALIZE
Phase 2 Bombing

**FRIENDLY FORCES
BOMBED BY 8 U.S.A.A.F.
8 AUGUST 1944**

1. 2 CDN CORPS AMMO
2. 5 A/tk
3. 31 FD COY
4. 7 MED REGT
5. 148 RAC ECH
6. 3 HY BTY
7. 28 HY BTY
8. NSR
9. 1/7 MX (MG)
10. HQ 3 CID
11. HQ 2CAB
12. FGH
13. PAD

Kilometres
0 1 2 3 4 5

0 1 2 3
Miles

N

DIRECTION OF PHASE TWO
BOMBING ATTACK

LEGEND

◯ Heavy Bomber Target Areas

◌ Bomb Plots

- - - Fighter Bomber Target Areas

dust from preceding attacks meant that the red smoke fired by 23 Field Regiment (SP), the yellow smoke burned for recognition purposes and the flares dropped by the Pathfinders could not be identified. As a consequence, the second wave was scattered and three of the 55 boxes dropped their bombs on friendly troops, one on British troops in the area of Thury-Harcourt, and the others on British, Canadian and Polish troops south of Caen.[35]

While other Fortresses droned through the flak to drop their bombs behind the German lines, a 12-plane formation veered off from its run and headed northeast towards Caen and the coast. This attracted the attention of Captain J.C. (Jamie) Stewart, a tall, athletic 24-year-old troop commander in 55 Battery of the 19th Army Field Regiment (SP), who had dismounted from his OP tank to chat with the officers of Major H.A. "Snuffy" Smith's* No. 3 Squadron of the Grenadier Guards to which Stewart was attached as a FOO. The squadron, which was second in the order of march behind Amy's No. 1 Squadron, was halted in cover waiting for the order to move forward. It was a warm afternoon and Stewart was enjoying a leisurely smoke with his comrades when he saw the bombs fall from the Fortresses and land in the southern suburbs of Caen. It was a shocking sight and one which observers could not comprehend. Stewart was sickened. After all, why would the Americans bomb our own troops? The question kept running through their minds: how had the Germans managed to capture all those Flying Fortresses?[36]

Indeed, other troops were asking the same question. The historian of the Algonquin Regiment of 10 Brigade, who fought as a major in TOTALIZE, wrote of the "belief, quite generally held that German intruders, in captured Fortresses, had joined the stream for a surprise bombing"[37] while in the North Shore Regiment of 8 Infantry Brigade, which saw a "cloud of dust, smoke and fire rolling toward them," the generally held impression was that "either the Germans were using captured American planes or a new secret weapon."[38] No sooner had the first errant group of bombers departed than a second group did the same thing. Their bombing pattern ran northeastward across Colombelles and Faubourg-de-Vaucelles, devastating troop concentrations, unit echelons, gun positions, the headquarters of the 3rd Division and 2 Armoured Brigade, and destroying about one third of the contents

---

* Snuffy Smith was a comic strip character of the time.

of the corps ammunition dump. Casualties were fairly high, even if localized, the North Shore Regiment losing nearly a company of men, while Major General Rod Keller, the commander of 3rd Canadian Infantry Division, was among the wounded. Other bombs fell near enough to Major General George Kitching and his staff in his tactical headquarters of 4th Armoured Division to force them into cover. The author of the 2nd Canadian Corps situation report for 8 August 1944 recorded, pen dripping with bitterness:

The great excitement today was the "precision" bombing of the Yanks ... ... We heard the bombers going towards [the] enemy just as we started lunch. A few minutes later they came back lower, and we crowded out to watch them. The sun glinted on their wings and they were a fine sight heading back to England, with their job well done (as we thought). Suddenly they opened bomb doors (there were 12 of them) and down came the bombs, and the rolling thunderclaps were all round us and lasted for four minutes, and it felt like 1½ hours. Their job well done they sailed on for England. Just as we were about to start lunch again we saw another 12 stream into sight. They were heading N[orth] E[ast] of us, but on seeing the billowing clouds of smoke and dust their pals had created they turned and made straight for CORMELLES letting us have it again. This we felt was anything but funny. We had visions of two and three thousands Forts unloading on us in lots of 12 all afternoon.[39]

The postwar myth is that the bombing seriously disrupted the advance of 4th Armoured Division and 1. *Dywizji Pancernej*, thus contributing to the slow progress that day. In fact, except for the light anti-aircraft regiment of the Polish division, which suffered 44 killed and wounded,[40] these formations were almost wholly untouched. But that is not to say that their advance was not impeded. The regiments of 2 Canadian AGRA and 9 AGRA were heavily hit, which affected the artillery support available, a point made by *Generał brygada* Maczek in his report on Operation TOTALIZE, and which was noted in the 10. *Brygada Kawalerii Pancernej* log at 1345 hours as, "*Bombardowanie pezycji NPLA przez wasne lotnictwo*," very roughly, "bombs dropped by the air force fell throughout the area of the AGRA."[41] 4 Medium Regiment of 2 Canadian AGRA was waiting to move forward with its guns hooked to their towing vehicles when it was bombed. Half of its guns were destroyed and it was only able to move the surviving eight weapons forward after some delay for reorganization. In 7 Medium Regiment, which was in action and firing, bombs fell across B Troop of the 12th Medium Battery. When the smoke and dust cleared, three guns had been knocked out (two by direct hits), while the sole remaining gun was still firing amidst the carnage that surrounded it.[42]

The question that must be answered is how effective was the American bombing? First, less than three quarters of the aircraft actually bombed, although that does not tell all the story. Targets 6 and 7 were hit on schedule with high explosive bombs from about 100 B-17s on each target. Later reports, including an assessment of Bretteville-sur-Laize by the 21 Army Group Operational Research Group, indicated heavy damage was inflicted on both targets.* Still, some of these bombers missed their targets; 1 Northamptonshire Yeomanry recorded that high explosive bombs fell on and near its squadrons in their battle positions near St. Aignan-de-Cramesnil.

In the second bombing about 70 aircraft were sent to Target 9; but none dropped their bombs on that target. Last, only about 250 aircraft actually released bombs on the Target 8 series. The actual wording used to describe the bombing in a postwar USAF study was "bombed in or adjacent to the target areas," which is not all that reassuring. That works out to an average of 33 aircraft or less than three boxes of bombers for each of the six targets. But even that assessment is misleading as only 16 groups, or roughly 192 aircraft, are assessed as having attacked the Target 8 series successfully, and that definition was rather broad. What this means is that only an average of 24 aircraft (two groups) actually attacked the target they had been assigned.

Did this attack by several hundred B-17s blast a way through the German defences. The short answer was that it did not. After all the planning and work and discussions, the American bombing was scattered and largely ineffective, other than for the destruction of two batteries of 2. *Bataillon, SS-Artillerieregiment* 12. In fact, it was more than ineffective; it was counter productive as two 12-plane formations hit the British, Canadian and

---

* The Operational Research report mistakenly attributed the bombing of Bretteville-sur-Laize to Bomber Command as part of the Phase 1 attacks.

Friendly fire
Allied bombers demonstrating to troops along the Route Nationale 158 that friendly fire isn't. While actual casualties to the two Phase 2 Divisions were negligible, the heavy damage caused to 2 Canadian AGRA contributed to the slow progress made by the Poles on 8 August. (NAC/PA 154826)

Polish forces concentrated south of Caen. Moreover, as we have seen, the most northerly targets submitted by Simonds had been rejected by the air forces as too close to friendly troops. As an alternate, First Canadian Army had requested that 2nd Tactical Air Force attack these targets with fighter bombers at the same time as the heavy bombers were hitting the remainder of the targets but this was not done, which was doubly unfortunate as the fighter bombers would have caught *Kampfgruppe* Waldmüller in the open in attack formation. Instead, the normal system of requesting aircraft to attack specific targets was used, but it seems the majority of targets were not hit because of target obscuration. (The bombers Meyer saw were attacking Bretteville-sur-Laize and St. Sylvain, not his troops between Cintheaux and Hautmesnil.) However, even if the bombing had been spot-on the target and effective, the survivors would have recovered from the effects and been prepared to engage the leading troops of 4 Armoured Brigade when they finally advanced shortly after 1600 hours on 8 August 1944.[43]

CHAPTER THIRTEEN

THE TANKS ADVANCE

"I could see through my binoculars a Panther tank off to the East about
1500 yards traversing his long barrel 75 mm gun on MY tank!"

SERGEANT AL HUBERT, CANADIAN GRENADIER GUARDS

Major Ned Amy, the commander of No. 1 Squadron of the Canadian Grenadier Guards, was doing his best to ignore the cries to get on as he attempted to find a way out of a tactical dilemma. The only way forward from his position near Point 122 was down a long, open forward slope, and he did not consider that a feasible operation, no matter who was yelling at him. Moreover, he had not slept in close to 36 hours and while he may not have been aware of this at the time, he was not operating at peak efficiency. Neither of course were his tank crews, all of whom had spent most of the last 36 hours in or near their tanks, either crawling forward or parked nose to tail at immediate readiness to move. A few days before this he had also seen about 30 burnt-out British tanks near Grentheville on the GOODWOOD battleground. While his troops had not seen what could happen to tanks that were caught in the open, it did influence his approach. With an open left flank – he was not aware of the presence of the British on his left – and no information on enemy locations, it was no time to be bold.[1] Moreover, the very man who could have given him an outline of what he faced and then supported his advance with the fire of his tanks, Major Sydney Radley-Walters of A Squadron, the Sherbrooke Fusilier Regiment, had moved his squadron away to the west after being ordered to support the Essex Scottish in their occupation of Caillouet.[2]

At this stage, with his relatively intact squadron halted behind a crest, while the attached company from the motor battalion was slowly working down the highway, he sensed that he was looking at a death trap for his squadron and was determined not to move over the ridge.* As he later wrote, he kept scanning the area to his left and front, but other than three burning German tanks to his left rear and two more on fire part way down the slope, he could see nary a trace of either friend or foe. And all the while, he was being bombarded by orders to "get cracking," "push on" and the like, until the next squadron commander in the column, Major H.A. Smith, was sent forward to tell him that Sunray (the title used to refer to commanders in radio transmissions, in this case Halpenny) and Big Sunray (Booth of 4 Brigade) and Big, Big Sunray (Kitching of 4th Division) and Big, Big, Big Sunray (Simonds of 2nd Canadian Corps) all wanted him to get going immediately. He replied with a pointed suggestion about what all those Sunrays of increasing orders of magnitude could do, especially as none of them seemed all that keen on coming up to the sharp end to demonstrate by personal example how to get going immediately.[3]

All the frenzied transmissions finally were too much for Lieutenant Craig Smith, a 26-year-old American and the troop leader of Amy's 3 Troop, who could hear them over the radio. Smith's tanks were deployed in "hull down" positions behind the crest. He moved over the crest and started down the slope at full speed. After a near miss by an anti-tank gun that fired from an orchard south of St. Aignan-de-Cramesnil, Smith began to zig-zag wildly and headed for the cover of one of the burning German tanks, while the tanks of his troop opened fire on the orchard. Smith's Sherman kept going down the hill but was holed twice, once through the turret, killing his gunner and loader-operator, and the other through the right sponson, which ignited the stowed ammunition. Smith managed to tumble from the turret of his burning tank despite his serious wounds and was dragged to cover by his driver and co-driver. The three Canadians crawled back through a potato field until they were picked up by the Argyll and Sutherland Highlanders of Canada of 10 Brigade, who were advancing southeast of the Route Nationale.[4]

With Amy's No. 1 Squadron, which had lost just about one third of its tanks, unable to advance from its present location, Lieutenant Colonel Halpenny ordered Major H.A. Smith to take over the lead. What followed

---

* It had lost three tanks to mines (Lieutenant Macdonald's as his squadron was moving up to the corps start line and two south of Rocquancourt).

HALPENNY FORCE
Canadian Grenadier Guards and Supporting Arms

Vanguard – AMY FORCE

NO. 1 SQUADRON – CANADIAN GRENADIER GUARDS

'C' COMPANY – LAKE SUPERIOR REGIMENT

3-INCH MORTAR
CARRIERS

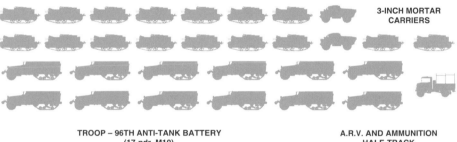

TROOP – 96TH ANTI-TANK BATTERY
(17-pdr. M10)

A.R.V. AND AMMUNITION
HALF-TRACK
CANADIAN GRENADIER GUARDS

TROOP – SHERMAN CRAB I FLAILS

SECTION – RECONNAISSANCE TROOP
CANADIAN GRENADIER GUARDS

RECCE OFFICER AND
NO. 2 SECTION R.C.E.

F.O.O. 23 FIELD REGT. (SP)
ARMOURED O.P.

This chart, which continues on the following three pages, demonstrates the size of an armoured battle group.

Main Guard – SMITH FORCE

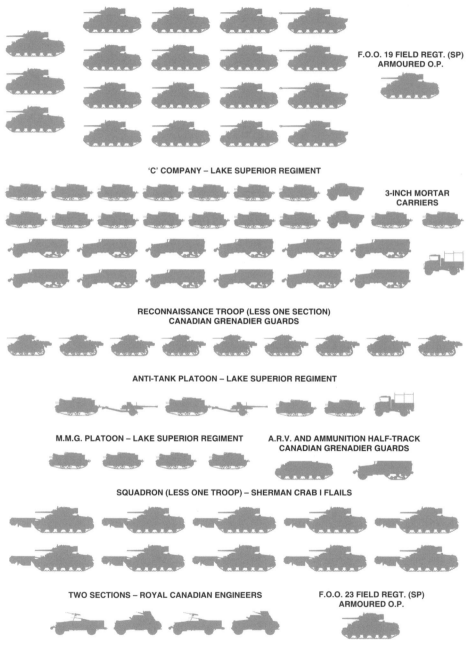

NO. 3 SQUADRON – CANADIAN GRENADIER GUARDS

F.O.O. 19 FIELD REGT. (SP)
ARMOURED O.P.

'C' COMPANY – LAKE SUPERIOR REGIMENT

3-INCH MORTAR
CARRIERS

RECONNAISSANCE TROOP (LESS ONE SECTION)
CANADIAN GRENADIER GUARDS

ANTI-TANK PLATOON – LAKE SUPERIOR REGIMENT

M.M.G. PLATOON – LAKE SUPERIOR REGIMENT

A.R.V. AND AMMUNITION HALF-TRACK
CANADIAN GRENADIER GUARDS

SQUADRON (LESS ONE TROOP) – SHERMAN CRAB I FLAILS

TWO SECTIONS – ROYAL CANADIAN ENGINEERS

F.O.O. 23 FIELD REGT. (SP)
ARMOURED O.P.

Advance Guard – HEADQUARTERS

R.H.Q. TROOP – CANADIAN GRENADIER GUARDS

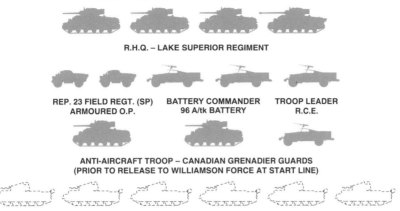

R.H.Q. – LAKE SUPERIOR REGIMENT

| REP. 23 FIELD REGT. (SP) ARMOURED O.P. | BATTERY COMMANDER 96 A/tk BATTERY | TROOP LEADER R.C.E. |

ANTI-AIRCRAFT TROOP – CANADIAN GRENADIER GUARDS
(PRIOR TO RELEASE TO WILLIAMSON FORCE AT START LINE)

Reserve – WILLIAMSON FORCE

NO. 2 SQUADRON – CANADIAN GRENADIER GUARDS

'B' COMPANY – LAKE SUPERIOR REGIMENT

3-INCH MORTAR
CARRIERS

ANTI-TANK PLATOON – LAKE SUPERIOR REGIMENT

M.M.G. PLATOON: LAKE SUPERIOR REGIMENT   SECTION – ROYAL CANADIAN ENGINEERS   F.O.O. 11 MEDIUM REGT.

BATTERY (LESS ONE TROOP) – 96TH ANTI-TANK BATTERY

ANTI-AIRCRAFT TROOP – CANADIAN GRENADIER GUARDS (AFTER RELEASE FROM ADVANCE GUARD HEADQUARTERS)

was an example of what could be accomplished by tanks as vulnerable as Shermans if they were permitted to make the best use of the terrain. In fact, the operation was so successful, one could only wish Halpenny had ordered Smith, or Amy for that matter, to attempt it earlier, instead of merely ranting on the regimental net. Mind you, it also would have helped if he had come forward to take a look for himself. Like Amy, Smith was no stranger to tight spots. He had won a Military Cross in December 1943 at Casa Berardi in the action in which Captain Paul Triquet of the Vandoos won the Victoria Cross.[5] Supported by the fire from No. 1 Squadron, Smith first tried to skirt the edge of Gaumesnil, but his tank and the Sherman of one of his troop leaders were knocked out. Before moving Smith had ordered the regimental reconnaissance troop, which was attached to his squadron, to proceed south parallel to the Route Nationale. There was no acknowledgement of this order from the troop leader, so Sergeant A. Hubert acknowledged it and the Stuarts began to advance. To Hubert's shock, as he passed Amy's squadron, he

> could see through my binoculars a Panther tank off to the East about 1500 yards traversing his long barrel 75 mm gun on *MY* tank! In a moment I could no longer see his gun and expected him to shoot at any second. The

37 mm gun on my Stuart would have been ineffective at that range. Then Guardsman* Red Holmes with 1 Squadron, who had been my gunner when I was with 1 Squadron, saw the situation and fired a 75 mm H.E. which exploded on the front of the Panther. The German did not return fire but turned and proceeded at high speed towards the South East. At the same time I saw a flash from a lower window of a building across the highway and Guardsman Barham returned a few bursts of Browning M.G. fire.

Meanwhile Sergeant Stafford continued on with his Stuart to the right of Lieutenant Smith's burning tank when he received a direct hit through the front of the tank between the driver and co-driver. This shot came from the southern part of Cintheaux. I did not see the flash of the gun but I saw the tracer of the shot. Sergeant Stafford was wounded in both legs while the rest of the crew was unhurt. Lieutenant Wright picked up most of the crew and brought them out of the field and into a building across the highway. Guardsman Thomas crawled through the grain and joined the rest of the crew after dark.

Clearly, the way ahead was not on the east of the highway. Smith took over another tank and leaving his second-in-command and one of his tank troops *in situ*, ordered Lieutenant Ivan Phelan to attempt to get ahead on the west through the gap between Gaumesnil and the railway line. What followed defied the imagination.

Lieutenant Phelan's troop was at this time in the woods at [the southwest corner of Gaumesnil] and was ordered to advance. Having observed flashes from the corner of the orchard [on the north edge of Cintheaux,] Lieutenant Phelan fired high explosive and advanced, finding he had shot up an 88 mm gun. Moving around the north of the orchard, he winged a 2 cm gun at the corner, and moving across to the buildings at [the northwest corner of Cintheaux] he got two more 2 cms. With his troop covering his advance, he dashed across to [an area in the field southwest of Cintheaux] which appeared to be a prepared position of some kind. Across the open stretch he was fired on by 88s from the hedge running south west from [the southern edge of] Cintheaux. This hedge was plastered with high explosive and co-

---

* In Commonwealth Guards regiments, the lowest enlisted rank was not trooper, if the unit was armoured, or private, if it was infantry, but guardsman.

axial by his troop sergeant and it was found to contain three 88 mm and one 2 cm, all of which were knocked out. On going over the mound [just in front of where his tank had halted] he saw 3 SP guns, two immediately to his front and one withdrawing [near the railway line 500 yards south of him.] All three were fired on and halted, one of the [closest two] going up on impact with a tremendous flash. Joined by the rest of his troop he proceeded to round up prisoners, and whilst dismounted so doing another SP gun exploded killing one man and wounding five others. Not daunted, they nevertheless rounded up 28 prisoners of war. About 15 dead men were counted around the gun positions. Two of his tanks had become X casualties [a casualty which is due to a temporary stoppage only, and which can be repaired by the crew of the vehicle without outside assistance]. A company of the Argyll and Sutherland Highlanders of Canada (Major Farmer) arrived on the scene and they took over the job of mopping up the town.[6]

Guardsman Al Page, who was driving Phelan's Sherman that day, had a slightly different recollection of the events that took place:

Moments after we parked Germans emerged, arms in the air. At this point I vaulted to the rear of our tank where I had strapped our Bren gun. I now had an unrestricted view of proceedings from a great vantage point. Page 264 of [the regimental history] is incorrect when it states Phelan was on foot when communications broke down. The fact is that Hurwitz's [the troop sergeant] tank had thrown a track and his entire crew were out of their tank at the time of the explosion, leading to one death and two injuries to his crew. Phelan was standing between Hurwitz's tank and our own, with pistol in the air, when the explosion occurred. The Germans just ran past him.[7]

Captain Jamie Stewart, the FOO attached to the Grenadiers, had accompanied No. 3 Squadron headquarters as they followed Phelan's troop around the woods. When Phelan's men dismounted to collect the prisoners, Stewart jumped down from the turret of his Sherman and ran over to collect a pistol he had spotted on the body of a dead German officer. He noticed several things when he examined the position. First, the 88s appeared to have been deployed in either an anti-aircraft or indirect fire role, rather than as anti-

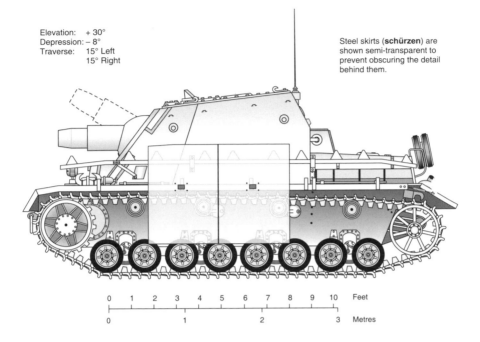

Elevation: + 30°
Depression: − 8°
Traverse: 15° Left
           15° Right

Steel skirts (**schürzen**) are
shown semi-transparent to
prevent obscuring the detail
behind them.

| 0 | 1 | 2 | 3 | 4 | 5 | 6 | 7 | 8 | 9 | 10 | Feet |
| 0 | | | 1 | | | 2 | | | 3 | | Metres |

Sturmpanzer IV – 155 mm assault infantry gun

Commonly known as the *Brummbär* (Grizzly Bear),
the Sturmpanzer IV was designed as a heavily
armoured, self-propelled howitzer to support
infantry engaged in street fighting. The vehicle
utilized the lower hull and chassis of the PzKpfw
IV and a box-like superstructure was built up from
angled armour plating. In the original design, the
Brummbär lacked a bow machine gun, which put
it at a distinct disadvantage in street fighting.
Later production vehicles were fitted with a ball-
mounted MG on the upper left side of the front
plate. The Sturmpanzer IV mounted a 155 mm
howitzer firing a high-explosive projectile which
weighed 83 pounds. A total of 38 rounds were
stored in the vehicle. This infantry howitzer had
a muzzle velocity of 787 feet per second with
a maximum range of 4,675 yards. Out of a total
production run of 40–60 vehicles, 28 saw service
in Normandy with *Sturmpanzerabteilung* 217.

Country of origin: Germany
Crew: 5
Length: 19 feet
Width: 9 feet 4 inches
Height: 8 feet
Weight: 32 tons
Engine: Maybach HL120TRM
Maximum speed: 25 mph
Range: 124 miles
Armament: 155 mm StuH43 L/12 gun,
     7.92 mm MG34
Armour – Maximum: 100 mm
           Minimum: 10 mm

Working for George
A Sherman of Headquarters 4th Canadian Armoured Division advancing on 8 August. What had been lush farm land is clearly the worse for war. An Auster Air OP aircraft is visible above the Universal Carrier in the centre of the photo, which indicates just how complete Allied control of the skies was. (NAC/PA 131373)

tank guns. Second, the enemy dead and prisoners were all in new uniforms with full battle order, with straps and pouches and the rest of the paraphernalia. Third, the officer had used his own pistol to commit suicide as his guns were being knocked out around him. Stewart, who had landed on D-Day as a FOO with D Company of the North Shore Regiment and had been almost continuously in the line ever since, although this was his first experience working with an armoured battle group, had another impression of 8 August 1944. He noticed that 4th Armoured Division, like 2 Canadian Armoured Brigade when they first landed, were reluctant to call for artillery fire as their natural inclination was to try to handle things themselves. However, he also realized that he had been remiss in waiting for orders to call for fire and should have been engaging targets on his own.[8]

While the engagement was hardly typical and the defenders were not what one would consider the *Wehrmacht*'s first team, Phelan's troop had managed to advance about a mile, in the process knocking out four 88 mms, four 20 mm light anti-aircraft guns and three lightly-armoured 150 mm self-propelled infantry guns. That probably explained why he had been able to cross the field and take on the self-propelled guns, which may have been trying

280

Humber scout cars
Humber scout cars CF 196754 and CF 196716 near Cintheaux 8 August 1944. The 54
unit sign on the right front of the nearest vehicle indicates it belongs to the Lake
Superior Regiment, the motor battalion of 4 Canadian Armoured Brigade. (NAC/
PA 113653)

to escape from their gun position. Without taking anything away from his achievement, it is unlikely his tank would have survived if three *jagdpanzers* had been in the same area, or if the 88s had been sited in an anti-tank role and manned by experienced detachments.

By this time it was past 1800 hours and there were at least three hours of good tank light remaining. Despite this, and the Grenadier Guard's mission of pushing on to Bretteville-le-Rabet, Halpenny gave No. 3 Squadron authority to first harbour at Cintheaux and then pull back to a regimental harbour near Gaumesnil. According to the unit War Diary

> It was then 2000 hours and it was considered that in view of the fact that darkness was rapidly approaching, the fact that some regrouping and the proper tying up [of] the next advance was necessary, that a dawn attack on Bretteville-le-Rabet would be most likely successful. The advance was tied up to continue at 0315 hrs.[9]

Simonds, of course, had instructed his divisional commanders that they must push on during the night. While the reason given by the Canadian Grenadier Guards, that the details of the advance required "tying up," made

Moving up

A column of Shermans, including a Firefly, third from left, driving along the Route Nationale. This shot was probably taken behind the Phase 2 start line as there are discarded jerry cans and signals wire visible in the foreground. (NAC/PA 140822)

some sense, Simonds probably would not have thought so, and it does have the ring of an excuse for inaction. Certainly the regimental history did not pull any punches in referring to the decision:

> This momentous decision – which granted Brigadeführer [sic] Kurt Meyer a respite of seven hours to rally the 89th Division and to deploy his 12th S.S. Panzer Division – vitiated Simonds' intention "to press straight on through the night." And disregarded his exhortation: "I want you to push on steadily regardless."[10]

While the Canadian Grenadier Guards had been attempting to advance east of the road, the vanguard of 10 Brigade, the Argyll and Sutherland Highlanders led by Lieutenant Colonel David Stewart with Major David Currie's C Squadron of the South Alberta Regiment, had been waiting for the Royal Regiment of Canada to secure Gaumesnil so it could advance and capture Cintheaux. All this was complicated by the lateral movement of the Grenadiers, but at 1800 hours two companies of the Argylls supported by two troops of C Squadron moved forward into Cintheaux. Lieutenant Gerry Adams commanded one of the tank troops and remembered that:

> I was told that I would support this company [A Company], go find the major and he would give me instructions. So I got out of my tank and I

found this major [J.A. Farmer] in a shell hole with his officers and giving orders and this was late in the day, about 5:30. He said "Who the hell are you?" – It really was amateur days. I told him who I was and that I had four tanks. So he said, "Here's your orders, do you want to lead or support?" and I said, "If it's okay with you, I'll support and I'll shoot you in." He said, "Okay, H-Hour is 6 o'clock" and I looked at my watch and it was quarter to six and that didn't leave much time

... ... So at six o'clock off we went. It was a very tame event, the infantry attacked the town, I didn't fire a shot and the whole thing was over in fifteen or twenty minutes.[11]

Lance Corporal Harry Ruch of 7 Platoon, A Company, the Argylls, wrote in his (highly illegal) personal diary that

we advance about two miles and line [sic] up in front of a place called Cyntheaux [Cintheaux] in preparation for the attack. At the signal we started across the wheat fields for the town. While going through the field we captured two Jerries that tried to say they were "Canadians" but we had heard that story before and sent them back to B[attalion]. H[ead]. Q[uarters]. It is a rather funny feeling going in on the attack. One don't know what to expect. Your owns shells whistling over your head, Jerry's landing in front, among and behind you. Everything seems confused. We took the town alright and captured or killed about 300 Jerries most of them still dazed from the bombing. We were rather fortunate in regard to casualties. One man wounded. One man killed. Bill Jones was killed. We dug in and prepared for the counterattack that did not come.[12]

While the tanks of the Canadian Grenadier Guards moved back into harbours, the Argylls continued down the axis and captured Hautmesnil, although the quarry to the south of it, which harboured the headquarters of *Kampfgruppe* Waldmüller, was not secured until first light, after the Germans had withdrawn.

> Meanwhile the other two companies [B and C] pushed on a few miles to Hautmesnil, actually a scattering of small buildings about a huge quarry. The C.O. decided that the quarry was too large to risk a one-company attack on it during the night. Accordingly "B" Company was ordered to contain it during the night and enter and capture it at first light.[13]

The day's work had cost the battalion from Hamilton, Ontario, one killed and 24 wounded. In turn they had captured 60 to 70 prisoners, 15 enemy vehicles, three 88 mm guns and a quantity of medical supplies. Although they did not know it, they had also reached the furthest point of the advance on the first day of TOTALIZE.[14]

And now the Polish army entered the battle to liberate Normandy. While 4th Armoured Division had been lining up in two great columns behind the corps start line, 1. *Dywizji Pancernej* had been moving into the 2nd Canadian Corps area from its concentration area near Bayeux. This move had commenced at 0230 hours on 8 August, although the forming up of the division into its columns had begun several hours earlier. Like the 4th Division, the division was to have closed up to the corps start line by "the morning" of 8 August. At this time the division was to be joined by the flails of the 22nd Dragoons, a British unit, and artillery representatives from 4 Medium Regiment of 2 Canadian AGRA.* *Generał brygada* Maczek's plan was straightforward and divided into two phases. In the first phase 10. *Brygada Kawalerii Pancernej* (the armoured brigade) was to seize the area south of Estrées-la-Campagne and Hill 140, while the infantry brigade (3. *Brygada Strzelców*) was to form a pivot in the area of Cauvicourt. In the second phase 3. *Brygada*

---

* 4 Medium Regiment was the only francophone artillery regiment in 2nd Canadian Corps. As many more Polish officers were fluent in French than in English, this grouping was logical and one that worked well.

was to take over the positions of 10. *Brygada*, which would then capture the division's final objectives north of Falaise. The divisional armoured reconnaissance regiment, 10. *Pułk Strzelców Konnych*, would provide left flank protection throughout. Unlike the 4th Division armoured reconnaissance regiment, the South Alberta Regiment, which was equipped with Shermans, 10. *Pułk Strzelców Konnych* had Cromwells, a British-designed cruiser tank which was even more vulnerable than the Sherman.[15]

While Kitching had opted to deploy his field artillery regiments in new positions in captured territory before his brigades advanced, Maczek seems to have decided to have one of his two field artillery regiments follow each of the brigades and deploy when needed. His detailed grouping was:

10. *Brygada Kawalerii Pancernej*	3. *Brygada Strzelców*
1. *Pułk Pancerny*	1. *Batalion Strzelców Podhalanskich*
2. *Pułk Pancerny*	9. *Batalion Strzelców*
24. *Pułk Ułanów*	2. *Pułk Artylerii Motorowej*
10. *Pułk Strzelców Konnych*	two batteries *Pułk Artylerii Przeciwpancernej*
8. *Batalion Strzelców* (from 3. *Brygada Strzelców*)	one battery *Pułk Artlerii Przeciwlotniczej*
22 Dragoons (flails)	11. *Kompania Saperów* less one platoon
1. *Pułk Artylerii Motorwej*	11. *Kompania Sanitarnia* (Medical Company)

one battery *Pułk Artylerii Przeciwpancernej*
one battery less 2 troops *Pułk Artylerii Przeciwlotniczej*
10. *Kompania Saperów*
10. *Lekka Kompania Sanitarnia* (Light Medical Company)

By 0630 hours on 8 August the head of 10. *Brygada* had reached the bridges south of Caen and continued forward to reach Bras at 0800. To comprehend the difficulties in moving an armoured division, remember that this move had originally commenced at 0230, and therefore it had taken four hours for the head of the column to move 20 miles. The infantry brigade reached the bridges over the Orne at 1300 hours followed by the main body of the division headquarters at between 1400 and 1500 hours. It had been a difficult move under black-out conditions over poor roads and hampered by clouds of dust that obstructed the vehicles in front. Moreover, the tasks had not been made any easier by the large numbers of troops from other formations in the area.

The arrival of Maczek's headquarters at Cormelles coincided with the Phase 2 bombing, including the attacks on the area south of Caen. He may have had difficulty expressing himself in English, or may still have been fuming, for he wrote on 13 August "at 1330 hours, the Air Force started the bombardment but, probably by mistake, instead of bombing the area of Cauvicourt–St. Sylvain, bombed the area South of Caen." He added

> As a result of this bombardment the Canadian AGRA suffered most losing a great number of men and much equipment, but our AA Artillery also lost 44 men (killed and wounded). The situation was extremely difficult as the area was packed with various munition dumps which exploded for 40 minutes after the bombing as a result of fires caused.

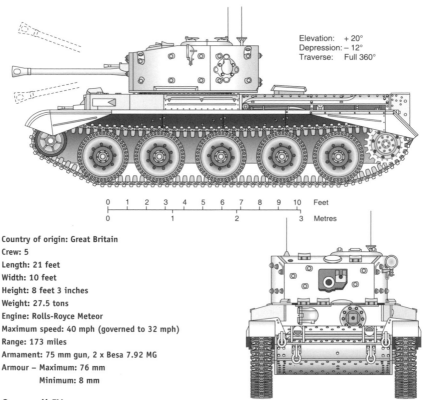

Elevation: + 20°
Depression: – 12°
Traverse: Full 360°

Country of origin: Great Britain
Crew: 5
Length: 21 feet
Width: 10 feet
Height: 8 feet 3 inches
Weight: 27.5 tons
Engine: Rolls-Royce Meteor
Maximum speed: 40 mph (governed to 32 mph)
Range: 173 miles
Armament: 75 mm gun, 2 x Besa 7.92 MG
Armour – Maximum: 76 mm
               Minimum: 8 mm

Cromwell IV

Although appreciated by its crew for speed and reliability, the Cromwell was a dated design that employed vertical, bolted-on armour plating together with a narrow hull that inhibited further up-gunning. It was outmatched by German tanks even before it entered service. The Cromwell equipped the armoured reconnaissance regiment of 1. *Dywizji Pancernej* in addition to other armoured regiments in British 7th and 11th Armoured Divisions and 6th Airborne Division.

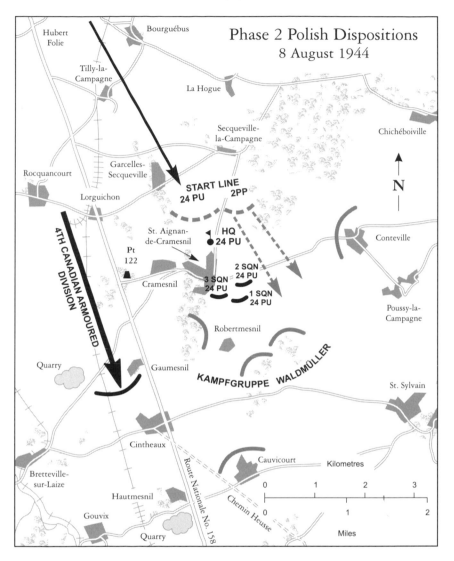

Phase 2 Polish Dispositions
8 August 1944

Despite myth propagated by a number of commentators on TOTALIZE, the bombing did no more stop the two leading regiments of 10. *Brygada* from crossing their start line at 1355 hours on time than did the counter-attack by 12. *SS-Panzerdivision*. The armoured regiments passed to the east of Tilly-la-Campagne and between Garcelles-Secqueville and Secqueville-la-Campagne. In fact, they approached the gap east of St. Aignan-de-Cramesnil while the Northamptonshire Yeomanry was still battling the tanks and SP guns of *Kampfgruppe* Waldmüller. At this point, things began to go terribly wrong. Meyer had directed the *Divisionbegleitkompanie* and a company of *SS-Panzerjägerabteilung 12* to occupy the woods between Robertmesnil and St. Sylvain, and they were reinforced later in the afternoon by the three surviving Tigers of *schwere SS-Panzerabteilung 101* commanded by the unit's medical officer, the senior surviving officer. These troops were sited in an ideal position to halt the Polish advance.

As was usually the case in engagements between German guns and Shermans unsupported by artillery and infantry, it was no contest . At 1425 hours 2. *Pułk Pancerney* reported that it had been halted by 20 German Tiger tanks, almost certainly a combination of Tigers and Mk IVs, firing from the area of the woods.[16] Shortly later, at 1500 hours, 24. *Pułk Ułanów* also met heavy fire from anti-tank guns, losing what its historian described as "a few tanks," while the commander of 1 Squadron, *Rotmistrz* (Captain in the cavalry) Marian Piwonski, was killed by artillery fire.[17]

Armoured Reconnaissance Regiment
1st Polish Armoured Division

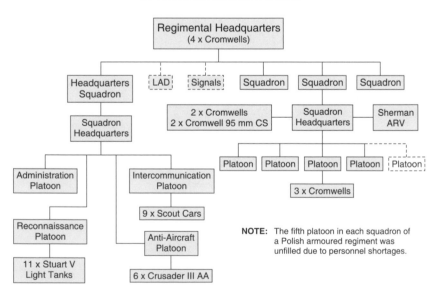

The armoured reconnaissance regiments in 21st Army Group were converted to the establishment of an armoured regiment. These units were expected to be able to either conduct reconnaissance operations or fight as an armoured regiment. The South Alberta Regiment, the armoured reconnaissance regiment of 4th Canadian Armoured Division, was equipped with Shermans but had not yet been issued Fireflys.

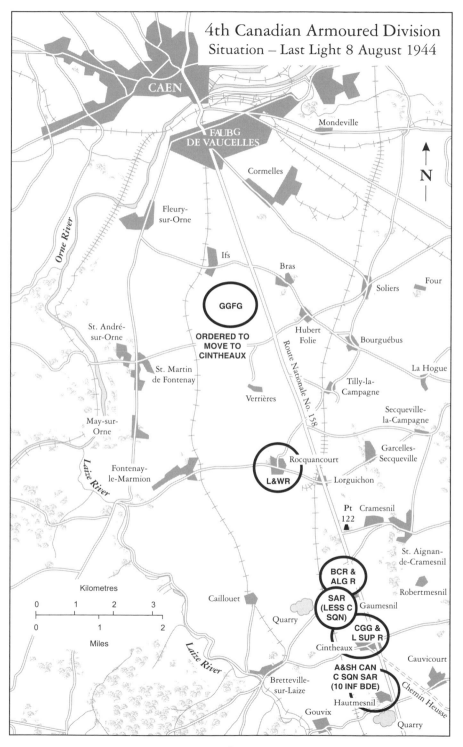

4th Canadian Armoured Division
Situation – Last Light 8 August 1944

N

CAEN

Mondeville

FAUBG
DE VAUCELLES

Cormelles

Orne River

Fleury-
sur-Orne

Ifs

Bras

Soliers

Four

GGFG

ORDERED TO
MOVE TO
CINTHEAUX

St. André-
sur-Orne

Hubert
Folie

Bourguébus

La Hogue

Route Nationale No. 158

St. Martin
de Fontenay

Verrières

Tilly-la-
Campagne

Secqueville-
la-Campagne

May-sur-
Orne

Laize River

Fontenay-
le-Marmion

Rocquancourt

Garcelles-
Secqueville

L&WR

Lorguichon

Pt
122

Cramesnil

St. Aignan-
de-Cramesnil

Kilometres

BCR &
ALG R

Robertmesnil

0   1   2   3

Caillouet

SAR
(LESS C
SQN)

Gaumesnil

0   1   2

Quarry

Miles

CGG &
L SUP R

Cinteaux

Cauvicourt

Laize River

A&SH CAN
C SQN SAR
(10 INF BDE)

Chemin Heusse

Bretteville-
sur-Laize

Hautmesnil

Gouvix

Quarry

289

Waiting to advance
Polish infantry and vehicles of other units waiting for the order to move forward on
8 August. (NAC/PA 128045)

Despite bringing artillery down on the German positions, the Polish regiments were unable to move forward. By 1520 hours German tanks were beginning to manoeuvre against the flanks of 2. *Pułk Pancerny*, but a countermove by 10. *Pułk Strzelców Konnych* blocked this German move. The situation was stalemated until last light, when 3. *Brygada* replaced 10. *Brygada* in the line. It had been a costly day; the armoured brigade recorded 57 tanks – nearly a third of its tank strength – as casualties, including 24 Z casualties, that is, requiring "extensive repair or replacement requiring evacuation."[18] While Simonds was critical of both division commanders for not getting on, he was especially critical of the Poles for their lack of progress, as was Kitching after the war.[19] Maczek put the blame, in my opinion correctly, on the ineffective bombing and a lack of artillery support. Given that his leading armoured regiments had moved off on time, but were stopped by enemy troops that he reasonably thought should have been neutralized by the bombing, he had a point. His general comments on the day included

The ground was difficult for an attack by armour, having severe small woods and high hedges. In spite of fairly difficult horizons, the ground was very favourable for the enemy's A[nti] T[an]k defence.

The enemy was not sufficiently neutralized by our own Air Force and

arty, so that the bde could attack without heavy losses (unfortunately the air force passed through our own forces, destroying not only a part of the art[iller]y, but also the am[munitio]n dumped for AGRA).

There was a constant threat to our left flank, which will be henceforth a menace to the div ops and my permanent worry.

The Crab regt was almost unemployed, since we did not find any mines.[20]

In one of his books, *A Fine Night for Tanks*, Ken Tout cited an account prepared after the war by a number of officers of the division that claimed that 24. *Pułk Ułanów* of 10 *Brygada* planned to pass between the Yeomanry and 144 RAC en route to its objective at Cauvicourt while 2. *Pułk Pancrny* was to loop around Robertmesnil and advance towards St. Sylvain and Estrées-la-Campagne. There are some difficulties with this version of events. First, the area between the two British regiments was very tight and the Polish regiment would have had problems shaking out as it passed to the west of the woods where 1 Northamptonshire Yeomanry was deployed. Second, this regiment suffered heavy tank losses that afternoon in an area that supposedly was within the axis of advance of 4 Armoured Brigade, but there is no mention of the appearance of other Shermans in any of the Canadian accounts. Third, while the redoubtable Captain Boardman of A Squadron of the Yeomanry recalled seeing tanks he later assumed to have been Polish to the west of the orchard, there is no evidence that they were other than those of Major Amy's 1 Squadron of the Canadian Grenadier Guards.[21]

CHAPTER FOURTEEN

THE GERMAN DILEMMA

*"The enemy has forced his way into the main line of resistance after aerial
preparation more intense than on 18 July. Starting last evening at 1000
hours and lasting throughout the whole night. With a very large number
of tanks, about 500."*

GENERAL DER PANZERTRUPPEN HEINRICH EBERBACH,

5. PANZERARMEE

The Canadian advance, of course, had still not taken place at about
1600 hours on 8 August when *General Der Panzertruppen* Eberbach at 5. *Panzerarmee* decided to order a withdrawal on the
army front to a line Moult (southeast of Vimont)–St. Sylvain–les
Moutiers (southeast of Grimbosq). At this time Eberbach still was considering committing 85. *Infanteriedivision* units piecemeal as they arrived in the
I. *SS-Panzerkorps* area. Accordingly corps headquarters ordered the *Hitlerjugend* to move to a line St. Sylvain–Bretteville-sur-Laize, although the latter
place would be the responsibility of 271. *Infanteriedivision.* Orders were also
issued for 85. *Infanteriedivision* to take up a defensive position on the general
line Condé-sur-Ifs to Grainville.

That the German high command in the west understood the gravity of
the situation only too well is demonstrated by the telephone conversations
between *Generalfeldmarschall* Hans von Kluge, the Commander-in-Chief
West, and Eberbach recorded in the 5. *Panzerarmee* war diary. The first conversation at 2100 hours entailed a review of the situation by Eberbach (EB)
and von Kluge (VK). It also shows that Eberbach still did not have a current
picture of events because of a general breakdown in communications across
the corps front.

EB: May I orient the Field Marshal on the situation? At the front of 86 Corps the enemy has attacked between Chicheboville and St. Aignan and has pushed forward into the area Conteville. Poussy and Conteville still in our hands. A number of enemy tanks knocked out.

With 1 SS Panzer Corps: There the enemy has forced his way into the main line of resistance after aerial preparation more intense than on 18 Jul. Starting last evening at 1000 hrs [2300 hours Allied time] and lasting throughout the whole night. With a very large number of tanks, about 500.

VK: What, 500?

EB: Yes, at Chicheboville alone there were 200 continuously throughout the whole day. The enemy has penetrated the main line of resistance there and pushed forward as far as St. Aignan, retaken in a counterattack. Then renewed area bombings, which crushed 12 SS Pz Div so that only individual tanks came back. The enemy pressed forward further south as far as Gaumesnil and is continuing his advance. 1 SS Panzer Corps has built up a battle line with anti-tank and flak guns, which has held so far. Whether this line will hold out until tomorrow if the enemy attacks more energetically is questionable. Actually, the new Infantry Division as well as the Hitler Youth Division [12. *SS-Panzerdivision*] are 50% knocked out. I shall be lucky if by tonight I am able to round up 20 tanks, including Tigers.

The onslaught continued throughout the whole day against 271 Inf Div.

Detachments of Hitler Youth Division were thrown in there. They had considerable casualties from enemy drum fire. 272 Inf Div: 2000 casualties, infantry very weak. No success in ejecting the enemy from Grimbosq. On the contrary, with new tanks which he is continuously bringing across the river, he has taken Brieux. On 74 Corps front the enemy has attacked energetically and so far, broken through the main line of resistance with 40 tanks in the direction of Cauville. La Plessis was captured by him, but since noon it is back again in our hands.

Located opposite 74 Corps: 7 Brit Armd Div, 8 Brit Armd Bde, 27 Brit Armd Bde, 50 and 53 Brit Inf divs. The opponent will, with good weather, again continue his attacks tomorrow and endeavour to push through in the direction of Falaise. I will commit, as second line, two Gren Bns, one Arty Bn and one 8.8cm Anti Tk Coy. I must confess quite frankly that I am looking forward to tomorrow with anxiety.

VK: I can understand that… That this would all go so quickly we too did not expect. But I can imagine that it did not happen so unexpectedly… I have always anticipated this and have always looked forward to the coming day with a heavy heart.[1]

While von Kluge's closing remark seemed somewhat banal, he was faced with an extremely difficult decision. If the Allies succeeded in breaking through north of Falaise, then all of 7. *Armee* and the left wing of 5. *Panzerarmee* were in grave danger of being trapped and destroyed in a giant pocket. (This, of course, had become apparent first to Bradley and Eisenhower, and then Montgomery earlier that same day.) As a last resort, troops would have to be taken away from the Mortain offensive, which was beginning to falter, in an attempt to prevent the incipient disaster. At 2330 hours German time von Kluge phoned Eberbach again.

VK: If you get back one of the Panzer Divisions which I had taken away from you, what then will you be short of most?

EB: Most of all, tanks are lacking.

VK: Have you a Commander who understands how to handle tanks? Where is the Commander of the Hitler Youth?

EB: The Hitler Youth Commander [Kurt Meyer] telephoned me this afternoon from St. Aignan; he was there to organize the resistance.

VK: That is "Rapid Meyer" (*der schnelle* Meyer). Have you had news from him since then?

EB: No news. That was before the carpet bombing.

VK: Early or during the night?

EB: I mean the bomb carpet which was laid down anew towards noonday. Since then, I have no further news from him.

VK: If I send you a tank formation, would that help you?

EB: Yes.

VK: Have you then a man who could lead them?

EB: Yes, Wünsche. [Commander *SS-Panzerregiment* 12]

VK: He is still there? Aha! I am considering whether I should still send you a Panzer Battalion.

EB: If it were possible.

VK: Perhaps another one from Alençon. During the night, naturally.

EB: If we are lucky with the fog. If they could come to Falaise? I would spot fuel there.

FM: Yes, I will call you up shortly.[2]

An hour later von Kluge called Eberbach for a third time to inform him that reinforcements, however meagre, were on the way.

VK: Has the situation deteriorated or got better?

EB: One cannot say improved, the opponent appears to arrange his formations afresh. All his attacks have been conducted with tanks without infantry. Since the Evening Report, I have the impression that everywhere, including 74 Corps, he is withdrawing tank forces to engage them too in the main area of penetration on the Caen road in the direction of Falaise. I believe that tomorrow he will attack perhaps even stronger still and on a wider front; from left flank 1 SS Pz Corps up to 86 Corps. Enemy has pressed forward from Hautmesnil with very strong elements through Langannerie. I hope that we succeed in destroying the enemy during the night at Langannerie where he is not supposed to be so strong (12 tanks), and hold the line St. Sylvain–Bretteville.

VK: With what forces will you do that?

EB: With elements of 86 Corps (battle groups), and elements of Hitler Youth Division. No contact with Meyer so far, only Wünsche is here.

VK: The tanks of 9 Pz Div will be sent off on the march from Argentan to Falaise, so that early tomorrow they will be half way on. That is a very weighty decision for me, a major abandonment of an order that has been given to me. I know of no other solution – have no further forces. If it goes on like this tomorrow, there will be no more stopping at all.[3]

In fact the Panther battalion of 9. *Panzerdivision* could only muster about a dozen battle-ready tanks, which was clearly inadequate. Therefore, while

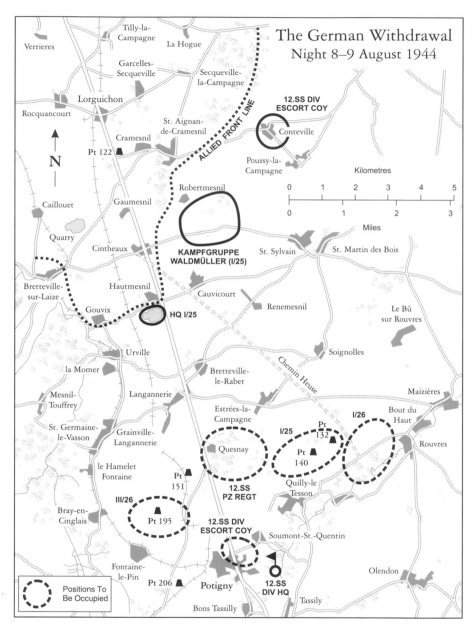

The German Withdrawal
Night 8–9 August 1944

2. *SS-Panzerkorps*, which was fighting west of the Orne, had been ordered to detach a panzer battalion from 9. *Panzerdivision*, at 0050 hours the corps headquarters advised that since the battalion was committed in action and could not be withdrawn, *schwere SS-Panzerabteilung* 102, with 13 serviceable Tigers, was being sent in its place.

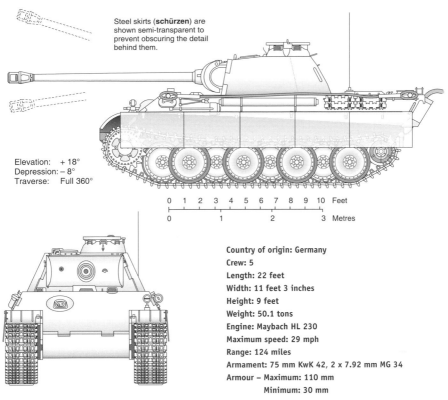

Steel skirts (**schürzen**) are shown semi-transparent to prevent obscuring the detail behind them.

Elevation: + 18°
Depression: − 8°
Traverse: Full 360°

| 0 | 1 | 2 | 3 | 4 | 5 | 6 | 7 | 8 | 9 | 10 | Feet |

| 0 | | 1 | | 2 | | 3 | Metres |

Country of origin: Germany
Crew: 5
Length: 22 feet
Width: 11 feet 3 inches
Height: 9 feet
Weight: 50.1 tons
Engine: Maybach HL 230
Maximum speed: 29 mph
Range: 124 miles
Armament: 75 mm KwK 42, 2 x 7.92 mm MG 34
Armour – Maximum: 110 mm
              Minimum: 30 mm

PzKpfw V – Panther Ausf. G

Widely regarded as one of the best tank designs of the war, the Panther boasted a finely tuned combination of thick, well-sloped armour, superior gunnery optics and a high-velocity 75 mm gun. The muzzle velocity of the KwK 42 was 3,066 feet per second and it fired a 15 pound AP projectile. The ammunition load was 79 rounds. The 75 mm gun, together with excellent armour protection in the frontal arc, allowed the Panther to sit back and engage Allied tanks from long range with impunity. While the Panther suffered from mechanical teething problems early in its service life, these were rectified for the most part and the tank earned a reputation for superiority in firepower, mobility and protection when compared to its Allied counterparts.

Protection in the Frontal Arc – A Comparison

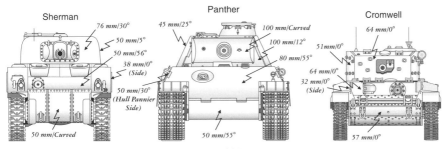

Sherman
76 mm/30°
50 mm/5°
50 mm/56°
38 mm/0° (Side)
50 mm/30° (Hull Pannier Side)
50 mm/Curved

Panther
45 mm/25°
100 mm/Curved
100 mm/12°
80 mm/55°
50 mm/55°

Cromwell
64 mm/0°
51mm/0°
64 mm/0°
32 mm/0° (Side)
57 mm/0°

While the Germans had blocked the advance by 1. *Dywizji Pancernej* and 4th Canadian Division, the situation was by no means favourable for the Germans. The advance by 10 Canadian Brigade that resulted in the capture of first Cintheaux and then Hautmesnil, along with that of 5 Brigade which had occupied and then abandoned Bretteville-sur-Laize, had turned the German line. In fact the Argyll and Sutherland Highlanders of 10 Brigade threatened the headquarters of I. *Bataillon, SS-Panzergrenadierregiment* 25, which was located just south of Hautmesnil at the intersection of the Caen–Falaise road and the track from Cauvicourt to Gouvix. Two thousand yards to the west, 3. *Batterie* of *SS-Werferabteilung* 12 had been attacked several times during the day in its position near Gouvix, but was able to extricate itself under the cover of darkness. Most important, *Kampfgruppe* Waldmüller's position south of St. Aignan had been rendered untenable, especially as it had lost nearly half its tanks during the day.

The German defence line south of Caen had been shattered and 89. *Infanteriedivision* driven back after suffering heavy casualties. To the west and south of the 2nd Canadian Corps area, the threat created by TOTALIZE had forced the Germans to withdraw *Kampfgruppe* Wünsche from the Grimbosq area and order its return to the area of the Route Nationale, conceding that bridgehead to the British. While the Polish Division had been unable to advance past the forward position of the Highland Division, after a slow start 4th Armoured Division had advanced another 2,500 yards past Gaumesnil to Hautmesnil. While Kurt Meyer fails to mention this in his memoirs, this seemingly insignificant advance threatened to cost the Germans dearly as it outflanked the *Kampfgruppe* Waldmüller position south of St. Aignan (despite what Eberbach thought, the Germans had not recaptured the village). Meyer's reluctance to raise this matter was understandable as he had written off the possibility of any Allied advance in that area as being impossible and, after all, German officers were no more likely than their Allied counterparts to write "I screwed up" in their memoirs. Moreover, while the day's fighting had cost 2nd Canadian Corps perhaps 70 tanks, it had cost the Germans at least a third as many plus a number of towed and self-propelled anti-tank guns. The simple fact was that the Allies could replace their losses and the Germans could not. The question now was if Simonds's corps could make the most of the opportunity?

In the meantime *Kampfgruppe* Wünsche arrived in the Potigny area at last after a long road move via Tournebu and Ussy. It was now preparing a defensive position along a "predetermined" line north of Potigny. While 5. *Panzerarmee* had directed that 12. *SS-Panzerdivision* would hold on the line St. Sylvain–Bretteville-sur-Laize, this was clearly impossible. Meyer appreciated that the next possible defensive position was on the high ground north of the Laison and he was able to build the framework of his defence around four manoeuvre units and establish a small reserve.

Kampfgruppe Waldmüller (reinforced I. *Bataillon SS-Panzergrenadierregiment* 25),[4] after it broke contact and withdrew, was to defend the hills north of Mazières, north of Rouvres, to Hill 140 inclusive, northwest of Assy. *Nr.* 1 *Kompanie* of *SS-Panzerjägerabteilung* 12 was attached to it. *Kampfgruppe* Krause (reinforced I. *Bataillon SS-Panzergrenadierregiment* 26) would defend the area astride the Caen–Falaise road from the hills north of Quilly to Hill 183. *SS-Sturmbannführer* Erich Olboeter's III. *Bataillon, SS-Panzergrenadierregiment* 26 was to defend the high terrain around Hill 195 northwest of Potigny and it was directed to absorb all stragglers from 89. *Infanteriedivision*.

SS-Panzerregiment 12 with attached *schwere SS-Panzerabteilung* 102 had the task of assembling in Quesnay Wood from where it was to carry out limited attacks to cover the setting up of defences and to prevent the enemy breaking through along the road to Falaise. *Aufklärungsgruppe* Wiencke was to establish and maintain contact with 272. *Infanteriedivision.* The *Divisionbegleitkompanie* was detached from *Kampfguppe* Waldmüller and ordered to move to Montboit, one mile west of Quilly-le-Tesson, where it would form the divisional reserve. *SS-Artillerieregiment* 12 and *SS-Nebelwerferabteilung* 12 would move to gun areas south of the Laison to cover the complete divisional area, while *SS-Flakabteilung* 12 was ordered to deploy its two 88 mm batteries astride the Route Nationale north of Potigny to destroy any tanks that had broken through. The light anti-aircraft battery and the attached 20 mm anti-aircraft company of *SS-Panzergrenadierregiment* 26 were available for air defence. Finally, division headquarters would remain at La Breche-du-Diable.[5]

At least that was the intention but the events of the next several hours would result in a quite different outcome. At first all went relatively well, although as can be seen by comparing this arrangement to the organization used for the counterattack on the afternoon of 8 August, considerable regrouping of forces was required. By 2300 hours the artillery and *Werfers* had redeployed and the panzer regiment had moved into Quesnay Wood. The men of I. and III. *Bataillonen* of *SS-Panzergrenadierregiment* 26 had moved to and were busily preparing their new defensive positions. During the night the guns of *SS-Flakabteilung* 12 and III. *Flakkorps* moved from the area south of Langannerie to new positions north of Potigny. However, in the case of Waldmüller's battle group the situation was quite different. The headquarters of I. *Bataillon, SS-Panzergrenadierregiment* 25, which had stood off attack from its position south of Hautmesnil, withdrew shortly before dawn to join the remainder of the unit near Soignolles.

The arrival of light brought an unpleasant surprise to the observers posted in the village church tower. The battle group, still consisting of I. *Bataillon, SS-Panzergrenadierregiment* 25, a company of Mk IVs, the corps and division *Begleitkompanien* and *Nr.* 1. *Kompanie, SS-Panzerjägerabteilung* 12 was encircled by Allied forces. When messengers sent by Waldmüller to division headquarters to report and request instructions had encountered Kurt Meyer on the Caen–Falaise road, he directed the battle group to defend in place until relieved by German panzers.[6] As we shall see, this plan did not survive renewed contact with the Allied forces.

Going nowhere
Captured German vehicles in the quarry at Hautmesnil. Two Canadians appear to be testing the cab of the truck for comfort, or perhaps looking for souvenirs. (NAC/PA 116526)

CHAPTER FIFTEEN

WORTHINGTON FORCE

"Last position given by the [British Columbia Regiment] was 105498
at 0624B hours. No further communications with them."

WAR DIARY, 4 CANADIAN ARMOURED BRIGADE

We have already encountered the series of frantic orders from Brigadier Leslie Booth, commanding 4 Canadian Armoured Brigade, during the late afternoon of 8 August and then, his sudden inexplicable silence. His superior, Major General George Kitching, after trying repeatedly to reach Booth by radio, finally went forward to contact him personally. To his horror, Kitching found Booth in his command tank more than two miles behind the front, apparently sound asleep. Kitching soon realized that the commander of his armoured brigade, an officer hand-picked to come from Italy to lead it, an officer who had won the Distinguished Service Order and Bar, and the officer he was counting on to make a rapid advance to the division's objective, was dead drunk. Kitching was irate and, ordering Booth from his tank, berated him for five minutes, reducing Booth to tears, and embarrassing Captain Kenneth Scott, the general's aide, who moved discreetly out of earshot.

For years after this event Kitching would only tactfully say that Booth was asleep,[1] but a few years before his own death, he admitted publicly that Booth was passed out on the floor of his tank.[2] George Kitching was a gentleman in the best meaning of the word, but it is still hard to understand why he did not immediately fire Booth and order him to report to Simonds forthwith, which would have been the end of Booth's career and would probably have resulted in a court martial. In 1943 Booth had barely survived a previous encounter with Simonds as a lieutenant colonel, when, contrary to orders, he had opened his unit's sealed orders for the invasion of Sicily before his ship had left dockside in the United Kingdom. On that occasion Booth had received a tongue-lashing of monumental proportions from Simonds and nearly lost his command. In a classic case of irony, he was saved by Kitching, who convinced Simonds that there was less chance of a security leak if Booth was at sea rather than in a transit depot in England.[3] This time he would be unlikely to get off so lightly. Why he allowed Booth to retain his command after this wretched example of dereliction of duty in the face of the enemy was something that Kitching was never able to explain adequately, especially as he admitted he had doubts about Booth's ability to control his drinking before TOTALIZE.[4] Unfortunately, one is left with the nagging suspicion that Kitching felt that it would not be quite "on" to subject a senior officer to the public humiliation of a court martial, or perhaps at the least, admission to a psychiatric hospital.

But Kitching did not remove Booth from command and at about 1830 hours Simonds ordered him to continue the advance during the night to secure Point 195, which was the approximate centre of 4th Division's final objective. At 2000 hours Kitching convened his orders group with his two brigade commanders, Booth of 4 Brigade and Jefferson of 10 Brigade, the commanders of his artillery, engineers and signals and his two principal staff officers at Jefferson's headquarters. He ordered Booth to push on through the night to capture first Bretteville-le-Rabet, and then Point 195, while Jefferson's 10 Brigade was to follow the armour and assist them after the capture of Bretteville-le-Rabet by taking the villages of Langannerie and Grainville-Langannerie.[5]

In the meantime Booth, who must have been a badly shaken man, had nearly initiated a tactical disaster. Captain C.J. Robertson, the commander

Brigadier Leslie Booth
A favourite of the anglophilic Simonds, the British-born officer was promoted to brigadier and returned from Italy to command 4 Canadian Armoured Brigade. Despite a fine record in the Italian theatre, Booth's performance in TOTALIZE was both professionally inadequate and personally disgraceful. (Courtesy First Hussars Museum)

of A Company of the Algonquin Regiment encountered Booth as Robertson led his company, which was first in the battalion order of march, past brigade headquarters northeast of Rocquancourt at about 1800 hours, probably shortly after Kitching had confronted the brigadier. Robertson recalled that Booth

> asked me to get my C.O. and bring him to his H.Q., which I did. After a few minutes the C.O. came over to my carrier and told me that the Brig. had told him that there was nothing between us and BRETTEVILLE LE RABET and to go there at once.
>
> We started forward. We came to a grain field that was supposedly mined as the engineers had taped a lane through it. The Gov. Gen. Foot Guards were feeding into it from a flank. I did not think it wise to go outside the tape even though we were in a hurry so stopped and reported to the C.O. I did not get an answer so went back to him. His set had broken. He also had a change in orders. We were to follow the G.G.H.G.'s [sic] to BRETTEVILLE. He told me to wait about seven minutes before pushing off as it would take him that long to get his set repaired.
>
> By the time we were underway again, the G.G.H.G.'s [sic] had disappeared. We went through the field, across the railroad track into a piece of bush. After much twisting and turning we came to the main CAEN-FALAISE Road. We went along it until we had reached the point where the centre line went to the east of the road. There wasn't a sign of anyone having been to that spot before us so I halted the column and reported the fact to the C.O. Again I didn't get an answer so I went back. His set was again out of order and there was another change of orders. He had to go back to Bde H.Q. at once. To make things more difficult, his Command Group, with the exception of himself, Sig[nals] Officer and I[ntelligence] O[fficer], along with B, C, and D Coys had become separated from our column. He left me in command of this group while he went back to the "O" Group. This was about 2200 hours.
>
> About 2400 hours the C.O. returned and briefed me on the new orders. I was to stay where I was until 1200 hours, 9 August, when I was to come under command G.G.F.G.'s along with the part of S[u]p[port] Coy that he was leaving behind. He gave me their location.[6]

This time Brigadier Booth essentially kept to his original plan, although he now decided to conduct a night advance with two battle groups. In one the Canadian Grenadier Guards with the Lake Superior Regiment would advance along the highway and capture Bretteville-le-Rabet. This advance would commence at 0315 hours. As the Grenadiers, less their No. 3 Squadron, which remained at Cintheaux, and its attached motor company of the Lake Superior Regiment were already in harbours on the north end of Gaumesnil, they would have been able to form up and move off with little difficulty other than that normally related with marshalling tanks at night. The situation faced by the other battle group was more daunting. Booth had decided that the British Columbia Regiment with the Algonquin Regiment (less its A and Support Companies) under command would move off at 0200 hours, advance south parallel to the Route Nationale, loop around Bretteville-le-Rabet and occupy Point 195. He planned to give his orders for this operation at about midnight at his headquarters located in the British Columbia Regiment harbour area about 200 yards west of the railway at a track junction with the road from Bretteville-sur-Laize to Cramesnil.[7]

The Algonquin Regiment, mounted in half-tracks and carriers and carrying extra ammunition and water, was still slowly making its way forward in a long snake of vehicles from Rocquancourt, and, as we have seen, at just about last light battalion headquarters and A Company missed the turn into the harbour area, which accounts for what Robertson termed their disappearance. The next sub-unit in the column, the troop of flame-thrower tanks of 141 RAC, made the turn and the rest of the battalion followed them. By happenstance the carrier of Major L.C. Monk, the commander of B Company, halted beside Booth's command tank. Lieutenant Colonel Donald Worthington, the commanding officer of the British Columbia Regiment, came over to Monk, informed him of the new plan and asked him to radio Lieutenant Colonel A.J. Hay, Monk's commanding officer, to tell him to report to Booth forthwith for orders.

While Hay was meeting with Booth and Worthington, the company and squadron commanders of the two units assembled near Booth's tank and waited. Meanwhile the half-tracks and carriers of the Algonquins rallied among the tanks and the troops dismounted. It was a quiet night, except for the distraction of a pesky but inaccurate German machine gunner, who loosed off a burst from over by the railway embankment every few minutes with little discernible effect until Lieutenant Thomas Alexander, the Algonquins' carrier platoon commander, grew tired of the disturbance and stalked and captured the lone German. Booth's orders group ended at about 0100 hours on 9 August and Lieutenant Colonels Worthington and Hay crawled out of Booth's tank. Worthington immediately gave his orders to the officers from both units, who circled around him in the dark. He began by telling them they would likely advance beyond artillery support, but that some tactical air might be available when daylight came. Even so, the force had a FOO from each of 19th and 23rd Field Regiments and 11th Medium Regiment of 9 AGRA. Monk of the Algonquins recalled being informed that the mission was to "seize and hold point 195 until the rest of our troops can reach us" and that Worthington described his plan thus:

Method – we will move out of this harbour, cross the highway about 300 yards south of where we are now, pass through the Lake Superior's [sic] who are dug in at this point, advance south on the east side of the highway, taking advantage of ground until opposite the objective, then re-cross the highway and assault the hill from the south-east [actually from the northeast].

The tanks will do the fighting on the way down. Keep moving; try to reach the objective before daylight. Marry up. B Company, Algonquin Regiment, B Squadron, C and D Companies, C Squadron, C.O. Algonquins will travel in my tank with me.

Move off in the following order – A Squadron, B Squadron, B Company, C Squadron, C Company, D Company.

A Squadron will clear the way.

Infantry, net your [radio] sets to the tank net, and use Squadron Code signs plus the letters A, B, C.

Zero [hour] in thirty minutes, and the start line [is] the highway.

The war diary of the British Columbia Regiment puts the matter somewhat differently. It indicates that the order of march was to be: C Squadron, Regimental Headquarters, B Squadron and A Squadron.[8] In matters of armoured detail, the material in its war diary along with the reports made by the participants of the squadrons will be used, especially in regards to the movement to the objective, where Monk was, by his own admission, no more than a passenger back in the column.

When Worthington asked for questions, someone brought up the matter of taking some 3-inch mortars along and Monk was directed to include two mortar detachments from Support Company with his company. Following the orders group, the company and squadron commanders got together to tie up as many details as possible in the limited time available. After locating the last tank in the BCR B Squadron column and agreeing with Major J.H. Carson, the squadron commander, that the latter would be responsible for navigation, Monk briefed his company officers and key noncommissioned officers by means of a flashlight under a blanket. Given the limited time before the column moved off, this was no more than a matter of showing them the objective and detailing the company order of march. Monk also emphasized that direction would be maintained during darkness by contact only – in other words there were no direction finding aids such as Bofors tracer or artillery flare shells, or even the tapes and lights laid by the AVRE crews for the troops who participated in Phase 1.

While the whole thing was obviously rushed, one does get the impression after reading the evidence that both units followed basic battle procedure and were able to maintain control of the preparations. The combined column moved off on time at 0200 hours on 9 August and crawled slowly nose-to-tail across the Route Nationale, then turned south. On its march the battle group passed through the Lake Superior Regiment without incident and then drove on through waist-high wheat. According to Monk,

> The chatter over the [radio] was incessant. We tried to figure out what was going on ahead, by what we heard over the [radio], but between the excited voices and considerable static, it was difficult. However, about 30 minutes after starting and during a short halt, we learned from the messages and the tracers that started to fly, that A [actually C] Squadron [of the BCR] were in contact and in action to their front and right. They were about 400 yards ahead and were firing at enemy infantry entrenched along long narrow tree line that ran east from the highway about opposite Cintheaux.

Captain M.A. Searle, the British FOO from 11th Medium Regiment, was detailed to travel with B Squadron. Shortly after moving off, his Observation Post tank provided by Headquarters Squadron, 4 Armoured Brigade, broke down. As he knew

> my presence up forward was vital, as only Medium Artillery could get the range. I therefore jumped on to the "B" Squadron Commander's tank, which was passing and asked him to take me along. His wireless was not working, so he displaced his operator for me and I took over gunner in his tank for the first phase, my wireless operator, Biggs, got a ride in another tank.[9]

Searle had actually flagged down the tank of Captain J.I. Hope, one of the squadron officers, whom he mistook for the squadron commander. While he stated he was in the gunner's position, it appears he meant the bow gunner's position. While Searle may have usefully occupied himself during the move by blazing away with the Browning machine gun, the restricted visibility from his seat in the tank meant that he would have been unable to follow the progress of the column on his map. Thus, an officer who could be expected to know his location at all times as a key element of his job, was unable to perform his assigned task and to pinpoint the location of any positions occupied.

After advancing perhaps a mile, the column came under fire from the direction of a few buildings that could only have been Cauvicourt. By this time the wheat, some of the buildings in that hamlet and a number of haystacks, some of which had exploded when hit, were burning furiously. While this light may have aided navigation, it also made the troops crowded in the half-tracks and carriers feel conspicuous and vulnerable as they drove through a storm of small-arms fire, but the tanks at least were able to fire their Brownings as they moved. As the going was fairly good, the column picked up speed and became spread out as it passed over rolling country and through more waist-high wheat. As the sky lightened, it sped up yet again until some of the vehicles farther back were literally driving at top speed.

It was about this time that the Grenadier Guards were observed advancing on Bretteville-le-Rabet; after debating whether he should wait for them to clear their objective before proceeding, Worthington ordered his force to "move on anyway, while we still have surprise." Next, high ground was sighted and RHQ and C Squadron made for it, engaging enemy soft-skinned vehicles,* armoured cars and half-tracks hidden in the woods on both flanks.[10] The regiment's history described the latter stages of the advance as a running battle:

> It's a truck this time, a Jerry soft-skin and we leave it blazing. Then another truck, and then an armoured car and some infantry. Things are going well. Nothing has altered our order of march. "C" Sqn. is still leading followed by RHQ, and "B" and "A." Down the valley we go headed for Hill 111 in the broad daylight. Daylight at last. Things should be better for the drivers can see and so can the gunners.
>
> The whole area shakes with blast, 88's fire from all angles. The air is streaked with tracer, smoke rises, tanks brew, crews bale out. Orders are shouted over the wireless, crew commanders strain their eyes through binoculars. The tail end of the regiment has been caught in the valley to Hill 111.[11]

By this time, the infantry had become separated from the lead two squadrons and the gap increased when B and C Companies attempted to follow fresh tank tracks through a gap in a line of trees. Here, as dawn was breaking, the half-tracks and carriers encountered trouble in the form of stumps and brushwood. The going got slow and a number of vehicles became stuck and had to be pulled free by carriers. To make matters worse, the infantry came under large-calibre direct fire, although with little effect. The advance continued across country, the troops returning small-arms fire by firing Brens from the moving half-tracks, which if nothing else did something positive for their morale. On the northern outskirts of what could only have been Estrées-la-Campagne the two Algonquin companies caught up with B Squadron of the BCR, whose commander, Major J.H. Carson, had dismounted from his tank and was studying his map with a puzzled look on his face.

While 10 Platoon of the Algonquins' B Company investigated the village, the three majors held an impromptu conference. Although Monk believed Major Carson was lost, in fact that officer had realized that the head of the Worthington Force column had veered off its route instead of heading towards Point 195, which lay to its right front, and he already had ordered 2 Troop to head for the correct objective, when Worthington came on the air

---

* Military jargon for unarmoured vehicles, i.e. trucks.

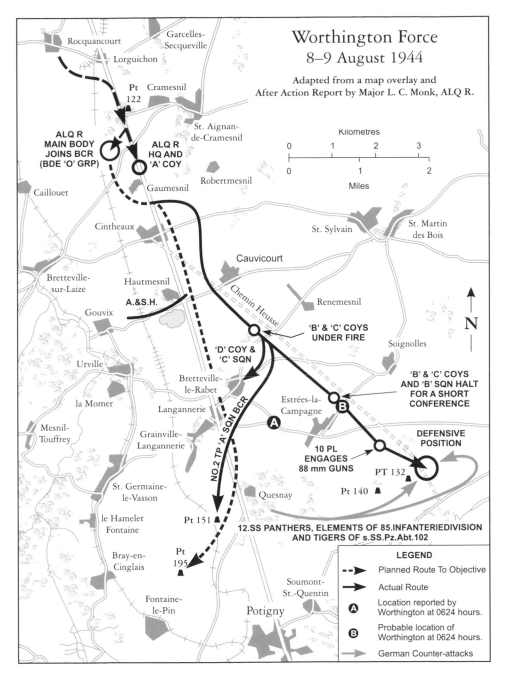

Worthington Force
8–9 August 1944

Adapted from a map overlay and
After Action Report by Major L. C. Monk, ALQ R.

Rocquancourt

Garcelles-
Secqueville

Lorguichon

Pt Cramesnil
122

ALQ R
MAIN BODY
JOINS BCR
(BDE 'O' GRP)

ALQ R
HQ AND
'A' COY

St. Aignan-
de-Cramesnil

Robertmesnil

Caillouet

Gaumesnil

Cintheaux

St. Sylvain

St. Martin
des Bois

Bretteville-
sur-Laize

Hautmesnil

Cauvicourt

Gouvix

A.&S.H.

Chemin Heusse

Renemesnil

Soignolles

'B' & 'C' COYS
UNDER FIRE

N

Urville

'D' COY &
'C' SQN

Bretteville-
le-Rabet

'B' & 'C' COYS
AND 'B' SQN HALT
FOR A SHORT
CONFERENCE

la Momer

Langannerie

Estrées-la-
Campagne

A

B

Mesnil-
Touffrey

Grainville-
Langannerie

DEFENSIVE
POSITION

NO.2 TP 'A' SQN BCR

10 PL
ENGAGES
88 mm GUNS

PT 132

St. Germaine-
le-Vasson

Quesnay

Pt 140

le Hamelet
Fontaine

Pt 151

Pt
195

12.SS PANTHERS, ELEMENTS OF 85.INFANTERIEDIVISION
AND TIGERS OF s.SS.Pz.Abt.102

Bray-en-
Cinglais

Soumont-
St.-Quentin

Fontaine-
le-Pin

Potigny

Kilometres

0   1   2   3

0   1   2

Miles

LEGEND

- – –► Planned Route To Objective

——► Actual Route

Ⓐ Location reported by
Worthington at 0624 hours.

Ⓑ Probable location of
Worthington at 0624 hours.

——► German Counter-attacks

and ordered him to "advance to high ground in front." The rest of the BCR B Squadron and C Company of the Algonquins left immediately, while B Company followed as soon as its 10 Platoon had returned from Estrées. In fact, 2 Troop of B Squadron actually kept on the correct route and reached a point about a mile and a half north of Point 195, where it was fired on by two German anti-tank guns. After knocking them out, the troop started back but was "hindered by scattered groups of enemy infantry trying to surrender."[12]

The tank tracks led into a valley, up the far side, past several rows of trees and finally into a rectangular field some 500 yards square surrounded by a shoulder-high hedge. Here Monk found B and C Squadrons less a few tanks that had been lost on the way, C Company and the two colonels. (The total fighting strength of the British Columbia Regiment at this location was 11 Shermans from B Squadron, 16 tanks from C Squadron, four tanks from regimental headquarters and one Stuart light tank of the BCR Reconnaissance Troop.)[13] As for the infantry, the better part of two Algonquin companies were on the objective but Monk found that he had lost his 10 Platoon somewhere along the route.

It was about 0530 hours and already quite light. Lieutenant Colonel Hay told Monk that the plan was to dig in and consolidate here and presumably wait for friendly reinforcements to arrive. C Company was already digging slit trenches in the hard, pebbly soil along the south side of the position. B Company was to defend the east side and part of the north, while D Company would be allotted the west and part of the north sides when it finally arrived. Monk briefed his two platoon commanders and then went in search of his lost sheep, which he found about 400 yards north back along the trail mopping up a German 88 mm gun position. As he later remembered, 10 Platoon was trailing the rest of the company by about 200 yards when it came under fire from the Germans, who may have been from III. *Flakkorps*, as they were not in the big league of *Wehrmacht* anti-tank gunners. Lieutenant Claire Durcher, the platoon commander, immediately charged with his two half-tracks, and his men leaped out of their vehicles with bayonets fixed and adrenalin pumping. It was no contest. The tough infantrymen from northern Ontario killed all but five of the 30 Germans on the position and destroyed the two guns. Monk added that the few surviving Germans were terrified, and with good reason for the Algonquins had used their bayonets freely.

Not surprisingly, the Germans reacted quickly to the sudden appearance of a mass of tanks and infantry behind their forward troops on a hill where they threatened to cut off the move of *Kampfgruppe* Waldmüller to its new position. Moreover it must have seemed to the German commanders that this was the opening stage of a tactical master-stroke that threatened to break through the hastily-occupied line of defences north of the River Laison, and it was far too close to the headquarters of 12. *SS-Panzerdivision* for comfort.[14] Perhaps the first concrete information came from *SS-Obersturmführer* Bernhard-Georg Meitzel, a member of the division staff attached to *SS-Panzerregiment* 12, who had been despatched from the regiment's location near Quesnay to establish contact with Waldmüller. As he later put it in his prisoner of war interrogation, "While scouting in the early morning east of my company's new position, my armoured car was all of a sudden shelled by tank guns but not hit."[15] To Meitzel's considerable surprise, he had run into Worthington Force, not *Kampfgruppe* Waldmüller, and wasted no time in returning to Quesnay to report to the regimental commander, *SS-Obersturmbannführer* Max Wünsche, who had already alerted his battle group to be prepared to move to counter what must have seemed to him to be the opening phase of another Allied armoured thrust.

At about the same time, Kurt Meyer, who had observed Meitzel's nearly fatal brush with the BCR, immediately telephoned Wünsche to pass on what he had seen and to ask for further information. When Meyer learned what Meitzel had to say, he immediately joined Wünsche. To his mind, the situation

On reconnaissance

This picture taken early in the campaign shows Meyer, then the commander of *SS-Panzergrenadierregiment* 25, mounted on a motorcycle with his divisional commander in the sidecar and the regimental medical officer climbing on behind Meyer. It is difficult to imagine that an Allied brigade commander would ever have attempted something like this. (Michael Reynolds Collection)

was critical and there was a real danger of an Allied armoured breakthrough in a sector that was almost completely undefended. In response Wünsche sent out two platoons of *Panzers* to destroy the enemy force and recapture its position.[16]

After he had briefed Wünsche, Meitzel drove back to the enemy position to gain more information about the Canadian penetration. Unfortunately for him, his armoured car was knocked out by Canadian fire and his arm broken when he was blown from the turret. He was taken prisoner by some Canadian tank crews, perhaps from those that had been sent out to the south of the position and whose tanks had been knocked out. These men had taken cover in a small woods a short distance away from the rectangular field and declined Meitzel's suggestion that they surrender. He could not fail to notice that he was repeatedly questioned as to the whereabouts of a "wide asphalt road," a fact that was clearly of importance to them.[17]

Meanwhile, in the position of Worthington Force, when Major Monk returned to the hill, he found the tanks had been deployed around the hedge facing in all directions. That the Germans were now aware of the Canadian presence became clear when the position came under fire from a small woods about 1,000 yards to the west. The Shermans returned fire but were unable to locate the guns. Worthington had delegated command of the tanks on the position to Major T.B. Baron, commander of the BCR C Squadron, who ordered B Squadron to secure a feature a few hundred yards south of the main position. In turn Carson decided to attack with Lieutenant Stock's troop, supported by fire by the troop of Lieutenant Scudamore. The two troops were able to complete the manoeuvre without cost, but when the squadron headquarters tanks attempted to join them, in the words of the war diary, "tanks began to brew-up" and all the Shermans that had moved forward, including those of both Major Carson and Captain Hope, were lost. The remaining troop of the squadron was placed under the command of C Squadron.[18] The FOO, Captain Searle, recalled

The time was about 0800 hours, when suddenly two of our tanks were hit and set ablaze, I did not see what happened to the crews, I hope they got out. I was transferred to another tank, and just as we moved off, up the field to take up a position where I could see some targets, a shell hit us and my tank was ablaze. I escaped through the escape hatch, the driver set the tank in gear, and we rolled clear. When I looked up I saw Captain Hope coming out of his tank, which had been hit, with his arm blown off, he was the only survivor of his crew. He reached the safety of our lines.[19]

Matters were not improved appreciably when two tanks from A Squadron made their way onto the position, especially after they reported that enemy armour and anti-tank guns had blocked the approaches.[20] Moreover, there was no sign of either the rest of the squadron, including its commander, or D Company of the Algonquins. Instead of a full armoured regiment and three companies of infantry, Worthington Force was now down to two companies of infantry and less than two squadrons of tanks. The situation was grim, but by no means desperate – yet. By 0800 hours the troops were pretty well dug in, and the enemy fire, while deadly accurate, was confined to anti-tank weapons and had not been particularly heavy. Besides the tanks that had ventured outside the hedge, several other tanks and a few half-tracks had been hit and were burning furiously. Worthington appeared calm but must have been concerned over the non-appearance of the rest of his force. His only possible course of action was to continue to hold until relief arrived.

Worthington's confidence would have received another blow had he been aware of the fate of the Algonquins' D Company and the rest of his A Squadron. As the tail elements in the column, they had lagged far behind especially when the lead tanks increased speed as visibility improved. The BCR War Diary later recorded:

After advancing for an hour in the dark, we stopped to orient ourselves, and decided that we were a mile west of Cauvicourt. On an order from the C.O. we swung east, and continued toward the objective. Infantry support in the form of one company of the Algonquin Regiment was directly be-hind us. All through, we were fired on by enemy machine-guns and snipers. Order of march was 2–[squadron headquarters]– 1–3, which later changed

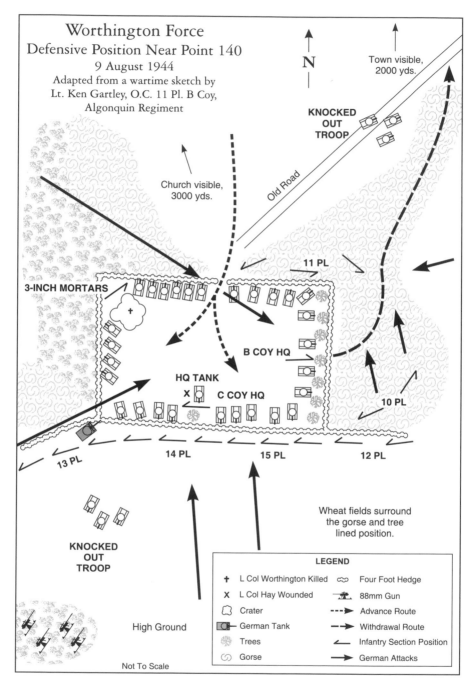

Worthington Force
Defensive Position Near Point 140
9 August 1944
Adapted from a wartime sketch by
Lt. Ken Gartley, O.C. 11 Pl. B Coy,
Algonquin Regiment

N

Town visible,
2000 yds.

KNOCKED
OUT
TROOP

Church visible,
3000 yds.

Old Road

11 PL

3-INCH MORTARS

B COY HQ

10 PL

HQ TANK

X   C COY HQ

14 PL   15 PL   12 PL

13 PL

KNOCKED
OUT
TROOP

Wheat fields surround
the gorse and tree
lined position.

High Ground

Not To Scale

LEGEND

+	L Col Worthington Killed	∞	Four Foot Hedge
X	L Col Hay Wounded	🔫	88mm Gun
☁	Crater	---▶	Advance Route
▣	German Tank	--▶	Withdrawal Route
✿	Trees	∠	Infantry Section Position
∽	Gorse	➡	German Attacks

to 1–[squadron headquarters]–2–3 by Major Sidenius, OC "A" Sqn, when one tank had a mechanical breakdown north of Estrées-la-Campagne. No. 1 Troop came upon two casualties, both "B" Sqn vehicles. At this point we were joined by No. 2 Troop, "A" Sqn from the right flank. Major Sidenius ordered his Sqn to advance toward Hill 143. At [a point about 1000 yards from the hill] Lieutenant L.D. Stevens reported unidentified tanks on the next hill, and was about to fire on them when they were recognized as the remainder of the regiment. He and his corporal proceeded onto open ground and [their tanks] were knocked out by a Tiger tank. Following this, a third tank of No. 1 Troop, and one of No. 2 Troop "B" Sqn were hit. One Tiger tank and one anti-tank gun were accounted for by this group. Meanwhile, No. 2 Troop "A" Sqn began to advance on Hill 143. Lieutenant McDiarmid and his sergeant only, reached the hill. Major Sidenius with his F[ighting] H[ead]Q[uarters] tanks, supported by No. 3 Troop, made a dash for the hill, but all three were hit within a few yards of their starting point. Major Sidenius was seen to start out of his turret, and then fall back again, The force left in the valley, pinned by the enemy, was as follows: No. 3 Troop "A" Sqn, 1 Tank No. 1 Troop "A" Sqn, 3 tanks No. 2 Troop "B" Sqn, and two vehicles from the Algonquins. More ammunition was sent to them on an Ack-Ack tank, but it was hit just before it reached them. The remaining tanks were knocked out after having accounted for another Tiger tank. The Algonquin vehicles were hit as they tried to withdraw.[21]

In fact, the account of this battle prepared by Major Keith Stirling of the Algonquins' D Company is remarkably similar. He wrote that they encountered enemy small-arms fire as they neared the area of Cauvicourt, but his men cleared the resistance and they pushed on behind the tanks, leap-frogging forward on the squadron commander's order. By the time they were clear of Cauvicourt, the sun had risen and the troops had lost the cover of darkness. Stirling recalled that,

When we came opposite and a little forward of Bretteville, our Squadron ran into heavy enemy resistance and the Squadron Commander [Major G.R. Sidenius] ordered D Company to hold back until he could clear the way with his tanks. The enemy which had been bi-passed [sic] by B and C Companies were now fully awake and with daylight on their side, soon made short work of our tanks, knocking out all but two, which got through to B and C Companies. The Squadron Commander was killed.

When D Company could no longer make contact with the Squadron we went forward to a position where we were heavily mortared and subjected to a great deal of anti tank gun fire. The company took up a defensive position in this area, while a reconnaissance party of one platoon went forward, but were driven back by fire from enemy tanks. We saw our tanks destroyed in front of us. We attempted to gain communication with battalion headquarters and B and C Companies, without result.

The company was later joined by a troop of Polish tanks, which attempted to get forward but was also driven back. Stirling then pulled his men back to a hill opposite Bretteville-le-Rabet where it dug in. A patrol sent into the village came under fire from the Lake Superior Regiment, which was clearing the place. After establishing their identity, D Company then helped complete the clearance of the village and dug in to await orders.[22] There can be no doubt that Stirling and his men had been lucky to get off comparatively easily.

At about 0930 hours a high explosive shell struck the side of a tank, badly wounding Lieutenant Colonel Hay, killing Company Sergeant Major A.J. Primeau of C Company and peppering the back of Major W. MacPherson, the company commander, with bits of gravel and shrapnel. By this time there were a fair number of wounded, including Captain Lewis, the RCASC officer in charge of the half-tracks, who suggested that he could lead the remaining 11 half-tracks loaded with the wounded back along the trail to safety. Accordingly the wounded were loaded, Lewis was told to be sure to tell Booth's Headquarters where the battle group was if he got through, and the vehicles made a dash for safety. One was hit but the remainder managed to reach 10 Brigade lines at 1030 hours,[23] where Lewis apparently reported that the Canadians were on Point 195. There was no reason for anyone to doubt him at this time, especially as that was what they expected to hear, or even for him to believe that he had been anywhere else. Later in the day Major G.L. Cassidy, the acting commanding officer of the Algonquins, after interrogating Lewis using a map and "avoiding all leading questions," was able to determine that the position was on high ground in the vicinity of Rouvres. (The actual position was about a mile northwest of Rouvres.)[24]

Up to the time when Hay was wounded, most of the fire had been concentrated on the tanks, and Lieutenant Kenneth Gartley, the commander of 11 Platoon, C Company, noted his men had yet to suffer any casualties.[25] As the day wore on, the German fire increased from all directions, but chiefly from the south and east. By 1030 hours about half of the Shermans were in flames. There was no sign of hostile ground troops so the infantry could only crouch in their slit trenches as their numbers were whittled down by shrapnel that reached into their pits from high explosive bursts in the trees and hedges. Majors MacPherson and Monk, the two infantry company commanders, while they had concluded they were not on the correct objective, decided that since they were under the command of the British Columbia Regiment, that was not their immediate concern. In the meantime, the orders remained to hold on, come what may.

A pair of Typhoons appeared overhead in the morning and first attacked the Canadian position – Monk called it being "Tyffied"– until warned off by yellow smoke. For the rest of the day, aircraft appeared at half-hourly intervals, rocketing and strafing the Germans around the Canadian position. There can be little doubt that this air support helped keep the Germans at bay and provided a notable boost to the Canadians' morale, who loudly cheered the aircraft whenever they came in sight, while heartily cursing the Germans.[26]

In the meantime, no one in the headquarters of 4th Canadian Armoured Division and 4 Canadian Armoured Brigade had the slightest idea where the battle group was. Radio contact had been lost before noon, although the artillery communications were still functioning. The assumption was that the British Columbia Regiment was on Point 195, which had been reported up the chain of command, but, as the battle progressed, reality began to replace optimism: Worthington Force had disappeared. Kitching suspected it had gone too far south and had swung toward Potigny; in fact Brigadier J.N. Lane, his Commander, Royal Canadian Artillery, went up in an Auster light aircraft to look for them along that route, although he could not proceed into enemy territory. Kitching was also aware of the sounds of a pitched battle to the east, but assumed it was coming from the Poles.[27]

One might ask, since Captain M.A. Baker, the 19 Army Field Regiment (SP) FOO with Worthington Force, still had communications with his regiment up to 1830 hours on 9 August when contact was lost after he reported "enemy attacking with heavy mortaring"[28] and presumably might have reported the friendly air attacks, why someone did not think to ask the artillery or the air force for information. Both Baker and Captain J.M. Donohue, the FOO from 23 Field Regiment (SP), were taken prisoner, although in the latter's case, only because he had decided to stay and fight as an infantryman after his tank had been knocked out, and he had ordered his men to make their way back to Allied lines.[29]

Several days later Gunner H.J. Horning, a member of Baker's FOO party, made his way back to Allied lines with a small group from the British Columbia Regiment to report that Baker's Sherman was one of the last in action and until the position was overrun had been engaging the attackers with its 75 mm and machine guns, while Bombardier G.K. Rankin "played havoc with German foot soldiers, using the 50 calibre Browning in the turret."[30] Captain Jamie Stewart, the 19 Army Field Regiment FOO with the Canadian Grenadier Guards, did not hear anything about the plight of Worthington Force during the day, but from his observation post west of Quesnay Wood, he later noticed some knocked-out tanks away in the distance and "wondered whose they were & figured they must belong to the Poles."[31] In response to an order from division headquarters to search for Worthington Force, Lieutenant Caswell's troop from C Squadron, 12th Manitoba Dragoons, probed southeast along the Laize until it was able to observe Point 195 and confirm that it was unoccupied.[32]

The inability of higher headquarters to locate Worthington Force accurately was tragic as all through the day the Germans wore down the Canadian position. By noon the force had no more than what Monk estimated as about seven tanks, while Searle put it at five. He had attempted to raise communications with his guns, but, as he put it, "on three occasions I went to tanks to use their [radio] sets, only to see them ablaze after a few minutes." He continued to attempt to raise his guns using tank radios, but without success. When he reported this to Worthington, the colonel replied, "Don't worry. I cannot get my set working either." Searle then took command of a party of Canadians defending a part (probably near the northwest corner) of the perimeter and was soon involved in heavy fighting in the unaccustomed role of infantryman.[33] If there was any reason why Worthington Force held out as long as it did, it might well have been the presence of the Typhoons overhead. At one stage the fighter bombers even broke up an infantry attack by two companies of 85. *Infanteriedivision* before they could close with the beleaguered position.[34] This happened sometime after 1400 hours, when Monk reckoned the British Columbia Regiment had only one tank still in action. On the other hand, when Worthington ordered his remaining tanks to make a run for safety at about 1500 hours, eight managed to reach friendly territory.[35]

At about 1500 hours, when it was obvious their situation was hopeless, the small party of Canadians that had captured Meitzel, two officers, including the BCR adjutant, Captain James Renwick, and 23 men, accepted Meitzel's offer and followed him into the German lines. It was only at this time that the Germans realized that the sudden appearance of the Canadians deep in their position was the result of a blunder and not a tactical master-stroke. Be that as it may, thanks to Worthington Force, *Kampfgruppe* Waldmüller was still isolated and unable to move to its defensive position

A large target
A comparison of this Sherman with the soldier standing by its rear provides an indication of the height of the lightly armoured tank. (NAC/PA 138646)

covering the Laison River.[36] While Meyer put the best possible light on it in the postwar period, the stark truth was that the Germans were in peril of being pushed back behind that river.

The remnants of Worthington Force now had a brief respite and an upsurge in their morale when they observed Shermans approaching from the north. This was correctly assumed to be the Poles, but when their tanks neared within about a mile of the Canadian position, the Germans shifted their fire to them. In turn, the Poles, 1. *Pułk Pancerny* of 10. *Brygada Kawalerii Pancernej*,[37] directed tank and artillery fire on the Canadians, until yellow smoke grenades – the signal for friendly troops – were set off. A Polish squadron was able to work within 300 yards of the position, in the process breaking up a force of German infantry who had managed to make their way unobserved into a depression some 500 yards east of the Canadians. However, the Polish tanks were eventually forced to withdraw with heavy losses and by 1730 hours no friendly tanks were in sight, and no Canadian tanks remained in action. Somehow, however, yet another enemy attack was driven off and it may have been that the Germans were content to sit back out of small arms range and methodically shoot the position to pieces. The result was inevitable.

By 1700 Gartley's Algonquin 11 Platoon had suffered fairly heavy casualties from continual shelling and mortaring with Lance Corporal J. Federation and Privates C.M. Grubb and C.A. Rogers killed and Sergeant R.C.K. Reynolds and Privates P. Palangio, W. Prus and R.H. Vanderlip wounded. Gartley felt that the situation in all the infantry platoons was similar. By then he recalled, "we were beginning to lose hope about seeing another day. Being late in the day and the friendly troops we had seen in the afternoon coming towards us, had evidently been halted."[38]

Worthington, who had been an inspiring leader all through the day, was killed by a mortar bomb just after he ordered his last three tanks to move forward to engage some Tigers which had appeared at close range. Monk put this at 1730 hours but Captain Searle, who was close enough to Worthington to witness his death and be dazed by the same explosion, fixed the time as 1945 hours, which seems more likely. At this time, with the Germans beginning to mop up the position, Searle decided that there was nothing to be gained by remaining, especially as his party's small arms ammunition was exhausted.

I shouted "Come on chaps, Crawl," and they followed me down to a wood. We passed a great number of dead Germans on the way, about thirty, I should say, extremely well turned out, S.S. Troops no doubt.

    We lay in the woods, but the Germans would not come in after us, they just shouted, "Come Comrade, not hurt you," but I said to our fellows, "They do not like you Canadians and they will shoot us," so we all lay still. At this stage we had no ammunition, if we had I believe the Germans would have had another fight on his hands [sic] as our chaps were all for it. We edged down the wood about a quarter of a mile to discuss our plans. I considered the best way to avoid capture was to lay up by day, and at night split up into pairs and each pair try to make for our own lines independently. We wished each other luck and went our own ways. I had an Algonquin from the mortars with me, an excellent companion.

After a perilous journey, Searle and the mortarman eventually made their way to the Canadian lines on 11 August, having picked up a wounded Algonquin on the way.[39]

    While it had been Worthington's intention to fight to the finish, the two Algonquin company commanders decided that there was nothing to be gained by a last stand. The Germans were closing with the position and by 2200 hours had overrun a corner of the field, capturing the survivors of Lieutenant Blais's 13 Platoon of C Company in the process. Monk, as the senior surviving officer (the other company commander, Major MacPherson, who had been in considerable pain from his wounds, had wandered into the open and had been killed by a burst of machine gun fire shortly after Worthington met his death), organized a withdrawal. He commanded the rear guard, holding the Germans at bay with a Bren gun until anyone able to move had made their escape. When he and Lieutenants Gartley and Saville, the last men off the position, abandoned the field, the Germans had closed to within 50 yards and Lieutenant Fraser, who had been with Monk and his party, was captured.

    By the dawn of 10 August 42 Algonquins and 10 members of the British Columbia Regiment had reached the Polish lines at Renemesnil and were sent back to 10 Brigade Headquarters at Cintheaux. Over the next two days, another 20 Algonquins, many of them wounded, made their way back to

Allied lines. On its first day in action during the Second World War the British Columbia Regiment had lost seven officers, including its commanding officer, and 33 men killed, five officers and 33 men wounded and four officers and 32 men missing, as well as losing 44 Shermans, two Stuart reconnaissance tanks, a Crusader anti-aircraft tank and a scout car. Included in this butcher's bill, besides the commanding officer, were all three tank squadron commanders, the adjutant, the three rear link captains and six subalterns.

The official casualty record compiled by the War Services Branch for the Algonquin Regiment on 9 August records 16 men killed, one officer and 20 men wounded and one man missing, a figure that is far too low.[40] The regiment itself recorded one officer and 35 men killed or died of wounds, two officers and 28 men wounded, and two officers and 50 men missing from the approximately 220 soldiers who fought on the hill.[41] It was a tragically gallant waste of life and a missed opportunity.

What had happened? First the entire operation was rushed and it seems no one thought to request aids to navigation such as tracer or artillery flares fired at designated points, although Simonds did apparently arrange some movement light. Second, the operation was late getting started – there were perhaps three hours of darkness left by the time C Squadron crossed the start line, and perhaps no more than an hour or two for the troops at the rear of what became a long disjointed column. Third, in its haste the column itself lost cohesion and contact between companies and squadrons broke down. The 4 Armoured Brigade log provides a clue as to what happened. At 0624 hours on 9 August the BCR rear link reported a location of grid reference 105498 (Point A on the map), and then at 0643, that the unit was 1,800 yards short of the objective and the tanks [A Squadron] were moving into assault formation[42]

As can be seen, Point A is on the road between Bretteville-le-Rabet and Estrées-la-Campagne and about 500 yards southeast of the former place, but it seems that Worthington was at Point B on the road between Estrées-la-Campagne and Soignolles, and about 500 yards from Estrées. An examination of the map shows that the distance and relationship between Bretteville and Estrées on one hand, and Estrées and Soignolles on the other, bear an uncanny resemblance to one another, as do the headings from the roads to the real and assumed objectives on the high ground that can be observed from both Points A and B.* Moreover, a wood lay to the left of both the correct and assumed axes. It is likely that Worthington had forced the ground to fit the map, an error many soldiers have made, including on at least one embarrassing occasion the author. (2 Troop of B Squadron had reached the correct objective, but finding itself on its own, it withdrew and was later destroyed fighting near Estrées-la-Campagne.) While night movement is always extremely difficult, and this often has been cited as the cause of the disaster, there had been little, if any, opportunity to practise cross-country movement by night or day in England, and it is a skill that can only be mastered through practice. Lack of training in cross-country movement and navigation in 4 Armoured Brigade, or perhaps ignorance of the pitfalls, played a major part in Worthington Force going astray.

There is a further point to be made. Because Booth had been incapable of exercising command in the late afternoon, several vital hours were lost. By the time Worthington Force moved off at 0200 hours, there were no more than two-and-a-half to three hours of darkness remaining. This meant that much of the advance was in daylight. Thus, even if the head of the column had not gone astray and had attempted to move onto Point 195, it would have had to pass between Grainville-Langannerie and Quesnay Wood at about 0630 hours, well after first light. As the wood was held by *Kampfgruppe* Wünsche of *SS-Panzerregiment* 12, which had moved into position on the previous evening, it seems likely that the lead squadron of the British Columbia Regiment would have been shot to pieces, and Point 195 would not have been captured, at least not that morning. Whether things might have been more successful if Worthington Force had moved off at last light seems unlikely as elements of the column would have been passing the wood as day broke. Even if Worthington Force had been able to move onto Point 195, it would have been counterattacked almost immediately by *Kampfgruppe* Wünsche. It is unlikely, however, that Worthington Force would have been wiped out and TOTALIZE might have ended diferently

---

* While there is high ground visible from both places, I confirmed by personal observation in May 2003 that the Point 195 feature is both higher and very much larger and more prominent than "Worthington Hill," which is on a long, flat ridge.

CHAPTER SIXTEEN

THE DAY OF
BURNING SHERMANS

*"Considerable speculative shooting was engaged in and the
tracer bullets were about as thick as snow in a snow-storm."*

WAR DIARY, CANADIAN GRENADIER GUARDS

T he fortunes of the remainder of 4 Canadian Armoured Brigade took a more favourable turn. As we have seen, the Argyll and Sutherland Highlanders of Canada and the tanks of the South Alberta Regiment were able to clear the Hautmesnil Quarry during the morning of 9 August, taking 25 prisoners and capturing many vehicles. Before this success, at 0330 hours the Grenadier Guards, less No. 3 Squadron, and the Lake Superior Regiment moved south on Bretteville-le-Rabet with No. 2 Squadron leading. Initially progress was good and by 0600 hours the leading tanks had reached low ground west of the objective. By this time, however, the defenders were aroused and there was a much small-arms fire, while the tanks blazed away with their Brownings and high-explosive from their main armament. (The Grenadier's war diary noted "tracer bullets were about as thick as snow in a snow-storm.") While Regimental Headquarters and No. 2 Squadron returned to the harbour area at Gaumesnil, No. 1 Squadron attacked the village from the north, 1 Troop commanded by Lieutenant McKinnon entering the village, covered by fire from the remainder of the squadron. The tanks and the motor battalion, assisted by Major Keith Stirling's D Company of the Algonquins, completed the clearance of the objective by 1500 hours, capturing 200 prisoners from *89. Infanteriedivision* and discovering that:

Scores of enemy had been killed by co-ax [machine guns] and high explosive, the gunners having a field day. High explosive rounds against single infantrymen was quite in order and speculative shooting on hedges and house flushed the enemy infantry who were then co-axed by the score.

No. 1 Squadron pulled back to the harbour at Gaumesnil shortly after 1700 hours, being replaced in the forward area by No. 2 Squadron in a mobile counterattack role.[1]

In the early afternoon, with the armoured brigade still mopping up Bretteville-le-Rabet, Kitching ordered Brigadier Jefferson to clear Langannerie and Grainville-Langannerie, placing the Lake Superior Regiment under his command. At 1415 hours the Lincoln and Welland Regiment passed through the Argylls and attacked Langannerie, supported by Major Arnold Lavoie's A Squadron of the South Alberta Regiment. After several hours of

Motor Battalion
The Lake Superior Regiment

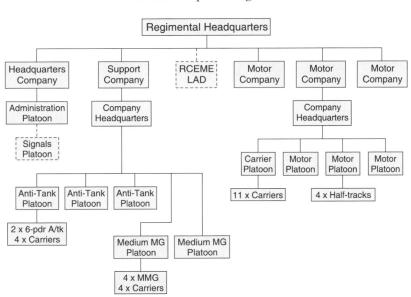

This unit was designed to support the three armoured regiments in the armoured brigade of an armoured division and was a bit of a hangover from the North African campaign. As a result it was light on infantrymen able to fight on foot and would experience difficulties coping with tasks such as village clearing and attacking dismounted.

Making a plan
Brigadier James Jefferson of
10 Canadian Infantry Brigade
(right) and Lieutenant Colonel
Gordon Wotherspoon of the
South Alberta Regiment study a
situation map near Hautmesnil.
(NAC/PA 163410)

heavy house-to-house fighting, which saw all four companies committed, the battalion managed to clear the village by late afternoon assisted by the Argylls and C Squadron of the South Albertas, which had been relieved in Hautmesnil by 9 Infantry Brigade of 3rd Canadian Infantry Division. By 1800 hours the village was secured, although a few isolated snipers were active into the early evening.[2]

While 10 Brigade was completing the clearance of the villages, and with the Canadian Grenadier Guards' battle group still mopping up Bretteville-le-Rabet and the British Columbia Regiment off who knew where, Booth's 4 Armoured Brigade was attempting to move onto Point 195 using its only uncommitted regiment, the Governor General's Foot Guards. (At this stage of the battle, Kitching's division was completely committed except perhaps for RHQ and one squadron of the South Alberta Regiment, and lacked a reserve for any unforeseen developments, a mortal military sin.) The Foot Guards, which had spent the night on the road as brigade reserve, moved into the area of Gaumesnil at 1100 hours. After what the regimental historian termed a "hasty lunch," the Commanding Officer, Lieutenant Colonel M.J. Scott, issued his orders at 1200 hours for the regiment's first attack.* The plan was for the unit, with A Company of the Algonquins, a platoon of heavy mortars and another of medium machine guns and a troop each of anti-tank guns

---

* While it is unclear exactly when Scott was directed to advance to Point 195, sheet 2 of the 4 Armoured Brigade log for 9 August contains an order from brigade headquarters to his unit at 1029 hours to "Tell your Sunray [Scott] to report here."

5th Anti-Tank Regiment
4th Canadian Armoured Division

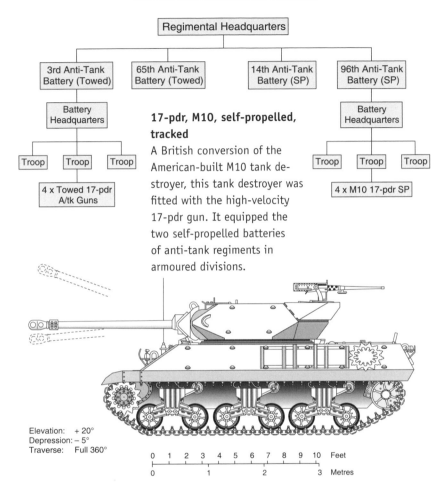

17-pdr, M10, self-propelled, tracked

A British conversion of the American-built M10 tank destroyer, this tank destroyer was fitted with the high-velocity 17-pdr gun. It equipped the two self-propelled batteries of anti-tank regiments in armoured divisions.

Elevation: + 20°
Depression: – 5°
Traverse: Full 360°

and AVREs, to loop east around Bretteville-le-Rabet, bypass all opposition and drive onto the objective, in other words, follow the route Worthington Force was thought to have taken.

In fact, the operation was rushed with an original H-Hour of 1330 hours, and the order to move was given before all the supporting arms had arrived, which did not reflect well on Brigadier Booth's ability to plan and organize operations. At 1430 hours the regiment swung off the highway and began to advance in squadron formations of three troops forward. Lieutenant N.F. Westheuser, the troop leader of No. 2 Troop of No. 1 Squadron, who was leading the advance, reported enemy in the wood when his troop had reached a hedge about 500 yards from Quesnay Wood. Intelligence was also faulty as the information received was that the wood was lightly held and may even have been cleared by leading troops, and therefore serious opposition was not expected. As we have seen, in fact the wood was occupied by *Kampfgruppe* Wünsche of *12. SS-Panzerdivision.* Westheuser's troop began to engage the enemy and No. 1 Troop swung up on his left, while No. 4 Troop did the same on his right.[3]

A bitter fight ensued. Westheuser's tank was knocked out by two shots through the right track; while his crew continued the fight, he dismounted and attempted to repair the damaged track despite the heavy artillery, anti-tank and machine gun fire. The squadron lost in turn Corporal D.G. Pecore's tank of No. 1 Troop, and then the Shermans of Sergeant N. Dennis and Corporal J.M. Corbeil, both of No. 2 Troop. Lieutenant Colonel Scott decided to clear the wood using A Company of the Algonquin Regiment, which indicates how desperate he must have considered the situation to be. The company commander, Captain C. Robertson, recalled that after the lead squadron had come under fire, his company

> retired over a knoll and worked farther west through the apple orchards until we again faced the wood about 1500 yards away. Anti-tank fire missed. The ground between us and the wood was very flat and sloped away from us toward the wood. The grain was cut but still on the ground.[4]

No. 1 Squadron then attempted to bypass the German position by working around the right flank, covered by 1 Troop, which soon lost its last two tanks, while Lieutenant Middleton-Hope's Sherman of No. 2 Squadron was knocked out after his squadron moved up into a hedge to provide further support. Meanwhile Sergeant McLean's Firefly of 4 Troop of No. 1 Squadron knocked out a tank near an orchard.[5] At about this time Lieutenant Colonel Scott issued what can only be termed an order based more on desperation than common sense. Captain Robertson of the Algonquins noted Scott

> wanted A Company to put in an attack on the wood. I discussed the matter with Major Laidlaw, their leading squadron commander. He wouldn't

give me any tank support; they were out of touch with Artillery so couldn't get any help for that source. Captain Stock [the commander of Support Company] had discovered D Company during our advance to Bretteville and had dropped out of the column so there was no help to be expected from the mortars. Taking the ground into consideration and no support available, I decided against the attack. While the reconnaissance was going on we saw Germans wandering around about 400 [yards] distant so a tank was rolled up and fired was opened. After the Germans had disappeared, Major Laidlaw and I started back to see the C.O. The Germans then opened fire and Major Laidlaw was killed.[6]

What was left unsaid in his report was the Laidlaw and Scott were prepared to let the Algonquins attack a strong enemy position across open ground without any artillery or armoured support, which does not reflect well on Booth's arrangements for the battle. Robertson, however, was not prepared to sacrifice his men in a futile operation, and his assessment of the situation was far superior to that of the Guards officers.

In what became a long, costly afternoon, the Foot Guards No. 1 Squadron lost 12 tanks, including Laidlaw's, in reply managing to claim only one concealed panzer knocked out by a Firefly, while the other squadrons lost another 14 Shermans between them. In other words, the Foot Guards had lost half its fighting strength in its first action and had achieved little in return; clearly Quesnay Wood was held by more than the light forces intelligence had estimated. As for the attached Algonquin company, Robertson had decided that the advance was going nowhere and "decided to put [his company] down in a defensive position. While looking over the area, we found enemy hiding in slit trenches so made a thorough search of the area and found several, all Russian, in German uniforms, according to their story." Unable to advance, the regiment took up defensive positions screened by outposts from Robertson's company facing Quesnay Wood as night fell. Clearly, contrary to what intelligence believed, the wood was the anchor of a strong defensive line.[7] More disturbing, in what after all was its first day and a half in action, the two guards armoured regiments of 4 Armoured Brigade had lost over a third of their total tank strength, and the situation of the British Columbia Regiment was still unknown.

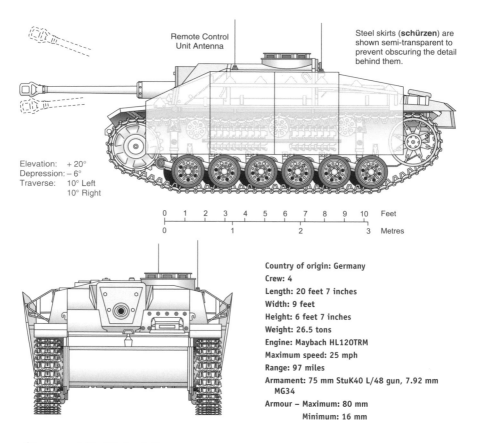

Remote Control
Unit Antenna

Steel skirts (**schürzen**) are
shown semi-transparent to
prevent obscuring the detail
behind them.

Elevation: + 20°
Depression: – 6°
Traverse: 10° Left
　　　　　10° Right

0　1　2　3　4　5　6　7　8　9　10　Feet

0　　　　　1　　　　　2　　　　　3　Metres

Country of origin: Germany
Crew: 4
Length: 20 feet 7 inches
Width: 9 feet
Height: 6 feet 7 inches
Weight: 26.5 tons
Engine: Maybach HL120TRM
Maximum speed: 25 mph
Range: 97 miles
Armament: 75 mm StuK40 L/48 gun, 7.92 mm
　　MG34
Armour – Maximum: 80 mm
　　　　　　Minimum: 16 mm

Sturmgeschütz III Ausf. G

The StuG III Ausf. G was the last in the line of German assault guns based on the
chassis of the PzKpfw III series. Originally developed as an assault gun for infantry
support, the Sturmgeschütz evolved into a dual-purpose assault gun and tank
destroyer. German tank production fell short of operational requirements as the war
progressed and the StuG III was often pressed into service to supplement the tanks
in panzer divisions. In contrast to American self-propelled tank destroyers equipping
British and Canadian units, the StuG III provided overhead protection for the crew,
together with a low silhouette. A shortcoming of the turretless design, though, was
restricted traverse for the main gun. The StuG III illustrated here has an additional
antenna indicating service in a *Funklenk* (remote control) company where it would be
the control vehicle for a Sprengladungstraeger demolition charge carrier.

The German situation was critical, and would remain so until Worthington Force was eliminated. The erstwhile *Kampfgruppe* Waldmüller – I. *Bataillon, SS-Panzergrenadierregiment* 25 and *Nr.* 1 *Companie of SS-Panzerjägerabteilung* 12 – had set up defences around Soignolles during the night of 8/9 August. The *Divisionbegleitkompanie*, which had been unable to withdraw to its reserve position near Montboit, deployed into a defensive position between St. Sylvain and the Château du Fosse, about a kilometre southwest of town, while the *Korpsbegleitkompanie* was sited to the left of its divisional counterpart. All hoped to be relieved by panzers soon, as promised by Meyer, but it was not to be. Wünsche and his tanks were occupied dealing with the British Columbia Regiment and Algonquin Regiment incursion that threatened to upset the German plans to establish a defensive line on the high ground north of the Laison River.

In the Polish division's area, 3. *Brygada Strzelców* had replaced the armour in the forward area on the evening of 8 August and prepared to capture Robertmesnil and the woods that had concealed the hornets' nest of tanks and anti-tanks guns by a night attack. When it advanced, however, it discovered the Germans had withdrawn and the brigade was able to clear as far south as the woods southeast of Robertmesnil, taking 48 prisoners while suffering only light casualties.[8]

That morning orders were issued at 0900 hours for 10. *Brygada Kawalerii Pancernej* to continue its attack to the south. The brigade attacked with two regiments, 1. *Pułk Pancerny* and 24. *Pułk Ułanów*, forward. The former regiment was to capture in turn Cauvicourt, Renemesnil and Hill 140, near where, unknown to the Poles, Worthington Force was fighting for its life. The Lancers were ordered to take the woods a half mile west of Renemesnil, the area of Estrées-la-Campagne and the copse to the east of the village. The divisional reconnaissance regiment was to consolidate the ground taken by the two armoured regiments while 2. *Pułk Pancerny* was in reserve behind 24. *Pułk Ułanów*. H-Hour was set as 1100 hours. In the meantime 3. *Brygada* was directed to capture St. Sylvain. This task was originally given to one battalion, but a second battalion was also committed when it was determined that the village was held in strength.[9] While far too late in kicking off, Maczek's plan was ambitious and perhaps depended on 4 Armoured Brigade being able to secure Bretteville-le-Rabet by the time the Polish advance reached the area of the village. Unwittingly the German reaction to Worthington Force and to the advance of 4 Armoured Brigade down the Caen–Falaise Road may have relieved some of the pressure on the Polish division.

Initially some good progress was made and by 1300 hours 1. *Pułk Pancerny* had reached the west edge of Cauvicourt while 24. *Pułk Ułanów* were at the woods west of Renemesnil. It was no cakewalk, though, as the Poles were opposed several times by what they described as tanks of Tiger type, numbering 10 to 15, and suffered losses as a consequence. It appears that they were able to make headway as by 1600 hours the former had captured Point 84, about a mile northwest of Soignolles, while two squadrons of 24. *Pułk Ułanów* had reached the north edge of La Croix, a hamlet on the west side of Estrées-la-Campagne. The unit then attempted to advance on Quesnay Wood but was repulsed by strong resistance from "dug-in Panthers and anti tank guns in fortified positions." The advance of 1 *Pułk Pancerny* made better progress, and it was this regiment which nearly raised the siege of Worthington Force, at least for a short period.[10]

As the tanks advanced, a battalion of 3. *Brygada* had relieved 10. *Brygada* in Cauvicourt and at 1930 hours another battalion started to clear St. Sylvain. This attack was preceded by artillery preparation and air strikes. Progress was slow but steady and by 2200 hours the area up to the church had been cleared, while St. Martin-de-Bois, on the east of the village was cleared by 2400 hours. By now Maczek had received orders to turn over the sector to 51st Highland Division, and the battalions were relieved by the Highlanders after midnight.[11] All things considered, the Poles had done well, even if this was not understood by Simonds. Southwest of St. Sylvain they had overrun and destroyed the *Korpsbegleitkompanie* of 1. *SS-Panzerkorps* and nearly did the same to the *Divisionbegleitkompanie*, forcing it to withdraw to the southeast. That evening the remnants of *Kampfguppe* Waldmüller and the *Divisionbegleitkompanie* both moved rearwards to the positions they had been unable to reach the previous night.[12]

CHAPTER SEVENTEEN

OPPORTUNITY LOST

"I was always up front ... You can't win battles being behind.
You've got to be there."

LIEUTENANT COLONEL DAVID STEWART,

ARGYLL AND SUTHERLAND HIGHLANDERS OF CANADA

t is now time to examine the general situation across the 2 Canadian Corps front as it stood at last light on 9 August. First, 51st Highland Division and 33 British Armoured Brigade had been transferred from Simonds's command to 1st British Corps at 1330 hours on 9 August. The inter-corps boundary now moved southward to include St. Sylvain and Soignolles within the British corps' area of responsibility. The Highlanders continued to expand their area to the south and east; by last light Conteville and Poussy between Secqueville-la-Campagne and St. Sylvain were in British hands. To the west of First Canadian Army, the British had expanded their bridgehead over the Orne from just north of Thury-Harcourt across to the northern edge of the woods to the Laize River opposite St. Germain-le-Vasson.[1] Within the Canadian area, 2nd Canadian Infantry Division continued to mop up its area and 5 Infantry Brigade had re-occupied Bretteville-sur-Laize and cleared the woods southwest of Quilly, in the process capturing three of the *Nebelwerfers* that had caused so much trouble the previous day. Throughout the day, 3rd Canadian Infantry Division had closed up behind 4th Canadian Armoured Division, its vehicles forming a long line inching down the RN. By noon 9 Brigade of the 3rd Division had relieved 10 Brigade of the 4th Division at Hautmesnil and expanded its hold west to occupy Gouvix and Urville. Last light found two battalions of 8 Infantry Brigade of 3rd Division at Bretteville-le-Rabet and Langannerie while Le

Régiment de la Chaudière had occupied La Bruyère just south of Cramesnil. The division's third formation, 7 Brigade, was concentrated just south of Cintheaux.[2]

The stage was now set for the closing stages of Operation TOTALIZE. Simonds could not have been happy with the results achieved on 9 August, especially by the 4th Division. It was true that the Poles had made good progress after their slow start on the previous day, in part because *Kampfgruppe* Waldmüller had been forced to withdraw by the loss of Hautmesnil to the Argyll and Sutherland Highlanders, but he must have begun to understand that the Germans had crafted an anti-tank screen along the hills north of the Laison, and Quesnay Wood was a hornet's nest of tanks and anti-tank guns. It was therefore time to adjust his plan.

Simonds ordered Kitching to continue his attack to secure the high ground south of Bretteville-le-Rabet as far south as Point 206 above Potigny, which was 4th Division's final Phase 2 objective, and then exploit towards Falaise on the west of the Route Nationale.[3] It seems that he intended to bypass Quesnay Wood with his armour and he probably believed it would be possible to avoid undue casualties and delay by keeping on the west slopes of the Point 195–Point 206 feature as much as possible. In the case of 1. *Dywizji Pancernej*, he changed its mission entirely, ordering it to clear Quesnay Wood with one battalion. Later in the day he cancelled that mission and ordered Maczek to capture Point 140 and the tank graveyard of Worthington Force, then seize a bridgehead over the Laison River between Montboit and Rouvres and clear the high ground west of Olendon as far south as Point 168, less than three miles north of Falaise.* The task of dealing with Quesnay Wood fell to the 3rd Infantry Division.[4] With the benefit of hindsight, Simonds had given Maczek a very tall order indeed, especially as he must have appreciated that the Germans had reinforced their defences

In the meantime, the 4th Armoured Division had continued its operations to capture Point 195. Throughout 9 August, three squadrons of 12 Manitoba Dragoons had been probing to the east, south and west. To the east a link-up with the Poles was achieved by B Squadron and Lieutenant A.B.

---

* This is an indication that Simonds, unlike Kurt Meyer, did not consider the Laison River to be a tank obstacle. This misconception would have serious repercussions a few days later.

Megaw's troop of D Squadron crossed to the west side of the Laize River but was forced to retire, although the east bank of the river was cleared for a considerable distance to the south. In the centre, C Squadron attempted to work its way forward but was held up by anti-tank guns and lost an armoured car to an 88 mm. Lieutenant W.S. McKeough's troop of this squadron also managed to cross the Laize and shot up some German positions before returning at last light. He also reported that 4 Armoured Brigade tanks had engaged him and that he had a few close calls trying to avoid their fire. The entry in the dragoon's war diary commented dryly that "some of our Armoured Corps troops, both tank crews and anti-tank crews have very limited knowledge of our own armoured fighting vehicles." However, the report from Lieutenant Caswell's troop, engaged in a fruitless search for Worthington Force to the south, that Point 195 was clear, had the most dramatic effect. Kitching immediately decided to seize it by a *coup de main* by sending a squadron each of armoured cars and tanks and a company of infantry to capture St. Hilaire Farm and the high ground south of the farm. Lieutenant Colonel J.A. Roberts, the Dragoons' commanding officer, detailed A Squadron for this task and he and Lieutenant Landreth, the intelligence officer, accompanied the squadron in their armoured cars. Unfortunately,

> The three formations were to meet at a given point and our squadron was the only one to arrive. Feeling we may have been wrong about rendezvous or late, A squadron proceeded to get onto high ground to cover the attack on St. Hilaire Farm by the tanks and infantry. We waited until last light and withdrew the squadron according to plan.
>
> The commanding officer went to 4th Canadian Armoured Division Headquarters to report on this apparent error and discovered that the squadron of tanks had been cancelled and the infantry were on their way then. We had not been advised about this change of plan which explained the absence of tanks and infantry at the rendezvous.[5]

The company of infantry, D Company of the Algonquin Regiment, had just finished helping the Lake Superior Regiment clear Bretteville-le-Rabet and were digging in near the town, when

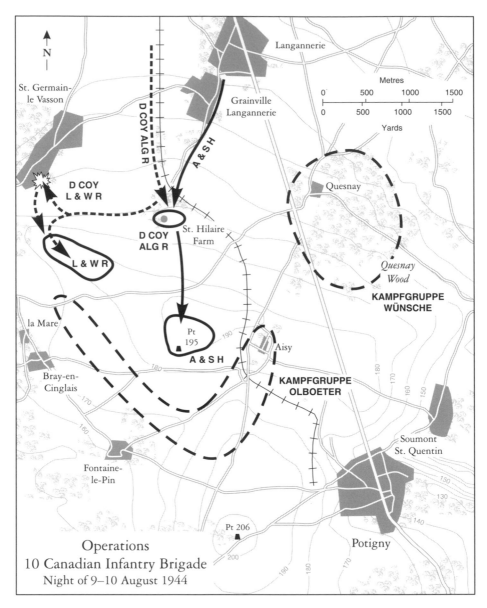

Operations
10 Canadian Infantry Brigade
Night of 9–10 August 1944

we received a message from Major Cassidy [the acting second in command of the Algonquins], who had taken over command after Lieutenant Colonel Hay had been wounded. The message was to move down the road to a railway and road junction where we were to meet the commanding officer of 18 Canadian Armoured Car [Regiment, 12th Manitoba Dragoons] who was to give us orders for an attack on St. Hilaire Farm opposite Quesnay Wood. We loaded the company on the carriers again and at 2200 hours on the 9th we were at the railway and road junction. The carriers returned to Bretteville-le-Rabet. There was no information of any kind. The only order was to move in and take the farm without any assistance. At 2330 hours Lieutenant McNairn arrived and told us we were to attack St. Hilaire Farm at once. We were to have no supporting arms, but A Company was to come along within the hour, also that the Regiment de la Chaudiere were to attack Quesnay Wood. [Lieutenant] Colonel Roberts of the 18th [Canadian Armoured Car Regiment] did not show up.

We formed up immediately and moved along the railway and into St. Hilaire Farm where we found no one. The enemy had left a few hours before. We took up our positions on the right of the farm. About 0800 hours in the morning Battalion Headquarters and A Company moved in on our left. The Chauds never did get to Quesnay Wood.[6]

The information that the back door onto Point 195 was open and unguarded, while not acted upon with the force and speed one should associate with an armoured division, set off a sequence of events that showed what could be accomplished by a combination of timely intelligence, audacious commanders and good troops.[7] While the second and third were more of a constant in the Allied armies in Normandy than some critics may care to admit, the three factors too often did not come together. The occupation of the Point 195 feature by Jefferson's Brigade, for it hardly qualified as an attack by Normandy standards, was one of these rare occasions. It is even more noteworthy because it stands in stark contrast to the repeated hammering against the front door by 4 Armoured Brigade that did little other than extract too heavy a cost in lives and tanks.

The first step in the 4th Armoured Division's operation was to clear the open ground south of St. Hilaire Farm down to Point 195. Kitching gave this task to Jefferson's 10th Brigade. Jefferson in turn ordered the Argyll and Sutherland Highlanders to capture Point 195 while the Lincoln and Welland Regiment were to take a spur of the feature that extended northwest towards St. Germain-le-Vasson. As we have seen, as late as last light the objective area had not been fully occupied by the Germans. Therefore, both battalions attempted to infiltrate onto their objectives by means of silent night attacks. In

Armoured Car Regiment
12th Manitoba Dragoons

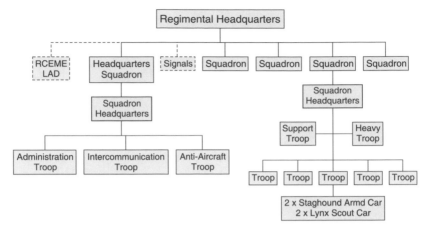

Note: Heavy Troop equipped with 37 mm Staghounds until replaced by the Staghound III in the last days of the war.

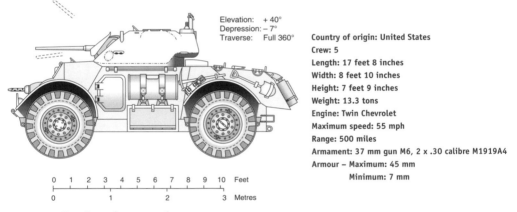

Elevation: + 40°
Depression: – 7°
Traverse: Full 360°

Country of origin: United States
Crew: 5
Length: 17 feet 8 inches
Width: 8 feet 10 inches
Height: 7 feet 9 inches
Weight: 13.3 tons
Engine: Twin Chevrolet
Maximum speed: 55 mph
Range: 500 miles
Armament: 37 mm gun M6, 2 x .30 calibre M1919A4
Armour – Maximum: 45 mm
Minimum: 7 mm

Staghound armoured car

Originally designed for the wide-open expanses of desert operations, the Staghound was a large and somewhat heavy armoured car. In Canadian service though, it proved popular due to the roominess of the design. It equipped the 12th Manitoba Dragoons throughout Northwest Europe.

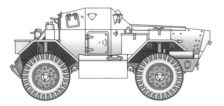

Lynx II scout car

The Lynx was a Canadian-built version of the British Daimler "Dingo" scout car. A compact, quick and manoeuvrable vehicle, the Dingo was a popular scout car. The Lynx was never as popular as the Dingo, due to persistent reliability problems. The Lynx served alongside the Staghound in the armoured car troop.

the case of the Lincoln and Welland Regiment, patrols from the unit's Scout Platoon were sent off in advance of the rifle companies to reconnoitre the tracks that led onto the spur.

The main body then moved out of Grainville-Langannerie at 2030 hours on foot guided by the scouts in the order D, A, B and C Companies and a small headquarters party. It was planned that the support company carriers and the attached troop of 17-pounder anti-tank guns would make their way forward separately, once the objective had been reached, and the FOO would join them at first light. Less than half a mile from the spur the guide lost his way and led D Company straight into St. Germain-le-Vasson, where it bumped into and wiped out a 12-man German patrol. All hell broke loose! D Company tried to extricate itself; two platoons were successful but the headquarters and the leading platoon experienced great difficulty breaking contact. The remainder of the dismounted battalion went to ground along the track when D Company first had met the enemy. A German machine gun opened up to their right rear while a woods near the road came under shell fire. In the confusion A and B Companies remained stationary while the headquarters and C Company made their way onto the correct objective, where they were joined by the support weapons and, towards first light, by the other rifle companies. It had not been a tidy operation, but it had worked.[8]

If the Lincoln and Welland Regiment attack had succeeded after initially going astray, the attempt by the Argyll and Sutherland Highlanders was a textbook example of how these things should be done. The Commanding Officer, Lieutenant Colonel Dave Stewart, was a very competent officer who took nothing for granted. He remembered that,

When we received the orders to take "Hill 195" it was late in the afternoon and two other regiments had tried but were misdirected and got off the track. I mentally wrote the Argylls off as well as myself.

I took the scout platoon with me and we reconnoitred the route I had chosen. On the way back I left members of the scout platoon at strategic points, to guide the Battalion, so I could lead them to the high ground.[9]

The main body of the battalion left Langannerie just after midnight on 9 August and marched through the dark in single file. It was perhaps a bit

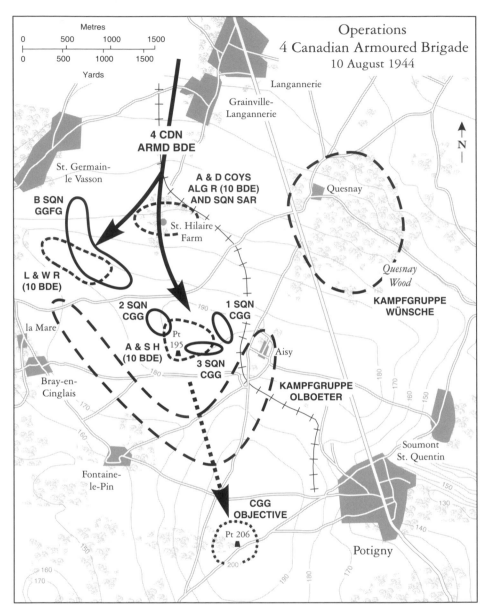

Operations
4 Canadian Armoured Brigade
10 August 1944

more than "Simply walking in single file to the hill, up its slopes to the top in and digging in there" but the attack succeeded without alerting the Germans dug in on another spur of the hill.[10] By dint of some good solid, basic infantry tactics, 10 Brigade had pushed the Canadian penetration ahead nearly another two miles. It is not too much to say that the majority of the ground gained by the 4th Division in TOTALIZE to date had been captured by the three marching infantry battalions of Jefferson's brigade ably supported by the tanks of Lieutenant Colonel Gordon Wotherspoon's South Alberta Regiment. Indeed a squadron of that regiment joined the Algonquin Regiment at St. Hilaire Farm shortly after the crack of dawn.[11]

Characteristically the Germans were neither slow nor reticent in reacting to the unexpected appearance of Canadian infantry on the Point 195 feature. While the Canadians had driven a deep wedge into the German line, this also meant that the Germans could fire on them from three sides, and they immediately began to plaster the battalion positions with shell and mortar fire and mounted a series of local counterattacks all through the blistering hot 10th day of August 1944.

In fact, with 10 Brigade now on Point 195, Kitching wasted little time in pushing 4 Armoured Brigade forward with orders to pass through the infantry and occupy the final objective, while deploying the Lake Superior Regiment, the motor battalion, on the Point 125 feature before first light to cover the division's right and rear. The British Columbia Regiment, which was rebuilding its strength and providing depth in the area of Langannerie, was able to field only 12 tanks, or a bit more than half a squadron, and was unable to play other than a supporting role in the operation.[12] Originally Halpenny's Grenadier Guards had been ordered to move onto the Point 180 feature at the end of the spur, but, when it was learned that the Lincoln and Welland Regiment was holding the spur, this unit was ordered to make directly for the brigade's objective, Point 206, southwest of Potigny. The plan was to move to Point 195, consolidate, and then mount an attack by one squadron down the forward slope between Fontaine-le-Pin and Soumont-St. Quentin and up the grade onto Point 206. By 1130 hours the Grena-

Major H.A. Smith, Canadian Grenadier Guards
On 8 August Smith's squadron outflanked the German defences at Cintheaux, and he later played a key role in the fighting at Hill 195. He took command of the Canadian Grenadier Guards in the fall of 1944.

diers were in the area of Point 195, with the loss of only two tanks as they passed St. Hilaire Farm. The unit now paused to consolidate before sending a squadron on to Point 206. The situation was not all that good. As we have seen, the Canadians were under fire from three sides, a tank that had moved a bit too far forward was ablaze and there were ominous reports that Point 206 was home to two dozen 88 mms.

Unfortunately the Germans, based on *Kampfgruppe* Olboeter, who had just returned from the area east of Vire,[13] mounted a counterattack at noon, the same time as Lieutenant Colonel Halpenny, the Grenadiers' commanding officer, had dismounted his commanders from their tanks and gathered them at his headquarters for an orders group. Captain Jamie Stewart, the ubiquitous FOO from 19th Army Field Regiment (SP), later wrote that

I had a dug-in O[bservation] P[ost] on the southside [of the feature,] looking up to Point 206. As I was walking back to the O[rders] G[rou]p when two things happened. First the sentry shot one of the people coming to the meeting and while we were gathering a mortar round [dropped] right in the open turret hatch of the 2i/c's tank. There was a bit of a delay, then Lieutenant Colonel Halpenny gave his orders, first of all stating that General Simmons [sic] had ordered the Grenadiers to go on to the next obj[ective Point] 206 or he would pull us out.[14]

The counterattack, which completely disrupted the plans for the attack and may have helped to convince the Canadian commanders that the Germans had established a third defence line that was too strong to overcome by a regimental or even a brigade attack, included the panzer grenadiers of III. *Bataillon SS-Panzergrenadierregiment 26*, several panzers and even a number of B IV "Goliath" remote-controlled miniature explosive-filled tanks of *Nr. 4 Kompanie, Panzerabteilung* 301,[15] whose "robot tanks" proved to be no more effective this time than they were when sent against the Royal Hamilton Light Infantry on Verrières Ridge on 31 July. While the Germans claimed they regained the hill, and Kurt Meyer characteristically both overstated and over-dramatized the results,[16] Point 195 remained firmly in Canadian hands all through that day, and all the days that followed, although the attack on Point 206 was cancelled, much to Captain Stewart's relief.[17]

A dead Sherman
A destroyed Sherman of the Canadian Grenadier Guards (unit sign 52) with Quesnay Wood in the background. (NAC/PMR 82-387)

Near Hill 195
A Sherman passing a destroyed vehicle near Hill 195 on 10 August 1944. (NAC/PA 132963)

In the meantime, Foot Guards had moved forward into the area held by the Lincoln and Welland Regiment.[18] The regiment deployed with its No. 2 Squadron covering the right flank, No. 3 Squadron looking south and No. 1 Squadron behind a railway embankment facing northeast.[19] As the situation developed, the Allied strength in artillery and air power began to make itself felt, one attack by Typhoons on Quesnay Wood resulting in a spectacular explosion and plume of smoke.[20] However the tank strength of the Grenadier Guards had been depleted by almost a third, seven or eight Shermans having been lost during the recent counterattack alone. It was apparent that 4th Division had reached the limit of its advance under the present conditions and the attack across the open ground into the 88s on Point 206 was postponed for the time being, although Booth issued orders to the Lake Superior Regiment, supported by the Foot Guards, to be prepared to "break through" to Point 206 if and when Quesnay Wood was captured.[21]

The attempt to outflank Quesnay Wood had failed. That was not surprising given the nature of the ground, and the time the Germans had been allowed to build up their anti-tank defences. It was now a case of holding on under heavy shelling and mortaring, and with the threat of counterattack by German tanks ever present.

In the left of the corps area, the Poles also had not been able to make much progress on 10 August. Simonds had ordered Maczek to seize a crossing over the Laison River. In fact the battalion of 3. *Brygada* that had taken over Soignolles was counterattacked from the northeast at 1055 hours, but repulsed the attackers. At 1520 hours, another counterattack developed against the feature northwest of Soignolles and was broken up by the Poles assisted by heavy concentrations from 2 Canadian AGRA. While under heavy pressure for most of the day, this battalion was able to actually push forward to the east from the village. Meanwhile 10. *Brygada* had been able to advance a short distance south and east from Estrées-la-Campagne, but were unable to advance to the river. Their freedom of movement was also constrained by Quesnay Wood, and Maczek decided to "wait until this strong point had been dealt with by 3rd Canadian Infantry Division before resuming an advance which so far had been costly enough."[22]

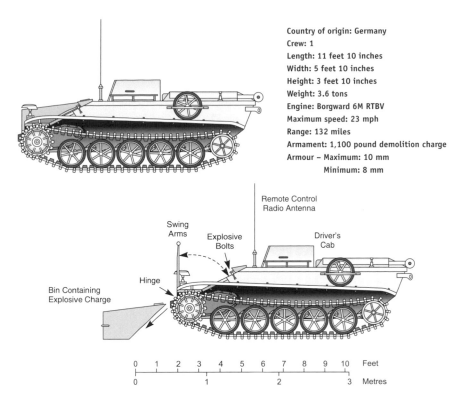

Country of origin: Germany
Crew: 1
Length: 11 feet 10 inches
Width: 5 feet 10 inches
Height: 3 feet 10 inches
Weight: 3.6 tons
Engine: Borgward 6M RTBV
Maximum speed: 23 mph
Range: 132 miles
Armament: 1,100 pound demolition charge
Armour – Maximum: 10 mm
           Minimum: 8 mm

Schwere Ladungsträger B IV b remote-control demolition charge layer

The Schwere Ladungsträger B IV b was designed to carry a demolition charge in a wedge-shaped metal bin. Arms on either side of the bin were hinged to extended horns on the nose of the vehicle. Hollow bolts containing explosive charges secured the explosive bin to the arms. In operational use, the Schwere Ladungsträger would be driven to a forward area by the lone crew member and would then be directed onto the target by remote control. The control vehicles were most often obsolete PzKpfw IIIs or Sturmgeschuetz III assault guns fitted with an additional antenna for the remote-control unit. Theoretically, when the Schwere Ladungsträger reached its target, the explosive bolts were fired by remote control and the arms were free to swing to a vertical position as the bin slid off the nose of the vehicle. After the demolition charge came to rest on the ground, the controller would guide the vehicle back to the German position before exploding the charge. The Schwere Ladungsträger equipped the 4th Company Panzer-Abteilung 301 (Funklenk) in Normandy.

CHAPTER EIGHTEEN

WITH A BANG,
NOT A WHIMPER

*"Although there was little information about the front, the general
impression was that the Hun had had enough and would surrender
on a show of force."*

COMPANY COMMANDER, THE NORTH SHORE REGIMENT

t was becoming clear that success in Operation TOTALIZE, which had
seemed so certain two days ago, was slipping from Simonds's grasp. All
now hinged on eliminating Quesnay Wood, the vital point that prevented any further advance to the south, although a successful advance
on either side of the woods would have rendered it untenable. At 1000 hours
on 10 August, Simonds had issued orders to his commanders for an operation which he hoped would restore momentum. The previously uncommitted 3rd Canadian Infantry Division, under the acting command of Brigadier Kenneth Blackader after the wounding of Major General Rod Keller
by American bombs, was given the main task. It, with 2 Armoured Brigade
under command, and supported by its own and the Polish divisional artillery as well as 2 Canadian and 9 AGRAs and even the flails of A Squadron,
1 Lothians and Border Horse firing their 75 mm main armament in an indirect role, as well as air strikes by Typhoons, was to push south-southeast
away from the Route Nationale and through Quesnay Wood to the Laison
River. The division's first objective was to seize crossings over the river east of
Potigny and then to push on to capture the commanding ridge west of Épan-
cy, in roughly the area of the original Polish objective. With Quesnay Wood
in Canadian hands, 1. *Dywizji Pancernej* was to capture Point 140, cross the
Laison and advance on Sassy. Simonds set the H-Hour at 1600 hours.[1]

That was less than eight hours away and did not leave much time for the infantry and tanks to complete their battle procedure, let alone for the artillery to work out the fire plan. However, it was still possible by reconnaissance and contact with the forward troops to determine that the woods was held in strength, although anyone who would have thought otherwise after the events of the past 36 hours could not have been paying attention, but somehow, as we shall see, the intelligence picture became horribly distorted. The first step remained the capture of Quesnay Wood and Blackader assigned this task to his old command, 8 Brigade, led in his absence by Lieutenant Colonel J.G. "Jock" Spragge[2] of the Queen's Own Rifles of Canada, who decided to attack with two battalions, the North Shore Regiment on the left and the Queen's Own on the right, tasked to clear the wood itself, with Le Régiment de la Chaudière, supported by the 1st Hussars, following the riflemen to clear the bend in the railway between Le Grange-de-Dime and the mine-workings to the southeast.[3]

Unfortunately, 8 Brigade was attacking directly against the keystone that anchored the German defences. While the Germans had perhaps 200 grenadiers and at most 23 tanks in Quesnay Wood, the position was intrinsically strong because of its size and the presence of a number of cleared spaces that would channel the attack.[4] This relatively low strength also failed to take into account the contribution of anti-tank weapons, mortars and artillery to the defence. Any attackers must approach the objective across flat, open fields, thus telegraphing the direction and strength of the assault, and the treed areas were cut up by roads and tracks and contained a number of glades and clearings that made excellent killing grounds, while making control difficult for the Canadian section, platoon and company commanders. When all things were considered, detailed information about the defences was limited. This was not the time for a hurried attack based on an ambitious plan, but that is precisely what Simonds had ordered.[5]

In fact, the plan was more than ambitious, it was plain foolhardy – with Quesnay Wood captured, D Company, the reserve company of the Queen's Own, was supposed to pass through the objective and seize the high ground overlooking Falaise. When this was announced, Major Cottrill, the company commander, laughed sardonically and someone remarked, "There must be a new boy on the staff who can't read maps. No one else would expect a single

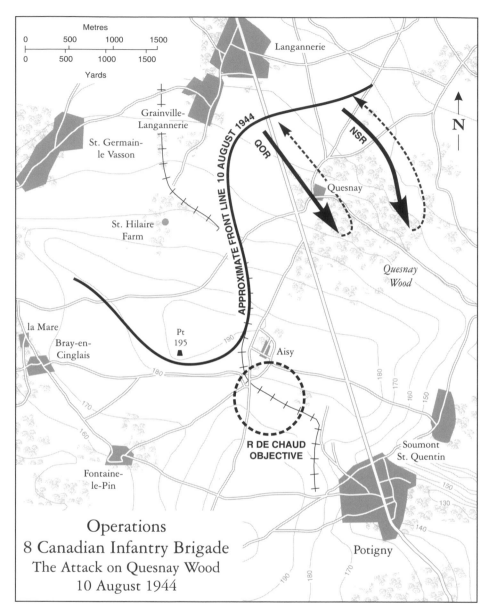

Operations
8 Canadian Infantry Brigade
The Attack on Quesnay Wood
10 August 1944

company without support to advance five miles through enemy held territory and then put in an attack."[6] Shades of Worthington Force.

Not surprisingly, given the demands of the battle procedure and fire planning processes, the actual attack was not mounted until 2000 hours, or four hours after the time Simonds had detailed in his orders group. At first it seemed to go well and the artillery support was reported as excellent, with no German retaliation. On the right the Queen's Own Rifles advanced with two companies, A and B leading, through farmers' fields divided by stone or dirt hedgerows two or three feet high with another seven feet or so of shrubbery on top of that. Many of the hedgerows were occupied and the riflemen moved forward while the Bren-gunners laced the foliage with automatic fire. Company Sergeant Major Charles Martin of A Company noted that, while the hedgerows provided good protection to the Germans, they also had poor fields of fire and often realized too late that the Canadians were upon them. Then, he added, they would give up rather easily, surprised that they were overrun.[7] A Company of the QOR had reached the last hedgerow before the woods, under fire as fierce as they had experienced at Carpiquet weeks before. Eventually a small party was able to work its way into the edge of the woods by crawling along a small furrow. On their left, B Company had taken heavy casualties but had also managed to get men into the trees and heavy undergrowth. These limited successes were reported to 8 Brigade through the fog of war as the battalion being on its objective.

Suddenly the Germans, who had been lying low in well-concealed positions, opened fire. The enemy armour, including one supposedly derelict tank that had been bypassed, rolled into action. The natural gloom of the forest

On the way up
A troop of 75 mm M10 anti-tank guns of the 3rd Anti-Tank Regiment RCA takes a break during Phase 2. (NAC/PA 192899)

Polish armour
Tanks of 1. *Dywizji Pancernej* wait for the order to advance. (NAC/PA 128955)

combined with the darkening sky along with uncertainty about the actual locations of their own troops made the artillery, the arm that often carried the day at this stage of the battle, ineffective. Lieutenant F.J. Lake had led the leading platoon of B Company through Quesnay village and into the forest, before he was wounded in both legs and most of his party killed or wounded. With the platoon cut off, the newly-promoted Corporal N. Zamaria took over and the remnants prepared to hold their ground. Around midnight they were joined by Lieutenant Robertson of the North Shore Regiment and a few of his men, who had been fighting to the left of the Rifles. Once Zamaria* explained the situation to him, Robertson left to see if he could guide the rest of B Company forward, but soon realized this was impossible. Returning to Zamaria and his group, he then organized the evacuation of the remaining men, including the walking wounded, and led them to safety.[8]

Meanwhile the party from A Company of the Queen's Own was down to its last three rounds of ammunition when it received orders to retire. By the time the QOR was able to make its way back to the Canadian lines, the regiment had suffered 22 killed and 63 wounded. Later that night, Major Lett, the acting commanding officer, sent out a search party of volunteers, including the Padre and Company Sergeant-Major Martin, both men who took their duties seriously, to collect the wounded. With the Germans close

---

* Zamaria received a well-deserved immediate Military Medal.

at hand and trigger-happy as they were anticipating another attack, the need for silence was paramount. When the Canadians came across a wounded man, they would give him a shot of morphine not only to ease his pain but to ensure his silence. Happily among the men located and rescued were Lieutenant Lake and the other wounded survivors of his platoon who were unable to walk.[9]

The other battalion, the North Shore Regiment, which had only three companies in the operation because of casualties from the American bombing on the 8th, looped around the tree line and entered the southern edge of the woods and began to clear it despite heavy mortar fire. The reality was a far different situation than that painted by Canadian intelligence, as one officer explained,

the 8th Brigade was ordered to attack Quesnay with the Q.O.R. on the right and to North Shore on the left, with the Chaudieres to follow through the Saumont St. Quentin. We were promised ample artillery support and although there was little information about the front, the general impression was given that the Hun had had enough and would surrender on a show of force.[10]

Another officer confirmed the rosy intelligence picture was completely at odds with the opposition they encountered as

the intelligence reports indicated that there were scattered machine gun nests facing us, and very light opposition. As soon as we crossed a rise and doubled down the slope facing Quesnay Wood, however, all hell broke loose. Very heavy mortar fire burst around us. The wood was very much more than lightly held. In fact, strong machine gun fire came from the small wood to which I was directing my platoon. As we got within 300 yards of it a tank moved out of the wood, crossed the face of the wood and down a small track. It got away before we could even fire at it with a P.I.A.T.[11]

Small groups of men from the rugged north shore of New Brunswick were able to actually fight their way into the southern end of Quesnay Wood, but were then hit by friendly artillery fire and forced to withdraw. The same Lieutenant Robertson that appears above in the Queen's Own account later recounted,

> from our position to the objective there was a succession of fields intersected by fences, cabbage patches, turnip fields and a huge potato crop. At zero hour we left our trenches to begin a steady course towards the wood, expecting every minute to be blasted by shells or mortar fire. The distance to the woods was at least 1,500 yards and we had gone at least 500 yards before Jerry began shooting. Four Tiger tanks appeared and sprayed our lines but we still moved on. My platoon reached the woods just as a tank rumbled out to fire point blank and I gave the order to charge. In the face of such fury most of the German defenders broke from their positions and ran. My platoon plunged on into the woods and found we were alone. I jumped into brush and landed in a trench with a German sergeant-major. He shot at me with his pistol and cut the chin strap of my helmet, allowing my helmet to fall over my eyes, but I lashed out with my foot and caught him so hard that he gave up the fight and was a prisoner. Taking his Luger, I plunged on into the woods and my platoon did a swell job of clearing out the area as we moved through. Soon we came upon an open space which proved to be the beginning of a village and a large football field. We approached the buildings and came upon the remnant of a company of the Q.O.R. which had attacked with us. We had reached our objective and now would face counterattacks but first we had to look after our wounded.
>
> Taking six men, I crawled forward and we applied first aid to thirty-seven wounded, and then I began organizing a move to a spot where I intended to spend the night. We then got organized and I found I had eighty men under my command but thirty of them were stretcher cases. Placing the wounded about a Bren carrier we found in the area, I arranged the fit men in a tight circular defence, and then took my batman to explore more of the woods. Only one burst of machine gun fire bothered us and we found another platoon of the North Shore in desperate straits like ourselves and brought them back to link up with us. By midnight we were all in one big group and settled down [to wait] the dawn but down

came our own fire and shells screamed in from all directions and the air was full of rock dust and the smell of cordite. Only one man was killed and none of the wounded cried out. I had a bottle of rum and crawled around giving many a taste of the pain-killer. Finally, at six-thirty, we were able to make our way back to the Chaudiere lines, then slept a little. When we finally joined the unit the next day I found myself and every man with me listed as missing.[12]

With the commanding officer, Lieutenant Colonel D.B. Buell, and two company commanders wounded, and communications within the battalion broken down, the North Shore was forced to returned to its start line, having suffered 22 killed and 58 wounded.[13]

With the providential benefit of hindsight we can see that Simonds did have another option rather than the assault on Quesnay Wood, and that was to bypass that strongpoint by a coordinated attack on Point 206 by 10 Brigade and the South Alberta Regiment, or perhaps the same by either the 2nd or 3rd Division supported by 2 Armoured Brigade. In fact late in the day on 9 August he had directed Kitching to capture Point 206 and then to exploit towards Falaise.[14] This operation, by the very troops that had achieved the only real successes in Phase 2 of TOTALIZE and supported by every bit of tactical air and artillery that could be mustered, might have worked, and in fact the Poles gained considerable ground here a few days later. If so, the attack would have not only turned the German position in Quesnay Wood, but would also have threatened the flank of the hard-pressed 271. *Infanteriedivision* west of the Laize River and forced a general withdrawal behind the Laison River. With the 3rd Canadian Infantry Division now in the line and with 2nd Canadian Infantry Division and 2 Canadian Armoured Brigade available now that the Phase 1 positions were mopped up, it was a feasible option, albeit one that may have been discarded by Simonds in favour of an attempt to salvage his original plan because of the casualties to 4 Canadian Armoured Brigade. By now the importance of trapping the German forces in the developing Falaise Pocket had become the focus of Allied operations, and he may have decided to seize the ground between Falaise and Ernes as a basis for further offensive operations to the southeast, followed by pursuit and exploitation towards the Seine.

The failure of the 8 Brigade attack on Quesnay Wood signalled the end of TOTALIZE. While another attempt might have succeeded, Crerar and Simonds seem to have concluded that the law of diminishing returns was now driving events. (It should be remembered that Amiens also had at first achieved spectacular results 26 years before, but then was cancelled for all intents and purposes on 11 August 1918 as Germans reinforcements threatened to halt the advance.[15] One should not take the comparison between Amiens and TOTALIZE too far, however as the results would hardly be flattering to Crerar, Simonds *et al*, especially as the Germans had little with which to reinforce their defence line along the Laison.) The hard-pressed defenders had been able to delay and then halt the Canadian offensive, while the bulk of 85. *Infanteriedivision* had now arrived and was taking up positions along the line of the Laison River. Last, the attack on Quesnay Wood might have succeeded had there been sufficient time for the 3rd Division to carry out proper battle procedure, and indeed perhaps adopt a different approach than the basic Mark I frontal attack. One is left with the impression that once again Canadian intelligence had failed to accurately assess the potential of the German forces to withstand another assault, and the cancellation of further offensive operations was premature.

Simonds, however, had not given up on continuing the push to Falaise; he cancelled all attacks on the morning of 11 August and issued orders for his two infantry divisions to replace the armoured divisions in the line, with the 2nd Division right and the 3rd Division left. While the 4th Division moved to the area of St. Sylvain to prepare for future operations, the Poles were to probe forward to the Laison valley in the Maizières area and attempt to seize a crossing. If that was unsuccessful, the 2nd Division would extend its front to take over the right portion of the 3rd Division's front. That division would then assault south and force a crossing over the Laison for the two armoured divisions to pass through.

While Eisenhower, Montgomery and Bradley had agreed on a change in emphasis in the Allied campaign plan on 8 August, this change in direction had not yet been communicated to the First Canadian Army; therefore as TOTALIZE developed, Crerar was still operating on the premise

SS-Obersturmbannführer Max Wünsche, **SS-Panzerregiment** 12
Wünsche was an experienced, brave and capable officer. His successful defence of Quesnay Wood convinced Simonds to halt TOTALIZE, perhaps prematurely. (Michael Reynolds Collection)

(Below) **Lorguichon**
An infantry battalion of 7 Brigade of 3rd Canadian Infantry Division passing through Lorguichon, in the area of one of the British Phase 1 objectives. (NAC/PA 129137)

that his formation would advance to Rouen and the Seine. Meanwhile the Americans had broken out of the west end of the beachhead and were sweeping to the east and south in a vast, swarming charge *à la* Jeb Stuart against negligible resistance through the German rear areas, while the right flank of Second British Army methodically moved forward against the steady resistance of 7. *Armee* and the newly-created *Panzergruppe Eberbach*. It was not until the afternoon of 10 August that Montgomery instructed Crerar to "swing to the east around Falaise and then south towards Argentan to link up with the Third U.S. Army."[16] In the meantime Simonds was still attempting to eliminate the German stronghold in Quesnay Wood, but with the failure of the 8 Brigade attack that evening, he cancelled any further offensive operations at 0830 on the next morning, adding that this would be "followed probably by regrouping."[17]

The arrival of the new directive from Montgomery (M 518) on the morning of 11 August confirmed that the focus of the campaign had shifted away from trapping the enemy against the Seine to the destruction of the German armies in Normandy in the giant pocket created by the insane counter attack ordered by the Führer. In his directive M 517 of 6 August Montgomery's intention had been to "destroy the enemy forces in that part of France" west of the Seine and north of the Loire.[18] While this ostensibly remained unchanged, in the new directive the emphasis shifted

Intentions

8. ... It must clearly be our intention to destroy the enemy forces between the Seine and the Loire.

The outline of the plan

9. For the moment, the plan outlined in M 517 will be modified as indicated below. We will now concentrate our forces in order to encircle the main enemy forces so that we can possibly destroy them in their present location.

First Canadian Army

10. The Canadian Army is to capture Falaise. That has first priority. It is vital that it happens quickly.

11. The Army will then capture Argentan with armoured and mobile forces.

12. A firm front line to the east between Falaise and the sea must be held.

Second British Army

13. The Second Army will advance its left wing to Falaise. That is of primary and vital priority. Sufficient forces will be made available to the Corps on the left to allow it to push forward, rapidly, to Falaise.

14. After Falaise has been taken, by either the Second Army or the Canadian Army, it will be held by the Second Army.

15. From Falaise, the Second Army will operate to the west and south...[19]

That afternoon (11 August) Crerar met with Simonds and Brigadier N.E. Rodger, his Chief of Staff, to discuss the forthcoming operation, which was originally designated TALLULAH but later was renamed TRACTABLE.[20] While TOTALIZE had gained nine miles and had broken the German hold on the ground south of Caen that had frustrated Allied commanders since Operations GOODWOOD and ATLANTIC in mid-July, Simonds and Crerar must have been more than a little frustrated by their failure to smash through the last defences before Falaise, and the former was seething at what he saw as a lack of aggressive spirit, if not something far worse, on the part of his armoured regiments. It may not be going too far to suggest that Simonds had concluded that his plan had been frustrated by subordinates unable to muster the requisite dash and skill to carry it through to fruition. Neither general seems to have questioned the cumbersome system of top-down tactical command and control – which fitted very well with Simonds's command style – and the great, bloody gap between the theories of doctrine based on experience in North Africa and the realities of combat in Normandy. That TOTALIZE had ended with a bang, not a whimper, mattered not at this time. The war must go on and both Crerar and Simonds were determined to prevail in their next attempt.

OPERATION TOTALIZE:
FACTS VERSUS MYTHS

"No plan survives contact with the enemy."

MILITARY MAXIM

There is one point that towers above all else: TOTALIZE was a successful operation of war – after all the Germans had been pushed back more than halfway to Falaise and their tank strength seriously depleted, while 89. *Infanteriedivision* had lost more than half of its fighting strength. Mistakes were made by both sides, but the simple truth is that the German hold on the plain south of Caen was broken at a heavy cost to their forces. Having said that, TOTALIZE revealed in vivid colour the strengths and weaknesses of the Canadian army in Normandy. While many of these were shared with the British, and perhaps to a lesser extent, with the American armies, it should not mask the reality that there were some that were uniquely Canadian. Above all else – and this must be confessed as a sweeping generalization – the standard of Canadian generalship and high-level staff work in Normandy was a cut below that of the other Allied armies, although Simonds certainly displayed vivid flashes of brilliance and would continue to do so throughout the war.

One must, however, question the recurring Canadian practice of failing to allot enough troops to tasks, considering the setbacks that resulted. When one has lived one's professional life in an atmosphere of military poverty that makes a virtue of stretching resources to the limit, it is tempting to point the finger of blame in this direction, but Canadian difficulties in Normandy may be more attributable to a lack of practical experience and a rather bureaucratic concentration on process, in itself a sign of an organization still groping to find its way.

As for the lack of cooperation between the infantry and the armour, especially in 4th Canadian Armoured Division, there was a tendency to rely on the British for guidance in all things military. While the British army was and still is a remarkably successful military institution, it had gone astray in matters of doctrine and tactics during the 1930s and 1940s, and the Canadian army marched in lock-step, largely as it had no other choice. However, in some areas Canada led the way – one need look no further than the introduction of the armoured personnel carriers in TOTALIZE, and there were other examples: the creation of the armoured engineer assault vehicle, the AVRE, after Dieppe in 1942; the use of field artillery in landing craft to supplement naval gunfire during amphibious landings; and the adoption of anti-aircraft rocket projectors for ground use.

At the unit level, where the actual fighting is done, there was little to find fault with, other than perhaps inexperience, and the artillery verged on excellent. Taking the 4th Canadian Armoured Division as an example, Algonquin Lieutenant Clair Durcher's platoon attack with fixed bayonets on the pair of 88's near Worthington Hill, Lieutenant Colonel Dave Stewart's infiltration of his Argyll and Sutherland Highlanders of Canada onto Point 195 and Canadian Grenadier Guards Lieutenant Ivan Phelan's troop assault near Cintheaux all demonstrate that most intangible of assets, the warrior spirit. One can find many other examples in the 4th Division and in the other Canadian formations in Normandy – Lieutenants Lake and Robertson and Corporal Zamaria of 8 Brigade at Quesnay Wood, for example. Within a few months of the events described in this book the gap in experience had been closed, but in Normandy there still was a way to go and the price was paid in time and blood.

A considerable mythology, what could be called the conventional wisdom, has grown around Operation TOTALIZE, and at this point I will compare some of the generally accepted beliefs about the operation with the facts as established by my research.

1. *The aim of* TOTALIZE *was to capture Falaise, thus closing the north flap of the Falaise Pocket, trapping the German armies in Normandy.* A variation of this tenet is that the failure to capture Falaise on 8 or 9 August 1944 was a

major reason for the Germans being able to extricate themselves from the pocket. While Crerar had, on 29 July, ordered Simonds "to draw up plans for an actual attack, axis Caen–Falaise, objective Falaise," the object of Simonds's TOTALIZE appreciation was to break through the German defences astride the Caen–Falaise road, and the final objectives of the operation were north of the city.[1] This same phrase, "to break through the German defences astride the Caen–Falaise road," was stated as the intention of the operation in the 2nd Canadian Corps operation instruction.[2] Indeed, the concept of the short envelopment which came to be known as the Falaise pocket did not originate until after TOTALIZE had commenced.[3] Furthermore, the gains made in TOTALIZE were unprecedented for the Commonwealth armies in Normandy, and at the time it was considered a major success.

2. *The night attack of 7/8 August was a shambles, with vehicles colliding or going astray and complete troops and squadrons losing their way; as a result, the tactical cohesion of the attackers was lost.* There was a great deal of confusion, a number of vehicles were destroyed by enemy action or lost in bomb craters, a rifle company and at least one troop of tanks as well as several individual vehicles ended up with other units, and two unit columns halted well short of their objective. It is important, however, to emphasize that the majority of the attacking tanks and infantry from two armoured and two infantry brigades drove through prepared positions held by six German infantry battalions and ended up on their objective areas relatively intact and able to fight, and after suffering remarkably few casualties in men and equipment, especially by the bloody standards of Normandy.[4]

3. *Two Allied armoured divisions waited on their start line for several hours, thus allowing the Germans to counterattack and foil the Phase 2 advance on 8 August.* This criticism seems to have originated with Kurt Meyer, who claimed to have observed an armoured division or two, depending how one reads his account, formed up and waiting on their start lines when he was on his reconnaissance shortly after first light on 8 August.[5] In fact, what he saw were the tanks and other armoured vehicles of the two armoured brigades that had spearheaded the Phase 1 attacks. The vanguard of 4th Canadian Armoured Division did not move forward of Rocquancourt until after 1230

hours, while the leading Polish tanks were still well north of the corps start line at 0800 hours.[6]

4. *The counterattack by a battle group of 12.* SS-Panzerdivision *broke up the attacks by 4th Canadian Division and 1.* Dywizji Pancernej. This is a variation of Number 3 above, and again is based on Meyer's statements.[7] In fact the German counterattack, which was against the Phase 1 forces, failed with heavy losses in men and armoured vehicles, something that the critics of TOTALIZE conveniently ignore. The delays encountered by the Canadian division resulted from a poorly-coordinated corps plan, as well as dereliction of duty by the commander of 4 Canadian Armoured Brigade.[8] The Polish advance was halted by a strong anti-tank defensive position established by both *Kampfgruppe* Waldmüller and the *Divisionbegleitkompanie* and a company of *SS-Panzerjägerabteilung* 12.[9]

5. *After having broken through the German defences, the Allies waited for Phase 2 on their start lines because Crerar and/or Simonds did not want to cancel the bombing after having gone through a protracted bureaucratic struggle to obtain the support in the first place.* While a breakthrough had been achieved, neither general was aware of it. Instead they were most concerned that the H-Hour for the bombing was confirmed with the air force, so that the operation could proceed, and this required that the air force be notified by 0800 hours, which meant First Canadian Army had to pass word to 83 Composite Group well before then.[10] The confirmation in fact was being passed at about the same time that Lieutenant Colonel Mel Gordon of the Sherbrooke Fusilier Regiment was telling his superior, Brigadier Robert Wyman, that the road to Falaise was open and requesting permission to push on.[11] As for the so-called bureaucratic struggle, nothing could be farther from the truth; except for Harris, the air force commanders had been for the most part cooperative and eager to assist throughout the planning, although their ability to deliver on their promises was entirely another matter.

6. *Kurt Meyer correctly identified the appearance of a lone bomber as the precursor of the Phase 2 bombing and ordered his counterattack to commence immediately. Later, when he sighted the approaching bombers, he directed his troops*

to move north from the villages into the fields, thus avoiding casualties from the attack. Meyer was correct in his appreciation that a heavy bombing strike was imminent, but the targets were Bretteville-sur-Laize and St. Sylvain, not Cintheaux, where he was controlling preparations for the counterattack.[12] Indeed, he and his troops were already well north of the area to be attacked by the following waves of aircraft, although he could not have known this, and given the self-admitted lack of accuracy of 8 USAAF, the village may well have been hit by some errant bombs. If, as he believed, he and his troops were in the target areas, to have left the protection of the villages and run into the fields was precisely the wrong thing to do, as the aircraft were loaded with fragmentation bombs and the normal pattern covered an area of some two thousand yards in diameter; furthermore Cintheaux was in full view of the Allied forces, and any exposure would have invited massive retaliation from the artillery.

7. TOTALIZE *did not achieve all its objectives because both Phase 2 armoured divisions were inexperienced and paused to clear centres of resistance rather than bypassing them.* This appears to have originated with Simonds, who rarely, if ever, admitted that his planning could have been in error; instead he characteristically blamed his subordinates for their inability to execute his brilliantly crafted plans. Not only did Simonds criticize the inexperience of his armoured divisions, but after the battle he assembled his armoured regimental commanders and accused them of cowardice and incompetence.[13] While the two divisions were inexperienced, that in itself is not the whole story and, as we have seen, Simonds later modified his views and castigated the Poles for being too aggressive.

In fact, Simonds had erred badly when he assessed the ground in his appreciation in that he failed to identify the importance of Quesnay Wood.[14] Even worse, his headquarters had managed to arrange affairs so that Gaumesnil, one of the Phase 1 objectives, lay inside the danger area for the Phase 2 bombing, so that it could not be occupied until after the bombing ended, which coincided with the Phase 2 H-Hour. As a result three brigades from two different divisions were essentially supposed to be attacking over the same piece of ground at the same time. In fact, the 4th Division delayed its advance until the village was captured by the 2nd Division. This wasted more than three hours and, while nothing is certain in war, the delay probably allowed the Germans time for *Kampfgruppe* Wünsche to move into Quesnay Wood and for the defenders of Bretteville-le-Rabet and Grainville-Langannerie to improve their positions. As well, even without the "friendly fire" incidents, the bombing plan had other serious shortcomings which resulted in the Poles advancing against a strong anti-tank screen without either air or artillery support.[15] Moreover, for Simonds's plan to succeed, the bombing had to be stunningly effective, and both attacking divisions had to capture all their objectives on time and in sequence. In other words, Simonds's plan was more of a staff college demonstration than a realistic operation of war.

But there is another factor that also contributed to a certain extent: his revision of his plan on 6 August simply gave too many tasks to Major General Charles Foulkes's 2nd Canadian Infantry Division. Foulkes, who had good reason to fear for his job, became fixated on accomplishing all of these tasks; as a result what should have been his top-priority task, expediting the passage of 4th Canadian Armoured Division forward, suffered. This could have been doubly disastrous if Simonds had decided to cancel the bombing and accelerate Phase 2. (In fact it would have been impossible to do so; in a variation of the "just in time"principle, the two armoured divisions only arrived in the forward areas shortly before H-Hour, and Simonds probably would not have been able to exploit the breakthrough in the morning if he had been disposed to do so.)

There is a time-honoured military adage that no plan survives first contact with the enemy. In August 1944 Lieutenant General Guy Simonds could be faulted for believing that no enemy would survive first contact with his plan, and not the other way round. His precise, scientific mind could not accept that human frailties or shortcomings in equipment or doctrine, let alone any action the enemy might take, could possibly interfere with the execution of his plans. (Unlike his patron Montgomery, Simonds never learned to simply keep repeating that his plans always worked exactly as designed.)* When things went awry, as they invariably do in war, it was always the fault

---

* Montgomery also was the first senior Allied commander to publish his version of events in *Normandy to the Baltic*, which appeared in 1947. This gave him an advantage that was not seriously challenged for nearly four decades, especially as his claims were echoed in both the British official history and the writings of members of his staff.

of others for not being able to execute his plan exactly as written. That is not to suggest that he was a knave or a fool, far from it. Guy Simonds was an intense man who was intellectually superior to most of his contemporaries; unfortunately his military education and experience had been largely theoretical, at least until he landed in Sicily in command of the 1st Canadian Infantry Division on 10 July 1943. It is often forgotten that his total experience of command in battle until his corps became operational on 11 July 1944 totalled less than three months.[16] Still, for his faults, real and imagined, Simonds clearly was by far the best Canadian senior commander of the war, and one whose performance does not suffer when compared to the best of his Allied contemporaries.

There are three other factors that bear on the results of TOTALIZE. One was luck; all the bounces went the German way. Again, luck can be more than a matter of statistical variables; the Germans did nearly everything right and, on the whole, they reaped the benefit. It also helped to have better weapons, equipment and doctrine, although this was offset by the limited mobility of their *Infanteriedivisionen* and the Allied superiority in artillery and air power. On the other hand, the inexperience of Simonds and his headquarters showed, as did the uncertain grip of the commander of 4th Canadian Armoured Division. Simply put, Major General George Kitching was just too nice a man to properly command that formation. He had failed to impress on his subordinates, particularly Brigadier Leslie Booth of 4 Canadian Armoured Brigade, the importance of maintaining the momentum, and Simonds's enjoinder that there must be "no holding back" went largely ignored. Worse, although he had first-hand evidence of Booth's dereliction of duty, Kitching chose to do nothing. Once things began to go amiss, the Canadian command structure, with its inflexible doctrine and cumbersome decision-making, was unable to regain control of the situation. Certainly Kitching should have jumped at the opportunity to shift the weight of the attack once the 12th Manitoba Dragoons found an unguarded way onto Point 195 on 9 August, and with all the force he could muster. One might ask rhetorically, what would Kurt Meyer have done if presented with the same opportunity?

Two, the Allied air forces, both tactical and strategic, proved to be woefully unable to live up to both the expectations of the army and their own exaggerated claims. This was partly a matter of air force doctrine, training and equipment and partly the result of the desire of senior RAF officers to maintain their independence on an equal footing with the Allied land forces. If 2 TAF had sent fighter-bombers to the area of the Phase 2 bombing targets as requested by the Canadians, the Typhoons and Spitfires would have caught *Kampfgruppe* Waldmüller in the open with what could have been catastrophic results for the Germans. Instead the enemy were largely north of where the bombs fell and were able to halt the Allied advance, thus allowing time for *Kampfgruppe* Wünsche to move into Quesnay Wood. As for the heavy bombers, the results were not worth the effort; in fact their contribution in Phase 2 of TOTALIZE was counter-productive. Again, this was the predictable result of using a force for purposes for which it was neither designed not trained, although this was not apparent to anyone in any of the Allied armies at the time. As an American general of a later generation put it, "hope is not a method."

Last and certainly not least, on 4 August Montgomery had asked if TO-TALIZE could be moved forward one day and Simonds had agreed. If he had held his ground to allow his Phase 1 divisions another day of sorely needed preparation, most of 12. *SS-Panzerdivision* would have moved west to join in the Mortain offensive on the night of 7 August, and therefore would not have been available to intervene along the Route Nationale. Now, this enters the realm of speculation, but it is possible that given another 24 hours, intelligence probably would have located both 12. *SS-Panzerdivision* and 1. *SS-Panzerdivision* fighting in the west, thus indicating that the Phase 2 objectives were at best weakly held. With 85. *Infanteriedivision* still some distance away and 89. *Infanteriedivision* shattered, there would have been little opposition once the Phase 1 objectives had been seized. It would have been a matter of motoring to Falaise and then onwards to Argentan and the Americans. (Remember that the decision to go for the short envelopment was taken on 8 August, which would have been before TOTALIZE began if Simonds had held his ground.) If Simonds had stood firm, it is quite possible that instead of trying to determine what went wrong, we would have spent six decades debating whether Montgomery, Crerar and Simonds were great generals, or just lucky ones, for capturing Falaise on 9 or 10 August and then linking up with the Americans and trapping the bulk of the German forces in Normandy, and perhaps ending the war in the west in 1944.

To sum up, TOTALIZE was successful, although it could and should have achieved more, more quickly. That it ultimately floundered on indecision and hesitation was due as much to cumbersome doctrine, inferior equipment and an unwieldy plan as it was to a few flawed commanders and the inability of the Allied air forces to follow through on their claims. However, it is indicative of the conditions under which the Allied armies fought in Normandy, that no one at the time thought that it was other than a successful operation of war.

THE DILEMMA OF NORMANDY

*"Mind you we don't have the right type of tank. We got Shermans
with the 75 and the 17-pounder and they've got a mix of PzKw4s
and a few Panthers and lots of SP guns."*

BRIGADIER GENERAL (RETIRED) S.V. RADLEY-WALTERS

A distinguished British general once remarked that his army always fought its battles uphill, in the rain and at the junction of four map sheets. Although written with tongue firmly in cheek, his wry comment is a metaphor for the reality of combat in Normandy. For the most part the Allies fought the campaign on the wrong side of a significant gap in tactical proficiency and in the quality of the weapons of war. While an in-depth examination of the whys and hows is beyond the scope of this work, there are three areas that merit discussion: battlefield cohesion; tactical doctrine; and equipment. The Allies were generally deficient in all compared to the Germans, and hence in overall battlefield performance, although there certainly were exceptions.[1]

The German army had been engaged in continual combat since the Balkans campaign of early 1941 and before that had overrun Poland, Denmark and Norway, the Low Countries and France with relative ease. Its early success, due at least in part to the ill-preparedness and incompetence of its opponents, has clouded the reality that the German army's performance revealed deficiencies that parallelled those of the Allies later in the war. By Normandy these weaknesses had largely been corrected in the testing ground of battle and the Germans had a significant advantage in the number of experienced, combat-proven officers and NCOs. In short, the German army knew how to fight and the Allies were learning as they went along.

How this came about provides an interesting confluence of circumstances. First, the German approach to training and military life, while tough and demanding, seems to have been free from much of the petty harassment and mindless routine that plagued Allied units, and this was not by accident. In the twenties, while the British returned to "real soldiering," the Americans retreated into isolationism, the French swung between self-pity and self-glorification, and the Canadians squabbled over battle honours, the Germans quietly got on with laying the foundations of an army to win the next war.

How this was done is an illuminating example of selection and maintenance of the aim, and the Germans took care to get the aim right in spite of, or perhaps because of, the conditions imposed by the victors. These included a manpower ceiling of 100,000 men, of whom no more than 4,000 could be officers. In a sharp break with European tradition and to avoid the creation of a mobilization base, the army was to be an all-regular force. Furthermore, no more than 5 per cent of the officers and troops could be released yearly by termination of their service, a move clearly designed to avoid the creation of a large reserve army.

While these restrictions would create difficulties during the expansion in the early years of Hitler's regime, there were unforeseen benefits in a tiny army that had clearly been intended to hold German militarism in check. Although the original establishment was filled from the ranks of veterans of the Great War, emphasis soon swung to attracting high quality recruits to develop an elite force, not only for its own sake, but also as a basis for expansion. The low turnover inherent in the long period of enlistment and the legally imposed ceiling on the annual release rate created unit cohesion modern armies could only dream of, and the Germans adopted a policy of recruiting locally to fill the battalions scattered about the country. Once in a unit, a soldier would probably spend his entire career with it, thus building both stability and ties with the community and resulting in a well-disciplined force that enjoyed the respect of the civilian population.[2] Of equal importance, the officers grew to realize the potential of soldiers developed in a system that encouraged initiative, self-discipline and the cohesion of the small unit.

Second, training was based upon doctrine derived from a study of the lessons learned from the war. General von Seekt, the first Chief of Staff, who served until 1926, believed that the infantry-artillery team supported by tanks and aircraft was the key to breaking away from the static conditions of trench warfare. While neither tanks nor aircraft were among the weapons allowed the army,* trucks fitted with wooden and cardboard superstructures could be used to simulate armour. If aircraft were *verboten* (and even stream-lined trucks were not very aerodynamic), the army could practise passive air defence and study the theories of air support.[3]

While the views of von Seekt and his successors reflected the conventional wisdom of the time, there were some who saw the tank as more than an in-fantry support weapon; it was, they argued, the other way around, and the tank was the first among equals in manoeuvre warfare built on the principle of all-arms cooperation. Influenced by the writings of Liddell Hart, Fuller and Martel – although the extent of that influence is a matter of debate – German officers, encouraged by Hitler after the Nazis came to power, devel-oped the armoured and tactical air forces that would lead to the spectacular victories in the early years of the next war.[4] While it was a long, frustrating struggle with many setbacks, the apostles of armoured warfare gradually made their point, and by the late thirties the German army not only had a number of panzer, light** and motorized divisions, but these formations were grouped into corps commanded by officers of the quality of Guderian, who was a leading proponent of the new way of warfare.[5] It must be added that these theories were vindicated in both the 1939 Polish campaign and the invasion of the Low Countries and France in 1940.

Last, a good deal of the foundation of the successes of the German mili-tary machine came from a desire to erase the stigma of the "stab in the back" excuse for the defeat in 1918. According to this theory the German army in the field had been let down by pusillanimous politicians and lily-livered civilians. All that was very well, but without the political will to erase the shame nothing would have been accomplished. The driving force behind Germany's military resurgence was a disgruntled First World War veteran with a very large axe to grind, Adolf Hitler. For understandable reasons his influence has largely been ignored when discussing German battlefield per-formance. Nowhere was his effect on the army greater than in his approach to military training and discipline, for he believed implicitly that Germany

---

* The Germans deliberately violated the terms of the Versailles Treaty by establishing an ar-moured cadre in the Soviet Union and developing the nucleus of an air force by encouraging young Germans to train as glider pilots and by creating a large state airline.

** A light division was a motorized division with an integral panzer battalion. It was planned to convert these divisions to panzer divisions as the number of tanks in service increased.

had lost the First World War because of a collapse of discipline and morale on the home front. At the same time there were some contradictions in his position for Hitler also considered that the training and discipline of the army in which he had served honourably and well as an infantryman had been deficient. In all, this resulted in his emphasis on *Volksgemeinschaft* – more or less, a sense of national camaraderie and purpose both in Germany as a whole and in the armed forces.[6]

Unlike the elected leaders in the democracies, who had to be sensitive to unduly harsh military treatment or political indoctrination of their young men, the Führer was determined to toughen the army's discipline and reshape both the armed forces and the nation in line with the tenets of National Socialism. Thus, what had been breaches of military discipline now became political crimes meriting harsh punishments: desertion and *Wehrkraftzeretzung* (undermining the fighting spirit of the troops) were considered an attack on the regime. In the Great War the Germans had executed 48 soldiers compared to about 346 British and approximately 700 French. In the Second World War, while the numbers of Allied troops executed dropped drastically, the Germans put as many as 20,000 officers and men to death, 75-80 per cent of whom had been found guilty of so-called political crimes.[7] Thus, while even the best of soldiers will falter under the prolonged stress of combat, the knowledge that the penal battalion or worse awaited those who might opt for self-preservation was a strong inducement to stand and fall with one's comrades. There was another factor that is often downplayed. Their letters home and their diaries reveal that most fighting men supported the Nazi regime wholeheartedly, because of both its strong appeal to German nationalism and its program of social welfare, full employment and elimination of class barriers which reflected the party's socialist roots.[8]

While most Allied soldiers – probably more than would ever have admitted it at the time – truly believed they were engaged in a struggle against evil, a sizeable number had little reason to be satisfied with the social conditions in their homelands. As well, after the first 18 months of the war a German invasion of the British Isles was increasingly unlikely and an enemy landing in North America never was a realistic threat. When all was said and done, there is a vast difference between waging war on foreign soil and fighting to defend one's homeland, family and way of life. That is not to say that morale was poor or that the Allied troops were not prepared to fight – far from it. The immutable fact, however, was that for the most part the soldiers were fighting for themselves and their buddies and the reputation of their unit, not for any inspirational theme or national goal.

As one would expect, German tactics were both simple and effective. There were two areas where Allied and German tactics diverged radically. The first was in the encouragement of the exercise of initiative and the use of mission-oriented orders by the Germans. Officers and men at all levels from infantry section up were expected to continually assess the situation and take immediate and decisive action in accordance with their commander's intention and without reference to any higher headquarters. This was in marked contrast to the Allies, who sincerely believed that chaos would result if their subordinates were allowed too much discretion in the execution of their orders. While the British and Canadian armies in particular taught that a commander's place was in his headquarters, where he could direct the battle based on intelligence derived from as many sources as possible, the Germans felt a commander's place was at the critical place on the battlefield, the *Schwerpunkt*, where he could assess the situation and make decisions based on what he could actually see for himself. An example of the difference in command philosophy occurred on the morning of 8 August 1944 during Operation TOTALIZE. From the German point of view the situation was extremely critical. The Allies had broken through the forward defences south of Caen astride the road that led to Falaise. The nearest German reserves were still several hours away and the collapse of the defences in Normandy threatened. With victory within his grasp, Lieutenant General Guy Simonds, commanding 2nd Canadian Corps, who had no idea whatsoever that a breakthrough had occurred, was ensconced in his headquarters far behind the lines discussing the next phase of the operation on the telephone with the chief of staff of First Canadian Army. Meanwhile *General Der Panzertruppen* Heinrich Eberbach, the commander of 5. *Panzerarmee*, was conferring with *Generalleutnant* Konrad Heinrichs of 89. *Infanteriedivision* and *SS-Oberführer* Kurt Meyer of 12. *SS-Panzerdivision* so close to the frontline that they could see Allied tanks sitting on the Phase 1 objectives. As a result, not only did Eberbach issue orders for counterattacks based on his personal assessment of the battle, but by his presence he gained several hours advantage over Simonds in the execution of his orders. In modern terms he got inside his opponent's decision curve, and, at the very least, delayed th inevitable for nearly a fortnight.

The Germans also held a decided advantage in the execution of coordinated all-arms operations, although this is a generalization and the *Waffen-SS* was inferior to the army in this regard. It may be too much to credit this advantage to *Volksgemeinschaft*, but clearly the Germans recognized that in war cooperation between arms and even between the army and the air force was vital. Even in the highly bureaucratic structure of the German government and military, this was generally true. While Hitler certainly doled out power and authority sparingly and tended to ensure that none of his subordinates ever became powerful enough to challenge his position, the fighting forces provided an example of cooperation based on doctrine, training and flexibility implemented by officers who led from the front.

Unlike the Germans, the British had largely avoided any examination of the lessons of the First World War, perhaps because of a reluctance to revisit the bloodbath in the trenches and perhaps, at least to some, because the armoured theories of Liddell-Hart and Fuller seemed to provide the revolution in military affairs that would substitute manoeuvre for pitched battle. All of this was very well and good, but without vision and leadership at the top – and the British army was saddled with some of the dimmest guiding lights in its long history through much the inter-war years – the whole exercise descended into petty squabbling and turf battles. As a result the various arms went their own way and the army came down firmly on all sides of the question. In Canada the situation was even worse. Not only was spending more than the bare minimum on defence political suicide, but the armed forces relied on the United Kingdom for guidance and direction in all matters military from tactics and doctrine and the provision of intelligence down to the smallest details of dress and parade square drill.

All this might still not have mattered if the sides had had a rough parity in the quality of their equipment. Alas, this was not the case. To adapt a piece of doggerel by Hilaire Belloc,

One thing is certain and it is that
They have the Eighty-Eight
and we do not.

One could substitute any sort of weaponry here – Tiger and Panther tanks, 75 mm anti-tank guns, MG 34 and 42 machine guns, *Sturmegeschütz* and *Jagdpanzer* assault guns, *Nebelwerfer* rocket projectors – and the equation always was the same. The Germans enjoyed a marked qualitative advantage, not least of all in the minds of the soldiers on both sides. For an explanation of just one example, the disparity in armour, refer to the first chart, The Allied Armour Dilemma, and then examine the next, which shows the ranges at which the Sherman Firefly, which at best totalled only one in five of the Commonwealth armour in Normandy, could knock out German armour. While there are any number of factors that affected the outcome of tank versus tank engagements, the grim truth was that the Allied tanks were terribly vulnerable. As one Canadian veteran put it,

So when you go to compare in your study and start looking at the forces, if you look at all the tanks, the 4th Armoured Division, the Poles, 2nd Armour[ed] Brigade and so on, and compare them to the Germans on the other side, there's no bloody comparison at all. Mind you we don't have the right type of tank. We got Shermans with the 75 and the 17-pounder and they've got a mix of PzKw4s and a few Panthers and lots of S[elf] P[ropelled] guns. And the Germans were always in their organization heavy in self-propelled guns and these self-propelled guns were on the chassis of Panthers and even on Pz4s and on other wheeled or tracked equipment with a very heavy gun on them and that heavy gun could take out a Sherman at 1,000 yards without any trouble at all. And consequently when you just put tank against tank it sounds as though we outweighed them considerably, which we did [numerically], tank versus tank, but the Sherman wasn't the tank that the Panther was and couldn't even come close to the Tiger and, consequently with this back up of SP guns which they had a lot of and some of them with 88 mm on them and some with the long-barrel[led] 75s, it only took a few of them to take on a big force and take it out. In other words 3 or 4 Jagdpanzers could take on a tank

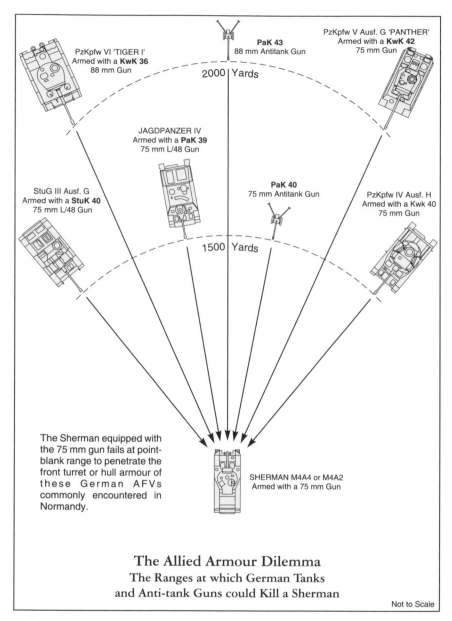

PzKpfw V Ausf. G 'PANTHER'
Armed with a **KwK 42**
75 mm Gun

PaK 43
88 mm Antitank Gun

PzKpfw VI 'TIGER I'
Armed with a **KwK 36**
88 mm Gun

2000 | Yards

JAGDPANZER IV
Armed with a **PaK 39**
75 mm L/48 Gun

PaK 40
75 mm Antitank Gun

StuG III Ausf. G
Armed with a **StuK 40**
75 mm L/48 Gun

PzKpfw IV Ausf. H
Armed with a Kwk 40
75 mm Gun

1500 | Yards

The Sherman equipped with the 75 mm gun fails at point-blank range to penetrate the front turret or hull armour of these German AFVs commonly encountered in Normandy.

SHERMAN M4A4 or M4A2
Armed with a 75 mm Gun

The Allied Armour Dilemma
The Ranges at which German Tanks and Anti-tank Guns could Kill a Sherman

Not to Scale

battalion and hold it up and destroy a lot of it. I was one of the lucky ones. I got 18 during my career. Wittmann with his Tiger and so on and the various areas in Europe, Russia and so on where he fought – I think he ended up with 139 which you can't really compare at all with what we had and consequently I think it's an uneven discussion, not a discussion, but an uneven way to weight the differences between a specialist weapon

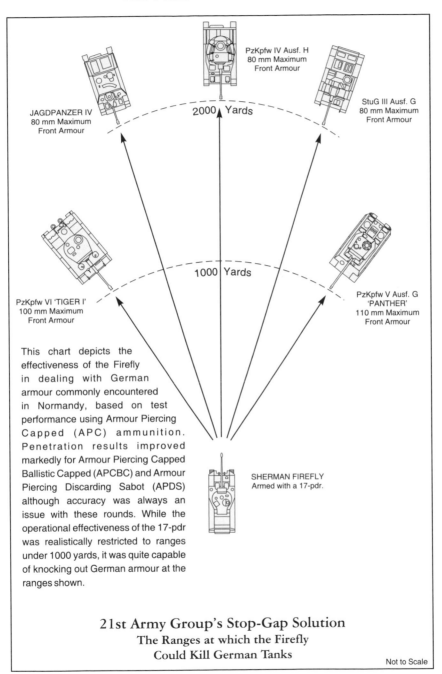

PzKpfw IV Ausf. H
80 mm Maximum
Front Armour

StuG III Ausf. G
80 mm Maximum
Front Armour

JAGDPANZER IV
80 mm Maximum
Front Armour

2000 Yards

1000 Yards

PzKpfw VI 'TIGER I'
100 mm Maximum
Front Armour

PzKpfw V Ausf. G
'PANTHER'
110 mm Maximum
Front Armour

This chart depicts the effectiveness of the Firefly in dealing with German armour commonly encountered in Normandy, based on test performance using Armour Piercing Capped (APC) ammunition. Penetration results improved markedly for Armour Piercing Capped Ballistic Capped (APCBC) and Armour Piercing Discarding Sabot (APDS) although accuracy was always an issue with these rounds. While the operational effectiveness of the 17-pdr was realistically restricted to ranges under 1000 yards, it was quite capable of knocking out German armour at the ranges shown.

SHERMAN FIREFLY
Armed with a 17-pdr.

21st Army Group's Stop-Gap Solution
The Ranges at which the Firefly
Could Kill German Tanks

Not to Scale

like the Tiger and a Sherman tank which was a useful weapon and so on and thank God we had lots of them and so on. But it was hard on people because not only when you were losing men but you were, after you were

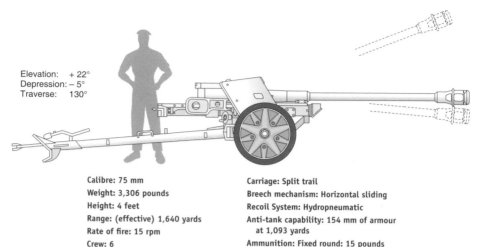

Elevation: + 22°
Depression: – 5°
Traverse: 130°

Calibre: 75 mm	Carriage: Split trail
Weight: 3,306 pounds	Breech mechanism: Horizontal sliding
Height: 4 feet	Recoil System: Hydropneumatic
Range: (effective) 1,640 yards	Anti-tank capability: 154 mm of armour
Rate of fire: 15 rpm	at 1,093 yards
Crew: 6	Ammunition: Fixed round: 15 pounds

Pak 40 anti-tank gun

Although the 88 mm dual-purpose gun is perhaps the best known German anti-tank gun of the Second World War, the Pak 40 was the mainstay of German anti-tank defences from 1942 on. The Pak 40 inherited many features of its predecessor, the 50 mm Pak 38, with improvements resulting from experience dealing with the Russian T-34 and KV-1 series of tanks. The recoil mechanism was improved, the gun shield was constructed of two spaced 4 mm armour plates and the horizontal sliding breach block was designed for semi-automatic loading. The Pak 40 was an easily concealed and effective anti-tank gun.

knocked out two or three times in a tank, you don't rush in and get into the fourth one very quickly, consequently there is a reaction to having a tank that can't stand up to an enemy tank.[9]

This disparity was not confined to tanks. The Germans understood that fire fights are won by the volume of fire, not necessarily by the number of rifles. Thus, not only did their medium and light machine guns have a cyclic rate of fire two to three times greater that the British and Canadian Brens and Vickers, but the ammunition scale of a German rifle company was more than twice as great as that of an American company, which was the most generous of the Allied armies. This in turn led to the ability to hold a position with a relatively small number of troops, freeing men to be able to manoeuvre against a threat and to mount immediate local counterattacks against Allied lodgements. A veteran who commanded a rifle company in

Normandy and ended the war on German soil as a battalion commander opined that Canada's army "went into action with some of the worst equipment on the battlefield. Allied tanks and machine-guns, for example, were usually inferior to what the Germans had." Furthermore, he added, "Our anti-tank weapon was one of the worst pieces of haywire ever put together. Our infantry equipment, without any question, was inadequate."[10] To put it bluntly, the British and Canadian armies found themselves in the position of the man who brought a knife to a gun fight.

All this, of course, has led to the common jibe that the Allies, unable to match the Germans man-to-man and tank-to-tank, fell back on technology and resorted to the use of massive amounts of artillery and air power to blast them out of their positions. This criticism often is phrased in such a manner as to imply that there was something unfair about this approach and that the Allies cheated their way to victory. While the Allies may have been unenterprising and perhaps on occasion even reluctant to slug it out, there is another, equally valid, way of assessing the situation. To put it bluntly, there is no room for fairness in battle. The aim is to maximize your own advantages, not your opponent's. The Allies' strength was in the mastery of the employment of their excellent artillery and, as any card player knows, you play to your strong suit. While the German artillery had some very good equipment, it was organized to support manoeuvre on a highly-decentralized basis and lagged in its ability to mass fire above the regimental and divisional level. The Allies, on the other hand, were able to both concentrate the fire of literally every gun within range on critical targets and then rapidly decentralize artillery to support manoeuvre warfare. In addition, the Allies outgunned the Germans in number of tubes by a factor of several times and enjoyed an advantage in ability to rapidly deliver ammunition directly to gun positions in tons their enemy could only dream of. Purists have sniffed at this approach to fighting for years, but it worked. It also must be acknowledged that as the Allied armies gained experience, the disparity in tactical ability between the two sides lessened and after Normandy the German advantage was never as great again.

ORDER OF BATTLE, FIRST CANADIAN ARMY/ 84 COMPOSITE GROUP, 7 AUGUST 1944

HEADQUARTERS, FIRST CANADIAN ARMY

General Officer Commanding-in-Chief	Lieutenant General H.D.G. Crerar[1]
Chief of Staff	Brigadier C.C. Mann
Colonel General Staff	Colonel G.E. Beament
Deputy Adjutant and Quartermaster-General	Brigadier A.E. Walford
Brigadier, Royal Armoured Corps	Brigadier N.A. Gianelli
Brigadier, Royal Artillery	Brigadier H.O.N. Brownfield
Chief Engineer	Brigadier A.T. MacLean
Chief Signal Officer	Brigadier J.W. Genet

84 Composite Group, Royal Air Force (operational 10 August)[*2]

Air Officer Commanding	Air Vice Marshal L.O. Brown

35 Reconnaissance Wing*
  2 Squadron*
  4 Squadron*
  268 Squadron*

123 Fighter-Bomber Wing*
  609 Squadron*
  198 Squadron*
  164 Squadron*
  183 Squadron*

131 (Polish) Wing
  302 (Polish) Squadron
  308 (Polish) Squadron
  317 (Polish) Squadron

132 Wing*
  66 Squadron*
  331 (Norwegian) Squadron

332 (Norwegian) Squadron
127 Squadron*

135 Wing*

222 Squadron*
485 (New Zealand) Squadron
349 (Belgian) Squadron
33 Squadron*

145 (French) Wing

340 (French) Squadron
341 (French) Squadron
329 (French) Squadron
74 Squadron*

146 Fighter-Bomber Wing*

193 Squadron*
197 Squadron*
257 Squadron*
263 Squadron*

ARMY TROOPS

2 Canadian Armoured Brigade

| Commander | Brigadier R.A. Wyman (wounded 8 Aug 44) |
| Deputy Commander | Colonel J.F. Bingham (assumed comd 9 Aug 44) |

6 Canadian Armoured Regiment (1st Hussars)
10 Canadian Armoured Regiment (Fort Garry Horse)
27 Canadian Armoured Regiment (Sherbrooke Fusiliers)

31 Armoured Brigade*

Commander   Brigadier G.S. Knight

7th Battalion, the Royal Tank Regiment
9th Battalion, the Royal Tank Regiment

33 Armoured Brigade*

Commander   Brigadier H.B. Scott

1 Northamptonshire Yeomanry
144 Regiment Royal Armoured Corps
148 Regiment Royal Armoured Corps

25 Canadian Armoured Delivery Regiment (Elgin Regiment)[3]

2 Canadian Army Group, Royal Artillery

Commander   Brigadier E.R. Suttie

3 Canadian Medium Regiment
4 Canadian Medium Regiment
7 Canadian Medium Regiment
15 Medium Regiment*
1 Heavy Regiment*

4 Army Group, Royal Artillery*

Commander — Brigadier H.A. Hambleton
    150 Field Regiment*
    53 Medium Regiment*
    65 Medium Regiment*
    68 Medium Regiment*
    79 Medium Regiment*
    51 Heavy Regiment*

9 Army Group, Royal Artillery*

Commander — Brigadier W.H. Crosland
    9 Medium Regiment*
    11 Medium Regiment*
    107 Medium Regiment*

74 Anti-Aircraft Brigade* (assigned to defence of 84 Composite Group airfields)

Commander — Brigadier J.M. Smith

107 Anti-Aircraft Brigade* (moving to the continent at the time of TOTALIZE)

Commander — Brigadier G.McL. Routledge
    16 Anti-Aircraft Operations Room RCA (still moving to continent)
    2 Canadian Heavy Anti-Aircraft Regiment
    108 Heavy Anti-Aircraft Regiment* (still moving to continent)
    109 Heavy Anti-Aircraft Regiment*
    344 Searchlight Battery*

661 Air Observation Post Squadron Royal Air Force*4

RCAF Army Headquarters Intercommunications Flight

2ND CANADIAN CORPS

Headquarters

General Officer Commanding — Lieutenant General G.G. Simonds,
Brigadier General Staff — Brigadier N.A. Rodger
Deputy Adjutant and — Brigadier H.V.D. Laing
    Quartermaster-General
Chief Signal Officer — Brigadier S.F. Clark

CORPS TROOPS

Canadian Armoured Corps
    18 Canadian Armoured Car Regiment (12 Manitoba Dragoons)

Royal Canadian Artillery
Commander   Brigadier A.B. Matthews
    6 Canadian Anti-Tank Regiment
    2 Canadian Survey Regiment
    6 Canadian Light Anti-Aircraft Regiment
    Corps Counter-Battery Office

Royal Canadian Engineers
Chief Engineer   Brigadier G. Walsh
    29 Canadian Field Company
    30 Canadian Field Company
    31 Canadian Field Company
    8 Canadian Field Park Company

661 Air Observation Post Squadron, Royal Air Force*

2ND CANADIAN INFANTRY DIVISION

General Officer Commanding   Major General C. Foulkes
General Staff Officer, Grade I   Lieutenant Colonel C.M. Drury
Assistant Adjutant and   Lieutenant Colonel L.A. Deziel
   Quartermaster-General

4 Canadian Infantry Brigade
Commander   Brigadier J.E. Ganong
    Royal Regiment of Canada
    Royal Hamilton Light Infantry
    Essex Scottish

5 Canadian Infantry Brigade
Commander   Brigadier W.J. Megill
    The Black Watch (Royal Highland Regiment) of Canada
    Le Régiment de Maisonneuve
    Calgary Highlanders

6 Canadian Infantry Brigade
Commander   Brigadier H.A. Young
    Les Fusiliers Mont-Royal
    Queen's Own Cameron Highlanders of Canada
    South Saskatchewan Regiment

Divisional Troops
    8 Canadian Reconnaissance Regiment (14 Canadian Hussars)

Royal Canadian Artillery
Commander   Brigadier R.H. Keefler
    4 Canadian Field Regiment
    5 Canadian Field Regiment
    6 Canadian Field Regiment
    2 Canadian Anti-Tank Regiment
    3 Canadian Light Anti-Aircraft Regiment

Royal Canadian Engineers
Commander   Lieutenant Colonel N.J.W. Smith
    2 Canadian Field Company
    7 Canadian Field Company
    11 Canadian Field Company
    1 Canadian Field Park Company

Tentacle, Air Support Signals Unit

Toronto Scottish (Machine Gun)

3RD CANADIAN INFANTRY DIVISION

General Officer Commanding   Major General R.F.L. Keller
General Staff Officer Grade I   Lieutenant Colonel J.D. Mingay
Assistant Adjutant and   Lieutenant Colonel E.A. Cote
    Quartermaster-General

7 Canadian Infantry Brigade
Commander   Brigadier H.W. Foster
    Royal Winnipeg Rifles
    Regina Rifles Regiment
    1st Battalion, Canadian Scottish Regiment

8 Canadian Infantry Brigade
Commander   Brigadier K.G. Blackader
    Queen's Own Rifles of Canada
    Le Régiment de la Chaudiere
    North Shore (New Brunswick) Regiment

9 Canadian Infantry Brigade
Commander   Brigadier J.M. Rockingham
    The Highland Light Infantry of Canada
    Stormont, Dundas and Glengarry Highlanders
    North Nova Scotia Highlanders

Divisional Troops
  7 Canadian Reconnaissance Regiment (Duke of York's Royal Canadian Hussars)

Royal Canadian Artillery
Commander   Brigadier P.A.S. Todd
  12 Canadian Field Regiment
  13 Canadian Field Regiment
  14 Canadian Field Regiment (still converting from 105mm SP to 25-pounder towed)
  3 Canadian Anti-Tank Regiment
  4 Canadian Light Anti-Aircraft Regiment

Royal Canadian Engineers
Commander   Lieutenant Colonel R.J. Cassidy
  6 Canadian Field Company
  16 Canadian Field Company
  18 Canadian Field Company
  3 Canadian Field Park Company

Cameron Highlanders of Ottawa (Machine Gun)

4TH CANADIAN ARMOURED DIVISION

General Officer Commanding   Major General G. Kitching
General Staff Officer Grade I   Lieutenant Colonel F.E. Wigle
Assistant Adjutant and   Lieutenant Colonel J.W. Proctor
  Quartermaster-General

4 Canadian Armoured Brigade
Commander   Brigadier E.L. Booth
  21 Canadian Armoured Regiment (Governor General's Foot Guards)
  22 Canadian Armoured Regiment (Canadian Grenadier Guards)
  28 Canadian Armoured Regiment (British Columbia Regiment)
  Lake Superior Regiment (Motor)

10 Canadian Infantry Brigade
Commander   Brigadier J.C. Jefferson
  Lincoln and Welland Regiment
  Algonquin Regiment
  Argyll and Sutherland Highlanders of Canada (Princess Louise's)

Divisional Troops
  29 Canadian Armoured Reconnaissance Regiment (South Alberta Regiment)

Royal Canadian Artillery
Commander   Brigadier J.N. Lane

15 Canadian Field Regiment
23 Canadian Field Regiment (Self-Propelled)
19 Canadian Army Field Regiment (Self-Propelled) (Attached from 2 AGRA)
5 Canadian Anti-Tank Regiment
8 Canadian Light Anti-Aircraft Regiment

Royal Canadian Engineers

Commander   Lieutenant Colonel J.R.B. Jones
   8 Canadian Field Squadron
   9 Canadian Field Squadron
   6 Canadian Field Park Squadron

10th Independent Machine Gun Company (The New Brunswick Rangers)

51ST HIGHLAND DIVISION*

General Officer Commanding   Major General T.G. Rennie

152 Highland Brigade

Commander   Brigadier A.J.H. Cassels
   2 Seaforth Highlanders
   5 Seaforth Highlanders
   5 Queen's Own Cameron Highlanders

153 Highland Brigade

Commander   Brigadier H. Murray
   5 Black Watch
   1 Gordon Highlanders
   5/7 Gordon Highlanders

154 Highland Brigade

Commander   Brigadier J.A. Oliver
   1 Black Watch
   7 Black Watch
   7 Argyll and Sutherland Highlanders

Divisional Troops
Royal Artillery

Commander   Brigadier W.A. Shiel
   126 Field Regiment
   127 Field Regiment
   128 Field Regiment
   61 Anti-Tank Regiment
   40 Light Anti-Aircraft Regiment

Royal Engineers
274 Field Company
275 Field Company
276 Field Company
236 Field Park Company

1/7 Middlesex Regiment (Machine Gun)

2 Derbyshire Yeomanry (Reconnaissance Regiment)[5]

C Flight, 652 Air Observation Post Squadron, Royal Air Force

1. *DYWIZJI PANCERNEJ* (1ST POLISH ARMOURED DIVISION)

General Officer Commanding	*Generał brygada* S. Maczek
No. 4 Liaison HQ Armoured*	Colonel J.H. Anstice

10. *Brygada Kwalerii Pancernej* (10 Armoured Cavalry Brigade)

Commander   *Pułkownik* T. Majewski
   1. *Pułk Pancerny* (1 Armoured Regiment)
   2. *Pułk Pancerny* (2 Armoured Regiment)
  24. *Pułk Ulanów* (24 Lancers)
  10. *Pułk Dragonów* (10 Dragoons (Motor Battalion))

3. *Brygada Strzelcow* (3 Rifles Brigade)

Commander   *Pułkownik* M. Wieronski
   1. *Batalion Strzelców Podhalanskich* (1 Rifles Battalion (Highland))
   8. *Batalion Strzelców* (8 Rifles Battalion)
   9. *Batalion Strzelców* (9 Rifles Battalion)
   Samodzielny Szwadron C.K.M. (1st Polish Armoured Division Machine Gun Company)

Divisional Troops
  10. *Pułk Strzelców Konnych* (10 Mounted Rifle Regiment (Reconnaissance Regiment))

***Artyleria Dywizyjna* (Divisional Artillery)**

Commander   *Pułkownik* B. Noel
   1. *Pułk Artylerii Motorowej* (1 Motorized Artillery Regiment)
   2. *Pułk Artylerii Motorowej* (2 Motorized Artillery Regiment)
   1. *Pułk Artylerii Przeciwpancernej* (1 Anti-Tank Regiment)
   1. *Pułk Artlerii Przeciwlotniczej* (1 Light Anti-Aircraft Regiment)

***Saperzy Sywizyina* (Divisional Engineers)**
  10. *Kompania Saperów* (10 Polish Field Company)
  11. *Kompania Saperów* (11 Polish Field Company)
   1. *Pluton Mostowy* (1 Bridging Platoon)
  11. *Kompania Parhkowa* (11 Polish Field Park Company)

ATTACHED FROM 79 ARMOURED DIVISION

22nd Dragoons (Sherman Crabs)
1st Lothian and Border Horse Yeomanry (Sherman Crabs)
141 Regiment RAC (Crocodiles)
79 and 80 Assault Squadrons (AVRE

1ST BRITISH CORPS (outline only)*

General Officer Commanding   Lieutenant General J.T. Crocker

CORPS TROOPS

Royal Armoured Corps
    The Inns of Court Regiment (Armoured Car)*

Artillery*
    62 Anti-Tank Regiment
    102 Light Anti-Aircraft Regiment
    9 Survey Regiment

652 Air Observation Post Squadron, Royal Air Force (less C Flight)*

6 (AIRBORNE) DIVISION*

General Officer Commanding   Major General R.N. Gale

3 Parachute Brigade
Commander   Brigadier S.J.L. Hill

5 Parachute Brigade
Commander   Brigadier J.H.N. Poett

6 Airlanding Brigade
Commander   Brigadier E.W.C. Flawell

1 Special Service Brigade (attached)

4 Special Service Brigade (attached)

49 (WEST RIDING) DIVISION*

General Officer Commanding   Major General E.H. Barker

70 Brigade
Commander   Brigadier E.C. Cooke-Collis

146 Brigade
Commander   Brigadier J.F. Walker

147 Brigade
Commander   Brigadier H. Wood

Belgian Contingent (approximately brigade-sized)

Netherlands Contingent (approximately brigade-sized)

NOTES

1. In all cases decorations are not shown.

2. * indicates a British formation or unit

3. Squadrons were deployed with corps and armoured divisions in Northwest Europe and Italy.

4. Air OP squadrons were assigned on the basis of one per army headquarters and one per corps. While the squadrons were air force units, the pilots were Royal Artillery officers.

5. While Canadian reconnaissance regiments were Canadian Armoured Corps units, the British allotted their reconnaissance regiments to a wartime creation, the Reconnaissance Corps, which ranked after the infantry in precedence.

REFERENCES

A. Stacey, *The Victory Campaign.*

B. Hastings, *Battle for Normandy.*

C. Grodzinski, *Operational Handbook.*

D. Anon, *BRA History.*

E. Jean Bouchery, *The British Tommy in North West Europe, 1944-1945*, vol. 2, Organisation, Armament and Vehicles (Paris, 1999).

F. Jean Bouchery, *The Canadian Soldier in North West Europe, 1944-1945* (Paris, 2003).

G. PRO: Air 25/709, 84 Group RAF Ops Record Book August 1944, "Allocation of Continental Airfields," p. 8, ser. 22, 10 August 1944.

GERMAN FORCES, CAEN–FALAISE SECTOR, 7 AUGUST 1944

PANZERGRUPPE WEST / 5. PANZERARMEE

Commander	*General Der Panzertruppen* Heinrich Eberbach
Chief of Staff	*Generalleutnant* Alfred Gause

1. SS-PANZERKORPS

Commander	*SS-Obergruppenführer* Josef "Sepp" Dietrich
Chief of Staff	*SS-Oberführer* Fritz Kramer

Korpsbegleitkompanie

12. SS-PANZERDIVISION
(Total strength 11,000-11,500 all ranks) (a)

Commander	*SS-Oberführer* Kurt Meyer
Chief of Staff	*SS-Sturmbannführer* Hubert Meyer

Divisionbegleitkompanie 12   *SS-Obersturmführer* Fritz Guntrum

SS-Panzerregiment 12

Commander	*SS-Obersturmbannführer* Max Wünsche
I. *Abteilung SS-Panzerregiment* 12 (9 Panther) (b)	*SS-Sturmbannführer* Arnold Jurgensen
II. *Abteilung SS-Panzerregiment* 12 (37 Mk IV)	*SS-Sturmbannführer* Karl-Heinz Prinz

SS-Panzergrenadierregiment 25

I. *Bataillon SS-Panzergrenadierregiment* 25

                              SS-Sturmbannführer Hans Waldmüller

SS-Panzergrenadierregiment 26

Commander	*SS-Obersturmbannführer* Wilhelm Mohnke
I. *Bataillon SS-Panzergrenadierregiment* 26	*SS-Sturmbannführer* Bernhard Krause

III. *Bataillon SS-Panzergrenadierregiment* 26   *SS-Sturmbannführer* Erich Olboeter
13. *Kompanie SS-Panzergrenadierregiment* 26
14. *Kompanie SS-Panzergrenadierregiment* 26
15. *Kompanie SS-Panzergrenadierregiment* 26
16. *Kompanie SS-Panzergrenadierregiment* 26

SS-Panzeraufklärungsabteilung 12   *SS-Sturmbannführer* Gerd Bremer
(approximately two armoured reconnaissance platoons only)

SS-Panzerartillerieregiment 12
Commander   *SS-Oberststurmbannführer* Oskar Drexler
  I. *Bataillon*   *SS-Sturmbannführer* Hagemeier
    (12 105 mm Wespe, 6 150 mm Hummel)
  II. *Bataillon*   *SS-Sturmbannführer* Gunter Neumann
    (18 105 mm LFH)
  III. *Bataillon*   *SS-Sturmbannführer* Karl Bartling
    (12 150 mm, 4 100 mm Kanon)

SS-Panzerjägerabteilung 12   *SS-Sturmbannführer* Jakob Hanreich
  (two companies *Jagdpanzer* IV, one company 75 mm PAK)

SS-Werferabteilung 12   *SS-Sturmbannführer* Willy Muller
  (four batteries 150 mm *Nebelwerfer*)

SS-Flakabteilung 12   *SS-Sturmbannführer* Rudolf Fend
  (12 88 mm, 9 37 mm)

SS-Panzerpionierbataillon 12   *SS-Sturmbannführer* Siegfried Muller
  (two companies)

Attached
  schwere SS-Panzerabteilung 101   *SS-Hauptsturmführer* Michael Wittmann
    (20 Tiger 1)
  4. *Kompanie Panzerabteilung* 301 (Funklenk)
    (36 B IV remote-controlled "tanks")
  schwere SS-Panzerabteilung 102 (from 9 August)
    (20 Tiger 1)
  II. *Abteilung Panzerregiment* 33 (9. *Panzerdivision*) (from 10 August)
    (24 Panther)

89. *INFANTERIEDIVISION* (b)
(Total strength 8,000 all ranks)

Commander   *Generalleutnant* Konrad Heinrich

Grenadierregiment 1055 (c)

Commander   *Oberst* Rossman

 I. *Bataillon Grenadierregiment* 1055
 II. *Bataillon Grenadierregiment* 1055
 III. *Bataillon Grenadierregiment* 1055
  13. *Kompanie Grenadierregiment* 1055 (d)
  14. *Kompanie Grenadierregiment* 1055

Grenadier Regiment 1056

Commander   *Oberst* Karl Roesler

 I. *Bataillon Grenadierregiment* 1056
 II. *Bataillon Grenadierregiment* 1056
 III. *Bataillon Grenadierregiment* 1056
  13. *Kompanie Grenadierregiment* 1056
  14. *Kompanie Grenadierregiment* 1056

Artillerieregiment 189

 I. *Bataillon Artillerieregiment* 189 (two batteries)
 II. *Bataillon Artillerieregiment* 189 (two batteries)
 III. *Bataillon Artillerieregiment* 189 (two batteries)

Panzerjägerabteilung 189

Fusilierbataillon 189

Pionierbataillon 189 (two companies)

Attached

 Sturmpanzerabteilung 217
  (13 *Sturmpanzer* IV 150 mm self-propelled howitzers)
 Artillerieabteilung 1151
  (12 Russian 122 mm howitzers)
 Artillerieabteilung 1193
  (12 Italian 149 mm howitzers)
 Werferbrigade 7
  Werferregiment 83
   (two *bataillon* 150 mm, one *bataillon* 210 mm)
  Werferregiment 84
   (two *bataillon* 150 mm, one *bataillon* 300 mm)

271. *INFANTERIEDIVISION*
(Total strength 12,621 all ranks)

Commander   *Generalleutnant* Paul Danhauser

Grenadierregiment 977

I. *Bataillon Grenadierregiment* 977
II. *Battaillon Grenadierregiment* 977
    13. *Kompanie Grenadierregiment* 977
    14. *Kompanie Grenadierregiment* 977

Grenadierregiment 978

I. *Bataillon Grenadierregiment* 978
II. *Bataillon Grenadierregiment* 978
    13. *Kompanie Grenadierregiment* 978
    14. *Kompanie Grenadierregiment* 978

Grenadierregiment 979

I. *Bataillon Grenadierregiment* 979
II. *Bataillon Grenadierregiment* 979
    13. *Kompanie Grenadierregiment* 979
    14. *Kompanie Grenadierregiment* 979

Artillerieregiment 271

(32 105 mm *LFH*, 9 150 mm *SFH*)

Panzerjägerabteilung 271

Fusilierbataillon 271

Pionierbataillon 271

(three companies)

272. INFANTERIEDIVISION
(Total strength 12,725 all ranks)

Commander   *Generalleutnant* Friedrich-August Schack

Grenadierregiment 980

I. *Bataillon Grenadierregiment* 980
II. *Bataillon Grenadierregiment* 980
    13. *Kompanie Grenadierregiment* 980
    14. *Kompanie Grenadierregiment* 980

Grenadierregiment 981

I. *Bataillon Grenadierregiment* 981
II. *Bataillon Grenadierregiment* 981
    13. *Kompanie Grenadierregiment* 981
    14. *Kompanie Grenadierregiment* 981

Grenadierregiment 982
   I. *Bataillon Grenadierregiment 982*
   II. *Bataillon Grenadierregiment 982*
      13. *Kompanie Grenadierregiment 982*
      14. *Kompanie Grenadierregiment 982*

Artillerieregiment 272
   (33 105 mm *LFH*, 9 150 mm *SFH*)

Panzerjägerabteilung 272

Fusilierbataillon 272

Pionierbataillon 272
   (three companies)

85. *INFANTERIEDIVISION* (from 9 August)
(Total strength 8,725 all ranks)

Commander   *Generalleutnant* Kurt Chill

Grenadierregiment 1053
   I. *Bataillon Grenadierregiment 1053*
   II. *Bataillon Grenadierregiment 1053*
   III. *Bataillon Grenadierregiment 1053*
      13. *Kompanie Grenadierregiment 1053*
      14. *Kompanie Grenadierregiment 1053*

Gremadierregiment 1054
   I. *Bataillon Grenadierregiment 1054*
   II. *Bataillon Grenadierregiment 1054*
   III. *Bataillon Grenadierregiment 1054*
      13. *Kompanie Grenadierregiment 1054*
      14. *Kompanie Grenadierregiment 1054*

Artillerieregiment 185
   I. *Bataillon Artillerieregiment 185*
      (8 105 mm *LFH* 18/40)
   II. *Bataillon Artillerieregiment 185*
      (8 105 mm *LFH* 18/40)
   III. *Bataillon Artillerieregiment 185*
      (12 150 mm *SFH*)

Panzerjägerabteilung 185
   (12 75 mm *PAK*)

Fusilierbataillon 185

Pionierbataillon 185
(two companies)

Miscellaneous

III. *FLAKKORPS* (e)
(Total strength approximately 12,000 all ranks)

Commander   *General Der Flaktruppen* Wolfgang Pickert

Flaksturmregiment 1
I. *Bataillon Flakregiment* 1
II. *Bataillon Flakregiment* 1

Flaksturmregiment 2
I. *Bataillon Flakregiment* 20
I. *Bataillon Flakregiment* 52

Flaksturmregiment 3
I. *Bataillon Flakregiment* 22
I. *Bataillon Flakregiment* 64

Flaksturmregiment 4
I. *Bataillon Flakregiment* 35
II. *Bataillon Flakregiment* 53
III. *Bataillon Flakregiment* 141
Flakabteilung 996

Flakabteilung 80
Flakabteilung 84
Flakabteilung 90
Flakabteilung 98
Flakabteilung 757
Flakabteilung II/*FAS* II
Flakabteilung zbV 11100

Flakkampfgruppe 11700
Flakkampfgruppe 12400 (?)
Flakkampfgruppe 13300

Panzerjägerabteilung 1344 (f)

NOTES

(a) The figures for total strength are on entering combat, except for 12. *SS-Panzerdivision*. In its case, this is the estimated strength and organization at end-July. The missing headquarters and units had been withdrawn for refitting, while the bulk of the remaining manoeuvre units had been organized into three battle groups. Both 271. and 272. *Infanteriedivisions* had suffered fairly heavy casualties and their effective strengths may have been under 10,000.

(b) The numbers of equipment in this table are take from the data for each unit or formation in Zetterling's *Normandy 1944*.

(c) The infantry divisions operated on two separate establishments: 85. and 89. *Infanteriedivisions* were organized with two regiments, each of three battalions, while 271. and 272. *Infanteriedivisions* had three regiments, each of two battalions.

(d) The companies in infantry regiments were identified using arabic numbers, with 1-4 in the first battalion, 5-8 in the second and 9-12 in the third, while 13 and 14 were allotted to the infantry gun and the anti-tank companies respectively. This system was used in both the two- and three-battalion regiments, with 13 and 14 reserved for the regimental companies, regardless of the number of infantry battalions. SS regiments had two additional regimental companies, 15 (reconnaissance) and 16 (anti-aircraft).

(e) The primary role of this *Luftwaffe* formation was air defence, with a secondary role of indirect fire because of the shortage of corps and army artillery units. Hence it was initially deployed in the area from the front line to the general area Falaise–Le Bény Bocage, while the eight independent *flakabteilungen*, all of which were equipped with light anti-aircraft guns, were sited farther to the rear. While the *flakkampfgruppen* were designed for ground combat (their training and equipment were inferior to the army anti-tank units), if enemy tanks broke through the forward defences the *flaksturm* units were also expected to engage them. Each *flakkampfgruppe* had four *flakkampftruppen*, each of two 88 mm *Flak* along with some lighter guns, while the *bataillons* of the *flaksturmregimenter* were organized with three batteries each of four 88 mm anti-aircraft, not dual-purpose, guns, and two batteries of 37 and/or 20 mm guns, except for *Flakabteilung* 996, which was a light anti-aircraft unit.

   While any model of the 88 mm could destroy any Allied tank, it must be emphasized that this formation's primary role was anti-aircraft, and its capability in an anti-tank role was limited. Two statistics bear this out: first, the *Flakkampfgruppen* claimed to have destroyed about 20 Allied tanks, while suffering the loss of 35 88 mm and 70 light flak guns; and second, III. *Flakkorps* stated that while it had shot down 462 aircraft, it had only knocked out 92 tanks (presumably including the 20 above) and 14 armoured cars during its tour in Normandy; of the tanks, 12 fell victim to *Panzerfaust* teams.

(f) While reference C states this unit did not serve in Normandy, 10 prisoners from *Panzerjäger-abteilung* 1344 passed through the First Canadian Army PW cage on 8-9 August 1944. During interrogation by Canadian intelligence, three of the prisoners provided details of the unit's organization and equipment. One stated he had been a member of an anti-tank gun crew, while the other two apparently had "been fighting as infantry."

REFERENCES

A. Hubert Meyer, *12 SS Panzer History.*

B. Reynolds, *Steel Inferno.*

C. Zetterling, *Normandy 1944.*

D. First Canadian Army Intelligence Summaries.

E. <www.feldgrau.com>

AIR POWER IN SUPPORT
OF THE LAND BATTLE
IN 21st ARMY GROUP

Both Crerar and Simonds had planned to use every available aircraft to break through the German defences covering the approach to Falaise. Therefore, to understand the contribution of the air forces, it is necessary to explain briefly the role and employment of the Allied air forces in the Normandy campaign, especially as most of the controversy surrounding the campaign has been centred on the land forces and the dynamics of the relationships between the senior commanders. While the armies did provide the majority of the manpower and resources, an essential part was played by the air forces, which at least in theory were equal partners with the armies under the overall stewardship of General Eisenhower. Eisenhower's Deputy Supreme Commander of the Allied Expeditionary Force was a British airman, Air Chief Marshal Arthur Tedder, while another RAF officer, Air Chief Marshal Trafford Leigh-Mallory, the commander of the Allied Expeditionary Air Force (AEAF), reported directly to SHAEF, as did both Montgomery and Royal Navy Admiral Sir Bertram Ramsey, the naval commander.[1]

Soldiers tended to think of the air force as a monolithic "light blue" cabal. In fact, the relationships among the senior Allied air commanders, dynamic individuals of strong personality and total devotion to the Allied cause all, were hampered by personal dislikes and distrust not only of the motives of the army but of one another. Moreover, to complicate matters the air forces had an extra level of command, that of the AEAF, over and above that of the land forces. Despite his appointment, Leigh-Mallory, who was responsible for concurrently supporting the land forces fighting in Normandy and providing the air defence of Great Britain, had no control over the heavy bombers of Air Chief Marshal Arthur Harris's Bomber Command and Lieutenant General Carl Spaatz's United States Strategic Air Force.[2] Leigh-Mallory became, in the words of Air Marshal Arthur Coningham,* the commander of Second Tactical Air Force (2 TAF), the commander of a "tiresome extra Headquarters in the chain of command."[3]

Leigh-Mallory further contributed to the muddle by delegating authority to Coningham for the operational control of the planning and operations of the tactical air forces. The original intention had been to appoint Coningham as Leigh-Mallory's deputy but this came to naught when General Lewis Brereton, commander of the Ninth United States Army Air Force, flatly refused to place himself under the command of Coningham, who had publicly disparaged American fighting qualities in the Mediterranean. To further complicate matters, both Eisenhower and Tedder had problems with Leigh-Mallory's command style and personality.** While the root of General Eisenhowers' displeasure seems to have been no more than a personality clash – Leigh-Mallory affected the patrician British accent and condescending manner that could be so irritating to North Americans – Tedder felt he was too inclined to subordinate the interests of the air forces to those of the armies.

If this was not enough, Coningham not only disliked Leigh-Mallory, but in common with Tedder detested General Montgomery. Coningham and Montgomery had enjoyed a close relationship in North Africa, where the headquarters of the Eighth Army and the Desert Air Force were co-located, but this changed after El Alamein, when Coningham grew to believe Montgomery had deliberately downplayed the role of the air force in order to hog all the credit for himself and his army. Tedder's aversion to Montgomery was more objective; after his experience in the Mediterranean theatre, he doubted the general's ability to make full use of air power, and much of the subsequent criticism of Montgomery's performance in Normandy is directly attributable to Tedder's deliberate campaign to undermine

---

* Coningham, who had a distinguished combat record, unfortunately tended to air his criticisms openly and indiscriminately. As a result, his position was weakened.

** A captured German intelligence assessment cited on p. 383 of Stephen Bungay's *The Most Dangerous Enemy, A History of the Battle of Britain* apparently described Leigh-Mallory as a "flying sergeant" because of his penchant for concentration on administrative details and his tendency to give his subordinates little scope for decisions.

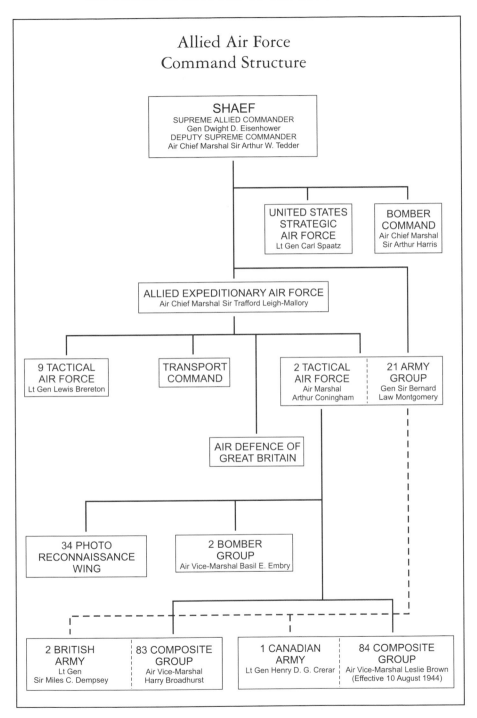

Allied Air Force Command Structure

SHAEF
SUPREME ALLIED COMMANDER
Gen Dwight D. Eisenhower
DEPUTY SUPREME COMMANDER
Air Chief Marshal Sir Arthur W. Tedder

UNITED STATES STRATEGIC AIR FORCE
Lt Gen Carl Spaatz

BOMBER COMMAND
Air Chief Marshal Sir Arthur Harris

ALLIED EXPEDITIONARY AIR FORCE
Air Chief Marshal Sir Trafford Leigh-Mallory

9 TACTICAL AIR FORCE
Lt Gen Lewis Brereton

TRANSPORT COMMAND

2 TACTICAL AIR FORCE
Air Marshal Arthur Coningham

21 ARMY GROUP
Gen Sir Bernard Law Montgomery

AIR DEFENCE OF GREAT BRITAIN

34 PHOTO RECONNAISSANCE WING

2 BOMBER GROUP
Air Vice-Marshal Basil E. Embry

2 BRITISH ARMY
Lt Gen Sir Miles C. Dempsey

83 COMPOSITE GROUP
Air Vice-Marshal Harry Broadhurst

1 CANADIAN ARMY
Lt Gen Henry D. G. Crerar

84 COMPOSITE GROUP
Air Vice-Marshal Leslie Brown
(Effective 10 August 1944)

him. Of the three senior British air force officers, Leigh-Mallory was the odd man out in that he held no great antipathy towards Montgomery, and unlike Tedder and Coningham had not served with him in North Africa and the Mediterranean. A cynic might wonder if, in the eyes of airmen, to know Montgomery was to hate him.

In turn, Montgomery, while claiming that as the ground force commander and the commander-in-chief 21 Army Group he had two air force opposite numbers – Leigh-Mallory, as the air commander-in-chief, and Coningham, who commanded 2 Tactical Air Force (2 TAF) which worked with 21 Army Group – actually ignored the arrangements by "dealing directly with Leigh-Mallory for heavy bomber support and with Air Vice-Marshal Harry Broadhurst [the commander of 83 Composite Group] on tactical air matters."[4] The tactical air support available to the land forces – 2 TAF for the British/Canadian armies and Nine Tactical Air Force (9 TAF) for the United States Forces – was a potent force of literally thousands of aircraft. Second TAF in turn was made up of No. 34 Photo Reconnaissance Wing, No. 2 Bomber Group of Boston, Mitchell and Mosquito light bombers, and Nos. 83 and 84 Composite Groups of fighter, fighter- bomber and reconnaissance squadrons that were allotted to support the Second British and First Canadian Armies respectively, some 80 squadrons in all. In fact, due to the failure of the Allied forces to expand the bridgehead, there was insufficient space to construct the planned number of airfields, especially in the Caen area, and the headquarters of Air Vice-Marshal L.O. Brown's 84 Group had not yet moved to the Continent by the time that First Canadian Army became operational on 23 July 1944. Eighty-four Group consisted of eight wings of Mustangs, Spitfires and Typhoons totalling some 29 squadrons; those that had moved to the continent had been placed temporarily under command of No. 83 Group.[5]

The lack of space for airfields lay at the root of many of the disputes between the senior RAF commanders and Montgomery. The latter had gone on record in the weeks leading up to the invasion as stating one of his key requirements was to gain sufficient space to permit the tactical air forces to operate from the continent. Thus the 83 Group Control Centre had landed in France on D-Day and was followed ashore in a matter of days by the group headquarters, while the first RAF aircraft servicing and airfield construction

Country of origin: Great Britain
Crew: 1
Length: 31 feet 4 inches
Span: 36 feet 10 inches
Height: 12 feet 7¾ inches
Weight: 5,610 pounds
Engine: Merlin 61 (1,565 hp)

Maximum speed: 408 mph at 25,000
feet
Rate of climb: 4,100 feet per minute
Service ceiling: 43,000 feet
Range: 100 miles

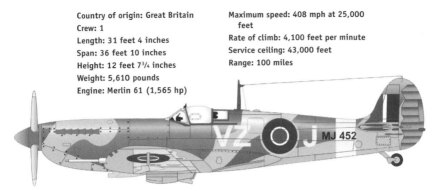

Supermarine Spitfire Mk IX
The main British fighter aircraft of the latter part of the war, it could also be employed to dive-bomb or strafe ground targets. This aircraft shows the identifying letters of 412 Squadron, RCAF. Spitfires from this squadron attacked and destroyed a German staff car on 20 July, knocking *Generalfeldmarschall* Erwin Rommel out of the war.

Country of origin: Great Britain
Crew: 1
Length: 31 feet 10 inches
Span: 41 feet 7 inches
Height: 15 feet 4 inches
Weight: 8,800 pounds

Engine: Napier Sabre II (2,200 hp)
Maximum speed: 417 mph at 20,500 feet
Rate of climb: 3,000 feet per minute
Service ceiling: 35,200 feet
Range: 510 miles (loaded)

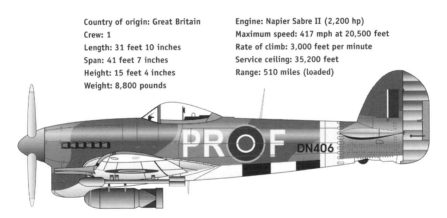

Hawker Typhoon
Originally designed as a high-altitude interceptor, the Typhoon was the major ground attack aircraft of 2nd Tactical Air Force. This "Tiffie," from 609 Squadron, somewhat unusually sortied armed with a bomb under the fuselage and 60-pound rockets under the wings.

units arrived on 7 June.[6] On 10 June three squadrons of RCAF Spitfires became the first Allied high performance aircraft to operate from an airstrip in France since 1940.[7] When his pledge to quickly seize space for the ten airfields required for 83 Group, let alone those for 84 Group, proved unattainable because of his failure to capture Caen, Montgomery put the matter out of his mind and pressed on with his altered strategy. It says much about Montgomery's increasingly autocratic and isolated command style that he neither discussed his reasoning with the air commanders nor explored alternatives with them. Still, the airmen must be faulted in that they failed to appreciate that at the time he might just have had other, more pressing things on his plate – like keeping the Germans from forcing the Allied armies back into the sea – that took priority over making space for airfields. After all, if the Allies could break the German ring formed around the bridgehead, space for the airfields would follow automatically.

While Montgomery was insensitive, all too prone to claim credit for the achievements of others and astonishingly rude on occasion, it does not follow that he did not appreciate the part played by the air force. On the contrary he was, certainly in his own mind, "air-minded." The historian John Terraine has noted that Montgomery could enunciate principles "as though he had not merely personally brought them down, like Moses, from the high mountain, but had also had a large hand in inscribing them up there." Montgomery's statement of principles of air cooperation as practised by the Eighth Army and the Desert Air Force was a masterly exposition of the realities of modern warfare. While it is too long to be repeated in toto, the last paragraph read

Fighting against a good enemy – and the German is extremely good, a first-class soldier – you cannot operate successfully unless you have the full support of the air. If you do not win the air battle first, you will probably lose the land battle. I would go further. There used to be an accepted term of "army cooperation". We never talk about that now. The Desert Air Force and the Eighth Army are one. We do not understand the meaning of "army cooperation". When you are one entity you cannot cooperate. If you knit together the power of the Army on the land and the power of the Air in the sky, then nothing will stand against you and you will never lose a battle.[8]

In a letter he signed to his three army commanders on 4 May 1944 Montgomery stressed once again the importance of air-ground cooperation in the upcoming battle for Normandy,

I feel very strongly on the whole matter, and I know that we can achieve no real success unless each Army and its accompanying Air Force can weld itself into one entity. . . The two HQ have got to set themselves down side by side, and work together as one team; that is the only way.

Regrettably, Montgomery failed to treat his senior air force colleagues as full partners, did not live up to his words and the application of coordinated land/air warfare in Northwest Europe suffered as a consequence.[9]

None of this really should have made much difference to the conduct of operations at the army/composite group level and below in Normandy. However, there was some spillover of the strained relations, unintentional or otherwise, and there were occasions when the Royal Air Force seemed to be more interested in demonstrating its independence than in responding to army requirements. On the other hand, it also seems clear that many senior army officers, among them Canadians, were not as conversant with the fine points of the employment of air power as they should have been, or as they believed themselves to be.

How was the air force to help the army win the land battle? In short, what was the doctrine used by the army and air force? It is important to remember that in 1944 the RAF was barely a quarter century old and considered itself still engaged in a struggle to continue as a separate service. Partly as a survival tactic and partly because it suited their own intellectual bent, a succession of senior RAF officers had embraced the doctrine of strategic bombing as the main function of air power and one that was a guaranteed war-winner. Wedded as it was to the primacy of the bomber, in the years leading up to the war the air staff was opposed to any attempt to involve the air force in support of the army except in a very limited and restricted manner. Even after the examples of the Spanish Civil War, where German pilots operated with the forward troops to direct aircraft unto targets, and the Blitzkrieg in 1940, the air staff stuck with its prewar doctrine and viewed with horror the emergence of joint army/air force operations in North Africa. In late 1942 the air staff stated that, with "the highest priority and sufficient energy [–] devoted to the development of a coordinated day and night bomber offensive [–] the war can certainly be won in 1944, and possibly in 1943."

While a joint RAF–British army team had developed workable tactical air doctrine as early as 1940, any suggestion that the air force might wish to support the army was dismissed coldly and contemptuously by the air staff, and it was not until mid-1943 that the air force accepted that strategic bombing alone could not win the war. That any concerted movement towards ground support emerged at all in the RAF must have been as near-momentous an event to the air staff as the Protestant reformation was to the Catholic Church. Still, and this is key, for many airmen were near-paranoid in their suspicion that the army was plotting to have its own "army air force," the air force retained a separate command structure which, below Eisenhower's headquarters, did not mesh with that of the ground forces. In short army commanders could only request, not order, air support.[10]

By 1944 it was too late to develop the armoured ground attack aircraft the RAF had refused to consider as far back as 1935 with a vehemence that was "apparently [based] on religious grounds, to judge by the fervour of their arguments."[11] Support to the army would have to come from fighter aircraft that were originally designed to kill other aircraft. With the once mighty *Luftwaffe* able only to intervene on a limited basis, much of the large Allied fighter force could be diverted to ground attack. Although flown with magnificent gallantry and great skill, the Spitfires, Mustangs and Typhoons were not as suited for the ground attack role as the air force claimed and the army (and the public) believed. The problem lay in both their vulnerability to ground fire and the inaccuracy of their bombs and rockets, which were not effective weapons when used to attack small targets such as tanks, although it would have been difficult to argue this point with German tank crews who found themselves on the receiving end of an air attack. On occasion the mere appearance of fighter bombers was enough to cause Germans to abandon their vehicles.* However, there also is some evidence that German commanders consistently overstated the effectiveness of Allied tactical air power for personal reasons, and that air attacks tended to be most effective on rear-area installations and troops. All that may have been subjective, but

---

* One could make the same argument about the relative inability of artillery to hit point targets but no one who fought in Normandy would argue that the Allied artillery was ineffective.

operational research studies done on the ground immediately after battles indicate that the claims of land target kills by Allied pilots were far too optimistic. Still, it is abundantly clear that regardless of statistical arguments developed by people who had not been on the receiving end of an air attack, tactical air support aircraft were not ineffective by any stretch of the imagination. Prisoner of war interrogations confirmed that the morale effect of air attacks was considerable and tactical aircraft were especially suited to the destruction of soft-skinned targets with their wing-mounted machine guns and cannon. Furthermore a very real indication of the effectiveness of the Allied air forces was the resources the Germans, who had severe manpower problems, devoted to anti-aircraft artillery, while the Canadian and British armies were able to reduce the number of their own light anti-aircraft guns and retrain the surplus personnel as infantry reinforcements.[12]

Still, by 1944 a workable doctrine had evolved which had the potential to meet the army's needs while recognizing the air force's status as a separate service – in other words, the air force could argue that it was not subservient to the army and thus, unlike the artillery, was not a supporting arm – while still fulfilling the majority of the army's requests for air support. The air force had the final say on which targets to attack based on its own assessment of the situation and the principle of concentration of air power on the most important targets. In early 1944 this doctrine was promulgated in two War Office pamphlets: *Army/Air Operations Pamphlet No. 1 – General Principles and Organizations*, and *Army/Air Operations Pamphlet No. 2 – Direct Support.*[13]

The application of air power was built on the principle of concentration of force. Aircraft could be switched rapidly from one part of the front to another and the whole assets of the two tactical air forces in Europe could be concentrated on decisive points, as was done in response to both the Mortain offensive and the Falaise pocket. To achieve this concentration, and conversely to avoid frittering away the air effort on unimportant targets, required centralized, independent control of air power. This was recognized by both services and it is noteworthy that it was the army author *of Army/Air Operations No. 2 – Direct Support* who wrote

The temptation to abuse the flexibility of air power by attacking targets that may appear to be favourable, but which in fact are not vital to the battle, must be resisted; otherwise the forces available may be dissipated and not used to the best advantage of the operation as a whole. The maximum effort must be concentrated at the decisive place.

Air support was divided into "indirect" and "direct" support. Indirect support was defined as "attacks on objectives which do not have an immediate effect on the land battle but nevertheless contribute to the land battle." The type of targets normally attacked included targets that we would call "infrastructure" today, that is, lines of communications, shipping and railways; in other words targets that supported enemy operations but did not directly contribute to the day-to-day tactical battle. Indirect support usually was provided by heavy or light bombers (the British "light" bombers were the same aircraft types as the American "medium" bombers) but fighter bombers could attack these targets as well. Direct support was defined as "attacks upon enemy forces actually engaged in the land battle." In fact, this definition was interpreted to include not only targets that were or soon could be engaged in combat, but also those behind the battle area that were of some tactical value. The latter were attacked by aircraft tasked for "armed reconnaissance," that is, ranging over a route or area behind German lines to collect intelligence and attack targets of opportunity with bombs, rockets or guns. Other aircraft were employed on artillery reconnaissance (Arty R) missions, that is, directing the fire of medium and heavy guns onto targets in the enemy's rear areas. "Direct support" was generally analogous to but slightly broader than the modern term "close air support," which was not used by the British at the time.[14]

Direct support missions were further categorized into "prearranged" and "impromptu" missions. The former had been assessed and arranged in advance, in some cases days or even weeks before, while the latter were flown in response to urgent requests submitted by the forward troops. Even in the most urgent of cases, the response to impromptu missions could be a matter of hours unless the planning staff had anticipated the request and had arranged a "cab rank" (named for the lines of waiting taxis found outside stations, hotels and theatres) of armed aircraft airborne and on call near the battle area. While the cab rank was popular with the army because of its speedy response, it was costly in terms of aircraft – to maintain a cab rank of between four and 12 Typhoon aircraft continuously on station required the resources of a complete fighter-bomber wing of three squadrons – and was reserved for those occasions when a response measured in minutes rather than hours was essential.

I n accordance with both doctrine and Montgomery's direction, the head-quarters of the army and the composite group were to be co-located. The air force organization was designed to enable the Air Officer Commanding to run his group without becoming immersed in the details of generating and controlling air operations. While the air force operated as an independent service, the operations of both services were coordinated in the Joint Battle Room located at the combined army/composite group main headquarters. The air support effort, especially the direct support program, was planned at the daily Joint RAF/Army conference held in this room. The conference began with a review of the day's operations followed by a briefing on the next day's operations. This led to an examination of the prearranged and other air support requirements along with any new army requests. A priority list of these requirements and the level of effort to be applied to each was then compiled. Finally the air staff developed a detailed air program from this list which was issued as orders by the commander of the composite group.

To support the air force control and reporting system, the army had de-veloped its own liaison organization in the form of Air Liaison (AL) Sections and the Air Support Signals Unit (ASSU). AL Sections were deployed at air-fields where specially trained army officers assisted in the briefing and de-briefing of aircrew and reported information to army HQ. The ASSU, made up of a headquarters and a number of mobile wireless detachments dubbed TENTACLES, was an independent signals network designed to pass messages relating to air action exclusively free of interference with other traffic.[15] TEN-TACLES were deployed to corps, division and brigade headquarters, and from time to time even as far forward as units. The ASSU also provided rear link communications for the AL sections at the airfields. This organization was designed to pass messages relating to requests for air support; unlike the German forces, there was no means of direct communications between the supported unit or formation and the aircraft tasked to carry out the attack.

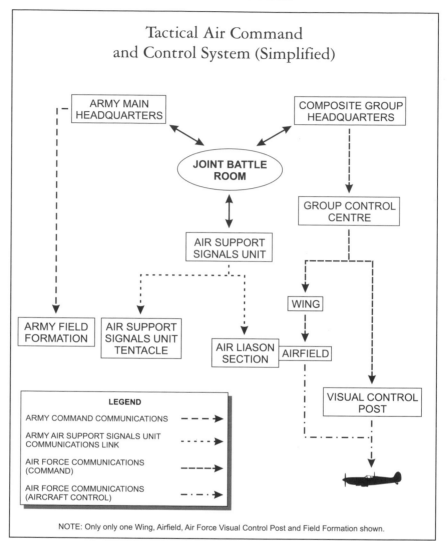

Tactical Air Command
and Control System (Simplified)

ARMY MAIN HEADQUARTERS

COMPOSITE GROUP HEADQUARTERS

JOINT BATTLE ROOM

GROUP CONTROL CENTRE

AIR SUPPORT SIGNALS UNIT

ARMY FIELD FORMATION

AIR SUPPORT SIGNALS UNIT TENTACLE

WING

AIR LIASON SECTION

AIRFIELD

VISUAL CONTROL POST

LEGEND

ARMY COMMAND COMMUNICATIONS - - - →

ARMY AIR SUPPORT SIGNALS UNIT COMMUNICATIONS LINK - - - - →

AIR FORCE COMMUNICATIONS (COMMAND) - - - - →

AIR FORCE COMMUNICATIONS (AIRCRAFT CONTROL) - - · - · →

NOTE: Only only one Wing, Airfield, Air Force Visual Control Post and Field Formation shown.

This was not an ideal situation and one which leaves the nagging thought that it may have been designed to emphasize the independence of the air force. Indeed, unlike the case with the American ground and air forces, it was not until later in the campaign that "contact cars" were introduced. A contact car was an armoured vehicle that carried an AL officer, an air force pilot and air force signallers and was used to control direct support aircraft.[16]

To complicate matters, as already noted when First Canadian Army became operational, the headquarters and many of the units of 84 Composite Group had not yet moved to France. It took a personal appeal from Crerar to Montgomery on 29 July before the group finally was able to commence operations on 10 August. In the meantime a liaison cell from 84 Group was attached to the Second British Army/83 Composite Group Joint Battle Room and all requests for air support were actioned there.[17] It was not an ideal situation and whether it functioned adequately was an open question.

Requests for air support that were beyond the capability of the composite group were passed up the chain to the headquarters of 2 TAF. Coningham's headquarters could approve and task requests for the light bombers of 2 Bomber Group or, after 84 Composite Group became operational on 10 August, provide additional fighters and fighter bombers from the other composite group. Any requests for additional aircraft would be forwarded to the headquarters of the AEAF. If the request could be met from within its own resources, for example 9 TAF, then orders would be issued to that formation. If, however, heavy bomber support was requested, then the request was submitted to SHAEF. Only after the approval of Tedder, acting for Eisenhower, had been obtained, would detailed planning commence. It was a cumbersome process, at least compared to tactical air, especially because of the extra approval step in the chain. On the other hand, diversion of heavy bombers to direct support of the army had not been contemplated prior to the invasion, and was a measure with which many airmen disagreed.

The effect of a massive strike of the strategic bomber force could be devastating. Either Bomber Command or the Eight United States Army Air Force (8 USAAF) had the ability to mount a raid with hundreds of four-engine bombers. The usual pattern for Bomber Command, regardless of the number of aircraft in the raid, was a circle of one thousand yards in diameter, with a very few bombs falling outside the area, while the American bomb pattern could cover a target area of up to twice that diameter. (The Americans usually bombed from a higher altitude than did the RAF.) Hence, the reluctance of the air force to engage targets close to our own troops with heavy bombers. Incidently, these comments should not be taken as criticism of the heavy bombers, but rather as a description of the nature of the weapon, which had been tailored for an entirely different set of circumstances – the bombing of German industry. Still, a pattern that could flatten a factory complex or several blocks of housing would leave much of a German zonal defence untouched.

When speaking of air support of ground forces, however, the usual bomb-load depended upon the mission requirement, but if destruction and cratering were desired, then 500- and 1000-pound high-explosive bombs with delay fuses were used. If, however, the objective was to inflict casualties on personnel and lightly-armoured material without impeding the movement of our own troops, then the load would consist of high-explosive bombs with instantaneous fuses or specialized fragmentation bombs weighing about 90 pounds each. In either case, the effect appeared to be what we would term carpet bombing, and the sudden spouting of hundreds of clouds of smoke and dirt into the air accompanied by the thunderous, pulsating roar was an awe-inspiring sight. In fact there were not enough aircraft to lay down a carpet of bombs on even a divisional objective area in a single lift, so specific targets had to be selected. Be that as it may, the visual effect of strategic heavy bombing was so impressive that the possibility that it could be ineffective seems not to have occurred to senior Allied army commanders in 1944.

While the supporting composite group was able to actually control attacking aircraft of the tactical air forces by ground-to-air communications, this was not the case for the strategic bombers. The heavy bombers were not fitted with radios that allowed them to communicate with the tactical air ground control stations or even tactical aircraft themselves. Instead, the only means of contacting the bombers in flight was to pass messages back through the tactical air chain of command to SHAEF, then across to the headquarters of either RAF Bomber Command or 8 USAAF. From there messages were relayed down the bomber chain to the individual airfields and then transmitted to the aircraft by radio. It was a long, clumsy process and one that lacked the flexibility to redirect or amend the bomber program to cater to developments in the ground situation. It also meant that not only was it impossible to warn the bombers if they were hitting friendly troops; it was impossible for the ground troops to receive any in-flight reports from the bombers while the mission was being flown. Friendly-fire incidents between tactical aircraft and ground troops were fairly common. Simonds recounted in a postwar interview of observing Typhoons attacking the Poles and how the ground troops, their patience exhausted after firing the appropriate recognition symbols to no avail, shot down one of the aircraft. Simonds collected the pilot and then contacted the air force, who replied that the attackers must have been German. "Isn't that interesting?" replied the general. "Would you like to speak to one of the pilots?" At which point he handed the phone to the airman.[18] Ostensibly this was not the case with the heavy bomber force, which may have created an aura of omnipotence around the bombers, although most likely the low reported incidence was because heavy bombers were rarely used in support of the ground forces and then only after considerable discussion and coordination of effort, rather than because of superior navigation and target identification skills on their part. In fact, despite the detailed coordination, close to half the heavy bomber attacks in Normandy resulted in friendly-fire incidents, causing well over a thousand casualties.

One cannot sum up the contribution of air power to the Allied victory in Normandy easily or in a few words. On one hand, the Allied air forces had knocked the *Luftwaffe* back on its heels before the invasion and freely ranged the skies above Normandy at will. Thus the ground forces were provided with a freedom of action that was largely denied to the Germans. The tactical air forces, supplemented by heavy bombers, wreaked havoc with the enemy forces, devastated the rear areas and effectively forced the Germans to restrict movement to the hours of darkness and poor weather. On the other hand, air power had not lived up to its advanced billing, although this was not generally known at the time. Some of these shortcomings were due to nothing more than the limitations of technology rather than any shortcomings on the part of aircrew, but others were a result of the aspirations of the air forces to retain their own independence, as opposed to providing effective close support to the armies. When all things are considered, however, the Allied ground forces could not have won the campaign by their own efforts alone, at least not without paying a much heavier price in blood.

WHO KILLED
MICHAEL WITTMANN?

A t approximately 1230 hours on 8 August 1944, seven Tigers of *schwere SS-Panzerabteilung* 101 attacked north along Route Nationale 158 as part of the 12. *SS-Panzerdivision* counterattack intended to block the Allied advance until 85. *Infanteriedivision* could arrive from the area of Trun. (An account of this action is found in Chapter 11.) Four of these Tigers, commanded by company commander *SS-Sturmführer* Franz Heurich, *SS-Untersturmführer* Willi Irion, *SS-Oberscharführer* Peter Kisters and *SS-Oberscharführer* Rolf von Westernhagen, were from *Nr. 3 Kompanie*, while the others were from the battalion headquarters. This attack was not a success; the Germans lost five Tigers, including the one commanded by *SS-Hauptsturmführer* Michael Wittmann, the acting battalion commander, who was killed in action sometime between 1230 and 1255 hours.[1] From the available evidence it appears that the only Tigers to survive were commanded by Heurich and von Westernhagen.

The death of a junior officer in itself would have been of little note had not Wittmann been the top-scoring German tank ace of the war, credited with the destruction of 143 Allied armoured vehicles, including about 25 of the 4th City of London Yeomanry and 1st Battalion the Rifle Brigade of 7th British Armoured Division on 13 June at Villers-Bocage.[2] It is not far off the mark to speculate that Wittmann's work at Villers-Bocage, which rocked the "Desert Rats"* back on their heels, may have put off the capture of Caen by several weeks. At the very least, it delayed the attack long enough for the Germans to build up enough forces to force the British to abandon the attempt to outflank the German defences. In recent years Wittmann has become a cult figure and the subject of more than one book and several web sites.[3] Part

---

* The divisional sign was a jerboa, a small rodent sometimes referred to as a desert rat. This had been adopted by the division as its identifying symbol when it was serving in North Africa, hence the nickname.

The Black Baron

SS-Hauptsturmführer Michael Wittmann, the top-scoring panzer ace of the war, was killed in action on 8 August 1944 while leading his unit in the 12. *Panzerdivision* counterattack. The circumstances of his death have never been fully explained. (Michael Reynolds Collection)

of his posthumous notoriety has its roots in the circumstances of his death. There is a Wagnerian overtone in the saga of a youthful commander suffering a noble martyrdom in combat. One could liken the manner of his passing to that of Tecumseh, Gordon of Khartoum, or even George Armstrong Custer for that matter.

While there has been speculation that a price might have been put on Wittmann's head and that he may have been hunted down and killed for the bounty, this is not supported by the evidence.[4] First, what did the Allies know of Wittmann and his exploits? In a word, nothing. While Wittmann was well known in Germany, and perhaps Allied intelligence was aware of his existence, the Allied troops actually doing the fighting had not heard of his accomplishments and celebrity status, and he therefore had not acquired the stature that Manfred von Richtofen, the Red Baron, enjoyed in the First World War, especially as there was nothing to distinguish his Tiger from others fighting in Normandy. To the Allies, a Tiger was a Tiger. No matter who was in the tank, be it Michael Wittmann or a scratch crew of clerks and mechanics, any Tiger was a lethal opponent to be destroyed by whatever means were available, and as quickly as possible. Further evidence that he had not been deliberately targeted is demonstrated by the fact that none of the available Allied documents pertaining to TOTALIZE refer to him, and his unit was treated as a normal Tiger battalion, that is, but one of a number of dangerous adversaries. Wittmann's name first appeared in August 1945 as part of a report of the interrogation of Kurt Meyer by Canadian intelligence.

In this action Capt Wittmann, of 101 Hy Tk Bn, was killed. This officer held the record for the number of tanks knocked out by one individual. Since 1943, on the Russian front, until the time he was killed in Normandy, he was officially credited with having knocked out 143 tanks of all kinds. At the time of his death he was part of the crew of a Tiger tank[5]

A two-part article in *The Canadian Army Journal* in 1950 based on the interrogation of *SS-Hauptsturmführer* Bernard-Georg Meitzel, an officer of 12. *SS-Panzerdivision*, who was captured near Falaise on 20 August, mentions his death, but only very briefly – "the Tiger commander, Wittmann, well known to all German Panzer men, was killed the same day"[6] – and without mentioning the reason for his fame. Even the Canadian official history published in 1960 only mentions Wittmann in passing as "a famous German tank officer, Capt. Michael Wittmann, commander of the 101st S.S. Heavy Tank Battalion, [who] was killed."[7] Brigadier General Sydney Radley-Walters, who as a major commanded A Squadron of the Sherbrooke Fusilier Regiment during TOTAL-IZE, has stated repeatedly that he had first heard of Wittmann in the mid-1980s when he was a participant on a Canadian Land Forces Command and Staff College battlefield tour of Normandy with Hubert Meyer, who had been the chief operations officer of 12. *SS-Panzerdivision*. Radley-Walters, who was credited with 18 kills of German armoured fighting vehicles, has consistently maintained that it mattered little who knocked out Wittmann's tank on 8 August 1944; what was important was that the German counterattack was defeated that day. Still, it soon becomes obvious in discussions with him that the rather cavalier dismissal by the British in recent years of any Canadian claims to have killed the German has raised his not-inconsiderable ire.[8]

There is an uncanny parallel with the death of the Red Baron, enough to have earned Wittmann the unofficial title of the "Black Baron" for the black uniforms that German tank crews wore. If much of the interest in Wittmann can be traced back to his status in the German forces as the leading destroyer of Allied armour and the near-mythological circumstances of his death, his actual killer, like that of von Richtofen, has never been pinned down beyond a reasonable doubt by an examination of all the available evidence. While early accounts pointed to a swarm of Shermans,[9] either Canadian or Polish, or even a Typhoon fighter bomber,[10] in more recent years the claim by a British

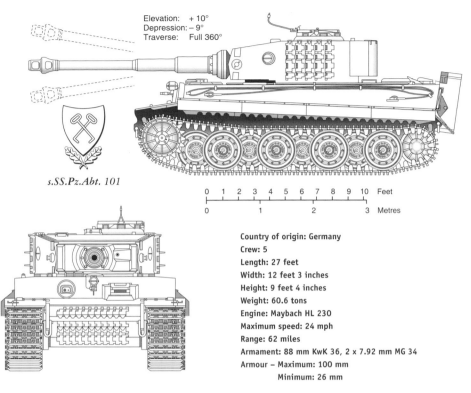

Elevation: + 10°
Depression: – 9°
Traverse: Full 360°

s.SS.Pz.Abt. 101

0 1 2 3 4 5 6 7 8 9 10 Feet

0   1   2   3 Metres

Country of origin: Germany
Crew: 5
Length: 27 feet
Width: 12 feet 3 inches
Height: 9 feet 4 inches
Weight: 60.6 tons
Engine: Maybach HL 230
Maximum speed: 24 mph
Range: 62 miles
Armament: 88 mm KwK 36, 2 x 7.92 mm MG 34
Armour – Maximum: 100 mm
Minimum: 26 mm

PzKpfw VI Ausf. E – Tiger I

In 1941, when the Germans received a bloody nose from Russian T-34 and KV-1 tanks, a specification was issued for a heavy tank equipped with a turret-mounted 88 mm gun and armour protection effective against all existing anti-tank guns. The result was the Tiger I, which entered service in the latter half of 1942. The Germans are thought to have used no more than 126 in Normandy, in independent battalions. Nevertheless, this tank commanded respect from its opponents. The combination of a high-velocity 88 mm gun with heavy armour made it superior to any Allied tank of the period. In particular, it was well suited to defensive fighting, where it could stand off at a distance and knock out advancing Shermans and Cromwells almost at leisure.

Protection in the Frontal Arc – A Comparison

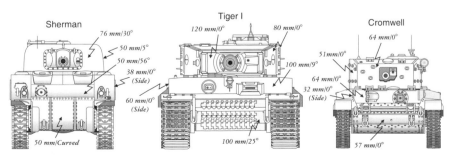

413

armoured regiment, 1 Northamptonshire Yeomanry of 33 British Armoured Brigade, that it knocked out Wittmann's tank has been widely accepted, and in fact, a Firefly of the regiment did destroy three Tigers of *schwere SS-Panzerabteilung* 101 in a matter of a few minutes that afternoon.[11] Having said that, far too much weight has been given to an entry in the British unit's war diary, which has gained the status of dogma by repetition rather than by passing rigorous analysis. That is not to say that the unit diary was incorrect, or that there was a deliberate attempt at deception. Indeed Wittmann may well have perished at British hands, and the unit does make a good case, but their claim that one of the Tigers knocked out by their Sherman Firefly was commanded by him is not ironclad.

The truth is that the Northamptonshire Yeomanry was not the only unit that engaged Tigers that August afternoon in 1944, but it was the only one whose claim was used by Les Taylor, himself an ex-member of the regiment, as the basis for his 1985 article in *After the Battle* magazine,[12] no doubt completely in good faith, although another British armoured regiment of 33 British Armoured Brigade, 144 RAC, claimed two Tigers destroyed in its war diary entry referring to the same engagement.[13] In Taylor's defence, examination of the evidence was made more difficult because no written record of the involvement of another main contender, the Sherbrooke Fusilier Regiment of 2 Canadian Armoured Brigade, has survived. The regimental headquarters half-track, which was sited with the main headquarters of 2 Canadian Armoured Brigade, was destroyed by a stick of fragmentation bombs dropped by a Flying Fortress of 8 USAAF between 1325 and 1355 hours on the same day, 8 August 1944, or within an hour of Wittmann's death.[14] Not only did the bombing destroy the vehicle, but the regimental intelligence sergeant was killed and all the radio logs and operational records were lost in the ensuing fire. To paraphrase an eminent Canadian military historian, it may come as a shock to some, but the first priority of the regiment in combat at the time was killing Germans, not reconstructing its records for posterity. Radley-Walters consistently has maintained that he moved part of his squadron, including two Fireflys, into an ambush position behind a stone wall in the area of Gaumesnil. In the ensuing engagement, one of the Fireflys knocked out a Tiger that was moving north just east of the Route Nationale, while he claimed a SP gun that was travelling along the road as destroyed.[15]

His first-person account will be discussed more fully below.

While Patrick Agte, author of *Michael Wittmann and the Tiger Command-ers of the Leibstandarte,* a biography of Wittmann, accepted the Northamp-tonshire Yeomanry's claim, he has included in that publication a number of eyewitness accounts which, on careful reading, raise some questions about his conclusion.* For example, the Yeomanry accounts indicate that the sec-ond Tiger destroyed burst into flames and exploded. Indeed, the statement in the regiment's war diary indicates that all three Tigers "brewed," although there is a chance that it may have been a case of jargon creeping into of-ficial use as a matter of habit. That, however, was not the case as first-hand accounts indicate that all three Tigers burned. At first glance, this account seems to be in agreement with a letter to Wittmann's widow written by *SS-Hauptsturmführer* Doctor Rabe, the medical officer of *schwere SS-Pan-zerabteilung* 101 who was following the advance. After leaving his vehicle and moving forward on foot, Rabe noted

> There was quite heavy anti-tank and artillery fire. I wanted to get to Michel's tank. When I had got to within about 250 to 300 meters I saw flames suddenly shoot from the tank and the turret fly off and fall to the ground. The tank then burned out completely...... It is unlikely that Michel got out before the hit, as I would have seen him.[16]

While Rabe did not report the status of the tank when he observed it, one could make the obvious interpretation from his statement that the flames shot out as a result of a hit *at that time.* However, why as a medical officer was he trying to get to Wittmann's tank? Was it to discuss the tactical situation with his commanding officer? That seems hardly likely as the tank was under heavy fire from artillery and anti-tank guns, and Wittmann would have had his hands too full to take time out for even the briefest of discussions. Or, and this seems to be the more likely case, was it because he knew the tank had been hit and he intended to aid any surviving crewmen? Were there other Ti-gers already burning and this tank was not, and therefore the only one which might have survivors still in it? Or was Wittmann's tank just the closest one

---

* There is no indication that Agte was aware of the claims by 144 RAC and the Sherbrooke Fusilier Regiment.

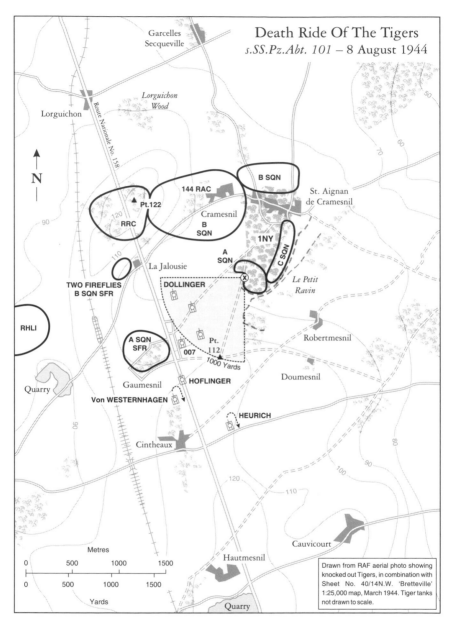

Death Ride Of The Tigers
s.SS.Pz.Abt. 101 – 8 August 1944

Drawn from RAF aerial photo showing knocked out Tigers, in combination with Sheet No. 40/14N.W. 'Bretteville' 1:25,000 map, March 1944. Tiger tanks not drawn to scale.

to the doctor, or perhaps it was the most important one in his eyes?

SS-Hauptsturmführer Hans Hoflinger, the operations officer of *schwere SS-Panzerabteilung* 101, who had accompanied Wittmann forward to Cintheaux, reported

Then we drove off, Michel right of the road and I left, four others with Michel (other Tigers, the author [Agte]) and the brother of von Westernhagen with me. Approximately 800 meters [900 yards] to Michel's right was a small wood which struck us as suspicious and which was to prove fateful to us. Unfortunately, we couldn't keep the wood under observation on account of our mission. We drove about one to one-and-one-half kilometres, and then I received another radio message from Michel which only confirmed my suspicions about the wood.

We began taking heavy fire from anti-tank guns and once again Michel called, but didn't complete the message. When I looked out to the left I saw that Michel's tank wasn't moving. I called him by radio but received no answer. Then my tank received a frightful blow and I had to order my crew to get out as it had already began to burn fiercely. My crew and I dashed toward the rear and got through. I stopped to look around and to my dismay discovered that five of our tanks had been knocked out. The turret of Michel's tank was displaced to the right and tilted down somewhat. None of his crew had got out...... I can state the exact time of the incident. It was 1255 hours, near the Caen–Falaise road in the vicinity of Cintheaux.[17]

It may be significant that the person who made the translation from the original German used the verb "displaced" to describe the condition of the turret. *The Concise Oxford Dictionary* defines that word as "shift from its place." This would indicate that something, perhaps an initial explosion, had unseated the turret, but the catastrophic explosion that blew the turret off to land several meters to the rear of the hull had not occurred when Hoflinger observed Wittmann's Tiger at 1255 hours. It is also significant that the *SS-Hauptsturmführer* made no mention of the Tiger burning.

Some weeks later the battalion signals officer, *SS-Untersturmführer* Helmut Dollinger, who had also taken part in the attack, recalled

On 8 August, at about noontime, we attacked the English, who had broken through south of Caen. The enemy secured his point of penetration through the massed employment of artillery, tanks, fighters and bombers. Nevertheless, we succeeded in advancing about three kilometers. Heavy anti-tank guns, which we could not make out at all at first, opened fire on us from excellent positions. The enemy succeeded in knocking out several tanks. As the leading tank, ours was hit and knocked out. I myself was wounded in the forehead. I lost consciousness for a few minutes, but before I did so I was able to give the order to bail out.[18]

Dollinger then recounted how he and his crew took shelter under the tank. He and one of his radio operators, *SS-Sturmmann* Alfred Bahlo, carried a mortally-wounded member of their crew on a makeshift stretcher out to the Caen–Falaise highway, where he was loaded on a *Kubelwagen*, which then drove off. Bahlo noted that "on the way we passed the knocked-out panzer of Hauptsturmführer Wittmann; the turret was blown off…"[19] At the very least these statements raise the possibility that Wittmann's Tiger did not explode and/or burn immediately when it was first hit and immobilized. However, British accounts indicate that all three Tigers burned and that the second one actually exploded when hit. If so, it could not have been Wittmann's, but this second tank that exploded is precisely the one that forms the foundation of the British claim. It does seem to be a bit of a leap of faith to suggest that perhaps Wittmann's tank exploded once with enough force to shift the turret partially off its mount so that it was tilted to the right, and then several minutes later exploded again with enough force to cause the turret to fly off the hull. In the meantime, the damage from the first explosion would have had to have been apparent enough to be evident to Doctor Rabe, but not severe enough to convince him that there were would have been no possibility of finding any survivors inside the Tiger, a somewhat doubtful proposition.

It is time to examine the competing Allied claims. First, the Poles: 1. *Dywizji Pancernej* was nowhere near the Cintheaux area, as it was preparing to assault to the south on the other side of St. Aignan at 1355, or just over an hour after the death of Wittmann.

Similarly 4th Canadian Armoured Division was still making its way forward and its vanguard, based on Major E.A.C. Amy's No. 1 Squadron of the Canadian Grenadier Guards, was in the area of Rocquancourt, several miles to the north and in dead ground to the ensuing engagement. At 1224 hours 4 Armoured Brigade Headquarters signalled "Rocqunacourt now clear. You can get cracking," and then at 1230 "Even despite your last inf[or]m[ation] [you] must speed on."[20] Thus, it is possible to conclude that neither formation played a part in Wittmann's demise.

Before proceeding further, it is time to a review the basics of tank gunnery as practiced by the armoured regiments of 21st Army Group in 1944. The equipment in use at the time was rather basic and simple compared to today's ensemble of laser range-finders, wind sensors, stabilizers, ballistic computers and the like. The sight in a Sherman used an engraved reticle pattern – a refinement on the cross hairs in a hunter's telescopic sight – that appeared in the gunner's field of view as a grid when he peered through his sight. He used this reticle for adjusting his point of aim, but the determination of range was by the Mark One Eyeball. The crew commander and gunner corrected the fall of shot based on observation of the impact of the round or the path of the tracer in relation to the target. The 75mm gun fitted to nearly four in five of the Shermans in a Commonwealth armoured squadron could not kill a Tiger unless a very daring crew could sneak up on an unwary victim and hit it in the side or rear at short range. The four Fireflys, one per troop, in a squadron could knock out a Tiger at up to 1000 yards with a hit on the front and up to 1,700 yards against the side and rear. However, there were serious accuracy problems with the 17-pounder gun and a hit on even a target as large as a tank was by no means a sure thing at ranges greater than 1,000 yards.[21]

Last but not least, armoured crews were trained to engage the most dangerous target first. This was usually the closest target and there is no reason to believe that any of the British or Canadian tank crews broke this golden rule of battlefield self-preservation. In summary, the Canadians would have engaged the Tigers farthest to the west first, while the British would have done the same to the eastern group of Tigers, and neither could have counted on an effective hit at ranges over 1,000 yards. Still, crews would have continued to engage any visible enemy tanks that had not been destroyed beyond a reasonable doubt – that is which had burned or exploded. Thus some already-knocked-out tanks might continue to be hit time and again until they finally burned. This could lead to more than one crew claiming hits and kills on the same tank and, as a result, unknowingly-inflated reports of enemy AFVs destroyed being passed upwards in the chain of command.

In the case of 144 Regiment RAC, the claim is based on the unit war diary entry[22] and the commanding officer's account in the history of the unit he wrote after the war. It is interesting that in his book he changed the original claim of two Tigers in the war diary to a Tiger and a Mk IV.

> In the afternoon the expected counter-attack developed. The enemy used about twenty Panther and Tiger tanks, with artillery and infantry support, in an attempt to outflank the Point 122 position from the east through the orchards and woods around St. Aignan de Cramesnil. The brunt of this attack fell on the 1st Northamptonshire Yeomanry on our left. Repeated attempts were made by the enemy to break into the St. Aignan position, but they were all beaten off, the enemy losing eleven tanks. Our B Squadron was also engaged, claiming one tiger and one Mark IV destroyed. B Squadron lost two Shermans.[23]

B Squadron was deployed southeast of Cramesnil as far west as the tree line and probably no farther forward then the track from the Caen–Falaise Road to St. Aignan-de-Cramesnil. From this area its tanks would have been able to score hits on the more northerly Tigers but probably not on Wittmann's tank, if it indeed was the one closest to the Caen–Falaise Highway. In any case, the "most dangerous tank principle" suggests that B Squadron's tanks would have fired on the other Tigers first, as they were much closer.

As for the Sherbrookes, as we have seen, any logged radio reports of the battle were destroyed when its regimental headquarters half-track was destroyed by an American bomb later that same afternoon. However the squadron commander, Major Sydney Radley-Walters, has recorded the events surrounding his squadron's part in the action of 8 August. His account begins after the series of local counterattacks which perhaps started as early as 0830 hours, were defeated.

> I decided that I should move forward to Gaumesnil and be in position to support the Royals [Royal Regiment of Canada] when they were ordered to capture the village. At approximately 1030 hours I left the woods and skirted the woods to the left until I reached the railway line, then turned south past La Jalousie until we reached the rear of Gaumesnil. I was able to get good cover during this move and had right flank protection from the

Royal Hamilton Light Infantry and my #1 Troop as I moved the Squadron south behind the bush at Gaumesnil. The village was small but at its eastern edge near the Caen [–Falaise] Highway was a large château with a tall stone and cement wall completely around the property, giving good fire positions to the east and south-east. That stone wall was still there the last time I visited Gaumesnil in 1993, however, the château was destroyed.

[T]o the rear there was a large wooded area which gave good protection from view. As best as I can remember, I had eight tanks left with me and two were equipped with 17-pounder guns. We took up defensive positions about the farm and made holes in the stone wall so we were covered from view but could observe any targets coming north on the Caen–Falaise Highway and in the fields to the east of it.

I recall the woods to the rear of the village and the hedgerows around the village gave good cover, so moving into this location and taking up positions behind the stone wall, and around the village was not a problem. It was approximately 1115 hours when the Squadron was settled in its position. Except for a few individual German stragglers, the village was not occupied.

At noon we could see movement to the east of Cintheaux. There was a long hedgerow that ran east from the village out into the fields and our artillery was shelling this area and the village when this movement was spotted. It is my recollection that it was somewhere between 1215 and 1230 hours when the attack started …… In our area around Gaumesnil the visibility, I recall, was thick with smoke and the German attack was supported by mortars and artillery as they moved parallel with the Highway towards Point 122. It is my recollection that the attack moved as a group with five Tigers leading the group well spaced with four at the front and the fifth leading a number of Mk IVs and half-tracks with Jagdpanzers.

One of the Tigers was running close to the highway beside Gaumesnil followed by two Jagdpanzers advancing on the main highway…

When we saw the German attack coming in, I just kept yelling, "Hold off! Hold off!" until they got reasonably close. We opened fire at about 500 yards. The lead tank, the one closest to the road, was knocked out. Behind it were a couple of SPs. I personally got one of the SPs right on the Caen–Falaise Road.

The other Tigers were engaged not only by my Squadron, but also by two Fireflys from B Squadron that had moved over to La Jalousie when the counter-attack started. Once we started to fire, the German column turned to the north-east and headed for the wooded area south of St. Aignan [de Cramesnil] ...... It is my recollection that we destroyed two Mk IVs before the rear of the German group veered too far to the east......When the action was over we claimed the Tiger beside the highway, a second Tiger which was at the rear of the advancing column, two Mk IVs and two SPs.[24]

It is important to note that the Tiger engaged and knocked out was the one that was travelling closest to the road, and Radley-Walters makes no mention of any hits on the other leading Tigers. The second Tiger he claimed was the one at the rear of the advancing column, perhaps that of *SS-Hauptsturmführer* Hans Hoflinger, which was destroyed after the four other Tigers lost in the engagement. Hoflinger stated that at the time he observed that five tanks had been lost, the turret on Wittmann's Tiger was still resting on the hull. Furthermore, he was emphatic that the time was precisely 1255 hours which suggests he looked at his watch. This was eight minutes after the second tank had exploded according to the British records.[25] While a difference of a couple of minutes in accounts would not be unusual, it is very unlikely that two competent military units, even if on opposing sides, would have had an eight-minute difference in the time set on their watches.

The claim by 1 Northamptonshire Yeomanry was three Tigers between 1240 and 1252 hours, although it would claim a total of 20 tanks or SP guns, including five Tigers, destroyed that day. The actual entry in the war diary regarding the engagement reads:

Three Tiger (IV) reported moving towards A Sq[uadro]n.; and were brewed up at 1240, 1247 and 1252 hrs, all without loss. Later 200 inf[antry] with 20 tanks in support formed up to counter attack and in a bombing attack which followed some bombs fell in our area.[26]

In 1946 the regiment published an account of its service in northwest Europe; the following extract deals with the engagement with the Tigers east of RN 158:

No. 3 Troop (Lieut. A. James) of "A" Squadron, the forward Troop covering the right flank, were the first to make contact. Sjt.* Gordon commanding a 17 pounder Tank reported three Tigers advancing slowly North, in line ahead, along the Falaise-Caen road. These were seen at a range of 1200 yards. On hearing Sjt. Gordon's report, Captain Boardman, the Squadron Second in Command, ordered him to hold his fire and moved over to the Troop position where he could control the shooting. When the range had closed to 800 yards Captain Boardman gave the order to fire. Sjt Gordon engaged the rear tank of the three. Two shots from Tpr. Elkins, the gunner set it on fire. Time 1240 hours. The second tank traversed right and fired three shots at Sjt. Gordon, but anticipating this he had already reversed into cover. Unluckily as he did so, either his turret flap hit a branch of an apple tree or it received a glancing blow from the enemy's shot; whatever the cause it came crashing down on the Serjeant's head almost knocking him out. Sjt. Gordon, completely dazed, climbed out of his tank and as he did so was wounded by shrapnel, for it must be remembered that the Squadron's position was continually under mortar and shellfire. Lieut. James dashed over to Sjt. Gordon's tank, took command, quickly moved into a new fire position and Tpr. Elkins fired one shot at the second tank. It exploded in a flash of flame. Time 1247. By this time the third Tiger was in a panic, milling about wondering how he could escape. To add to his confusion, Captain Boardman peppered away with 75 mm A.P. [armour piercing], which stopped him but did not put him on fire. Two shots from Tpr. Elkins settled the matter and this Tiger also started to burn. Time 1252. Three Tigers in twelve minutes is not bad business. Captain Boardman later described it as "rather like Practice No. 5 on the ranges at Linney Head."[27]

This was the basis, along with supporting statements by eyewitnesses such as those of Boardman and his gunner, for the Yeomanry's claim that it killed Michael Wittmann. Everything that has come later, including a series of books by Ken Tout, merely repeats the basic story. It may be significant that in his latest book, which was published in 2000, after a visit to Canada and interviews with a number of veterans, including Radley-Walters, Tout,

---

* Sjt. is an abbreviation for serjeant, an alternate spelling of sergeant that was in favour in some circles at the time. See the OED.

who was a gunner and then crew commander in C Squadron of the regiment during TOTALIZE, acknowledged *for the first time* that other units besides his had engaged Tigers and did not claim Wittmann specifically for the Northamptonshire Yeomanry.[28]

A recent German publication reinforced the British claim, at least at first glance. However, it seems this book was written long after the war to provide a quick reference on the combat record of Tiger-equipped units, and relies heavily on secondary sources. For example, it credited five, not three Tigers, to [the Firefly of] 3 Troop, which is clearly in error as this tank was brewed up itself later that afternoon after adding a Mk IV to its score. The Yeomanry did not claim any further Tigers for this tank.[29]

There is another piece of evidence which has proven to be very useful. An RAF vertical air photo taken on 9 August identifies four knocked out Tigers in the area between the Route Nationale and the woods and orchard southwest of St. Aignan-de-Cramesnil. In fact this photograph appeared in Taylor's 1985 article.[30] Three of the Tigers lie in a rough line running from southeast to northwest within 800 yards of the woods and orchard where A Squadron of the Yeomanry was deployed. The fourth is 1,100 yards from the orchard, but is within 200 yards of the highway and 400-500 yards of the position where the Sherbrooke Fusiliers' tanks were concealed. Furthermore, the location of the mass grave where the remains of Wittmann and his crew were discovered in 1983 is adjacent to this last Tiger, and the forensic evidence in fact indicates that this was their common grave. The obvious conclusion is that the tank closest to the highway was the Tiger commanded by Michael Wittmann. After all, it would have made little sense for whoever first buried the crew to have carried the cadavers, which may have been badly burned and/or mutilated, several hundred yards before interring them, especially as it seems only the remains of Wittmann's crew were later recovered. Brutal as it sounds, the bodies were likely thrown in the nearest convenient crater and covered over. This tank was photographed a few months after the battle and the markings on the Tiger's turret, "007," that is, the commanding officer's tank are clearly visible.[31] Thus, it must be assumed this was Wittmann's tank.

As additional proof, A Squadron of the Northamptonshire Yeomanry reported sighting three tanks, no more and no less, and in 1999 this was confirmed in a rather forceful letter to Brigadier General Radley-Walters from Lord Tom Boardman, the Yeomanry A Squadron second-in-command, who made it clear that he was also quite sure from the evidence he had seen that Wittmann was in one of the three tanks engaged by his squadron, especially as no other tanks were visible from the British position.[32] This begs the question of how the Yeomanry could then claim five Tigers destroyed, and contradicts both Radley-Walters's account and the evidence of the air photograph. Unintentionally, Boardman's statement supports the argument that the Sherbrooke Fusiliers knocked out Wittmann's tank, since if the Yeomanry were unable to see it, they could not have engaged it.

One last point that should be mentioned, if for no other reason than it will clear the air, is the subject of the main Canadian positions on the RN. Radley-Walters stated that, at the time of the engagement, the Royal Regiment of Canada had seized Point 122, which was east of the road.[33] This was disputed by Lord Boardman, who noted that the road was the inter-division boundary and therefore the Canadians could not have been where Radley-Walters claimed.[34] However, the Royal Regiment of Canada's history confirms the unit captured Point 122 prior to moving forward towards Gaumesnil. Furthermore, when the company commanders went forward on their reconnaissance, they found Canadian tanks sitting on their start line and were told by the armoured commander that his tanks had been all around the village.[35] This places Radley-Walters's squadron in the area of Gaumesnil in the early afternoon of 8 August.

After pondering all the above evidence and considering the competing claims, unfortunately there is one more bit of evidence that threatens to throw all the work so far into the circular file. Monsieur Serge Varin, a resident of Caen, who viewed the wreckage of Tiger 007 several months after the battle, reported that there were no signs of any penetration of the turret or hull by any Allied weapons other than a large hole on the back deck on the left air intake grill immediately behind the turret and forward of the engine cover. Even this hole has been described as being caused by an internal explosion and therefore not an "entry wound," but any signs of a penetration might have been obliterated by the explosion. In some accounts the engine was reported to be intact and/or undamaged while other versions have an explosion occurring in the engine and fighting compartments. (As the area was littered with destroyed Allied and German armoured vehicles, presumably these civilians had developed a certain amount of expertise in determining what kind of weapon had destroyed what tank.) In fact, the single hole was the original basis of the suggestion that a Typhoon had knocked out Wittmann's tank, although this premise was first suggested by the presence on an unexploded Typhoon aerial rocket in the area. The unanswered question is if there was no sign of any penetration by any weapon or projectile at all, why then should we accept that a rocket from a Typhoon destroyed Tiger 007 rather than any other weapon?

No hole, no hit. That seems to rule out Wittmann falling victim to an Allied tank or perhaps an anti-tank gun, especially as the latter would have been firing at extreme range. However, there are no records that indicate that any Typhoons were active over the area during the time of the counterattack on 8 August. *SS-Untersturmführer* Helmut Dollinger, the signals officer of *schwere SS-Panzerabteilung* 101 was the only source who mentioned fighters at all (see above) when he claimed that "[t]he enemy secured his point of penetration through the massed employment of artillery, tanks, fighters and bombers." However Kurt Meyer made a point of remarking on the Allies' failure to use their tactical fighters on the morning of 8 August. In support of Meyer's recollection, the 2 TAF records do not include any reports of Typhoons destroying enemy tanks in the Caen area on 8 August, although two tanks were claimed as destroyed and one as damaged by Typhoons on armed reconnaissance in the area Mézidon–Falaise–Flers–Argentan. In actual fact, these were the only tank claims logged by 2 TAF that day. 84 Composite Group should have been supporting First Canadian Army, however its move to the continent had been delayed and its operations record book entry for 8 August 1944 reads, "Operational control of aircraft is still maintained by 83 Group but it is understood that 84 Group will assume control of the Group aircraft at 0001 hours on 11 August, giving air support to First Cdn Army sector."[36] In the case of 83 Group, Air Vice Marshal Broadhurst's headquarter's operations record book logged

> The principle task was close support to the Canadians south of CAEN. Two châteaux used as H.Q. between BRETTEVILLE and FALAISE were destroyed in addition to a large number of gun and mortar positions and concentrations of troops and vehicles which were attacked.

Decapitating A Tiger
The Destruction of Tiger 007

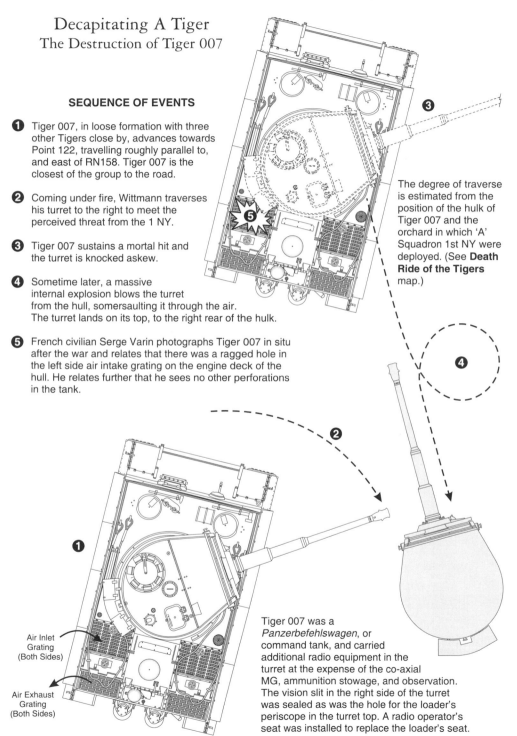

SEQUENCE OF EVENTS

❶ Tiger 007, in loose formation with three other Tigers close by, advances towards Point 122, travelling roughly parallel to, and east of RN158. Tiger 007 is the closest of the group to the road.

❷ Coming under fire, Wittmann traverses his turret to the right to meet the perceived threat from the 1 NY.

❸ Tiger 007 sustains a mortal hit and the turret is knocked askew.

❹ Sometime later, a massive internal explosion blows the turret from the hull, somersaulting it through the air. The turret lands on its top, to the right rear of the hulk.

❺ French civilian Serge Varin photographs Tiger 007 in situ after the war and relates that there was a ragged hole in the left side air intake grating on the engine deck of the hull. He relates further that he sees no other perforations in the tank.

The degree of traverse is estimated from the position of the hulk of Tiger 007 and the orchard in which 'A' Squadron 1st NY were deployed. (See **Death Ride of the Tigers** map.)

Air Inlet Grating (Both Sides)

Air Exhaust Grating (Both Sides)

Tiger 007 was a *Panzerbefehlswagen*, or command tank, and carried additional radio equipment in the turret at the expense of the co-axial MG, ammunition stowage, and observation. The vision slit in the right side of the turret was sealed as was the hole for the loader's periscope in the turret top. A radio operator's seat was installed to replace the loader's seat.

427

This sketch illustrates the hull of Wittmann's Tiger (viewed from above) with the major components under the rear deck shown in outline. The stylized explosion is in the area of the damage noticed by Varin. There are three observations that spring to mind if this damage was indeed the signature of the fatal hit. First, the round could not have come from the Yeomanry tanks firing from the area of the orchard as the Tiger's turret and hull would have masked the shot. Second, the projectile – whatever it was – could only have come from an arc ranging from approximately east-southeast to west-northwest. Third, and this is most important, it would have been impossible to determine what the nature of the projectile was as the damage to the rear deck destroyed any physical evidence.

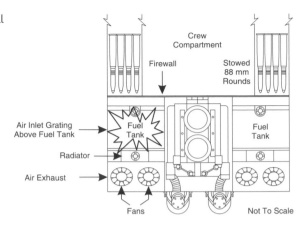

Compared with yesterday's score, the number of tanks and M[otorized] E[nemy] T[ransport] was bound to appear small. In all 2 tanks were destroyed and 1 damaged and the score for MET was 49 – 26 – 50.[37]

The 2 Tactical Air Force record book entry provides considerably more detail,

> Immediate Support: 243 Typhoons carried out attacks on Headquarters, gun and mortar positions, tanks, woods, troop concentrations, strong points and barges. Claims 2 MET destroyed, 4 damaged, several barges destroyed and damaged. 2 aircraft and pilots missing. 24 Spitfires attacked targets on the Seine. Claims 5 barges and 1 tug destroyed, 1 tug and 12 barges damaged. No losses.
>
> Armed Recce: 179 Spitfires attacked scattered MET in the Mézidon–Pont L'Eveque–Elbeuf–Falaise–Alençon–Dreux–Laigle and Bernay areas. Claim 23 MET destroyed and 30 damaged. In the vicinity of Alençon, Argentan, Flers and Falaise a considerable number of ambulances and lorries with red crosses attached were seen. In one instance troops jumped out of one of these lorries. Claims in these areas: 7 MET destroyed and 11

damaged. No losses. 47 Mustangs in the Holbec–Gourney–Dreux–Bernay–Alençon–Argentan areas claim 4 MET damaged. 69 Typhoons in the Mézidon–Falaise–Flers–Argentan area claim 6 MET and 2 tanks destroyed, 3 MET and 1 tank damaged. One aircraft and pilot missing.[38]

It is clear that no tanks were claimed destroyed or damaged in the forward areas by immediate support aircraft and that the only tanks claimed were by Typhoons on armed reconnaissance missions in areas away from the actual battle. Therefore Wittmann and his crew almost assuredly did not fall victim to an attack from the air.

Then, what happened? Study of the available photographs of the scene indicate that Wittmann's tank was facing more or less parallel to the Caen–Falaise Road, perhaps inclined a bit towards Cramesnil. As the only damage to the tank that could have caused the explosion was on the left rear of the hull, this rules out both of the British armoured regiments, even if they could have observed or even hit that tank from their positions. We have already eliminated both the 1st Polish and 4th Canadian Armoured Divisions, an attack from the air, and a direct hit by Allied or German artillery would have been an unlikely, although not impossible, occurrence. A spontaneous internal explosion, an event as improbable as winning the lottery, would probably not have caused the hole in the hull top, although it could have caused the turret to fly off. By elimination, that leaves the Sherbrooke Fusilier Regiment as the only unit to have been in a position to have been actively engaging Wittman's Tiger. The principle used in awarding claims by the air forces was that if an enemy aircraft crashed or exploded while being engaged, credit for the kill went to whoever was actively engaging or pursuing it at the time of its demise. For example, on 8 August four Spitfires from 443 Squadron RCAF shared a claim of a German fighter without firing a shot, the official record noted that "they found a lone FW.190 whose pilot, as soon as our aircraft turned towards him, baled out without argument."[39]

After an examination of the available evidence, the most likely conclusion is that a Sherman Firefly of the Sherbrooke Fusilier Regiment destroyed the Tiger commanded by *SS-Hauptsturmführer* Michael Wittmann at some time between 1230 and 1255 hours 8 August 1944. This, of course, is not a certainty, and the matter will no doubt be debated for years. Before leaving the subject, it should be emphasized that the truly important thing is that British and Canadian soldiers destroyed five Tigers as well as a number of other AFVs, thus defeating the left wing of *SS-Oberführer* Kurt Meyer's counterattack. The death of Wittmann was no more than an incidental result of the battle. It may be more than coincidence that this was the only area were the Phase 2 forces were able to make any substantial gains later this afternoon.

One last point – and an important one – the accident of fate that saw Wittmann fall prey to a Sherbrooke Fusilier tank does not mean that 1 Northamptonshire Yeomanry and 144 Regiment RAC were in any way inferior to the Canadian unit in skill or training. It was a case of pure blind chance that the path Michael Wittmann chose led into the sights of a Canadian Sherman. Given the slightest of changes in circumstances, he could just as easily have fallen prey to a British tank.

BRON PANCERNA:
A BRIEF HISTORY OF THE
1st POLISH ARMOURED DIVISION

by John R. Grodzinski

To fully understand the formation, employment and ultimate fate of the 1st Polish Armoured Division, or 1. *Dywizja Pancerna*, one must appreciate that it constituted part of a recognized Polish state in exile, based in the United Kingdom. The Polish Government in Exile was originally formed in France after the fall of Poland, and then moved to London, just before France fell in 1940. It included a president, prime minister, cabinet and most ministries associated with any government, including an armed forces, all of which were expected return to Poland after its liberation. The Polish Forces in the West would therefore constitute the nucleus of the new Polish army, air force and navy. By 1945, the Polish Armed Forces in the West numbered over 228,000 men and women organized in two army corps, a parachute brigade, 15 air force squadrons with 300 aircraft of various types and a navy with one cruiser, six destroyers, three submarines, six torpedo boats and three interned vessels. There were also many schools, training establishments, administrative units and staff organizations, while a number of Poles were also found in British and allied units throughout Europe, the Mediterranean and the Far East. Despite the fact that Poland fell in October 1939, her soldiers, sailors and airmen were found in every theatre of the war thereafter.[1]

Three naval vessels[2] became the first Polish units in the west when they left Poland for Great Britain in September 1939. The same month, the first army units began forming at Coëtquidan,[3] in Brittany, France, which eventually grew to four infantry divisions, two independent infantry brigades (one based in French Syria), an armoured cavalry brigade, several independent anti-tank companies[4] and a number of training establishments. The Poles also formed several air force squadrons and flights in France, while a large group of airmen went to Great Britain. By the spring of 1940, there were 7,661 officers and 74,600 non-commissioned officers and men in all three services. Most of these units participated in the campaigns of 1940, fighting in France and Norway. As the fighting drew to a close, one infantry division was interned in Switzerland,[5] while 19,500 men were evacuated to Britain and the brigade in Syria moved, against the wishes of the French, into British-controlled Palestine.[6]

Following the French campaign, the Poles had once again to restructure their forces in Britain. In September 1940, the I. *Korpus Polski* (1st Polish Corps) was formed in Scotland,[7] consisting of six brigades and corps troops, while the infantry brigade in Palestine moved to Egypt. The corps had 3,492 officers and 10,885 soldiers, which increased to 4,158 officers and 13,570 men by mid-1941.[8] Several armoured units were also formed; they were not brigaded until the 16. *Brygada Pancerna,* with three tank battalions, was formed in September 1941. On 13 November 1941, another armoured formation was created when the 2. *Brygada Strzelców* was renamed the 10. *Brygada Kawalerii Pancernej*[9] and included three cavalry regiments.[10]

Relations with Britain and the Soviet Union and Polish perceptions of future Allied strategy influenced subsequent Polish military plans. Following the German invasion of the Soviet Union, a Polish–Soviet military cooperation treaty was signed on 14 August 1941, which not only addressed the future of Poland, but also the fate of 200,000 Polish prisoners of war and thousands of civilians in Soviet camps, who would also provide a valuable source of reinforcement. By the spring of 1942, Polish forces were based in the United Kingdom, the Middle East and the Soviet Union, the latter constituting the largest group, with some 46,159 personnel in four divisions. For *Generał* Władysław Sikorski,[11] the Prime Minister of the Polish Government in Exile and the Commander in Chief of the Polish Armed Forces, it became imperative to determine where these dispersed forces should be concentrated to achieve Polish aims, particularly since Allied strategy to defeat Germany had now evolved significantly.

Until the winter of 1941-1942, Polish units in the United Kingdom had been on anti-invasion alert. With that threat removed, a new source of personnel available from the Soviet Union and the Allied offensive strategy against Nazi Germany about to implemented, Sikorski understood the necessity of preparing Polish forces to support these plans. As a result, Sikorski met with his senior commanders in London to plan the future force structure and held similar meetings with Churchill and Stalin.[12]

Sikorski called the first meeting with his service chiefs and senior commanders in London, on 14 April 1941. Three different options were put forward by his commanders: first, to maintain the status quo with units based in Britain, the Middle East and the Soviet Union; second, placing the majority of Polish troops in the United Kingdom, thus linking them to western Allied plans for the liberation in Europe; and third, concentrating all troops in the Middle East, where they could eventually return to Poland via the Soviet Union or the Balkans, should the Allies utilize that route. *Generał dywizji* (Lieutenant-General) Władysław Anders, commanding the army in Russia, held that cooperation with the Soviets was essential to ensure the release of Poles from the camps and for the future liberation and security of Poland. Anders believed that if his units left, the Soviets would create their own "Polish Army." When his 115,000 troops and civilian personnel were forced to leave the Soviet Union for the Middle East during the summer of 1942, a Soviet-controlled Polish Army was indeed formed.[13]

At a second meeting on 27 April 1942, a compromise was reached[14] whereby 8,000 troops would reinforce the I. *Korpus Polski* in Scotland, while the majority would remain in the Middle East, in what Sikorski hoped would become a Polish field army of two corps. Thus while the political centre for Polish aspirations rested in Britain, military power was concentrated to the Mediterranean.[15]

While the establishment of armoured formations was included in all Polish plans, Generał Sikorski was opposed to establishing an armoured division, as the British Commander in Chief Home Forces insisted having "absolute discretion regarding its operational employment."[16] This would in effect divide control[17] of Polish forces.[18] Sikorski finally agreed, albeit with strong reservations, emphasizing that I. *Korpus Polski* must be "fully capable of independent operations"[19] and include, as a minimum, an armoured division, plus one or two independent mechanized infantry brigades. On 28 October 1941, Sikorski addressed these plans to the Chief of the Imperial General Staff and decided upon organizing an armoured division with the following timetable:

1 July 1942 – Preliminary training of personnel not at present constituted as armoured units commences.

1st October to end of December 1942 – Conversion of the existing Polish Army Tank Brigade to an armoured brigade; followed by the conversion of the remaining units and formation of the second armoured brigade. Concurrently with these conversions, the formation of the necessary units for the support group and smaller units will take place.[20]

By February 1942, the plans were further refined and the formation of the division was set to occur in two phases: the first included the creation of the divisional headquarters, two tank brigades and certain divisional units; while phase two would see the integration of reinforcements from the Soviet Union, and bringing the "division up to full strength." During this period of reorganization, the Polish corps was also expected to maintain responsibility for a smaller defensive sector along the Scottish coastline.[21]

As a result of these decisions, the organization of I. *Korpus Polski* was set at one armoured division of two armoured brigades and a support group, an independent infantry brigade, a parachute brigade, corps reconnaissance, artillery and engineer units and supporting troops. The Polish 1st Armoured Division, or 1. *Dywizja Pancerna,* was formed on 25 February 1942, with two existing armour formations, the 10. *Brygada Kawalerii Pancernej*[22], 16. *Brygada Pancerna,*[23] a support group[24] and divisional units.[25]

British experience in the Middle East found the current armoured division structure to have too many tanks and too little infantry and artillery support. An armoured division would now have one armoured and one infantry brigade. The Poles initially refused to comply with these changes, as they intended to split the division into two, each based on one of the existing armoured brigades. However with available manpower sufficient to man only one division, the proposed changes were eventually accepted, but took time to implement, as a new infantry brigade, two artillery regiments, a reconnaissance regiment and additional support units had either to be raised or re-rolled from existing units.[26]

These changes led to a general reorganization of the corps in September 1943. As one of the armoured brigades was initially planned to be disbanded, the 10. *Brygada Kawalerii Pancernej* and 16. *Brygada Pancerna* were temporarily regrouped as the 10/16. *Brygada Pancerna*,[27] while debate raged between members of the cavalry-dominated 10. *Brygada Kawalerii Pancernej* and the "tankers" of the armoured brigade as to which formation should remain on the order of battle.[28] In the end the name 10. *Brygada Kawalerii Pancernej* was retained, but since the commander and staff of the 16. *Brygada Pancerna* were more experienced, the brigade headquarters squadrons were exchanged and a number of units were exchanged between the two brigades.[29] One of the cavalry regiments in 10. *Brygada* was re-roled as the divisional reconnaissance regiment[30] and another[31] was transferred to the reorganized 16. *Brygada Pancerna* (which was now to remain in the corps); they in turn were replaced by two armoured regiments (the 1st and 2nd) from 16. *Brygada Pancerna*.[32] The 16. *Brygada Pancerna* was reorganized using the remaining regiments and was grouped with another infantry brigade to form the 2. *Dywizja Grenadierów-Pancery (Kadrowa)* (2nd Grenadier-Armoured Division (Cadre)).[33]

In its final structure, 1. *Dywizja Pancerna* included 10. *Brygada Kawalerii Pancernej*, the 3. *Brygada Strzelców* (3rd Rifle Brigade) and divisional troops. One of the three infantry battalions for the rifle brigade already existed within the division, while another came from elsewhere within the corps. Formation of the third infantry battalion, the 9. *Batalion Strzelców* occurred in 1943. A squadron of the corps reconnaissance regiment was re-roled as the machine gun company, thus rounding out all the units needed for the rifle brigade. A corps heavy artillery unit was also reorganized as the 2. *Pułk Artylerii Motorowej*, which was also given a battery from the 1. *Pułk Artylerii Motorowej*. The division was still short 900 personnel, most of which were made up by transferring personnel from the Middle East. Finally, as a result of these changes, I. *Korpus Polski* was renamed I. *Korpus Pancerno-Motorowy* (1 Armoured-Motorised Corps) on 31 August 1942.[34]

In its final form, the detailed order of battle for 1. *Dywizja Pancerna* was as follows:

Dowódcy Dywizji (Divisional Command Group)

Kwaterna Glowna Dywizji (Headquarters)
    Sztab (Staff)
    Szwadron Sztabowy (Headquarters squadron)
    1. *Szwadron Regulacji Ruchu* (1 Traffic Control Squadron)

No. 4 Liaison HQ (British)

10.*Pułk Strzelców Konnych* (divisional recce regiment)

10. *Brygada Kawalerii Pancernej* (10th Armoured Cavalry Brigade)
    1. *Pułk Pancerny* (1st Armoured Regiment)
    2. *Pułk Pancerny* (2nd Armoured Regiment)
    24. *Pułk Ułanów* (24th Lancer Regiment)
    10. *Pułk Dragonów* (10th Dragoon Regiment; motor battalion)

3. *Brygada Strzelców* (3 Rifle Brigade)
    Batalion Strzelców Podhala ńskich (Podhole Rifle Battalion)
    8. *Batalion Strzelców* (8 Rifle Battalion)
    9. *Batalion Strzelców* (9 Rifle Battalion)
    1. *Samodzielny Szwadron C.K.M.* (*C.K.M.* means heavy machine gun)

Artilleria Dywizyjna
    1. *Pułk Artylerii Motorowej* (1 Motorised Artillery Regiment)
    2. *Pułk Artylerii Motorowej* (2 Motorised Artillery Regiment)
    1. *Pułk Artylerii Przeciwpancernej* (1 Anti-Tank Regiment)
    1. *Pułk Artylerii Przeciwlotniczej* (1 Anti-Aircraft Regiment)

Saperzy Dywizyjna
    10. *Kompania Saperów* (10 Engineer Company)
    11. *Kompania Saperów* (11 Engineer Company)
    1. *Pluton Mostowy* (1 Bridging Platoon)
    1. *Kompania Parkowa* (1 Field Park Company)

1. *Batalion Łączności* (1 Signals Battalion)
    1. *Szwadron Łączności* (1 Signals Squadron)
    2. *Szwadron Łączności* (2 Signals Squadron)
    3. *Szwadron Łączności* (3 Signals Squadron)
    10 *Szawdron Łączności* (10 Signals Squadron)

    Kompania Warsztatowa 10 *Brygada Pancerney* (10 Armoured Brigade Workshop
      Company)
    Kompania Warsztatowa 3 *Brygada Strzelców* (3 Rifle Brigade Workshop Company)

Supply and Transport
    3. *Kompania Zaopatrywania* (3 Supply Company – supplies/fuel)
    10. *Kompania Zaopatrywania* (10 Supply Company – ammo)
    11. *Kompania Zaopatrywania* (11 – rations)
    Kompania Przewozowa Piechoty (Infantry Transport Company)

Medical
    10. *Lekka Kompania Sanitarnia* (10 Light Medical Company)
    11. *Kompania Sanitarnia* (11 Medical Company)
    1. *Polowa Stacja Opatrunkowa* (1 Field Operating Station)
    1. *Polowa Higieny Polowie* (1 Field Hygiene Section)

1. *Park Materiałowy* (1 Material Park)
8. *Sąd Polowy* (8 Field Court)
Poczta Polowy (Field Post)
1. *Szwadron Czołgów Zapasowych* (1 Tank Delivery Squadron)[35]

Provision of vehicles and equipment occurred slowly, as British authorities insisted it not receive its proper scales until "all the British Armoured Divisions have not only completed but have a large reserve of tanks standing behind them." For example, in November 1941, the Polish armoured brigade had only 48 tanks and it was expected this figure would climb to 100 tanks by March 1942, still short of the required brigade total of 178 tanks.[36] Problems with the supply of tanks were only overcome following personal intervention by the British Prime Minister, who told the Chief of the Imperial General Staff that "the Poles should be treated on this footing equally with British Divisions."[37]

Before continuing, an examination of Polish experience with armour is necessary. The first Polish armoured forces were created in 1919 and by 1930 a separate armoured branch had been formed, but its growth and development as an independent manoeuvre arm was limited by financial and technical factors. French influences dominated Polish doctrine and staff college training that placed undue emphasis on employing tanks in support of infantry, but it was planned to motorize four cavalry brigades. Designs had also been made of a new family of armoured vehicles and trials of French and British tanks were also conducted.[38] By 1939, total armour holdings included 1,134 vehicles, most of which were light tanks supporting infantry divisions or cavalry brigades. There were also 52 Vickers E light tanks,[39] two battalions and a company with a total of 169 7TP light tanks,[40] a battalion with 53 French built R-35 tanks and three battalions with 67 obsolete Renault M-17 FT, plus 100 armoured cars and 11 armoured trains. The role of the latter was to provide mobile artillery support to infantry and cavalry units. Despite this progress, the September 1939 campaign demonstrated that Polish armour was too light, under-gunned, lacking prolonged sustainability and doctrinally subordinate to other arms to have any appreciable affect on the outcome,[41] although Polish tanks fought in several notable actions, such as at Tomaszow Lubelski from 17-20 September 1939.[42]

The 1. *Dywizja Pancerna* owes its origin to these prewar aspirations and the formation of the 10. *Brygada Kawalerii Pancernej* in 1937. With two regiments of motorized cavalry,[43] recce, motorized artillery, anti-tank and armour units, the brigade was officially listed as "armoured-motorized formation." However, it was hardly "similar to corresponding formations of the German, Russian and French Armies … the proportion of armoured to motorized components was so insignificant that it amounted to no more than the ordinary equipment of an infantry or cavalry unit with armoured reconnaissance vehicles."[44] Nonetheless, it possessed considerable defensive firepower and was ably handled in southern Poland during the September 1939 campaign as part of *Armia Kraków* and later *Armia Karpaty*, where it faced intensive combat against the XXII *Panzer Korps*. By mid-September, it was in the Lwów area and was soon ordered into Hungary, from where the majority of its personnel escaped to France. Once there, the brigade was reformed as part of the Polish Armed Forces in Exile in 1940.[45] Despite insufficient training, the French insisted the brigade be committed piecemeal to action in June 1940, and after 10 days of fighting, its personnel were split into small groups with orders to make their way to British and Polish transports to the United Kingdom, where the brigade was once again reformed.

Returning to the story of the 1. *Dywizja Pancerna,* one important unit ignored by historians was No. 4 Liaison Headquarters, which was a British unit assigned to the division. Given the number of non-English speaking Allied army contingents within 21st Army Group that did not employ British staff procedures, several liaison headquarters were allotted to Belgian, Polish, French, Czech and Royal Netherlands[46] units to eliminate or reduce problems stemming from linguistic problems, staff technique or doctrinal differences. For the Poles, the unit provided "remembrancers" for staff "so at to ensure smooth working and the proper application of Staff Duties as between … Corps and 1 Polish Armd Div."[47] No. 4 Liaison Headquarters was created when the 1. *Dywizja Pancerna* was formed and the commander often shadowed the divisional commander and also attended most meetings regarding the establishment and organization of the division.[48] The most important function of the headquarters was its responsibility for contact between British and Allied contingents; passage of all correspondence, routine orders, reports and messages, ensuring their comprehension and passing back of any correspondence or messages to higher headquarters. Operational documents were not passed through the Liaison HQ, but they were provided with duplicate copies. No. 4 Liaison HQ was commanded by a colonel and had an establishment of 35 officers, 150 other ranks, 43 vehicles and 21 motorcycles. The first test of the liaison HQ concept was first exercised during Exercise LINK, in September 1943, which will be discussed below.[49]

Experience in Normandy found that No. 4 Liaison HQ had too many personnel to operate effectively and the anticipated method of operation did not hold true once operations commenced. Originally, all orders and instructions were to have been passed from the corps commander through the commander of the liaison HQ, but it was found that "in operations the corps commander prefers to deal directly with the division commander] and that assistance, *owing to language difficulties, is not now required* (my italics) from the Comd 4 Liaison." Rather than mirror the divisional commander, the liaison staff should be integrated with the divisional staff where they would ensure proper compliance to orders. Consequently, the establishment of No. 4 Liaison HQ was reduced to 23 officers and 93 other ranks, while the number of vehicles was halved. The commander was also reduced by one rank to lieutenant-colonel, however, as 1. *Dywizja Pancerna* was the largest Allied contingent in 21st Army Group, efforts to have the commander's rank to upgraded to colonel proved unsuccessful.[50]

Much of the literature dealing with the Normandy campaign has centred on the quality of the training received by Canadian, British and other Allied formations before their arrival in France. Surprisingly, none has examined the training of the 1. *Dywizja Pancerna* or when it has, it has simply assumed it was the same as that for other formations within 21st Army Group. When the division was first formed, sufficient training areas were close to its garrison locations or would be "made available." The division was later moved "to obtain more suitable conditions for training the armoured units."[51] Throughout its stay in the United Kingdom, individual training was thorough, as was unit-level collective training, while brigade and division collective training exercises occurred on several occasions. 16. *Brygada Pancerna* held its first exercise in September 1942, but these became more difficult due to the continual divisional reorganizations and the need to train a large number of new recruits recently transferred from camps in the Soviet Union, who in many cases required convalescence from their ordeal before they could even commence training.[52]

The division appears to have only participated in two divisional level exercises within a corps context. The first of these was Exercise SNAFFLE held in the Newmarket area in 1943. 1. *Dywizja Pancerna* opposed 4 Canadian Armoured Division in a scenario in which each was the main striking force for a fictitious country. The other exercise, was LINK, held 13-18 September 1943 and designed to "practice HQ 2 Cdn Corps, 61 Inf Div and 1 Polish Armd Division in a full scale exercise with tps involving various phases of battle and including the org and sp with live firing by RA units and the dropping of sups by air." The second object was to "try out draft establishments of Liaison HQs with certain allied contingents."[53]

Generally, the Polish division performed well, at least according to the reports, particularly in river crossings, where "its advance had been more rapid than was anticipated," but in some cases, opportunities were lost, as "an excellent piece of work which should have resulted in the gaining of considerable time by British forces" was not exploited. Passages of lines, march discipline and traffic control were generally well conducted, particularly on 17 September, when "a move along very narrow and twisting roads, was exceptionally good." However, congestion proved a continual problem and created delays in movement on several occasions, sometimes predicated by the unnecessary movement of A and B echelon vehicles. This was as much a problem for this exercise as it was for later operations.[54] Despite the presence of No. 4 Liaison HQ, which was responsible for the passage and interpretation of information and orders with all higher and flanking units, and to aid the smooth working of the divisional headquarters, problems in the passage of information to the Polish division persisted. The exercise final report makes regular reference to the keenness demonstrated throughout the division and offers the following caution:

> The Poles are so keen and work at such high pressure, that one cannot help feeling that while their efficiency may be unimpaired for the period of an exercise serious consequences might result from a prolonged series of action unless every opportunity is taken of rest.[55]

Unfortunately, most of the experience gained was lost as shortly after the exercise, 1. *Dywizja Pancerna* was reorganized with the new British armoured division establishment.

The division was brought up to full strength until 19 March 1944, when its final mobilization was ordered preparatory to its moving to the continent. This took about a month to complete and following several moves it commenced its final exercise cycle,[56] in the Scarborough area, where it underwent a number of regimental/battalion and brigade level collective exercises, which also allowed the integration of all services for the first time. On 4 June, a three-day divisional exercise known as Exercise NIEMEN, put battlegroups against one another, such as when the 24. *Pułk Ułanów* exercised against the remainder of 10. *Brygada Kawalerii Pancernej*, while from 21-25 June, a number of schemes were held with the 2nd French Armoured Division. Thus the division appears to have received more formation-level collective training than 4 Canadian Armoured Division, but the true quality of this training is difficult to assess due to the lack of adequate documentation.[57]

As for individual training, some 1,470 officers attended tactics, armoured fighting vehicle and various technical courses, while 11,114 soldiers received a variety of automotive, driving, radio, weapons, technical and other training. Of the total number of officers listed above, 452 received specialized training in tactics, staff technique and other subjects at the Polish Central Armour School in Scotland, while during 1942 and 1943, 159 attended the Senior Officers Tactical Course[58] and other staff training offered by the British army.[59] Individual training was indeed thorough and comprehensive.

Finding replacement personnel also plagued the Polish Army in the West, particularly once units were committed to battle, as it was cut off from the primary source of replacements. During 1941 and 1942, considerable reinforcement was provided when over 100,000 Poles were evacuated from the Soviet Union. While most of them were allocated to the II *Korpus Polski* in the Middle East, some 10,000 were sent to reinforce all Polish units in the United Kingdom, of which 5,500 joined the 1. *Dywizja Pancerna*. The division achieved its peak of training and manpower, just before moving to France, in July and August 1944. For example, on 31 July 1944, 24.*Pułk Ułanów* reported 627 soldiers or 81 per cent of its personnel as having come directly from Poland, while another 147 had either been evacuated from other countries (France, 129; Belgium, 8; Rumania, 3; and Lithuania, 1) or recruited from Poles living elsewhere (Argentina, 3; England, 1; and Canada, 2). Of the personnel, 21 per cent had served with the regiment in Poland in

1939 and another 30 per cent had served with it in France in 1940.

In Normandy, the division suffered 2,327 casualties and making up these losses proved difficult. Casualties outstripped available reinforcements and by December 1944 the division was short 2,298 personnel, while serious training deficiencies forced 21st Army Group to take it out of the line for further training. The Ardennes offensive quickly terminated these plans and by January 1945, after the division had resumed operations, Lieutenant-General Crocker noted the deficiencies had worsened due to a high proportion of reinforcements being Poles who had, until recently, been prisoners of war, having been forced to serve in the *Wehrmacht*. These personnel lacked training and suffered from a myriad of medical and other problems, leading Crocker to recommend the division be withdrawn for retraining. General Crerar refused to support Crocker, as this would necessitate replacing the Poles in the line with 4th Canadian Armoured Division, thus affecting the Canadian division's participation in the upcoming Rhineland battles, known as Operation VERITABLE.[60]

As a small army, the Polish army had a small but capable group of officers to command formations and units and fill key staff positions. For example, *Generał brygady* Stanisław Maczek[61] commanded the 10. *Brygada Kawalerii Pancernej* from October 1938 to 1942 and then the 1. *Dywizja Pancerna* from 1942 to 1945, and is closely associated with the development of Polish armoured forces during the war. He is buried in the United Kingdom. *Pułkownik* Franciszek Skibiński served as deputy commander of the 10. *Brygada Kawalerii Pancernej* until 22 August 1944, when he took over the 3. *Brygada Strzelców* on 25 August 1944, after filling in as commander of the divisonal reconaissance regiment for three days.[62] He then took command of the 10. *Brygada Kawalerii Pancernej* from January until July 1945. When Skibiński took over the brigade, his deputy was *Pułkownik* Antoni Grudziński, who remained there until July 1945.[63] *Pułkownik* Marian Wieroński[64] commanded the 3. *Brygada Strzelców* until replaced by Skibiński, who in turn was succeeded by *Pułkownik* Władysław Dec in January 1945. Dec had earlier served as deputy commander of the brigade before taking it over. The divisional artillery commander was *Pułkownik* Bronisław Noel, who went on to be the deputy divisional commander in 1947. Three officers occupied the post of divisional chief of staff. *Podpułkownik* Jerzy Levit-toux was the division's first casualty when he killed near Caen on 18 July

1944.[65] His replacement was *Podpułkownik* Ludwik Stankiewicz,[66] who was promoted from a headquarters *10. Brygada Kawalerii Pancernej* staff position on 20 July 1944. He remained in that position until 26 September 1945, when *Podpułkownik* Zbigniew Dudziński replaced him.[67] Stankiewicz filled the position once again from July 1946 to June 1947.[68]

Following its exercise cycle, the division was finally concentrated in Aldershot during the second half of July 1944. During the spring and summer, the division had also received several high-level visits from Władysław Raczkiewicz, the President of Poland, *Generał* Kazimierz Sosnkowski, the Polish Commander in Chief (who replaced Sikorski after his death in 1943) and General Eisenhower, while on 13 March 1944 General Montgomery paid a visit. The division then moved to ports at London, Dover and Southampton, arriving in Normandy on 30 July 1944, almost four years after many of its members had left France. After moving to Bayeux, the division came under command of 2nd Canadian Corps and final preparations commenced for the division's first operation, including a detailed briefing of the headquarters officers by General Montgomery on 5 August 1944. Rear HQ First Canadian Army reported the division 100 per cent complete with vehicles and equipment on 7 August 1944 with 129 Sherman V, 25 Sherman VC, 33 Stuart and 59 Cromwell tanks. Each armoured/cavalry regiment had three squadrons, with four Sherman tanks in the squadron headquarters, and four "platoons" (note the Poles did not use the term "troop"), each of three tanks.[69]

While historians note the losses suffered by the 1. *Dywizja Pancerna* due to Allied bombing in August 1944, the result of the division's first casualties in July 1944 is rarely recounted. Prior to moving to France, Maczek sent his two principal staff officers, *Podpułkownik* Jerzy Levittoux, the Chief of Staff, and Major Mieczysław Rutkowski, the divisional Assistant Adjutant and Quartermaster General, plus an officer of No. 4 Liaison HQ, Major William Willis (or Wills, accounts vary) and two drivers, to Normandy to learn of fighting conditions there and to liaise with the British 11th Armoured Division. Two days after arrival, during the night of 18 July 1944, the group was driving back to the British divisional headquarters when several German planes began dropping flares and anti-personnel bombs. When the attack ended, Rutkowski found both Levittoux and Willis were mortally wounded. Thus before being committed to operations, the Poles had lost a critical staff officer, along with an important member of the Liaison HQ. Rutkowski returned to Aldershot to report on what happened and was soon back in Normandy with another operations officer from the divisional headquarters and another member of No. 4 Liaison HQ, while Major Ludwik Stankiewicz, from 10. *Brygada Kawalerii Pancernej*, was promoted and took over final detailed planning for the division's first operations in Normandy, which is recounted in this book.[70]

Following the Normandy campaign, 1. *Dywizja Pancerna* crossed the Seine, pursuing the enemy, and in nine days covered 400 km to Ghent. In late September 1944, it took the Belgian cities of Axel, Hulst and Terneuzen. Throughout much of October, it occupied defensive positions and was then given the task of taking Breda, which fell on 29 October. It eventually reached Moerdijk, where it received a well deserved halt for rest and reconstitution. As a result of the Ardennes offensive, 1. *Dywizja Pancerna* was given an additional frontage of 50 km to defend and also participated in the early attacks against Kapelsche Veer, which was eventually taken by the 4th Canadian Armoured Division. On 7 April 1945, the division went into action again, alongside the 2nd Canadian Division and 4th Canadian Armoured Division, crossing into German territory on 8 April. Five days later, one Polish Sherman, along with a scout car, one jeep and a motorcycle from the 2. *Pułk Pancerny* liberated 1,500 Polish women from a camp at Oberlangen. The Küsten Canal was crossed on 19 April and on 22 April, after reaching Leda, the division was given the task of taking the naval base at Wilhelmshafen. After the division's two brigades linked up at Leer on 1 May, they reached the outskirts of Wilhelmshafen three days later. While preparing to assault the city, confirmation came of the ending of hostilities and on 5 May 1945, *Pułkownik* Antoni Grudziński, Deputy Commander of the 10. *Brygada Kawalerii Pancernej* moved into Wilhelmshaven with the 2. *Pułk Pancerny* and 8. *Batalion Strzelców*, where he accepted the surrender of the city and port. Throughout most of its operational history, 1. *Dywizja Pancerna* was under Canadian command, either as part of 2nd Canadian Corps or other corps under First Canadian Army.[71]

After the war, the division served with the British occupation forces in Germany. During its 287 days of fighting to help liberate Northwest Europe, the 1. *Dywizja Pancerna* lost a total of 5,098 men, of whom 1,294 were killed.[72] In 1947, its personnel were transferred to the Polish Resettlement Corps in the United Kingdom, from where most found new homes there, western Europe or in North and South America. The last elements of the division were demobilized in 1949. All that remains of its history are the memories of the few remaining veterans, memorial markers in the United Kingdom, France, Belgium and the Netherlands, and the graves of soldiers who were lost between July 1944 and May 1945, which are in a number of cemeteries throughout Northwest Europe.

Polish Rank Titles – A Comparative Table

British	Polish	Contraction
Field Marshal	Marszałek Polski	Marsz.
General	Generał broni[1]	Gen.
General of Division (Lieut.-Gen.)	Generał dywizji[2]	Gen. Dyw.
General of Brigade (Maj.-Gen.)	Generał brygady	Gen. Bryg.
Colonel	Pułkownik (Pułk = regiment)	Płk.
Lieutenant-Colonel	Podpułkownic (pod = under)	Ppłk.
Major	Major	Maj.
Captain	Kapitan (Rotmistrz in the cavalry)	Kpt./Rtm.
Lieutenant	Porucznik[3]	Por.
Second-Lieutenant	Podporucznik	Ppor.
Warrant Officer	Chorąży[4]	Chor.
Staff Sergeant	Starzy Sierżant (Starzy can be "old" or "senior")	St. Sierż.
Lance Sergeant	Sierżant	Sierż.
Corporal	Plutonowy	Plut.
Lance Corporal	Kapral	Kapr.
Private	Starszy Szeregowiec	St. Szer.
Private	Szeregowy or –iec	Szer.

NOTES

1. *Generał* is pronounced as Gene Hackman did in the film *A Bridge Too Far:* "g" as in gun; "ł" as "w".
2. "j" sounds like "y".
3. "cz" = "ch" as in chair
4. "ch" has an "h" sound; "ą" pronounced as "on"

Polish officers also followed European practice by having higher staff training or professional association designations, such as engineers (*inż*), or with medical degrees or doctorates (dr.) between their rank and name. For example, in the case of *Pułkownik dypl.* Bronisław Noel, the *dypl* indicated completion of the Polish Army War College.

The various arms also had unique rank titles depending on the type of unit. For example, there were several equivalent titles for private, such as *ułan* in a lancer regiment, *dragonów* in the 10. *Pułk Dragonów, stzelec* in a rifle unit, *kanonier* in the artillery, *saper* in the engineers and so on. Similar distinctions continued up to and including the rank of *starzy sierżant*.

ENDNOTES

Introduction

1. The only recent work that was both in-depth and largely based on original research was Jody Perrun's examination of the development of the TOTALIZE air plan. Jody Perrun, "Missed Opportunities: First Canadian Army and the Air Plan for Operation Totalize, 7-10 August 1944" (MA Thesis, Carleton University, 1999).

2. In 1968 a writer for *Canadian Magazine*, a broadsheet insert included every Saturday in several Canadian newspapers, accompanied Simonds on a tour of the area between Caen and Falaise. It was during this visit that he stated, "But [the Poles] were impetuous and anxious to get going, and when they moved out of cover, the German tanks in that wood over there opened up on them." David Carmichael, "How Canada Smashed the Germans," in *Canadian Magazine* (Toronto, 5 Oct 1968), 19.

Prologue: The Cramesnil Spur

1. NAC, RG 24 Vol. 14,046, Reel T-10652, War Diary 2 Canadian Armoured Brigade, "Op 'Totalize' An Account of Ops by 2 Cdn Armd Bde in France 5 to 8 Aug 44," Aug 1944, 7.

2. In fact, he was correct in his assessment. There were elements of at least six German infantry battalions behind them, while there could have been no more than a complete battalion along with stragglers and scattered detachments spread across the front facing two British and two Canadian brigades on their objectives. Letter, Gordon to Colonel G.W.L. Nicholson, Director of the Historical Section, 1 February 1960 (copy in author's collection); Transcript of taped narrative prepared by Brigadier General (retired) S.V. Radley-Wal-

ters, June 2001 (author's collection).

3. NAC, RG 24 Vol. 13,624, Operations Log, First Canadian Army, Sheet 6, Serial 36, 8 Aug 1944.

Chapter One: The Canadian Army

1. Major General Sir Archibald Macdonell, quoted in Stephen Harris, *Canadian Brass: The Making of a Professional Army, 1860-1939*, 143.

2. John English, *The Canadian Army and the Normandy Campaign: A Study of Failure in High Command*, 19-20; John Macdonald, "In Search of Veritable: Training the Canadian Army Staff Officer, 1899-1945" (MA Thesis, Royal Military College of Canada, 1992), 81; DHH, Historical Section (G.S.), Report No. 22, "The Reorganization of the Canadian Militia, 1919-1920" (Ottawa, 1949).

3. Donald E. Graves, "Fists of Mail, Walls of Steel, Armoured Warfare, 1914-1945" (unpublished paper, 1995), 20.

4. C.P. Stacey, *Official History of the Canadian Army in the Second World War, Volume I: Six Years of War: The Army in Canada, Britain and the Pacific*, 33.

5. Harris, *Canadian Brass*, 167-171.

6. Barry Hunt, "The Road to Washington: Canada and Empire Naval Defence, 1918-1921" in James Boutilier (ed.), *RCN in Retrospect 1910-1968*, 44-61; English, *Canadian Army*, 20.

7. John Marteinson and Michael McNorgan, *The Royal Canadian Armoured Corps: An Illustrated History*, 46-47.

8. George Stanley, *Canada's Soldiers: The Military History of an Unmilitary People*, rev. ed., 339-340.

9. DHH, "The Reorganization of the Canadian Militia, 1919-1920," 26.

10. Philip Ventham and David Fletcher, *Moving the Guns: The Mechanisation of the Royal Artillery 1854-1939*, 23-24.

11. Lieutenant General E.W. Sansom (1890-1982) joined the militia in 1906 and saw considerable service in the Great War. He held a variety of command and staff positions in the permanent force after the war and in 1939 went overseas in a staff appointment with the 1st Canadian Division. He commanded 5th Canadian Armoured Division and then 2nd Canadian Corps, but was replaced by Lieutenant General G.G. Simonds prior to the Normandy Campaign. He retired in 1945.

12. J.L. Granatstein, *The Generals: The Canadian Army's Senior Commanders in the Second World War*, 45.

13. G.W.L. Nicholson, *Gunners of Canada: The History of the Royal Regiment of Canadian Artillery*, Volume 2, 1919-1967, 12-16; Larry Worthington, *'Worthy' A Biography of Major-General F.F. Worthington, C.B., M.C., M.M.*, 135; Marteinson, *RCAC History*, 68.

14. Marteinson, *RCAC History*, 62.

15. Tony Foster, *Meeting of Generals*, 87-88; Marteinson, *RCAC History*, 72-75; Graves, "Fists of Steel," 25.

16. Lieutenant General Eedson Louis Millard Burns (1897-1985) was born in Westmount, Quebec, and graduated from the Royal Military College in 1915. He served in the Royal Canadian Engineers on the Western Front and was awarded the Military Cross. After the First World War he distinguished himself by developing advanced aerial survey methods and attended the Quetta Staff College and the Imperial Defence College. At the outbreak of the war he served in Canadian Military Headquarters in London and in Ottawa. He then commanded 2nd Canadian Division in England and 5th Canadian Armoured Division and 1st Canadian Corps in Italy. He was relieved from the latter position in the fall of 1944 and spent the rest of the war in rear area appointments. After the war he served in the Department of Veterans Affairs and then in 1954 returned to duty as the commander of the United Nations Truce Supervisory Organization and in 1956 the United Nations Emergency Force, both in the Middle East. He retired in 1959.

17. Lieutenant General Guy Granville Simonds (1903-1974) was born in England but emigrated to Canada with his family at an early age. He graduated from the Royal Military College in 1924 and was commissioned in the Royal Canadian Artillery. In the prewar years he successfully completed the Long Gunnery Staff Course and the Staff College Course, both in the United Kingdom. He commanded 2nd Canadian Corps throughout the campaign in Northwest Europe, except for a period as acting commander of First Canadian Army because of the illness of Lieutenant General H.D.G. Crerar. After the war he served as chief instructor of the Imperial Defence College in the United Kingdom and commandant of the Canadian National Defence College before being appointed Chief of the General Staff in 1951. He retired in 1955.

18. Harris, *Canadian Brass*, 203-205.

19. Government of Canada, *Defence Forces List Canada (Naval, Military and Air Forces) Part I* (Ottawa, 1938), 126-130, 132-134.

20. Harris, *Canadian Brass*, 197-198; Goodspeed, *Battle Royal*, 349.

21. Anon, *The Regimental History of the Governor General's Foot Guards*, 40; D. Goodspeed, *Battle Royal: A History of the Royal Regiment of Canada 1862-1962*, 352; 163; Brereton Greenhous, *Semper Paratus: The History of The Royal Hamilton Light Infantry (Wentworth Regiment) 1862-1977*, 163; R. Rogers, *History of the Lincoln and Welland Regiment*, 2nd ed., 92; Gerald Cassidy, *Warpath: From Tilly-la-Campagne to the Kursten Canal*, 18; DHH, Historical Section (G.S.), Report No. 57, "A Summary of Major Changes in Army Organization," 22 December 1952, 17.

22. Greenhous, *Semper Paratus*, 160-161.

23. Major General Harry Wickwire Foster (1902-1964) graduated from the Royal Military College in 1924 and was commissioned in Lord Strathcona's Horse (Royal Canadians). He was attending the British Army Staff College in 1939 when war was declared and joined the 1st Canadian Division on its arrival in the United Kingdom in December. Foster took command of the 4th Canadian Armoured Division in late August 1944 and then was transferred to the 1st Division in Italy in December of that year. He presided over the court martial of SS-*Brigadeführer* Kurt Meyer in December 1945 and served in Canada until

his appointment to the Commonwealth War Graves Commission in 1950.

24. Foster, *Meeting of Generals*, 74-76; DHH, Historical Section (G.S.), Report No. 64, "Reorganization of the Canadian Militia, 1936, Appendix "O."

25. English, *Canadian Army*, 47; Harris, *Canadian Brass*, 206-208.

26. Charles Stacey, *Arms, Men and Governments: The War Policies of Canada 1939-1945*, 12-13; John Grodzinski, *Operational Handbook for the First Canadian Army, 1944-1945: Formation Organization, Staff Technique and Administration*, 1.

Chapter Two: Canada Goes to War

1. Graves, "Fists of Mail," 24-25.

2. Goodspeed, *Battle Royal*, 356-360.

3. It should be added that during the period in which Eberbach was critical of the Canadian high command, First Canadian Army had not yet been activated, although Crerar with a small headquarters cell had moved to Normandy on 18 June. The Germans had assumed incorrectly that Crerar was commanding the eastern portion of the bridgehead. USNA, RG 338, MS # B-840, Heinrich Eberbach, "Report on the Fighting of Panzergruppe West (Fifth Pz Army) from July 3–9 Aug 1944," 45-46.

4. In this regard the state of the Canadian formations probably was little different from that of the other Commonwealth countries at the same time. Study of the experience of the Australian and New Zealand forces in Greece and Crete reveals severe shortcomings in the performance of many senior officers, including Brigadier James Hargest, a frequently cited critic of British performance in Normandy. DHH, Canadian Military Headquarters Reports 11, 13, 23, 34, 49, 73 and 94 covered a number of major exercises held in the period 1941-1943, while Report 46 dealt with the supply of equipment up to September 1941. All are available on the DHH website.

5. Macdonald, "In Search of Veritable," 79.

6. Foster, *Meeting of Generals*, 77-78.

7. Granatstein, *The Generals*, en279.

8. The cavalry suffered even more than the rest of the army from tiny officer establishments. In 1938 there were 23 regular cavalry captains and lieutenants; four of the captains were Great War veterans, while one lieutenant had

been commissioned in that year. Government of Canada, *Defence Forces List 1938*, 126, 127.

9. Macdonald, "In Search of Veritable," 97-98, Appendix III, 271-272.

10. English, *Canadian Army*, 14; Government of Canada, *Defence Forces List 1938*, 38-44, 126-144; Government of Canada, *Defence Forces List 1938*, 50-55, 131-145.

11. General Andrew George Latta McNaughton (1887-1966) was born in Moosomin, Saskatchewan, and studied engineering at McGill University in Montreal. He joined the militia in 1906 and went overseas in 1915 with the 4th Field Battery, Canadian Field Artillery. McNaughton rose rapidly in rank and by 1917 was the Counter Battery Staff Officer of the Canadian Corps, in which position he distinguished himself by his organization of the very successful counter-battery program during the battle for Vimy Ridge. He ended the war as a brigadier general in command of the Canadian Corps Heavy Artillery and then served in the permanent force after the war, including as Chief of the General Staff from 1929 to 1936, after which he was seconded to head the National Research Council. During the Second World War McNaughton commanded in turn 1st Canadian Division, 7th Corps, the Canadian Corps and First Canadian Army. Unfortunately he proved unable to master command of an army and was relieved in December 1943. McNaughton later served as the Minister of National Defence and had a distinguished postwar diplomatic career.

12. Harris, *Canadian Brass*, 208.

13. John Ellis, *The Sharp End: The Fighting Man in World War II*, 348-349.

14. General Henry Duncan Graham Crerar (1888-1965), a native of Hamilton, Ontario, attended the Royal Military College and joined the militia before the First World War. He served overseas in France and Flanders, rising to the rank of lieutenant colonel and replacing McNaughton as Counter Battery Staff Officer. After the war Crerar attended both the British Army Staff College and the Imperial Defence College and was a colonel (temporary brigadier) commanding the Royal Military College when war was declared in 1939. He was posted to London, England, in October to set up Canadian Military Headquarters and then returned to Canada in

1940 to become Vice Chief and then Chief of the General Staff. Crerar proceeded overseas again in December 1941 to command 2nd Canadian Division, although in reality he commanded the Canadian Corps on an acting basis because of McNaughton's absence on sick leave. He commanded 1st Canadian Corps in Italy and succeeded McNaughton in command of First Canadian Army, holding that position until the end of the war in Europe.

15. English, *Canadian Army*, 128-136.

16. Dominick Graham, *The Price of Command: A Biography of General Guy Simonds*, 55-57; Grodzinski, *First Canadian Army*, 14, 22, 30, 32, 44.

17. Grodzinski, *First Canadian Army*, 35, 39-40, 43, 48.

18. DHH, Historical Section (G.S.), Report No. 37, "The Policy Governing the Finding and Selection of Officers for the C.A.S.F. (later C.A.(A))" (Ottawa, 1950), 2-3.

19. DHH, Report No. 37, 3.

20. DHH, Report No. 37, 4, 5.

21. English, *Canadian Army*, 71; George Blackburn, *Where the Hell Are the Guns?*, 148-153.

22. Stacey, *Six Years of War*, 138.

23. Stacey, *Six Years of War*, 72.

24. Stacey, *Six Years of War*, 72-77.

25. Stacey, *Six Years of War*, 78-80.

26. Grodzinski, *First Canadian Army*, figure facing p. 4.

27. Stacey, *Six Years of War*, 87-88.

28. Stacey, *Six Years of War*, 88-91; Grodzinski, *First Canadian Army*, 3.

29. Stacey, *Six Years of War*, 93-94.

30. Stacey, *Six Years of War*, 94-95.

31. Stacey, *Six Years of War*, 95-97.

32. A similar proposal to expand the Canadian Corps into a two-corps army had been successfully resisted by its commander, Lieutenant General Sir Arthur Currie, in the First World War, although it almost certainly would have meant his promotion to army commander. He argued that the expansion would not materially increase the CEF's fighting strength, while the overhead in terms of staff officers and supporting units would be beyond Canada's ability to provide and maintain. As a result the CEF retained its four strong divisions for the remainder of the war, while the other British and Empire forces reduced the size of their divisions and their fighting power substantially. Stacey, *Six Years of War*, 98-99.

33. Given McNaughton's strong preference for not splitting the army, it seems likely that he was attempting to enlist British support for maintaining the army structure. Stacey, *Six Years of War*, 100-101.

34. Stacey, *Official History of the Canadian Army in the Second World War, Volume III: The Victory Campaign, The Operations in North-West Europe 1944-1945*, 275; English, *Canadian Army*, 136.

35. Foster, *Meeting of Generals*, 310.

36. G.D. Adams, interview with Donald E. Graves, 22 November 1995. Donald E. Graves collection.

37. DHH, CMHQ, Report No. 46, "Situation of the Canadian Forces in the United Kingdom, Summer, 1941: IV The Problem of Equipment," Appendices A and B (Ottawa,).

38. DHH, Historical Section (G.S.), Report No. 66, "Training of First Cdn Army (less 3 Cdn Inf Div and 2 Cdn Armd Bde), December 1943–May 1944" (Ottawa, 1954).

39. DHH, Historical Section (G.S.), Report No. 43, "Training of the 4th and 5th Armoured Divisions in the United Kingdom, October 1941–July 1944" (Ottawa, 1951).

40. DHH, Report No. 66, "Training First Cdn Army," 1-2.

41. DSS, Report No. 43, "Training 4th and 5th Armoured Divisions,"10.

42. Adams interview, Donald E. Graves collection.

43. Stacey, *Arms, Men and Governments*, 214.

44. Stacey, *Victory Campaign*, 274.

45. Stacey, *Victory Campaign*, 47.

46. Norman R. Donogh, correspondence with the author, 29 January 2004.

Chapter Three: First Canadian Army in the Field

1. Stacey, *Victory Campaign*, 103-105, 107-108, 128; Meyer, *The History of the 12. SS-Panzerdivision Hitlerjugend*, 41-42.

2. Any reference to this order was omitted from the division's history, although it appeared in Meyer's narrative prepared when he was a prisoner-of-war for the U.S. Office of the Chief of Military History, which was cited by Stacey. Stacey, *Victory Campaign*, 130; Meyer, *12 SS History*, 36-40.

3. In at least some circles in the German forces, while the British were called Tommies, the Canadians were known as "the Tommy SS" and it was believed that "Canadians would not take prisoners, they'd shoot them." A. Baker, interview with Donald E. Graves, 25 November 1995.

4. Stacey, *Victory Campaign*, 150-151.

5. Stacey, *Victory Campaign*, 143.

6. Stacey, *Victory Campaign*, 146.

7. Stacey, *Victory Campaign*, 152.

8. Stacey, *Victory Campaign*, 153-155; English, *Canadian Army*, 214-217; Meyer, *12 SS History*, 134-138.

9. Major General Rodney Frederick Leopold Keller (1900-1954) was born in England and graduated from the Royal Military College in 1920. Commissioned in the PPCLI, he went overseas in 1939 with the 1st Canadian Division and assumed command of the 3rd Canadian Division in 1942. Keller was wounded in August 1944 and evacuated. He never really recovered from his wound and died on a pilgrimage to his old battlefields.

10. Brigadier Kenneth Blackader (1897-1967) was a militia officer and First World War veteran who was commanding the Black Watch of Montreal when Canada mobilized in 1939. On 20 January 1942 he was appointed commander of 8 Infantry Brigade.

11. Stacey, *Victory Campaign*, 157-158; Terry Copp (ed.), *Montgomery's Scientists: Operational Research in Northwest Europe – the Work of No. 2 Operational Research Section with 21 Army Group, June 1944 to July 1945*, 71-77.

12. English, *Canadian Army*, 221, 226-227.

13. Stacey, *Victory Campaign*, 159-162, 164; Meyer, *12 SS History*, 145-149.

14. Stacey, *Victory Campaign*, 166.

15. George Kitching, *Mud and Green Fields: The Memoirs of Major-General George Kitching*, 101.

16. General John Crocker (1896-1963) was a veteran armoured officer who had served as brigade major (chief operations staff officer) of Hobart's armoured brigade in 1936. In 1940 Crocker commanded 3 Armoured Brigade in France, followed by a succession of armoured commands in the Middle East and the United Kingdom. In 1942-1943 he led 11th Corps in Tunisia and was then appointed to command 1st British Corps for the invasion, an appoint-ment he retained throughout the campaign in Northwest Europe.

17. The state of affairs in the division was of such concern to some senior members of the division, most of whom are now deceased, that it remained fresh in their minds half a century later. Over the past 20-plus years a number of these officers used the privileged platform of the Canadian Land Forces Command and Staff College to describe the situation in extremely blunt and forceful language. I was provided with the information by a former senior member of the college staff on the condition that I disclose neither their names nor the specifics of their comments. (Other sources have confirmed this information, again on the same condition.) English, *Canadian Army*, 190, 227, 247-252 and *Lament for an Army: The Decline of Canadian Military Professionalism*, 38-39; Stacey, *Victory Campaign*, 27; Kitching, *Mud and Green Fields*, 189; Graham, *Price of Command*, 280.

18. Stacey, *Victory Campaign*, 165.

19. The Canadian official history devotes two and a third pages to discussing the varying expectations of GOODWOOD, and cites both the complete version of Montgomery's instruction to Dempsey of 15 July, the third paragraph of which read "Generally to destroy German equipment and personnel, as a preliminary to a possible wide exploitation of success," and the Second British Army intention as defined in the 2nd Canadian Corps Operation Instruction No. 2 of 16 July, "To draw enemy formations away from First U.S. Army front by attacking southwards with 1, 8, 12, 30 and 2 Canadian Corps." Stacey, *Victory Campaign*, 166-168.

20. Stacey, *Victory Campaign*, 170-176; English, *Canadian Army*, 225-230.

21. General Charles Foulkes (1903-1969) was born in England and came to Canada as a youth. After briefly attending university, he joined the militia in 1922 and in 1926 transferred to the Royal Canadian Regiment in the permanent force. Foulkes attended the British Army Staff College and went overseas in 1939 with the 1st Canadian Division. He led the 2nd Canadian Division in Normandy, commanded 2nd Canadian Corps briefly in an acting capacity, and then commanded 1st Canadian Corps in Italy and Northwest Europe.

After the war he held the position of Chief of the General Staff from 1945 to 1951 and then headed the Chiefs of Staff Committee until he retired in 1960.

22. Major General Charles Foulkes quoted in the Canadian official history. Stacey, *Victory Campaign*, 276.

23. Max Hastings, *Overlord D-Day and the Battle for Normandy 1944*, 351; English, *Canadian Army*, 191-194; Stacey, *Six Years of War*, 416; *Victory Campaign*, 196-198; *Arms, Men and Governments*, 223-224.

24. Stacey, *Victory Campaign*, 181-182.

25. Stacey, *Victory Campaign*, 196.

26. Major General C. Churchill Mann (1904-1989) was educated at the Royal Military College and served in the Royal Canadian Dragoons in the permanent force. In 1939 he was a student at the British Army Staff College when war was declared. He served in a number of command and staff positions – including a key role in planning the 1942 Dieppe Raid – culminating in chief of staff at First Canadian Army throughout the campaign in Northwest Europe.

27. Stacey, *Arms, Men and Governments*, 223.

28. Stacey, *Arms, Men and Governments*, 224.

29. Stacey, *Victory Campaign*, 196-198.

30. Crerar, unlike British officers, was not afraid to stand up to Montgomery, not least of all because, as he remarked to Stacey, "Monty would always go through a yellow light; but when the light turned red, he stopped." Stacey, *A Date with History*, 235-236.

31. Stacey, *Victory Campaign*, 181-182.

32. Stacey, *Victory Campaign*, 183.

33. Hastings, *Overlord*, 297-298.

34. Hastings, *Overlord*, 298-302; Robin Neillands, *The Battle of Normandy 1944*, 281-289.

35. Stacey, *Victory Campaign*, 185; Michael Reynolds, *Steel Inferno: 1 SS Panzer Corps in Normandy*, 190-191; DHH, Historical Section (G.S.), "Report No. 50, The Campaign in North-West Europe, Information from German Sources," 14 October 1952, 81.

36. War Diary Fifth Panzer Army, 25 July 1944, cited in DHH, Report No. 50, 82-83.

37. Graham, *Price of Command*, 279-280.

38. Major General George Kitching (1910-1999) was born in Canton, China, and educated at the Royal Military Academy, Sandhurst, in the United Kingdom. He served in the British

army until 1938, when he emigrated to Canada. In September 1939 Kitching joined the Royal Canadian Regiment after the outbreak of war. He was removed from command of 4th Canadian Armoured Division in late August 1944 and appointed Brigadier General Staff, Headquarters 1st Canadian Corps. After the war Kitching remained in the army, eventually being promoted major general again and he retired in 1965.

39. Kitching, *Mud and Green Fields*, 162-176.

Chapter Four: Making the Plan

1. Hastings, *Overlord*, 345.

2. The remarks were recorded in note form by Major A.T. "Gus" Sesia, RHLI, the commanding officer of 2 Field Historical Section. A.T. Sesia, "Resumé of Remarks by Lieut.-General G.G. Simonds, CBE, DSO" in RG 24, Vol. 17506, War Diary 2 Field Historical Section, July 1944.

3. Stacey, *Victory Campaign*, 204.

4. Reynolds, *Steel Inferno*, 200.

5. Stacey, *Victory Campaign*, 204; Reynolds, *Steel Inferno*, 200.

6. Stacey, *Victory Campaign*, 205-206; Nicholson, *Gunners of Canada*, Vol. II, 307-308.

7. Stacey, *Victory Campaign*, 201.

8. Stacey, *Victory Campaign*, 205; NAC, MG 30 E 157, Crerar Papers, Vol. 2.

9. Stacey, *Victory Campaign*, 206.

10. Reynolds, *Steel Inferno*, 202.

11. The next time the battalion commander's name appears in the history is when he was officially replaced as commanding officer on 13 August. R. Rogers, *Lincoln and Welland Regiment*, 135; English, *Canadian Army*, 253.

12. Stacey, *Victory Campaign*, 206; Nicholson, *Gunners of Canada*, Vol. 2, 308.

13. English, *Canadian Army*, 253.

14. USNA, Eberbach, "Panzergruppe West (5 Pz Army)," 22.

15. DHH, "Information from German Sources," 88-89.

16. DHH, "Information from German Sources," 89.

17. DHH, "Information from German Sources," 90.

18. DHH, "Information from German Sources," 90-91.

19. DHH, "Information from German Sources," 92.

20. Meyer, *12 SS History*, 165-166

21. Eberbach's report included "On 3 Aug Gen-Arty Warlimont from OKW paid us a visit ..." and the record of the meeting in the war diary is of the same date. USNA, Eberbach, "Panzergruppe West (5 Pz Army)," 41-42; DHH, "Information from German Sources," 94.

22. The translation in Meyer's history of 12 SS Panzer Division does not differ extensively in meaning from that in the Army Historical Section's Summary of German sources reproduced in the text. DHH, "Information from German Sources," 94-95; Meyer, *12 SS History*, 166.

23. Stacey, *Victory Campaign*, 208; War Office. *Field Service Pocket Book, Part 1 – Pamphlet No. 4, Appreciations, Orders, Messages, and Intercommunication*, 1944, 5.

24. 21 Army Group M516, 4 Aug 1944, quoted in English, *Canadian Army*, 267.

25. Although the study is anonymous, the cover page indicates it was prepared under the direction of G (Training) HQ British Army of the Rhine with the assistance of the Canadian Army Historical Section. G (Training), *British Army of the Rhine, Battlefield Tour, Operation Totalize*, 9.

26. Stacey, *Victory Campaign*, 207; English, *Canadian Army*, 267.

27. These include J.L. Granatstein, Desmond Morton and Carlo D'Este, who arguably spent nearly as much space using secondary sources to criticize the Canadian conduct of operations as discussing the battle itself in his study of the Normandy campaign. Popular historians such as Denis and Shelagh Whitaker, Richard Rohmer and Alexander McKee also misstated Crerar's and Simonds's intentions, while Roman Jarymowycz's repeated claim that Crerar or Simonds should have ignored Montgomery's direction and launched a wide sweep towards Paris cannot be treated as serious comment. However, those who took the care to get the aim right include C.P. Stacey, George Stanley, Reginald Roy, Donald E. Graves, John Keegan, John English and George Blackburn. J.L. Granatstein and Desmond Morton, *Bloody Victory: Canadians and the D-Day Campaign 1944*, 166; Carlo D'Este, *Decision in Normandy: The Unwritten Story of Montgomery and the Allied Campaign*, 427; Denis and ShelaghWhitaker, *Victory at Falaise: The Soldiers' Story*,109; Alexander McKee, *Caen: Anvil of Victory*, 357; Richard Rohmer, *Patton's Gap: An Account of the Battle of Normandy 1944*, 183; Roman Jarymowycz, "Canadian Armour in Normandy: Operation 'Totalize' and the Quest for Operational Maneuver," *Canadian Military History*, Vol. 7, No. 2, Spring 1998, 34; *Tank Tactics: From Normandy to Lorraine*, 163-164; and "On Doctrine – A Brief Comment" in *The Army Doctrine and Training Bulletin*, Vol. 4, No. 3, Fall 2001, 58; Stacey, *Victory Campaign*, 207; Stanley, *Canada's Soldiers*, 373; Reginald Roy, *1944: The Canadians in Normandy*, 147; Donald E. Graves, *South Albertas: A Canadian Regiment at War*, 109; John Keegan, *Six Armies in Normandy*, 252; English, *Canadian Army*, 263; George Blackburn, *The Guns of Normandy*, 310-311.

28. Reynolds, *Steel Inferno*, 199.

29. First Canadian Army INTSUM Number 38, 6 Aug 44.

30. Roy, *Canadians in Normandy*, 149.

31. *General der Panzertruppen* Heinrich Eberbach, the commander of *Panzergruppe West* and then *5. Panzerarmee*, although generally critical of the Canadian high command in Normandy, wrote approvingly of the Canadian use of night attacks. Crerar has been criticized by Major General Chris Vokes, who commanded 1st Canadian Infantry Division in Italy at the time, for advocating a "Great War approach" at a conference of the senior commanders of the Eighth Army, which was fine if he was speaking of the Somme. Vokes also claimed Crerar had served as a junior officer, that is a lieutenant or captain, in that war, while in fact he had ended the war as a lieutenant colonel. Crerar, who first saw action in 1915, had served in the Canadian Corps in France and Belgium during "Canada's Hundred Days" in 1918 when the corps enjoyed a string of spectacular successes in open, manoeuvre warfare. It is likely that he was referring to the Canadian Corps's use of innovative tactics, and not to the British penchant for frontal attacks on fortified positions. It is unlikely that Vokes, who was not a deep thinker at the best of times, could have made the distinction, although he claimed to have liked Crerar. The British officer corps had been so repelled by their experiences in the war that, unlike the Germans, they had

refused to consider any of the positive lessons that could be drawn from a study of it. With the benefit of hindsight, it would have been politic for Crerar to have kept his mouth shut, especially as the only result of raising the issue was to damage his reputation. Still, while Crerar may not have been a military genius, he was not as bad a general as Montgomery made him out to be and his handling of his army in 1945 was first class. One should also note that Montgomery tended to disparage the abilities of others, perhaps to emphasize his own brilliance, and that the severest criticism of Crerar and the Canadian army in Normandy appeared after critical eyes were beginning to examine Montgomery's generalship, and that some of the earliest and harshest critics of the Canadians were ex-members of the field marshal's staff at Headquarters 21st Army Group. USNA, Eberbach, "Panzergruppe West," 32; English, *Canadian Army*, 268.

32. Stacey, *Victory Campaign*, 201, 207; English, *Canadian Army*, 263; Historical Section(G.S.). "Report No. 65: Canadian Participation in the Operations in North-West Europe, 1944. Part III: Canadian Operations, 1-23 August" (Ottawa, 1953), 7; Murray Johnston, *The Story of the Royal Canadian Electrical and Mechanical Engineers and of the Land Ordnance Engineering Branch*, 64

33. Stacey. *Victory Campaign*, 207-208; English, *Canadian Army*, 263.

34. NAC, Crerar Papers, Vol. 2, Simonds to Crerar, Outline Plan, 1 Aug 44. Unless otherwise noted, all details of the plan are taken from this document.

35. Graham, *Price of Command*, 67-68; English, *Canadian Army*, 266-267.

36. There is one significant difference between El Hamma and TOTALIZE; in the former battle the British forces looped around the German defences to attack from a flank. In Normandy there were no open flanks to exploit and Simonds essentially mounted a frontal attack. Shelford Bidwell, *Gunners at War: A Tactical Study of the Royal Artillery in the Twentieth Century*,187-190; Shelford Bidwell and Dominick Graham, *Fire-Power: British Army Weapons and Theories of War 1904-1945*, 270-272; Francis de Guingand, *Operation Victory*, rev. ed., 213-217.

37. CDL was the abbreviation for Canal Defence Light, a powerful searchlight mounted in a tank turret. The name was a cover story for a device designed to support night attacks by dazzling the enemy's vision. It was one of those unique brainwaves, like the Edsel, New Coke or the 1968 unification of the three Canadian services for that matter, that seem to be strikingly brilliant and go rolling along with increasing momentum past the sublime and into the ridiculous. An astonishing total of 1,850 tanks were converted to CDL during the Second World War, none of which were used in TOTALIZE. Despite the major effort devoted to develop and bring the specialized vehicle into service, its only operational use ever was by one squadron during the Rhine crossing. All in all, CDL was a colossal flop. Still, Simonds could not have known that in August 1944, as can be seen from the request. The reader may be excused for pondering on the result if the same resources had been devoted to developing an armoured personnel carrier. A. Smithers, *Rude Mechanicals: An Account of Tank Maturity During the Second World War*, 100, 231.

38. Stacey, *Victory Campaign*, 210n.

39. A. Smithers, *A New Excalibur: The Development of the Tank 1909-1939*, 183; Gerald Nicholson, *Canadian Expeditionary Force 1914-1919*, 405; Roy, *Canadians in Normandy*, 54; C. Lucas-Phillips, *Alamein*, 249.

40. BAOR *Battlefield Tour*, 32.

41. BAOR *Battlefield Tour*, 32; Nicholson, *Gunners of Canada*, 310-311; NAC: RG 24 C3 Vol. 41314, War Diary HQ RCA 2 Cdn Corps 1 Aug 44; George Ruffee, *The History of the 14 Field Regiment, 1940-1945*, 33.

42. Stacey, *Victory Campaign*, 210; Johnston, *RCEME History*, 64-65; NAC: RG 24 C17 Vol. 13658, War Diary AQ First Canadian Army, Infm Sup by Brig Laing, DA & QMG 2 Cdn Corps, n.d.

43. This worked out to an output of about 2.5 vehicles per hour. Thus, the attacking divisions could not have received the last of their allotment of 30 carriers each until late on 5 August, or more likely early the next morning. NAC: RG 24 C3 Vol. 2460, Reel T 12748, War Diary D Sqn 25 Armoured Delivery Regiment, 3 Aug 1944; Stacey, *Victory Campaign*, 210; Johnston, *RCEME History*, 64-65; NAC: WD AQ, Laing Report.

44. The Canadian Armoured Carrier Regiment History noted that it appears that Captain F. S. Corbeau, who later commanded the independent First Canadian Armoured Personnel Carrier Squadron and then A Squadron in the carrier regiment until he was wounded on 26 February 1945, was in charge of this organization, while the other officers were Lieutenants St. Germain, Combe, Kaiser, Power and Blackadar, all of the Elgin Regiment. It seems possible that each officer commanded a group of carriers supporting one of the six attacking infantry battalions. Keith Ramsden, *The Canadian Kangaroos in World War II*, 4; Perrun, "Missed Opportunities," 138.

45. Blackburn, *Guns of Normandy*, 315, 323.

46. BAOR *Battlefield Tour*, 25.

47. BAOR *Battlefield Tour*, 32; NAC, RG 24 Vol. 13712, WD GS 2 Cdn Corps, 1 Aug 44.

48. NAC, WD GS 2 Cdn Corps 3, 4 Aug 44.

49. Graham, *Price of Command*, 148.

50. NAC, WD GS 2 Cdn Corps, 1 Aug 44.

51. BAOR *Battlefield Tour*, 32; Alan Jolly, *Blue Flash: The Story of an Armoured Regiment*, 38-39.

52. Stacey, *Victory Campaign*, 210 and n.

53. Stacey, *Victory Campaign*, 210-211.

54. NAC, RG 24 vol. 10978, Rodger Diary.

55. Stacey, *Victory Campaign*, 207.

56. NAC, Rodger Diary.

57. Stacey, *Victory Campaign*, 207; Historical Section, G.S., Report No. 65, 15.

58. Simonds had been authorized access to Ultra at the request of Crerar. He was the only Canadian army officer below Headquarters First Canadian Army who was cleared for the product. In this case the intelligence disseminated by Bletchley Park did not alert Crerar and Simonds, among others, to the extent of the forthcoming Mortain counter-offensive; if more information had been available to them, they might have drawn a different conclusion regarding the withdrawal of the panzer divisions facing First Canadian Army, and especially the whereabouts of 1. *SS-Panzerdivision*. David O'Keefe, Compilation of Ultra material (n.p, n.d) (author's collection).

59. Ralph Bennett, *Ultra in the West: The Normandy Campaign of 1944-45*, 7.

60. Bennett, *Ultra in the West*, 7-24.

61. D'Este, *Decision in Normandy*, 420-421.

62. Major General Charles Richardson (1908-

1994) filled a number of key staff positions during the Second World War.

63. Richardson had been loaned to First Canadian Army to assist in the planning of TOTALIZE. There was no evidence, as was claimed by Max Hastings, that his attachment was resented by Crerar and his staff NAC, Crerar Papers, Vol 2, *Record of Tele Conversation, Col GS and Brig Richardson, BGS Plans 21 Army Gp, on behalf of Brig Mann, C of S First Cdn Army, from Main Army HQ to HQ AEAF*, 5 Aug 44.

64. NAC, RG 24 Vol. 12342, First Canadian Army Final Intelligence Report: Introduction, Jun 45.

65. Graham, *Price of Command*, 149.

66. NAC, RG 24 Vol. 13712, WD, G.S. 2 Cdn Corps, 5 Aug 44.

67. English, *Canadian Army*, 268.

68. David O'Keefe, "The Double-edged Sword: Intelligence and Operation 'Totalize' Normandy, August 8, 1944," (author's collection).

69. Stacey, *Victory Campaign*, 214; First Canadian Army Intelligence Summary No. 38 6 Aug 44, part 1, General, Para. 2.

70. NAC, Crerar Papers, Vol. 2, letter Crerar to Crocker and Simonds, 6 Aug 44.

71. Historical Section, GS, Report No. 65, 16.

72. BAOR *Battlefield Tour*, 10-11.

73. NAC, Crerar Papers, Vol. 2, letter Simonds to Crerar, Operation "Totalize," 6 Aug 44.

74. BAOR *Battlefield Tour*, 76.

75. BAOR *Battlefield Tour*, 79.

76. NAC, Crerar Papers, Vol. 2, letter Wright to Crerar, 1320 hrs 7 Aug 44.

77. NAC, Crerar Papers, Vol. 2, Notes on Telephone Conversation with Comd 2 Cdn Corps at 1745 hrs 7 Aug 44, Operation "Totalize."

Chapter Five: Bullets and Bombs – The Fire Plan

1. At the risk of being accused of falling into the trap of relying on one's own experience rather than the historical record, I was responsible as Chief Instructor in Gunnery at the Canadian School of Artillery for personally preparing and delivering the lectures on the artillery appreciation and allotment and fire planning at divisional level and above. I have, however, relied on primary and reliable secondary source material as much as possible, although

my own professional training and experience has made the task much easier.

2. Major General A. Bruce Matthews (1909-1991) was a militia officer who rose rapidly from the rank of major in 1939 to become the CRA of the 1st Division in Sicily and Italy before returning to England as CCRA of 2nd Canadian Corps for the campaign in Northwest Europe. On 10 November 1944 he replaced Foulkes in command of the 2nd Division.

3. Grodzinski, *First Canadian Army*, table following p. 11.

4. BAOR *Battlefield Tour*, 96.

5. Anon, *The History of the Brigadier Royal Artillery Branch of Headquarters First Canadian Army*, 41.

6. BAOR *Battlefield Tour*, 100.

7. This figure seems to have been for 2nd Canadian Corps only. Pemberton cites the total ammunition as 282,200 rounds. Blackburn, *Guns of Normandy*, 317-318; A. Pemberton, *The Development of Artillery Tactics and Equipment*, 228.

8. Stacey, *Victory Campaign*, 215.

9. Major General George Kitching, the commander of 4th Canadian Armoured Division, had served as the GSO 1 of 1st Canadian Infantry Division in Sicily and then commanded 11 Canadian Infantry Brigade in Italy. He was not a fan of the barrage and wrote in his memoirs that Simonds's "rather stubborn use of the barrage was about the only thing for which General Simonds could be criticized during the whole Sicilian campaign." He also noted that 1st Canadian Infantry Division stopped using the barrage as its preferred method of providing fire support after Simonds moved to command 5th Canadian Armoured Division. Kitching, *Mud and Green Fields*, 154, 173; Pemberton, *Artillery Tactics and Equipment*, 235.

10. BAOR *Battlefield Tour*, 95.

11. BAOR *Battlefield Tour*, 93.

12. An accepted density for a barrage was one gun per 20 to 25 yards of attacking front. The figure for TOTALIZE was one gun per 12 yards. However the rate of advance was at least three times the normal rate. Therefore the total rounds fired on each line was much less than normal. Pemberton, *Artillery Tactics and Equipment*, 279.

13. DHH, Report No. 65, 17.

14. *BRA History*, 41.

15. By analysing the deployment layout and the shelling activity of enemy guns by type and area, divisional, regimental and even battalion boundaries could be located quite accurately. Similarly any change in the deployment layout or the shelling activity could provide indications of the enemy's intentions. BAOR *Battlefield Tour*, 6.

16. BAOR *Battlefield Tour*, Royal Canadian Artillery 2nd Canadian Corps Counter Battery Policy – Operation Totalize, 98.

17. BAOR *Battlefield Tour*, 11.

18. BAOR *Battlefield Tour*, 96.

19. *BRA History*, 38.

20. NAC: RG 24 v. 13645, First Canadian Army Intelligence Summary No. 33. Part 1, Paragraph 7. 1 Aug 1944; NAC: RG24, Vol. 14332, WD HQ RCA 4 CAD, 8 Aug 1944, Sheets 3 and 4.

21. NAC, Crerar Papers, Simonds to Crerar, "Outline Plan," 1 Aug 1944, 3-4.

22. NAC: Crerar Papers, Vol 2, "Memorandum of Points Arising at Conference Held at HQ First Cdn Army at 1700B hrs 4 Aug 44," 5 Aug 44, 2-3; "Operation 'Totalize' Request for Air Support Part III – Air Plan," 4 Aug 44.

23. While Jody Perrun has written that this call resulted from wishful thinking on the part of Canadian officers based on Ultra intelligence and the recent move of *12. SS-Panzerdivision*, as we have seen there was more to it than that. NAC: Crerar Papers, Vol 2, "Record of Tele Conversation, Col GS and Brig Richardson, BGS Plans 21 Army Gp, on behalf of Brig Mann, C of S First Cdn Army, from Main Army HQ to HQ AEAF," 5 Aug 44; Perrun, "Missed Opportunities," 106.

24. NAC: Crerar Papers, "Record of Tele Conversation, C of S First Cdn Army and Col GS First Cdn Army, from HQ AEAF to Main Army HQ at approx 052130 B Hrs, on the Decisions taken at a Joint Army/RAF Conference at HQ AEAF this afternoon," 5 Aug 44

25. NAC: Crerar Papers, Vol 2, "Record of Tele Conversation," 5 Aug 44; AEAF/TS/13165/Air, 6 Aug 44.

26. AEAF/TS/13165/Air, 6 Aug 44.

27. NAC: Crerar Papers, Vol 2, "Record of Tele Conversation," 5 Aug 44.

28. Stacey, *Victory Campaign*, 212.

29. Stacey, *Victory Campaign*, 212-213.

30. NAC, Crerar Papers, Vol 2, "Memo of Telephone Conversation between C of S First Cdn Army, Speaking from HQ Bomber Command and Comd First Cdn Army, Commencing at 1213 Hours 6 Aug 44," undated but obviously 6 Aug 1944.

31. Anon, *BRA History*, 40; PRO WO 171/259 Vol 88825, Ops Log 1 Br Corps, Ser 702, 6 Aug 44.

32. NAC: Crerar Papers, Vol 2, 6-1-5/Ops, "Minutes of Conference" 1100B hrs 7 Aug 44; Message HQ Bomber Command to First Canadian Army (Main) AC 531 1240 hours 7 Aug.

33. The weather forecast issued by HQ 1 Cdn Army Met Gp for the battle area for 8 Aug 44 included local thunder showers in the early afternoon with 4-7/10 cloud cover at 2000 to 3000 ft. NAC: RG 24, C17 Vol 13624, Ops Log 7 Aug, Ser 63; Transcript of message prepared by Brig Richardson, 7 Aug 44.

34. DHH 81/849 mfm, U.S. Air Force Historical Study No. 70, "Tactical Operations of the Eighth Air Force, 6 June 1944-8 May 1945" (Air University, 1952), 57-58.

35. Perrun, "Missed Opportunities," 113 n; DHH 86/285, Air Ministry Historical Branch, RAF draft narrative, "The Liberation of North-West Europe Volume IV: The Break-Out and Advance to the Lower Rhine, 12 June to 30 September, 1944," 92.

36. It is evident that Crerar and/or Simonds had realized the implications of not hitting targets 8A and 8G. It is not certain that 83 Group shared their assessment of the importance of these targets. NAC: Crerar Papers, Vol. 2, Record of phone conversation Richardson on behalf of Col GS to G/C Rosier at 83 Gp RAF, 7 Aug 44.

37. PRO Air 24/1496, HQ 2 TAF Operations Record Book, 7 Aug 44, 27.

38. NAC: RG 24 C17 Vol 13624, First Cdn Army Op Instr No. 12, 7 Aug 44, para 8.

39. NAC, Op Instr No. 12, para 11; Blackburn, *Guns of Normandy*, 322, 326.

40. This section has been modified slightly from the original in the interest of clarity. DHH, Historical Section (G.S.), Report No. 74, "Offensive Air Support of First Canadian Army During Operations in North-West Europe" (Ottawa, 1955), 37-38.

Chapter Six: Preparing for Battle

1. Major General Thomas Rennie (1900-1945) had served with the division as a battalion and brigade commander in North Africa and Sicily before being appointed to command 3rd British Division for the invasion. He was killed in action on 24 March 1945 just after he had crossed the Rhine with the Highland Division.

2. H. Essame, *The Battle for Germany*, 185.

3. Lucas-Phillips, *Alamein*, 111-112; Graham, *Price of Command*, 72; D'Este, *Decision in Normandy*, 132-133, 274-275.

4. BAOR *Battlefield Tour*, 86-87.

5. After Normandy, 148 RAC was broken up to provide armoured replacements and was replaced in the brigade by the East Riding Yeomanry from 27 Armoured Brigade. On 18 January 1945 33 Armoured Brigade was transferred to 79th Armoured Division and re-equipped with Buffalo amphibious troop carriers. Jean Bouchery, *The British Soldier in North West Europe, 1944-1945*, 26-27.

6. BAOR *Battlefield Tour*, 14, 91.

7. BAOR *Battlefield Tour*, 13-14.

8. The tasks as eventually allotted were: to capture the forward objectives, an infantry brigade, an armoured regiment and the divisional reconnaissance regiment; to capture May-sur-Orne, Fontenay-le-Marmion and Tilly-la-Campagne and to mop up the area west of the Caen–Falaise Road to the River Orne, one infantry brigade; and to restore the momentum of the attack and finally, on order to advance between the lanes of the armoured columns and then to capture Bretteville-sur-Laize, one brigade. The alternate assessment of tasks was: to capture the forward objectives, a reinforced infantry brigade and an armoured brigade; to capture May-sur-Orne and Fontenay-le-Marmion, an infantry brigade; to capture Tilly and Rocquancourt and to reinforce if necessary and mop up behind the leading infantry brigade, an infantry brigade; and finally to secure Bretteville-sur-Laize, a minimum of two infantry battalions, which means an infantry brigade less one battalion

9. Brigadier Robert A. Wyman (1904-1967), a militia officer from Edmonton, had gone overseas in 1939 in command of the 3rd Field Regiment RCA. He took command of the Divisional Support Group of 1st Canadian

Armoured Division (later 5th Canadian Armoured Division) on 18 July 1941, and then moved to command 1 Canadian Armoured Brigade on 2 February 1942. He commanded the brigade in Sicily and Italy until he returned to England to take command of 2 Canadian Armoured Brigade on 15 April 1944. Wyman landed on Juno Beach on D-Day and had been in action almost continuously ever since. In 2nd Canadian Infantry Division Brigadiers Megill of 5 Canadian Infantry Brigade and Young of 6 Canadian Infantry Brigade were regular signals officers, while Brigadier Ganong of 4 Canadian Infantry Brigade had just assumed his appointment on 3 August. Grodzinski, *First Canadian Army*, 35, 46, 48; Nicholson, *Gunners of Canada*, 50-51, 93.

10. Grodzinski, *First Canadian Army*, Charts, Independent Armoured Brigades.

11. BAOR *Battlefield Tour*, 81.

12. The organization and command arrangements in this and following paragraphs are taken from the 2 CAB after action report, except where otherwise indicated. NAC, War Diary 2 CAB, "Op 'Totalize,'" Aug 44.

13. BAOR *Battlefield Tour*, 13.

14. Intelligence Section, *8 Canadian Reconnaissance Regiment (14 Canadian Hussars) Battle History*, 6; BAOR *Battlefield Tour*, 13.

15. NAC, War Diary 2 CAB, sheets 9, 7 Aug 44 and 11, 8 Aug 44.

16. NAC, War Diary 2 Cdn Corps, Page 2, 5 Aug 44.

17. Stacey, *Victory Campaign*, 201.

18. Roy, *The Canadians in Normandy*,138.

19. NAC, War Diary 2 CAB, Pages 4-6, 1-5 Aug 44.

20. Greenhous, *Semper Paratus*, 253.

21. Goodspeed, *Battle Royal*, 435.

22. PRO, WO 171/640, War Diary HQ 33 BAB, Sheet 1, 3 Aug 44.

23. BAOR *Battlefield Tour*, 13.

24. BAOR *Battlefield Tour*, 13.

25. NAC, War Diary 2 CAB, "Op Totalize," Aug 44.

26. Major Radley-Walters commanded A Sqn, 27 Canadian Armoured Regiment in Totalize, author interview, 16 Jan 2002.

27. NAC, War Diary 2 CAB, "Op Totalize," Aug 44.

Chapter Seven: Phase One Totalize

1. When researching this chapter, I was surprised to find a significant number of veterans who did not recall this operation as TOTALIZE. Instead, they referred to it as "the night push."

2. First Canadian Army staff intended to confirm that the operation would commence that evening with Bomber Command by 2000 hours. One can only imagine the result if the operation had been postponed after the assaulting brigades had formed up in their assembly areas.

3. BAOR *Battlefield Tour*, 39.

4. BAOR *Battlefield Tour*, 17.

5. DHH, 145.2R14011(D4), "Account of the Attack on Pt. 46 - 8 Aug 44 by RHLI as given by Lt- Col Maclachlan," 10 Aug 44.

6. Anon, *8 Reconnaissance Regiment History*, 7.

7. Blackburn, *Guns of Normandy*, 321.

8. NAC, War Diary HQ 2 CAB, 9, 7 Aug 44.

9. BAOR *Battlefield Tour*, 40.

10. BAOR *Battlefield Tour*, 17, 38-39; Ken Tout, *A Fine Night for Tanks: The Road to Falaise*, 55.

11. Tout, *Fine Night for Tanks*, 55-56.

12. BAOR *Battlefield Tour*, 17-18.

13. Brigadier Eliot Rodger, the chief of staff of 2nd Canadian Corps, as well as other staff officers, also briefed the press. During the war Ross Munro covered Canadian troops extensively from the Battle of Britain, through the occupation of Spitsbergen, Dieppe, Sicily, Italy, Normandy and the long advance into Germany. His account is interesting and provides a sense of the times, but is a bit too uncritical to be reliable history. Ross Munro, *Gauntlet to Overlord: The Story of the Canadian Army*, 169.

14. For two vivid accounts of the atmosphere on a gun position at this stage in the battle procedure, see Lucas-Philips, *Alamein*, 149-152, and Blackburn, *Guns of Normandy*, 324-326.

15. G Int, HQ Cdn Forces in the Netherlands, *"Special Interrogation Report Brigadeführer Kurt Meyer, Comd 12 SS PZ Div 'Hitler Jugend' (6 June 1944–25 August 1944),"* 7, 9, 10, 24 Aug 1945.

16. NAC, Crerar Papers, vol. 2, letter, Wright to Crerar, 7 Aug 44; War Diary 2 CAB, 2 CID Intsum No. 8, 6 Aug 44.

17. NAC, War Diary 2 CAB, "Notes on 89 Inf Div," First Cdn Army Int Summary No. 38, 6 Aug 44, published in 2 CID Intsum No. 8, 6 Aug 44.

18. Tout, *Fine Night for Tanks*, 126; Niklas Zetterling, *Normandy 1944: German Military Organization, Combat Power and Organizational Effectiveness*, 237.

19. Zetterling, *Normandy 1944*, 134, 136, 142, 152-159, 184-187.

20. Extract from captured appreciation by Comd, 89 Inf Div, 6 Aug 44, FCA Intsum No. 42, 10 Aug 44 (Donald E. Graves collection).

21. Tout, *Fine Night for Tanks*, 127.

22. Extract from 1056 GR Op Order, 4 Aug 44, FCA Intsum No. 43, 11 Aug 44 (Donald E. Graves collection).

23. FCA Intsum 40, 8 Aug 44, 41, 9 Aug 44 (Donald E. Graves collection); BAOR *Battlefield Tour*, 6, 7; Tout, *Fine Night for Tanks*, 126.

24. Zetterling, *Normandy 1944*, 134, 136, 142; BAOR *Battlefield Tour*, 6, 7.

25. NAC, Crerar Papers, vol. 2, Message AC 531 071240 [hrs] Aug, HQ Bomber Command to HQ FCA (Main) re confirmation of bombing arrangements. 7 Aug.

26. DHH Air 15-721, Air Ministry, "Tactical Bulletin No. 42, Night Operations by Bomber Command in Close Support of the Army, Caen Area, 7/8 Aug, 1944," 1-2.

27. Simonds, quoted in Carmichael, *Canadian Magazine*, 18.

28. Copp (ed.), "Report No. 8, Operation 'Totalise' RAF Heavy Bombing on the Night of 7/8th August 1944" in *Montgomery's Scientists*, 95-96.

29. DHH Air 15-721, "Tactical Bulletin No. 42," 4.

30. Stacey, *Victory Campaign*, 213, 218.

31. The operational researcher team may have ventured into speculation when, in comparing the attacks on Rocquancourt, Fontenay-le-Marmion and May-sur-Orne, they concluded "the last two were bombed and they proved difficult to take; the first was not bombed but the infantry was assisted by an artillery barrage and reached their objective more easily." The poor results due to inaccurate bombing rather than the choice of bombing itself over shelling probably was the root cause of the difficulties. Copp, "Report No. 8, *Montgomery's Scientists*, 95-98.

32. Anon, *History of the Third Canadian Light Anti-Aircraft Regiment From 17 August, 1940 to 7 May, 1945, World War Two*, 28.

33. BAOR *Battlefield Tour*, 40; Jolly, *Blue Flash*, 42.

34. Jolly, *Blue Flash*, 42; Interview, Radley-Walters, 16 Jan 02.

35. BAOR *Battlefield Tour*, 40.

36. Blackburn, *Guns of Normandy*, 326.

37. Guns from 2 CID, 4 CAD, 51 HD, 2 Cdn AGRA, 9 AGRA and two regiments of 4 AGRA fired on the barrage. The ammunition allotted for support of the attack was 400 rounds per gun (rpg) for 25-pounders and 105 mm and 200 rpg for the mediums. This totalled 216 field and 144 mediums. BAOR *Battlefield Tour*, 95, 100.

38. Blackburn, *Guns of Normandy*, 327-328.

39. Alan Wood, *The Falaise Road*, 34-35.

40. BAOR *Battlefield Tour*, 41.

41. Tout, *Fine Night for Tanks*, 59.

42. Radley-Walters, interview, 16 Jan 02.

43. E.A.C. Amy, "Normandy, 1 Squadron Canadian Grenadier Guards," 5.

44. BAOR *Battlefield Tour*, 21.

45. PRO, WO 171/1807, War Diary, 79 Assault Squadron RE, Report on Operation Totalize, 9 Aug 44; WO 171/1690, War Diary, 80 Assault Squadron RE, sheets 3-5, 7/8 Aug 44; Radley-Walters, interview, 16 January 2002.

Chapter Eight: The 51st Highland Division Advance

1. PRO, WO 171/831, War Diary, 22 Dragoons, Sheet 9, 8 Aug 44; WO 171/1690, War Diary, 80 Assault Squadron RE, Sheets 3, 4, 7-8 Aug 44; WO 171/1265, War Diary, 1 Black Watch, 7 Aug 44.

2. Tout, *Fine Night for Tanks*, 62-63.

3. Tout, *Fine Night for Tanks*, 126.

4. According to the regimental history, the "tanks" actually were a battery of 150 mm self-propelled guns. R. Neville, *The First Northamptonshire Yeomanry in Northwest Europe*, 26-27; Tout, *Fine Night for Tanks*, 14-15..

5. While the battlefield tour credits the Black Watch with capturing 40 prisoners, the war diary claimed 79 were taken. PRO, War Diary 1 BW, 8 Aug 44; BAOR *Battlefield Tour*, 22; Tout, *Fine Night for Tanks*, 19.

6. Tout, *Fine Night for Tanks*, 63.

7. PRO, WO 171/878, War Diary 144 RAC, Sheets 4-5, 7 Aug 44; BAOR *Battlefield Tour*, 41; Jolly, *Blue Flash*, 42-44.

8. Jolly, *Blue Flash*, 44.

9. Tout, *Fine Night for Tanks*, 63; *The Bloody Battle for Tilly, Normandy 1994*, 145.

10. PRO, WD 144 RAC, Sheets 4-6, 7 Aug 44; WD 80 Assault Squadron RE, Sheet 3, 7-8 Aug 44; WO 171/1267, War Diary 7 Argyll and Sutherland Highlanders, Page 4, 8 Aug 44; BAOR *Battlefield Tour*, 21-22, 41-42, 45; Jolly, *Blue Flash*, 45-48.

11. PRO, WO 171/880, War Diary 148 RAC, Appx D, "Report on Operation Totalize," 8 Aug 44; WO 171/1267, War Diary 7 Black Watch, Sheet 5, 8 Aug 44; BAOR *Battlefield Tour*, 22.

12. BAOR *Battlefield Tour*, 23-24.

13. BAOR *Battlefield Tour*, 86.

14. BAOR *Battlefield Tour*, 53.

15. BAOR *Battlefield Tour*, 53, 54.

16. BAOR *Battlefield Tour*, 54.

17. BAOR *Battlefield Tour*, 55.

18. BAOR *Battlefield Tour*, 56, 57.

19. BAOR *Battlefield Tour*, 58.

20. PRO, WO 171/674, War Diary 152 Inf Bde, 7 Aug 44; BAOR *Battlefield Tour*, 23.

21. PRO, War Diary 152 Inf Bde, 7 Aug 44; War Diary 148 RAC, Appendix D, 8 Aug 1944.

22. PRO, War Diary 152 Inf Bde, 7 Aug 44; BAOR *Battlefield Tour*, 24.

Chapter Nine: The Canadian Advance

1. Tout, *Bloody Battle for Tilly*, 144-145; PRO, WO 171/858, War Diary 1 Lothians and Border Yeomanry, Appendix J/5, Sheet 2, 1, 7 Aug 1944.

2. Intelligence Section, *8 Reconnaissance Regiment History*, 8.

3. NAC, RG 24 Vol 13751, Ops Log, 2 CID, Sheets 365-367, 8 Aug 44; BAOR *Battlefield Tour*, 50.

4. Larry Zaporzan, *Rad's War: A Biographical Study of S.V. Radley-Walters in the Normandy Campaign* (MA thesis, University of New Brunswick, 2000), 234.

5. Goodspeed, *Battle Royal*, 441-442.

6. Blackburn, *Guns of Normandy*, 331.

7. DHH, 145.2R14011(D4), "Account of the Attack on Point 45 (0655) 8 Aug 44 by RHLI as Given by the Adjt RHLI," 10 Aug 44; BAOR *Battlefield Tour*, 21.

8. PRO, War Diary, 1st Lothians &Border Yeomanry, Appendix J/12, 7 Aug 44.

9. DHH, Historical Section (G.S.), Report No. 65, *Canadian Participation in the Operations in North-West Europe, 1944*, 23 Dec 53, 25.

10. DHH, Report No. 65, 27.

11. Blackburn, *Guns of Normandy*, 333.

12. BAOR *Battlefield Tour*, 82.

13. Stacey, *Victory Campaign*, 207.

14. The operational research report claimed 791 1000 lb and 321 500 lb bombs were released by 89 Halifaxes and 3 Lancasters. The researchers mistakenly suggested that Bretteville-sur-Laize had been attacked in error. In fact it was bombed by the USAAF as part of the Phase 2 bombing. Copp, *Montgomery's Scientists*, 96-97.

15. DHH, Hist Sect, "Report No. 65," 26; 145.2F1011(D4), "Account of the Attack and Capture of May-Sur-Orne by FUS MR, night of 7/8 Aug 44, Given by Maj Brochu and Capt Lamothe to Capt Engler at Etavaux and May-Sur-Orne," 12 Aug 44, 1; BAOR *Battlefield Tour*, 23.

16. DHH, "Account by Brochu and Lamothe," 2.

17. Copp, *Montgomery's Scientists*, 95-96.

18. DHH 145.2Q1011(D8), "Account by Maj Cavanagh, "A" Coy, Camerons of Canada, of the Attack on Fontenay-le-Marmion, Night 7/8 Aug 44," Given to Capt Engler at Fontenay-le-Marmion, 10 Aug 44.

19. DHH, Hist Sect, Report No. 65, 26; "Account by Maj Cavanagh"; 145.2Q1011(D5), "Account of the Attack by the Camerons of Canada on Fontenay-le-Marmion Night 7/8 Aug 44 Given by Lt John Graham to Capt Engler at Fontenay-le-Marmion," 11 Aug 44, 1.

20. DHH, "Account by Maj Cavanagh."

21. Pearce was awarded the Distinguished Conduct Medal. Nicholson, *Gunners of Canada*, 316; DHH, "Account by Lt Graham," 1.

22. DHH, Hist Sect, "Report No. 65," 26; Stacey, *Victory Campaign*, 219-220.

23. DHH, "Account by Lt Graham," 2.

24. DHH, 145.257011 (D6), "Account of the Attack by the S Sask R on Rocquancourt 8 Aug 44 given by Maj Courtneay, "A" Coy, S Sask R, to Capt Engler," 10 Aug 44.

Chapter Ten: 8 August 1944 – The German Reaction

1. *SS-Sturmbannführer* Erich Olboeter (1917-1944) was noticeably younger than his contemporaries in 12. SS-*Panzerdivision*. He had served in the invasion of the west, in the Balkans and on the Eastern Front. On 2 September 1944 he died of wounds suffered when he was caught in an ambush by the Belgian resistance.

2. *SS-Obersturmbannführer* Max Wünsche (1914-1995) joined the *SS-Verfunungstruppe* in 1934 and was commissioned in 1936. He was a "poster boy" for Aryan manhood – tall, blond and muscular – and served as an orderly for Hitler during the invasion of Poland, much to his chagrin. Wünsche commanded a panzer grenadier company in the west, where he was wounded. He then served as divisional adjutant in the Balkans and commanded an assault gun battalion on the Eastern Front. He was transferred to 12. *SS-Panzerdivision* on its formation as commander of *SS-Panzerregiment* 12, which he led through the Normandy campaign. In the subsequent retreat he was wounded and captured.

3. Meyer, *12 SS History*, 170.

4. DHH, Report No. 50, 101.

5. While Kurt Meyer claimed in his interrogation that the tanks of *Kampfgruppe* Krause had arrived on the morning of 8 August and participated in the counterattack and subsequent operations, this is at odds with the divisional history and the version of events on pp. 158-160 of the English edition of his memoirs. The available evidence suggests that Krause's *bataillon* was part of *Kampfgruppe* Wünsche. DHH, "Special Interrogation Report Brigadeführer Kurt Meyer, Comd 12 SS Pz Div 'Hitler Jugend' (6 June 1944–25 Aug 1944)," 24 Aug 45, 7-8; H. Meyer, *12 SS History*, 172; Kurt Meyer, *Grenadiers*,

6. Meyer omitted a company of *Jagdpanzers* of *SS-Panzerjägerabteilung* 12 from the list in his memoirs. Kurt Meyer, *Grenadiers*, 158.

7. *SS-Brigadeführer* Kurt Meyer (1910-1961) was one of those rare individuals with an almost instinctive ability to read a battle. Although he suffered from a foot injury that required an orthopedic shoe, he joined the Nazi party in 1925 and the police force in 1929 and then transferred to the *Leibstandarte* in 1934. Meyer fought as the company commander of the 14th and then the 15th companies in Poland in 1939 and in the west in 1940. That August he was promoted to *SS-Sturmbannführer* and given command of a reconnaissance battalion, which he led in the Balkans campaign of April 1941 and in the invasion of the Soviet Union. He was promoted *SS-Obersturmbannführer* on 11 November 1942 and transferred to 12. *SS-Panzerdivision* in 1943 on its formation.

Meyer led *SS-Panzergrenadierregiment* 25 in the early days of the Normandy campaign and then took command of the division when its commander was killed. Unfortunately while a regimental commander, soldiers under his command murdered a number of Canadian prisoners in separate incidents at his headquarters. In December 1945 Meyer was convicted in complicity in these crimes and sentenced to death by a court-martial, although this was later commuted to life in prison. He was released in 1954.

8. *Generalleutnant* Kurt Chill (1895-?) had served in the infantry in the First World War and rejoined the *Wehrmacht* in 1937. He assumed command of I. *Bataillon, Grenadierregiment* 1 on 1 September 1939 and then served as a tactics instructor during most of 1940. Chill then led 122. *Infanteriedivision*, originally as an *Oberst*, before taking command of 85. *Infanteriedivision* on 1 February 1944. In the Scheldt fighting he commanded *Kampfgruppe* Chill with considerable skill, which led to his appointment to lead LV. *Armeekorps* on 5 February 1945.

9. *SS-Sturmbannführer* Max Waldmüller (1912-1944) served in the 1941 Balkans campaign and on the Eastern Fromt before his transfer to 12. *SS-Panzerdivision*. He was ambushed and killed by Belgian partisans on 8 September 1944 in the Ardennes as the division withdrew back to Germany.

10. *SS-Standartenführer* Wilhelm Mohnke (1911-?), a native of Lubeck, joined the Nazi party in September 1931 and the SS two months later. He was commissioned in 1933 and commanded *Nr.* 5. *Kompanie* of the *Leibstandarte* in the Polish campaign and in the opening stages of the attack in the west. Mohnke took command of II. *Bataillon* on 28 May after the CO was wounded. He commanded the battalion in the Balkans campaign, where he lost his foot during a Yugoslavian air attack. He did not return to active service until early 1942 but was transferred to the replacement battalion in March. Mohnke was posted to 12. *SS-Panzerdivision* on its formation as a regimental commander, led his unit in Normandy and took command of 1. *SS- Panzerdivision* in late August 1944. Promoted to *SS-Brigadeführer* on 30 January, 1945, he was wounded once again in an air raid and evacuated. Follow-

ing his recovery, he commanded the defence of the Reichs Chancellery and was captured by the Russians, remaining in captivity until 1955. Mohnke was implicated in the murder of British prisoners in May 1940 and Canadian prisoners, chiefly from the Royal Winnipeg Rifles, in June 1944, but was never brought to justice, dying a few years ago.

11. Kurt Meyer, *Grenadiers*, 157.

12. Kurt Meyer, *Grenadiers*, 157.

13. A more dramatic version of events may be found in Hubert Meyer's history of 12. *SS-Panzerdivision.* Unfortunately the interrogation report suffers in that the author did not differentiate between Meyer's statements and his own summary and editorial comments. DHH, "Meyer Interrogation Report," 7; Meyer, *12 SS History*, 172.

14. *SS-Hauptsturmführer* Michael Wittmann (1914-1944) was the leading panzer "ace" of the war with 143 kills of Allied armoured vehicles to his credit. He had enlisted in the SS on 1 November 1936 and transferred to the *Leibstandarte* five months later. Although originally an infantryman, Wittmann served in the Balkans and in the invasion of the Soviet Union as a crewman in a *Sturmgeschütz* unit commanded by Max Wünsche. Wittmann was commissioned on 12 December, 1942 and served in Tigers for the rest of his career.

15. Meyer, *12 SS History*, 172.

Chapter Eleven: Mopping Up

1. Letter, Gordon to Col G.W.L. Nicholson, 1 Feb 60 (copy in author's collection)

2. English, *Canadian Army*, 274; Jarymowycz, "Canadian Armour in Normandy" in *Canadian Military History*, Spring 1998, Vol. 7, No. 2, 22-23.

3. Kurt Meyer, *Grenadiers*, 158-159; Hubert Meyer, *12 SS History*, 172.

4. NAC, War Diary 2 CAB, "Op 'Totalize'," Aug 44.

5. 2 CID HQ was notified by 4 CIB at 0745 hrs. NAC, RG 24 Vol. 14093, Reel T 11417, Ops Log, 4 CIB, Sheet 146, Sers 239, 243, 8 Aug 44.

6. NAC, RG 24, Vol 13624, Main HQ FCA Ops Log, Sheet 6, Serial 36, 8 Aug 44.

7. Zetterling, *Normandy 1944*, 184-185.

8. English, *Canadian Army*, 271-272.

9. NAC, Ops Log, 4 CIB, Sheet 146, ser. 241, 8 Aug 44.

10. Intelligence Section, *8 Reconnaissance Regiment History*, 8.

11. NAC, Ops Log, 4 CIB, Sheet 147, Ser 251, 8 Aug 44.

12. NAC, Ops Log, 4 CIB, Sheet 148, Sers 257, 260, 261, 264, 265, 266, 8 Aug 44.

13. NAC, Ops Log, 4 CIB, Sheet 151, Sers 300, 302, 8 Aug 44; BAOR *Battlefield Tour*, 25.

14. BAOR *Battlefield Tour*, 50.

15. DHH, 145.2F2011(D4), "Account of the Attack and Capture of May-sur-Orne by Fus MR, Night of 7/8 Aug 44, Given by Maj Brochu and Capt Lamothe to Capt Engler at Evaux and May-sur-Orne," 12 Aug 44., 2.

16. DHH, 314.009(D324), "Report on Emp of Flame Throwers in Attacks on May-sur-Orne and Secqueville La Campagne on 8 Aug 44."

17. DHH, Account by Brochu and Lamothe, 2.

18. DHH, 141.4A6011(D1), "Account of "C" Squadron, 6 Cdn Armd Regt, Action at Fontenay-le- Marmion Given by Lt-Col A.D.A. Marks to Capt J.W. Monahan at Historical Section, C.M.H.Q., Acton," 17 Jun 46.

19. DHH, 145.2Q1011(D5), "Account of the Attack by the Camerons of Canada on Fontenay-le- Marmion Night 7/8 Aug 44 by Lt John Graham to Capt Engles at Fontenay-le-Marmion," 11 Aug 44, 2.

20. NAC, Ops Log, 4 CIB, Sheet 148, Sers 259, 260, 261, 263, 264, 8 Aug 44.

21. DHH, 145.2R14011(D4), "Account of the Attack on Pt 46 – (0655) 8 Aug 44 by RHLI as Given by Adjt. RHLI," 10 Aug 44, 2.

22. Goodspeed, *Battle Royal*, 442; Transcript of Radley-Walters taped narrative, Aug 2001; Blackburn, *Guns of Normandy*, 335-336.

23. Hubert Meyer, *12 SS History*, 173.

24. Kurt Meyer, *Grenadiers*, 152-153.

25. Kurt Meyer, *Grenadiers*, 158-159.

26. Letter, Gordon to Nicholson, 1 Feb 66.

27. BAOR *Battlefield Tour*, 26.

28. PRO, WO 171/640, War Diary HQ 33 BAB, Sheet 4, 8 Aug 44.

29. NAC, War Diary 2 CAB," *Op 'Totalize';*" Appx 7, Aug 44.

30. Zaporzan, *Rad's War*, 241-242.

31. Neville *First Northamptonshire Yeomanry*, 29.

32. Jolly, *Blue Flash*, 48.

33. Neville, *First Northamptonshire Yeomanry*, 28.

34. Marc Milner, "Reflections on Caen, Bocage and the Gap: A Naval Historian's Critique of the Normandy Campaign," *Canadian Military History*, Spring 1998, Vol. 7, No. 2 (Waterloo, 1998), 17.

35. DHH, "RAF Narrative," fn (1), 95.

36. Patrick Agte, *Michael Wittmann and the Tiger Commanders of the Leibstandarte*, 430.

37. Kurt Meyer, *Grenadiers*, 158-159.

38. Meyer, *Grenadiers*, 159.

39. Ken Tout, *Tank!*, 134-135.

40. Neville, *First Northamptonshire Yeomanry*, 29.

41. Neville, *First Northamptonshire Yeomanry*, 29-30.

42. Zaporzan, *Rad's War*, 248-249.

43. Jolly, *Blue Flash*, 51.

44. Neville, *First Northamptonshire Yeomanry*, 30-33.

45. Neville, *First Northamptonshire Yeomanry*, 33-34.

46. PRO, WO 171/859, War Diary, 1 NY, Sheet 3, 8 Aug 44.

47. PRO, War Diary 1 BW, 8 Aug 44.

48. BAOR *Battlefield Tour*, 26.

49. Stacey, *Victory Campaign*, 225.

50. DHH, 145.2R6011(D2), "Account of the Attack on Quilly 8 Aug 44 by the R de Mais as given by Lt-Col H.L. Bisaillin, CO, to Capt Engler at Quilly," 11 Aug 1944.

51. BAOR *Battlefield Tour*, 26; Stacey, *Victory Campaign*, 220.

Chapter Twelve: Phase 2 Commences

1. *Generał dywizji* Stanisław Maczek (1892-1994). Active service in First World War in Hapsburg army as a company and battalion commander and formation operations staff officer. Fought in Bolshevik War 1919-1920 as operations officer, 5 Infantry Division and battalion commander, 26 Infantry Regiment. Staff College, 1923-1924. Deputy Commander 76 Infantry Regiment, Commander 81 Infantry Regiment; Infantry Commander (arms advisor) 7 Infantry Division. Longtime apostle of mobility who worked hard to improve same in Polish army. Commander 10 Cavalry Brigade (Motorized), Poland 1937-1939. Escaped to France and commanded 10 Cavalry Brigade 1939-1940. Made his way to UK. Commanded 10 Cavalry Brigade UK 1941-1942. Commanded 1st Polish Armoured Division, UK and NWE 1942-1945. Commanded 1st Polish Corps UK 1945-1946. Retired 1949. Information provided by Major John Grodzinski, LdSH(RC), October 2002.

2. NAC, WD 4 CAD, Sheet 4, Aug 1944, 6-7 Aug; letter, Kitching to Brigadier General (retired) EAC Amy, 14 July 1988.

3. In the letter to Amy, Kitching wrote, "Guy was convinced we would meet heavy opposition in Cintheaux and would not change his plan. There was some doubt in his mind also whether he would be able to call off the bombing mission in time." Kitching, *Mud and Green Fields*, 192-193; letter, Kitching to Amy, 14 July 1988.

4. Reginald Roy seems to have relied, at least in part, on a paper written for him by General Kitching in 1980 or 1981. Roy, *The Canadians in Normandy*, 192-193; DHH 81/150, letter, Roy to Dr. W.A.B. Douglas, Directorate of History, with attached Kitching paper, 29 January 1981.

5. English, *Canadian Army*, 271.

6. Marteinson, *RCAC History*, 263.

7. NAC, Crerar Papers, Vol. 2, letter GOC 8-3, Simonds to Crerar, 6 Aug 44.

8. Marteinson, *RCAC History*, 263.

9. Kitching, *Mud and Green Fields*, 192.

10. NAC, RG 24 Vol 13712, War Diary 2 Cdn Corps, 1, 3 Aug 44.

11. NAC, Crerar Papers, Vol. 2, Outline Plan, 1 Aug 44.

12. NAC, RG 24, Vol. 10942, File 245.P1.013(D1), "Operational Report, C.O. 1 Polish Armd Div Fighting During the Period From 7-12 Aug 1944.," 13 Aug 44.

13. BAOR *Battlefield Tour*, 33.

14. BAOR *Battlefield Tour*, 33.

15. NAC, War Diary 2 Cdn Corps, Page 2, 5 Aug 44.

16. David O'Keefe, Compilation of Ultra Messages 30 July–8 Aug 44, author's collection.

17. This letter was signed at 2100 hrs, or 11 hours after Simonds had issued his orders. NAC, Crerar Papers, Vol 2, letter Simonds to Crerar, Operation "Totalize," 6 Aug 44.

18. Kitching, *Mud and Green Fields*, 193.

19. NAC, RG 24 Vol. 14156, Reel T12391, War Diary 10 CIB, Page 5, 7 Aug 44.

20. NAC, RG 24, Vol. 14255, Reel T12722, War Diary 21 CAR, 8 Aug 44; Vol. 14260, Reel T12727, War Dairy 22 CAR, Page 3, 7 Aug 44.

21. RG 24 Vol. 14248, Reel T12714, War Diary 18 CACR, Sheet 5, 8 Aug 44.

22. Brigadier Leslie Booth (1906-1944), who was born in the United Kingdom, was a militia officer in the 1st Hussars of London, Ontario. He commanded the Three Rivers Regiment (12th Canadian Armoured Regiment) in the United Kingdom, Sicily and Italy before being named to command the 4th Armoured Brigade.

23. Marteinson, *RCAC History*, 263; Terry Copp, *Fields of Fire: The Canadians in Normandy*, 194.

24. Extracts from letter Kitching to Brigadier EAC Amy, 14 July 1986, author's collection.

25. *Military Training Pamphlet No. 41: The Tactical Handling of the Armoured Division and its Components, Part 2, The Armoured Regiment*, 1943, 22.

26. E.A.C. Amy, "Normandy, 1 Squadron Canadian Grenadier Guards Phase 2 Operation Totalize 7/8 August 1944" (unpublished ms), 21 Feb 93, 2, author's collection.

27. NAC, RG 24, Reel T-17277, War Diary 22 CAR, Page 3, 7 Aug 44; Amy, "1 Squadron Canadian Grenadier Guards," 2-3.

28. NAC, War Diary 22 CAR, Page 3, 7 Aug 44; Amy, "1 Squadron Canadian Grenadier Guards," 3-4.

29. Amy, "1 Squadron Canadian Grenadier Guards," 4, iii, iv.

30. NAC, RG 24, Vol 13624, Main HQ FCA Ops Log, Sheet 6, Serial 36, 8 Aug 44.

31. Robert Spenser, *History of the Fifteenth Canadian Field Regiment*, 100-101; NAC, RG 24, War Diary, HQ RCA, 4 CAD, Sheets 3, 4, 8 Aug 44; War Diary, 23 Fd Regt (SP), 8 Aug 44; War Diary, 19 Army Fd Regt (SP), 2, 8 Aug 44 (both author's collection).

32. D'Este, *Decision in Normandy*, 426.

33. The log entry reads "4 Armd Div will take care of GAUMESNIL and lay on fire plan through RCA 4 Div. To Comd Post – Advised that 4 Div would look after GAUMESNIL. We will neither attack nor send in patrols because bomb line located to NORTH of it." NAC, War Diary 2 CID, Sheet 374, Serial 4421, 8 Aug 44

34. NAC, RG 24, Vol. 13712, Operations Log, 2 Canadian Corps, Ops Log, Sheet 10, Serial 75.

35. Goodspeed, *Battle Royal*, 443.

36. Zaporzan, *Rad's War*, 253; Goodspeed, *Battle Royal*, 443.

37. NAC, War Diary HQ 4 CAD, Ops/Int Log Sheets 2 and 3, Serials 46, 51, 73, 76 and 77, 8 Aug 44.

38. DHH 81/849, mfm, "Tactical Operations of the Eighth Air Force 6 June 1944 – 8 May 1945," U.S. Air Force Historical Study No. 70, Air University, 1952.

39. DHH 86/285, "The Liberation of North-West Europe, Volume IV, The Break-Out and the Advance to the Lower Rhine, 12 June to 30 September, 1944," 95; 81/881, mfm., "The Employment of Strategic Bombers in a Tactical Role, 1941-1951," U.S. Air Force Historical Study No. 88, Air University, 1955, 82.

40. Captain J.C. Stewart, unpublished account of operations in Normandy, author's collection.

41. Cassidy, *Warpath*, 97.

42. <http://collections.ic.gc.ca/chp12a.htm>

43. Sitrep, 2 Cdn Corps, 8 Aug 44, quoted in Perrun, "Missed Opportunities," 133.

44. The number of casualties was taken from the Polish operational report, while 4 Liaison war diary reported, "Main Div HQ and A2 echelon bombed by Fortresses while passing Caen. No Polish cas[ualties.]" NAC, Operational Report, CO 1 PAD, 2; PRO, WO 171/3465, War Diary No. 4 Liaison Headquarters Armoured, August 1944, 2, 8 Aug 44..

45. Polish Institute and Sikorski Museum, C. 10/I, Operations Log, 10 Armoured Cavalry Brigade, Sheet 2, 8 Aug 44.

46. NAC, RG 24 vol. 14401, War Diary, 7 Canadian Medium Regiment, August 1944, 2, 8 Aug 44.

47. Research showed that the neutralizing effects of heavy bombing had largely disappeared an hour after the last bomb was dropped. Copp, "Report No. 14, Heavy Bombing in Support of the Army," in Copp, *Montgomery's Scientists*, 99-106.

Chapter Thirteen: The Tanks Advance

1. Amy, "1 Squadron, CGG," 7.

2. Zaporzan, *Rad's War*, 253-254.

3. Amy, "1 Squadron, CGG," 6.

4. Craig Smith, quoted in Amy, "1 Squadron, CGG," ii-iii; quoted in Fred Gaffen, *Cross-Border Warriors: Canadians in American Forces, Americans in Canadian Forces, From the Civil War to the Gulf*, 125-127.

5. Marteinson, *RCAC History*, 169-170.

6. NAC, RG 24 Vol 14260, Reel T 12727, War Diary 22 CAR, Page 5, 8 Aug 44; *Military Train-*

ing Pamphlet No 41: The Armoured Regiment, 48.

7. Al Page, quoted in Amy, "1 Squadron, CGG," vii.

8. Stewart, unpublished account.

9. NAC, War Diary 22 CAR, Page 5, 8 Aug 44.

10. Fortescue Duguid, *History of the Canadian Grenadier Guards 1760-1964*, 264.

11. G.D. Adams, interview.

12. Private diary, Lance Corporal Harry Ruch, cited in Robert Fraser, *Black Yesterdays: The Argylls' War*, 223-224.

13. Fraser, *Black Yesterdays*, 224.

14. NAC, RG 24, War Diary, HQ 10 CIB, Page 5, 8 Aug 44; Graves, *South Albertas*, 113.

15. Unless otherwise noted, the material on 1 PAD operations is taken from the division's report on operations. NAC, "1 PAD Operational Report," 1-2, 13.

16. Although the unit reported the Germans as 20 Tigers, the panzers undoubtedly were a combination of types. "*2. Pulk zatrzmany przez 20 Tygrysowcw rej. 108556.*" Polish Museum and Sikorski Institute, C. 10/1, Log 10 Armoured Cavalry Brigade, Sheet 2, 8 Aug, 1944.

17. Anon, *24 Pulk Ulanow* (Germany, 1947), 36.

18 .War Office, *Field Service Pocket Book, Part I – Pamphlet No. 1, Glossary of Military Terms*, 10.

19. Kitching, *Mud and Green Fields*, 196.

20. NAC, 1 PAD Operational Report, 3.

21. Tout, *Fine Night for Tanks*, 111-113.

Chapter Fourteen: The German Dilemma

1. Hist Sect, "Information from German Sources," 104-105.

2. Hist Sect, "Information from German Sources," 106-107.

3. Hist Sect, "Information from German Sources," 107-108.

4. The statement on p. 176 of Hubert Meyer's history of 12. *SS-Panzerdivision* that the battle group was based on I. *SS-Panzergrenadierregiment* 26 is in error.

5. Meyer, *12 SS History*, 176.

6. Meyer, *12 SS History*, 176.

Chapter Fifteen: Worthington Force

1. Kitching, *Mud and Green Fields*, 195.

2. Transcript of interview, Major General (retired) George Kitching with Donald E. Graves, Edmonton, 23 May 1998, author's collection.

3. Kitching, *Mud and Green Fields*, 145-146.

4. When pressed by Graves, who was possibly the last historian to interview Kitching before his death, as to why he did not immediately relieve Booth of command, Kitching said that Booth had not yet done anything to warrant his relief. When Graves responded by asking what Kurt Meyer would have done under similar circumstances, Kitching replied that Booth would never have achieved his command in 12. *SS-Panzerdivision*, which, to be fair, was accurate. Kitching also admitted that on at least two previous occasions (neither in action), he had seen Booth totally incapacitated because of over-indulgence in alcohol, but the brigadier had reassured him that he never drank in the field. Last, Kitching added that he had been taken aback when Simonds suggested that Booth take command of 3rd Canadian Infantry Division when he first heard Keller had been wounded on the afternoon of 8 August. Kitching Interview, 23 May 1998.

5. Kitching, *Mud and Green Fields*, 195-196.

6. C. Robertson, "An Account of the Battle Experience of "A" Company Algonquin Regiment, August 8 to 11, 1944," Aug 44, 2, author's collection.

7. This location is taken from the sketch map prepared by Major L.C. Monk of the Algonquin Regiment as part of his report on the action. Unless otherwise noted, the description is taken from his account. DHH, "Report No. 65," 33; L. Monk, "An Account of the Battle Participation of the Algonquin Regiment between August 6 and August 11, 1944," Aug 44, author's collection.

8. NAC, Reel T-12764, War Diary British Columbia Regiment, Aug 1944, Sheet 6.

9. PRO, WO 171/1265, War Diary, 11 Medium Regiment, RA, Appendix B, "Account of an Armoured Battle on 8th August 1944 by Capt. M.A. Searle, 11 Med. Regt. R.A. F.O.O.," Aug 1944, 1.

10. NAC, War Diary British Columbia Regiment, Aug 1944, Sheet 6.

11. Anon, *The Story of the British Columbia Regiment 1939-1945*, no pagination.

12. NAC, War Diary British Columbia Regiment, Aug 1944, Sheet 7.

13. NAC, War Diary, British Columbia Regiment, Aug 1944, Sheet 6.

14. Kurt Meyer, *Grenadiers*, 162; Hubert Meyer, *12 SS History*, 177.

15. "Meitzel' is the spelling used in Hubert Meyer's *The History of the 12. SS-Panzerdivision Hitlerjugend*, while "Meitzell" appeared in the *Canadian Army Journal* articles. Bernhard-Georg Meitzel, "Caen-Falaise" Part Two, *Canadian Army Journal*, May 1950 (Ottawa, 1950), 71.

16. Hubert Meyer, *12 SS History*, 177; Kurt Meyer, *Grenadiers*, 161-163.

17. Kurt Meyer, *Grenadiers*, 163.

18. NAC, War Diary, British Columbia Regiment, Aug 1944, Sheets 6.

19. PRO, Searle Account, 1.

20. NAC, War Diary, British Columbia Regiment, Aug 1944, Sheet 7.

21. NAC, War Diary, British Columbia Regiment, Aug 1944, Sheets 8-9.

22. Keith Stirling, "An Account of the Battle Experience of "D" Company, Algonquin Regiment, Aug. 8, 9, 10, 11, 12, 1944," Aug 44; G.L. Cassidy, "Outline of Events (A, D, HQ and Sp. Coys, Algonquin Regiment, Aug. 9-12, 1944," para 4 (both author's collection).

23. DHH, "Report No. 65," 36.

24. Cassidy, "Outline of Events" para 5.

25. Ken Gartley, "The Algonquins First Battle Experience," Aug 44, 2 (Author's Collection).

26. War Diary, The Algonquin Regiment, Appendix A, L. Monk, "Eye witness account of battle at Hill 140 near BRETTEVILLE LE RABET, NORMANDY Aug 8-9 1944," 2, Aug 1944 (author's collection).

27. Kitching, *Mud and Green Fields*, 196; Kitching's statement is in a videotaped record of 4 Allied Tactical Air Force Canadian Officers' Tour of Normandy, 1991, loaned by Donald E. Graves, who was present.

28. NAC, War Diary, 19 Army Field Regiment (Self Propelled), 3, 9 Aug 44.

29. Nicholson, *Gunners of Canada*, 319; NAC, War Diary 23 Field Regiment (SP), 10 Aug 1944.

30. Anon, *19 Canadian Army Field Regiment RCA: Regimental History September 1941–July 1945* (Deventer, 1945), 46-47.

31. Stewart, Normandy ms, 9.

32. NAC, RG 24, vol. 14248, reel T 12714, War Diary 18 Canadian Armoured Car Regiment, 7, 9 Aug 44.

33. PRO, "Searle Account," 2.

34. Michael Reynolds suggests the infantry were from *Kampfgruppe* Krause. Kurt Meyer, *Grenadiers*, 162 and Reynolds *Steel Inferno*, 241.

35. The 4 Armoured Brigade Log includes a report from the second-in-command of the British Columbia Regiment that seven tanks had made their way back to his location near Gaumesnil. DHH, Report No. 65, 36; NAC, 4 Canadian Armoured Brigade Log, Sheet 2, 9 Aug.

36. Kurt Meyer, *Grenadiers*, 163.

37. NAC, "1 Polish Armoured Division Operational Report," 3; K. Jamar, *With the Tanks of the 1st Polish Armoured Division*, 66-67.

38. Gartley, "First Battle," 2; Cassidy, *Warpath*, 116.

39. PRO, "Searle Account," 2-3.

40. DHH, "Report No. 65," 37.

41. Cassidy, *Warpath*, 115-116.

42. NAC, War Diary 4 Canadian Armoured Brigade, Ops/Int Log, Sheet 1, 9 Aug 1944.

Chapter Sixteen: The Day of Burning Shermans

1. DHH, "Report No 65," 37; NAC, War Diary 22 Canadian Armoured Regiment, Pages 5, 6, 9 Aug 1944; Stirling, "Battle Experience of D Company," Aug 1944.

2. DHH, "Report No. 65," 37-38; Rogers, *Lincoln and Welland Regiment*, 141; Graves, *South Albertas*, 115.

3. Anon, *Governor General's Foot Guards*, 100-101; NAC, War Diary, 21 Canadian Armoured Regiment, 9 Aug 1944; Robertson, "Battle Experience of A Company," Aug 1944.

4. Robertson, "Battle Experience of A Company," Aug 1944.

5. Anon, *Governor General's Foot Guards*, 102-103.

6. Robertson, "Battle Experience of A Company," Aug 1944.

7. Anon, *Governor General's Foot Guards*, 101-104; Robertson, "Battle Experience of A Company," Aug 1944.

8. NAC, 1 Polish Armoured Division Operational Report," 3, Aug 1944.

9. NAC, "1st Polish Armoured Division Operational Report," 3, Aug 1944.

10. NAC, "1st Polish Armoured Division Operational Report," 3-4, Aug 1944; Anon, *24 Pulk Ulanow*, 36.

11. NAC, "1st Polish Armoured Division Operational Report," 4, Aug 1944.

12. Meyer, *12 SS History*, 178.

Chapter Seventeen: Opportunity Lost

1. USNA, RG 338 MS B-256, Paul Danhauser, "Commitment of the 271 Infantry Division" (Eng trans.), Encl 8, 1 Oct 1946,

2. DHH, "Report No. 65," 38-40.

3. DHH, "Report No. 65," 40.

4. NAC, First Canadian Army Operation Logs, Sheet 22, Serial 131, 9 Aug 1944; "1st Polish Armoured Division Operational Report," 4, Aug 1944; DHH, "Report No. 65," 40, Aug 1944.

5. NAC, War Diary, 18 Canadian Armoured Car Regiment, pp. 6, 7, 9 Aug 1944.

6. Stirling, "Battle Experience of D Company," Aug 1944.

7. NAC, War Diary, 10 Canadian Infantry Brigade, p. 5, 9 Aug 1944.

8. Rogers, *Lincoln and Welland Regiment*, 142.

9. Fraser, *Black Yesterdays*, 227.

10. Stacey, *Victory Campaign*, 229.

11. DHH, Hist Section, *Report No. 65*, 40; Cassidy, *Warpath*, 112; Graves, *South Albertas*, 115.

12. DHH, "Report No. 65," 41.

13. Hubert Meyer, *12 SS Panzer History*, 179; Kurt Meyer, *Grenadiers*, 164.

14. Stewart Papers, "Sidelines on TOTALIZE," 8-9.

15. While Zetterling claims that the battalion as such did not fight in Normandy, the fourth company was attached to 2 Panzer Division. Another B IV company, *Panzerkompanie 316*, also saw action in Normandy. Canadian intelligence summaries during TOTALIZE included reports of prisoners from 301 Panzer Battalion. Meyer, *12 SS History*, 179; Zetterling, *Normandy 1944*, 188, 189.

16. Kurt Meyer, *Grenadiers*, 164; Hubert Meyer, *12 SS History*, 179; Stacey, *Victory Campaign*, 229.

17. Stewart, "TOTALIZE," 9.

18. DHH, Hist Section, "Report No. 65," 41.

19. Anon, *Governor General's Foot Guards*, 105.

20. Rogers, *Lincoln and Welland Regiment*, 143, Stacey, *Victory Campaign*, 230; Cassidy, *Warpath*, 112-113.

21. Once again, 4th Canadian Armoured Division was attempting to use tanks unsupported by infantry to advance on and capture an objective, in this case point 206. Not only that, the key ground around the point 195 feature had 4 Canadian Armoured Brigade superimposed on top of 10 Canadian Infantry Brigade. Stacey, *Victory Campaign*, 230; NAC,

22. War Diary, 4 CAB, Aug 1944, 10 Aug 44, 5.

22. NAC, "1st Polish Armoured Division Operational Report," 4; DHH, "Report No. 65," 42.

Chapter Eighteen: With a Bang, Not a Whimper

1. Stacey, *Victory Campaign*, 230; PRO, War Diary 1 Lothians and Border Yeomanry, Appendix J/2, Sheet 2, 6 Aug 1944.

2. After the conclusion of the Normandy campaign, Spragge would move sideways to take command of 7 Brigade, an appointment he would hold until 20 February 1945 when he was relieved for his failure to take Moyland Wood.

3. DHH, "Report No. 65," 43.

4. Hubert Meyer, *12 SS History*, 180.

5. Roy, *The Canadians in Normandy*, 227.

6. W. Barnard, *The Queen's Own Rifles of Canada 1860-1960*, 215.

7. Charles Martin, *Battle Diary: From D-Day and Normandy to the Zuider Zee and VE*, 55-56.

8. Barnard, *Queen's Own Rifles*, 216-217.

9. Martin, *Battle Diary*, 57-58; Stacey, *Victory Campaign*, 230-231; Barnard, *Queen's Own Rifles*, 217.

10. <http:collections.ic.gc.ca/regiment/chp13a.htm>

11. <http.collections.ic.gc.ca/regiment/chp13.ahtm>

12. <http://collections.ic.gc.ca/regiment/chp13a.htm>

13. Stacey, *Victory Campaign*, 230-231.

14. NAC, First Canadian Army Operation Logs, Sheet 22, Serial 131, 9 Aug 1944.

15. Gerald Nicholson, *Canadian Expeditionary Force 1914-1919*, 418.

16. Stacey, *Victory Campaign*, 236.

17. NAC, First Canadian Army Operations Log, Sheet 4, Ser 27, 11 Aug 1944.

18. Stacey, *Victory Campaign*, 232.

19. Stacey, *Victory Campaign*, 234; Hubert Meyer, *12 SS History*, 182.

20. Stacey, *Victory Campaign*, 231.

Epilogue: Operation Totalize: Facts versus Myths

1. Stacey, *Victory Campaign*, 201.

2. BAOR *Battlefield Tour*, 25.

3. D'Este, *Decision in Normandy*, 424.

4. BAOR *Battlefield Tour*, 21-22.

5. Kurt Meyer, *Grenadiers*, 158-159.

6. NAC, Ops/Int Log 4 Armoured Brigade, Sheet 1, Serial 14, 8 Aug 1944; *Operational Report, C.O. 1 Polish Armd Div*, 2, 13 Aug 44.

7. See, for example, his memoirs. Both John English and Roman Jarymowycz appear to have bought into his argument completely, in the former's case at least as pertains to the Polish division, while Michael Reynolds, although still accepting the gist of it, is more circumspect. Kurt Meyer, *Grenadiers*, 159-160; English, *Canadian Army*, 278; Jarymowycz, *Tank Tactics*, 170-172; Reynolds, *Steel Inferno*, 236-237;

8. Interview, Kitching with Graves, 23 May 1998.

9. Kurt Meyer, *Grenadiers*, 160.

10. NAC, Main HQ FCA Ops Log, Sheet 6, Serial 36, 8 Aug 44.

11. Letter, Gordon to Nicholson, 1 February 1966.

12. Kurt Meyer, *Grenadiers*, 159.

13. BAOR *Battlefield Tour*, 32-33; Graves, *South Albertas*, 120.

14. BAOR *Battlefield Tour*, 9.

15. NAC, *1 Polish Armd Div Operational Report*, 3.

16. The Sicilian campaign lasted 38 days, while he only commanded his division in Italy from 3 to 22 September before falling prey to jaundice, and he had resumed command in October for no more than a fortnight before he was appointed to command the 5th Canadian Armoured Division on 1 November 1943. He did not lead the armoured division in battle before he was promoted and returned to England to take command of his corps.

Appendix A: The Dilemma of Normandy

1. This is an complex matter which is subject to subjective interpretation and selective uses of sources. Zetterling attempts to conduct an objective discussion to prove that the German army had the edge on the Allies and is largely successful. For an example of an argument that takes the opposite tack and sometimes reverts to emotional appeals, see *Fields of Fire* by Copp. Neillands sums up the situation succinctly in *The Battle of Normandy, 1944* while conceding German battlefield superiority. Zetterling, *Normandy 1944*, 87-99; Copp, *Fields of Fire*, 5-13; Neillands, *Normandy*, 407.

2. Robert Kennedy, Department of the Army Pamphlet No. 20-255, *The German Campaign in Poland (1939)*, 8-10.

3. Kennedy, *Campaign in Poland*, 11-12.

4. For recent analysis of the extent of British armour theorists on the interwar German army, see Robert M. Citino, *Quest for Decisive Victory. From Stalemate to Blitzkrieg in Europe*, and James S. Corum, *The Roots of Blitzkrieg. Hans von Seeckt and German Military Reform*; Heinz Guderian, *Panzer Leader*, 20.

5. Guderian, *Panzer Leader*, 45-46, 49.

6. Stephen Fritz, *Frontsoldaten: the German soldier in World War II*, 159.

7. Fritz, *Frontsoldaten*, 90.

8. Fritz, *Frontsoldaten*, 237-238.

9. Radley-Walters, taped narrative, August 2001.

10. Lockhart Fulton, in "I'm not sure how, but somehow we've lost direction," Richard Foot, *Ottawa Citizen*, 25 September 2004.

Appendix D: Air Power in Support of the Land Battle in 21st Army Group

1. U.S. historian Carlo D'Este devotes a chapter to discussing the air command structure and its relationship with both the land forces and the strategic air forces. While acknowledging that Montgomery had attempted to foster cooperation in principle, he paints him as the culprit for the strained relations between the services. D'Este, *Decision in Normandy*, 212-231.

2. John Terraine, *The Right of the Line, The Royal Air Force in the European War 1939-1945*, 608-609.

3. Terraine, *Right of the Line*, 609.

4. Montgomery, with his usual immodesty, claimed that "Not only did I have two badges in my beret: I was wearing two berets," referring to his positions as the overall commander of Allied ground forces and as the commander of 21st Army Group. Terraine, *Right of the Line*, 610-611.

5. Grodzinski, *First Canadian Army*, 111, 116-121.

6. Terraine, *Right of the Line*, 633.

7. Terraine, *Right of the Line*, 637-638.

8. Terraine, *Right of the Line*, 380-381.

9. Letter, Montgomery to Dempsey, 4 May 1944, D'Este, *Decision in Normandy*, 515-516.

10. In recent years two articles on the provision of air support to 21st Army Group have ap-

peared. Christopher Evans, "The Fighter-Bomber in the Normandy Campaign: The Role of 83 Group" in *Canadian Military History*, Vol. 8, No. 1, Winter 1999, 21-31; Paul Johnston, "Tactical Air Power Controversies in Normandy: A Question of Doctrine" in *Canadian Military History*, Vol. 9, No. 2, Spring 2000, 59-71; see also Bidwell, *Fire-Power*, 262.

11. McKee, *Caen*, 283.

12. Evans, "Fighter Bomber," 24; Zetterling, *Normandy 1944*, 42-45.

13. Johnston, "Tactical Air Power," 62.

14. Johnston, Tactical Air Power," 62-63.

15. War Office, *Field Service Pocket Book, Part I, Pamphlet No. 1, Glossary of Military Terms*, 9.

16. Grodzinski, *First Canadian Army*, 113-115.

17. Stacey, *Victory Campaign*, 202.

18. Simonds, quoted in Carmichael, *Canadian Magazine*, 19.

Appendix E: Who Killed Michael Wittman?

1. Agte, *Wittmann*, 423.

2. The total loss of British armoured vehicles at Villers-Bocage, after the leading British troops had been surrounded by German tanks and infantry, was 25 tanks, 14 half-tracks and 14 carriers. McKee, *Caen*, 108-111.

3. I located three websites devoted to Michael Wittmann on 5 May 2002 without much effort. At that time the titles and addresses were "Michael Wittmann (April 22, 1914–August 8, 1944)" <www.achtungpanzer.com/gen3. htm>, "Michael Wittmann" <www.sonnet. com/usr/aaron/witt.html> and "Michael Wittamnn" <http://users.pandora.be/dave. depickere/text/wittmann.html>.

4. The question was raised sometime after his death as a captured 49 (WR) Division situation report of July 1944 allegedly included "[a] reward is offered for *SS-Obergruppenführer* Sepp Dietrich, the notorious commander of the 1st SS Panzer Corps, dead or alive." The phrase used by Agte to describe this was "degenerate practice." Agte, *Wittmann*, 429-430.

5. This interrogation report was a combination of what appear to have been verbatim statements by Meyer and summaries of his words by the unnamed interrogator. No differentiation seems to have been made by the author as examples of both often appeared in the same paragraphs, without the use of quotation marks. While it cannot be stated with absolute certainty, this paragraph appears to have been a summary of Meyer's actual words. DHH, "Meyer Interrogation," 8.

6. This account erroneously puts the date of Wittmann's death as 9 August. Bernard-Georg Meitzell [sic], "Caen–Falaise," Part Two, in *Canadian Army Journal*, (Ottawa, May 1950), 73.

7. Stacey, *Victory Campaign*, 222.

8. Author's interview with BGen Radley-Walters, January 2002.

9. D'Este, *Decision in Normandy*, 459.

10. Agte, *Wittmann*, 430.

11. The entry in the unit war diary reads "Three Tiger (VI) reported moving towards A Sqn: and were brewed at 1240, 1247 and 1252 hours, all without loss." PRO, War Diary 1 Northamptonshire Yeomanry Sheets 2 and 3, 8 Aug 44; Hastings, *Overlord*, 351.

12. The extract from the diary shown on page 47 of the article in fact is a montage of two pages. The first line of the entry dealing with the destruction of the Tigers is on the bottom of one page, the remainder on the second. Les Taylor, "Michael Wittmann's Last Battle," in *After the Battle*, Number 48, (London, 1985), 46-53.

13. The claims of both units are also recorded in the brigade war diary. PRO, War Diary 144 RAC, sheet 6, 8 Aug 44; WO 171/640, War Diary HQ 33 Armd Bde, Sheet 4, 8 Aug 44.

14. "All regt records on hand were destroyed." A report of a survey of the site by 21 Army Group Operational Analysis personnel may be found in Copp, *Montgomery's Scientists*. NAC, War Diary 27 CAR, 8 August 1944; Copp, "Report No. 9, The Effect of 90 lb Fragmentation Bombs" in *Montgomery's Scientists*, 279-282.

15. Author interview, Jan 2002.

16. Agte, *Wittmann*, 429.

17. Agte, *Wittmann*, 424.

18. Agte, *Wittmann*, 429.

19. Agte, *Wittmann*, 429.

20. NAC, HQ 4 Cdn Armd Bde, Operations/Intelligence, Sheet 1, Serials 14-15, 8 August 1944.

21. NAC, RG 24 vol. 10457, Report No. 14, 1 Canadian Field Research Section, First Canadian Army, 14 Jun 45.

22. PRO, WO 171/878, War Diary 144 Regiment Royal Armoured Corps, sheet 6, 8 Aug 44

23. Jolly, *Blue Flash*, 51.

24. This account was compiled by Lieutenant Colonel Larry Zaporzan, RCAC, as part of his masters thesis on the career of Brigadier General S.V. Radley-Walters, CMM, DSO, MC, CD. I am grateful for his permission to use his work. Zaporzan, *Rad's War,* 241-249.

25. Agte, *Wittmann,* 424.

26. Neville, *First Northamptonshire Yeomanry,* 35, 29-30.

27. This change apparently occurred after a series of interviews on a 1999 research trip to Canada. Tout, *Tank!,* 125-127; *Fine Night for Tanks,* 89; *Bloody Battle for Tilly,* 151.

28. Schneider, *Tigers in Combat, Vol. II,* 259; Tout, *Fine Night for Tanks,* 90.

29. Taylor, "Michael Wittmann's Last Battle," 48.

30. Agte, *Wittmann,* 289.

31. Lord Thomas Boardman, letter to Radley-Walters, 13 Jun 99. Copy provided by BGen Radley-Walters, Jan 2002.

32. Zapozan, *Rad's War,* 241.

33. Boardman, letter to Radley-Walters, 13 Jun 99.

34. BAOR *Battlefield Tour Operation,* Map 5, 8.

35. Goodspeed, *Battle Royal,* map facing 438, 440-442.

36. PRO, Air 25/709, 84 Group RAF Operations Record Book August 1944, p. 8, Serial 18, 8 August 1944.

37. PRO, Air 25/698, 83 Group RAF Operations Record Book August 1944, no p., no ser.

38. PRO, 2 TAF Operations Record Book, Sheet 28, 8 Aug 44.

39. PRO, 83 Group Operations Record Book, 8 Aug 44.

Appendix F: Bron Pancerna: A Brief History of the 1st Polish Armoured Division

1. "Organizacja Polskich Sił Zbrojnych na Zachodzie n dzień 1.1. 1945 r;" Witold Biegański. *Wojska Polskiego Na Zachodzie: Formowanie, Działania, Bojowe,* Warszawa, 1967, 84-86; Stanisław Komornicki et al, *Wojsko Polski, 1939-1945,* Warszawa, 1984, 55, 56. Beginning in 1941, in a programme similar to CANLOAN, a number of Polish officers were assigned to British colonial units, joining British regiments in Eastern Africa and Burma.

2. These were the destroyers *Błyskawica, Grom* and *Burza.*

3. The future commander of the *1 Dywizja Pancerna, Generał brygady* Stanisław Maczek, was

commander of this camp.

4. Eight anti-tank companies were formed and each was attached to a French infantry division.

5. In 1944 most of these personnel escaped their exile and moved into France, providing a valuable reinforcement to Polish units in the west.

6. See *Polskie Sily Zbrojne w Drugiej Wojnie Swiatowey Tom II Kampanie Na Obczyz Czesc 1, Wrzesień 1939-Czerviec 1941.* Londyn, 1959, 37-58, 144-145. This multi-volume study was published by the Sikorski Institute in London, covered the operations of Polish forces throughout the war and, as a new regime was installed in Warsaw in 1945, is closest to being an "official" Polish history of the Second World War.

7. The corps was responsible for defending the coastline along the Firth of Tay and Firth of Forth in eastern Scotland from Arbroath–Dundee–Perth–Leuchars–St. Andrews, around Fife to Rosyth. See *Polskie Sily Zbrojne w Drugiej Wojnie Swiatowey Tom II Kampanie Na Obczyz Czesc 2.* Londyn, 1975, Map 19.

8. The large number of officers was a result of the number of headquarters personnel that had been evacuated from Poland and their were insufficient positions to employ them all. Various schemes attempted to employ surplus officers as "soldiers" during the day, such as their being used as crews for 12 armoured trains. Naturally, this created a host of other problems.

9. Soldiers in this brigade sported a black left epaulette on their battledress tunics, commemorating the black leather jackets worn by the 10. *Brygada Kawalerii Pancernej* from 1937-1940. In 1943, this dress distinction was extended to entire division. See Józef Dembinok et al, *Oznaki i Odznaki Polskicy Sił Zbroynych Na Zachodzie,* Katowice, 1984, 26.

10. Bieganski, *Wojska Polskiego na Zachodzie,* 47-48.

11. *Generał* Władysław Sikorski, 1881-1943, assisted in the creation of several Polish patriotic organizations in Austria during the First World War. During the Russo-Polish War of 1918-1920, he commanded the 5th Army and in 1921 became Chief of the General Staff, after which he served briefly as Prime Minister of Poland. From 1925-28 he was Commander

of the Lwów Military District and between 1928 and 1939 devoted himself to political and military studies, writing a number of books, one of which, *Modern Warfare*, was translated into English and French. Following the September 1939 campaign, he arrived in France and was appointed Prime Minister of Poland and Commander in Chief on 7 November 1939. He was responsible for the establishment of naval, military and political cooperation treaties with Great Britain, the Czech Government in Exile, the Comité National Française and later the Soviet Union, and worked diligently to gain American support for the Polish cause. He also oversaw the creation of the Polish Armed Forces in the West. Sikorski was well respected by all wartime leaders and his tragic death in an aircraft crash off Gibraltar on 4 July 1943 was a setback for Polish post-war aspirations. His successors never developed the same rapport with western leaders. See Bohdan Wroński, et al, *Generał Sikorski: Premier, Naczelny Wódz*, Londyn: Instytut Polski I Muzeum Im. Gen. Sikorskiego w Londynie, 1981.

12. Dr Michael A. Peszke, "The Creation and Disposition of the Polish Armed Forces in Exile: A Brief Review of Significant Polish Literature," unpublished manuscript, 31-32.

13. Peszke, "Creation and Disposition of Polish Armed Forces," 33.

14. Other provisions such as the organization to be adopted for forces in the Middle East were also reached, but are not germane to the evolution of the 1st Polish Armoured Division.

15. Peske, 35, 36, 40.

16. Factors Affecting the Formation of a Polish Mechanized Corps," 4 November 1941, WO 216/19, File 38026, 4C.

17. The same situation would later arise with the command and control of the Polish Parachute Brigade, which was originally under the direct command of the Polish Commander in Chief, but passed to the General Officer Commanding British Parachute Forces.

18. "Factors Affecting the Formation of a Polish Mechanized Corps," 4 November 1941, WO 216/19, File 38026, 4A.

19. Sikorski to Churchill, 28 October 1941, WO 216/19 File 38026, 1A; "Notes of a Conversation with General Ragoulski, Polish M.A. and Colonel Galisz, Head of the I Bureau, Polish GHQ, 31 October 1941," WO 216/19, File 38026, 2A.

20. Brooke to Churchill, 4 December 1941, WO 216/19, File 38026, 2.

21. Sikorski to Brooke, February 1942, WO 216/19, File 38026, 20a.

22. The brigade included the following cavalry regiments: 10 *Pułk Strzelców Konnych,* 24 *Pułk Ułanów,* 14 *Pułk Ułanów* and a motorized battalion, the 10 *Pułk Dragonów.*

23. This brigade included the following armoured regiments: 1 *Pułk Pancerny,* 2 *Pułk Pancerny,* 3 *Pułk Pancerny,* and a motorized unit, the 16 *Baon Dragonów.*

24. The support group included: 1. *Pułk Artylerii Motorowej,* 1. *Pułk Artylerii Przeciwpancernej* (1 Anti-Tank Regiment), 1 *Pułk Artylerii Przeciwlotniczej* (1 Anti-Aircraft Regiment) and the 1 *Boan Strzelców* (1 Rifle Battalion).

25. Among these were the 1 *Pułk rozpoznawczy* (1 Reconnaissance Regiment), four communications squadrons, two engineer companies, a field park company, a movement control unit, a military police squadron and logistical support units.

26. *Polskie Siły Zbrojne w Drugiej Wojnie Swiatowey Tom II Kampanie Na Obczyz Czesc 2,* 132-133.

27. Commander in Chief Order 1220/org 43, dated 21 September 1943.

28. The Poles, like those in most other armies, found that the introduction of armour had created a rift between the cavalry, who had given up their horses for tanks, and the armoured units, which were "pure" tank units, created after the introduction of armour. This often led to wasteful argument over which branch should control armour matters.

29. This was also done during the reorganization of the 2nd and 3rd Canadian Army Tank/Armoured Brigades during 1943, when the more experienced formation headquarters and units were exchanged between the two. See Grodzinski, *First Canadian Army.*

30. This was the 10. *Pułk Strzelców Konnych,* or the 10th Mounted Rifle Regiment.

31. This was the 14 *Pułk Ułanów.*

32. Marian W. Żebowski, *Polska Broń Pancerna: Zarys Historii, 1918-1947,* 174, 409, 410.

33. In late 1944, the armoured brigade became an independent brigade, while the 2 *Dywizja Grenadierów-Pancery (Kadrowa),*

was reorganized as an infantry division in February 1945. It was preparing to deploy to the continent just as the war ended. Thus, had the war continued, I *Korpus Polski* would have moved to the continent and included one armoured division, one infantry division and an armoured brigade, plus certain corps level troops.

34. *Polskie Sily Zbrojne w Drugiej Wojnie Swiatowey Tom II Kampanie Na Obczyz Czesc 2*, 127.

35. Throughout the Normandy campaign, the division received replacement vehicles from E Squadron, 25 Canadian Armoured Delivery Regiment.

36. Bond to D.S.D., 8 November 1941, WO 219/19, File 38026, 8A.

37. Churchill to Brooke, 18 December 1941, WO 216/19, File 38026, 13A.

38. In 1939, one French R-38 and one British Matilda infantry tank had been received for trial.

39. These were equipped either with a 47 mm gun or twin machine guns.

40. Like the Vickers, there were two models of this tank. The 7TPdw had two turrets each with a 7.92 mm machine gun, while the 7TPjw had a 37 mm Bofors gun.

41. The 217 German tanks lost in the campaign were largely the result of anti-tank and artillery fire rather than encounters with other tanks.

42. Żebowski, *Polska Broń Pancerna*, 274-278; Steven Zaloga and Victor Madej, *The Polish Campaign 1939*, New York, 1985, 65.

43. Two units, the 10 *Pułk Strzelców Konnych* and the 24 *Pułk Ułanów* were the primary manoeuvre elements of the brigade and they would remain part of the brigade structure in France and England.

44. F.S. Kurcz (translated by Peter Jordan), *The Black Brigade*, Harrow, 1943, 4. The name given for the author, who is described as having been Chief of Staff of the 10th Mechanized Cavalry Brigade in Poland and France, was a pseudonym for Major Franciszek Skibiński, the actual Chief of Staff of the brigade, later holding several key appointments in 1 *Dywizja Pancerna*, although there is no evidence he wrote the book.

45. In France, members of the brigade took to wearing a poppy as a brigade symbol as the brigade commander's name, Maczek, means "poppy."

46. The allocation of Liaison HQs was as follows: No. 2(Belgian), No. 4 (Polish), No. 20 (French), No. 22 (Czech) and No. 23 (Royal Netherlands).

47. EXERCISE "LINK" Method of Working with 1 Polish Armd Div," RG 24, Volume 10,728, File 21C1.009(D80), 104.

48. "Minutes of Meeting Held on 7 November 1941 to Discuss Factors Affecting the Formation of a Polish Armoured Division," 9 November 1941, WO 216/19, File 38026, 7A.

49. "Liaison – Allied Contingents," 21 AGp/1987/G(SD), 6 June 1944, RG 24, Volume 10,604, File 215C1.(D86) Org. Polish Forces; WE – HQ No. 4 Liaison Armd (XIV/1233/1), 20 September 1944, RG 24, Volume 10,604, File 215C1.(D86) Org. Polish Forces, 32.

50. WE – HQ No. 4 Liaison Armd (XIV/1233/1), 20 September 1944, RG 24, Volume 10,604, File 215C1.(D86) Org. Polish Forces; WE – 4 Liaison HW (Polish Forces), 27 November 1944, RG 24, Volume 10,604, File 215C1.(D86) Org. Polish Forces, 14.

51. "Minutes of a Meeting Held on 7 November 1941, To Discuss the Factors Affecting the Formation of a Polish Armoured Division," 9 November 1941, WO 216/19, File 38026, 7C; Sikorski to Brooke, February 1942, WO 219/19, File 38026, 20a.

52. Żebowski, *Polska Broń Pancerna*, 409.

53. Stanisław Maczek, *Od Pdwody do Czogla*, Londyn, 1984, 140; Exercise "Link" – Preliminary Instrs, 60-5-26/Trg HQ First Cdn Army, 14 August 1943 NAC RG 24 Volume 10,728 File 219C1.009(D80), 1 and Index 1, 1.

54. EXERCISE "LINK" Preliminary Instruction," 14 August 1943, RG 24 Volume 10,728, Filed 219C1.009(D80); "Eastern Command Exercise "LINK" Director's Notes," RG 24 Volume 10,728, Filed 219C1.009(D80).

55. Eastern Command Exercise "LINK" Director's Notes," RG 24 Volume 10,728, Filed 219C1.009(D80), 17.

56. Antoni Grudziński, *1 Dywyzja Pancerna: Zaryz Historii Wojenny*, 67.

57. Grudziński, *I Dywizja Pancerna*, 67; Maczek, *Od Podwody do Czolga*, 146; Komornicki, *24 Pułk Ułanów*, 239; Dec, *Nawik I Falaise*, 194; *10. Pułk Strzelców Konnych*, Belgium, 1945, 16.

58. This training was offered at Catterick Camp, Farnborough and Sandhurst.

59. Żebowski, *Polska Broń Pancerna*, 431-434.

60. Crocker to Crerar, 11 January 1945; Crerar to Crocker 14 January 1945, both NAC MG 34 E157 Vol 2, File GOC-in-C 1-0-4/1.

61. Maczek was born in 1892 and die in the United Kingston in 1994.

62. Skibiński also commanded the 10. *Pułk Strzelców Konnych* from February 1942 to November 1943.

63. Grudziński also commanded the *Samodzielny Szwadron C.K.M.* during 1942 and 1943.

64. This officer commanded the *Batalion Strzelców Podhalańskich* during 1942.

65. Maczek, *Od Podwody do Czolga*, 148.

66. Stankiewicz commanded the 10. *Pułk Dragonów* from September 1945 to July 1946.

67. Dudzinski commanded the divisional machine gun battalion, the *Samodzielny Szwadron C.K.M.*, from August 1942 to March 1944.

68. This list comes from a detailed record of the divisional order of battle, comprising details of key appointments, movements, casualties, awards and insignia, in Grudziński, "1 Dywyzja Pancerna," 127-153.

69. Grudziński, *1 Dywizja Pancerna*, 67; "Polish Armd Div," 7 August 1944, RG 24, Volume 10,718, File 215C1.99(D11); Maczek, *Od Podwody do Czolga*, 146-147. "Memo on WE Pol Armd Div," Aug 1944, RG 24 Volume 10,992 File 275P1.015(D1), 6.

70. Maczek, *Od Podwody do Czolga*, 148-149; Władysław Dec, *Narawik i Falaise*, Warszawa, 1958, 200-201.

71. The sources for this synopsis include Grudziński, *1 Dywizja Pancerna*, and Maczek, *Od Poswody do Czolga*.

72. A complete 58-page list of the division's casualties and a map of cemetery sites and memorials is available in *1 Dywizja Pancerna: Polegli na Polu Chwały w Drodze do Polski*, Londyn, 1964.

BIBLIOGRAPHY

Unpublished Sources.

Amy, E.A.C., "Normandy, 1 Squadron Canadian Grenadier Guards."

Canadian Land Forces Command and Staff College Library, Kingston.

      Worthington Force collection.

Directory of History and Heritage, DND, Ottawa.

      Air 15-721, Air Ministry, "Tactical Bulletin No. 42, Night Operations by Bomber Command in Close Support of the Army, Caen Area, 7/8 Aug, 1944."

      Air 86/285, Air Ministry Historical Branch, RAF draft narrative, "The Liberation of North-West Europe Volume IV: The Break-Out and Advance to the Lower Rhine, 12 June to 30 September 1944."

      Canadian Military Headquarters Reports.

      Current Reports from Overseas.

      Defence Forces List Canada (Naval, Military and Air Forces) Part I (Ottawa, 1938 and 1939).

      Historical Section (G.S.) Reports.

      First Canadian Army Intelligence Summaries.

      Interrogation Reports.

      Narratives Collected by Historical Officers.

      Various Correspondence.

Donogh, Norman, Correspondence with the author.

Duguid, Fortescue, *History of the Canadian Grenadier Guards 1760-1964* (Montreal, 1964).

Graves, Donald E, "Fists of Mail, Walls of Steel, Armoured Warfare, 1914-1945" (unpublished paper, 1965).

—— Transcripts of interviews.

Grodzinski, John R., Various material on 1. *Dywizji Pancernej.*

Macdonald, John, "In Search of Veritable: Training the Canadian Army Staff Officer, 1899-1945," (MA Thesis, Royal Military College of Canada, 1992).

National Archives of Canada, Ottawa.

      Manuscript Group, MG 30 E 157, Crerar Papers.

      Records Group 24, Records of the Department of National Defence.

O'Keefe, David, Compilation of Ultra Material.

—— "The Double-edged Sword: Intelligence and Operation 'Totalize' Normandy, August 8, 1944".

Perrun, Jody, Missed Opportunities: First Canadian Army and the Air Plan for Operation Totalize, 7-10 August 1944," (MA Thesis, Carleton University), 1999.

Peszke, Michael A., "The Creation and Disposition of the Polish Armed Forces in Exile: A Brief Review of Significant Polish Literature," unpublished manuscript

Polish Museum and Sikorski Institute, various material on 1. *Dywizji Pancernej.*

Radley-Walters, Sydney, unpublished narrative and interviews with the author.

Stewart, James, unpublished narrative.

United Kingdom National Archives (UKNA) (formerly Public Records Office (PRO)).
    War Office and Air Ministry Records.
United States National Archives (USNA).
    Records Group 338, Narratives by Senior German Officers.
Zapozan, Larry, "Rad's War: A Biographical Study of S.V. Radley-Walters in the Normandy Campaign," (MA Thesis, University of New Brunswick, 2000).

Published Sources.

Agte, Patrick, *Michael Wittmann and the Tiger Commanders of the Leibstandarte* (Winnipeg, 1996).
Air University (U.S.), U.S. Air Force Historical Study No. 70, "Tactical Operations of the Eighth Air Force, 6 June 1944-8 May 1945," (Air University, 1952), found in DHH mfm 81/849.
—— "The Employment of Strategic Bombers in a Tactical Role, 1941-1951," (Air University, 1955).
Anon, *British Army of the Rhine, Battlefield Tour, Operation Totalize* (Germany, 1947).
—— *History of the Third Canadian Light Anti-Aircraft Regiment From 17 August, 1940 to 7 May, 1945* (Holland, 1945).
—— *19 Canadian Army Field Regiment RCA: Regimental History September 1941-July 1945* (Deventer, 1945).
—— *The History of the Brigadier Royal Artillery Branch of Headquarters First Canadian Army* (n.p., 1945).
—— *Polskie Sily Zbrojne w Drugiej Wojnie Swiatowey Tom II Kampanie Na Obczyz*, 3 vols (London).
—— *The Regimental History of the Governor General's Foot Guards* (Ottawa, 1948).
—— *The Story of the British Columbia Regiment 1939-1945.*
Barnard, W., *The Queen's Own Rifles of Canada 1860-1960* (Toronto, 1960).
Bennett, Ralph, *Ultra in the West: The Normandy Campaign of 1944-45* (New York, 1979).
Bidwell, Shelford, *Gunners at War: A Tactical Study of the Royal Artillery in the Twentieth Century* (London, 1970).
—— and Graham, Dominick, *Fire-Power: British Army Weapons and Theories of War 1904-1945* (London, 1982).
Biegański, Witold, *Wojska Polskiego Na Zachodzie: Formowanie, Działania, Bojowe* (Warsaw, 1967).
Blackburn, George, *The Guns of Normandy* (Toronto, 1995).
—— *Where the Hell Are the Guns?* (Toronto, 1997).
Bouchery, Jean, *The British Solider in North West Europe, 1944-1945* (Paris, 1999).
Carmichael, David, "How Canada Smashed the Germans," in *Canadian Magazine*, (Toronto, 1968) 5 October 1968.
Cassidy, Gerald, *Warpath: From Tilly-la-Campagne to the Kursten Canal* (Markham, 1980).
Copp, Terry, *Montgomery's Scientists" Operational Research in Northwest Europe – the Work of No. 2 Operational Research Section with 21 Army Group, June 1844 to July 1945* (Waterloo (Ont.), 2000).
—— *Fields of Fire: The Canadians in Normandy* (Toronto, 2003).
D'Este, *Carlos, Decision in Normandy: The Unknown Story of Montgomery and the Allied Campaign* (London, 1983).
De Guingand, Francis, *Operation Victory* rev. ed. (London, 1960).
Dembinok, Józef, et al, *Oznaki i Odznaki Polskicy Sił Zbroynych Na Zachodzie* (Katowice, 1984).
Ellis, John, *The Sharp End: The Fighting Man in World War II* (New York, 1980).
English, John, *The Canadian Army and the Normandy Campaign: A Study of Failure in High Command* (New York, 1991).
—— *Lament for an Army: The Decline of Canadian Military Professionalism* (Toronto, 1998).
Essame, H., *The Battle for Normandy* (New York, 1969).
Foster, Tony, *Meeting of Generals* (Toronto, 1986).
Fraser, Robert, *Black Yesterdays: The Argyll's War* (Hamilton, 1996).
Fritz, Stephen, *Frontsoldaten: the German soldier in World War II* (Lexington, Ky., 1996).

Gaffen, Fred, *Cross-Border Warriors; Canadians in American Forces, Americans in Canadian Forces, From the Civil War to the Gulf* (Toronto, 1995).

D. Goodspeed, *Battle Royal: A History of the Royal Regiment of Canada 1862-1962* (Toronto, 1962).

Graham, Dominick, *The Price of Command: A Biography of General Guy Simonds* (Toronto, 1993).

Granatstein, Jack, *The Generals: The Canadian Army's Senior Commanders in the Second World War* (Toronto, 1993).

Granatstein, Jack and Morton, Desmond, *Bloody Victory: Canadians and the D-Day Campaign 1944* (Toronto, 1984).

Graves, Donald E., *South Albertas: A Canadian Regiment at War* (Toronto, 1998).

Greenhous, Brereton, *Semper Paratus: The History of The Royal Hamilton Light Infantry (Wentworth Regiment) 1862-1977* (Hamilton, 1977).

Grodzinski, John R., *Operational Handbook for the First Canadian Army 1944-1945: Formation Organization, Staff Technique and Administration* (n.p., 1996).

Grudziński, Antoni, *I Dywizja Pancerna: Zaryz Historii Wojenny* (London, 1964).

Guderian, Heinz, *Panzer Leader* (London, 1974).

Harris, Stephen, *Canadian Brass: The Making of a Professional Army, 1860-1939,* (Toronto, 1988).

Hastings, Max, *Overlord D-Day and the Battle for Normandy 1944* (London, 1985).

Hunt, Barry, "The Road to Washington: Canada and Empire Naval Defence, 1918-1921" in James Boutilier (ed.), *RCN in Retrospect 1910-1968* (Vancouver, 1982).

Intelligence Section, *8 Canadian Reconnaissance Regiment (14 Canadian Hussars) Battle History* (Holland, 1945).

Jamar, K., *With the Tanks of the 1st Polish Armoured Division* (Hengelo, 1946).

Jarymowcz, Roman, "Canadian Armour in Normandy: Operation 'Totalize' and the Quest for Operational Maneuver," *Canadian Military History*, Volume 7, Number 2, Spring 1998.

—— *Tank Tactics from Normandy to Lorraine* (Boulder, 2001).

—— "On Doctrine – A Brief Comment" *The Army Doctrine and Training Bulletin*, Volume 4, Number 3, Fall 2001.

Johnston, Murray, *The Story of the Royal Canadian Electrical and Mechanical Engineers and of the Land Ordnance Engineering Branch* (n.p., n.d.,).

Jolly, Alan, *Blue Flash, The Story of an Armoured Regiment* (n.p., n.d.).

Keegan, John, *Six Armies in Normandy* (New York, 1982).

Kennedy, Robert, Department of the Army Pamphlet No. 20-255, *The German Campaign in Poland (1939)* (Washington, 1956).

Kitching, George, *Mud and Green Fields: The Memoirs of Major-General George Kitching* (St. Catharines, 1993).

Komornicki, Stanisław, et al, *Wojsko Polski, 1939-1945* (Warsaw, 1984).

Kurcz F.S., (trans. Peter Jordan), *The Black Brigade* (Harrow, 1943).

Lucas-Phillips, C.E., *Alamein* (London, 1962).

Maczek, Stanisław, *Od Pdwody do Czogla* (London, 1984).

Marteinson, John and McNorgan, Michael, *The Royal Canadian Armoured Corps: An Illustrated History* (Toronto, 2000).

Martin, Charles, *Battle Diary: From D-Day and Normandy to the Zuider Zee and VE* (Toronto, 1994).

McKee, Alexander, *Caen: Anvil of Victory* (London, 1966).

Meitzell [sic], Bernhard-Georg (interrogation report), "Caen-Falaise," Part Two, *Canadian Army Journal* May 1952, (Ottawa, 1952).

Meyer, Hubert, *The History of the 12. SS-Panzerdivision Hitlerjugend* (Winnipeg, 1994).

Meyer, Kurt, *Grenadiers* (Winnipeg, 1994).

Milner, Marc, "Reflections on Caen, Bocage and the Gap" A Naval Historian's Critique of the Normandy Campaign," *Canadian Military History*, Spring 1998, Vol. 7, No. 2 (Waterloo, 1998).

Munro, Ross, *Gauntlet to Overlord: The Story of the Canadian Army* (Toronto, 1945).

Neillands, Robin, *The Battle of Normandy 1944* (London, 2002).

Neville, R. *The First Northamptonshire Yeomanry in Northwest Europe* (n.p., n.d.).

Nicholson, Gerald, *Canadian Expeditionary Force 1914-1919* (Ottawa, 1962).

—— *The Gunners of Canada: The History of the Royal Regiment of Canadian Artillery, Volume 2, 1919-1967* (Toronto, 1967).

Pemberton, A., *The Development of Artillery Tactics and Equipment* (London, 1950).

Ramsden, Keith, *The Canadian Kangaroos in World War II* (Cavan, Ont., 1998).

Reynolds, Michael, *Steel Inferno: 1 SS Panzer Corps in Normandy 1944* (London, 2002).

Rogers, R., *History of the Lincoln and Welland Regiment*, 2nd ed. (St. Catharines, Ont., 1979).

Rohmer, Richard, *Patton's Gap: An Account of the Battle of Normandy* (Toronto, 1981).

Roy, Reginald, *1944, The Canadians in Normandy* (Toronto, 1984).

Ruffee, George, *The History of the 14 Field Regiment, 1940-1945* (Amsterdam, 1945).

Smithers, A., *A New Excalibur: The Development of the Tank 1909-1939* (London, 1989).

—— *Rude Mechanicals: An Account of Tank Maturity During the Second World War* (London, 1989).

Spenser, Robert, *History of the Fifteenth Canadian Field Regiment* (Elsevier, 1945).

Stacey, Charles P., *Official History of the Canadian Army in the Second World War, Volume I, Six Years of War: The Army in Canada, Britain and the Pacific,* (Ottawa, 1957).

—— *Official History of the Canadian Army in the Second World War, Volume III, The Victory Campaign* (Ottawa, 1960).

—— *Arms, Men and Governments: The War Policies of Canada 1939-1945* (Ottawa, 1970).

—— *A Date with History* (Ottawa, 1982).

Stanley, George, *Canada's Soldiers: The Military History of an Unmilitary People*, revised edition (Toronto, 1960).

Terraine, John, *The Right of the Line, The Royal Air Force in the European War 1939-1945* (Ware, Herfordshire, 1977).

Tout, Ken, *The Bloody Battle for Tilly* (Stroud, 1994).

—— *A Fine Night for Tanks: The Road to Falaise* (Thrupp, 1998).

Ventham, Philip and Flectcher, David, *Moving the Guns: The Mechanisation of the Royal Artillery 1854-1939* (London (UK), 1990).

War Office (UK), *Military Training Pamphlet No. 41: The Tactical Handling of the Armoured Division and its Components, Part 2, The Armoured Regiment* (London, 1943).

—— *Field Service Pocket Book, Part I – Pamphlet No. 1, Glossary of Military Terms* (London, 1944).

—— *Field Service Pocket Book, Part I – Pamphlet No. 4, Appreciations, Orders, Messages and Intercommunications* (London, 1944).

Whitaker, Denis and Shelagh, *Victory at Falaise: The Soldiers' Story* (Toronto, 2000).

Worthington, Larry, *'Worthy': A Biography of Major-General F.F. Worthington, C.B., M.C., M.M.* (Toronto, 1961).

Wood, Alan, *The Falaise Road* (Toronto,1944).

Wroński, Bohdan, et al, *Generał Sikorski: Premier, Naczelny Wódz* (London, 1981).

Zaloga, Steven, and Victor Madej, *The Polish Campaign 1939* (New York, 1985).

Żebowski, Marian W., *Polska Broń Pancerna: Zarys Historii.*

Zetterling, Niklas, *Normandy 1944: German Military Organization, Combat Power and Organizational Effectiveness* (Winnipeg, 2000).

INDEX

Battle studies by Brian A. Reid also appear in...

Fighting for Canada
Seven Battles, 1758-1945

Edited by Donald E. Graves

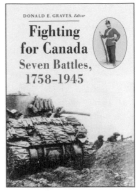

It is a popular myth that Canada is a peaceable kingdom and Canadians are an unmilitary people. Canada was created by armed conflict, or the threat of conflict, and throughout their history Canadians have proved to be a more warlike people than many would like to believe. *Fighting for Canada* and *More Fighting for Canada* are devoted to battles fought either to defend Canada or by Canadians overseas on behalf of their nation. The actions described are:

- **Ticonderoga, 1758**: The French defeat the British in the bloodiest military action fought in North America before the Civil War – *Ian M. McCulloch*
- **Queenston Heights, 1812**: General Brock's outnumbered but professional army defeats an American invasion – *Robert Malcomson*
- **Ridgeway, 1866**: Fenians invade the Niagara Peninsula and embarrass the Canadian militia – *Brian A. Reid*
- **Leliefontein, 1900**: Gallant rearguard action in the Boer War – *Brian A. Reid*
- **Moreuil Wood, 1918**: Rare and disastrous cavalry action in the First World War – *John R. Grodzinski & Michael R. McNorgan*
- **Le Mesnil-Patry, 1944**: Enthusiasm and courage unavailing in the face of the ruthless Waffen SS in Normandy – *Michael R. McNorgan*
- **Kapelsche Veer, 1945**: Unnecessary and costly battle for a boggy Dutch island that should never have been fought – *Donald E. Graves*

448 pages • 6.75 x 9.75 inches • about 160 illustrations and maps • appendices, endnotes, bibliography, index • 2000 • 1-896941-15-x hardcover • 1-896941-16-8 paperback

More Fighting for Canada
Five Battles, 1760-1944

Edited by Donald E. Graves

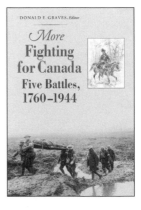

- **Sillery, 1760**: The French and the English meet again eight months after the Battle of the Plains of Abraham, and the outcome is different – *Ian M. McCulloch*
- **Cut Knife Hill, 1885:** A Canadian force is surprised by the aboriginal peoples in the Northwest Rebellion – *Robert Caldwell*
- **Paardeberg, 1900**: The Royal Canadian Regiment attacks an entrenched enemy across open ground swept by rifle fire – incredible bravery or incredible stupidity? – *Brian A. Reid*
- **Iwuy, 1918**: A mixed force of Canadian cavalry and armour encounters a stubborn German rearguard position near the village of Iwuy – *Michael R. McNorgan*
- **Melfa Crossing, 1944**: A surprise crossing of the heavily-defended Melfa River, a major breakthrough in the Italian Campaign – *John R. Grodzinski*

368 pages • 6.75 x 9.75 inches • about 120 illustrations and maps • appendices, endnotes, bibliography, index • 2004 • 1-896941-36-2 hardcover • 1-896941-37-0 paperback

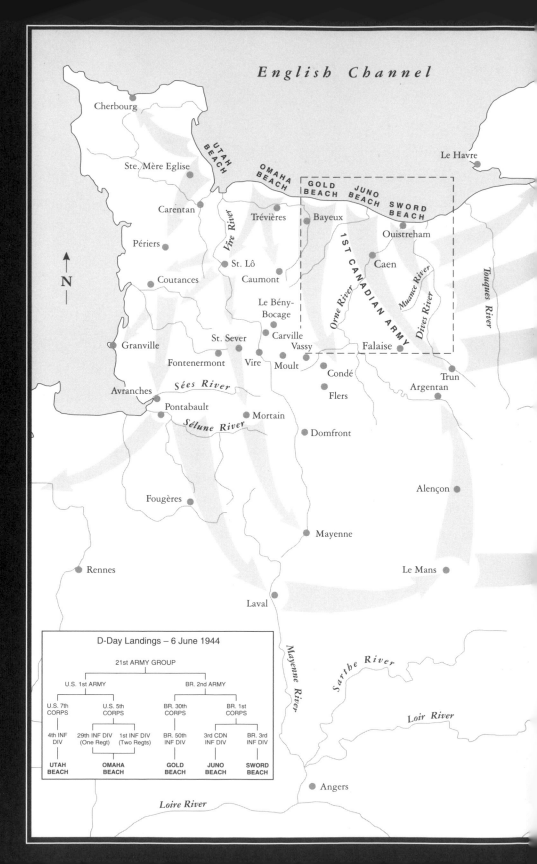

English Channel

Cherbourg

Ste. Mère Eglise

Carentan

Périers

Coutances

N

Granville

St. Sever

Fontenermont

Avranches

Pontabault

Fougères

Rennes

UTAH BEACH

OMAHA BEACH

Trévières

Bayeux

GOLD BEACH

JUNO BEACH

SWORD BEACH

Le Havre

Ouistreham

Vire River

St. Lô

Caumont

Le Bény-Bocage

Carville

Vassy

Vire

Moult

Condé

Flers

Caen

1ST CANADIAN ARMY

Orne River

Muance River

Dives River

Touques River

Falaise

Trun

Argentan

Sées River

Sélune River

Mortain

Domfront

Alençon

Mayenne

Le Mans

Laval

Mayenne River

Sarthe River

Loir River

Angers

Loire River

D-Day Landings – 6 June 1944

21st ARMY GROUP

U.S. 1st ARMY · BR. 2nd ARMY

U.S. 7th CORPS · U.S. 5th CORPS · BR. 30th CORPS · BR. 1st CORPS

4th INF DIV · 29th INF DIV (One Regt) · 1st INF DIV (Two Regts) · BR. 50th INF DIV · 3rd CDN INF DIV · BR. 3rd INF DIV

UTAH BEACH · OMAHA BEACH · GOLD BEACH · JUNO BEACH · SWORD BEACH

"The color of the skin is in no way connected with the strength of the mind or intellectual powers."

— BENJAMIN BANNEKER

BENJAMIN BANNEKER

By Melissa Maupin

The Child's World®

GRAPHIC DESIGN
Robert E. Bonaker / Graphic Design & Consulting Co.

PROJECT COORDINATOR
James R. Rothaus / James R. Rothaus & Associates

EDITORIAL DIRECTION
Elizabeth Sirimarco Budd

COVER PHOTO
Portrait of Benjamin Banneker / Banneker Douglass Museum

Library of Congress Cataloging-in-Publication Data
Maupin, Melissa, 1958-
Benjamin Banneker / by Melissa Maupin.
p. cm.
Summary: Describes the life and accomplishments of Benjamin
Banneker in the fields of science and architecture, as well as
his impact as one of the pioneers in promoting equality.
ISBN 1-56766-618-3 (library : reinforced : alk. paper)

1. Banneker, Benjamin, 1731-1806 — Juvenile literature.
2. Astronomers — United States — Biography — Juvenile
literature. 3. Afro-American scientists — United States —
Biography — Juvenile literature.
[1. Banneker, Benjamin, 1731-1806. 2. Astronomers. 3. Afro-
Americans — Biography.] I. Title

QB36.B22M38 1999
520'.92 — dc21
[B]
99-18148
CIP

Contents

The Bannaky Family

Benjamin Banneker's grandmother set sail for America in 1698. She was an English woman named Molly Walsh. After a long journey, she arrived in Maryland. Molly had worked on a farm in England. One day while she milked a cow, it kicked over a bucket of milk. Molly tried to explain to the farmer what had happened, but he did not believe her. He thought she had stolen the milk.

The farmer decided to punish Molly. He sent her to the British *colonies* as an *indentured servant.* Once she arrived in Maryland, Molly had to work for seven years without pay.

At the time, Europeans had just begun to settle in America. Much of the land was still free. Settlers could claim a piece of property for themselves. When Molly finished her seven-year sentence, she wanted to start a farm. She found a pretty piece of land next to a creek. She claimed it as her own.

Molly knew that it would be difficult to survive by herself. She needed help to clear the brush, to find food, and to build a house. Over time, Molly managed to save a little money. *Slavery* was legal in many parts of the colonies. With the help of a slave, Molly thought she could run a small farm.

CORBIS/Historical Picture Archive

IN ENGLAND, BENJAMIN'S GRANDMOTHER MOLLY WORKED AS A DAIRYMAID. SHE CAME TO AMERICA IN 1698.

CORBIS/Richard T. Nowitz

EUROPEAN SETTLERS TRAVELED TO AMERICA ON LARGE SHIPS THAT COULD CROSS THE OCEAN. THE TRIP WAS NOT AN EASY ONE. MANY PASSENGERS BECAME ILL. SOME DIED BEFORE THEY REACHED THE COLONIES.

CORBIS/Bojan Brecelj

No one knows for sure how many Africans were kidnapped from their homeland and taken to America. Slavery was legal in the United States until 1865.

Slavery meant that human beings could be owned. Slave traders kidnapped African people from their homeland. They took them away from family and friends. They sent them to America on ships. The traders sold them to white Americans. Then the slaves were forced to work without pay. Molly did not believe slavery was right, but she needed help.

Most Africans did not know English when they first arrived. They did not understand the ways of white people. They were angry, scared, and homesick. Many slave owners preferred not to buy the new slaves. Molly had little money to spend. New slaves cost less than those who had been in America longer. She chose two young men who had just arrived on a slave ship.

A WHITE FARMER EXAMINES A SLAVE BEFORE BUYING HIM. SLAVES WERE TREATED LIKE A PIECE OF PROPERTY, NOT LIKE HUMAN BEINGS.

One of the slaves was named Banna Ka. Other slaves told stories about him. Many believed he was an African prince. He was a proud man who once had servants himself. At first, Banna Ka refused to work for Molly. Slowly, he began to change his mind.

CORBIS

Banna Ka liked to hunt. He began to bring home game for Molly to cook. After a while, she and the two men learned to communicate. Molly remembered her own life as an indentured servant. She knew it was wrong to force people to work without pay. She decided to free the two slaves.

As they cleared the land and built a cabin, Molly and Banna Ka grew closer. They fell in love and decided to marry. People began calling Banna Ka by the name "Bannaky". From then on, it was the only name he ever used. Bannaky and Molly lived a comfortable life on their farm. They raised four children together.

One day while he was hunting, Bannaky's life came to a tragic end. A terrible rainstorm swept into the county. A lightning bolt struck an oak tree, splitting it in two. When the tree crashed down, it struck and killed Bannaky. Molly never remarried.

Soon after Bannaky's death, his daughter Mary turned 16. Molly thought it was time for her to marry. Like her mother, Mary bought a male slave. His name was Robert. She freed him, just as her mother had freed her father. Soon, she fell in love with Robert. The young couple married, and Robert took Bannaky as his own last name. Their first child was born in 1731. Robert and Mary named him Benjamin.

TO BE SOLD,
A Likely negro Man, his Wife and Child ; the negro Man capable of doing all forts of Plantation Work, and a good Miller : The Woman exceeding fit for a Farmer, being capable of doing any Work, belonging to a Houfe in the Country, at reafonable Rates, inquire of the Printer hereof.

CORBIS/Bettmann

A NEWSPAPER ADVERTISEMENT OFFERS A FAMILY OF SLAVES FOR SALE.

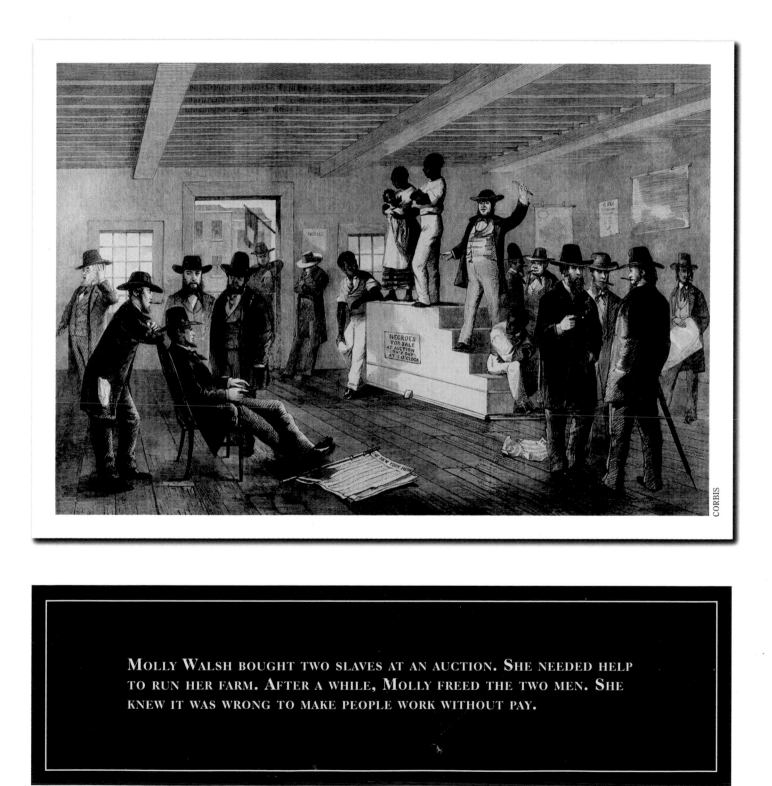

CORBIS

MOLLY WALSH BOUGHT TWO SLAVES AT AN AUCTION. SHE NEEDED HELP
TO RUN HER FARM. AFTER A WHILE, MOLLY FREED THE TWO MEN. SHE
KNEW IT WAS WRONG TO MAKE PEOPLE WORK WITHOUT PAY.

CORBIS/Peter Harholdt

A MARYLAND FARMER TENDS HIS LIVESTOCK. MANY PEOPLE WHO CAME TO THE COLONIES HOPED TO FIND A BETTER LIFE. THEY WANTED TO WORK ON THEIR OWN FARMS INSTEAD OF LABORING FOR SOMEONE ELSE.

Benjamin the Student

Life in the 1700s was very different from today. In Maryland, many people lived on farms. They planted gardens to feed their families. They also raised chickens, hogs, and cattle to eat. Some people raised crops to sell. Sometimes farmers traded their crops for other goods, such as fabric to sew clothing or wood to build a cabin.

Few black families owned farms in those days. In Maryland, most blacks were slaves. The Bannakys were fortunate. They wanted their farm to be successful. Everyone in the family worked hard. Benjamin split wood for the stove. He also fed the chickens. When he was old enough, he helped *harvest* the tobacco crop. He even tended the fires in the smokehouses where they dried the tobacco leaves.

Life was simple and slow. There were no cars or buses. There were no supermarkets. Benjamin traveled to a small general store on horseback. His father hauled goods in a horse-drawn wagon.

Everyone in the family lived in Molly Walsh's cabin. There was no electricity. Cabins of the day had wood stoves or a fireplace. Families used fires to cook and to stay warm. Candles and gas lanterns supplied light. Benjamin and his sisters could not watch television or go to the movies. Instead, they played simple games. Benjamin also enjoyed hunting and fishing, just as his grandfather Banna Ka had done many years before.

At the end of the day, the Bannaky family gathered together to eat. Grandmother Walsh read to the children before bedtime. She told them stories from the Bible. It was the only book the family owned. She also taught Benjamin and his sisters to read. Benjamin learned quickly. He could read and count by the time he was six. He loved to solve math problems in his head. Soon it was Benjamin who read the Bible to his family.

As the family grew, the cabin became crowded. Mary and Robert decided to build their own home. Over the years, other settlers had claimed some of Molly's land. Robert decided to buy back 120 acres. The settlers wanted 7,000 pounds of tobacco in exchange.

In 1737, the Bannakys harvested enough tobacco to purchase the land. First, they dried the tobacco. Next, they packed it into round, wooden barrels. Robert and his helpers rolled the barrels toward the town of Joppa. Six-year-old Benjamin followed behind. Joppa was about 40 miles from their farm. It took several days to reach the town on foot.

Once they arrived, Robert purchased the land. He put both his name and young Benjamin's on the deed of ownership. At age six, Benjamin was a landowner! The family finally owned their own farm.

THE BANNAKYS GREW TOBACCO ON THEIR FARM. AT THE TIME, FEW BLACK FAMILIES WERE LUCKY ENOUGH TO OWN THEIR OWN LAND.

CORBIS

CORBIS/Colin Garratt; Milepost 92

AFTER THE BANNAKYS DRIED THEIR TOBACCO, THEY PUT IT IN BARRELS. THEN THEY TOOK IT TO THE MARKET TO SELL.

CORBIS/Bettmann

IN COLONIAL AMERICA, BLACK CHILDREN WERE RARELY ALLOWED TO GO TO SCHOOL. MANY WHITE CHILDREN ALSO STAYED HOME TO HELP THEIR PARENTS.

Soon the family built a cabin. They planted the tobacco fields. Crops grew well on their farm. Many years before, Banna Ka used a clever idea he remembered from Africa. He dug *channels* in the ground. The channels carried water from a creek to the crops. He also built *dams* to control the water flow.

Robert Bannaky did the same thing on his own farm. Neighbors called the farm Bannaky Springs because there was so much water. The Bannaky's *irrigation* system kept their crops green and healthy.

One of their new neighbors was a white man named Peter Heinrich. He was a farmer, but he also planned to start a school for boys. It probably surprised Heinrich to learn that a black family owned the farm next door. At the time, most black people in the area were slaves who worked on large *plantations*.

One day, Heinrich discovered that Benjamin could read. Most black children were never taught such skills. Heinrich realized that Benjamin was bright. He wanted to help him learn even more. When Heinrich opened his new school, he asked Benjamin to attend.

Benjamin was eager to go to school, but he may have felt strange on the first day. It was rare for black children to attend school. Benjamin was the only black child in his class. His sisters did not attend school. At the time, even white girls usually stayed home and learned to run the household.

No one knows when Benjamin first used the name Banneker. After he went to school, it became his last name. Perhaps Heinrich first spelled it "Banneker" as he wrote it on the chalkboard. Benjamin may have copied the name just as the teacher wrote it.

Benjamin continued to work on the farm. He attended school in the winter when there was less work to do on the farm. He enjoyed his classes. Learning new things made him want to know even more. In addition to math and reading, he learned to play the flute and the violin.

As he grew older, Robert Bannaky needed more help from Benjamin. He had difficulty walking. His back ached from years of hard work. Benjamin was a strong young man. He was willing to do all he could for his family. His parents decided they needed his help all year long.

Benjamin had to leave school, but he never quit learning. He often stopped by to talk with Peter Heinrich. His former teacher often gave Benjamin books to read. Sometimes he even found mistakes in the math books he borrowed.

When he went to town, Benjamin always took the time to visit with his neighbors. Farmers in the area knew he was very good at math. They often asked for his help with their accounts. He was a friendly young man who enjoyed helping others. He also liked to create math puzzles to see if the townspeople could solve them.

"THE PUZZLE OF THE COOPER AND THE VINTNER"

A cooper and a vintner sat down for a talk,
Both being so groggy that neither could walk;
Says cooper to vintner, "I'm the first of my trade,
There's no kind of vessel but what I have made,

And of any shape, sir, just what you will,
And of any size, sir, from a tun to a gill."
"Then,' says the vintner, "you're the man for me.
Make me a vessel, if we can agree,

The top and the bottom diameter define,
To bear that proportion as fifteen to nine,
Thirty-five inches are just what I crave,
No more and no less in the depth will I have;

Just thirty-nine gallons this vessel must hold,
And then I will reward you with silver or gold—
Give me your promise, my honest old friend."
"I'll make it tomorrow, that you may depend!"

So, the next day, the cooper, his work to discharge,
Soon made the new vessel, but made it too large;
He took out some staves, which made it too small.
And then cursed the vessel, the vintner, and all.

He beat on his breast, "By the powers" he swore
He never would work at his trade any more.
Now, my worthy friend, find out if you can,
The vessel's dimensions, and comfort the man!

THIS IS ONE OF THE MATH PUZZLES BENJAMIN BANNEKER WROTE. IT IS CALLED "THE PUZZLE OF THE COOPER AND THE VINTNER." A COOPER IS A CRAFTSMAN WHO MAKES WOODEN BARRELS AND TUBS. A VINTNER MAKES WINE.

When he was 21, Benjamin went into town one morning. He met a traveling salesman named Josef Levi. Mr. Levi had traveled all over the colonies and in Europe. As the two men talked, the salesman took out his pocket watch to check the time. The ticking gold watch amazed Benjamin. He had never seen one before. How did it work? Levi loaned the watch to Benjamin. He said he would pick it up the next time he came to town.

Benjamin took the watch home and carefully took it apart. He made notes and drawings of each piece. He studied how all the parts worked together. Benjamin decided he could build a clock by carefully copying the watch. He began to make all of the parts, carving them out of wood. He made them bigger than the tiny ones in the watch. He made calculations to tell exactly how much bigger each part should be.

With only a few metal pieces, Benjamin built a large wooden clock. He continued to work on it for several years. He wanted it to be perfect. When he was finally finished, Benjamin's clock kept perfect time for the rest of his life.

This was no ordinary clock. Benjamin made it chime every hour. After a while, the chiming bothered him. He changed it so that it chimed only on the hours of twelve and six. Benjamin's clock may have been the first one ever built in America.

People came from all over the county to see the clock. Word spread about the young inventor. Some people even hired him to repair their own clocks and watches. Benjamin was happy to help them.

AN ANTIQUE POCKET WATCH. BENJAMIN WAS FASCINATED BY THE WATCH HE BORROWED FROM MR. LEVI. HE DECIDED TO BUILD ONE OF HIS OWN. THE CLOCK HE MADE WORKED PERFECTLY THROUGHOUT HIS LIFE.

In the Stars

As Benjamin Banneker grew older, he lived alone. He never married, and his parents and grandmother had died. Benjamin found company with friends who lived nearby. He was especially close to the Ellicott family. The Ellicotts ran a flour mill and general store near Benjamin's farm.

Benjamin had helped them build the mill. Over the years, he often stopped by to visit the family. He was particularly fond of George Ellicott, who was 19 years younger than Benjamin. The two shared an interest in mathematics and science.

George Ellicott enjoyed *astronomy* and *surveying*. He introduced these sciences to Benjamin. George let him borrow a telescope and other equipment. Benjamin spent his nights looking at the stars and planets. He even put a skylight in the roof of his cabin. Then he could stargaze from inside his house on cold, winter nights.

Benjamin did not just admire the stars and planets. He also studied them. He recorded their movements each night. As he observed the sky, he learned a great deal. He could tell when the sun would rise and set. He could also predict when an *eclipse* would occur. On April 14, 1789, Benjamin predicted a solar eclipse. Even well-known scientists did not expect the eclipse. George suggested that Benjamin publish such useful information. Benjamin agreed. He started to write an *almanac*.

Benjamin enjoyed a peaceful life. He worked on his farm during the day. He studied the sky at night. At the same time, there was trouble growing in the colonies. The *colonists* wanted to rule themselves. Great Britain wanted to keep control of the new land. Finally, the colonists decided to *rebel*. The American Revolution began in 1775.

THE FIRST SHOTS OF THE AMERICAN REVOLUTION WERE
FIRED BETWEEN COLONIAL SOLDIERS AND BRITISH TROOPS
AT LEXINGTON, MASSACHUSETTS ON APRIL 19, 1775.

CORBIS/Bettmann

THOMAS JEFFERSON READS THE DECLARATION OF INDEPENDENCE TO BENJAMIN FRANKLIN. FRANKLIN WAS ONE OF THE FOUR MEN WHO HELPED JEFFERSON WRITE THE DOCUMENT.

In 1776, five men, led by Thomas Jefferson, wrote the *Declaration of Independence*. This important document ended all ties between the colonies and Great Britain. It stated that the United States was a free nation. The colonists vowed to fight until Great Britain gave up.

The war ended in 1783. The United States had won its freedom. Several years later, the new country still had no *capital city*. President George Washington had a location in mind, however. It was a plot of land on the Potomac River. It covered about 10 square miles. In 1790, President Washington and the United States Congress agreed to create a *federal territory*. It would later be called Washington, D.C.

The government needed experts to build the capital city. President Washington appointed a famous French *architect* named Pierre L'Enfante. He also appointed George Ellicott's relative, Major Andrew Ellicott, to the project.

That winter, George delivered an important letter to Benjamin. Major Ellicott had told the president about him. President Washington wanted Benjamin to help build the capital city. He became the first *African American* to receive a *presidential commission*. The team appointed him as the scientific assistant to the project. Benjamin was now 60 years old.

AMERICANS DECIDED TO CALL THE NATION'S CAPITAL WASHINGTON, D.C., IN HONOR OF THE COUNTRY'S FIRST PRESIDENT.

CORBIS/Bequest of Mrs Benjamin Ogle Tayloe

CORBIS/Bettmann

MARYLAND COLONISTS WORK WITH A SURVEYING INSTRUMENT IN
1730. SURVEYORS PLANNED THE CITY OF BALTIMORE NEARLY
70 YEARS BEFORE BENJAMIN WORKED IN WASHINGTON, D.C.

The following year, Benjamin traveled to the new capital. He used Major Ellicott's instruments. They were the finest available. At night, he used the stars to determine which direction was north. During the day, Benjamin used his knowledge to lay out straight, even streets.

As work continued on the capital city, there was a problem. Pierre L'Enfante had a bad temper. People found it difficult to work with him. Eventually the team fired him. He returned to France, taking his plans with him. Unfortunately, the job was not done. It looked as if the team would have to start over again.

Some people believe that Benjamin saved the day. One story says that he drew the plans for the new capital city from memory. The team could finish the project, and the job was finished on time. Today no one is certain whether Benjamin actually did duplicate the plans. Nonetheless, his skill and intelligence became famous. News of his abilities spread across the young nation.

CORBIS

THE ORIGINAL PLANS FOR THE FEDERAL TERRITORY. GEORGE WASHINGTON AND THOMAS JEFFERSON HELPED PLAN THE CAPITAL CITY. THEY WANTED IT TO BE A CITY OF TREE-LINED STREETS, GREEN PARKS, AND BEAUTIFUL ARCHITECTURE.

Schomburg Center for Research in Black Culture

BENJAMIN WORKED ON THE CAPITAL CITY FOR SEVERAL MONTHS IN 1791. WHEN HIS WORK WAS DONE, HE RETURNED TO HIS MARYLAND FARM.

A Plea for Freedom

Benjamin worked on the capital city project for several months. When he returned to his farm, he was more interested in the stars than ever. He soon finished his almanac. He sent copies to a few well-known publishers. He also sent a copy to another important man, Thomas Jefferson.

Jefferson was now the *secretary of state.* Years earlier, he had written the Declaration of Independence. In that important document, he wrote that all men are created equal. Unfortunately, he did not believe that black men were the equals of whites. Benjamin knew this was wrong. He wrote a letter asking Jefferson to rethink his beliefs. He sent a copy of the almanac to show him what black people could do.

Benjamin asked Jefferson to help end *prejudice.* Perhaps Jefferson could make a difference. Perhaps he could make white people see that blacks were human beings just as whites were.

The following are Benjamin's own words: "I apprehend you will embrace every opportunity to eradicate that train of absurd and false ideas and opinions, which so generally prevails with respect to us [blacks]; and that your sentiments are concurrent with mine, which are, that one universal Father hath given being to us all; and that he hath not only made us all of one flesh, but that he hath also, without partiality, afforded us all the same sensations and endowed us all with the same faculties."

Jefferson sent the almanac to European scientists. They studied and learned from it. They told Jefferson the information was correct. Unfortunately, this was not enough. Jefferson was a slave owner. It was difficult for him to agree that blacks could be the equals of whites.

Still, Jefferson believed in freedom. He saw that Benjamin was an intelligent and good human being. The secretary of state wrote a short letter back to Benjamin. He thanked him for the almanac. He even agreed that blacks deserved better treatment. In the letter, Jefferson wrote:

"No body wishes more than I do, to see such proofs as you exhibit, that nature has given to our black brethren talents equal to those of the other colors of men; and that the appearance of the want of them, is owing merely to the degraded condition of their existence, both in Africa and America."

Jefferson's words mean that he wanted to believe what Benjamin said. Perhaps the almanac proved that black people were as intelligent as whites. Perhaps blacks seemed different only because others treated them so badly.

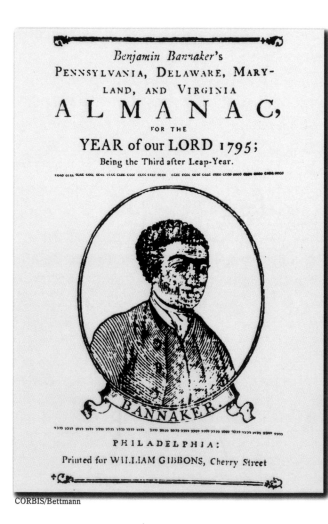

Benjamin Bannaker's
PENNSYLVANIA, DELAWARE, MARYLAND, AND VIRGINIA
ALMANAC,
FOR THE
YEAR of our LORD 1795;
Being the Third after Leap-Year.

BANNAKER.

PHILADELPHIA:
Printed for WILLIAM GIBBONS, Cherry Street

BENJAMIN PUBLISHED HIS ALMANAC FOR FIVE YEARS. SCIENTISTS IN THE UNITED STATES AND EUROPE RESPECTED HIS ACCURATE WORK.

CORBIS/Bettmann

BENJAMIN KNEW THAT THOMAS JEFFERSON WAS AN IMPORTANT AND INTELLIGENT MAN. HE ALSO KNEW THAT JEFFERSON DID NOT BELIEVE BLACKS AND WHITES WERE EQUAL.

Schomburg Center for Research in Black Culture

TODAY BENJAMIN BANNEKER IS CONSIDERED AMERICA'S FIRST BLACK INVENTOR AND SCIENTIST.

In 1792, two printers published the almanac. They called it *Benjamin Banneker's Pennsylvania, Delaware, Maryland, and Virginia Almanac and Ephemeris*. (An ephemeris is a scientific table that lists information.) It listed all of the *celestial bodies* that people knew about. It also told readers where they could find them in the sky. The almanac sold well. A growing number of scientists and teachers noticed Benjamin. He continued to publish the almanacs every year until 1797.

As he grew older, Benjamin sold part of his land. He wanted to spend less time farming. He hoped to write more about astronomy and the natural world around him. He wrote books about bees. He also wrote about another insect, the locust. He wrote essays against slavery and war, too.

THE TITLE PAGE FROM BENJAMIN'S 1795 ALMANAC. BANNEKER PUBLISHED HIS FINDINGS UNTIL 1797.

Benjamin Banneker died in his cabin on October 25, 1806. His famous wooden clock still worked. Sadly, his cabin burned down two days later. The fire destroyed most of his belongings. His notes, the clock, and his tools were gone. What little was left went to Benjamin's closest friend, George Ellicott.

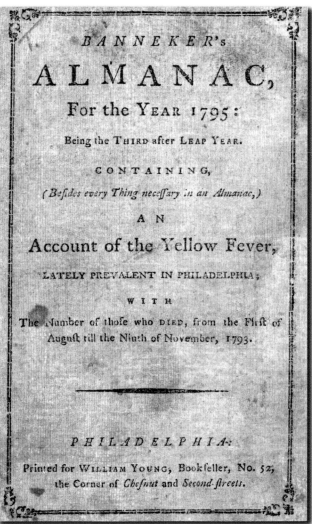

BANNEKER's
ALMANAC,
For the YEAR 1795:
Being the THIRD after LEAP YEAR.
CONTAINING,
(Besides every Thing necessary in an Almanac,)
AN
Account of the Yellow Fever,
LATELY PREVALENT IN PHILADELPHIA;
WITH
The Number of those who DIED, from the First of
August till the Ninth of November, 1793.

PHILADELPHIA:
Printed for WILLIAM YOUNG, Bookseller, No. 52,
the Corner of Chesnut and Second-streets.

Benjamin Banneker has long been known as the first black man of science. Most of what he knew, Benjamin taught himself. Some historians have called him a genius. Many schools across the country are named in honor of Benjamin Banneker. In 1998, the Banneker Historical Museum and Park in Baltimore County, Maryland, opened to celebrate his accomplishments.

Banneker helped to change the way whites thought about black people. He never allowed the color of his skin to prevent him from achieving his goals. Benjamin Banneker was living proof that black people had the same natural intelligence as white people. He believed that all people should be free. He believed everyone could succeed — all they needed was an equal chance.

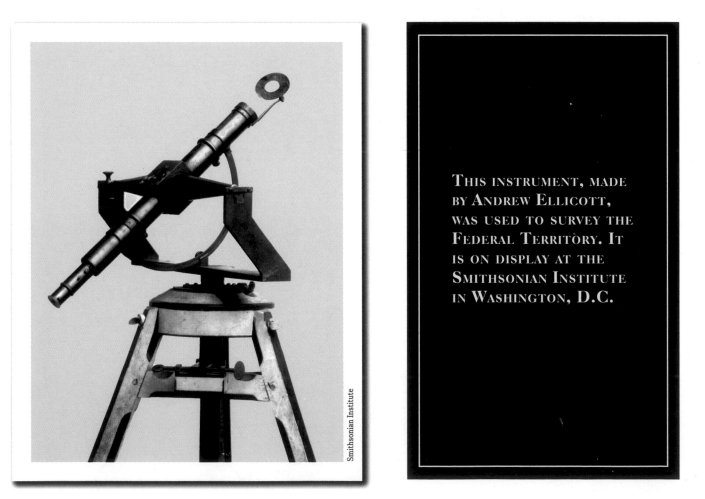

Smithsonian Institute

THIS INSTRUMENT, MADE BY ANDREW ELLICOTT, WAS USED TO SURVEY THE FEDERAL TERRITORY. IT IS ON DISPLAY AT THE SMITHSONIAN INSTITUTE IN WASHINGTON, D.C.

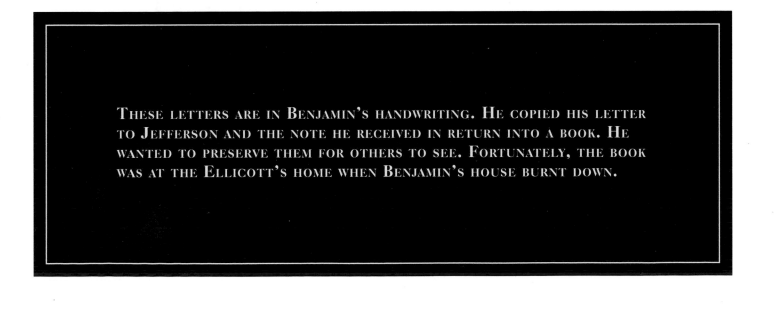

THESE LETTERS ARE IN BENJAMIN'S HANDWRITING. HE COPIED HIS LETTER TO JEFFERSON AND THE NOTE HE RECEIVED IN RETURN INTO A BOOK. HE WANTED TO PRESERVE THEM FOR OTHERS TO SEE. FORTUNATELY, THE BOOK WAS AT THE ELLICOTT'S HOME WHEN BENJAMIN'S HOUSE BURNT DOWN.

Timeline

1698 Benjamin's grandmother, Molly Walsh, arrives in Baltimore as an indentured servant.

1700s Molly Walsh buys two slaves and later frees them. She marries one of the former slaves, a man named Banna Ka.

1731 Benjamin Banneker is born to Molly's daughter Mary on November 9.

1737 Benjamin learns to read and write. Robert Bannaky and Benjamin become landowners.

1746 Benjamin stops going to school to work on his family's farm.

1752 Benjamin begins work on his wooden clock. It may be the first clock ever built in the United States.

1775 The American Revolution begins on April 19.

1776 The United States declares its independence from Great Britain.

1783 The American Revolution ends. The United States wins its freedom.

1789 Benjamin Banneker is the only scientist to predict a solar eclipse.

1790 Congress passes an act to establish a federal district. Banneker receives a presidential commission to survey the new capital.

1791 Banneker joins Major Andrew Ellicott's surveying team in Washington, D.C. Benjamin writes a letter to Thomas Jefferson. He asks him to help end prejudice.

1792 Two printers publish Banneker's almanac.

1797 The last edition of Benjamin's almanac is published.

1806 Benjamin Banneker dies in his cabin on October 25.

1998 The Banneker Historical Museum and Park is opened near his homestead.

Glossary

African American
(AF-ri-kan uh-MAYR-ih-kan)
An African American is a black American whose ancestors came from Africa. Benjamin Banneker was an African American.

almanac
(ALL-muh-nak)
An almanac is a yearly publication with information about weather, tides, sunsets, and sunrises. Almanacs also contain items such as stories, history, recipes, and advice.

architect
(AR-kih-tekt)
An architect is a person who designs buildings and then tells workers how to construct them. Pierre L'Enfante was an architect.

astronomy
(uh-STRAH-no-mee)
Astronomy is the study of stars, planets, and other celestial bodies. Benjamin Banneker liked to study astronomy.

capital city
(KAP-eh-tall SIT-ee)
A capital city is the place where most of a country's government is located. Washington, D.C., is the capital city of the United States.

celestial bodies
(seh-LESS-tee-yull BAH-dees)
Celestial bodies are the sun, moon, stars, planets, and other objects in the sky. The study of celestial bodies is called astronomy.

channels
(CHA-nullz)
Channels are long, narrow grooves used to transport water. Banna Ka made channels in his fields to bring water to his crops.

colonies
(KALL-uh-neez)
Colonies are territories that are governed by another country. Great Britain governed the original thirteen American colonies.

colonists
(KALL-uh-nists)
Colonists are people who live in colonies.

dams
(DAMZ)
Dams are barriers that block the flow of water. Banna Ka built dams to stop water from flowing to certain areas of his field.

Declaration of Independence
(deh-kluh-RAY-shun of in-dee-PEN-dens)
The Declaration of Independence is a document that was written in 1776. It announced the independence of the United States of America from Great Britain.

eclipse
(ee-KLIPS)
An eclipse is when one celestial body partially or completely covers another. During a solar eclipse, the moon covers the sun so people on Earth cannot see it.

Glossary

federal territory
(FEH-deh-rull TAYR-ih-tor-ree)
A federal territory is land that is set aside for the government of the United States.

harvest
(HAR-vest)
To harvest is to gather or pick crops. The Bannakys worked hard to harvest their crops each year.

indentured servant
(in-DENT-churd SER-vent)
An indentured servant is a person who works for someone else without being paid. Years ago, some people became indentured servants as punishment for a crime.

irrigation
(eer-ih-GAY-shun)
Irrigation is a system used to supply water to crops. Banna Ka used irrigation to keep his crops healthy during the dry summer months.

plantations
(plan-TAY-shunz)
Plantations are large farms that grow crops, such as tobacco or cotton.

presidential commission
(pre-zih-DENT-shull kuh-MIH-shun)
A presidential commision is when someone is given permission by the president to perform certain tasks. Benjamin Banneker was given a presidential commission to help build the capital city.

prejudice
(PRED-ju-diss)
Prejudice is a bad feeling or opinion about something or someone without good reason.

rebel
(ree-BELL)
When people rebel, they disobey a government or ruler. The colonists rebelled against British rule in the late 1700s.

secretary of state
(SEH-kreh-tayr-ree of STATE)
The secretary of state is the person who is in charge of the relations between the United States and other countries.

slavery
(SLAY-ver-ree)
Slavery is the practice of forcing human beings to work without pay.

surveying
(sur-VAY-ing)
When someone is surveying something, he or she is using math to tell how big a piece of land is. George Ellicott introduced surveying to Benjamin Banneker.

Index

Further Information

Books

"Benjamin Banneker," *The Grolier Library of North American Biographies, Vol. 7*. Danbury, CT: Grolier Education Corporation: 1994.

Ferris, Jeri. *What Are You Figuring Now?* Minneapolis, MN: First Avenue Editions, 1990.

Pinkley, Andrea Davis. *Dear Benjamin Banneker*. San Diego, CA: Gulliver Books, 1994.

Pollard, Michael. *The Clock and How It Changed the World* (History and Invention). New York: Facts on File, 1995.

Web Sites

General Information:
http://tqd.advanced.org/3337/banneker.html

To view a Library of Congress exhibit on the letter to Benjamin Banneker written by Thomas Jefferson:
http://www.loc.gov/exhibits/treasures/trr022.html